THE TECHNOLOGY AGE CLASSROOM

TERENCE CANNINGS

PEPPERDINE UNIVERSITY

LEROY FINKEL

SAN MATEO COUNTY OFFICE OF EDUCATION

FRANKLIN, BEEDLE & ASSOCIATES INCORPORATED
8536 SW St. Helens Drive, Suite D
Wilsonville, Oregon   97070
(503) 682-7668

Publisher	Jim Leisy
Production Coordinator	Lisa Cannon
Interior Design and Production	Jon Jacob
Production Assistant	Tom Sumner
Cover Design	Neo Nova
Proofreader	Eve Kushner

Selected clip art on cover courtesy of Imageline, Inc. All rights reserved.

Selected clip art on cover courtesy of Click Art® EPS Illustrations by T/Maker Company. All rights reserved.

Rights and Permissions
Franklin, Beedle & Associates, Inc.
8536 SW St. Helens Drive, Suite D
Wilsonville, Oregon 97070

Library of Congress Cataloging-in-Publication Data

Cannings, Terence R.,
    Technology age classroom / Terence R. Cannings, LeRoy Finkel.
      p.   cm.
    Includes bibliographical references and index.
    ISBN 0-938661-44-2
    1. Computer-assisted instruction. 2. Computer literacy.
    3. Computers and children 4. Education--computer programs-
-Evaluation. I. Finkel, LeRoy. II. Title.
LB1028.5.C355 1992
371.3'34--dc20
                                    92-22963
                                       CIP

PREFACE

Many members of the educational technology field—teachers and students alike—have expressed a need for a book that contains articles selected from the hundreds available on the subject and features the best few in one volume. As a lifelong trainer and learner, I have wanted the same. That's why I was excited when I discovered *The Information Age Classroom* (1986) by Terry Cannings and Stephen Brown, an anthology of articles on using technology in the classroom.

However, after using that book and its updates for four years, I found the material was becoming dated—it became clear that I was going to have to supplement the original volume with current material. That meant returning to reading umpteen journals, newspapers, monographs, etc. to find good current materials for my technology in education students.

One day during a conversation with Terry Cannings and publisher Jim Leisy (a former student of mine), we decided that it was time to publish a new book, including more sides of the picture. They invited me to be a co-author, and a new book idea was born. Now it was our job to do the massive search through the literature to find the best of the articles written on the subject of technology in education, place them in sensible order, and put them all in one volume.

That's what this book has become—a collection of readings across a wide variety of educational topics. Not all the articles paint a rosy picture of what is happening in the schools, because (as you will read) not everything is as wonderful as some would have you believe. We have provided a positive view along with the negative, so hopefully you will get a balance of reality and fantasy.

This book was designed to be used in teacher training courses at the undergraduate and postgraduate level, or as reading for inservice programs in the well-organized school districts that offer such programs. It can and should also be used by anyone who takes lifelong learning seriously and who wants to keep up to date on a topic that has been "hot" for a number of years.

We would like to thank the people at Franklin, Beedle & Associates for their patience and persistence in helping make this book a reality, and to James Wiebe and Don Ritchie, whose reviews and comments were invaluable to us.

LeRoy Finkel
Terry Cannings

Related Books from FRANKLIN, BEEDLE & ASSOCIATES INCORPORATED

AppleWorks for Students
Patti D. Nogales

AppleWorks for Teachers
Carol McAllister and Patti D. Nogales

Computer Tools and Problem Solving in Mathematics
James Wiebe

DOS 5 Fundamentals
Carolyn Z. Gillay

DOS 5 Principles with Practice
Carolyn Z. Gillay

Introduction to the Personal Computer
Keith Carver and June Carver

Macintosh and You: The Basics
Patricia L. Sullivan

Quattro Pro 4.0: A Hands-on Introduction to Spreadsheets
Keith Carver and June Carver

Technology Tools in the Information Age Classroom
LeRoy Finkel

We Teach with Technology
Greg Kearsley, Mary Furlong and Beverly Hunter

Works for Students
Patti D. Nogales

WordPerfect for Windows
Jane Troop and Dale Craig

CONTENTS

Chapter Three

Applications In The Classroom   102

CHAPTER FOUR

TECHNOLOGY USE ISSUES FOR THE TEACHER   233

CHAPTER FIVE

CLASSROOM MANAGEMENT STRATEGIES AND TEACHING TECHNIQUES FOR THE TECHNOLOGY AGE CLASSROOM   340

CHAPTER SIX

TECHNOLOGY AND STUDENTS WITH SPECIAL NEEDS   381

Chapter Seven

Emerging Technologies   459

CHAPTER EIGHT
VISIONS OF FUTURE
EDUCATIONAL ENVIRONMENTS   567

WHAT ARE THE BENEFITS OF USING TECHNOLOGY IN THE CLASSROOM?

1. "Luddite Schools Wage a Wasteful War." Lewis J. Perelman. *Wall Street Journal*, Sept. 10, 1990.
2. "Computers Failing As Teaching Aids." William Bulkeley. *Wall Street Journal.*
3. "Memories: A Ten-Year Retrospective." LeRoy Finkel, Don Rawitsch, and Holly Brady. *Classroom Computer Learning*, May/June 1990.
4. "The Politics of Educational Change: Cautionary Tales from the Past." Gail Marshall. *CUE Newsletter*, Sept./Oct. 1989.
5. "Educators Must Ask Themselves Some Important Questions." Mary-Alice White. *Electronic Learning,* Sept. 1989.
6. "Albert Shanker: A Man With Provocative Ideas about Educational Reform." Jon Goodspeed. *Electronic Learning,* Sept. 1989.
7. "In the Midst of Restructuring, Our Only Hope Is a Knowledgeable Teacher." Jon Madian. *Electronic Learning*, March 1990.
8. "In Search of A Computer Curriculum." Priscilla Norton. *Educational Technology.*, March 1988.
9. "Does Programming Deserve a Place in the School Curriculum?" Karin Wiburg. *The Computing Teacher,* Oct. 1989.

For the uninitiated, the title of this chapter might conjure up visions of wonderful technology applications created from readings you might have done, from television news stories you might have seen, or from things you have heard from friends. The initiated, on the other hand, might respond, "It's about time they asked that question!" It all depends on your perspective and your experiences.

Another way to approach the subject is to reread the title. Is the emphasis on WHAT the benefits are or should emphasis be on what are the benefits (?), implying that maybe there *are not* benefits to using technology in the classroom. Again, your personal response will depend on your perspective and your experiences.

To provide readers with a common base of experiences, we are starting this book with a series of articles about what others are saying about the application of technology to the classroom, followed by articles by educators on the same subject. A careful reading will make you wonder if both groups are talking about the same subject.

Practitioners of other-than-education tend to view technology as a wonderful solution to the education woes of our country, just as technology has been a solution, (albeit partial) for keeping American industry ahead of foreign competitors. Most would like to apply the industrial model of solving problems to schools, expecting the same result that model has had in industry.

Educators, on the other hand, heap praise on the *possibilities* that technology holds, but are not willing to view technology as the total solution to our woes until some hard questions have been asked and answered. This questioning of what technology can *really* do to help education is a refreshing change from the rhetoric of the day.

To put this in still another way, there is lots being said today about education, educators, and technology's role in education. Most of what we hear is said by non-educators and most of what they are saying is negative. The thing that frightens us, as educators, is that the farther away from the classroom the source of the comments, the *more positive* the attitudes are about technology. People who have experience using technology, though not with school-age children, are much more positive about the possibilities than are classroom teachers who use technology with their students every day. What we can't figure out is on what grounds these non-educators are basing their positive comments—"It's worked with adults, therefore it will work with young children, too." It's very confusing.

Despite all these remarks, you are sure to complete these readings with a more thorough understanding of what others are saying about the application of technology to schools—good and bad. The first article, "Luddite Schools Wage a Wasteful War" comes to you from the *Wall Street Journal* —it was written for and read by the business leaders of the world. The author, Lewis Perelman, is the director of something called Project Learning 2001 at the Hudson Institute. Perelman has received lots of press recently as an advocate of change, proclaiming the ills of public education with the solution(s) being the application of technology, as well as offering institutions of choice, where parents and kids select the school that they wish to attend. This article is one of many in a similar theme that Perelman has published. He is not alone in his beliefs, and you will read similar remarks made by others.

Another *Wall Street Journal* article, "Computers Failing as Teaching Aids," again takes the negative side of the issue and provides some explanation as to why things are not working well in schools with technology. It's hard to argue with most of what Bulkeley says. His report only highlights the failure of schools to provide *enough* resources when they try to implement change, unlike industry, which spends enough to provide adequate training along with hardware and software. Our concern about articles like these is that the positive side of technology use in the classroom doesn't get printed in the *Wall Street Journal*. Those articles are published in technology journals and education journals. As a result, businessmen read negative articles and sales figures in the *WSJ*, while educators read testimonials in their periodicals.

Not much happens these days without political process or intervention—the application of technology to schools is no exception. "The Politics of Educational Change: Cautionary Tales from the Past" shows us that things haven't changed much in 25 years. Gail Marshall reminds us of the lessons learned from the book, *The Politics of Educational Innovation* by Ernest House, and applies what he said back in 1974 to what is happening today with technology in the classroom. Not much changes over time.

And then come the questions! Educational technology tends to raise more questions than it claims to answer. But asking questions seems essential to the planning process as well as the implementation process. We can't just *assume* all this stuff "works" just because someone says it does. Mary-Alice White starts asking some of those good questions in her article, "Educators Must Ask Themselves Some Important Questions." She goes back to basic issues such as, "What is its educational value?" and "Is this the best medium to present the material?" While these questions sound very fundamental, they are seldom asked. Most people just jump on the technology bandwagon without hesitation or question.

That gives you the background that we want you to have, but before you proceed further, here's another approach to using technology in the classroom.

There is a whole "other" world of technology use that we have not dealt with so far. That has to do with preparing students for the Year 2000—giving them the skills they will need to survive in a technological age. Translation: providing students with a curriculum in "computer literacy" or "computing" or some other like title. We could have provided a raft of articles explaining all the current thinking. Fortunately for all of us, we came upon one that serves to summarize the past and describe the present. "In Search of A Computer Curriculum," by Priscilla Norton, is a long, scholarly piece, but it does cover the topic accurately and in depth. It will give you perspective on what has been, what is now, and what may be the future.

And for those who still want to beat the "should-we-teach-programming-horse," we provided the current thinking on that subject in the article "Does Programming Deserve A Place in the School Curriculum?"

If you're wondering about who is right or wrong, there are no simple answers to most of the questions that are raised by educational technology. So much depends on *local* concerns which involve politics more than what might be right or make good sense. That's why we tried here to give you a broad perspective of what is being said and done so you can compare it to your own local situation.

Questions for Discussion

1. How can educational technology serve the needs of schools-of-choice advocates?
2. Discuss some of the reasons why change can happen quickly in business, but takes more time in education.
3. Discuss the practical reality of what you can do with only enough computers to allow students 20 minutes per week for each.
4. Discuss alternative strategies for using one computer with 30 kids.
5. Discuss strategies a teacher or administrator could take to slow down the "jump on the technology-bandwagon" attitude that may be held by teachers, administrators, and/or school board members.
6. What does White mean by TITO, trivia in, trivia out?
7. Discuss the current status of computer literacy education and computer programming education in your community. What are the differences between nearby communities?

Questions from the Readings

1. "School is a process not a building" says Lewis Perelman. How can this process change the way we presently operate our schools?

2. List four reasons why computers are failing in the classroom according to Bulkeley's article in the *Wall Street Journal*.
3. Who are the other "key players" who influence change, according to the Marshall article?
4. What common attributes do all the projects have that are described in the White article, "Educators Must Ask Themselves Some Important Questions"? Why does she like these attributes?
5. Interview the computer literacy and/or computer programming teachers at your school or a neighboring school. Find out *why* a topic is taught. Ask how long it has been since the content was changed. What skills are being taught, and why?

Luddite Schools Wage a Wasteful War

Perhaps the most pernicious myth thwarting progress in education today is the shibboleth that "Technology will never replace the classroom teacher." The truth: It already has.

I recently witnessed a demonstration of a computer program that can teach any student of any age to read English up to any level of proficiency—without the aid of a human teacher. The product, to be marketed next year by a California company, Periscope Software, was pilot tested in public schools and produced reading gains far superior to conventional classes.

This is an exciting but not unique example. Two decades of research show that computer-based instruction produces at least 30% more learning in 40% less time at 30% less cost compared to traditional classroom teaching. Other research demonstrated 125 technologies and methods that proved to at least double the productivity of teaching—yielding at least twice as much learning for each unit of labor, cost, or time.

These tools—as well as the VCR, television, and even the telephone—are almost totally unused in U.S. schools and colleges. The cost to the U.S. economy of academia's successful resistance to technological innovation is at least $100 billion a year. The country simply can no longer afford this kind of waste. A technological revolution now is totally transforming the role of learning and teaching in the modern economy. As a result, the "Yak in the Box" model of instructional technology—the 1,000-year-old lecturing classroom professor—will have as much place in the 21st century's learning enterprise as the blacksmith shop has in today's transportation system.

By
Lewis J.
Perelman

Better Results at Less Cost

There is nothing the education establishment can do to stop this revolution, except on its own turf—it's happening everywhere outside the schools. For instance, corporate education departments are spending at least 300 times more on computer-based instruction than public schools are, as a share of their total budgets. Companies like Unisys and IBM are restructuring employee education programs to replace the great bulk of classroom teaching with instruction delivered by computers and telecommunications—to achieve better results at less cost.

Classrooms and teachers are far too costly and slow to meet the Information Age's exploding demand for learning. Increasingly learning is built into both production systems and consumer products. For example, in the past decade the U.S. went from having nearly no personal computers to having some 45 million PCs in use, which means that some 60 million people learned how to use PCs. We know that almost none of this economically and socially crucial learning took place in schools. It was "delivered" by vendors, manuals, tutorial software, videos, telephone hot lines, user groups, books, magazines, electronic bulletin boards, built-in "help" systems, much trial-and-error and a great deal of schmoozing. And many parents and

5

teachers will testify that kids often led adults in climbing up the PC learning curve.

Many business leaders are eager to see education embrace leading-edge technology. But few seem to recognize that, in the absence of wide-open choice and competition, the school-of-the-future and the classroom-of-tomorrow will continue to be the meretricious hoaxes they always have been. On the other hand, restructuring advocates inside and outside the school system who rightly see "choice" as the key to educational *perestroika* often don't seem to realize that technology is essential to the success of such a policy. For teachers to become the high-tech professionals they need and increasingly want to be, the agendas of technology and choice need to be melded into a single platform for change.

> The market is the essential solution to the "one best system" fallacy that has yielded, among other disasters, the dumbing down of the school textbook to perfect idiocy.

U.S. public schools and colleges are technologically stuck in the Middle Ages for the same reason Soviet collective farms are: a complete lack of accountability to the consumer and total insulation from competitive, market forces. Central, bureaucratic, "command" management provides no incentive—and a thicket of discouragements—for productivity, and hence for innovation. Russian grocery stores are not barren because Soviet farmers are ignorant of the potential of hybrid seed, fertilizers, and so forth to increase food production. It just doesn't pay any better for the collective farmer to grow corn than just to grow old.

American teachers and schools are trapped in the same political quagmire.

A friend of mine tried to sell a marvelous interactive video system for building the basic skills of sub-literate adults to the adult-education division of a major urban public school district. He argued that the system would virtually pay for itself by increasing productivity at least 30%—students could get through the curriculum with better achievement about a third faster. "You don't understand," the division director said. "The district pays us for attendance, not achievement. There's no reward for getting students through here faster; if anything, my ADA [average daily attendance] might go down and my budget could get cut."

Similarly, when I did a study a couple of years ago for one of the country's most affluent school districts to find out why the vast majority of teachers had shown no interest in participating in a multimillion-dollar program aimed at expanding computer-based instruction, one teacher I interviewed could have spoken for thousands when she said: "Why should I do anything different next year from what I did last year? Who cares?" Changing to new ways of teaching takes time, effort, risk and money. The bureaucracy was offering nothing even to cover these costs to her, much less any reward for success.

Only when schools have to earn their revenues in the marketplace by competing to serve consumers who are free to choose where to take their business (and money) will schools and teachers have the incentive to adopt productive technologies. And only when schools are free to operate as autonomous enterprises—with true "school-based management"—will educators have the opportunity to use their own resources to acquire the technologies they judge to work best.

The latter point is often overlooked. We need choice and competition in education not only to goad technical innovation but to provide quality control. The market is the essential solution to the "one best system" fallacy that has yielded, among other disasters, the dumbing down of the school textbook to perfect idiocy.

Also overlooked is how crucial technology is to the success of the policy called "choice"—which, to work effectively, must include the freedom for teachers to choose how to design and run their schools as well as the freedom for students to choose what schools and programs to attend. Technology blows away many of the key objections to choice programs: That "choice" is phony when all schools are essentially the same. That successful schools will be filled up and leave many students stuck in bad schools. That distance and geography limit actual choices.

'Sameness' Is Obsolete

First, computer-based, multimedia and other advanced technologies now provide not only great diversity in instructional designs, but enable us to custom-make programs to meet each student's individual needs, abilities and goals. So "sameness" is obsolete.

Moreover, "distance learning"—the use of telecommunications to deliver instruction from anyone, anywhere to anyone anywhere—virtually eradicates spatial barriers to choice. Once we recognize that "school" is a process not a building, it's clear that we can now de-liver as many different schools as cable TV channels, to wherever there is an adequate terminal. In the U.S., that's just about everywhere. Every student can have access to the best teachers and instruction available in every subject. Distance learning can liberate minorities from the knowledge ghetto.

Techno-choice is an essential strategy to save education from economic irrelevancy—and the American workforce from disastrous impoverishment. But it requires wholesale replacement of lecturers and classrooms with silicon chips and glass threads.

The obsolescence of the job of "classroom teacher" need not be a threat to the people who now hold that position. They won't be thrown on the scrapheap or sent to the glue factory. Indeed, the learning revolution is opening a golden age for professional educators who are truly dedicated to serving the consumer. But "more of the same" is not an option. Teachers now must decide what role they will play in this revolution: vanguard or victim, leader or Luddite.

Article #2
Computers Failing As Teaching Aids

HERALDED REVOLUTION FALLS SHORT DUE TO LACK OF MACHINES, TRAINING.

By
William
Bulkeley

The computer revolution in education was supposed to be here by now.

Enthusiasts in the early 1980s predicted that children soon would be learning more from desktop computers than they ever had from teachers. The Carnegie Commission said computers would have to be added to the three R's. And many expected computers to squeeze out Big Chief notepads and flashcards.

But now, even after spending more than $2 billion on an estimated 1.7 million personal computers, educators are hard-pressed to spot the heralded revolution in the schoolhouse.

"The computer-learning revolution predicted back in the early 1980s just hasn't happened," says education professor Henry Kepner Jr. of the University of Wisconsin at Milwaukee. Marc Tucker, president of the National Center on Education, a Washington research group, says, "A lot of kids in this country now distinguish between a computer and a telephone . . . I think we should expect a great deal more."

What Happened?

What derailed the revolution? Educators have a long list of reasons: School computers remain scarce. The early computers that schools bought weren't very good, and the software for teaching is still lousy. Most teachers never get adequate computer training. And using computer programs to teach classes has turned out to be much more difficult than expected. "The mistake was thinking that if we put in a lab or two, com-

8

puter education would happen by magic," says Joseph Arangio, headmaster of Mario Umana High School of Science in Boston. His school has four computer labs for its 900 students, but only five of the 75 teachers use them. "We had real high expectations that it was going to be the solution to all sorts of problems," he says.

Most educators and researchers remain convinced that computers eventually will find a place in the schools. And in the few cases where schools already are regularly using computers to teach various subjects the results have been encouraging. Most studies show that students using computer-aided instruction will achieve mastery of a subject 10% to 30% faster says Charles L. Blaschke, president of Educational Turnkey Systems Inc., a technology consulting firm in Falls Church, Va. Computers work especially well in special education, remedial education for dropouts and gifted children, he says.

Adds Allen Glenn, an education professor at the University of Minnesota: "In my heart, I think there is tremendous potential and opportunity. But we can't answer yet whether it changes the score on the SAT" college-entrance exams.

The biggest stumbling block has been the shortage of computers in schools. While 96% of all U.S. public schools have computers, most of them simply put 10 to 20 of the machines in a single computer laboratory, which various classes share. Because of the limited number of machines, even the minority of science and math classes that used computers average less than 15 minutes of daily use for each student, according to a Research Triangle Institute study for the National Science Foundation; most other subjects used computers even less.

"There's perhaps one computer for every 35 to 38 students — barely one per classroom," says John Schram, a senior vice president of educational publisher Houghton Mifflin Co., Boston. "That has had as big a limiting effect as anything."

Moreover, sharing the labs among several different subjects and teachers makes scheduling difficult. And often the distribution of computers doesn't match the need. Washington D.C. put labs with 10 computers each in every school — enough machines, perhaps, for one of its elementary schools with 300 pupils but not for a high school with 1,500 students.

The shortage isn't likely to disappear any time soon. Despite steadily dropping prices, personal computers remain daunting investments for school systems used to buying one new $15 textbook a year for each student. At the same time, school systems are under pressure to spend more to raise teacher's salaries and cut class sizes. Says Richard Riley, Maine's educational technology coordinator: "Total student expenditures in Maine are around $2,700 a year per student. If you purchase a computer that's half the budget for a student."

Similarly, in Pittsfield, the school board approved spending $180,000 to boost the number of computers next year, but the mayor rejected the entire plan. "It's easy to cut, because in their minds it's considered almost a luxury item," says Irene Vassos, the school system's computer specialist.

Meanwhile, schools that jumped on the bandwagon early may have to replace obsolete machines before even thinking about adding more computers. Jeanelle Leonard, director of computer-literacy training in the Washington, D.C., schools, says that this year, instead of expanding the number of machines, the school system will replace five-year-old Commodore computers because of soaring repair costs.

Frustrations Over Software

Another big hurdle is the lack of software suitable for teaching. Because the market is less lucrative than for commercial software, there are fewer education programs to choose from and the products aren't as fast or as easy to use as business software.

"You need resources before you get a package as good as a spreadsheet," says Alan Lesgold, a professor of psychology at the University of Pittsburgh. "You don't see venture capitalists trying to corner the market on third grade education." The educational-software market amounted to only $153 million last year, the Software Publishers Association estimates, out of total software sales of $2.9 billion.

Robert Pease, a computer enthusiast who heads the science department at Conard High School in West Hartford, Conn., says, "For most (software) packages teachers have to reinvent the wheel. They have to learn (how to use it) themselves first and then tailor it for their activity. It increases class-preparation time."

The problem isn't only getting computers and software, though; it's also knowing how to use them. Researchers say many schools merely teach students the basics of using computers rather than putting the machines to work as tools for studying other subjects. That's like requiring courses in pencils instead of in writing, says Celia Einhorn, a computer-education coordinator in Albuquerque, N.M.

As a result, computer familiarity is all most students get. Educational Testing Service reported in April that a survey of 24,000 students found that 87% of 11th graders had used a computer, and more than 95% could identify pictures of a floppy disk and a keyboard. But when it came to completing tasks with a computer, students apparently hadn't learned much. For questions about using spreadsheets and data bases, for instance, the scores barely topped random guessing.

Training for Teachers

Getting teachers to use computers in their courses has been a big problem too. Few teachers publicly criticize computers for fear of appearing technologically backward, but many ignore the machines after one or two frustrating experiences. "It takes a tremendous amount of time to become familiar" with the computers; says a high-school language teacher in Newton, Mass: "I've been too busy teaching to integrate the computers."

An Educational Testing Service survey found that 32% of the computer-education coordinators in elementary schools were uncomfortable with computers.

Yet, schools aren't giving teachers the computer access they need to feel at ease using the machines. "We'd hoped to put a computer into every teacher workroom," says Ms. Einhorn, the Albuquerque computer instructor. "But the school board said 'Work with the kids first.'" As a result, most of the teachers didn't get the chance to become familiar with the computers on their own before having to use them in the classroom.

Ms. Leonard of the Washington, D.C. schools says: "We expected the teachers to really embrace the technology and take off with it." Instead, three years after the first computers were installed, the school district had to begin requiring that educators take computer courses.

Adding to the problem is that few colleges require education students to use computers or to take courses on using them to teach. And teachers who haven't been taught with computers often don't see ways to use them. Iris Weiss, a Chapel Hill, N.C., researcher, recalls a seminar on computer education where one man said, "If these methods are good, how come none of my teachers at Harvard teaches this way?"

Memories: A Ten-Year Retrospective

By
LeRoy
Finkel,
Don
Rawitsch,
& Holly
Brady

Let's take a little trip back in time. We're not going too far—just ten years or so. Ronald Reagan has not yet moved into the White House. The headlines are full of stories about Americans held hostage in Iran and about OPEC's role in the oil crisis. *Ordinary People* has won the Oscar for Best Picture, but you can't find it in your local video store because there aren't any local video stores. In fact, VCRs are quite expensive, and as a consequence they are still scarce in the home. Nor are there fax machines in offices, nor cellular phones in cars. Record stores are full of 12-inch LPs—not compact discs. And the popular CB radio is giving way to a new technological fad: the boom box.

But we're not going to talk about politics or pop culture or popular electronic gadgets. We're going to focus on technology in the schools. We're simply going to take a measure of how far we've come in the uses of technology in education over the past ten years.

The Early Years

The year 1980 was crackling with energy for teachers interested in technology. The education community was abuzz with stories about the potential of microcomputers in the classroom. It had been less than four years since Jobs and Woz had introduced the Apple I at the Homebrew Computer Club in Palo Alto, California, and yet clearly there were more than a handful of teachers who had appropriated the technology and spirited an Apple II (which debuted in 1977) into their classrooms. Many of these teachers had been teaching programming on mainframe or minicomputers since the '60s or '70s. All were eager to discover how the new "portable" computers could be used with kids.

By 1980, the market was flooded with microcomputers, and educators had a wide variety to choose from. The cover story of the first issue of *Classroom Computer Learning* (then *Classroom Computer News*), which premiered in September of that year, covered many of them—including the Apple II, the Commodore PET, The Texas Instruments 99/4, the Atari 400 and 800, the Exidy Sorcerer *(the Exidy Sorcerer?!?)*, and Radio Shack's TRS-80. Most of these computers were designed to be hooked up to TV sets, and software was stored on cassette tapes.

By September 1981 when *Electronic Learning (EL)* debuted, educators had begun to zero in on a select group of computer brands that seemed to offer the most for schools. In *EL's* first cover story, three educators laid out what computers they would buy if given the money to develop technology centers for their schools. One chose the 16K PET (because of its array of "excellent software"), another the 16K TRS-80 Model I (its revolutionary 64-column line was "much more usable" than the standard 40 columns of most other computers), and the third chose the "quite sophisticated" 48K Apple II with its "high-resolution" color graphics. The IBM PC—IBM's first en-

11

Reprinted by permission of: *Technology & Learning* (Formerly Classroom Computer Learning)
© 1992 Peter Li, Inc. 2169 East Francisco Blvd., Suite A4, San Rafael, CA 94901

try into the microcomputer market—was announced just as the issue went to press.

Of course, there was not much in the way of educational software to run on these machines. Consequently, educators used what they had—BASIC in ROM—to develop simple programs that could be used in the classroom. These homebrewed programs—some of which were educational only for people with good imaginations—often found their way into collections of public domain software that were distributed free throughout the country. One of the early missions of Computer-Using Educators, Inc., a California-based organization for professional educators, was to set up a software exchange, later named SoftSwap, to identify the better titles and clean them up with a consistent user interface.

But educators wanted more. Those who had worked with mainframes and minis were familiar with some of the early education programs such as *Oregon Trail, Star Trek, Hangman, Stock Market (STOCK),* and *Adventure* that ran on the larger machines. These educational pioneers began to reprogram the oldies to run on micros, and some even created small companies to produce better software for schools.

Minnesota Educational Computing Consortium (MECC) was probably the first and certainly the largest organization to produce a sizable number of programs for microcomputers. Disks with such prosaic names as Elementary Volume 1 (including *Hurkle),* Elementary Volume 6 (including *Oregon Trail)*, and Math Volume I (including *Bagels* and *Snark)* became the most popular programs in use in schools.

A short time later, a small New York educational media company named Sun-

burst Communications hired away some of MECC's talent and hit it big with one of the first "problem solving" programs, *The Factory.* Around the same time, a Massachusetts junior high school teacher named Tom Snyder convinced McGraw-Hill to publish the simulation software he had created for his classroom—a program which later became widely known as the *Search Series*—and went on to publish many other popular titles under his own name.

On the opposite coast, a college English professor and professional tutor named Jan Davidson rented space in an empty school building and produced her first product, *Speed Reader,* under the Davidson & Associates label. And 700 miles north, an educator and young mother named Ann Piestrup, bolstered by an Apple Foundation Grant, started a little company to market her first program, *Rainbow.* She and others went on to produce such early software classics as *Gertrude's Secrets, Gertrude's Puzzles,* and *Rocky's Boots* under The Learning Company label.

But such programs filtered into the classroom slowly. In the meantime, nearly every technology-literate teacher was teaching programming to students—usually BASIC because that was the language that came with their machines. The prevailing theory was that all students would need programming skills in the work world of the 21st century.

With the publication of Seymour Papert's *Mindstorms* in 1981, Logo became another popular choice of programming languages, and the rationale for teaching programming shifted: We began to believe that it was a good way to promote problem solving skills among our students. A short time later, the Educational Testing Service forced educators to consider yet another programming language when it announced that its Advanced Placement computer science exam would test students' skills not in BASIC or Logo, but in Pascal. Most educators at the high school level soon shifted to that language.

The Machines
Get More Powerful

In November 1983, IBM officially entered the education market with the introduction of the PC Junior. Nicknamed "Peanut," the machine offered 128K of RAM—64K more than most other computers found in the schools at that time. For various reasons, the PCjr was not well received (IBM chose to take it off the market a year and a half later), but it did serve to raise educators' expectations regarding minimum memory for a school-targeted machine. Within the next year and a half, Apple, Commodore, and Tandy all introduced machines that offered a minimum of 128K—notably, the Apple IIc, Commodore 128, and Tandy 1000. Educators also began to retrofit older machines with additional memory.

These new 128K machines allowed software developers to publish new kinds of programs. A small West Coast home software publisher with the unlikely name of Brøderbund blundered into the education market with a program called *The Print Shop*. The program spawned an entire new genre of software designed to produce banners, greeting cards, and posters. The success of *The Print Shop* encouraged Brøderbund to market other programs in the schools, including the enormously popular *Carmen Sandiego* series.

Another significant trend in software occurring about this time was the new emphasis on the use of productivity tools in the classroom—word processors, databases, and spreadsheets. While educators had for several years adopted for classroom use business programs such as *Wordstar, AppleWriter,* and *Visicalc*, it took a partnership between Scholastic Software and Bank Street College in 1982 to produce *Bank Street Writer*, the first widely distributed word processor specifically designed for kids. *Bank Street Writer* was followed by such education-specific tool programs as *Magic Slate, FrEdWriter, Bank Street Filer, Talking TextWriter,* and *EduCalc*. When minimum memory in the installed base of machines increased to 128K, *AppleWorks* began to find its way into the classroom. Today the *Works* package, available for three computer platforms—Claris' *AppleWorks, Microsoft Works for the Macintosh,* and *Microsoft Works for the PC*—is perhaps the most popular productivity tool in the schools.

Shake Out

The computer industry took a sharp downturn in 1985. Apple laid off 1200 people in one day, and the continuing power struggle between Steve Jobs and John Sculley finally ended in the ouster of Jobs. IBM's withdrawal of the PCjr pulled the plug on countless third-party software projects and killed at least one magazine start-up. And Commodore, already in turmoil from internal problems, was unable to follow through in marketing plans for its advanced new Amiga computer, introduced in mid-1985.

Nonetheless, schools kept acquiring hardware and software, and educators organized to support technology in the schools. The best-known of the grassroots organizations include CUE in California, TCEA in Texas, MACUL in Michigan, and NCCE in the Northwest. Some states rewarded pioneering teachers by providing support programs. Notable among them were MECC and TIES in Minnesota, the BOCES offices in New York, Educational Service Centers in Texas, and the short-lived TEC Centers in California. One national professional organization, the National School Boards Association, created a district support program, the Institute for the Transfer of Technology to Education (ITTE).

Back on Track

In July 1986, Tandy/Radio Shack introduced the Tandy 1000EX and SX family of computers. This relatively low-cost group of machines offered a number of attractive features to schools—including selfbooting ROMs (which meant that educators would not have to load DOS into their machines each time they used a new program) and built-in speech capabilities. To accompany the launch of these machines into the school market, Tandy stepped up its support of third-party software developers.

Tandy's announcement heralded two new trends. First, it generated serious interest among educators in the purchase of MS-DOS computers for student use in the schools. In April 1987, when IBM debuted its new family of PS/2 computers, that interest increased, in part because IBM had once again upped the ante for memory capacity. IBM's new machines offered a minimum of 512K of RAM, more than twice that of most other computers in the schools. Moreover, the machines also offered exceptionally high-resolution color screen displays. With both the Tandy and the IBM platforms thriving, software publishers began to increase their stock of MS-DOS titles, not only by converting

existing Apple II programs to MS-DOS formats, but also by creating new titles that took advantage of the special features offered by the MS-DOS machines.

The other trend accelerated by the introduction of the Tandy 1000 was the increased number of educational software programs that "talked." Until this time, teachers who wanted to use programs with speech synthesis had to purchase special adaptive equipment—the Echo and Cricket speech synthesizers were two popular choices. But software developers were often reluctant to develop programs that required the user to purchase special peripherals. When the Tandy 1000 was announced, developers began to create more programs with speech capabilities, secure in the knowledge that the Tandy machines could run their programs without additional equipment. The Apple IIGS, introduced three months after the Tandy 1000, provided the same kind of built-in speech capabilities, and further spurred the development of "talking" educational software.

Connecting the Machines

As the number of machines increased in the schools, networks began to proliferate. Because of Tandy's long history with educational networks and its cost-competitiveness, the company enjoyed early success in this area. What's more, in mid-1986 Tandy teamed up with ESTC, a relatively young publisher of integrated learning systems (ILSs), in a partnership that delivered a good number of networked curriculum systems to the schools.

At the same time, IBM was enjoying significant success setting up networked PS/2 labs in elementary schools to run various integrated learning systems and later its popular *Writing to Read* program.

These networking successes led to one of the recent major trends: the rebirth of integrated learning systems. While companies such as Computer Curriculum Corporation, Control Data Corporation, New Century, WICAT, Wasatch, and Ideal Learning Systems had been offering basic-skills curricula via technology for many years, most school districts had not been entirely receptive to such comprehensive systems. But with the increased number of networks in the schools, realignment of ILS curricula with state-developed curriculum frameworks, and greater technical sophistication among teachers and administrators, the ILS market became reenergized.

New companies, such as Jostens Learning (which brought together ESC and Prescription Learning Centers) began competing with the older ones for the infusion of federal dollars often used to purchase such systems. And because federal dollars were involved, many of the newly purchased systems found their way to populations of at-risk and minority students.

The Beginnings of a New Decade

What will the '90s bring? Surely none of us is rich enough in imagination to produce a truly accurate picture of schools ten years from now. But we can look at some recent events of significance, and take our guesses.

One of those recent events is surely the introduction of the Apple Macintosh to schools. For the first four years of its life, the Macintosh was marketed to the business community only: the Apple II, Apple claimed, was the computer for the schools, and "Apple II Forever" was the slogan for that computer. But by the summer of 1988, Apple had rethought its position, and the company quietly began to promote the Macintosh to schools as well as in the corporate world.

The Macintosh, when equipped with *HyperCard,* became the first machine to demonstrate clearly the promise of the multimedia technologies that will certainly play a large part in education in the '90s. Projects from National Geographic, Lucasfilm, WGBH Nova, and ABC Interactive/Optical Data began appearing during the summer of 1989. These new educational programs were the first truly to combine computer text and graphics with full-motion video images—and the results were often quite powerful.

IBM's *LinkWay* system, which appeared not long after the *HyperCard* prototypes, provided equally intriguing multimedia capabilities in the MS-DOS world. IBM spawned such video-rich products as the Target Interactive Project, an interactive simulation that focuses on substance abuse; and WorldScan, a learning station designed to provide students with news footage of significant historical events of the 20th century.

And Commodore's re-emergence in the education market—with a *HyperCard*-like authoring system and a family of Amigas that offers powerful multimedia capabilities—may provide educators still another option for the '90s. Another seminal development for the '90s was the introduction of CD-ROM technology. Apple, Hitachi, and others marketed external CD-ROMs for several years before Tandy and newcomer Headstart Computer (a division of Philips) announced machines with built-in CD-ROM drives. (Similar machines from IBM, Apple, and others are rumored in the pipeline.) CD-ROMs offer new potential not only for the storage of massive amounts of data (Apple's CD-ROM can store as much as 270,000 pages of typewritten information), but also for the enhancement of the multimedia capabilities of the computer. CD-ROMs allow developers to incorporate into their programs top-quality speech and music, a large number of still images, advanced computer animation and some video motion sequences. One of the first successful educational applications of CD-ROM has been delivery of complete encyclopedias on CD-ROM discs—including the first multimedia encyclopedia from Jostens Learning and Encyclopedia Britannica.

Perhaps even more significant, IBM is working with others to perfect the DVI (digital video-interactive) technology that will allow full-motion video to be delivered over CD-ROM. If and when this occurs, software developers will be able to deliver full-motion video with computer text and graphics from a CD-ROM drive, and computing as we knew it in the '80s will be left in the dust.

Clearly, we have come a long way in ten years. We have moved through many stages, and we have learned many things about the uses of technology with children. And yet, we are still just beginning. Twenty years from now, we will look back on these days and wonder how the early pioneers of the '80s sustained themselves on the meager equipment of the day. We'll wonder where we got the stamina to continue our fight for funds, our evangelizing for the use of technology in the schools, our support of colleagues interested in becoming a part of the movement. We will have to admit that what kept us going most was little more than our *visions* of what education could be, and the relatively small successes that caused us to know we were, indeed, on the right track.

LeRoy Finkel is editor of the CUE Newsletter. *Don Rawitsch, after a 15-year career at MECC, is currently an independent consultant in search of new opportunities. Holly Brady is editor-in-chief of* Classroom Computer Learning.

Article #4
The Politics of Educational Change: Cautionary Tales from the Past

By
GAIL
MARSHALL

Today, many educational critics say that school computer use is in trouble. *PC Computing* recently devoted space to a special report, "PC's in the Schools—An American Tragedy" (January 1988), that lamented low implementation rates of school computers. The article provided data on federal funding, presented stories of schools judged to be successful users of technology, and cited many software products. But the article didn't grapple with a major problem—creating the climate for educational change required by the computer revolution.

Educational change isn't easy. Research reports often tell us that computer use doesn't yield increased achievement. Teachers and administrators who have worked with change efforts read the reports and comment that the innovative practices might have been a good idea, but they never survived from the drawing board to the classroom. And the same teachers and administrators can point to roadblocks in that compromised any chance of success.

If computer educators want to improve their chances of success *The Politics of Educational Innovation* by Ernest House (McCutchan Publishing Corporation, Berkeley, CA, 1974) should be daily reading. House has been an evaluator of federal and state funded projects for many years, and his book is an analysis of the problems change agents encounter.

Most research studies fail to describe the setting in which the innovation occurred; they fail to tell you about the obstacles to be overcome and the strategies that failed. Instead, they provide a few cursory words about the site, the students and the procedures. Then they show a few tables or charts designed to show the impact on students. In most cases, the charts list a few f-ratios and then caution that more research is necessary. House's book is refreshingly different. It tells how projects were undermined by political infighting, how attempts at teacher training were poorly conceived and poorly timed, and how planning failed to account for the necessary fiscal and human resources.

Many of the projects House reports on are not computer projects, but every case study he presents provides a cautionary tale for the computer educator. For example, in discussing problems with the implementation of a large scale CAI product during the '70s House says the project planners sent the teachers to a university to be trained a full year before the project was to be implemented. Even at that, he says, there wasn't enough time for the teachers to learn the necessary skills. Project staff underestimated demands placed on teachers by the proposed change and little help was provided by school administrators. In his concluding remarks on the CAI project, House says that the attempt at innovation is costly, especially for teachers who receive no recompense for the effort. So costly that participating teachers shy from future innovation efforts.

House analyzes the roles of other key players in the innovation effort. He dis-

17

tinguishes between "career bound" and "place bound" superintendents. Career bound superintendents, he says, focus on becoming superintendents early in their careers and they look forward to moving from small school districts to large ones (and maybe even to business or universities) on the strength of their success. They bring many innovations into the schools, but they seldom stay to see the innovations through. While they can "unfreeze" existing bureaucracies, they don't sustain the change efforts associated with the unfreezing. Place bound superintendents work their way up in the district and they tend to be more cautious about introducing innovations, but they also tend to stay around long enough to observe the consequences of change.

Central Office Staff activities in the change effort are also described by House. He says the inhibition of change is a function of many central administrators, and toward that end they can cut down on communication among key players, "stack the deck" by making sure they hold the most votes during decision making, and they "line up the ducks" by supporting their candidates for newly advertised positions.

The federal government's role in change efforts during the '60s and '70s is analyzed by House. The government's efforts, he says, were not designed to stimulate innovation, but to control it. They sought a single strategy, which can be transferred in top down fashion, and in order to create educational products that can easily be transferred from one state to another they've produced uniform sets of materials for training or classroom use. The Research, Development and Diffusion model proposed to spread innovations means top down control of the innovation. And that, says House, depends on a "passive consumer,"

the teachers, at the end of the innovation chain. In his concluding remarks, House questions if teachers will accept top down models of change or if they will call for a greater role in the change process, from an innovation's inception through to its institutionalization. Given the calls for increased support for technology at the state and federal levels, House's book is worth reading if we want to avoid the problems associated with earlier federally supported change efforts.

The innovative process demands that everyone involved constantly learn new skills. In addition to the hardware and software skills demanded by the computer revolution, computer advocates need to acquire or develop political savvy.

Since the factors House describes affect planning, implementing, evaluating and funding of computer projects, it's worth change makers' time to review problems in the politics of computer innovation. Here are a few factors that make a difference:

• **Personal contact speeds up the change process.**

When people work together and talk about the innovation, the effects of the project spread. Beware of a staff member who doesn't comment on the innovation. According to House, those "passive adopters" limit planned change.

How can you and your school district increase personal contact to improve computer use in your schools? Do you know who the "passive adopters" of computers are? How can they become more involved?

• **Geography affects the spread of an innovation.**

A school that is successfully implementing an innovation may contribute to another school's decision to adopt. If an innovation saturates an area, personal contact is likely to be increased, so the innovation is even more likely to be successful. In contrast, innovations that exist in isolation tend to languish after a while. In a few years, innovation activities disappear.

What strategies can you and others in your town or region use to improve computer activities? Are there computer projects worth highlighting that are in danger of being abandoned for lack of attention?

• Superintendents are key players in the innovation process.

Superintendents who move from district to district are likely to bring many innovations with them and are likely to stimulate enthusiasm for the innovation in their new districts. But, beware, highly mobile superintendents don't remain in place long, and after they leave, local support for the innovation may disappear.

Is your Superintendent involved in planning for computer use? and what would happen to computer use if the current Superintendent moved to another district? Who in the district would be an advocate if your Superintendent left?

• Central Office Staff can affect the scope and support for computer use.

Central Office Staff can throw considerable logistical support behind an innovation and speed up the change process. They have access to funds, equipment and personnel that can make the change process easy. On the other hand, the COS can slow down or hide the innovation, lobby for resources to be diverted to other projects, and mount campaigns for the adoption of projects more closely related to their own interests.

Are Central Office resources committed to computer use in your district? What strategies can you use to increase computer planning and implementation?

How can COS take ownership for computer use?

• Entrepreneurs can make a difference.

An "entrepreneur" in favor of the innovation can be a powerful agent for change. Entrepreneurs can be administrators or teachers who initiate, organize, publicize, and protect computer projects. They can find the necessary resources and promote enthusiasm where commitment has been lacking. But beware, entrepreneurs usually flourish in fragmented or loosely organized bureaucracies. And when a school district is re-organized or a new superintendent is hired, the entrepreneurs' mobility is likely to be limited.

• Teachers usually aren't regarded as key change agents by school district planners.

Teachers' access to information is likely to be limited, so finding out about innovations and routinely discussing problems with innovations is problematical. Rewards for teachers' participation in innovations are unlikely, so many teachers who might volunteer decide not to. This limits the opportunities for teacher-to-teacher discussion.

How much access do teachers have to information about the district's plans for computers? Are computer activities initiated by teachers receiving the attention needed to sustain a high level of computer use? What strategies would increase teachers' commitment to computer use?

• Innovations often fail because no one knows a project is in trouble until it's too late to resuscitate the project.

Since classrooms are isolated, problems with the innovation aren't likely to be noticed by anyone other than the teacher. If the district loses interest in the innovation but the teachers remain committed to it, support from the top is unlikely to be significant or sustained.

Are computer applications being nurtured and monitored? Does everyone approach the evaluation of computer projects with a positive attitude?

• **Expectations for computer use have been unreasonable, prompting discouragement and even waste.**

Many of the innovations from the '60s and '70s were oversold. Technology projects promised large increases in student achievement and many promoted the idea that teachers weren't essential to the teaching process. But, when schools tried the technology innovations, they found that hardware wasn't ready on time, software wasn't written, and frequent mechanical breakdowns occurred. The overselling of technology convinced many school staffs that technology in the schools was a pipe dream, and equipment was often junked.

Is the memory of earlier technology trouble holding back current computer use? If so, how can those impressions be changed? Does everyone in the district have a set of short term goals for computer use? Is planning based on the knowledge that delays in delivery and installation are to be expected, and that the delays shouldn't signal failure?

• **Previous technology projects were often costly failures.**

The technology wave of the '60s and '70s cost far more dollars than planners anticipated. Many of today's administrators and policy makers tend to be cautious about technology today because they carry memories of cost overruns.

• **Federal programs for change were often based on a "This year you get it, next year you don't" funding formula.**

During the '60s and '70s the federal government distributed dollars for change on a large scale. Many of the projects were ill-conceived, others were under-funded for the scope of work involved, while others were allowed too short a time for accomplishing their goals.

To compound the problem, the politics of government agency staffing and the changing agendas of successive presidential administrations meant that funding goals changed frequently. Politically astute school administrators quickly learned to follow government dollars, even when that meant abandoning support for successful projects in their districts.

Does your school district have a backup plan that details what happens if funding sources dry up? Does your district have a long range commitment to computer use, no matter what?

Change isn't always a positive experience for school staff. Many teachers and administrators have been burned out by negative experiences with innovations. The complexity of dealing with school problems compounds efforts at change. The loss of dollars, both federal and state, for routine educational expenditures maximizes frustration in trying to keep abreast of the computer revolution. But change can be a positive process and House's case studies, reading like whodunits, can actually make the process enjoyable. And reading about earlier innovation efforts may cast problems with current computer implementation in a broader, more positive perspective.

Article # 5
Educators Must Ask
Themselves Some Important Questions

WHAT IS THE EDUCATIONAL VALUE OF CERTAIN TECHNOLOGIES? WHAT ARE THE CRITICAL
TECHNOLOGIES THAT BEST SERVE EDUCATION? THESE AND OTHER QUESTIONS ARE EXPLORED.

BY
MARY-ALICE
WHITE

In conference after conference, in trade journals, and in the national media, we hear more and more about new developments in technology and less and less about their educational benefits. I would like to see that ratio reversed. If we asked ourselves certain questions, we could help to change that emphasis.

Question One

The first question we should ask of any technological development is: "What is its educational value?" Metaphorically speaking, we have tigers in technology but mere insects in instruction. We use marvelous electronic systems for filing, storing, and retrieving information—but they are no better than the information itself. We said about mainframe computers GIGO, or "garbage in, garbage out." In educational software, we should say TITO, or "trivia in, trivia out." A new system can be a teacher's dream, but the content is often trivial in terms of its real educational value.

We should be asking the same question about the educational value of the proposal by Whittle Communications to beam a free news program by satellite into public schools. The controversy surrounding Whittle's Channel One has focused on the program's commercial advertising. But the more important question to ask is: "What is the educational value of a television news broadcast?" We have one answer to that from a recent survey (*New York Times,* June 6, 1989) of American adults which shows that after 40 years of television news, American adults know little more about current affairs than they did 40 years ago. Television news is not intended to be educational; it is intended to be entertaining.

One broadcasting company has created a videodisc that contains its news programs on the topic of the 1988 presidential campaign, which it hopes schools will buy for teachers to use. This wonderful videodisc technology can bring up whatever film or text the viewer wishes, on demand. The question that remains is the same important question: "What is the educational value of the content?"

Laser discs are marvelous. But TITO, in the case of this particular product, still reigns. The information brought up is trivial. Television news does not provide a basis for an informed classroom discussion of the issues. Television news is entertaining; it provides quick images that can shape opinion, but it is not a reliable source for understanding what lies behind today's headlines.

So this is one example of a tiger in the technology—the laser disc hooked to a computer and a remote controller for instant retrieval of still and motion film, tape, text, and sound—but the content, in my opinion, is an insect of instructional content.

There is a great deal of media attention now on what is called multimedia.

21

What is usually meant by such terms is that information in the near future will come in the form of moving and still color pictures, graphics, sound, text, and some or all of this information will be under the control of the user to change or rearrange. This mix of information modes will be delivered on an interactive screen, controlled by a computer, and possibly communicated through a phone. There is nothing wrong with this idea except that it is based more on the hype about the technology than on a thoughtful notion of how the media will present such information.

Question Two

Who is asking this second question: "What type of information is best presented through which medium?" Print is a wonderful piece of technology, but not everything is understood most easily when learned in print. Most tasks that are manual, for example, are more easily learned through pictures or videos. Graphics simplify and clarify some kinds of information, such as comparisons and trends, but are useless in understanding poetry.

A model of educational multimedia that sets high standards for matching information with the appropriate medium is "The Voyage of the Mimi," by Sam Gibbon, which is designed for 10- to 13-year-olds. Film was used to develop a narrative that would interest young students about sailing in search of whales. This subject was chosen because whales interest both girls and boys. (This choice is significant because so much software is male-driven, using competitive games, speed-paced trials, outer space travel, castles, dragons and treasures—all of which are unappealing to most girls.)

The Mimi narrative leads the viewers into filmed interviews with scientists on relevant topics. In the classroom there are computer tools for related student projects, such as testing water temperature. And there are classroom print materials. Here is a model of different media presenting information that best suits each medium.

A model of a student-controlled information search tool is the Palenque visual information base developed by Kathy Wilson at Bank Street College of Education in New York. The student viewer can conduct his or her own visual exploration of a Mayan ruin in any sequence: going down the steps into the underground repositories, walking along the paths, or climbing the steps to the top of the temples. At any point the student can choose to listen to Mayan music, bring up print archives, or visit a museum. This is an example of visual technology putting relevant information into the hands of the user, a marriage of quality between technology and instruction.

A good educational tool in science enables students to ask questions, find relevant and non-trivial information, gather data, analyze trends, and make predictions. A model for this kind of interactive science tool is Kids Network, which was designed by Bob Tinker of TERC (Technical Education Research Center, Cambridge, Mass.).

In Kids Network students form a team

> So much software is male-driven, using competitive games, speed-paced trials, outer space travel, castles, dragons and treasures—all of which are unappealing to most girls.

with other schools to collect scientific data. Using a computer and a modem, students collect data on such topics as acid rain in their community and send the data into a central computer. The students are then sent, from that central computer, plots and maps for the whole country showing trends in acid rain which they can try to explain in terms of smokestack emissions, wind currents, and topography.

> If we educators can be thoughtful about curriculum—if we can be thoughtful about instruction—can we not be thoughtful about the tools we need to improve learning?

What is especially appealing about this Kids Network project is that the students are behaving like scientists themselves by collecting original data and analyzing trends, rather than replicating classical experiments which so often fail to replicate in the school science laboratory. This project is under the supervision of an experienced acid rain scientist who is finding that the students are not only collecting accurate data, but are able to produce far more observations than the federal Environmental Protection Agency can produce with its own limited staff.

Another quality educational tool is Weather Machine, which was developed by the National Geographic Society. In this program students receive, via a modem, the daily national weather reports—exactly the same data professional weather forecasters receive. Highly colorized maps on an Apple IIGS show the data visually in terms of wind direction, precipitation, barometric pressure, and warm and cold fronts.

The students deal with real data in real time, from which they can predict local, regional, or national weather. The students are not playing at science; they make real predictions which they can check against tomorrow's weather.

They are also being exposed to data analysis and the graphic presentation of trends in the way many scientists today are dealing with quantitative data. They learn that weather, like much of science, consists of many finite observations forming a visual trend that makes events more predictable. Children of this age can begin to have a sense of the regularity of natural events so that some part of life becomes more understandable.

Models of learning tools such as these suggest new developments in technological tools for education. Instead of those toy-like and look-alike games with perceptually confusing graphics, these are serious tools for developing and analyzing information. Children here are being taken seriously as *partners* in the search for knowledge. Such models give us great hope for what the technologies could do for exciting, quality education.

Question Three

The third question is: "How will we get more tools for education that combine quality technology with quality education?" One way is for schools to invest in such tools so that the market becomes more appealing.

Question Four

Which leads to the fourth question: "What *are* the critical tools for education?" Who is identifying them, pointing out what we need with appropriate standards of quality? We know that the financial world lives on spreadsheets, modems, and information bases. We know that lawyers find a legal data base indispensable to searching for legal precedents. And that physicians depend on medical data bases.

A conference of educators called to deal with this subject could be extremely helpful in identifying the tools necessary for education, thereby motivating the technology industry to produce them. If we cannot say what we need and want, then we must expect the industry to produce a variety of software, good and bad, to find out what the educational market will buy.

If we educators can be thoughtful about curriculum—if we can be thoughtful about instruction—can we not be thoughtful about the tools we need to improve learning? Why don't we take the lead in calling for the tools to improve learning and teaching? Why don't we define the kind of tools we want: tools that are easy to use, empower the student, treat the student as a colleague in the search for knowledge. Tools that bring up meaningful information, not trivia.

If we ask these questions, can we not answer them for education? If we do not, then who will?

Mary-Alice White, Ph.D, is professor of psychology and director of the Electronic Learning Laboratory at Teachers College, Columbia University, New York., NY.

Albert Shanker: A Man with Provocative Ideas about Educational Reform

THE PRESIDENT OF THE AMERICAN FEDERATION OF TEACHERS BELIEVES TECHNOLOGY CAN PLAY AN "ESSENTIAL" ROLE IN EDUCATION IF SCHOOLS ARE RADICALLY CHANGED.

BY
JON
GOODSPEED

Editor's Note: *Long a stalwart of school restructuring, Albert Shanker was a keynote speaker at the National Educational Computing Conference in Boston this June, where he spoke of technology's role in that restructuring. Shanker, who has a daily and weekly schedule that would tire even Hercules, met with* Electronic Learning *editor Jon Goodspeed in a cab from Logan Airport en route to the convention. Below are some excerpts from that interview.*

EL: Do you believe that computers and technology can play an important role in education?

SHANKER: I think computers and technology can play more than an important role; they can play an essential role in education. It is very clear from the results that we are getting in our schools, which are much more shocking and disappointing and disastrous than the general public knows at this time, that we need a radical transformation within our schools.

Technology is indispensable to that radical transformation in two ways. We can see that because there have been previous efforts to transform the schools, and it was the absence of computers and technology, essentially, which resulted in the failure [of those attempts at change].

These two essential elements are that, one, you need to devise a system of education in which kids can be active during their learning, rather than passive. You need a system of learning in which a student can proceed at their own pace rather than having to follow the average of a class, where some are bored and others are left behind. And you need a system of learning in which different students can learn in different ways.

You also need a system of learning in which the mistakes that one makes while learning, which are inevitable, are not exposed to the public of one's peers, resulting in humiliation. You need a system in which these mistakes can be made in a relatively private atmosphere. Technology is absolutely indispensable for the accomplishment of all of these.

The second part of the essential nature of technology is that in order to develop many different ways of learning the same thing, many different [teaching] approaches are necessary. It's impossible for an individual teacher, or even a group of teachers within a school, or even the teachers within one school system, to develop all of these different ways. That's one of the reasons why teachers continue to rely on the lecture; it is easier to develop one lecture than it is to sit down the night before and say, "For each lesson I'm giving today, I'm going to figure out five different ways in which the kids can learn."

25

Essentially, information technology makes it possible for the creation of a national, and even an international, peer review panel that would try out different things and develop either a national or international data base or files of best cases, best systems.

Teachers might just go to the computer [data base] and find that when they are teaching about the Declaration of Independence, in the opinion of social studies teachers across the country, the best computer program is the following, the best video tape is the following, the best three audio tapes are the following, the best simulation games are the following.

EL: According to estimates, fewer than 20 percent of all teachers actively use computers as part of their instructional program. What do you believe needs to happen so that a majority of teachers use computers on a regular basis, if you do indeed believe that they should be used on a regular basis?

SHANKER: Since teachers obviously are going to come to school to lecture every day, then the uses for the computer are much more limited than for the kind of schooling that I am talking about.

What I am talking about is a radical restructuring. I would like to give an assignment to teachers and say, "For the next three years I want you to prohibit lecturing; any lecturer will be punishable by...." But the teachers have to get the kids to learn the same things that they always wanted them to learn.

Now if you do that, you'll have to think of ways of getting the kid to be active and you'll have to think of all types of technology, not just modern technology, but old-fashioned models— maps, pictures, all sorts of things. You

have to get people within education to see that all sorts of things that were not possible before, are now possible—things that they always knew in theory were more effective.

I think teachers have to have a vision of a different type of schooling. I think that if large numbers of teachers and administrators or school board members were to see this vision, were to see that something is better and be more willing to take enough time and energy to change their habits, then not only will they be changing habits but they will be changing all sorts of current conditions in the schools.

In the business world people are constantly scanning the environment to see whether their competitors are about to use more objective ways of doing things, because if they don't get there at least at the same time their competitors do, they may very well be out of business.

We need to develop incentive systems within our schools, otherwise people won't change. The current moves for "school choice" are really aimed at that. The people who are pressing for it are saying, "Well, if a lot of the parents felt the school was ineffective, they would pull their kids out." That would be, in effect, the going-out of business.

If there were "winners" and "losers" in terms of school effectiveness or school system effectiveness, just as there are "winners" and "losers" in businesses, then you and I wouldn't have to run around talking about the virtues of using technology that's available; the people in those places would say "damn it, we can't afford to be without it because our competitor [another school] may get it first." And so I think we need to deal with the question of incentives; until we deal with that, trying to bring about change by delivering sermons to people doesn't work well.

EL: Robert Pearlman, in his article "Technology's Role in Restructuring Schools" [*Electronic Learning,* June 1989], discussed the St. Paul's Saturn School of Tomorrow. Do you hold that up as a model school using technology?

SHANKER: The name "Saturn School" and the idea came from a speech that I gave and a column that I wrote where I talked about the Saturn project which General Motors and the United Auto Workers are involved in. They are building a totally different type of plant where employees will work in teams and where the relationships between labor management are totally different, in an effort to put out a better car than the Japanese.

At the end of my column I raised the question: If in an industry that's as traditional as the auto industry, both the industry and the labor side can get together to do something like the "Saturn Project," why can't there be a Saturn Project in the schools? The superintendent and the union at St. Paul, Minn., picked that up.

I wish that there were more than one school in the country that decided that they would take the cue from one of the more innovative practices within business and industry. After all, the schools, as they are now operating, are largely the way they are because of the factory system. [Frederick] Taylor's scientific management methods became the bible of the industry. [Those methods] moved immediately to Teachers College, at Columbia University, and other schools where administrators were educated, and they started saying, "Well, if facto-ries are the most efficient way of organizing a productive system, how can we model a school after the factory?" Now that we see old-fashioned factories can no longer compete with new styles of management that use technology—which is essentially what the Japanese have shown us— it's time that we not only rethink our factories, but we rethink our human factories: our schools.

EL: One popular use of telecommunications technology is to allow students to communicate with other students in countries around the world. Do you think it is important that this type of exchange continue? Is it important for students to think in a global manner?

SHANKER: I think it's important for students to think in a global manner, but I also think it's important for students to think in a national manner. I am very concerned that we are jumping into global education as a way of saying that it is not important to know

> "I am very concerned that we are jumping into global education as a way of saying that it is not important to know much about our own country."

much about our own country. [We are afraid we might become] supernationalistic or ethnocentric. I don't think we'll understand much about the world unless we understand something about ourselves and our own history.

The second thing is, I don't think we ought to [learn about the rest of the world] with any sense of neutrality. Up until two months ago, we had all kinds of educational materials in this country that said that we in the United States are very ethnocentric because we think that everybody in the world wants democracy.

Now, of course, a whole bunch of Chinese students in Tiananmen Square taught us a lesson that we were being ridiculous when we said that they weren't interested in freedom or democracy. They just weren't able to express that because they were living at the point of a gun.

I think one of the things that the Chinese students have shown us is the power of fax machines and computers to help people communicate with each other, even where there is a totalitarian system in place. They are much more likely to get honest communication through technology than almost any other form, because once it's used on a mass basis, it's unlikely the governments will spend the amount of time, energy, and money necessary to monitor everybody.

EL: The term "distance-learning," which is using telecommunications to bring classroom instruction to a remote area, is occurring in some areas of the U.S. One problem is this: a teacher who is certified in one state may not be certified in the state into which he or she is being "beamed." This problem has led many to call for national certification in core-curriculum areas—math, science, languages. What is your opinion of national certification?

SHANKER: I am on the National Board for Professional Teaching Standards. Today the states license teachers; that is, they provide the minimum qualification, whereas we [the board] are trying to create board certification much in the way that states license doctors. There are professional boards that have a higher form; that is, they certify for excellence in a given field.

Now I don't have much sympathy for those who say [a teacher cannot teach] if he or she doesn't meet the licensing requirements in one state, because there isn't any one of those states that doesn't hire unlicensed people right now whenever there is a shortage.

So if they are hiring unlicensed people, then why not allow for an outstanding presentation by a licensed teacher from some other state to be beamed into that state.

As long as they are engaged in a wholesale violation of their own laws, they can't have a "holier-than-thou" attitude about a teacher who happens to come in via satellite, rather than one who comes in because there is a teacher shortage there.

In the Midst of Restructuring, Our Only Hope Is a Knowledgeable Teacher

TEACHERS WHO FIRST USE BASIC COMPUTER APPLICATIONS, SUCH AS WORD PROCESSING, WILL BE BETTER PREPARED TO HELP SHAPE CURRICULUM REFORM AND USE MORE ADVANCED TECHNOLOGY.

BY
JON
MADIAN

Educators from all disciplines agree that our current curriculum is in a process of renewal, and that the emerging curriculum should empower students to learn and think creatively. Moreover, many educators envision that computers and multimedia technology will be major players in the reorganization and delivery of the new curriculum. Some see in these new technologies, and the curricula they will support, channels for student and teacher problem-solving and expression—the primary ingredients of empowerment.

As clear as the need and momentum are for the new curriculum, it is equally clear that we are having a difficult time planning for this change and envisioning it in detail. To arrive at a destination of our choosing, we need a calculus that measures where we are and where we believe we are going. There are several parameters that need to be plotted: What is the essence of the new curriculum? Should we continue to buy basals and textbooks? What kind of computer systems and audiovisual equipment should we invest in? What kind of staff development do we need? How can we achieve a sensible three-year plan?

As the saying goes, "Anyone who feels these questions are answered easily hasn't understood the problem." In this case, the underlying problem is: How do you change a large system that has a long history of doing things in prescribed ways? In addition, the technology central to educational change is costly and still in its infancy, albeit changing rapidly, while future forms and costs are highly uncertain. No wonder educators who are working to plan, design, and implement the new curriculum feel like they are riding a narrow raft in a pitching sea.

Since the answers are not yet upon the horizon, perhaps, to paraphrase Rainer Maria Rilke, all we can do is live the questions fully, so that in the not too distant future, we will live our way into the answers.

The New Curriculum

In science, mathematics, language arts, and social studies, the emphasis is upon learning as a process: Students are encouraged to ask difficult questions and explore possible answers rather than memorize simple facts or rules.

The question, for example, in social studies is not: When did Columbus cross the Atlantic? Instead, the emphasis shifts to questions such as: What were the forces that motivated Columbus and his backers to undertake the exploration? What is the role of vision, politics, courage, fortitude, religion, patriotism, economics, and hubris in such undertakings?

New curriculum ideas in language arts are reflected in the whole language

29

movement, literature-based instruction, and the theory of composition known as the writing process. Simply a design process no different from the steps taken by an architect, painter, or sculptor to compose a piece of work, the writing process is also not too different from the methods used to develop ideas in science: question and brainstorm, formulate, test, revise and retest, and finally publish. The creative process in any field ultimately leads to a new level of peer feedback, dialogue, and questioning.

Which Technologies?

Since the heart of this new curriculum is wholeness and process, many people question whether we should continue to buy (or even use) basals and textbooks, which emphasize skills and facts at the expense of process and problem solving. Instead, should we begin investing in literature, field trips, multimedia materials, and technology-based systems that support problem solving and student expression?

Clearly, purchasing more basals and/or textbooks is questionable, although those currently in use do have valuable stories, poetry, lessons, and information that can be used as part of the instructional process. Some schools and districts are shifting textbook funds toward literature and primary source materials; this shift is in step with the new curriculum concepts. Likewise, it seems sensible to use textbook dollars to invest in technology for curriculum delivery and as a tool for student expression.

Multimedia and hyper environments are the most promising, as well as the most speculative and expensive, technologies. There's little doubt that these environments are where we're heading

in the new curriculum. At this stage, however, we do not know what this curriculum and the supporting technologies will look like when they reach maturity—or at least adolescence—years from now. So far there are only a few curricula available for these media.

Since the new multimedia technologies are so new and fast-changing, and since only a few teachers per school are successfully integrating simple technological applications like word processing and video into the curriculum, it seems that it is too early to think clearly about the design, delivery, and staff development for interactive multimedia. If this is the case, then we have a hard job ahead—that of resisting the mounting pressure from the computer and multimedia manufacturers and the educational technocrats who want us to join the technology "revolution" with the latest and greatest applications. Rather, we might better set the pace of our own curriculum/technology "evolution."

A Path to Wisdom

How can educators set their own pace? An educated staff's understanding of curriculum options and technology is the only assurance that they will understand how to choose and use the increasing power of technology to give expression to our best curriculum.

Teachers need time to explore the new curriculum ideas, learn how to handle the technology, and effectively integrate technology into the curriculum. This kind of staff development requires hands-on experience, and opportunities for experimentation and sharing information with colleagues trying to solve the same kinds of problems at the same grade level. In short, if teachers are to empower students to work with a stimulating, problem-solving curriculum, they too need to live the process by creatively solving their own curriculum and technology problems in their own schools. Seen in this light, staff development parallels curriculum development—teachers, rather than textbook publishers, become the curriculum designers and refiners.

Staff Development

In the past, staff development was too often a "training" process in which teachers were conditioned to "use" or "deliver" a prescribed curriculum in prescribed ways. This training, orchestrated by basals and textbooks, focused upon the teacher as a technician. Delivery of the training usually followed the expert-lecturer format with teachers playing the role of passive students.

During the next few years staff development should provide teachers with time and expert support that will enable them to reflect upon and refine their curriculum while working in cooperative curriculum design groups.

Since teachers, like students, learn from modeling, more time must be devoted to master teachers conducting demonstration lessons, team teaching, and mentor teachers providing feedback to colleagues.

Curriculum Evolution

Emphasis should be upon integrating a process-oriented curriculum, particularly in reading, literature, writing, and social studies. Even science and math should be connected to each other and to the social studies and literature curricula through studying the history of scientific and mathematical ideas and related inventions. Within this context, we will be challenged to devise strategies to teach skills.

Technology Plan

Since most of public education is devoted to language arts in one form or another, and since current pedagogy fits so snugly with word processing, a sensible three-year plan will set as its goal the effective use of word processing by students and teachers to support all phases of the writing process in all curricular areas.

The technology plan should emphasize computers and peripherals that support word processing—large monitors, networks, scanners, modems, and (most importantly) a sufficient number of work stations for students and teachers to have ample access to the technology. What is ample daily access for students and teachers? Defining and achieving this goal is of primary importance.

> The technology plan should emphasize computers and peripherals that support word processing...

Such a plan, simple as it is, will focus teachers and students upon important instructional activities while they use the computer in ways that will improve their thinking and expression skills. In a number of years, when sufficient equipment and an excellent curriculum supported by word processing is in place, teachers will be ready to apply their curricular and technological skills to sort out the issues and possibilities in multimedia. By that time, multimedia technology and curriculum will have made important advances. (The most technologically savvy computer coordinators and teachers will have been using multimedia all along.)

How relatively simple it would be if we set the easily definable and attainable goal of everyone using word processing effectively. Once this goal is realized, it may be deceptively easy to take the next steps because the teachers will thoroughly understand process-based curriculum and how the computer, through word processing, can support instruction.

Summary

The history of educational change is littered with carcasses of textbooks, machines, and dittos left by overly zealous sales people and by hopeful yet despairing educators. One fad gives way to another when the educational community responds to exaggerated expectations and the resulting disappointments. Whenever we fail to thoroughly understand and explore the roots of educational problems and the ideas and technologies offered to remediate them, we will be the victims of superficial thought and undisciplined good intentions.

The only guarantee against faddism in the coming decade of expected unprecedented change is that we invest in a thorough evaluation and ongoing refinement of our instructional process, and that we provide first-rate staff development and support. Our efforts will require a total commitment of time, energy, patience, intelligence, and love—a total involvement of the whole educational and business community.

Jon Madian is the founding editor of The Writing Notebook, *a publication devoted to creative word processing in the classroom. He is also a children's author, language arts consultant, psychotherapist, and software designer.*

By
Priscilla
Norton

With the introduction of microcomputers into schools has come a series of curriculum questions which are still largely unanswered. What do students need to know about a computer? Do computers constitute a separate subject area, a tool, a mechanism for teaching problem-solving, or a new form of literacy? Can computers really be more than sophisticated electronic workbooks or flashcards? How do teachers fit computers into an already full curriculum? Is the computer a subject or a vehicle of instruction? Why does education need computers at all? The history of attempts to answer these and similar questions has taken a variety of routes as educators have searched for an appropriate computer curriculum. Yet, all of the computer curricula proposed so far have failed to capitalize on the unique potentials for innovative educational practice that the computer offers.

Existing Computer Curriculum Models
The Programming Curriculum

When schools first began purchasing microcomputers, often at the insistence of anxious parents, the teaching of programming became the mainstay of the computer curriculum. The programming curriculum generally consists of an identified set of concepts associated with programming (data input, looping, logical operations, etc.) usually taught in a special "programming class." This line of curricular reasoning generally rests on two assumptions: jobs of the future will involve computers, and computer programming is the essential skill for mastery or control of the computer.

As the computer programming hysteria has begun to wane, however, educators are recognizing the fallacies underlying these assumptions. Relevant to programming as a vocational necessity, experts now suggest that only about seven percent of all new jobs between 1980 and 1990 will be genuinely high technology occupations. Although it has been estimated that 75 percent of all jobs will involve the use of computers in some way, in most cases, they will require computer *use* not computer programming (Anderson, 1981). In the real world, most people *use* programs rather than write them. Furthermore, the demand for computer programmers will be in the tens of thousands as compared to the 40 million students who will soon be seeking employment (Bernstein, 1983).

Programming gives students "control" over the computer according to the second argument supporting a computer programming curriculum. Proponents of this viewpoint feel that someone who has not learned to program is "being controlled" by the computer. Programming, however, neither insures control nor is it the only way to exercise control. Students who make effective use of spreadsheets or word processors, for instance, have precise control for getting the system to do what they wish. Any knowledge they might have of a computer language lends nothing to their control of the computer in using such tools (Bork, 1985).

33

While these objectives cast doubt on computer programming as the mainstay of the computer curriculum, they do not suggest that programming as a part of the curriculum should be abandoned. Rather, educators must ask, what is it that students are expected to do with the programming skills they acquire? The strongest argument for learning to program may be related to the study of particular disciplines. Thus, a student studying science, computer science, mathematics, or the social sciences may use programming as one technique for mastering aspects of a particular subject.

The Computer Literacy Curriculum

The second curricular agenda to develop for computers in education was the computer literacy model. Although there are as many definitions of computer literacy as there are curriculum designers, the term generally embraces computer awareness as well as previously identified computer programming skills. Bitter's (1982) computer literacy scope and sequence includes such areas as computer vocabulary, computer ethics, how a computer works, and advantages and disadvantages of computers as well as an introduction to computer programming. Bork (1985) includes social implications of the computer, strengths and weaknesses of computers, the ability to learn more about computers, and common applications as computer literacy essentials.

Like the computer programming curriculum, the computer literacy curriculum has also come under criticism. Harvey (1983) has questioned the assumption that there is anything about computers which belongs in the school experience of every student. He states that it is not possible to identify any universally required computer experience. Rather, the wide range of computer uses is so varied that it is impossible to teach all of them to every student. Likewise, he states, most computer use has little if any relation to the commonly identified skills. For instance, to operate the computerized cash register at McDonald's, workers do not need to know anything about input, output, memory, or programming.

Most curricular experts are not willing to go as far as Harvey. Instead, critics of the computer literacy curriculum take the position that knowledge of computers and the use of computers cannot be viewed as a separate curricular area. The most important parts of the computer literacy curriculum, they suggest, are best learned in other classes or perhaps in nonclassroom environments such as libraries or homes. Thus students should encounter word processing where writing is done, such as in the English class. Spreadsheets and graphic capabilities should be introduced in arithmetic, mathematics, and science contexts. Databases should be part of sociology courses, political science courses, and other courses where data are important. Paint programs have a natural home in art and industrial design classes. In such situations, students see a meaningful application relevant to what they are doing, and the computer is not presented as an isolated device.

It has been said that the problem of the computerized society will be solved by teaching computers and programming to everyone. The real problem is elsewhere.... How should we educate and train people to make the best use of these increasingly powerful tools? There lies the real challenge for education (Hebenstreit, 1983).

The Computer as Tool Curriculum

A more recent development in computer curriculum has been an emphasis on the computer as tool model. This computer curriculum views the computer as a tool which extends human intellectual power as other tools have extended human physical powers. Included in the computer as tool curriculum is the teaching of skills associated with the use of a variety of applications software including word processors, database managers, spreadsheets, and graphics tools. As recently as 1986, Westley referred to a curriculum which emphasized the role of tool applications as "forward-looking."

The problem with the computer as tool curriculum, however, is twofold. The first hides behind the often unarticulated assumption that computers are neutral, that they are just another tool. Tools are never neutral, however, but "create a culture of tool users who have to operate them on the tool's terms" (Davy, 1985). Computers are having and will continue to have an impact on culture and society. A computer curriculum must not only consider skills enabling users to identify what the computer can do *for* us but must also include what it is doing *to* us. A computer curriculum must make certain that students study what the computer's effects will be, not just how to use computers.

The second problem is similar to that leveled against the computer literacy curriculum. Specifically, knowing how to use a word processor is of little use unless one has something to write about; learning to use a database is important only if one has a need to organize data. Tools are often more interesting to in-

structors than to students, since instructors have backgrounds which supply motivations students cannot be expected to have. Weizenbaum (1976) has stated that the computer can be a powerful metaphor for understanding many aspects of the world. Yet, he states, it enslaves the mind that has no metaphors and few resources to call on—the mind that has been educated with only "facts" and "skills." Tool applications are worthwhile only when students are prepared to use them to solve problems which have meaning and applicability to their needs. "Every intellectual tool must be demonstrated to be educationally useful, to contribute in some way to the learning process." (Bork, 1985)

The Problem-Solving Computer Curriculum

Most educators are cognizant of the fact that the current emphasis in schools on the acquisition of knowledge will be ineffective in handling the "information explosion" and the need to cope with rapid change. Most understand that students will need to be independent learners and problem solvers. The problem-solving computer curriculum rests on the belief that computers can facilitate students' ability to problem-solve. Students are assigned or choose problems to solve in a computer environment under the assumption that they will learn to be better problem-solvers in real world situations.

One of the leading proponents of the problem-solving computer curriculum is Seymour Papert, the inventor of LOGO. He feels that by taking advantage of educational opportunities to master the art of deliberately thinking like a computer, the learner becomes able to articulate what thinking is. Working in a LOGO environment, he suggests, teaches students to think about thinking. He has written "... obviously, I believe this to be a good thing in that the ability to articulate the processes of thinking enables us to improve them." (Papert, 1980:158) D'Ignasio (1986) has further elaborated this concept by stating that working with a variety of computer programs allows the learner to build "computers in their mind," meaning that one is able to internalize the thinking processes modeled in computer use and apply them to non-computer situations.

There is little quantitative research to support the broad claims made for the problem-solving computer curriculum. Although it is premature to discard the model completely, caution should be exercised in using this curricular model as the exclusive frame for planning a computer-oriented educational curriculum. Research in general problem-solving suggests that problem-solving procedures need to be made evident to students and then practiced and practiced again. Thus, links between computer use and problem-solving need to be made explicit and practiced independent of a computer environment. While the computer may introduce problem-solving strategies, it is probably insufficient to think of the problem-solving computer curriculum as the final answer in teaching problem-solving and critical thinking.

Having examined each of these curricular approaches, it is evident that none of them can be adopted as a single model. One might combine the four models and attempt to find a place in the curriculum for each of them. It is unlikely, however, that an already overloaded curriculum can accommodate the demands of each of these approaches as single elements. It is also unlikely that when added together the sum of the four will comprise a single unified approach to computers in the curriculum. The direction in which these models point, as curricular arrows for action, does not lead to a viable educational path for devising a computer curriculum.

Integration: An Evolving Curricular Model

Integration of computers with existing curricula is taking a central role in the search for a computer curriculum. As early as 1982, Bitter suggested that many of the goals of a computer literacy curriculum could be achieved within traditional curricular areas. Hunter (1984) has devised a K-8 curriculum which illustrates this idea. Pogrow's (1985) Higher Order Thinking Skills (HOTS) program was also designed to work with aspects of the current curriculum. First-year results from this program suggest that it is possible to use computers to improve the higher order thinking skills of elementary students while also improving their basic skills. Norton and Resta (1986) have investigated the impact of a variety of software programs on the reading achievement of elementary students. Their findings indicate that students who use problem-solving and simulation software score significantly higher on measures of reading comprehension and problem-solving abilities. In addition, *Electronic Learning* has published a "Software Side by Side" feature since early 1985 which takes a comparative look at different software packages within the content area of "Computers in the Curriculum."

These examples illustrate what has become the critically important question in the search for a computer curriculum: "Given the curriculum objectives for a particular discipline, what kind of software would be most desirable as a means of increasing instructional effectiveness?" (Schiffman, 1986). The computer appears to be most beneficial when ways are found to use it to support existing curriculums. Therefore, given the curriculum objectives for a particular subject/grade level, the best computer curriculums are those which determine where and how the instructional capability of the computer can be beneficially "infused" into lessons designed to help students achieve the objectives of an established curriculum.

At first glance, the computer integration curriculum seems promising. It appears to embrace all the components originally identified by the programming, literacy, problem-solving, and tool curriculum. Each of the skills elaborated as part of these curriculums can be accomplished within the frame of the computer integration curriculum. Literacy skills can become part of computer use. Technical skills, vocabulary, social implications, and ethics can be mastered as the computer is used in support of more traditional curricular goals. Programming can be taught as an example of mathematical principles or as examples of scientific principles. Tools such as a word processor or a database can facilitate faster writing or more efficient information collecting. Problem-solving strategies may be introduced within the frame of discipline related tasks.

In addition to its inclusiveness, the computer integration curriculum appeals because of its manageability. Rather than adding additional classes or competencies to an already crowded teaching schedule, the computer integration curriculum fits nicely into an already existing curricular structure. The computer becomes a necessary and sometimes motivating "instructional resource." The computer becomes intertwined with other audiovisual devices like tape recorders, filmstrips, and educational television and videocassettes. It becomes one more component of the overall teacher designed and implemented lesson plan.

However, the arrow still points in the wrong direction. Like the earlier computer curriculums, the computer integration curriculum carries with it a set of unspoken assumptions which fail to recognize the unique potentials of the computer and current changes in society. All the proposed computer curriculums rest on a concept of learning and education which emphasizes the mastery of a set of basic skills and basic knowledge held to be important for full participation in society.

The computer integration model defines learning and education as content specific and content oriented and presupposes an existing curriculum that is best left unchallenged. To be educated is to have mastered a discrete body of knowledge and to be able to execute an established set of skills.

There can be no doubt that a fundamental knowledge base and set of skills form an essential ingredient in learning, but a truly innovative computer curriculum which sheds the limiting assumptions of the traditional curriculum has the potential to push curricular goals beyond their current boundaries. The search for a computer curriculum presents educators with the opportunity and the vehicle for reinventing curricular goals not just integrating the computer with current curricular goals.

Reinventing Curricular Goals

The first step in reinventing the curriculum begins with an assessment of the demands the larger social context places on the curriculum. Just about everyone is now familiar with the literature which suggests that contemporary society has moved from an industrial to an information age. What this means in everyday terms is that the majority of people living and working in Western countries are engaged in the production, distribution, and interpretation of information. There is a risk, however, that we may drown in this information while remaining starved for knowledge. Western cultures are in jeopardy of becoming "blip cultures." Members of such a culture are constantly bombarded by "short, modular blips of information—ads, commands, theories, shreds of news, truncated bits and blobs that refuse to fit neatly into pre-existing mental files." (Toffler, 1980) In the midst of all this information, students must be prepared to bring order to the chaos of information and give value to data that would otherwise be useless. Demands on the curriculum, therefore, become less dependent on particular, established contents and rest, instead, on processes for making sense of a wide range of information.

Stating current needs within a different frame, John Naisbitt has written in *Reinventing the Corporation* (1985) that the new basics for an emerging literacy-intensive society should lead to thinking, learning, and creating—what he calls TLC. He does not mean, however, that reading, writing, and arithmetic should not be taught. Rather, he believes that these are necessary but insufficient processes to equip students with the ability to function in the classroom and the corporation.

The first basic, thinking, is the ability to synthesize and make generalizations, to divide into categories, to draw inferences, to distinguish between fact and opinion, to put facts in order to analyze a problem, to arrange and rearrange information to make decisions, solve problems, create opportunities, and raise human potential. The second basic, learning how to learn, is essential in a world that is constantly changing. There is no one subject, says Naisbitt, that will serve one for the foreseeable future, let alone the rest of life. If an individual knows how to learn, he or she can adapt and change no matter what technological, social, or economic permutations occur. The last of his three basics is creativity. Our schools, says Naisbitt, are models of rationality, but as decision loads become more complex and the problems we face unique, creativity—seeing new solutions—becomes a prized ability.

In a study released in 1985, the Committee for Economic Development reported the results of a survey of both large and small corporations which indicated that a general high level of literacy, a sense of responsibility, the ability to work in teams, the ability to continue to learn, and the ability to problem solve were the top-ranked attributes for potential employees. Like Naisbitt's TLC, these abilities demonstrate an attitude toward educational needs which do not reflect a preoccupation with a particular content or a specified set of skills but with processes for making sense of experience and information.

The second step in reinventing the curriculum is to frame a concept of the learning process. There are many approaches to learning including the behavioral, the cognitive, and the developmental. One perspective particularly useful for designing a computer curriculum incorporates elements of all three of these. This model, developed by Robert Karplus (1985), views the learning process or learning cycle as being comprised of three phases. The first is the experiential phase where students play with phenomena, building intuition and insight through a series of experiences relevant to a subject area. The second stage in the learning cycle is the process of learning ideas and elaborations of content. The third stage in the learning cycle is learning what to *do* with what is learned. This last phase is oriented toward applications, toward using knowledge.

The most familiar phase of this learning cycle is the second one. Most curriculums stress this aspect of learning. Examining most curriculum guides reveals a list of concepts to be taught and learned. Associated student activities usually encourage memorization, practice, and evaluation of a student's mastery of these identified concepts. Rarely do these guides emphasize provisions for expanding student's experiences or for doing things with what has been taught.

The third step in reinventing the curriculum centers on identifying the unique potentials inherent in introducing computers into the curriculum. Computers are much more than sophisticated drill and practice machines. They are much more than systems for managing and planning instruction. Instead, they offer to educators the potential for both introducing students to experiences beyond the restrictions of contemporary classrooms (the first phase of the learning cycle) and for providing opportunities for "doing" things with mastered content (the third phase of the learning cycle).

Computer simulations, for example, can provide students with experiences impossible to gain otherwise. A computer simulation on nuclear power plants can provide the experiences necessary for developing intuition and insight into the complex problems associated with nuclear energy. Likewise, using databases in a geography class permits students to go beyond collecting information relevant to the study of the states.

Instead, students may find answers to questions concerning geographical features and attempt to draw conclusions and generalizations about how people organize themselves in communities, going beyond studying geography to "doing" geography. Using computers in education, therefore, permits curriculum designers to expand their concepts of the curriculum—to emphasize processes for acquiring experiences and applying knowledge (doing) as well as content to be mastered.

At the Heart: Process

Computers enable parents and educators to pass along a set of processes for solving unknown problems and creating possibilities. Among the processes that can be effectively transmitted and used by each successive generation are those associated with computer use, that is, processes for using symbols to represent and structure experiences and ideas in ways that provide order and meaning in our lives.

> Process is more important than goals are to the continuing development of society. Obviously goals are extraordinarily important to the human being and his social organization—there has to be a reason "for." But processes transcend particular goals, particular times, and particular societies. They are transferable from generation to generation almost without being dragged down by semantic details. In a very real sense, they are the purest objects we can pass on to our descendants, because they aren't clouded by our search for advantage (McCorduck, 1985).

The search for a computer curriculum, then, is not a search that should focus on the computer but, rather, should focus on the curriculum. It is not a search for a set of computer experiences or computer familiarity or computer skill, but the search for a curriculum that puts *processes* for acquiring experiences and applying knowledge at the center. In doing this, the curriculum designer does not abandon content specified by the traditional curriculum. Instead, the curriculum designer, coordinator, and teacher views content as a vehicle for teaching process rather than an end in itself.

Computers provide the perfect learning environment for emphasizing process, since their uniqueness lies in their ability to process symbols. A computer has the power to process print symbols, mathematical symbols, and graphic symbols. Add a voice recognition unit, and it can also process spoken language symbols. The ability to process each of these symbol systems permits the computer user to devise descriptions about qualities of their experience. When these symbol systems are combined by drawing on the power of the computer, the computer user can describe a larger array of those qualities.

When interacting with a computer, however, the user is able to do more than just use symbols to describe experiences and ideas. They are able to bring these descriptions to life, to model the processes these symbols describe. Beyond the capacity to use symbols for describing, computer use permits one to experiment with process. Process is the heart of the computer.

> Computers provide the perfect learning environment for emphasizing process, since their uniqueness lies in their ability to process symbols.

So that is what a computer is—a symbol processing environment with the power to both describe and to model process. A curriculum which uses the computer as a learning environment for teaching process capitalizes on the unique potential of the computer. It teaches processes for creating order of experience expanding, not replacing or adding to, the traditional content curriculum. The traditional content curriculum becomes the vehicle for incorporating process.

A Computer Using Curriculum

Instead of objectives which stress understanding, knowing, recalling, demonstrating, identifying, and recognizing, a computer using curriculum adds finding, locating, evaluating, judging, modeling, doing, being, becoming, creating, exploring, discovering, and reporting. Once students "know" and "understand" the milestones of the American Revolution, they can become historians, sorting through accounts, judging their credibility, comparing different perspectives, creating interpretations, exploring variables, predicting outcomes, and reporting their interpretations. Once students have "discussed" and "analyzed" poetry, they can become poets, creating insights and institutions, sharing feelings, and communicating ideas. Once students "understand" genetic principles, they can become scientists, experimenting with genetic combinations, controlling variables, hypothesizing outcomes, and testing generalizations.

Books are good for accumulating knowledge, for understanding concepts, for learning facts, and assimilating how others have made sense of scientific, economic, historical, and literary experiences. Yet, no one has designed a "book curriculum." Computers, on the other hand, provide an excellent tool for exploring systems, for discovering insights, for experimenting with interpersonal communication, for writing, for processing information. The computer provides a perfect environment for assuming the role of biologist, chemist, physicist, mathematician, geographer, economist, or historian. Yet, there is no need to write a "computer curriculum." Rather, the traditional content curriculum should reflect changes which enable the educator to capitalize on the potentials of this new tool.

A computer using curriculum begins with the traditional curriculum, but it does not attempt to integrate or "infuse" the computer into the curriculum. It does not use the computer to provide drill and practice in math or reading; it does not use the computer to present rote concepts through tutorials; it does not use computers to chronicle historical dates or scientific facts. Instead, the traditional curriculum serves as a springboard to processes for making sense of the world we live in. Therefore, to the traditional content emphasis, a computer using curriculum adds, to overall educational objectives, such competencies as:

- Using computers and content as vehicles, students will discover ways to talk about and direct their thinking and problem-solving strategies.
- Using computers and content as vehicles, students will explore techniques for working cooperatively while attacking complex content related problems.
- Using computers and content as vehicles, students will become communicators modeling strategies for sending and receiving messages using a variety of symbol systems (linguistic, print, mathematical, musical, and visual).
- Using computers and content as vehicles, students will create meaning from information by using processes modeled during a variety of computer applications for searching, sorting, evaluating, and reporting information.

A look at three curricular areas may serve as examples of how these general objectives may be translated into specific subject matter objectives.

Language Arts

The traditional language arts curriculum is concerned with such things as grammar, spelling, punctuation, vocabulary, and letter writing. The computer using curriculum, however, turns students into writers. As students learn to formulate their ideas through writing and to share those formulations with a reading audience, grammar, spelling, punctuation, poetry, and essays come alive. They learn what to do with language arts content. The writing process changes from a mechanical operation to a vehicle for thinking. Much of writing is reformulation—making significant changes in overall organization, structure, and clarity. Reformulation is a form of creative play, requiring intuition, experimentation, and the reconstruction of patterns of thought. The writer asks a series of what-ifs, testing alternative structures.

Writing in a computer environment both suggests and provides writing environments more conducive to reformulation than more static print environments. Therefore, to the traditional language arts curriculum, a computer using curriculum adds such competencies as:

- Students will use writing as a vehicle for shaping understandings derived from studying the social sciences and the physical and biological sciences.
- Students will be able to reflect on their feelings through creative writing, and literacy experiences.
- Students will reflect on their thinking through prewriting, writing, editing, and publishing their ideas.

The Social, Biological, and Physical Sciences

An idea played out in a computer environment is regulated by systems of ideas whose range is bounded only by the limitations of human imagination. The computer is a tool which enables students to act out any idea they can imagine. Computer programmers, whether 5 or 40, are creators of kingdoms for which they alone are the lawgivers. Universes of virtually unlimited complexity can be created, and a system so formulated and elaborated can be acted out according to selected laws. Computer users, the business executive forecasting profit and loss margins or the fourth grader managing *The Whatsit Corporation,* become participants in a dynamic universe. With the computer as tool, they can experiment with the possibilities of that universe, test their intuitions, and create, understand, and evaluate patterns of relationship. A computer environment modeling a social system, a biological system, or a physical system permits students to see how complexity and structure derive from observed laws and to formulate and test avenues of possible action. This capacity provides the foundation for a computer using curriculum in the content areas.

A computer using curriculum in the social, biological, and physical sciences encompasses two areas. The first uses computers to involve students with software designed to model processes and decisions in these sciences. In these "microworlds," students are able to explore, evaluate, and judge criteria for effective decision-making. Examples abound. *Forecasting* encourages students to enter information about the weather and then test their predictions about weather outcomes. *President Elect* places students in the role of a presidential candidate managing campaign funds and planning strategies for winning electoral votes. *Where in the World Is Carmen San Diego* places students in the role of a detective tracking a criminal by following clues based on geographic references. *T-Rex* lets younger learners control variables like food, energy, health, temperature, and water to discover what might have killed the dinosaurs and to discover whether or not they can keep the dinosaurs alive. All of these programs encourage students to transfer knowledge of content gained from their textbooks to simulations of real-world situations.

The second area for computers in the social, biological, and physical sciences curriculum relates to information organizing and processing strategies modeled through computer use. These environments encourage students to become historians, economists, geographers, politicians or biologists, chemists, physicists, engineers. They become searchers, sorters, creators, and reporters of information relevant to the solution of problems in these content areas. Therefore, a computer using curriculum would add such competencies as the following:

- Students will become historians, geographers, economists, and politicians exploring decision making and then judging and evaluating the parameters for those decisions.

- Students will become biologists, chemists, engineers, and physicists exploring biological and physical phenomena relevant to how these systems work.
- Students will learn processes modeled in a computer environment for collecting and organizing information relevant to problems in the sciences.
- Students will learn processes modeled in a computer environment for using information to develop concepts and relationships relevant to problems in the social sciences.
- Students will learn processes modeled in a computer environment for using information to develop concepts and relationships relevant to problems in the sciences.

The Arts

Society is becoming increasingly reliant on the visual image. The more obvious examples are television and films. Yet, there are many more subtle examples. Many complex concepts are best represented using the visual image. The old adage "a picture is worth a thousand words" is increasingly relevant to the expression of many of the complex ideas developing in the social, biological, and physical sciences. A concept like recursion or reductionism in mathematics and science is easily communicated through computer graphics but complex to read and write about.

Working with visual images in a computer environment provides the user with the ability to represent their understanding in a different way. Many children and adults as well often talk about *Print Shop*—even when no computers are available. Those who do not

traditionally think of expressing themselves with visual images often report thinking of things they would like to do with *Print Shop* if only they had a computer. They have taken processes from the computer environment and used them as models for thinking about their world. Recognizing the potential of the computer to model processes for visually representing experiences of the world, a computer using curriculum adds art to the curriculum in new and unique ways. The following represent some of these ways:

- Students will explore and discover graphic and spatial relationships.
- Students will learn to represent their aesthetic and emotive understandings using processes modeled in a computer environment.
- Students will learn to integrate graphic and textual material to express ideas and concepts more completely.
- Students will use processes modeled in a computer environment to communicate information about content areas.
- Students will use processes modeled in a computer environment to enhance and publish subject area projects.

Conclusion

Since computers were introduced into the educational process, educators have been in search of a viable and appropriate computer curriculum. This search has seen the proposal of a programming curriculum, a computer literacy curriculum, a computer literacy curriculum, a tool-using curriculum, and a problem-solving curriculum. Most recently, the search for a computer curriculum has led to proposals for a computer integration curriculum designed to identify computer uses which support the established curriculum. Yet, all of these curriculums have failed to capitalize on the unique potentials computers offer to educators.

The focus in these curriculums has been on the computer rather than the curriculum. Previous attempts to create a computer curriculum have emphasized particular, established contents and skills for mastery of the computer. These curriculums have failed to recognize that the computer offers the opportunity to place processes for making sense of experience and a wide range of knowledge at the heart of the curriculum. Devising a curriculum which capitalizes on this unique potential offers the possibility of using traditional content not as an end in itself but rather as a vehicle for emphasizing processes for incorporating "doing" to expand students' experiences of complex systems.

Recognizing these unique potentials creates possibilities for expanding the curriculum in ways which push learning toward new horizons. In the search for a computer curriculum, educators must avoid limiting themselves to emphasizing computer use or supporting traditional curricular goals and, instead, use the unique potentials of the computer as a vehicle for *reinventing the curriculum*.

References

Anderson, H., Lampert, H., Young, J., and Malamud, P. "Where the Jobs Are—and Aren't." *Newsweek,* November 23, 1981.

Bernstein, H.T. "The Information Society: Byting the Hand that Feeds You." *Phi Delta Kappan,* October 1983.

Bitter, G.G. "The Road to Computer Literacy: A Scope and Sequence Model." *Electronic Learning,* September 1982.

Bork, A. *Personal Computers in Education.* New York: Harper and Row, 1985.

Committee for Economic Development. *Investing in Our Children,* New York: Committee for Economic Development, 1985.

Davy, J. Mindstorms in the Lamplight. In D. Sloan (Ed.), *The Computer in Education: A Critical Perspective.* New York: Teachers College Press, 1985.

D'Ignasio, F. "Building Computers in Your Mind." Presentation at the Arizona State Computer Users conference, October 1985.

Editorial, "Technically Speaking... An Occasional Column of Editorial Opinion." *Educational Technology,* February 1986.

Harvey, B. Stop Saying "Computer Literacy." *Run: Computer Education,* Dennis Harper and James Stewart (Eds.) Monterey, CA: Brooks/Cole Publishing Company, 1986.

Hebenstreit, J. "Computers in Education—The Next Step." Paper delivered at International Federation of Information Processing TC3 Conference, Delft, The Netherlands, June 1983.

Hunter, B. *My Students Use Computers.* Reston, VA: Reston Publishing Company, 1983.

Karplus, R., as quoted in Alfred Bork, *Personal Computers in Education.* New York: Harper and Row, 1985.

McCorduck, P. *The Universal Machine.* New York: McGraw-Hill and Company, 1985.

Naisbitt, J. *Reinventing the Corporation.* New York: Warner Books, 1985.

Norton, P., and Resta, V. "Investigating the Impact of Computer Instruction on Elementary Students' Reading Achievement." *Educational Technology,* March 1986.

Papert, S. *Mindstorms: Children, Computers, and Powerful Ideas.* New York: Basic Books, 1982.

Pogrow, S. "Helping Students Become Thinkers." *Electronic Learning,* April 1985.

Schiffman, S.S. "Software Infusion: Using Computers to Enhance Instruction." *Educational Technology,* February 1986.

Toffler, A. *The Third Wave.* New York: William Morrow and Company, 1980.

Weizenbaum, J. *Computer Power and Human Reason.* San Francisco: W.H. Freeman, 1976.

Westley, J. "How Texas Made History with the New Literacy Texts." *Classroom Computer Learning,* February 1986.

Priscilla Norton, a frequent contributor to Educational Technology, *is Assistant Professor, Department of Curriculum and Instruction in Multicultural Teacher Education, University of New Mexico, Albuquerque, New Mexico.*

Article #9
Does Programming Deserve a Place in the School Curriculum?

By
Karin M.
Wiburg

At a recent demonstration of *HyperCard* stackware, the sales representative suggested that this new Macintosh environment "would replace programming." This comment reflected assumptions made by many educators—that programming is a relatively useless enterprise of value only to future programmers. Such assumptions are based on experience with older programming languages, for example BASIC, designed only for general purposes, as well as an older instructional model that suggested teaching programming might improve problem solving, but was certainly not relevant for learning about other academic content.

It has become commonplace to criticize the teaching of programming and to suggest that there is very little evidence that programming activities can improve students' problem solving skills (Ohler, 1987). This lack of evidence is often used to support the position that programming is not of enough educational value to deserve a place in the curriculum.

I would argue that the newer programming languages, a broader view of programming, and an instructional model whereby programming is used to support learning other content should cause us to rethink programming's place in the curriculum.

While researchers agree that studies relating programming and cognitive gains have yet to show conclusive results (White, 1985), significant gains in both problem solving and academic achievement have been reported when programming activities are skillfully integrated with school curricula (Fire Dog, 1985; Clements, 1985; Clements, 1986; Shore, 1986; Wiburg, 1987; Au, Horton, and Ryba, 1987). These new studies emphasize the use of programming as a tool for exploring concepts across the curriculum. In addition, the educational programming languages used today are significantly different and easier than the types of languages used in earlier research studies. In fact it could be suggested that the changes are so significant, in both the languages available and the instructional applications possible, that previous research on the cognitive impact of programming may no longer be relevant.

What made programming so difficult for students in the past was the need for extensive planning and the writing of long sequential text-oriented code before one could even try out the program. New programming environments, such as the Apple Macintosh's *HyperTalk* and L.C.S.I's *LogoWriter*, provide easily learned user control over not only text, but also sound, image, and video, as well as the opportunity to create and try out small procedures and then stack together the ones that work. Using these interactive programming languages feels more like creative design than the repetitive mathematical coding required by programming in the old days.

A Broader View of Programming

I remember asking my son, at 14, to give me a definition of programming. He said,

46

"getting a computer to do what you want it to do." His answer suggested what I consider the essential aspect of programming—that of user control over the computer. Most simply, a program is a set of coded instructions that control the processing and output of a computer. This definition includes coding in BASIC, writing "macros" to control a spreadsheet's functions, adding printer codes to a word processing program, and creating a *HyperCard* stack.

This broader perspective on programming has been articulated by Gerald Balzano (1987). Balzano designed several programmable tools to assist students in learning to compose music. The tools use both icons (pictures) and text to control computer processing. Balzano has suggested that current conceptions of programming are in a state of flux and that his concept of design-oriented computing environments is a crucial component in redefining programming.

Any serious control over the operation of a constrained but rich environment requires an expressive power that approaches a "programming language." The language is just another name for the organization of control over that environment, the structure of the various "handles" the user has on that environment, both alone and in combination with one another. This organization can have a linguistic "feel" to it or it can be more iconic (p. 105).

Balzano goes on to suggest that what has made programming so difficult is the extensive need for planning when using traditional languages, before being able to effectively interact with the computer. With the proper programming environment, which he refers to as "concrete programming," the process of programming could become more like designing than programming. In such an educational environment the program evolves from a series of student explorations. Lines of code are easily connected, becoming holistic procedures, which are easily tried out, stacked in any order, edited and manipulated by the user until they do what the user wants.

The Merging of Applications and Programming

The programming process generally involves four steps: planning, coding, testing, and then debugging or revising the program. Writing with a word processor also involves planning, typing (coding), testing (critically evaluating the written output), and then revising. The difference between programming and word processing is in many ways a matter of degree. Programming provides a broader range of control over the computer output, particularly when the language used allows control over more than one modality. As mentioned earlier, languages such as *HyperTalk* have the capacity to control text, graphics, video, and sound.

The availability of these new educational environments suggest a redefining of educational computing beyond the traditional framework of "tutor, tool, and tutee." (Taylor, 1980) Instead, one sees a convergence of applications involving programmable tools, and programming languages that come with excellent editors and graphics tools. Bork (1985) suggested the merging and interdependence of applications and programming in a recent article. He and his colleagues called for good word processors as part of optimal programming environments. Vice versa, serious applications users can type in a series of "macros" to customize a spreadsheet program or program their own unique fonts for a desktop publishing project.

Perhaps an even more profound implication of new educational programming environments is their potential impact on learning by allowing users simultaneous control over multiple media. Hypermedia (Dede, 1987) provide new ways of thinking about our world that may be superior to a previous information delivery system tied to the linear world of the printed textbook. Dewey (1938) long ago suggested art as an integrative experience that forms the basis for long term retention of learning. Elliot Eisner (1982), in a series of lectures on the "cognitive curriculum," wrote about the potentially positive impact on student cognitive abilities when students work with multiple representations of concepts. Newer brain research suggests that presenting concepts in visual, auditory, and kinesthetic modes increases the probability of learning, since students possess a variety of learning styles. While Dewey and Eisner never considered the cognitive implications of computer use with its opportunity for exploration in multiple modalities, their theories offer strong support for the educational potential of newly available programming tools.

We are only beginning to develop the applications of new programming languages for both learning and the creation of teacher-developed software. To suggest that programming has little importance in the curriculum is based on assumptions that are no longer true, specifically that programming is difficult and developmentally inappropriate for children and that it is not relevant to learning or teaching about content outside of programming. As it becomes possible to click on icons and easily put together a sequence of effects that produce a personalized product, programming, like printing, can become part of every user's desktop. (In fact, we might call this new type of programming *desktop programming.)

Until recently there was inadequate hardware and software in schools for us to evaluate the impact of computer use on learning. Limited access time to computers has been the major reason given in numerous studies for inconclusive findings related to programming and problem solving. We have not had good programming environments, skilled programming teachers, or good instructional models for integrating programming within the school curriculum. With new programming tools and better models for integrating programming with the content of school curricula, the promise of programming to help students think may yet be demonstrated.

An Instructional Model for Educational Programming

We used an instructional model for facilitating problem solving in computer based learning environments (Gallini, 1985) in a collaborative university/school district research project involving the integration of the educational programming language *LogoWriter* with the school curricula (Wiburg, 1987). Gallini (1985) has suggested that two conditions are crucial if teachers are to develop successful computer-based problem solving environments. First, students should use programming to ask and answer questions about the content they are currently studying. Secondly, students must be helped to learn and articulate the problem solving process in which they are involved while investigating problems in such an environment.

Traditionally, programming has been taught as a separate subject, not as a design tool or as a means for investigating concepts across the curriculum. In addition, misunderstandings of Papert's intentions in providing Logo microworlds led to well-meaning teachers leaving inadequately prepared students floundering at computers. Teachers like myself have learned that many students, particularly inner-city children, do not come to the computer motivated and excited about problem solving. However, research has shown that problem solving skills can be taught. Shore (1986) found that when Logo was taught using a "guided discovery" approach, students learned significantly more, especially in terms of higher level skills, than when students were left to discover Logo either on their own or in small groups.

Therefore, our collaborative research involved 1) making sure students were engaged in programming activities that were about the content they studied during the rest of their day in the regular classroom, and 2) directly teaching students both problem solving and programming strategies.

After talking with the teachers about what they planned to teach, elementary school computer teacher Maria Wilson and I chose a number of topics we believed could be better understood with the use of programming activities. The topics included fractions, symmetry, word problems, whales, the Gold Rush, and United States geography. Students were asked to use a programming language to design products that exhibited understanding in chosen content areas. The emphasis on design is significant, and reflects an important perspective on the goals of the curriculum, as well as an optimal application of the new programming tools.

Eisner (1985) has suggested that if we want to teach problem solving behavior, we must develop problem solving objectives. Such problem solving objectives, like the design projects we suggested to students, provide criteria for successful solutions, but do not dictate the form in which students might reach those solu-

tions. For example, students were asked to design a scene from the Gold Rush using *LogoWriter*. They were given a goal, and taught some specific strategies for both problem solving and programming. As problem solvers they learned to make lists of the events around the Gold Rush, described the environment to each other in which the miners lived and worked, and brainstormed different solutions to problems the miner must have faced. (One of the more successful projects was the design of a giant flowchart by the whole class that showed the branches of an adventure story about the Old West.) In addition to mastering flowcharts and other planning procedures, students learned to write Logo procedures to control the presentation of different scenes in their stories, to program graphics and animation and to customize their own shapes for use in story scenes.

During our study a control group continued to participate in the regular weekly computer program at the elementary school, in which all students received approximately one hour per week of work in the computer lab. The regular group program offered students opportunities to use a variety of computer applications, but emphasized problem solving software such as that available from Sunburst and MECC. Students also normally got some Logo instruction, although during the months of this research, the control group was deliberately not given any Logo programming opportunities. In addition, the computer activities offered to the control group were not integrated with other classroom learning activities.

Results of this research were quite positive, involving evaluation of both student products and growth in cognitive processing skills, and showing significant gains in cognitive abilities by the programming group as compared to a control group (Wiburg, 1987). Studies such as this suggest that programming, when skillfully integrated with school curricula, might be a powerful educational tool, especially as we recognize the need to teach problem solving in addition to facts and concepts.

In conclusion, it seems premature to discount "programming" as of little educational value. On the other hand, it is not too soon to begin thinking about the sort of curriculum that would support student exploration of content in such an environment.

References:

Au, W. K., Horton. J., & Ryba, K. (1987). "Logo, teacher intervention, and the development of thinking skills." *The Computing Teacher, 15* (3), 12-16.

Bork, A., Pomicter, N., Peck, M., & Veloso. (1985, September/October). "Toward coherence in learning to program." *The Monitor,* pp. 16-18.

Balzano, G. J. (1987). "Reconstructing the curriculum of design." *Machine Mediated Learning, 2* (1-2), 83-109.

Clements, D. (1985, January). "Logo programming: Can it change how children think?" *Electronic Learning,* pp. 28, 74-75.

Clements, D. (1986, August). "Effects of Logo and CAI environments on cognition and creativity." *Journal of Educational Psychology, 78,* 309-318.

Dede, C. (1987). "Empowering environments, hypermedia and microworlds." *The Computing Teacher, 15* (3), 20-24, 61.

Dewey, J. (1938). *Experience and education.* New York: Macmillan.

Eisner, E. (1982). *Cognition and curriculum: A basis for deciding what to teach.* New York: Longman.

Eisner, E. (1985). "The educational imagination—On the design and evaluation of school programs (2nd ed.)." New York: Macmillan. London: Collier.

FireDog, P. (198 5, September). "Exciting effects of Logo in an urban public school system." *Educational Leadership,* pp. 45-47.

Gallini, J. (1985, February). "Instructional conditions for computer-based problem-solving environments." *Educational Technology,* pp. 7-11.

Ohler, J. (1987). "The many myths of programming." *The Computing Teacher, 14* (8), 22-23.

Papert, S. (1980). *Mindstorms: Children, computers and powerful ideas.* New York: Basic Books.

Shore, A. (1987). *Improved higher order thinking skills through guided problem solving in Logo.* Unpublished doctoral dissertation. University of Southern California, Los Angeles, CA.

Taylor, R. (Ed.) (1980). *The computer in the school: tutor, tool, tutee.* New York: Teachers College Press.

Wiburg, K. M. (1987). *The impact of different types of computer-based learning environments on fourth grade students' cognitive abilities.* Unpublished doctoral dissertation, United States International University, San Diego, CA.

Dr. Karin M. Wiburg, School of Education. United States International University, 5 Pomerado Rd. San Diego, CA 92131.

WHAT DOES THE RESEARCH SAY? Chapter

2

1. "What's the Research Telling Us?" Daniel E. Kinnaman. *Classroom Computer Learning*. March 1990. pg. 31.
2. "New Survey Summarizes What Top Technology Teachers Have Learned." Holly Brady. *Technology and Learning*. January 1991. pg. 38
3. "Computer Applications have 'Undeniable Value,' Research Shows." M.D. Roblyer, W.H. Castine, and F.J. King. *Electronic Learning*. Sept. 1988. pg. 38.
4. "Claims of Improved Academic Performance—The Questions You Should Ask." Richard Alan Smith. *The Computing Teacher*. May 1988. pg. 42.
5. "Computers and Learning: The Research Jury is Still Out." Gerald Bracey. *Electronic Learning*.
6. "Computer Education Myths and Realities." Gail Marshall. *CUE NewsLetter*. Jan/Feb 1990. pg. 1.
7. "Let's Do a Better Job Of Exploring Important Questions." Saul Rockman. *THE Journal*. Sept. 29, 1989.
8. "Design Experiments: A New Kind of Research." Center for Technology in Education (CTE). *Technology & Learning*. March 1991.
9. "Young Children, Literacy, and Computers." Linda Polin. *The Computing Teacher*. Nov. 1990. pg. 34.
10. "Individual Learning Styles Disregarded By Computer-Based Instruction." Gerald Bracey." *Electronic Learning*. Sept. 1989.
11. "Technology Integration for Mainstreamed Students." Mary A. Anderson. *The Computing Teacher*. Dec/Jan 90–91. pg. 6.

Having read the articles in Chapter 1, you now have a fairly firm grasp on what people are saying about the use of technology in schools—both positive and negative. It seems appropriate now to take the scholarly approach and review the research base to seek out some "truths" about the application of technology to school. Does it work? What does it do well? Are there things technology does better than teachers? Does it work better with some kids? Is it better in some subjects and not others? These are all legitimate questions—let's see if we can find the answers.

You would think that after 20-plus years of using technology in schools, there would be overwhelming evidence of its worth as a learning tool. If you think that, you're wrong—there is no *overwhelming* evidence of the value of technology. There is some evidence; there are research results; there are anecdotal remarks by myriad teachers; there are hundreds of articles about thousands of studies; there are stories of improved attitude, improved attendance, and "saving" of large numbers of students at risk. But for every positive item you read, you can find a contrarian who has found the opposite effect. Or more to the point, you can find someone who has looked *carefully* at the existing studies and found most of them to be wanting in terms of research design.

Much of the ambivalence of research results has to do with the different expectations of what role technology can play in the classroom. Those who expect technology to improve test scores have to create test situations that will measure that. Those who expect technology to change student attitudes towards school have to attempt to measure and report on their findings. Those who expect to use technology to teach *about* the technology have to measure that. And somehow, all of this data has to be analyzed and reported in a clear, meaningful manner. Do you get the picture? The reporting mechanism is confused because different people are reporting different things, but all the results are being grouped into one common basket. We've reprinted a series of articles that talk about the results as well as talk about the problems with the results. You'll find them good reading.

Daniel E. Kinnaman's article, "What's the Research Telling Us?" starts by telling us what's wrong with all the research projects (mostly design problems) and then in sidebar articles goes on to describe where technology research is being conducted and describes some of the studies. It's a good state-of-the-art article for the early 1990's and sets a nice stage for the articles that follow.

One year later, the same magazine (now with a new name) that featured Kinnaman's article published the results of a federally funded research survey by Bank Street College. This article focuses on what technology-using teachers have found as they attempt to integrate technology into their classrooms. This is one of very few reports we could find that dealt with the *process* of using technologies and the struggles to implement them.

In a similar vein, "Computer Applications have 'Undeniable Value,' Research Shows." by M.D. Roblyer, W.H. Castine, and F.J. King reports on their book, which reviews nearly all the significant research done on the subject over the last 25 years. This is recommended reading for those who want to devour this topic in more detail. Like Kinnaman, Roblyer et al have much to say about the quality of the research design used by many of their research colleagues. Nonetheless, using the principles of meta-analyses they are able to draw conclusions about the value of technology in the classroom and report their findings in this brief article.

To sharpen your analytical skills, Richard Alan Smith offers a primer on asking questions in his article, "Claims of Improved Academic Performance—The Questions You Should Ask." Reading between the lines, like so many others, Smith appears to be skeptical about research result reporting and suggests a series of "second" questions that need to be asked of the research reporter. How you get the opportunity to ask these second-line questions is another matter—but they are good questions to ask.

As you read through these articles, you might come to the conclusion that we intentionally only picked articles that raise questions about the quality and results of technology research. But actually, our hope was to give you a realistic picture of the state-of-the-art, and the state-of-the-art is a skeptical attitude about the availability of good, qualitative research.

Gail Marshall reports on the anthropological research done by her graduate students in the article, "Computer Education Myths and Realities." The disparity between what is said and what is actually done in the classroom (as discovered by her students) gives cause for alarm. The study methodology is one you might want to use to verify the status of educational technology in your community.

When you confront technology-using teachers with the evidence of confusion that the previous articles elucidate, they will usually respond with, "But the tests don't measure what technology is teaching my students." While this may be true, it also raises questions about what technology is teaching kids and what relationship that learning has to the curriculum that teachers are 'supposed to be' teaching. Another issue is how we can change what is being tested. Some writers are just now beginning to realize that it's time to start asking different and better questions in order to bring about changes in schools via technology.

We thought we might include some straight reporting articles on research, similar to those you will find as you do your normal professional reading. "Young Children, Literacy, and Computers" and "Technology Integration for Mainstreamed Students" will provide you with that perspective and give you insight into research that likely was not included in any of the previous articles. Don't let our heavily skeptical leanings bias your reading of these three articles.

Questions for Discussion

1. If you sat the authors Kinnaman, Roblyer, and Smith down in the same room to discuss research, do you think they would agree on any specific areas where technology definitely works?
2. Why do you suppose research studies are so often flawed in their design or implementation?
3. How would you respond to a school board member who asks, "*Show me* that using technology can improve the learning or behavior of students"?
4. How would you propose to measure the impact of the Hawthorne effect on children using technology? How would you eliminate the effect from your measurement?
5. Your Superintendent and Technology Committee are using research reports to justify large future expenditures on technology to your school board. You know that one of the school board members has read this book and this chapter. What do you do?
6. Why should computer-effectiveness studies done 15-20 years ago be eliminated from the research base that we review to help us make future decisions?
7. What are some of the untested concepts that are taught by technology but not measured by standardized tests?

Questions from the Readings

1. What did Kinnaman mean when he said, "They fault the comparative research paradigm for its failure to distinguish adequately between the *media* and the *message*"?
2. After reading the survey results from the Bank Street College article, what sense did you get about the ease of implementing technology into the classroom? What are the barriers? What support factors must be provided?

3. What are the "General Findings of Effectiveness" described in the Roblyer et al article?
4. Based on what you have read, are you willing to share these results with colleagues to help you make your point that technology can be effective to teach kids?
5. Can you think of other second-level questions to ask beyond those described in the Smith article?
6. Looking at Marshall's article and the results of her "anthropological" studies, why do you suppose there is such disparity between myth and reality? What could cure the problem(s)?
7. From Polin's article, what are the results of using computers in early literacy?
8. What did Polin report about IBM/John Henry Martin's Writing-to-Read early literacy program?

What's the Research Telling Us?

AFTER A DECADE OF STUDIES, WE CAN DRAW CERTAIN CONCLUSIONS—BUT THERE'S STILL WORK TO BE DONE.

By
Daniel E.
Kinnaman

During the 1980s, more than two million microcomputers made their way into America's classrooms. The number of schools that own computers jumped from approximately 25 percent in 1981 to virtually 100 percent by the end of the decade. And over half the states began requiring or recommending preservice technology programs for all prospective teachers. The "information age" has clearly arrived, and in the '90s the educational use of computer technology will surely continue to grow.

But what has the research shown so far about our use of technology in the classroom? A concise, yet thorough, answer to this question was recently offered at the 1989 annual meeting of the American Educational Research Association. At that conference, researchers Carol Williams of Eastern Connecticut State University and Scott Brown of The University of Connecticut presented a paper entitled "A Review of Research Issues in the Use of Computer-Related Technologies for Instruction: An Agenda for Research." The paper examined the research syntheses of Kulik and Kulik (1987), Niemiec and Walberg (1987), and Becker (1988), who themselves collectively synthesized the results of more than 500 research studies.

These researchers found that many of the studies of the past decade comparing computer-based instruction with conventional classroom instruction have been plagued with problems in design. From the ones that were not, they drew the following generalizations:

• students learn more in classes where they have some form of computer assistance;
• students like instruction more when they have instructional help from a computer;
• computers do not seem to change attitudes significantly toward subject matter; and
• gains in achievement are fairly consistent when CAI is used to supplement regular classroom instruction: achievement results are mixed in studies in which CAI is substituted for traditional instruction.

On the basis of their review, Williams and Brown conclude that while there is "some evidence that well-designed computer-assisted instruction can be more effective than traditional instruction, the findings to date can be described only as 'moderately positive.'"

What's Wrong With the Research

Does this mean that computer technology isn't effective enough to warrant its cost to the education community?

Not necessarily, say Williams and Brown. They suggest that the lackluster results may be attributed to researchers' preoccupation with the "comparative research" paradigm—the research model that pits CAI against traditional instruction.

They fault the comparative research paradigm for its failure to distinguish adequately between the *media* and the

55

Reprinted by permission of: *Technology & Learning* (Formerly *Classroom Computer Learning*)
© Peter Li, Inc. 2169 East Francisco Blvd., Suite A4, San Rafael, CA 94901

message. Under the comparative paradigm, researchers have a tendency to view technology as an experimental variable, independent of the instructional context in which it is employed: "Unless one's goal were to replace all classroom teachers with a superior and cheaper technology, [this model] provides [only] marginal information to guide the development of improved instructional enterprise."

Instead, they suggest "a number of potentially fruitful lines of research" to investigate the potential of computer-related technologies to enhance *and change* the way teachers teach and the way students learn. For instance, they suggest that future researchers:
• investigate innovative ways to use special features of computers and other interactive media to create a set of conditions for optimally effective learning;
• conduct more "prototype" research which demonstrates "the effectiveness of relatively small-scale, high-quality projects, carried out under well-controlled conditions and treated like experiments guided by theoretical ideas about teaching and learning";
• investigate the potential of computers to emphasize procedural knowledge ("knowing how") as opposed to declarative knowledge ("knowing that"). This includes research regarding student use of "real data," and the study of the effectiveness of "computer laboratories that simulate real situations";
• study the effects of expert systems and artificial intelligence in the classroom.

An Agenda for the '90s

Fortunately, the direction that Williams and Brown suggest for educational research in the '90s is already being pursued in a number of newer research projects. As you read the results of the individual studies noted on the next few pages, you will see significant progress in the research being conducted in the field of educational technology. New research centers have been established and, increasingly, researchers are going beyond the comparative paradigm to investigate the potential for using computers to create new opportunities for teaching and learning that might otherwise be educationally unattainable. It will be interesting to follow such research through the next decade.

Becker, H.J. "The Impact of Computer Use on Children's Learning: What the Research Has Shown and What It Has Not." Center for Research on Elementary and Middle Schools, The Johns Hopkins University, Baltimore, MD.

Kulik, J.A., and C.L.C. Kulik. "Review of Recent Research Literature on Computer-Based Instruction." *Contemporary Educational Psychology*,12, pp. 222-230.

Niemiec, R., and H.J. Walberg. "Comparative Effects of Computer-Assisted Instruction: A Synthesis of Reviews." Journal of Educational *Computing Research. 3,* pp. 19-37.

Daniel E. Kinnaman is news editor of Classroom Computer Learning *and coordinator of the computer education and dropout prevention programs for Windham public schools in Willimantic, Connecticut. He is currently completing a Ph.D. in Curriculum and Instruction at the University of Connecticut.*

Special Centers for Research in Educational Technology

Apple Classrooms of Tomorrow (ACOT)

ACOT is a long-term research project investigating the impact of high-computer-access (HCA) environments on teaching and learning. Directed by Apple's Advanced Technology Group, ACOT is designed to serve as a prototype for technology-based educational reform. Each of the five ACOT sites (Blue Earth, Minnesota; Columbus, Ohio; Cupertino, California; and Memphis and Nashville, Tennessee) independently determines how technology will be used, based on its own educational goals and methods.

There are currently about three dozen studies underway throughout ACOT to explore, develop, and demonstrate the potential of technology. For each of these studies, students and teachers have been provided with almost unlimited access to high-quality computer technology in the classroom, and in some cases, at home. Here's a sampling of the various research projects.

Writing. The focus of this study is to determine the impact of high computer access on students' development as writers. Researchers have found that:

• students write more and better in an HCA environment;

• the quality of instruction is more significant than access to computers in learning to write;

• writing regularly with computers can make a substantial difference among low-achieving students.

Student Thinking. Focusing on the influence HCA has on students' thinking, this study found that:

• student planning strategies are influenced by the flexibility of the computer;

• revisions in written work are more substantial in the HCA environment;

• students report that they don't learn differently in an HCA environment, but that they learn more advanced material and that learning is more challenging.

Student Empowerment. This study investigates the impact of the HCA environment on students' perceptions of themselves as responsible for, in control of, or as the source of their own learning (i.e., empowerment). Four classroom conditions were identified that positively affect the level of student empowerment: involving students in shaping tasks, working on large tasks such as constructing a model, working on tasks that are cognitively and socially complex, and providing feedback that is task-related rather than person-related. The study found that HCA environments encourage activities that meet these four criteria, and therefore facilitate student empowerment.

Center for Technology in Education

A little over a year ago, the U.S. Department of Education awarded a five-year grant to a consortium led by the Bank Street College of Education to establish a national Center for Technology in Education (see *CCL* "Newsline," March, 1989). The CTE's mission is to study, design, and demonstrate the roles that technology can play in improving student learning and achievement in schools. Its efforts are based on recent research in the cognitive, social, and instructional sciences, which have shown that "learning is an active, constructive process, in which the development of content knowledge and cognitive skills are integrally related." The following are among the many research and development projects the CTE has initiated during its first year.

Performance Assessment. By taking advantage of the capabilities technology brings to the testing environment (e.g., simulation), the research group aims to develop "project-based" assessments that measure higher-level thinking skills. A primary goal of the project is to develop "new testing situations [that will] create new goals for learning," and thereby induce curriculum change.

Women and Technology—A New Basis for Understanding. Preliminary research for this project involved conducting interviews with men and women judged to be "technology experts." The focus of the project is to explore possible gender-related differences in how seasoned computer users "understand and relate to technologies." Initial results show the importance of a "technological imagination" to being an "active shaper" rather than a "passive recipient" of technology. The second phase of the project includes development of a HyperTalk-based prototype learning environment, called *Imagine*, in which users can assume the role of designers and create machines for whatever purposes they wish. The project aims to provide the tools and the encouragement needed to help girls develop their "technological imaginations."

MECC/UM Center for the Study of Educational Technology

To promote research in educational computing and to make research results more readily available, MECC and the University of Minnesota recently established the MECC/UM Center for the Study of Educational Technology (see *CCL* "Newsline," April 1989). Thus far, the Center has released two "research bulletins" which together cover fourteen studies. Research Bulletin #3, covering seven new studies, is scheduled for release at the end of April 1990. In addition to their own studies, the Center also seeks to help disseminate quality research from other sources (e.g., ACOT). Below is a sample of the Center's work.

Lending Computers and Software to At-Risk Students. This project resulted from Minnesota's Assurance of Mastery (AOM) legislation. Students with identified "mastery deficiencies" received computers and software to use at home. Training sessions were provided for students and their parents to attend together. Initial results show that the computer loan program had a positive impact on students' progress toward mastery, and that parents' involvement increased students' participation in the project.

Computer Graphics and Student Performance. This study, involving 120 eighth graders, examined the influence of graphics on student performance in computer-based simulations. Results indicate that the more realistic the graphics, the faster students initially work (is faster better?), but that the influence of graphics decreases with repeated use of the simulation.

Project Explore. In January 1990, several hundred middle schools were able to incorporate into their classroom activities real data transmitted via modem from an international expedition across Antarctica (see *CCL* "Newsline," February 1990). The MECC/UM Center is doing a follow-up study among ten of the sites to determine "the viability of realtime data in the curriculum." Some of the data for this study were also collected on-line by participating teachers and students. A full report will be released in late April 1990.

A Sampling of
Current Research

What Computer Coordinators Need in Order to Become Effective Agents of Change

This investigation focused on computer coordinators who are attempting to effect change in the uses of educational technology while working on a "part-time basis" (e.g., "provided with release time to facilitate computer implementation in the schools").

Results indicate that, along with knowledge of instructional computing, effective coordinators must have interpersonal and organizational skills to facilitate staff development. "Tenacity" and "initiative-taking" are also important.

The study suggests that the most effective strategies for coordinators include 1) showing understanding and concern for the burden that change places on teachers, and 2) initially providing a high level of technical support, and gradually "weaning" teachers from dependency on the coordinator.

It also found that an effective coordinator produced greater student comfort with computers; improved teacher skills, self-esteem, and readiness for further growth; and teacher satisfaction with the program.

Source: Strudler, Neal and Gall, Meredith. "Successful Change Agent Strategies for Overcoming Impediments to Microcomputer Implementation in the Classroom." Paper presented at the annual meeting of the American Educational Research Association, New Orleans, April 1988, ERIC #298938.

Can Technology Help Restructure the Curriculum?

The "recitation paradigm" is still the rule in American education. Teachers present facts in sequence; learning is assessed by how well students can recall them. Increasingly, educators stress the need for a new approach for learning environments focusing more on guided inquiry than on "teaching as telling."

This study investigated the experiences of five teachers as they "tried to shift their instruction toward guided inquiry with the use of the computer software program *Geometric Supposer*."

Results showed that although computer technology is quite useful for teaching by guided inquiry, there are many obstacles that prevent teachers from using technology in that way. These include the need to design new teaching materials, to adopt new classroom management techniques, to restructure units of instruction, to develop new methods of assessment, and to reconcile new teaching styles with school policies that favor "discipline and central authority over individual initiative and invention."

To make the transition from recitation to guided inquiry successfully, teachers must want to do it, they must be given sufficient time to work through obstacles, and they must have lots of support, especially from each other and from an experienced advisor. As the teachers in this study worked through the transition process, "they found more ways to integrate the old and new approaches rather than having to choose between them."

Source: Wiske, Martha and Houde, Richard. "From Recitation to Construction: Teacher Change with New Technologies," Educational Technology Center, Cambridge, MA, ERIC #303371.

Learning From Student Evaluations of Educational Software

Though much has been published about evaluating educational software, only a few projects have investigated the value of student evaluations. One such study published in 1988 offers some interesting insights into the features students find most valuable in educational software.

The project involved 291 teachers and more than 2,300 students in evaluating 135 software packages. The following are among the conclusions reached by the researchers:

• student evaluations were based more on "difficulty" and "interest" than on "concepts" and "new ideas" learned from the software;
• there were no significant differences between evaluations by students with little educational software experience and those with experience with ten or more programs;
• only weak correlation existed between high student ratings and programs teachers said "should arouse student interest";
• simulations received high ratings more frequently from students than from teachers;

• tutorials and educational games received high ratings more frequently from teachers than from student evaluators;
• teachers and students agreed more on programs rated extremely low than on those with extremely high ratings.

Source: Callison, Daniel and Haycock, Gloria. "A Methodology for Student Evaluation of Educational Software," Educational Technology, v. 28, no. 1, pp. 25-32, January, 1988.

Computer Networking for Collegial Exchange Among Teachers

For several years the Educational Technology Center (ETC) at Harvard has been studying the potential of microcomputer-based electronic networks to promote professional interaction among teachers. In a 1989 report, researchers presented findings from two networks involving secondary science teachers.

Although the frequency of network use varied widely among users, the vast majority of the participating teachers reported that their network was a very valuable resource.

Researchers found that teachers were motivated to participate by both "social needs" and "task needs," and that the network was a "successful vehicle for exchange of information on specific topics." They also found that teachers sought information they could "apply immediately to their teaching work."

The report concludes that such networks are a viable means of promoting interaction but warns that a network "provides only the medium for activities." Activities must be customized to "to meet teachers' interests and to support the demands of their work."

Source: West, Mary Maxwell and

McSwiney, Eileen. "Computer Networking for Collegial Exchange Among Reseachers: A Summary of Findings and Recommendations," Educational Technology Center, Cambridge, MA, ERIC #303374.

Zaps, Booms, and Whistles In Educational Software

This study offers interesting findings to the debate over the relative merits of four types of reinforcement in educational software. Having the computer simply flash the word "correct" as reinforcement for a correct response was the control. The other reinforcements were black-and-white graphics, sound, and color graphics combined with sound. For each of these three types, the reinforcement grew progressively more elaborate with each correct response.

Effectiveness of the reinforcement was based on how long it held students' attention. For the first few correct responses, each of the three reinforcement types was significantly more effective than the control. However, by the tenth correct response, none of the three types was more effective than the control, and only one (black-and-white graphics) was as effective.

The software used for this study also demonstrated the correct answer for students whose responses were incorrect. Possibly the most interesting finding was that students spent significantly more time on demonstrations of correct answers than they did with any of the reinforcement types.

Source: Jaeger, Michael. "Zaps, Booms, and Whistles in Educational Software." The Computing Teacher, v. 15, no. 6, pp. 20-22, March, 1988.

Article #2
New Survey Summarizes What
Top Technology Teachers Have Learned

By
Holly
Brady

Who are the teachers working with technology in schools nationwide? What works in their classrooms and what doesn't? How do they manage their scarce resources? And what kinds of barriers and incentives have affected their work? A new survey conducted by the federally funded Center for Technology in Education offers some answers.

What have we learned over the past decade about using computers with our students?

That's a question that a lot of educators—both administrators and teachers—would like to have answered.

The Center for Technology in Education (CTE), a federally funded research center located at Bank Street College of Education in New York City, has just published the results of a national survey aimed at answering such questions. *Accomplished Teachers: Integrating Computers Into Classroom Practice* reports on a 16-page survey distributed nationally to 1,200 teachers chosen because of their accomplishments in integrating technology into their teaching. Respondents—over 600 of them—represent a wide range of subject areas in grades 4–12 nationwide. They come from public schools across the country in which geographic location, size, and economic level

Figure 2.2.1

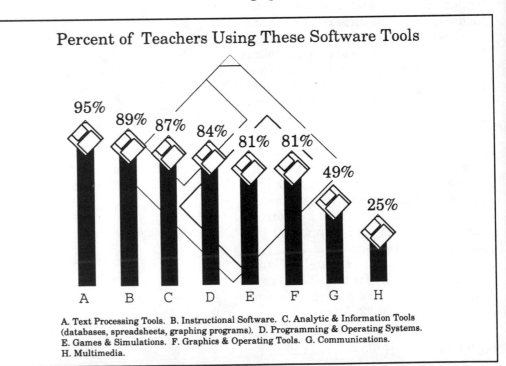

Percent of Teachers Using These Software Tools

95% 89% 87% 84% 81% 81% 49% 25%

A   B   C   D   E   F   G   H

A. Text Processing Tools. B. Instructional Software. C. Analytic & Information Tools (databases, spreadsheets, graphing programs). D. Programming & Operating Systems. E. Games & Simulations. F. Graphics & Operating Tools. G. Communications. H. Multimedia.

62

mirror national norms. They are not a cross section of all teachers; rather they are a special group recognized for their significant accomplishments with technology.

Below are some of the findings from the survey.

What Kinds of Teachers Have Embraced Technology?

• Effective computer-using teachers work in schools that have extensive technology resources. The average number of computers in schools where these technology-proficient teachers work is 59, compared with 26 reported in a recent random survey of U.S. schools. When broken out for various grade levels, the survey reveals that elementary schools average 39 computers, middle schools 53, and high schools 83 (as compared to averages of 19, 26, and 45 computers respectively in the random sampling of schools.)

In addition, these schools seem to be well on their way to investing in more sophisticated technologies: 56 percent of them have hard disk drives, 37 percent have laser printers, 33 percent have videodisc players, 33 percent have voice synthesizers, and 23 percent have optical scanners.

• These teachers have spent much time mastering computer-based practices and approaches—fully five to six years on average. The teachers included in this unique group turned out to be a mature and experienced bunch, with more than half between the ages of 40 and 49. Three-quarters have been teaching for 13 years or more. Most (73%) have used computers in their teaching for five years or more, with some using the technology for more than nine years.

Where have they gotten their training? Interestingly, 90 percent say that they are to some degree self-taught. Close to 80 percent have taken in-service courses offered by their district and/ or at school. They get information from software catalogs, computer education, magazines, and general computer magazines. They also attend conferences related to computer education. More than 80 percent have computers at home for their use.

• **These teachers are not working in a vacuum.** As motivated as they are, this unique group of educators also receives a significant amount of local support. Most (77%) report that they have continued access to on-site support and advice. This includes help from other teachers, from a school computer coordinator or from a district computer coordinator, or aide from a district computer coordinator, or from another consultant. What's more, almost half (42%) of their teaching colleagues at school are also using computers for instruction.

How Do They Use Technology?

• **These teachers use computers not as single-use machines, but rather as multi-purpose tools.** One of the most striking results of the study is the number of different uses teachers report for their machines. On average, these teachers use computers for between 14 and 15 different applications, with word processing being the most popular. (See graphs.)

What's more, these teachers use computers for a number of different educational tasks, from demonstrating an idea in front of the class to remediation. The most popular educational task, engaged in by about 60 percent of the respondents, is having students use the computer to make their own products—including reports, newsletters, and magazines.

• **The computer-based practices of this group of teachers have shifted over time.** The survey reveals clear patterns of use over time for certain types of software. For example, the use of word processors and databases tends to increase as teachers gain more experience with technology, and then levels off at about 5-6 years. So also does the percent of teachers whose students create their own products with the computer.

In contrast, the percent of teachers who frequently use computers for enrichment, remediation, and drills declines slowly with years of experience. About 30 percent of the group have abandoned their teaching of BASIC and Logo over time. Another 15 percent no longer use keyboarding, computer authoring tools, or recreational programs and games.

When it comes to future plans, about half the group report an interest in trying out telecommunications, videodiscs, and robotics with their students. About 40 percent say they would like to try on-line services, on-line databases, commercial mail systems, outliners and idea processors, music composition programs, and statistical programs. And about one-third would like to try computer-aided design, lab interfaces, and Hypertalk.

What Are the Barriers?

• **Although barriers to the integration of computers have lessened for most of these teachers over the years, significant barriers still remain.** It used to be that teachers' lack of interest in and weak knowledge of computers were seen as very significant barriers to better integration of technology into the curriculum. Now, however, this is rarely mentioned as an important concern. Rather, these teachers see lack of enough time to develop computer-based lessons as a major barrier.

Moreover, these teachers believe that there is not enough hardware—computers, printers, and other peripherals for

Figure 2.2.2

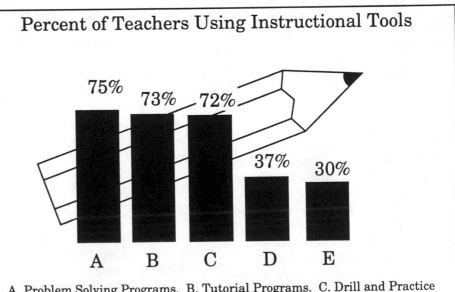

Percent of Teachers Using Instructional Tools

75%   73%   72%   37%   30%

A   B   C   D   E

A. Problem Solving Programs. B. Tutorial Programs. C. Drill and Practice Programs. D. Software Accompanying a Textbook. E. Conceptual Tools

them to be able to continue their accomplishments with technology. And they cite certain administrative barriers—including lack of financial support and too little help in supervising computer use—as factors in making them less effective as technology-using educators than they would like to be.

In summarizing the results of the survey, CTE researchers Karen Sheingold and Martha Hadley ask two important questions: Is it possible for the accomplishments of these teachers to be realized in fewer than five to six years? And can they be implemented on a much wider scale?

Their answers are clear: "We are skeptical," they say, "that the process can be made to happen quickly, although perhaps [it can be accomplished] in less than five to six years. To become expert in anything takes a good deal of time, and these teachers have had both to master the technology and figure out how to teach with it. In time, of course, increasing numbers of people will enter the teaching profession already proficient in computer use. They will bring with them the technical expertise and comfort [levels] that current teachers have to learn on the job."

As to whether the accomplishments of these teachers can be realized on a wider scale, Sheingold and Hadley believe so, "but only under circumstances in which there is enough...technology for teachers to have regular access, ample support, and time for teachers to learn how to use it...and a school structure and culture in which teachers are encouraged and expected to take a professional and experimental approach to their work."

For a full copy of the report, send $5 (check or money order, made out to Bank Street College of Education) to Laura Bryant, Center for Technology in Education, Bank Street College of Education, 610 W. 112 St., New York, NY 10025.

Holly Brady is editor-in-chief of Technology & Learning.

Figure 2.2.3

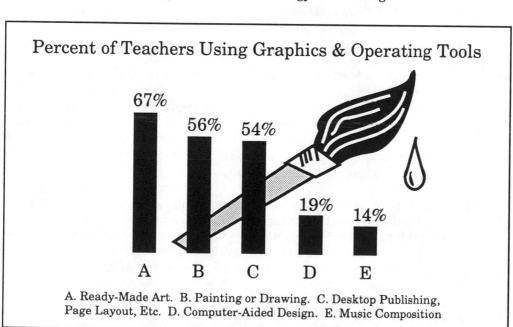

Percent of Teachers Using Graphics & Operating Tools

67% 56% 54% 19% 14%

A   B   C   D   E

A. Ready-Made Art. B. Painting or Drawing. C. Desktop Publishing, Page Layout, Etc. D. Computer-Aided Design. E. Music Composition

Article #3
Computer Applications Have "Undeniable Value," Research Shows

AN IMPORTANT AND COMPREHENSIVE, NEW RESEARCH REVIEW PROVIDES
SOME POSITIVE, THOUGH TENTATIVE, ANSWERS TO THE QUESTION: ARE COMPUTERS WORKING?

BY
M.D.
ROBLYER.
W.H.
CASTINE,
AND F.J.
KING

Editor's Note: *The following excerpt is from Assessing the Impact of Computer-Based Instruction: A Review of Recent Research to be published this fall by Haworth Press, Inc, New York, N.Y. as a special issue of* Computers in the Schools, *Volume 5, Numbers 3 & 4.*

The children of our society will never again know schools without computers. While technology's rapid evolution makes it difficult to predict its exact role in our future, the Computer Age has already had an irrevocable impact on our educational system.

School offices, like business offices, have achieved greater efficiency through computerizing clerical and administrative functions. Teachers depend on computer tools to help relieve their paperwork burden. Students learn practical computer skills as preparation for college work and for life in a technological society. And, while there are no measures for this kind of impact, such benefits have earned computers a unique and permanent place in our educational system.

If the hundreds of articles written since 1980 are any indication, classroom instruction has also changed as a result of computer applications. Teachers appear to be more willing than ever to consider using high technology in their teaching methods. The literature is rich with claims of unique effects for various computer-based methods, and some authors maintain that the new kinds of learning which computers make possible are actually changing the goals and curricular structure of education.

The result: a new, more effective education for the citizens of a modern information society.

However, society currently has some very specific measures for the effectiveness of its educational system: student achievement, attitudes, dropout rate, learning time. After nearly twenty-five years of use in instruction, the impact of computer applications on these measures remains largely an unknown quantity.

Educators Ask Urgent Questions

As educational decision-makers grapple with the fiscal demands of maintaining and expanding the instructional computing movement, they have urgent questions about the impact of computer-based instruction and other computer applications:

• Can computer applications help improve student performance in basic skills and other key areas?

• For what specific skill areas, grade levels, and content areas are computer applications most effective?

• Which kinds and levels of students seem to profit most from using computers to learn?

66

• Can computer applications improve students' attitudes toward school, learning, and their abilities to learn?

• Will improved attitudes translate into better performance in school and lower dropout rates?

Although computers have been in use in instructional roles since the early 1960s, the answers to these questions remain largely unanswered, and the questions themselves are often unasked. But up to now, lack of effective data has not curbed educators' enthusiasm for microcomputers. Since their introduction in the late 1970s, microcomputer use in education has increased dramatically despite the lack of clear evidence of the contributions to teaching and learning.

Educational leaders at all levels acknowledge the necessity of increasing research in this field if we are to make any progress in determining the unique role of technology in improving educational quality. In the meantime, it seems essential that we listen to and apply the results of research that we have.

The purpose of this review is to provide as complete and up-to-date a picture as possible of trends in both research topics and findings, and of the contributions of instructional computing applications to educational effectiveness.

Approximately 200 complete reports were gathered, although over half of this number had to be discarded due to insufficient data or methodological problems. Of the total number, 38 studies and 44 dissertations were able to be included in the analysis.

General Findings On Effectiveness

Available data indicate that computer applications have been effectively used in education, but more effectively in some areas than in others. The following sections provide tentative answers to some questions about the general usefulness of computer applications in various grade levels, content and skill areas, and with various types of students.

• **Computer applications and grade level.** The data results indicate that the effectiveness of computer applications varies significantly from level to level. At this time, however, it appears that computer applications have a higher probability of meeting with greater success at college and adult levels than at elementary and secondary levels.

• **Computer applications and content.** Again, some surprising and unprecedented trends emerge from this review. Use of computer applications in math, reading, and cognitive skill areas all reflected similar effects while science effects were nearly twice as great.

• **Computer applications and certain kinds of students.** A commonly held belief in the literature about computer applications is that they are dramatically more effective with low achievers than with regular or high achieving students. While this hypothesis has been substantiated in part by some past reviews, this study found no evidence of statistically significant differences between students on the basis of ability levels.

...Up to now, lack of effective data has not curbed educators' enthusiasm for microcomputers.

Another common hypothesis is that boys learn more with computer media, perhaps because it is socially more acceptable for them to use machines in other areas. Again, as the results of analysis for these groups indicate, there is no support for this hypothesis in the data from 1980 to present.

• **Student attitude and the use of computers**. An analysis of results reported on three groups of variables: self-confidence in learning (or attitudes toward self), attitudes toward school or subject matter, and attitudes toward the computer as a medium of instruction. Results of studies which presented statistical data indicate that computer use has a positive impact on students' attitudes toward school and learning. Since so few studies with data were located which measured student preferences for computer media and the impact on students' self-concept of using computer applications, results are unclear in this area.

Educators should not expect to justify the purchase or use of computer systems by effects on attitudes. This is especially true since no relationship has been established between attitudes toward computers and achievement. Results, to date, are simply not that convincing that students are more motivated by computers, and the relationship of student attitudes to achievement and to decreasing dropout rate remains unknown.

• **Differential effects with males and females**. While evidence is inconclusive that females learn less than males with computer applications, one trend seems clear: females tend to have considerably less experience with computers and desire for such experience.

Effectiveness In Content Areas and Student Groups

It is worth mentioning again that the sketchy nature of the available data makes all these findings tentative at this time.

• **Computers and the teaching of mathematic skills.** Results indicate that computer applications are about equally effective with both lower level and higher level skills: computation versus math and problem solving.

• **Computers and the teaching of reading/language skills.** Computer applications seem most effective in the area of word analysis skills such as phonics, followed by higher level reading and language skills.

• **Computers and the teaching of science**. Results in the science area were especially promising, even though only four studies were located to include in the meta-analysis.

• **Computers and ESL.** The overall picture in studies of CAI with Spanish-speaking students suggests that CAI does not seem to have advantages for them over other methods of learning English skills.

• **Word processing and writing skills**. While effects seem small at this time in this area, more work must be done on ways of maximizing effects on quality of students' written work. More studies also need to focus on measuring attitudes toward writing as a result of word processing and the impact of these

> One trend seems clear: females tend to have considerably less experience with computers and desire for such experience.

attitudes on how much students actually write.

• **Computer and *Logo*.** *Logo* shows promise as a method of enhancing cognitive skills of various kinds, and results look especially good in comparison with unstructured, discovery-learning CAI applications.

Conclusion

Revolutions have a way of mandating change while glossing over logistical details of how to implement that change. This has certainly been the case with the Microcomputer Revolution in education during the last 10 years. Research is the tool which can help make sure the revolution has practical implications for schools. The results of this review have indicated clearly that more is not necessarily better; newer, not always an improvement. The findings have also made it clear that computer applications have an undeniable value, and an important instructional role to play in classrooms in the future. Defining that role is the task of the next decade.

M.D. Roblyer is Professor of Computer Education and Co-Director of The Panhandle Center of Excellence, Florida A&M University, Tallahassee, Fla; W.H. Castine is Professor and Department Chairperson, Secondary Education and Foundations, Florida A&M University; and F.J. King is Professor of Educational Research, Florida State University, Tallahassee, Fla.

Article #4
Claims of Improved Academic Performance—The Questions You Should Ask

By
Richard
Alan
Smith

"Reading proficiency increased by over 22%!
Math skills increased by 21%!
Writing skills by 21%!
Our product was the
only variable!"

Accountability is an increasingly important factor in education, so there has been a big rise in the number of advertisers claiming that the educational products they sell will have a positive impact on students' academic achievement. This is especially true in the field of computer assisted instruction, where claims of effectiveness range from nebulous statements of "superior achievement" to selected research findings, such as, "30% gain in languages and 59% gain in mathematics." But before you purchase any system that appears to produce large achievement gains, you should examine the claims of improved academic performance found in the advertisements. Once you know what questions to ask and what answers to expect, you can interpret evaluation results presented in the never-ending effort to separate you from your money.

You will not need a detailed knowledge of statistics to discover whether, in an effort to make results look stronger, advertisements are reporting non-scientific evaluations in deceptive language. Researchers use specific terms to establish facts or principles; PR people often use the same terms just to make their products look good. By evaluating the claims critically, you may discover that no statistical analysis was actually conducted or that only selected findings were reported. You will also be able to determine whether the reported findings can be extended to your students.

Your first step is to obtain a copy of the complete evaluation report from the company. A written request on your school's letterhead directed to the company's representative or nation sales manager should get you a copy of the report. Use the following basic questions as a guideline for interpreting the report. If a copy of the complete evaluation is not readily available, then pose these questions directly to the salesperson.

Who did the evaluation?

Was the report done by the vendor, or was it done by a company or university specializing in evaluation? Any report done by the company selling you the product is immediately suspect. After all, the company has a vested interest in demonstrating good results. If the company did do the evaluation, the results may be biased because of factors such as the following:

• How students were selected for evaluation. Were they students in a special magnet school program, or were they in an average school?

• How the results were measured. Were teachers asked to rate the software as to its effectiveness, or are the results from test scores?

70

In any event, you should be more comfortable with a report done by an independent university scholar or a consulting firm specializing in determining the effectiveness of new school programs on student achievement.

Was the project used by students who are similar in academic ability and socio-economic background to the students you teach?

If the students whose grades improved are not similar in background to your students, do not assume that your students will achieve the same levels of success. It is like giving the same medicine to two groups of people suffering from a different illness, and expecting both illnesses to be cured.

Was a simple pretest/posttest design used without a comparison group?

Any evaluation that uses the simple pretest, posttest model should be regarded with a great deal of caution. Among researchers, this model is known as a preexperimental design, and it is not likely to measure skill improvement attributable to the program. One key weakness is that the pretest itself may cause students to perform better on the posttest with or without any other kind of instruction due to the practice effect. If no comparison group was used, it is not correct to claim that positive results observed are due solely to the exposure to the program under consideration. A comparison group might very well have exhibited the same positive results without having undergone computer assisted instruction. In such a case, the change in the level of accomplishment could be attributable to other factors such as the students' natural maturation or the type of learning experiences they underwent

aside from computer assisted instruction.

If a comparison group was used, were the students in it similar to those in the sample group?

This is related to the last principle mentioned. Consider the following scenario: If students in the comparison group (the group that does not get exposure to computers) are low achievers, and those who *do* get exposure to computers are average achievers, we're likely to see a difference in achievement, not necessarily due to the fact that computers were used. The same point could be argued with rich kids versus poor kids, private school students versus public school students, and so on.

Were the students in the study chosen randomly?

Random selection of students will increase the reliability of the results. A simple example of a random selection procedure is to write on separate pieces of paper the names of all students in a school. Next put the names into a container then shake the container and pick, without looking at the paper, 35 names. The students thus selected would be studied. (A simple computer program could also be developed to randomly choose names.) An example of a nonrandom selection would be when the school principal or a teacher decides which students should participate in the study.

Have you checked for the famous Hawthorne effect?

You probably remember from college psychology courses that the Hawthorne effect is produced when the people under study realize they are subjects of study. The subjects try to produce the experimental effect they believe the researcher expects. In general, this phenomenon produces a positive effect. The positive results are, of course, only temporary and not truly due to the use of (for our purposes) computers or any other planned intervention. Check on this effect by asking how the students performed long after the study. The follow-up test should have occurred after a time span longer than the initial program itself lasted. (A year or two after the program would not be too long.) The point is to give the test when students are no longer aware that they are subjects of a study.

Is the novelty of the computers producing the positive results?

Especially in schools where few out-of-the-ordinary events take place, the mere novelty of introducing something new will produce enough interest and enthusiasm to generate a positive effect. This is true with computers or any other educational innovation. Check the student scores over time to see whether they are consistently higher. Also see whether any applications of the program were put into schools where variety is more common. In these situations it is likely that student achievement levels will not be as high as in more conservative settings.

Were any other educational projects going on at the same time, or consecutively, with the same group of students?

If so, beware. When the same group of students is exposed to more than one educational project at the same time, or consecutively, it is impossible to be sure that any positive results are due to either one of the projects alone.

If a gain over time is claimed, have you inspected the scores?

Look at these Iowa Test of Basic Skills mathematics percentile scores. They are from a school in a middle-class, suburban community. The scores were published in a set of evaluation reports distributed by an educational computing company hoping to sell its product.

Test Date	Percentile Score
Fall 1981	59
Spring 1982	89
Fall 1982	75
Spring 1983	83
Fall 1983	77
Spring 1984	80
Fall 1984	82
Spring 1985	87
Spring 1986	94

On the basis of these scores, the company claimed that from fall 1981 (the date of the first use of the computer system) to spring 1986 the percentile score for the school increased from 59 to 94—a 59% increase, or an average of 12 percentile points per year.

Close examination of the scores indicates that you should not expect a steady gain of 12 percentile points each year that the system is in use. Rather, you might expect a great deal of gain the first year with modest gains and some fluctuation in following years.

Studying this group's scores should lead you to question why there was such a rapid gain during the first year of the program's use. Was this the novelty effect in operation?

Were any other educational programs put into place at the same time? If so, it would be difficult to identify which caused the increase in student gains and which did not contribute.

Also, it would be a good idea to find out why the scores appeared to be so low the first year. In this case, a written explanation provided by the company stated that the fall 1981 ITBS tests were hand scored rather than machine scored. It further explained, "It is possible that there may have been some measurement error introduced" through hand scoring. All later tests were machine scored, eliminating "several potential sources of measurement error." Thus we have discovered a potential source of error caused by the nonuniformity of the measurement technique.

By the way, those of you who are familiar with the ITBS are aware that it is generally administered once a year. When the ITBS is administered twice a year, as in the study under question, the results of the second administration should be closely inspected. The preexperimental design warning is applicable here. Specifically, the first administration of the ITBS may cause students to perform better on the second administration of the ITBS because of the practice effect.

Do the charts say what they mean?

Often graphic presentations are used in reporting the results of an evaluation, especially those evaluations that summarize the student test scores. Question what is being reported. For instance, slopes of lines may look like sharp increases in one set of axes and like a flat line on another, depending on the scales used (see Figures 2.4.1 and 2.4.2).

If average scores of students are reported as significant gains, make certain that the evaluation report notes a test of significance.

When the difference in the tested group's scores is higher than what could be attributed to random chance, statisticians call the results significant, or more precisely *statistically significant.* So the use of the word *significant* in an adver-

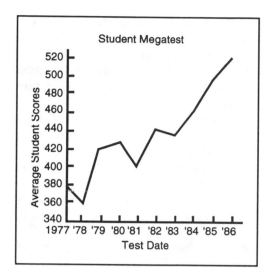

Figure 2.4.1
Notice that on this chart, the scores seem to have risen sharply.

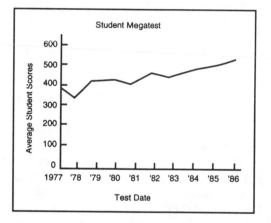

Figure 2.4.2
This chart shows the same scores but seems to present less student progress due to the smaller range of the vertical scale.

tisement is not to be taken lightly. For example, statisticians say results are significant if there is a probability of 5% or less that an ineffective program could have produced positive results. (5% is a standard measurement; some researchers permit as much as 10% error while others hold it to as little as 1%). Accordingly, you need to check the evaluation report to see whether a test of significance was done. These tests are difficult to identify and interpret if you don't know what you're looking for, so you may need to get someone experienced in statistical analysis to identify and explain them to you.

Has an estimate of the cost-effectiveness been offered in addition to the costs cited for the project under evaluation, the control group, and any alternative projects with the same goals?

Frequently you will see *"cost-effective!"* tossed into an advertisement for a computer assisted instruction system. The simplest measure of cost-effectiveness is the amount of money it takes to raise the average student's score a single point on a standardized test when compared to the amount spent on a similar group exposed to a different method of instruction with the same objectives.

Keep in mind that you can have a measure of cost-effectiveness only when you are comparing different systems of instruction with the same goal. For example, a good comparison would be a videodisc-based approach to teaching fractions as compared to a computer assisted instruction system to teaching fractions. A system to teach fractions cannot be compared to a system to teach grammar.

Make certain that the costs cited are comprehensive and include such items as maintenance and training in addition to the cost for the computer system alone. Bias may be present in the costs cited in the advertisement or reports of the company. Try to have the costs verified independently by asking the vendor for the name of a school that has installed the program. Ask the teachers there whether their costs have varied from what they expected; whether there were any surprises.

Has the project under evaluation been used as an addition to or in lieu of teaching presently offered?

Believe it or not, it is common to find claims of effectiveness when a new computer based instructional system (or any novel instructional system) is implemented in addition to the instruction that normally takes place in the school. The problem is that the gains in student performance are more likely attributable to the additional instructional time than to any intrinsic value of the computer instruction offered.

Are the vendors willing to guarantee you the same results that they advertise, or give you your money back?

This is the bottom line. Ask. The answer the salesperson offers will indicate what results you can reasonably expect from the computer assisted instruction system being sold.

Article #5
Computers and Learning:
The Research Jury Is Still Out

RESEARCH EVIDENCE STILL DOES NOT COME CLOSE TO PROVIDING PRESCRIPTIVE
DATA FOR DECIDING WHETHER AND HOW TO USE COMPUTERS AS ADJUNCTS FOR INSTRUCTION.

What is the evidence available to us in the fall of 1988 that computers can be effective, general-purpose learning tools? A recent report by Henry J. Becker of Johns Hopkins University attempts to bring together all available research related to this question.

Teachers Have Positive Perceptions

Becker begins by summarizing his own survey research conducted over the past five years, the most recent survey involving some 8,000 teachers and principals. Computer-using teachers perceived computers as "helping students to enjoy their school experience more and motivating them to pay attention to academic work." Four out of ten believed that student enthusiasm in school subjects for which they used computers was "much improved" because of computers.

They also saw computers as being highly useful to special populations— gifted students and special education students. Most did not, however, perceive that computers had been useful, at the time of the survey, to the average student. Only seven percent judged that learning in the usual curricular areas was "much improved" for average students.

In schools with a high proportion of available computer time devoted to word-processing, teachers perceived more

learning by above-average students than in schools with smaller amounts of time devoted to word processing. Drill and practice, on the other hand, was seen as beneficial primarily to lower achieving students. The amount of time spent in programming activities was not seen as contributing to improved learning outcomes in school subjects.

Earlier Studies Irrelevant Today

As Becker notes, the large number of teachers involved lend plausibility to the findings. Still, these are only perceptions of benefits, not direct measures of them. To get those direct measures we must turn to more rigorous experimental studies which compare the achievement of students using computers to those not using computers. This is what Becker does for the rest of his report.

This, of course, is not the first such undertaking, although it may well be the most thorough and most thoughtful. Becker points out that most studies in the past are in many ways not relevant to us now. Many of the early studies used mainframes and minis, not micros. In many of the early studies, those who had control of the computer and its software were researchers, not classroom teachers. Most of the software was primitive compared to what is available now. And, finally, the whole instructional milieu was quite different—word pro-

By
GERALD
BRACEY

75

cessing now takes 15 percent of all computer time, but was non-existent in the earlier studies. We might well expect different outcomes under the changed circumstances.

Yet, the literature that reports on computer-assisted instruction, which usually does so favorably, continues to draw on these older studies. "All except two of the more than 200 studies contained in the Kulik, Kulik and Bangert-Drowns, and Niemiec and Walberg meta-analyses were published prior to 1983," states Becker's study. "Even more significantly, studies involving microcomputers constitute only one out of 64 studies in the two most recent Kulik, et al, reviews and only two out of 224 studies in the Niemiec and Walberg meta-analysis." I would add that those two studies in the Niemiec and Walberg meta-analysis produced improbable results.

Becker Eliminated 34 out of 51 Studies

Becker thus sets out to look only at what the research literature says about the effectiveness of microcomputers. For his examination, he employs a technique known as best-evidence synthesis. Like meta-analysis, best-evidence synthesis generates a statistic called effect size. Effect sizes of .4 to .5 are considered substantial while those of .2 to .3 are considered valuable if they are consistently found. Negative effect sizes would mean, in this instance, that students learning from traditional instruction learned more than students using computers.

Becker limited his search to reports produced after 1984, which used microcomputers and which had achievement measures as one of the outcomes. Searching various sources of data, he turned up eleven dissertations, thirteen reports from school district evaluations, fifteen published articles and fifteen unpublished. Eleven studies had to be discarded because they did not compare learning with computers to traditional learning. Another eight were tossed out because they had no measure to determine how comparable the groups were when the study started *nor* did they randomly assign students to the comparison groups. (In experimental design, group comparability and random assignment are both important; studies lacking both are fatally flawed.)

Another seven studies were removed because they lasted fewer than eight weeks. This time-limit is arbitrary, but it is a characteristic of best-evidence synthesis to specify criteria for other researchers to accept or reject. I prefer longer treatments, at least a semester, while other researchers will opt for treatments even shorter than eight weeks in order to "see what is feasible." They argue that if you can't produce an effect in the short term, it is unlikely to appear in the long run. Finally, eight other studies were discarded because they had so few students.

Eliminating 34 out of 51 studies may seem harsh, but I don't think so. The methodologically weakest studies are likely to be biased toward favorable outcomes. In addition, I have found that many, perhaps most, people who conduct research on various aspects of computers are more comfortable with the issues of computers than they are with the issues of research methodology. That is, I find more weak studies in the area of computer research than I do in a number of other areas, and I don't find the editors of computing research journals particularly astute at detecting problems.

Results: Evidence of Effectiveness Scanty

The findings? The best study that Becker turned up compared mathematics instruction in grades 3 and 5. In this experiment, the effect size was +.48 in the third grade and +.31 in the fifth. As quoted earlier, this effect size is considered educationally significant.

The next best study was a "comprehensive typing, reading, and language arts program conducted in grades 1-6. As evaluated using the Metropolitan Achievement Tests, the effect sizes for this study are huge, averaging +1.00," according to Becker's report.

For most of the rest of the studies, the effect sizes are much smaller and some are even negative. Most of these though, also have problems either with the study or with the reporting of the study—important details of what was done are not described; important statistics are omitted, etc.

What are the implications of all the studies? Becker notes that most of the studies reviewed, flawed and unflawed, have to do with math, reading and language arts in the upper elementary grades, but that even if all of them were considered "to be without damning flaws, *together they do not come close to providing prescriptive data for deciding whether and how to use computers as adjuncts for instruction in these subjects* [emphasis added]."

Becker concludes that "the existing evidence of computer effectiveness is very scanty if we prudently refuse to collapse [consider together] such disparate studies as a system-wide effort to raise Chapter I students' math and reading scores, a writing project of a single junior high English teacher, and an evaluation of computer programming's effects on problem-solving abilities of

above-average achieving 5th graders." (These studies would be "collapsed"—thrown into one hopper—in a meta-analysis.)

Becker thinks we need a new model of research in order to build a systematic body of research that will tell us under what conditions and circumstances we can expect computers to be effective, and when we should look elsewhere. He spends the last three pages of the report describing a national study that he is undertaking to provide such information, or, at least, the beginnings of such a systematic body of knowledge. The study is expected to take three years to complete and cover numerous grades and subjects.

Footnotes

1. Kulik, James, Kulik, Chen-Lin, and Bangert-Drowns, Robert. "Effectiveness of computer-based education in elementary schools." *Computers in Human Behavior, 1,* 59-74, 1985.
2. Niemiec, Richard, and Walberg, Herbert. "Computers and achievement in the elementary schools." *Journal of Educational Computing Research, 14,* 435-439, 1985.

Reference

The Impact of Computer Use on Children's Learning: What the Research Has Shown and What It Has Not, Henry J. Becker, Center for Research on Elementary and Middle Schools, The Johns Hopkins University, 3505 N. Charles Street, Baltimore, Md. 21218: April 1988; inquire about price.

Gerald Bracey, Ph.D., is the director of research and evaluation for the Cherry Creek Schools in Englewood, Colo.

Article #6
Computer Education Myths and Realities

By
GAIL
MARSHALL

Myths are traditional stories, ostensibly true, whose origins have been lost. They are explanations of phenomena, and when we read them we're aware the events depicted may have occurred. But we're never quite sure. Larger than life, myths perplex us because they mirror reality, but a reality with twists and turns of fate.

Myths engage our attention because we want to anchor their themes and outcomes here and now by finding out how much is true and untrue. In the 1920s Margaret Mead decided to check the reality of a pervasive myth, the myth of the turbulence during teen years. Were adolescents around the world as mercurial and feckless as American teenagers? Margaret Mead wanted the answer. So the fledgling anthropologist moved to Samoa, then untouched by American culture and customs. Living among the Samoans gave her insights into the Samoan culture, but also sharpened her perceptions of American life. Anthropological investigations do that. By watching how others live anthropologists begin to question the assumptions of their own cultures. The result is a healthy examination of fundamental beliefs and perplexing issues.

Drill and practice has assumed mythic proportions in American education. Almost every educational reform proposal stresses the need for increased emphasis on basic skills. Drill and practice is proposed as a means of raising students' level of performance. So software developers have designed drill and practice software, schools have purchased the software, and teachers have scheduled students for drill.

In spite of the public belief in drill and practice's efficacy, research results are often equivocal. In a major analysis of computer-based instruction, (Assessing the impact of computer-based instruction. *Computers in the Schools* Vol. 5, Nos. 3/4, 1988) M.D. Roblyer, W.H. Castine and F.J. King said that if we're really going to understand the impact of computers on students we must stop looking at the results of studies and start looking at what has occurred in the classrooms being studied. So for several weeks a group of us looked at classrooms and examined myths.

To act like anthropologists we started examining the fundamental ideas about computers that shape our day-to-day use. We talked about how we use computers, why we use them, and what we expect children to learn. We found that our statements were shaped by our own philosophies of education as well as by our previous classroom experiences, both as students and then as teachers. We also realized we were shaped by the example of powerful teachers, and by the media articles and ads that depicted the ideal computer environment. We also found that we disagreed with one another. One person's ideal computer plan ran contrary to another's. What seemed to work in one computer setting was reported to have failed in another setting. And so we became "computer anthropologists" visiting local classrooms, observing what was happening with drill and practice software use, interviewing

78

the teachers, and reexamining our policies and perceptions.

After our time "in the field" we reported back our findings. All the "anthropologists" were teachers, most in traditional schools; some conducted training for industry and some provided educational activities for social service agencies. All were familiar with computer hardware and software, and were familiar with the instructional goals of drill and practice. We chose drill and practice use for several reasons. First, many of the "anthropologists" used drill and practice, were moderately dissatisfied with its impact, and were looking for clues to improve their classroom practice. Others, who had read research articles and meta-analyses of drill studies, had developed personal theories about why drill didn't seem to make an impact. They wanted to test their theories by observing teachers' use of the drill and practice software, just as Margaret Mead wanted to compare her observations of American teenage behavior by looking at another culture's teenagers. We wanted to examine the myths about drill and practice, observe the classroom cultures, pool our data, and see if there were constant realities that could explain our individual mythic perceptions.

Just as Margaret Mead's data served as a corrective to the myth of universal teenage turmoil the data collected by our "anthropologists" re-shaped our ideas about the implementation and assessment of drill and practice. The data provided a counter-point to the media vision, and surprised our "anthropologists." Holding their own viewpoints about the efficacy of computer-based drill and practice and having specific ideas about what works and doesn't work in their own computer classrooms, they weren't prepared for the range of implementation strategies and the differences between their own points of view and the views of other teachers. Looking over the shoulder of someone else's student sharpened their awareness of what students need in order to make sense of computer-based learning. They concluded that drill and practice use is not uni-dimensional. Drill and practice is scheduled in different ways by different teachers. Use of features, including analysis of student performance, is variable. So is teachers' behavior in the computer room. Above all, the field workers questioned whether drill has the strong, positive impact on all students that the myths have conditioned us to believe.

> In computer classrooms all students worked at the same task (multiplying three digits by three digits, for example) whether or not they had mastered that skill.

We offer several caveats about the data: Unlike Margaret Mead, who spent many months on Samoa, our visits were limited to a day or so; like Margaret Mead we brought our own assumptions about the way computer classrooms are supposed to work. What we observed has caused us to re-assess how we approach the delivery of computer-based instruction and, for many of us, has demythologized drill and practice. As one field worker said, "When you take away the hype and you substitute rigorous questioning of teachers and students, you begin to find people questioning how effectively they're using drill, and whether it is making a difference."

Now let's look at our findings:

• **Myth 1:** Drill and practice software publishers stress that regular classroom instruction should precede drill and practice computer use. They also recommend that classroom instruction follow the drill provided by the computer.

• **Reality:** We found that links between computer-based drill and practice and traditional practice were serendipitous. Teachers reported they used traditional texts and workbooks in the classroom, and covered the content sequences mapped by those instructional materials. In computer classrooms all students worked at the same task (multiplying three digits by three digits, for example) whether or not they had mastered that skill. The teachers' need for uniform delivery of computer instruction mandated that all students used the same software—and the alignment between what was being drilled in the computer room and what was being taught in the regular classroom was haphazard. Those teachers reported it was too complex to align the traditional classroom in order to provide a match with computer-based instruction.

• **Myth 2:** Computer classroom drill and practice use is matched to students' diagnosed learning deficits, and by using the drill and practice software students improve their performance.

• **Reality:** Many teachers reported they use the software available in their schools. Sometimes the available software isn't designed to remediate specific student learning difficulties, but teachers use what's available in order to maximize computer room use. When software is available, and this is especially true when schools have purchased the Alphabet City array of products, many teachers report that they assign an entire class of students to a strand of software, even though a significant proportion of students may not need the remediation. The teachers work on the wide-scale assignment principle because it makes better scheduling sense.

• **Myth 3:** Principals and other top level administrators are in charge of the schools' computer plans and they work closely with teachers to implement the plan.

• **Reality:** One of our "anthropologists" asked an elementary school principal for permission to observe drill and practice use. "We don't do drill in this school," said the principal. And, in fact, the school system has a comprehensive curriculum and the curriculum emphasizes LOGO and tool use.

But the observations showed a pattern of drill and practice use. Students worked on drill while the teacher corrected papers in the rear of the classroom. Interviews with teachers confirmed that little attention was paid to the district's curriculum because teachers' evaluations were based in part on the standardized achievement test performance of their students. Teachers were reluctant to "experiment" with tool use for fear it wouldn't produce learning gains.

• **Myth 4:** The large scale drill and practice software (programs provided by the Alphabet City publishers) advertise their training programs as one of the strengths of their products. In fact, school district personnel have commented that the training provided strengthened not only computer classroom training, but also teaching provided in the traditional classroom.

Many of the software publishers have developed one, two or three days worth of training to familiarize teachers with the software content and hardware operation. The training also shows teachers how to interpret the diagnostic printouts, tailor instruction to the printout information, and assess student progress.

• **Reality:** Many teachers said that while the training was helpful as an overview it was too hurried. Two or three days isn't sufficient to learn how to make decisions about assigning students to software strands, interpret diagnostic data, and align traditional classroom instruction. They also said that most training is provided just before computer use begins. Teachers reported they fail to understand the importance of many of the techniques and strategies discussed when training occurs, but appreciate the need for that information once they're working with the computers and students.

Some districts discourage teachers from requesting follow up training; other districts re-assign teachers who initially received the training. Instead of staffing the computer room with teachers trained by the software companies, paraprofessionals, who haven't received the training, are hired to staff the computer rooms. A major problem that results is diminished attention to the diagnostic reports. When teachers don't work hands on, they tend to discount records of student performance.

• **Myth 5:** Drill and practice software tests skills which students have acquired, provides feedback as a corrective when students make mistakes, and supplies teachers or students with a report on performance.

• **Reality:** Our "anthropologists" were more distressed with the reality of computer provided feedback than with any other aspect of computer-based drill and practice. They observed several problems with feedback. Many drill and practice programs graded a problem correct

or incorrect, but provided no feedback on how to solve the problem correctly. The result? Many students continued to apply the wrong algorithms, so they practiced their mistakes during the drill session.

In some cases our "anthropologists" watched the software provide the answer and demonstrate how to correctly apply the algorithm to get the correct answer. But our field researchers also saw the "Huh?" look on students' faces. In many instances the computer-presented solutions didn't register with students, and, as a result, the students didn't change their strategies for solving the problems, a prerequisite for improving knowledge. As a result, the fieldworkers concluded that many students spend the 10-30 minutes of drill sessions practicing their mistakes.

• **Myth 6:** The hardware and software provide a coherent framework for the systematic delivery of carefully designed instructional sequences.

Reality: Since teachers are human beings they act from sets of assumptions about the way classrooms should work. They hold fundamental beliefs about how to teach and how to energize learning. They transform the content and processes of educational practices to fit their own definitions of the teaching-learning process. If teachers don't believe in the instructional value of instructional sequences, they'll skip over them. If teachers don't believe young children can reflect on their learning or don't believe in the efficacy of allowing children to use their own language to learn more about language use, then they'll alter the design of integrated software sequences.

One of our field workers observed the contrasting styles of teachers in a Writing to Read school. Differences were noted in the teachers' provision for writing time, quiet spaces for speaking and listening, and hands on exploration. One teacher's room was quiet. As a result, students were able to discriminate between different vowel and consonant sounds. They wrote and listened to one another's writing. The other teacher didn't seem to discourage noise. The principal activities were physical. Students acted out stories, and shouted words aloud, but there was little fine tuning of their vowel and consonant discriminations. Words presented by the computer were consistently mispronounced by the students.

Thus the reality of schools' use of drill is complex, varied and often unpredictable. Teachers use drill software extensively when their schools' plans call for its occasional use. Actual use is at variance with published recommendations and key features (the feedback mechanisms, for example) were often disregarded. When used they didn't seem to be consistently successful in changing and improving students' adoption of correct algorithms.

Schools are complex. Using drill and practice software may be an appropriate educational solution for students' learning problems. But our "anthropologists" showed us that drill and practice adoption, implementation and evaluation (both formal and informal) must acknowledge the realities, and re-examine the myths of computer use.

If schools are going to use drill and practice (or any other type of software for that matter), then all the players—Board of Education, administrators,

teachers, students and parents—must have a voice in what's needed.

Administrators can't decide to purchase the software, contract with the publishers, schedule the training, send teachers to the training and then redraw the plans without expecting a problem with implementation.

School administrators need to acknowledge that drill use, like any other form of computer instruction, requires cooperative planning at every level. If top level administrators want drill, they must examine every implication of its adoption, implementation and evaluation.

If drill software is chosen the adopters should be prepared to show the match between the software and its actual impact on students of similar skills and learning styles. The adopters should be prepared to show how drill use is thought to be superior to other forms of instruction, and be prepared to examine impact data to test their assumptions.

Schools need to acknowledge that drill, like any other form of computer instruction, is susceptible to personalization. School staff must decide how they're going to monitor implementation, and how they're going to guide teachers to use implementation strategies that promote learning.

School administrators, teachers and others must decide the value of the diagnostic data provided by the software, and decide how they're going to use the data. One dramatic means of diagnosing impact is MBWA, management by walking around. Everyone in the district who has a policy-making role, and that means

> One dramatic means of diagnosing impact is MBWA, management by walking around.

parents and students as well as teachers and administrators, should be encouraged to become an anthropologist for a day or so. Walking around the computer room, looking over students' shoulders, and watching teachers' decision-making after they've analyzed the data should be the basis for analyzing what works and what doesn't work.

Finally, a commitment to review the data should be made. Just as teachers often fail to analyze student data generated by the computer, so administrators often fail to pay attention to teachers' and students' comments about computer use. If teachers start asking pointed questions about problems with training, or students say they don't see a fit between what's happening in the computer room and the regular classroom, then it's time for administrators to listen to the comments and act on them. Nor should the software developers be exempt from the data analysis and midcourse correction process. Asking teachers what works and what doesn't work in the training process should be an inevitable outcome of training. Looking over teachers' and students' shoulders should be part of the effort to improve the software design, and should be directed toward suggestions for successful implementation strategies. Then, having demythologized drill, maybe we can decide its role in the educational process.

Article # 7
Let's Do a Better Job of Exploring Important Questions

By
Saul
Rockman

Educational researchers who study the effects of technology in schools and colleges have been saddled with answering the questions: "does technology work: does it make a difference?" In a society that's looking for easy answers, that answer almost always lies with standardized test scores. But looking for the answers just in student achievement scores prevents us from exploring the less obvious but more exciting changes taking place.

Those of us who research the use of technology in education have important and difficult jobs ahead of us. First, we must learn to ask better questions so that we can identify important outcomes in classrooms—even if they are hard to measure. Our challenge is to get to the heart of what is actually being accomplished with computers.

Second, we must encourage the use of technology in ways that are central to education if we expect changes to occur and be accurately measured. That means that the data we collect must reflect what is really happening in the classroom and in what context teachers and students are using the computer.

Finally, we have to make a persuasive case to school boards, regents and other educational decision-makers that the information we have collected—even if it isn't a test score—may be sufficient and appropriate to understanding the role and impact of computers in schools.

There are research studies that examine the impact and effects of comput-

ers used for education and instruction for almost every grade level and for almost every subject area. If education and its implementation was a science, a few systematic studies that achieved consistent positive outcomes would be sufficient to persuade us that we should use computers to enhance education in our schools. We have that evidence. We know that the use of computers can increase scores on achievement tests; we know that interactive technologies can substantially increase efficiency in learning; we know that at-risk students can master higher-order thinking skills through the use of technology.

Unexplored Territory

But there are other questions left unexplored. How are students and teachers becoming empowered through the use of technology? How are essential social skills and cooperative behaviors developed through the use of computers? How are highly constrained classrooms changed by placing several computers in them? And how are relationships and roles within classrooms changing because of technology?

We should look at how computers can encourage cooperative learning or improve the attitude of students toward school and toward specific subjects. We should explore why dropout rates are reduced in some programs that emphasize the use of technology for instruction and why many burned-out teachers be-

84

come renewed and invigorated in their teaching after incorporating computers in their work.

These questions deal with central issues in education. They move beyond test scores and focus on how we want to define learning and learners in our society.

To deal with these questions effectively, researchers must define the instructional context sufficiently, so that they and others can understand exactly what is going on in the classroom. Perhaps the best way to explain the importance of the instructional context in research is to look at what happens when it is not well-defined. Let me give an example.

One study examined the effects of a computer program on higher-order thinking skills. Students worked on the computers for only an hour over a week's time, and yet the researchers expected measurable changes on year-end standardized tests. How much impact could an hour's instruction have on a comprehensive test? That amount of time is only five percent of one school week, with 38 other weeks to influence what happens on the final test.

In a study of the impact of computers on writing, the context was described by stating: "Students used word processing on the computers for 20 minutes, three times a week for a month." And from that description, the reader was supposed to arrive at conclusions about the impact of technology on writing in schools.

Which word processing program was used? How much training was provided? What kinds of writing instruction took place? Did teachers encourage collaborative efforts? Is four hours, over the course of a month, sufficient time to progress in a writing program? What kinds of students participated? Were students familiar with process writing or computers before the study? Was the time in the computer lab spent on writing or on teaching keyboarding?

The answers to these questions, and to many others, help define an instructional context for understanding what went on in the school. Only then can researchers—and educational decision-makers—draw meaningful conclusions from the study.

It takes time and an understanding of technology to take this next step. And we are getting closer to what is important. In an Apple Computer study of early literacy, researchers are asking questions about more than 40 variables in an effort to define what is going on in classrooms. Some questions focus on the school and classroom setting and the attitudes of administrators and parents; some look at leadership and support. Others look at the different instructional programs in the school that might influence what the focus classes are doing. Still other questions examine the beliefs, attitudes, skills, and knowledge of the participating teachers—their perspectives on the curriculum, the computers, and the teaching and learning styles.

> Our challenge is to get to the heart of what is actually being accomplished with computers.

There are questions about program implementation, such as what software is used in which classes, for how long and with which students. There are questions about the demographics and background characteristics of the students, their English proficiency, their reading and writing skills.

When added together, these questions help describe and define what is going on in the classrooms. Without specific information on the instructional context of the research, we cannot draw strong conclusions about the effects of computers on the curriculum and the way technology can enhance student skills, knowledge and attitudes.

Our society is asking tough questions about schools and is seeking to change the existing educational system. Technology can play an important role in that change process and in achieving highly-valued educational goals. However, if technology is going to play a meaningful role, we must help decision-makers understand that continuing to ask the same questions and expecting answers from the existing measures will be a barrier to change.

Asking better questions about technology's impact will focus our attention on answers that are salient to helping schools change. Researchers can help by doing a better job of gathering, reporting, and defining the data. But more importantly, we can lead by example and help other educators ask better questions and interpret the answers to those questions.

Article #8
Design Experiments:
A New Kind of Research

By
THE STAFF
OF THE
CENTER FOR
TECHNOLOGY
IN
EDUCATION

In a middle school in Rochester, New York, 30 eighth graders spend one day each week exploring the city of Rochester from scientific, mathematical, historical, cultural, and literary perspectives. Working in groups, these students conduct original research on topics ranging from weather to industry to theater to employment. They learn to use a variety of strategies in their work, including library research, telephone and face-to-face interviews, field observations, and experimentation. Later they develop a *HyperCard* exhibit for the Rochester Museum and Science Center, an exhibit that includes text, audio, graphics, maps, and music.

In a Boston area school, fifth- and sixth-graders who are studying the seasons collect shadow data during the year and record them in a computerized database. Later they exchange their information over an electronic network with students in New York and Japan and try to make sense of the differences. They also use a simulation program called SunLab to study the relationship between the earth and the sun in many different parts of the world at different times of the year.

What do these two examples have in common? They are both design experiments in a school-based research program conducted by the Center for Technology in Education—a program that goes significantly beyond previous research on technology in schools. Each design experiment in our study incorporates a number of high-quality interactive technologies that are feasible for school use today. Each involves the close collaboration of researchers and teachers. And each is taking place over a period of several years. There are now design experiments in New York City; Boston; Providence, RI; and Rochester, NY.

Analyzing the Learning Environment

Over the past decade several innovative research and demonstration projects have explored the use of interactive technologies in schools. However, much of the research has tended to look at the consequences and effectiveness of particular prototypes or products. Does the product get used? Can students and teachers understand it? Does it fit in with or alter the curriculum? What do students learn from using it?

We are attempting to produce school-based research that goes beyond particular pieces of technology or technology-supported curricula—research that actually analyzes *technology-integrated learning environments.*

To conduct such an analysis, we must be able to work over a period of time in schools and classrooms where technologies are incorporated into teaching and learning. We must also be able to look across these classrooms, schools, and technologies in order to compare them. We want to know: what constitutes an

87

effective technology-infused environment for students? How do different uses of technology for teaching and learning in classrooms influence how teaching and learning take place in a classroom? With a broader view, we can investigate how different constellations of technology, instructional purposes, classroom activities, and organization combine to create an effective learning environment for students.

What Is a Design?

In our design experiment research, the design is a plan, or blueprint, for how to integrate technology into the classroom structure, instructional goals, and learning activities. The plan, however, is not static. As plans are implemented, classrooms are closely observed. If a particular aspect of the design isn't working, it is changed. The entire process is then documented as the design evolves and is revised

For example, in the Boston school mentioned above, students who were trying to make sense of the shadow data from Tokyo and New York generally worked on their data in groups. Each group had a leader, a student whose job it was to report the group's views to the whole class. As the activity progressed, it became clear to our researchers that only the leaders of the student groups were benefiting; the other students in the group were not participating. So the teacher and researchers reorganized the activity, asking each student to use the *SunLab* software to collect relevant information from a different place in the world. Then a class discussion was initiated in which each student reported on his or her data. This turned out to be a much more successful way of getting all of the students to grapple with these complex and difficult ideas.

This process of design and redesign makes sense only if there is a set of criteria against which we measure our designs. Through our observations and the other information we collect, we are currently evaluating the experiments in terms of seven criteria. We believe these criteria are in evidence in the best technology-infused classrooms, and we hope that in publicizing them we give practicing educators new ideas for evaluating their own work. The criteria are as follows:

1. In effective technology-infused classrooms, thinking is stressed. We look for evidence that all students in a classroom engage in activities that require them to think deeply about significant problems and issues. Do students apply the knowledge and ideas they are learning rather than simply acquire inert information?

2. Students and teachers help each other to learn. It is important that students and teachers see learning as a generative and cooperative—rather than a competitive—exercise. To do this, they must work together and coach each other, in addition to doing independent work.

3. Students are motivated and are genuinely involved in learning. We look for evidence that activities are organized to engage students in work that they care about, to allow them to put energy and significant time into the

> It is important that students and teachers see learning as a generative and cooperative—rather than a competitive—exercise.

topics and projects of their schoolwork and to enable them to present the work publicly and to revise it based on audience reactions.

4. Assessment practices reflect the development of complex thinking and reasoning skills. Current testing practices, such as multiple choice tests, are often inappropriate for measuring student progress in this context. We look for evidence that progress is sensitively and appropriately assessed through performance-based tests, portfolio reviews, and similar techniques.

5. The learning environment is responsive to students. The learning environment—which comprises teachers, materials, and activities—needs to be responsive to the ideas, needs, and misconceptions of a variety of students so that they are helped to learn in appropriately individualized ways. For example, when a student raises a question in a discussion, this new idea may reorient or expand the discussion. We see whether teachers incorporate their students' contributions.

6. Students learn flexibly and well across different domains and disciplines. We are interested in determining what students learn and how they learn it. We use different measures in different experiments to assess effects that various learning environments have on student achievement.

7. The innovation positively influences existing practices over a sustained period of time. To be fully successful, the project needs to be incorporated into the school beyond the life of the research. We are examining how this takes place in the different settings.

Through our design experiments, we are hoping to learn how different designs contribute to effective learning and to effective environments for learning. We anticipate that there will be multiple ways to be successful, and that the various designs will produce different visions of technology-enhanced education.

The Center for Technology in Education is located at Bank Street College of Education, in partnership with Bolt Beranek and Newman, Inc.; Brown University; and Harvard University. Its core funding is provided by the U.S. Department of Education, Office of Educational Research and Improvement. For more information, write: Center for Technology in Education, Bank Street College. 610 West 112 Street, New York, NY 10025.

Article #9
Young Children, Literacy, and Computers

By
Linda
Polin

This month's column offers a closer look at one of the research topics briefly mentioned in the September issue summarizing the 1990 American Educational Research Association meeting. That issue is *emergent literacy*. There are three studies of early childhood computing to report on in the context of emergent literacy, though not all are directly focused on that issue. One study describes results of a survey of preschool computer use, and reveals in its findings the limited vision of computing held by many early childhood educators (Donohue, Borgh, & Dickson, 1987). In contrast, the Computers in Early Literacy (CEL) project is a multi-faceted project specifically investigating emergent literacy in kindergarten and first grade students (Olson & Johnston, 1989; Olson & Sulzby, 1990). And, because it is simply not possible to discuss early childhood literacy and computing without reference to the IBM Writing to Read project, evaluation findings for it are also included.

Emergent Literacy

In the 1970s and early 1980s a number of research studies explored the amount and kind of knowledge pre-literate children had about literacy. Some investigations examined children's awareness and understanding of environmental text such as public signs and product labels. Others studied children's book handling behaviors, invented spellings, and the drawing and texts children produced. They found that very young children actually know quite a bit about literacy activities and behaviors. Children make use of the environment to make sense of public signs and product labels. Children know that print has a communicative purpose, flows in a direction, involves patterns, and corresponds to speaking (Goodman, 1986; Mavrogenes, 1986). The phrase emergent literacy is used to describe the variety of reading-like and writing-like behaviors that children engage in before they are actually able to read and write, usually before age six (Teale & Sulzby, 1986).

Researchers examined children's literacy behaviors to determine where they came from, what supported their development, and how they related to later reading and writing. For example, Rowe (1989) discovered the manner in which social interaction between adults and children, and between children, influenced the development of children's literacy. Adults were able to model conventions of reading and writing by doing writing for which children were the audience, and by doing reading of children's writing, i.e., being an audience. He carefully documented elements of the teacher's talk and behavior that later found their way into children's reading and writing behaviors. He described the importance of establishing a literacy community and its function as a place where children could try out ideas about the forms and functions of literate behavior.

This perspective stands in contrast to the "reading readiness" view in which children become ready to read when

90

they have mastered prerequisite subskills (e.g., in visual perception). Emergent literacy also disputes earlier theories that proposed a developmental sequence in which reading preceded writing. "We now have substantial evidence to indicate that there exists a dynamic relation between writing and reading, because each influences the other on the course of development, and that reading comprehension is engaged in during writing (through reading one's own writing) and is not a trivial matter" (Teale & Sulzby, 1986).

Many of the ideas associated with emergent literacy have their roots in the whole language movement in writing and reading (Goodman, 1986). Both emphasize the need for students to experience writing and reading in a variety of contexts and forms, but always complete and meaningful. Both emphasize the interdependence of reading, writing, speaking, and listening. For further reading, Cathy Gunn has published an annotated bibliography of readings on whole language (Gunn, 1990).

Computers in Early Literacy

The most promising piece of research on young children, literacy, and computers is still in process; only preliminary results from the first year's pilot study have been released. The CEL project (Computers in Early Literacy) is important because it provides the theoretical basis and research support for the use of computers with young children, specifically as a tool for engaging children in emergent literacy activities.

The project provided an Apple IIGS to a kindergarten and three GS machines to a first grade classroom. The kindergartners used *Color Me* graphics software and the *Muppet Slate* word proces-

sor; the first graders used *Magic Slate*. Students were free to choose time at the computer center just as they might choose time at any of the other centers in the classroom. Interestingly, there was a sharp distinction in the attractiveness of the computer center. Approximately one-third of the children sustained a strong interest in the computer, using it several times (4-8) a week; the balance of the class rarely used it.

In both classrooms students engaged "in a variety of patterns of use and forms of writing" at the computers. They used the graphics programs to draw, but also to "enact stories" and create illustrations for paper and pencil stories. They used the word-processing software to generate letter strings, whose patterns tended to echo the keyboard layout or environmental print in the room. Some letter strings were described as part of "playing typist" and others represented stories.

When compared with paper and pencil activities, the computer versions showed some interesting differences. Students composed stories on the word-processor just as they might with paper and pencil, but where the letter forms were often scribbles or inaccurate reproductions of letters when done by hand, on computer, these stories were composed of real letters. This seemed to please the children. The researchers also noticed that children made use of the space bar to indicate words, and the shift key to explore the upper and lower case values of letters. Also, children sounded out or pronounced letter names much more often when on computer, paused to reread more often, and generally revised their typing more often too. The researchers caution that these differences may be functional artifacts of computer use. For example, pausing to reread may serve to relocate one's place on screen; naming letters may help students remember as they search the keyboard for the right key. Nevertheless, these are important elements of early literacy, and their abundance in the computer center is taken as a real computer advantage. One important source of literacy activities for young children is collaboration, either with adults or peers, through sharing and watching. A lot of interaction took place at the computers, little of it true collaboration. Most talk involved a waiting student who might provide audience commentary, or technical assistance.

First graders developed and made use of a culture of computer expertise in which "any student could be a resource. Whenever one child discovered a new function...the news spread quickly." Despite their resident experts, students experienced some problems with the more advanced word-processing software, largely due to confusions of overchoice. They also found any command involving extensive cursor movement in the text to be difficult to track. Word-wrap and text scrolling off screen made them uncomfortable. Nevertheless, students on computer wrote longer stories than with pencil. They also stopped to reread and alter text, although revision was almost always done in process rather than by recalling and editing a saved document. Researchers attribute many of these observations to the influence of paired work at the computer, suggesting that "while the roles varied from one pairing to the next, there were almost always opportunities for each member to scaffold the other in one aspect or other of the writing process." When asked which they preferred, computer or pencil, students gave a slight edge to the computer (20 to 15), attributing greater ease, efficiency, and aesthetic quality to their computer-generated work.

Survey of Early Childhood Computing

In the opening of their article, Donohue, Borgh, and Dickson (1987) report little "hard research" on the impact of computers in early childhood education, but a plethora of opinions about the possible contribution computers can make. "...Some of the strongest arguments for preschoolers' use of the computer emphasize gains to be made in the area of socio-emotional development, which are then linked to cognitive development." Donohue et al. ask and leave unanswered the question of whether or not "there are any meaningful problems or projects for young children that can best be solved by using a computer?"

Apparently many share this skepticism; computer use among young children is still fairly uncommon. When Donohue and his colleagues surveyed 124 preschool programs in one county of Wisconsin, they found only 24 programs that actually had computers, and only 18 of those (14.5%) allowed students to use the computers. Surprisingly, those eighteen were fairly representative of the socioeconomic and ethnic variation in the county. Children in wealthier neighborhoods did not have disproportionately greater access to computers than children from low income areas.

Directors of the eighteen computer-using programs were interviewed about their programs. They indicated that children most often worked in pairs at the computer as one of many free choice activities. Time available for computer activities varied widely across programs. It is not clear whether the researchers did not choose to ask or the directors did not have information on the nature of

the computer activities students participated in. Perhaps because the researchers chose to speak with program directors rather than teachers, the responses
they got focused on teacher training,
supervision, scheduling, and security.
The main software concerns were difficulties finding age appropriate software,
the relatively high cost of software given
the program budget, and resources for
finding out about good programs. Fortunately, the Project High/Scope (Perry
Preschool) Cognitive Curriculum, a
dominant influence on early childhood
programs, has recently published a critical review of early childhood software
(High/Scope, 1989).

Longitudinal Data on Early Computing and Literacy

Writing to Read, based upon the work of
Dr. John Henry Martin, argues that
children can write what they can say
and read what they can write. To serve
this view of literacy learning, Writing to
Read sets up five centers for a variety of
activities: a computer station where children listen and talk; a work journal
station where they record new words in
their journals and learn new words with
similar sounds; a listening library station with tapes of Caldecott award winning stories and songs; a typing station
where children may generate their own
prose about anything they choose; and a
make words station that contains materials for art project constructions involving words.

The data from the annual and longitudinal views of Writing to Read projects
look very good. In 1984, Educational
Testing Service concluded that students
who had been through the project in
kindergarten outperformed their comparison group peers in writing (by writing sample) and reading (standardized

test), and were comparable (neither better nor worse) than peers on spelling
tests. The spelling information was important to educators who worried that
invented spellings might somehow last
in children's minds as correct spellings.
When project graduates were compared
in first grade with peers who had not
experienced the program, advantages
remained in writing, but not in reading.
The 1989 report released by IBM con-
tends that these initial findings extend
through second grade. Nevertheless, the
evaluation data reported by ETS and
IBM have come under fire by a few
critics who argue that the research methods were questionable, the demonstrated
gains of relatively little importance, and
the costs prohibitive to other means of
achieving the same effects (West, 1990).

The IBM project does enact a good bit
of what emergent literacy proponents
find important for young children to
experience. It mixes reading, writing,
listening, and speaking as mutually reinforcing literacy processes. It provides
models and sharing of literacy activities; it allows invented spellings. However, there are some places the project
departs from emergent literacy, especially in its belief that "using 42 phonemes (letter-sound combinations) as
building blocks, children discover that
the sounds of speech can be made visible
in writing." This decoding/encoding view
of reading and writing is not found among
the views held by emergent literacy and
whole language educators.

*We welcome your help in locating ap-
propriate research to summarize in
this column. To send copies of papers or
reports, or for further information about
the studies in the column, contact Linda
Polin, Pepperdine University - GSEP.
400 Corporate Pointe, Culver City, CA
90230*

Article #10
Individual Learning Styles
Disregarded By Computer-Based Instruction

WHILE SOME STUDENTS BENEFIT FROM COMPUTER-ASSISTED
INSTRUCTION, MANY OTHERS WITH DIFFERENT APTITUDES DON'T.

By
GERALD
BRACEY

American psychological and educational research has been characterized by two main approaches. In one approach, researchers have looked for general laws; Freud, Piaget and Clark Hull, for example, looked for laws of personality, child development, and learning that applied to all people.

In the other line of study, researchers have looked at individual differences. They argue that "general laws" are really conditional laws and affect people differently depending on whether those people are introverts or extroverts, impulsive or reflective, have a high IQ or low IQ, etc.

Although researchers interested in individual differences have dominated educational research in general, much, if not most, work concerning computer-assisted instruction (CAI) has been of the general law variety.

Researchers have asked: "Does CAI work better than traditional instruction?" Seymour Papert, among others, has railed against looking for *the* effect of *the* computer (the general law approach). But it seems to me that there are more studies looking for the effect of the computer than those looking for differential effects on different groups. As one recent article put it: "Research about computers in schools often treats this subject as if it were a unitary issue, ignoring the differences among students that may make learning with computers highly effective for certain individuals,

and quite ineffective for others."

This column takes a look at a recent study that shows how CAI approaches, which don't take into consideration the different learning styles of children, help some students but hinder others.

Many past studies have focused on the differential impact of drill and practice on students of different abilities. Here, as is so often the case in research, the results show a mixed bag. There is a slight trend to indicate that drill-and-practice CAI programs are effective for low-achieving students but not for high-achieving students. But there may be a bias in these studies. Many people in the field of computer research feel that drill and practice is a useful tool for low-achieving students and tend to study only that student group, missing the useful comparisons with high-achieving students.

The Study

A recent study approached the problem differently. In this study the same CAI system provided instruction to students of all achievement levels, but the students did not use the same level of instruction.

Children were examined from the end of third grade to the end of sixth grade, and those who were defined as high achievers at the start of the experiment gained anywhere from 1.8 to 2.6 times as much as did the low-achievers. These

94

results, writes the author, "show that good students progress in solving difficult problems about two times faster than poor students progress in solving relatively easy exercises. The result is that the discrepancy in the levels between students with extreme abilities attending the same class grows continually with the years of CAI practice."

To this point, there is nothing surprising in the results. In many instances, high-ability students do more with a given set of experiences than low-ability students. Indeed, the differential learning rate between the groups is probably the best definition of ability. But now the researcher embarked on a different path than usual: she set out to find out *why* there were differential results for the groups.

She sat down next to the students while they used the computer and often conducted short interviews after they had finished. She plotted their progress over time and looked for patterns in their answers.

High-Achieving Students

Some high-achieving students did well because they were good at making online deductions as they progressed through a strand of problems, using the solutions of easier problems to allow them to deduce the answer to the harder ones. Others were aided by their ability to better remember problems they had solved, and their willingness to seek help from teachers, parents, or peers outside the lab concerning problems they couldn't solve.

Low-Achieving Students

Unlike the high-achieving students who showed direct advancement from level to level or only occasional regressions to lower levels, low-achieving students had different patterns of success and failure.

They were more likely to oscillate between two consecutive levels for several sessions, and to regress two or more levels in consecutive sessions. This would mean that while these students had apparently "mastered" a particular skill or set of skills in one session, when they returned, the "mastery" had disappeared.

Observation of low-achieving children revealed several patterns of errors. They were less able to deduce answers from the problem or from seeing a correct answer, and were less able to remember a given algorithm over time.

One common error was to reverse the right sequence for entering answers (typing 45 instead of 54). Beyond this there were idiosyncratic problems such as one student who had a tendency to daydream while at the terminal and missed the time deadline for entering answers. Another talked to himself and to other students. A third tended to "play" the keyboard like it was a piano, often sliding over several keys before hitting the intended one and entering the wrong answer unintentionally. Some of these students showed higher achievement when assessed by paper and pencil tests than when tested using the computers.

> Some of these students showed higher achievement when assessed by paper and pencil tests than when tested using the computers.

Conclusions

"When a student begins work with the computer system," the author writes, "he or she has to make an 'internal switch' from the regular mode of work with paper and pencil to the special mode of computer work. It appears that our low-achievers were not able to regularly make that type of on-and-off switch. These students showed less flexibility than high-achievers, thus making more software- and hardware-related errors."

After teasing out some characteristics of inefficiency in dealing with the computer, the researcher and the teacher tutored one child for a few hours on a strand where the child was stuck. The tutoring was done with paper and pencil exercises. The child solved all of the problems she could not solve at the computer as well as problems several levels above that strand. When she returned to the computer, she became stuck on the lower level again. "We may therefore conclude that her child-machine problems overpowered all remedial efforts," says the author.

"As long as a CAI system for individualized learning works in a uniform mode for all students," the author concludes, "there will always be students who benefit from some particular type of work while other students, with different aptitudes and styles of learning, will face problems working in that particular mode."

Reference

Nira Hativa, "Computer-Based Drill and Practice: Widening the Gap Between High- and Low-Achieving Students," *American Educational Research Journal,* Fall, 1988.

Gerald Bracey, Ph. D., is the director of research and evaluation for the Cherry Creek Schools in Engelwood, Colo.

Technology Integration for Mainstreamed Students

BY
MARY A.
ANDERSON

In 1986 the U.S. Department of Education, Office of Special Education Programs (OSEP) called for research to improve the integration of technology, particularly to assist students with mild handicaps in mainstreamed classrooms. OSEP asked for studies to investigate school-based examples of successful integration of technology and to develop models for local education agencies (LEA) to use in classrooms that include students with mild handicaps.

The student with mild handicaps typically spends the majority or a significant amount of the school day learning academic subjects in the mainstreamed classroom. Both regular and special education teachers are responsible for his or her education. The student may have learning disabilities, mental handicaps, or behavioral or emotional disorders.

This article highlights teacher practices in successful integration of technology found in three studies performed by Johns Hopkins University researchers, Education Development Center, Inc. and Technical Education Research Center (EDC/TERC), and Macro Systems, Inc. (Macro). Because each of the studies focuses on a different school level, I also elaborate on some of the specific findings from each of the research projects.

What Is Integration of Technology?

All three studies agree that the entire school system needs to commit to using technology to deliver the curriculum and to develop and nurture academic skills at successive grade levels. Many classroom teachers use computers and other forms of technology in their classrooms. However, technology integration is more than this. It must include administrative policies and procedures that support and communicate active commitment to technology. EDC/TERC defined successful technology integration as:

• teachers' applications of technology in a sustained way to promote and support all students' participation and progress in learning; and

• technology application occurring across a number of classrooms and content areas over time, and a school-based effort rather than the special interest of an individual teacher.

Teacher Practices

Recommendations for teachers derive from the findings of all three research projects.

- Consider curriculum objectives and individual student needs.
- Be actively involved in technology-based lessons.
- Structure lessons so that students work together in groups.
- Take advantage of technology training opportunities.
- Collaborate with other teachers for lesson ideas and improvement.

Objectives and Student Needs. The first practice for successful computer lessons is to correlate the software used with curriculum objectives and student needs. One project stated that teachers have the "responsibility and choice to

97

apply technology to the pursuit of learning objectives." The knowledge that the teacher brings or can obtain about the strengths and potential of the student, especially the student with mild handicaps, will assist in selecting appropriate technology-based lessons. Consulting the individual educational plan (IEP) for the student helps identify student needs and prepare effective instruction involving technology.

Active Teacher Involvement. The teacher can focus the student on learning. By providing the student with an introduction to the software and by guiding students when using the program, as well as extending students' understanding of the material, the teacher makes the students' experience with technology more meaningful.

Group Learning. Teachers can direct students to work in groups as well as individually at the computer. Working with a partner or in small groups encourages practice of social skills and problem solving skills while learning academic content. Working cooperatively promotes participation from all members of the group.

Teacher Training. Ongoing staff development provides the teacher with knowledge as well as emotional support. Special and regular education teachers as well as others involved with technology integration can come together to view suitable software. Demonstrations of curriculum and EP goals that correlate with software and suggestions of technology applications are useful. This is an opportunity to view software program options and learn ways to modify programs. Exposure to technology and ways it can be integrated into the curriculum results in more frequent use of the technology by teachers.

Support of Colleagues. One teacher working with another helps the process of planning and trying out technology-based lessons. Peer coaching is a practical way for teachers to help one another. The school principal has an important role in scheduling time for teachers to get together for this collaboration.

Johns Hopkins University: The Elementary School Level

Johns Hopkins conducted 16 studies with an emphasis on the teaching/learning process and how that process is supported. Fifty elementary classrooms were involved in their research effort, which focused on the teacher and the classroom.

The studies found the teacher's role to be critical. Teachers control decisions about grouping students, introducing the software program, and using the program to assist student progress. Does the teacher need to introduce the software program? The studies showed that younger students working with tutorial software learned faster and were correct more often when there was a teacher introduction. In addition, teachers can make lessons more effective if they:

*   explain the activity's purpose,
*   detail what is expected of students,
*   outline roles to facilitate use of the software,
*   monitor and assess students, and
*   point out how the program relates to situations off the computer.

Technology can assist the monitoring of student progress. The computer's consistent monitoring was particularly beneficial for students with mild handicaps. Students with mild handicaps may be inactive, inefficient learners. To counteract these tendencies, teachers can instruct students to pay attention to the program's directions, hints, feedback, and scoring. Student use of these program features aids in self-monitoring and personal performance evaluation.

Several studies by the Johns Hopkins University team involved students working individually, with a partner, and in groups of three. It was found that students who worked individually and with a partner when using computer assisted instruction (CAI) were more on-task than triads. With problem solving software both individual and group work was on-task. Group work resulted in positive interactions and collaborative strategies. Cooperative grouping during CAI increased peer interaction and involvement in the task. Students needed direct instruction in social skills, as well as the necessary time to work out problems in groups. It was observed that peer tutoring, especially between handicapped and non-handicapped students, was a benefit of group work.

It was observed that peer tutoring, especially between handicapped and non-handicapped students, was a benefit of group work.

EDC/TERC: The Middle School Level

EDC/TERC carried out their study in four diverse middle schools by observing in classrooms, collecting materials, and interviewing and talking informally to teachers, administrators, technology specialists, and students. The research team wrote 23 case studies that served as the basis for defining successful technology integration and for identifying sixteen findings about what promotes successful technology integration. The sixteen findings fall into five categories: teacher knowledge and practice, communication and collaboration, teacher development, technology resources, and school-based facilitation.

These findings focus on the actions, knowledge, and thought processes of teachers who successfully integrate technology into their classrooms. Teachers need to be actively involved with students' use of all types of software; they need opportunities to continually reflect on and to evaluate practice; and they need to draw on knowledge about students, the potential contribution technology can make, curriculum, instructional strategies, assessment strategies, and hardware/software.

Teachers benefit from working together to try out software. Regular and special education teachers need to engage in frequent, ongoing communication about curriculum goals, instructional strategies, and student needs. Novice technology users need to have someone to turn to for knowledge as well as emotional support. In-service workshops are insufficient in helping teachers learn to integrate technology successfully. Instead, training needs to include ongoing school-based support and structures for collaboration and communication.

School-based facilitation deals with the kind of organizational supports administrators and other school-based specialists need to put in place to support teachers' efforts. These include taking the next step after a decision has been made; the need for a vision of the value and potential of the computer in meeting students' needs: and the need for policies and procedures that promote links between special and regular education programs. In addition, someone needs to take responsibility for ensuring that hardware is kept in good working condition. Administrators and/or specialists need to establish a mechanism so that teachers can narrow down choices of software.

Macro Systems, Inc.: The High School Level

Macro worked with mildly handicapped students and staff and faculty at nine high schools in two school districts. Their goal was to identify a model and refine practices in needs assessment, software selection, in-service training, and school communication. The focus was on CAI software. Macro examined the decisions, actions, and outcomes of administrators, teachers, and other staff. Hardware and software resources and classroom instructional activities were also studied through interviews, observation, and review of documents.

The overall plan for technology use and integration developed by an active technology committee for the school or district provided a better guide when it incorporated in a regular and significant way the input of teachers and other end users of the technology at the school and classroom level. It was found that the work of the technology committee was enriched when the committee included representatives with differing backgrounds and perspectives. The committee facilitated communication not only between regular and special education teachers and between classroom teachers and computer teachers, but also between teachers and administrators. A committee structure enabled teachers to become more involved in higher level technology decisions, especially in decisions about the availability of computers and other technology resources.

Macro Systems found that what works on the school and district levels seems to work in the classroom. Thus, the emphasis on communication and input from technology users that enhances technology integration at school and district levels also seems to encourage successful technology use within the classroom. Communication between teacher and students before, during, and after applications of technology in instruction enhances success. In addition, involving students in planning for use of computers, especially in organizing the class, can promote the integration process.

When regular and special educators collaborated, positive attitudes and interactions were found to increase. Decisions made together were easier, and resources were found to be better utilized. While it was often difficult for teachers to find the time for this collaboration, communication about student needs, instructional strategies, and software selection resulted in teachers feeling comfortable about using computers and discovering more ways to use them.

Teachers will do a better job of integrating technology into classroom instruction if systematic resources organized at the school and district level are available to them. Clearly identified and routinely available assistance in equipment and software identification, selection, acquisition, and operational use appears to substantially benefit the integration process.

Conclusions

These three studies confirm the key role the teacher plays when using technology to deliver instruction. Practices suggested for teachers reflect what is generally considered good instruction; it is valuable to know they are substantiated by research. The mildly handicapped student in the mainstreamed classroom can participate in and benefit from computer experiences. As more and more regular and special education teachers, as well as school districts, become committed to the value and benefits of technology-based lessons, these experiences should become more widespread.

This material was developed under Contract No. 300-87-0115 with the U.S. Department of Education. The content does not necessarily reflect the position or policy of OSEP/ED, and no official endorsement of the material should be inferred.

Research Models (Products in Development)

Macro Systems Model. A multipart manual with resources, guidelines, and discussion of issues and options for implementing and maintaining technology integration. Available 1991 from Macro Systems, Inc., 8630 Fenton St., Silver Spring, MD 20910.

MAKE IT HAPPEN! A manual with a school-based approach that guides principals, a school-based management team, and an interdisciplinary team of teachers through their part in accomplishing technology integration. Available 1991 from Education Development Center, Inc. 55 Chapel St., Newton. MA 02160.

Teacher Technology Resource Guide and *The Principal's Assistant.* A user's guide for technology in education. Available 1991 from Center for Technology in Human Disabilities, The Johns Hopkins University, 2301 Argonne Drive, Baltimore, MD 21218.

References

Hanley, T.V., Appell, L.S., & Hams, C.D. (1988). "Technological innovation in the context of special education systems: A qualitative and structured research approach." *Journal of Special Education Technology, 9 (2),* 98-108.

Morocco, C. & Zorfass, I. (1988). "Technology and transformation: A naturalistic study of special students and computers in the middle schools." *Journal of Special Education Technology, 9 (2),* 88-97.

Panyan, M.P., Hummel, J.H., Steeves, K.J. & Givner. C. (in press). "Report of technology integration project research." *International Journal of Special Education.*

Storeygard, I. & Simmons, R. (1989). Middle school research report. *Teaching and Computers,* 7(3), 20.

Zorfass, I.M., Persky, S.E., & Remz, A.R. (1990). *Promoting successful technology integration: Contributions of technology specialists.* Paper presented at the annual meeting of the American Education Research Association, Boston, MA.

Mary A. Anderson, Center for Special Education Technology, Council for Exceptional Children, 1920 Association Drive, Reston, VA 22091. For additional information, contact the Center at (800) 873-8255.

Chapter 3 APPLICATIONS IN THE CLASSROOM

1. "Art and Music." Laurie Beckelman. Excerpts from *Instructor's Big Book of Computer Activities*. Page 134.
2. "Computers Help Students See Art in a Different Hue." Gwen Solomon. *Electronic Learning*.
3. "Computers in Music Education." Laurie Beckelman. Excerpts from *Instructor's Big Book of Computer Activities*. Page 143.
4. "How to Get Better Scores: Use Computers to Help Teach Music." Gwen Solomon. *Electronic Learning*.
5. "Computers and English: Future Tense... Future Perfect?" Stephen Marcus. *CUE Newsletter*. Dec. 88/Jan 89. Page 1.
6. "English/Language Arts: A Focus on Literature." Stephen Marcus. *Electronic Learning*. Oct. 1989. Page 38.
7. "Process Writing in the One-Computer Classroom." Kathy Pon. *The Computing Teacher*. March 1988.
8. "A Writing Class Taps Into a World of Knowledge." Gwen Solomon. *Electronic Learning*.
9. "Observations on Electronic Networks: Appropriate Activities for Learning." James Levin, Al Rogers, Michael Waugh, and Kathleen Smith. *The Computing Teacher*. May 1989. Page 17.
10. "Manipulatives and the Computer: A Powerful Partnership for Learners of All Ages." Teri Perl. *Classroom Computer Learning*. March 1990. Page 20.
11. "Software That Helps Develop Critical and Analytical Math Skills." Ann Corcoran. *Electronic Learning*.
12. "Techniques and Technology in Secondary School Mathematics." Gary G. Bitter and Harold Frederick. *NASSP Bulletin*, October 1989. Page 22-28.
13. "Algebra Tools: The New Generation." Jonathan Choate. *Classroom Computer Learning*. April, 1989. Page 24.
14. "Dinosaur Roundup." Leslie Eiser. *Classroom Computer Learning*. April 1990. Page 27.
15. "Technology and the Science Class: Going Beyond the Walls and the Disk Drive." Jeff Holte. *Electronic Learning*.
16. "Ideas for Integrating Videodisc Technology Into the Curriculum." John Phillipo and Sandy Martin McCarty. *Electronic Learning*. April, 1990.
17. "National Geographic Kids Network: Real Science in the Elementary Classroom." Dr. Candace L. Julyan. *Classroom Computer Learning*. October 1989. Page 30.

18. "Hands-On Science Projects With Help from On-Line Networks." Gwen Solomon. *Electronic Learning*. April 1989.

19. "Learning to Save the Environment." Leslie Eiser. *Technology & Learning*. March 1991. Page 18

20. "The Computer-Infused Social Studies Classroom." Robert Vlahakis. *Classroom Computer Learning*. Nov./Dec. 1988. Page 58.

21. "Presidents, Politics, and Campaign Issues." Carol Holzberg. *Classroom Computer Learning*. Sept. 1988. Page 46.

22. "Microsoft at Work." Alice Jagger and Bob Veeck. *Microsoft Works in Education*. Oct. 1989. Page 16.

23. "Women in the News." Beth White. *Teaching and Computers*. March/April 1990. Page 42.

24. "Using *Carmen Sandiego* to Teach Reference Skills." Lynn Myers. *The Computing Teacher*. October, 1989. Page 12.

25. "LEGO Meets LOGO." Marian Rosen. *Classroom Computer Learning*. April 1988. Page 50.

26. "Electronic Lesson Plans: Food Files." Beth Smith. *Teaching and Computers*. Sept. 1989. Page 38.

Now for the *hard core* chapter of this book. We've given you some background information telling the whys, the why nots, and the results of many years of research. This chapter will show you some (though not all) of the applications of technology in real classrooms. Here's what people are *really* doing with technology in their classrooms.

If you consider yourself a "single-subject" educator, you may only want to read those articles that are about your subject (assuming we included some). But we'd like to encourage you to read all the articles as cross-disciplinary teaching is a recurring theme throughout them. This is a concept we support, and we are pleased to see that the use of technology seems to encourage it.

Let's begin with the arts. Amazingly, for a variety of reasons, teaching the arts seems to be gradually disappearing from our schools—some associated with costs, some with waning interest. Can technology play a role in expanding interest in the arts? In reducing costs? In integrating arts education into other curriculum areas?

The first reading, "Art and Music" was published in a special edition of *Instructor, a* magazine designed to provide elementary grade teachers a comprehensive introduction to how computers can be used in schools. This article provides the basic introduction to the arts and to "arty" uses of computer technology. We deleted the sections about computer hardware for the arts since those change about every six months. Those purists, for whom the mere notion of using technology in the arts would be an abhorrent behavior, will be pleased to note that in the conclusion the article *clearly* states, "The computer will not replace the traditional media of artistic expression. . . ." And we hope that remains true forever.

Back to the basics, "Computers in Music Education" comes from the same issue of *Instructor* that provided the arts basics. The article describes all the things you can do musically with a computer including teaching music keyboarding, composition, music theory, and technical music.

This time the basics are the 3 R's (plus science and social science). To begin, we offer the article, "Computers and English" by Stephen Marcus, who takes a look into what he sees as the future uses of technology in teaching the language arts. How far into the future? Part of the article deals with changes "during the next 15 years," so it's hard to say exactly when they will happen. In Part 2 of the same article, Marcus recommends some readings that you might like to pursue.

The Marcus article is followed by another Marcus article, this one focusing on teaching literature with technology (yes, Marcus is a very prolific writer, and a very good one). He describes what he calls "rough software categories" for studying literature and then offers recommended examples of software to use when teaching literature.

For the basic primer on using computers in the writing class, we have included, "Process Writing in the One-Computer Classroom." This article covers all the bases with some specific tips for teachers who want to try it.

The final article in the language arts subject describes how a writing class uses telecommunications to communicate (in writing) to fellow-students throughout the world. Similar activities are becoming quite popular these days, if not commonplace, and at many different grade levels. The impact on student writing is interesting to observe.

To illustrate the expanding role of electronic networks in teaching, we included the article, "Observations on Electronic Networks: Appropriate Activities for Learning." This article, co-authored by well-known, experienced pioneers in the use of telecommunications, provides more insights into how this exciting technology can be used beyond just simple written communication between schools of the world.

Surprisingly, the use of technology in mathematics classrooms for anything more than simple drill has been slow in coming. Perhaps, with the emergence of new trends in mathematics teaching and articles such as the ones we have included here, which clearly show the relationship between technology and the new trends in teaching mathematics, this situation will change. Teri Perl's article, "Manipulatives and the Computer" should be listed as a classic article on the subject. Perl, long an advocate of using manipulatives in math education, has combined that interest with her (also long term) interest in computers and has written an excellent article on how and why the two work so well together.

Technology advocates have said for years that computers and software help develop critical thinking and analytical skills, but few have been able to prove it (see Chapter 2). In her article on that subject, Corcoran both defines the situation in terms of the new NCTM standards, but recommends specific pieces of software that help achieve the kinds of learning advocated.

"Technology and the Science Class: Going Beyond the Walls of the Disk Drive" offers the reader an overview of a number of ways to use technology in science classes—from software to multimedia to telecommunications to probeware to simulations.

Combine the resources and experience of the National Science Foundation with National Geographic Society and Technical Education Research Centers (TERC) and what you get is the most talked-about telecommunications program available today. The NGS "Kids Network", as it is known, is described in depth in Julyan's article. How to effectively use telecommunications technology to link children throughout the country (now expanded to the world) in a common science learning activity. As you read the article you will see why this system is discussed so much. You'll be happy to learn that modules for additional grade levels and different activities have been added to the Network and are being added all the time. Very exciting stuff.

From science to social science—"The Computer-Infused Social Studies Classroom" provides you with the overview on the topic. There are a wide variety of uses of technology in the social science classroom; this article only touches on some of them.

For the next presidential campaign, or for smaller political campaigns that may be conducted in your region (or neighborhood), the article "Presidents, Politics, and Campaign Issues" will prepare you and your students for how to study the election using technology. There are lots of different activities described along with software recommendations to match.

Microsoft *Works* (or most any program with the name Works in it) is becoming a standard tool for studying any number of subjects from writing to science to math to social studies. This article describes how to use the database tool to do an in depth study of the world or any of the 50 states. These are really basic bread-and-butter applications of a readily available software program in most schools. And this article only touches the tip of the iceberg-potential of *Works*.

No article series would be complete without an article about Logo—our choice is an article about LEGO and Logo. The product LEGO TC has captured the attention of teachers and kids very quickly. Add the versatility of Logo programming and you have a technology combination of endless uses. This article describes just some of them. There are many others, more than the imagination can believe.

And to conclude this chapter, we have included a lesson plan showing how to use computers in a foods class or other class studying foods—nutrition, for example.

Questions for Discussion

1. Do you feel that using technology such as computers contradicts the whole notion of hands-on arts instruction?
2. With the emphasis today on teaching basics at the expense of the arts, how will teachers of the arts gain access to the limited technology resources on most campuses? Where will they get the money for appropriate software and other materials?
3. In his future-oriented article, Marcus identified changes that *will* take place in the next 15 years. Which of these changes have already taken place?
4. From the Marcus article, what other changes do you foresee happening because of technology changes or other things that have occurred since the article and the list were prepared?
5. What do you suspect are the problems that might arise when using telecommunications in a classroom?
6. Discuss how using software contradicts the notion of using manipulatives in math education.

7. The use of spreadsheets in math education was described in the articles. Can you think of ways to use a spreadsheet tool to improve math education?
8. Why is the NGS Kids Network receiving so much attention? What's good about it? What's different about it?

Questions from the Readings

1. Describe the specific ways computers can be used in art education.
2. Why might computer art appeal to some children who are otherwise not interested in art?
3. From the Futures article by Marcus, what was the common theme of the books he recommended reading? Why did he include them in an article about language arts?
4. In the Marcus article on literature, what are the "rough categories" of software he describes for studying literature?
5. From the Perl article, why is the use of manipulatives considered to be an important ingredient in math education today?
6. From "Technology and the Science Class," what is the difference between simulations and laboratory probes? How are they different?
7. Which tool(s) seems to be the most popular to use in social science classrooms? Why might each be popular?

Introduction

At first glance, computers and the creative arts may seem an odder couple than Walter Matthau and Jack Lemmon. After all, what can an electronic number-cruncher bring to fields in which emotion is the basis of excellence, fluidity and nuance the prerequisites of successful expression? The answer is, a lot. The computer's essence is plastic in the truest sense of the word. It is more malleable than fingerpaints, less ephemeral yet as changeable as a piano chord. It offers a unique combination of impermanence and replicability, encouraging that basic of all artistic basics: messing around.

Your students can create works of visual or aural art on a computer, save them forever, and at the same time experiment to make them better. Their mistakes fade faster than an arcade asteroid; their successes are safely stored. In the end, they might have three or four or more pieces that might or might not appear to be related—and all of them would hold the same potential for alteration as the original. Herein lies the premier value of computers in your art or music classroom. The freedom of expression your students discover at the computer keyboard may well infuse their work with more traditional mediums.

But freedom of expression is, of course, only half of what your students need to reach their creative potential. Discipline is equally important. Here, too, the computer can help. Indeed, the malleability that encourages experimentation also encourages discipline. The more easily students can change their work, the more willing they may be to go the rounds of revision necessary to perfect their creation. And the computer exacts discipline in another way as well. If students are to save their successes and banish their failures, they must follow the lock-step procedures for saving, changing, and erasing computer-generated art. No room for sloppiness here!

To these global advantages of the computer as a creative medium, we can add several others. Motivation, for example. Computer buffs who would never consider themselves capable of drawing or of composing worthwhile music may discover untapped creative potential when the computer, not a paint brush or piano, is their medium. On the other hand, an artistic but technophobic child might overcome computer anxiety when using the machine to explore familiar talents.

Computers also offer excellent opportunities to integrate art and music into the rest of the curriculum. Students can illustrate stories, either their own or those they have enjoyed reading. They may explore the mathematical relations between the elements of music, making both music and mathematics seem more worthwhile. And when they write programs to create visual or aural art, programming itself becomes more real—students see their labors at the computer producing something they and others can relate to readily and comfortably.

BY LAURIE
BECKELMAN

107

But perhaps most important, computers make entirely new forms of expression available to your students. Musical composition itself may be one. No longer must students master the complex language of musical notation in order to create their own songs. With software such as *Music Maker* (Sublogic Corporation), the computer does the notating while the student maestro at the keyboard concentrates on perfecting the tune. In the visual arts, the computer makes possible a level of precision and exact repetition of form impossible without the most sophisticated drafting tools.

> Versatility is what differentiates the computer from traditional media. Computer art is infinitely variable and instantly erasable.

4. A completed form can be "exploded" into fragments or doubled on itself in a mirror image.

5. Series of works can be played back, like a slide show, or a single work can be animated, introducing your students to forms of artistic creation ordinarily beyond the resources of the classroom.

6. In addition, the versatility of the computer enables students to use this single tool to simulate many artistic techniques, including drawing, painting, creating patterns or collages, experimenting with colors, and even "sculpting," with software that has three-dimensional capabilities.

Why Use Computers In Art Education

What can a computer do that a paint brush can't? Consider the following:

1. It takes almost no skill at the computer to draw perfect geometric shapes, to repeat lines at precise intervals, to repeat preprogrammed forms to make patterns, even to replicate kaleidoscopically a pattern or drawing around a focus. Such capabilities provide a wonderful basis for lessons on composition, perspective, texture, pattern, and proportion.

2. Students may be able to enlarge a portion of their work to draw fine details more easily, or reduce a portion to preserve proportion or composition.

3. They may store parts of drawings separately from the whole work and use them later in another work, or each artist can store a shape table of favorite or recurring forms.

Versatility Makes the Difference:

This versatility is what differentiates the computer from traditional media. Computer art is infinitely variable and instantly erasable. Since your students cannot make an irreversible error on the computer, they are freed from fear of mistakes to experiment. They can work and rework their pieces until they have the pictures they want. And if you suggest a way to improve the work, they can try your suggestion without having to start from scratch.

In some ways, painting with the computer is similar to working with the more familiar materials of visual artistic expression. With even basic hardware and software, you can:

• Draw and paint in black and white or in various colors.

• Vary the width of your line (brush stroke) and the colors of lines and backgrounds.

• Color large areas.

• Save your creation and bring it out to look at later.

But there is a fundamental and all-important difference: Painting with the computer is like working with paint that is simultaneously wet and dry. Students need not wait for blue paint to dry before changing it to red; they need only specify a new pen color and refill the offending area. Indeed, with many software packages, students can try any number of color relationships and save just the ones that are most satisfying. Similarly, an image is never cast in stone. If Jared decides that the horns look funny on the rhinoceros' head, or that the Rolls Royce really shouldn't be flying a Jolly Roger, he can change just the horns or the flag, retaining the portion of his drawing with which he was satisfied.

And, there is less police work for you! No paints to spill or clean up. No brushes to soak in turpentine or paste to remove from sticky fingers. As the clock ticks on toward the end of class, you needn't become commandant of the clean-up patrol. You will need to spend some time saving students' creations, especially if you have many computers and want to save everything on one disk. But you can give most of your attention to supporting your students' artistic endeavors and to providing advice and supervision, eliciting the excitement and creativity that make teaching worthwhile.

Integrating Art Education and Other Subjects:

You can also use the computer to integrate art education with education in other subject areas, emphasizing the connections between art and other areas of activity. The computer's capacity for drawing perfect geometric designs and curves, or for making perfectly scaled geometric models, allows students to recognize both the order and the beauty of mathematical concepts. Students can practice mapmaking, or illustrate changes of climate, migration patterns, or crops discussed in social studies class.

Or, you can have children illustrate stories they have read or written. Many students may find story structure easier to understand through pictures. In early education, the computer is especially useful for teaching colors and shapes; in science it can create perfectly symmetrical optical illusions or can demonstrate theories of color perception. Even basic graphics packages can be used to graph statistics or to diagram functions.

Finally, because the computer is so much a part of the students' own culture, it can prompt discussions of the historical relations between art and society. When students can see their own art as a reflection of their times, the times of other artists become more real and more meaningful. As have many schools of art before it, computer art also raises the question of what really is art. Do the capabilities of the medium make computer art any less the product of the individual artist's vision and skill? Out of such discussions comes a deeper and more authentic knowledge of aesthetics.

Summing Up

The computer will not replace the traditional media of artistic expression, but it is a powerful medium with great potential for opening the satisfaction of artistic creation to your students. When students work intelligently with any visual medium, they learn how to see better. And the computer, through its ability to erase, enlarge, reduce, or reproduce line, shape, or pattern, can focus their "seeing" on specific aspects of style and composition. Further, students can easily see the effects of changes in their conception or execution of a work.

In the last analysis, it is no easier to produce fine computer art than it is to master any medium, but students may be able to produce something "artistic" with the computer much sooner than with other media. Their pride of accomplishment may lead to further exploration in this and other artistic media, and to the commitment that supports refinement of skills.

Computers Help Students See Art in a Different Hue

WITH THE COMPUTER AS PALETTE, ART CLASSES HAVEN'T BEEN THE SAME
AT DUPONT MANUAL HIGH, A MAGNET SCHOOL IN LOUISVILLE, KY.

"When you create art you always think, 'What if...' " says Suzanne Sidebottom. "The biggest value computers have is that they let you try 'What if.' You're free to try that shape change or color difference. You can always get back the original."

Sidebottom is a visual arts teacher at Louisville, Ky.'s only magnet school, duPont Manual High. She teaches two computer art courses in addition to her regular pottery classes.

Computer as Art Tool

The art computer lab has seven Amiga and two Macintosh computers plus dot matrix, ink-jet, and laser printers. If nine computers seems like too few, the lab opened with a single Amiga three years ago. A parent art-support group realized the value of technology and bought that first computer. Since then, the Board of Education has supplied the others and installed a complete, 32-station Macintosh laboratory that's shared by all of the departments in the school.

Visual Arts serves 150 of the 1,250 student population and is one of five magnet programs at duPont Manual High School. There are also majors in Performing Arts, Math/Science, Technology, Communications, and High School University (a program for gifted students). Visual Arts students take a full academic program and share classes with all of the other students in the school.

In addition, the art students take 16 state-approved courses in their major. They start with a basic core group of art courses and progress to advanced studio classes. To take so many classes, the state lets students attend the school for an extra hour a day. Some even return for regularly scheduled, three-hour evening meetings to work on projects. "They're a real dedicated group of students," says Sidebottom. "They're there because they want to be, and they really want to learn."

Sidebottom's lab is project-oriented. Students use the Amigas and Macs to plan the layout for textiles and paint media, create animations, and develop commercial applications for their art. Computers allow the students to experiment. However, the computer is only one of many art tools the students use.

Scholarships and Awards

After graduation, 93 percent of the students continue their education. About half go on to college; the rest attend specialized art schools. "the best art schools in the country," says Sidebottom. These students, who were accepted into Manual High School on the basis of their portfolio, leave the school with awards, exhibit experiences, and scholarships listed on their resumes.

This past year, for example, 25 Visual Arts graduates won $225,000 in scholarships. "The students who wanted and

By
Gwen
Solomon

111

needed scholarship money got it." Sidebottom says.

Awards to students are numerous, too. Beth Torstrick and Gregory King won Computer Learning Foundation awards for work submitted during Computer Learning Month in October 1988.

John Dennis won first place and Alan Lett second place in this year's Pratt Institute's National Talent Search; both created computer graphics. Last year, another duPont Manual student took first place.

Another competition, "The Art of Science," sponsored by Dow Chemical and funded by the New York Academy of Sciences and the National Science Foundation, is a travelling exhibit of 50 pieces of student art from all over the country. Of these 50 pieces, the cover piece was created by John Dennis, and two others were created by Manual students Gregory King and Jason Noble. All were computer graphics. John Dennis also displayed his work at Pratt Institute in New York during National Science and Technology week.

Animation

Students learn fine art techniques, but also explore commercial art forms. When they learned animation techniques, for example, they used genlock technology to combine half-inch video tape and computer graphics. Their equipment had limitations, so they took their Amiga to the school's Broadcast Studio and hooked it up to sophisticated film devices. There they created two minutes of animated images on three-quarter-inch tape that they could edit.

One group's animation opened with a digitized sequence of a sink in the studio. From this sink came small digitized drops of water. As the drops grew larger,

objects appeared inside. Each group member added a vision inside a droplet. There were racing cars, a fireplace, a mouse, snow, and a fish. The fish fell into a fishbowl, which splashed droplets back up and let the students' images come back out.

A School Resource

The Visual Arts students often use their talents to advertise school programs. Sidebottom's students produced a bumper sticker for the statewide gifted program. They scanned-in and perfected the school's crest for the student newspaper. They also designed a poster for the Kentucky School Boards Association that had an oil landscape on one side and information about a conference on the other. They used computers for lettering and layout and planned the oil painting with computer-generated transparencies. They create brochures for the Honor Society awards ceremony and other functions.

Other Projects

Students also try out ideas on the computer that they ultimately create with other media. For example, Jennifer Pittenger created the model for an 8-foot tall geometric sculpture that she later crafted out of plywood. It stands in the student cafeteria. Wendy Hawkins designed a wood sculpture that incorporated three-dimensional batiked areas.

Some of these projects are expensive. The Board of Education provides most of the funds; the students pay a materials fee to offset some of the costs; parent and student groups conduct fund raising, and Sidebottom's students put their talents to use. They create paper and porcelain jewelry that is sold in galleries around town and at local crafts fairs.

Students also learn to use computers for purposes other than art. A Senior Seminar class began a data base on the Macintosh to keep track of all colleges that offer art programs and art schools. They list how large each school is, what scholarships are available, major areas of study, tuition, cost of housing, and more. Most important, they list the Manual graduates who go there.

Students are shaping the future of the Visual Arts program by taking up the challenge of art educator Joan Truckenbrod from the Chicago Art Institute. "When Truckenbrod addressed the school," Sidebottom says, "she challenged us to take images and send them by satellite dish or modem. It's taken us two years, but now we're doing that."

Images now travel to the Board of Education headquarters, the Computer Education Center, two other high schools, and around Jefferson County by satellite. "We transmit images to their computers or printers. Next year we'll also use modems," Sidebottom says, "and we want to run a line into the broadcast studio."

An Unlikely Background

Sidebottom claims she has an unlikely background for the computer work she teaches. With a major in Fine Arts and experience teaching art to elementary- and middle-school children, Sidebottom was selected by the district to learn about computers six years ago. She went through the training and was required to train other teachers as well. She wasn't satisfied with the results. "I could draw a better square with a pen than with a *BASIC* or *Logo* program."

When it was required that her students use the computers, too, Sidebottom ordered Koala tablets and had her students draw instead of teaching them programming. Her ideas worked well not only with these students but also with mainstream and special education children.

By the time duPont Manual's Visual Arts program needed a computer graphics teacher, Sidebottom was prepared. She designed the computer graphics courses and began teaching them. "I came into it through the back door, though," she says. "I'm a potter. But this is a very exciting and rigorous environment. Being here has made me grow as a teacher."

"Students get caught up with it, too, and one thing just leads to another," she adds. "That's what learning is all about."

Article #3
Computers in Music Education

FROM *THE INSTRUCTOR'S BIG BOOK OF COMPUTER ACTIVITIES*

BY LAURIE
BECKELMAN

You needn't have used much software to know that computers can create sound. The variety of blips and beeps, the sounds of alien planes exploding, the triumphant victory theme or dirge of defeat are almost a requisite part of software, educational or entertainment, designed for kids.

But this primitive auditory vocabulary of reward and reinforcement is just the beginning. The same microcomputers that beep success in math, science, social studies, and English drills have some truly amazing capacities as musical instruments and as tools for teaching music. The ways in which your students can make music on a computer have direct bearing on such musical activities as singing, eurhythmics, music appreciation, or mastering the technique of another musical instrument. They can influence virtually all facets of music education.

For example:

1. Many programs that teach composition use the piano keyboard as a screen icon; some even require a plug-in piano keyboard for playing music at the computer. Other programs actually teach basic chords or fingering on such string instruments as the banjo, guitar, ukelele, and mandolin, or on the brass instruments.

2. By combining aural and visual drill, the computer can also help train students in various skills associated with music theory: ear training, sight singing, reading rhythm and notes, understanding scales and chords, and learning musical form and terms.

3. Perhaps most dramatically, the computer can give students at literally all levels of musical training opportunities to express themselves creatively through musical composition. This opens the world of music to a whole new group of students and makes those already at ease in that world even more capable. The computer can perform endless transpositions, splicing, and repetitions, allowing students who are just acquiring a formal musical background to experiment with sound. As students experience the excitement of creating and playing their own music, they may also become more responsive to lessons on notation, form, and theory.

4. Finally, as with visual computer art, computer-made music is a new form in itself. Students are already continually exposed to music created on computers, moog synthesizers, or other electronic media—consider the emotionally compelling, Academy Award winning theme from the movie *Chariots of Fire*. Because of the way it makes sound, the computer has capabilities that are quite different from those of traditional musical instruments. As your students experiment with these capabilities, they create the music of their future.

Why Use Computers In Music Education

As in other subject areas, the computer has a valid place in music education just for presenting tutorials and drills in music theory skills. It can present drills in recognizing intervals and rhythm patterns, in key signatures, in major and minor scales and chords. It can quiz students on naming notes that are displayed on the staff, that are sounded, or both; it can display and perform notes simultaneously, challenging students to determine which notes are different; it can test students' understanding of musical terms and demonstrate the differences between terms.

Students working at their own pace with the computer can ask for numerous repetitions of a drill. They can get immediate feedback, determine for themselves the length and difficulty of quizzes, and they needn't fear seeming dumb. Your students can drill alone on sight reading but still have their wrong responses corrected.

And the computer can add a dimension to the drills you do choose to supervise. It can provide simultaneous visual and auditory cues in dictation or sight reading drills for an individual, a small group, or a whole class. By allowing you to play and replay the same melody with variations of form, key, harmony, or rhythm, the computer can enable you and your students to experiment with chords and keys, to hear the differences between major and minor keys, to discover dissonance, and to see how these elements can be used in music to create a mood.

Finally, there is the familiar issue of motivation. Most students today love computers and are eager to be involved with them. The computer gives instant gratification for success and privacy in failure. For you, relegating the time-consuming and repetitive drills to the computer frees class time for the more interesting and creative elements of music education, the things that require your special human or musical contribution.

Well over 50 programs available today will turn a classroom computer into a musical drillmaster. Unfortunately, some of the best require special (and often expensive) music boards or peripherals to work. The Syntauri Corporation, for example, produces a wide range of tutorial and drill programs for use with its alphaSyntauri music synthesizer. But even if your school isn't flush enough to afford a computer dedicated to the music room, or an upgrade for one that is shared, you can find good programs. The Minnesota Educational Computing Consortium, known for its excellent teacher-created and -tested software, produces four disks of music theory drills that combine graphics and sound to cover everything from terms and notation to rhythm, pitch, intervals, scales, and chords. Although music theory programs tend to be geared to upper-elementary, junior high, or higher levels, you will find programs that introduce younger students to such musical basics as pitch and rhythm. For example, Temporal Acuity Products' *Magic Musical Balloon Game* helps young children learn melodic discrimination as they decide whether a brief melody goes up, down, or remains the same. Again, graphics reinforce the aural lesson.

Composition: But the benefits of a computer for drilling music theory pale against the computer's potential to open the world of the composer to every student. Even a toddler (chronologically or musically) can sit down at the computer, play a series of notes, listen to it, and edit it again and again until it becomes music. Through this kind of experimentation, with support from well-designed software and a creative teacher, students can learn the musical methods that will help them make even better music.

Indeed, music composition software is one of the hottest types of software being produced today. This is good news for you. It means that many good, inexpensive programs are available for use in your classroom. This software does for music what word processors do for words. Sarah can sit down with a program such as Scarborough Systems' *Songwriter* and create, edit, and play her own music. Using the arrow keys, she moves the cursor up and down a picture of a piano keyboard that appears on the screen, listening to notes (by pressing the return key) as she goes. When she hears one she likes, she records it by simply pressing the space bar. The number keys let her change the length of her note.

Working like this, Sarah can enter, change, or delete a note. She can play her composition backward or forward, either phrase by phrase or note by note. Further, she can define a motif of up to 100 notes, save it, recall it with a single keystroke, and insert it anywhere in her composition. Finally, she can save her opus for later performance or revision. What power!

You can use such software not only to foster open-ended experimentation but also to further more specific music education goals. Once students have composed a melody, have them change the tempo to explore rhythm, or the key to experiment with mood. Introduce younger students to high and low sounds by having them write short high or low "songs" of their own; help older students understand the power of a musical idea through the composition and repetition of their own motifs. The possibilities are almost endless.

When you select composition software for your students, you should consider their present level of musical knowledge, as well as how much you want them to learn of traditional composition methods and standard musical notation. Because of the computer's memory limitations, much of the composition software does not display actual note values, but uses other kinds of graphics. Some programs show a piano keyboard on the screen, indicating the corresponding typewriter keys to make notes. Such software may be most appropriate for composers who already know either musical notation or the piano keyboard. But even those who don't can use such software to gain familiarity with these traditional musical images. Because of the auditory reinforcement, their ignorance of keyboard or notation needn't restrict their creativity.

Programs may also show some graphic representation of rising and falling tones, but without reference to standard musical notation. *Songwriter* shows a "player piano" roll on the screen, along with the piano keyboard. *Music,* a program created by the Lawrence Hall of Science for children from preschool to second grade, uses bars of varying colors and lengths, and the numbers from 1 to 8 to differentiate notes in its graphics.

Some software, such as Electronic Arts' *Music Construction Set,* does display the traditional staff and notation. Students select from a collection of icons on the display screen—clefs, notes, time signatures, accidentals, and other elements of traditional musical notation—

> This software does for music what word processors do for words.

and place them on the staff using an input device such as the keyboard, a touch pad, or a joystick. At any point, the composer can sound a single note or play any portion of the work to hear the sounds represented by the notation. By using *Music Construction Set* with a fairly inexpensive peripheral such as Sweet Micro System's Mockingboard (a small chip that plugs into the inside of the computer), students can hear up to six notes simultaneously *and* see the musical notation on the screen.

Whatever their level of sophistication, students composing music on the computer are free to experiment and to discover what music can say. There is no right or wrong; they needn't worry about writing something that will sound awful when performed. The instrument is accessible and the rewards are immediate. And if you're lucky enough to have access to 15 or more computers, your students can play, compose, and rehearse all at once without deafening the class. Imagine the sound of 15 pianos, trumpets, or drums!

Further, students can do things with the computer that are impossible in traditional musical forms. They can record and edit improvisation. With appropriate software, they can write multipart music and hear it performed immediately, without rounding up an instrumental ensemble. Through such experimentation, your students are more likely than ever before to develop "the eye that hears and the ear that sees."

Music in a Unified Curriculum: Using computers in your music classroom has one additional benefit: it ties music more closely to other realms of your students' study and lives. Programming methods for composition tie rhythm and scaling to math skills, using numbers and notes to reinforce one another.

Students can use their musical skills to "hear" a computer program or a picture. Indeed, through the computer they can synchronize music with other artistic media of all types with relative ease. This puts the "eye that hears and ear that sees" in a whole new context and gives you the opportunity of making music a truly integral part of your students' lives.

Summing Up

If you're beginning to believe that the silicon soul of this new machine can unleash the creative soul of all your Johnnys and Jills, you may just be right. Certainly the computer's flashy way with numbers has too long eclipsed its equally protean and impressive way with pictures and sound. It's time for the computer-as-creative-medium to come out of the closet. And with your enthusiasm, creativity, and guidance, it can—for a whole generation of lucky students.

Article #4
How to Get Better Scores: Use Computers to Help Teach Music

AT MIAMI'S NEW WORLD SCHOOL FOR THE ARTS, MARK HILL USES
COMPUTERS TO LET MUSIC STUDENTS CREATE, SEE, AND HEAR THEIR OWN MUSIC.

BY GWEN
SOLOMON

Miami's New World School for the Arts, a magnet school, houses specialized programs in visual arts, theater, dance, and music. One third of the school's population consists of music students who audition to get in. One hundred and twenty are high school students; 30 others are first- and second-year college music students in a selective conservatory program.

Mark Hill, director of the Digital Music and Computer-Assisted Instructional Music (CAIM) Laboratory, is chair of the music department. Some of his duties include classroom teaching, determining curriculum, and more mysterious tasks such as correlating software to music theory. "We use technology not for its own sake," Hill says, "but as a tool for getting a good, solid music education."

In this unique cooperative venture, the Dade County Public Schools, Miami-Dade Community College, and Florida State University run the school together. "I think it's the only program like it in the country," says Hill. Students take academic courses in the morning with the regular academic faculty and then participate in the "Arts Block" for three hours each afternoon.

The Music Lab

The CAIM Lab contains four IBM PS/2 Model 30s with the IBM Music Feature Card, four Apple IIGSs, and two Macintosh SEs, all with Musical Instrument Digital Interfaces (MIDI) and two printers. In addition, there are six Yamaha, Roland, and Korg synthesizers, and a Yamaha Drum Machine.

In Hill's lab, students receive individualized computer instruction correlated with what they learn in music theory classes. Students in the 10th and 11th grades take college level courses for college credit, and Hill schedules them 10 at a time into the lab.

Hill's 12th-grade students continue to learn theory, but they also use the computers for MIDI applications. This means they do their own composing, arranging, and sequencing on a computer. MIDI is a music-industry standard that lets computers communicate with synthesizers such as keyboards, drum machines, and expanded boxes. Students use software that lets them compose for the synthesizer, see the score on the monitor, play the piece, edit their work, and even print out the score.

For the college students, there's more of an emphasis on ear training. They listen to music and learn to take dictation. They learn the different components of music: the melodies, harmonies, and rhythms. Hill serves as a facilitator, working with students one at a time. "It's almost like having private lessons; students use a variety of approaches on computers to reinforce concepts in music, and I supervise them," Hill says. "There's never really been a way for students to practice music theory

118

before. Computers offer a way to interact with music theory, to reinforce different concepts."

New Way to Learn

Traditionally, students attend class and read books on music theory. Software adds the ability to practice, get immediate feedback, and improve comprehension. The two basic types of programs are sequencers and note editors. With sequencers, students compose on the synthesizer keyboard, record the notes as a data file, and play back their work on any MIDI device. With note editors, students write the score on-screen and then play it through the MIDI device. Some software combines features of both.

When students learn about chords, for example, their lab sessions involve several pieces of software, each of which approaches the concept in a slightly different way. With a program such as Electronic Courseware Systems' *Functional Harmony Series,* students get a visual and aural approach. They see harmony on the screen in regular music notation and hear the harmony. Then they are asked to identify the harmony, see how the harmony fits into the scale that the piece of music is based on, and analyze how the chord functions.

Student Albert Suarez, for example, auditioned for admission to the school on his French horn; he was accepted but lacked some fundamental music skills. By spending extra time in the CAIM lab one summer, Suarez concentrated on scales, key signature, and other basics. Hill saw exactly what skills Suarez lacked and supplied software to reinforce those concepts. In particular, Suarez improved his understanding of modal scales by using software that let him identify and build the scales on screen.

Software Collection

The CAIM lab opened in November 1987. "Since then," Hill says, "we've accumulated the most comprehensive collection of computer-assisted software in writing theory and ear training in the country." In the last two years, they invested about $10,000 in single copies of software that students take turns using. With 450 software lessons available, students have a variety of ways to approach each topic. Hill calls this method "individualized prescriptive music instruction."

When students want to learn to play a difficult musical passage on their instrument, for example, they use the computer to help them hear how the piece sounds. They type in the score with note-editing software and listen as the synthesizer plays the passage over and over again. Hopefully, students come to understand not only the passage but also numerous variations.

If Hill sees that students don't understand a particular concept, he makes sure they are exposed to slightly different presentations with each new piece of software. They continue to try alternative approaches until the concept is clear. Recently, students Ellen Stone, Gwen Burney, and Carisa Wilson worked together at one computer to reinforce the concept of secondary dominants. They used tutorial software correlated to their textbook and then worked with other software programs to identify harmony on the screen and decide how it fits on a key.

"The variety of approaches motivates students," Hill says. "Learning never ends. The students could study theory the rest of their lives and never put a dent in it."

Hill's background is in music theory. With degrees from the University of

Miami School of Music, Hill became interested in computers because he felt they were the perfect tool for learning. "If it weren't for music, I wouldn't be involved at all," he says. Hill received *Electronic Learning's* Certificate of Merit for 1989-90 for his accomplishments.

No Holding Back

Now that this lab is complete, Hill wants to set up a full MIDI applications lab with eight stations. This will include eight computers, eight sound modules, eight master keyboard/synthesizers, and recording equipment so students can tape their work and analyze it later. Hill wants to have every computer networked so any student can play and hear any other keyboard instrument or sound module in the room through headphones.

The advantage to a MIDI applications lab is that students can hear music in different keys, tempos, and pitches. They can experience—actually see—the variations. MIDI gives students the chance to try "What if..." What if the harmony is different? What if the pitch is lower? Since students can change the variables, they can create and experiment.

Hill wants a recording studio for performing groups as well. Instead of just rehearsing, students will come in to record the session, listen to it, and evaluate the performance. With it, Hill's program will provide total technical support for music in a combination of traditional and high-tech areas. Performing ensembles will have a place to get quality recordings of their work to use as an evaluative tool. Music directors will be able to listen to the performance and work on any area that needs improvement.

At graduation, many students at the New World School for the Arts win schol-arships to major music institutes. Hill's students are at a distinct advantage. With so much theoretical preparation, they are ready for future careers as serious musicians—they already know the score.

BY
STEPHEN
MARCUS

Part 1

Efforts to predict the future of computer technology are particularly chancy, given its rate of change. To paraphrase Al Bork at UC Irvine: by the time it's free of bugs, it's obsolete. So you can make a monkey out of yourself trying to predict the future of computers in the teaching of English. Since that's what I regularly spend time doing, I suppose I should take some comfort in knowing that at least I'm in good company—for the ancient Egyptians, the god of text and writing took the form of a baboon.

Mentors aside, I tried about three years ago to identify changes (either positive or negative) that might occur during the next 15 years, resulting from the impact of technology on the teaching of writing. It's interesting to see to what degree I'm already behind the times. What follows is a shortened version of my list. In Part 2, below, I'll suggest some ways to anticipate previous crises and make the most of the inevitable.

- People will stop confusing real paper with virtual paper. Most of us still think of a word processor as merely a means of producing a printed document. That's like thinking film as a way to document plays, which after all don't have montage, closeups, split screens, etc. Hypermedia "documents" exist as process, not product. At the very least, William Miller predicted to the Modern Language Association,

"scholarly publishing...will [move] to a paperless, computerized mode, [and] university administrators will shake their heads in wonder at the antiquated humanists who insist that a large share of the library's resources be spent on books and magazines so clearly doomed to physical extinction."

- Grading will become more dependent on the kind of data available from style checkers. All the controversy about style checkers doesn't seem to deter efforts to develop more of them. Some research suggests that teachers grade papers on completely different dimensions of writing; nevertheless, style checkers will continue to be a particularly "easy sell" to those who have a penchant for quantifying information.

- More education will take place in the home through instructional databases and telecommunications networks. Many of these will be provided by commercial sources, not educational institutions. These developments will be intensified as companies take such savvy approaches like AppleLink Personal Edition, in which a telecommunication system is presented within an entertainment metaphor.

- Writing labs will become like studio art courses, in which instructors can monitor and give immediate feedback on students' developing texts—and have their advice almost as quickly incorporated into the emerging documents. This may sound pretty good,

121

but some teachers are troubled by the consequences. They think students become too dependent on easy access to teachers' help in all stages of the composing process. In addition, some teachers who want to see discrete "drafts" of students' writing complain about no longer being sure how to define such a "draft," given the rapidity with which students revise their work. Other teachers aren't sure who should be getting the grade in such "collaborative" writing environments.

- Software that generates its own text will change the nature of writer-text-reader relationships. Early plans for IBM's EPISTLE project envisioned the computer's reading incoming letters, taking note of key words, and generating memos based on the stored writing style of the person responsible for the reply. While this work remains uncompleted, it has in its own way been anticipated by the automatic signature machines already widely used.

- Spelling and style checkers will make it even harder to convince students to learn many of the basic skills. Unfortunately, just as a great many teachers are still unsure about the power relationships between computers and people, students themselves are prone to thinking that the machines will solve their problems. This is an issue of attitudes and expectations as much as technology.

- Handwriting will degenerate for more students. In general, it will develop as one of the fine or applied arts. There are reasonable people who question the need for students' learning handwriting (as opposed to printing) in the first place. The increasing accessibility of software that allows and encourages people to "design" their documents may lessen many people's willingness to depend on—or develop—their handwriting, the legibility of which is most probably a source of indifference or shame.

Readers may want to fine-tune, omit, or add certain items—as well they should. It is, in fact, less important whether such predictions are accurate than that by concentrated efforts to articulate them, they aid any novice oracle in applying focused attention and insight to a problematic but fascinating field.

The future of literacy—that is, the nature and proficiency of reading and writing skills—is as uncertain now as it has always been. Pessimists note that history provides ample evidence for questioning the desirability of "technological progress." In fact, when I first started working in the field, most English teachers proudly turned their backs on the future, ignored the present, and faced the past with hope and determination.

The optimistic view, of course, is that computers and related technologies are providing new and increasingly rich environments that both enhance and transform students' capacities. The stability and vitality of the profession depend on talented teachers who acquire an informed exuberance (and you know who you are). As usual, they'll be a major force in making the most of what the technology and their students offer them.

Part 2

In Part 1, I predicted some effects of technology on the teaching of English. Here in Part 2 I'll deal with more general questions, beginning with brief descriptions of compelling speculations about the foundations of our future. This is a partial reading list for those who wish to understand the source, nature, and direction of trends in hardware, software, and "neural wetware" (i.e., our own brains). Each book could be described in the same terms Sherry Turkle uses to characterize the "holding power" of computers. These books fascinate, they disturb equanimity, they precipitate thought.

• *Are Computers Alive?* by Geoff Simons (Birkhauser). Even if you're familiar with typical discussions of artificial intelligence (AI) development, you may experience some difficulty with notions of computer chips made not from silicon but from carbon-based life forms, with questions of robotic sexuality and reproduction, with debates about civil rights for computers, and with calls for computer liberation. Simons is Chief of England's National Computing Centre. His "central thesis [is] that computers and robots...can be properly regarded as emerging life forms...The arguments against computer life... have been outflanked by events." Simons' book is at times hard to like and difficult to accept, but it is a valuable resource and protection against easy answers to difficult questions. "We will soon not be asking whether computers and robots are alive, but w*hat sort* of life they represent."

• *Robots of Dawn* by Isaac Asimov (Doubleday). This is a science fiction novel, and on its own, it wouldn't necessarily stand out as a guidepost to the future. In the context of Simons' book, however, it provides an intriguing vision of a society trying to resolve its attitudes about technological life forms; in fact, it deals with most of the very issues that Simons raises. As a kind of murder mystery, Asimov's book deals in part with question of whether a robot can be said to have been "killed"—as opposed to merely destroyed, damaged, or demolished. The story is filled with events in which robots are victims of a kind of "racism." Yet, insofar as robots are treated as second-class citizens, they are by that very fact taken to be in some meaningful way alive. Asimov's and Simons' books make a fascinating pair. Reading Simons, you might feel that "by no stretch of the imagination could this guy's ideas be taken seriously." Asimov's imagination, however, is more than equal to the task, and he does us a service by exercising it with his usual story-telling power.

> "We will soon not be asking whether computers and robots are alive, but w*hat sort* of life they represent."

• *Machines Who Think* by Pamela McCorduck (W.H. Freeman and Company). Can machines think? Well... can human beings fly? The answers to both questions depend on the level of abstraction at which they're asked and on the historical moment in which they're posed. McCorduck addresses the issues of AI at a variety of levels. She explores the major objections to the very notion of AI and provides a fascinating history of attempts to refute them. She traces AI's roots in philosophy, ethics, religion, literature, psychology, and the arts (as well as the sciences), noting that AI practitioners are "as lively a group of poets, dreamers, holy men, rascals and assorted eccentrics as one could hope to find—not a dullard among them." Her account tells us as much about our own intelligence as about the capacities of our artifacts to mirror, or mock, or surpass us.

• *The Second Self* by Sherry Turkle (Simon and Schuster). Turkle provides a Piagetian study of people and computers. Her focus is on "the machine as it enters social life and psychological development... The question is not what will the computer be like in the future, but what will *we* be like? What kind of people are we becoming?" While McCorduck's work focuses more on the major figures in AI development, Turkle provides extremely rich and provocative insights into the broader computer-using culture—including the kids in our classes. She identifies stages and qualities of people's concerns with computer technology. Her writing, like McCorduck's, is informed with intelligence, sensibility, and humor.

• *The Man Who Mistook His Wife for a Hat* by Oliver Sacks (Harper & Row). If you're familiar with this book, you may well wonder why I've included it here. It deals, after all, not with artificial intelligence but with aberrations in real intelligence, with the "inconceivably strange...world of the neurologically impaired." These patients are "travellers to unimaginable lands—lands of which otherwise we should have no idea or conception... The scientific and the romantic in such realms cry out to come together...." This book does not relate directly to the future impact of technology. Instead, it serves both to remind us how fragile and precious are our capacities for consciousness and thought, and to keep us humble as we presume to decide what the future (or for that matter, the present) can or can not hold. Sacks' accounts illustrate the tenuous nature of how "what makes sense" depends to a great extent on the idiosyncrasies of what we're using to make sense w*ith*.

Even with such provocative and illuminating resources like those described above, we have the problem of deciding how to focus our attention. How do we structure our reading of current events and developing trends—particularly as we shift our attention from the somewhat distant future to the more immediate present, as we attempt to understand and make good use of developing technology.

William Paisley and Martin Chen provided one useful device while at Stanford University. These researchers framed a series of questions about the effects of present and future technologies on literacy. Their overall question was this: who learns what, from which technology, with what effects on other learning and behavior, and when does this all take place?

This framework is useful for organizing and understanding the developments we see reported everywhere—in newspapers, newsletters, and professional journals and in our everyday experience. In elaborating their framework, Paisley and Chen discussed the following clusters of questions:

• WHO? That is, what socioeconomic groups are acquiring access to the technology? In what gender ratios? Which groups are using public access systems? Within social groups, what are the roles and personality types of those making greater or less use of the systems? Are different groups or individuals showing a preference for specific technologies?

• LEARNS WHAT? That is, what levels and kinds of learning are being attained? What benefits are being derived from casual versus directed use of the systems? What unintended learning outcomes are evident?

• FROM WHICH TECHNOLOGY? That is, which of the *available* technologies are actually being used?

• WITH WHAT EFFECTS ON OTHER LEARNING? Is the technology reinforcing or conflicting with other modes of learning? (Are students coming to expect a teacher to have Pause, Review, and Fast Forward functions?)

• WITH WHAT EFFECTS ON BE-HAVIOR? How are the technologies affecting students' personal adjustment, social development, and patterns of interaction with other students and adults?

• IN WHAT TEMPORAL FRAME OF REFERENCE? Are the questions above being asked at the time of students' initial or later use of the technology? Is the technology itself in an early or later stage of development? (And is the *teaching* of the technology in an early or mature stage?)

This is a daunting set of questions, not all of which will be relevant to a given situation. Taken as a whole, however, they provide the kind of consolidating device that helps bring order to a wealth of disparate events. They give us a handle on the blooming, buzzing, beeping confusion we too often experience around us. These questions, useful as an organizing framework for establishing research directions, can also direct even our informal observations and discussions about how computer technology is shaping the quality of life and learning in the classroom. It's not that they'll make our future perfect, but they can help our present be less tense.

Stephen Marcus, Ph.D., is Associate Director, South Coast Writing Project, Graduate School of Education, University of California, Santa Barbara. This article is based on earlier work appearing in the September and November, 1987, issues of the English Journal.

Article #6
English/Language Arts: A Focus on Literature

WANT TO ENHANCE THE TEACHING OF LITERATURE IN GRADES K-12?
HERE ARE ALMOST A DOZEN SOFTWARE PROGRAMS THAT HELP BRING LITERATURE ALIVE.

BY
STEPHEN
MARCUS

We've come a long way since the days when a major educational computing conference had only one language arts presentation to put on its schedule. (The presentation was offered three times. Twelve people showed up!)

Since those ancient days (1981), English and language arts classrooms have played a major role in teachers' efforts to integrate technology into school curricula. These teachers have had an enormous influence on the quantity and quality of time that students have spent using computers in instructional settings.

Although drill-and-practice software continue to flourish, word processors and other composition aids (like prewriting software and style checkers), and desktop publishing setups have probably received the most attention from computer-using teachers. This shouldn't be surprising, since this software supports the "writing process" approach that is much in favor in language arts instruction.

A Literate Society

Another current trend for shaping the language arts curriculum places literature at its core. If the goal is to develop "a literate, thinking society, then surely the means to that end must be devising for students meaningful encounters with the most effective sources of human expression." It is literature that has the "capacity to move the human spirit in any age, to involve and motivate learning with its appeal to universal feelings and needs, and to elevate common experiences to uncommon meaning ... Literature reminds us of the best in the human character, the most admirable in human values, and the most articulate in human speech." (*English-Language* Arts *Framework,* California State Department of Education, 1987.)

These are lofty goals and may seem far removed from tales of how Jimmy's boa ate the wash or whose "Who" Horton heard. Nevertheless, the love of literature is nurtured at all levels of instruction by a combination of texts and teaching that allows and encourages students to "lose themselves in a good book." In addition, the long-accepted relationship between frequent reading and the development of writing skills adds particular value to the literature-centered classroom.

The point here, however, is not to promote a particular approach to language arts instruction nor, in the listing below, to market any particular software. The point is to indicate that for those who require it, there is ample justification for focusing on literature, and there is a rapidly growing body of courseware that derives its emphasis from this approach and is in turn being shaped by the best practices developed in successful literature instruction.

It's also reassuring to note that new developments are allowing new kinds of technological integration into the whole

126

language arts spectrum of reading, writing, speaking, and listening. Sound digitizers and synthesizers, video overlay cards, and other multimedia applications allow students to see and hear, to illustrate and animate their own and others' texts, and they can do all this in instructional settings that have the interactive, flexible nature that derives from computer-based applications

Categories

There are some rough categories of software that are useful for studying literature. *Tutorials* are interactive programs that help students think and write about what they're reading or do their own creative writing. There are *word processing files* that contain assignments to help students do similar tasks. Though such material doesn't have the interactive nature of tutorials, it can be structured to carry on a dialogue of sorts with the student. There are also *data base* applications that either provide research material or allow students to construct their own thorough activities based on their reading.

Numerous *creative writing programs* let students write and sometimes illustrate (and even animate) their work. And there is interactive *fiction,* in which the particulars of story line and (occasionally) plot and character development result from the reader's choices in the course of using the software—turning the reader, in a sense, into an author. More generalized *utility programs* can aid in creating references and notes on favorite books or for preparing research papers.

There are some very popular and successful programs—like *The Children's Writing and Publishing Center* from The Learning Co., or the series of literary analysis aids from MECC—that can aid students in writing about literature. What is somewhat new is the approach pioneered by companies like Humanities Software, in which the courseware includes, or has as its primary focus, classic children's and adult literature.

Numerous Programs

The 1989 National Educational Computing Conference, held in June in Boston, provided a marked contrast to the conference referred to at the start of this discussion. An extraordinary array of English and language arts software was on display, both in sessions and on the exhibit floor. The few products mentioned below merely suggest the wide range of aids and features becoming available for studying, writing about, and creating literature.

The descriptions of software programs in the accompanying box do not constitute a "best of" list, nor are they meant to evaluate the products—that should be left to individual teachers. Of course, by virtue of being included here, it is implicit that these are products worth taking a look at. (Note: Prices are retail for single copies. Check for discounts and lab packs.)

> ". . . Literature reminds us of the best in the human character, the most admirable in human values, and the most articulate in human speech."

A Sampling of Literature Software

Title: THE BOARS EXPLORE
Description: After reading animated adventures, students can use graphics, animation, and text to create their own adventures. First title in the series is *The Boars in Camelot*.
Grades: 2-6
Computers: Apple II family
Publisher: Pelican Software
Learning Lab Software Publ. Inc.
21000 Nordhoff St.
Chatsworth, Calif. 91311
(800) 222-7026 (in Calif.);
(800) 247-4641
Price: $49.95

Title: CREATIVE WRITER
Description: Two packages, Picture Plots and Transportation Tales, contain a word processor and a graphics library for students to use to create scenes and stories.
Grades: 1-5
Computers: Apple II family
Publisher: Silver Burdett & Ginn
4343 Equity Drive, P.O. Box 2649
Columbus, Ohio 43216
(614) 876-0371 (call collect in Ohio, Alaska, and Hawaii);
(800) 848-9500
Price: $49.95/package

Title: CULTURE 1.0
Description: A multimedia data base and guide to more than 3,700 years of literature, art, history, music, philosophy, and religion. Included are images, melodies, and essays, along with student writing utilities. The optional workbook provides interdisciplinary lessons and worksheets.
Grades: 9-12 (and college)
Computers: Macintosh
(requires hypercard)

Publisher: Cultural Resources, Inc.
7 Little Falls Way
Scotch Plains, N.J. 07076
(201) 232-4333
Price: $175.00 (optional workbook, $35)

Title: EXPLORE-A-CLASSIC
Description: Illustrated and animated interactive fiction, with options for students to write their own and create puzzles, mazes, masks, and puppets based on the stories. Current titles include *The Three Little Pigs*, *Stone Soup*, and *The Princess and the Pea*.
Grades: Pre K-3
Computers: Apple, IBM, Tandy 1000
Publisher: William K. Bradford Publishing Co.
P.O. Box 1355
Concord, Mass. 01742
(800) 421-2009
Price: $75.00/title

Title: JOSHUA'S READING MACHINE
Description: Uses music, graphics, and text to develop reading skills in the context of 37 Mother Goose rhymes, children's songs and Aesop's Fables.
Grades: K-2
Computers: Apple, IBM and MS-DOS compatibles, Macintosh, Tandy
Publisher: Compu-Teach
78 Olive Street
New Haven, Conn. 06511
(203) 777-7738 (in Conn.);
(800) 44-TEACH
Price: $39.95

Title: NEWBERRY ADVENTURE SERIES
Description: Students read the award-winning books, then work through the

programs, participating in major decisions required to complete the plots. Understanding of the work is encouraged through questions geared to vocabulary, understanding of main ideas, and recall of specific events. Progress through the story depends on correct answers in the proper sequence.
Grades: 3-8
Computers: Apple II family, Commodore 64
Publisher: Sunburst Communications
39 Washington Dr.
Pleasantville, N.Y. 10570
(800) 431-1934
Price: $65.00

Title: READING MAGIC
Description: Illustrated interactive stories. Current title: *Jack and the Beanstalk* (a "whimsical retelling...set in the future on another planet") and *Flodd, the Bad Guy*.
Grades: K-1
Computers: Apple II family, IBM Tandy 100 and compatibles
Publisher: Tom Snyder Productions
90 Sherman St.
Cambridge, Mass. 02140
(617) 876-4433
Price: $44.95

Title: THE READING WORKSHOP
Description: Along with literary selections (included with courseware) the students are involved with any of 10 reading, writing and language arts activities, which are modifiable using the Teacher ToolKit. Selections range from *The Chocolate Touch* and *The Wizard of Oz* to *The Necklace* and *The Tell-Tale Heart*. Different reading-level materials are provided for each grade level.
Grades: 4-9
Computers: Apple II family, MS-DOS
Publisher: Mindscape Inc.
3444 Dundee Rd.

Northbrook, Ill.   60062
(800) 221-9884
Price: $150/Reading Level

Title: THE STORYTELLER
Description: A collection of fables, folk tales, legends, and fairy tales read by a variety of graphic animated story tellers. Includes a word processor and writing aids for creating, editing and printing additional stories or having them read by the animated figures.
Grades: 3-12
Computers: Amiga, Apple IIGS, IBM, Macintosh
Publisher: First Byte
from Electronic Arts
P.O. Box 7530
San Mateo, Calif. 94403
(800) 245-4525 (product info.);
(415) 571-7171 (site licensing and lab packs)
Price: Variable, depending on version

Title: SUCCESS WITH LITERATURE
Description: A software-text combination, focusing on classic literature like *The Red Badge of Courage, Romeo and Juliet, Walden*, and *A Tale of Two Cities*. Includes a customized word processor and booklets to guide students in their reading and the writing of book reports or literary essays.
Grades: 7-12 (and freshman college)
Computers: Apple II family, MS-DOS
Publisher: Scholastic Software
P.O. Box 7502
2931 East McCarty St.
Jefferson City, Mo. 65102
(800) 392-2179 (in Mo.)
(800) 541-5513
Price: $29.75 (additional student booklet and one disk, $9.95)

Title: WRITE ON!
Description: A literature-based collec-

tion of word processor files that contains prepared lessons geared to well-known children's and adult literature, ranging from *Where the Wild Things Are* to *Crime and Punishment*.

Grades: K-12
Computers: Apple II family, IBM, Macintosh (word processors)
Publisher: Humanities Software
P.O. Box 950
Hood River, Ore. 97031
(509) 493-1395
Price: $70/title (includes site license)

Process Writing in the One-Computer Classroom

As a K-6 computer teacher, I know I have the time and energy to teach the specifics of word processing as well as to design and carry out writing activities that incorporate the steps of the writing process on a daily basis. In working with the staff at my school and in talking with other teachers, I am also aware that most regular classroom teachers, particularly those with only one computer in their rooms, are more limited as to the time they can spend on these endeavors. However, it wasn't too long ago that I was a regular classroom teacher. I know that there are management and educational techniques that a classroom teacher can use to orchestrate the writing process and the vehicle—word processing itself—and still keep from going crazy.

First of all, a teacher must have a mindset of what steps of the process he or she intends to focus on. For me, although there are seven specific steps, I find it easier to break the process into four: prewriting, writing, editing/revising, and publishing. Second, I make a conscious decision that all of the steps will not be performed at the computer in every writing assignment. The computer has its place in all of these steps, but each teacher will have to make personal decisions about when its use is appropriate and convenient. There isn't time for a teacher with 30 students and one computer to put all of the kids on it for every step of the writing process for every writing activity assigned throughout the year. But there are times when using the word processor is appropriate and effective.

Prewriting

There are many different kinds of prewriting a teacher may choose to do with students. These range from brainstorming or clustering ideas to researching and participating in sensory experiences. Prewriting may be done in groups, with the whole class, or individually. It can be done with the conventional classroom tools or it can be done on the computer.

I find brainstorming the easiest to do on the computer because students can simply toss out ideas instead of worrying about their classifications. Further, it works well when the class as a whole is sitting in front of the monitor while the teacher or one individual types the ideas generated. Then the teacher need only print the list of ideas, make copies. and distribute it to the class. Now students have their own idea-specific wordbank in front of them, which is particularly helpful for younger kids.

Individual brainstorming files may be created by the teacher. A disk containing directions is loaded into the computer when each student goes for his or her turn. For example:

List six qualities of a good friend. Then, write some ideas telling about a good friend you've had or would like to have. When you save your list, save it with your name in the following way: Kathy, friend.

By
Kathy
Pon

131

Each individual saves his or her work on a file disk; the next student simply loads the original directions and continues with the activity.

Clustering is another form of prewriting. It is a way of listing ideas, but grouping them in categories. The computer is well suited for this activity because of its inserting capacity. For example, a student might generate ideas that have to do with autumn. A good place to start is with a few topics such as the following:

Thanksgiving
The Weather
Things in Nature
The Harvest

The student can list ideas under each topic, jumping around from group to group without having to worry whether there is room to add more—there is! This activity is good cognitive skill practice for all students. It can be used in a more advanced way for older students by letting them move text around as their lists grow, putting terms that belong together in groups and then naming the groups. I like to tie this activity in with grammar. Having students cluster terms by nouns, verbs, and adjectives is one way to do this (see Figure 3.7.1).

Tying prewriting to what is being studied in grammar is an excellent use of the computer. The following tasks are useful because they are short and they

Figure 3.7.1

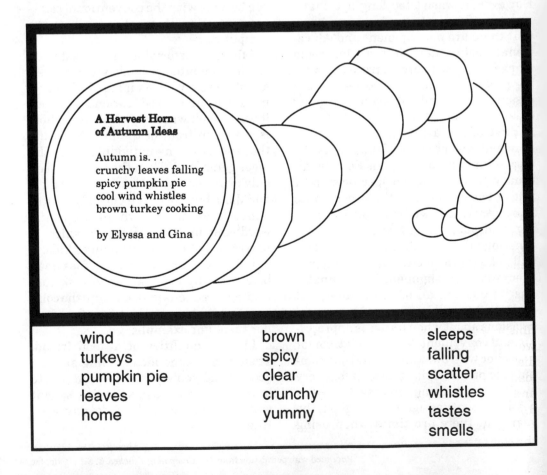

A Harvest Horn
of Autumn Ideas

Autumn is. . .
crunchy leaves falling
spicy pumpkin pie
cool wind whistles
brown turkey cooking

by Elyssa and Gina

wind	brown	sleeps
turkeys	spicy	falling
pumpkin pie	clear	scatter
leaves	crunchy	whistles
home	yummy	tastes
		smells

don't tie up the computer for long amounts of time.

List five words to use for "said." (This list would be printed for groups or individuals studying quotation marks and conversations. They would use the words while writing a conversation.)

Write five nouns that are names of things you see in the cafeteria. (This might be used as a basis for a creative story that focuses in on nouns.)

List five words that have the prefix *bi*. (This might be used for writing a poem that uses words with prefixes.)

It's a good idea to keep the computer open with specific tasks such as the following, which are also forms of prewriting:

Write one or two facts you remember about butterflies.

Write one fact you've learned about Mr. Lincoln.

The resulting lists can be combined into a class fact list and printed as a resource for students researching and writing reports.

Finally, an effective way to use the computer at the prewriting stage is to write story starter questions and save them in a story starter file. Students can put their cursor in the insert mode and write their answers right after the questions without erasing the rest of the text. Questions would address the major components of the story to be written, such as "Who is the hero or heroine?" "Where does the story take place?" and "What good things happen in the story?" When finished, students would again save their work under their own names on a file disk so that the next student need only load up the original task and questions and begin answering them (see Figure 3.7.2).

It cannot be emphasized enough that the computer is an excellent tool for use

---

Figure 3.7.2

More Ideas for Writing at the Computer

A Science Fiction Story Starter
Directions: Make sure your cursor is in the insert mode. Then, put your cursor on the first arrow after each question and answer it. When you are finished, move your arrow key to get to the next question. Save your work under your name + Sci (Kathy.Sci).

1. Where on earth or in the universe is the setting of the story?

2. Who is the main character of the story? Describe him or her or it.

3. What happens to the character?

4. Who or what stands in the way of the character?

5. How does he or she or it solve the problem?

6. How does the story end?

---

at the prewriting stage. However, when there is only one tool and 30 students, the teacher will need to decide when it will be used at this point (versus another time in the writing process) so as not to tie up valuable classroom time.

Writing

Some would say that when the computer is used at the writing stage, its tool capacity is greatest. After all, students have at their fingertips an instrument that encourages fluency as they write or delete text easily, bypassing horrible eraser marks and crossed out sentences.

However, most elementary students don't have the keyboarding skills needed to generate text very quickly. Moreover, most teachers who have one computer in their classrooms don't have the time to allow students onto the computer for very long periods. (If each student took 30 to 40 minutes at a time for writing at the computer, it might be months before assignments were finished.) Therefore, I advocate for the one-computer classroom that most writing at this stage be done with paper and pencil.

At some point during the school year students should generate text directly on the computer so that they see how easily the writing stage can be done. However, with one computer in the classroom and 30 students, a teacher will be doing well to take the entire class through this stage just once.

But there are some one-computer activities I consider sensible and appropriate at this stage in the writing process. Here is my favorite: Have typed into the computer a short poem, ditty, or nursery

Figure 3.7.3

City sidewalks, busy sidewalks,
Dressed in holiday style.
In the air there's a feeling of
Christmas.
Children laughing people passing,
Meeting smile after smile,
And on every street corner you'll
see. . .
Silver bells, silver bells,
It's Christmas time in the city.
Ring-a-ling, hear them ring!
Soon it will be Christmas Day.

rhyme with certain sentence parts underlined. Also give students a hard copy of the piece. Their task is to replace the underlined parts with their own words

to fit a certain theme. To save time, students first work on their hard copies, then enter their work on the computer. In Figure 3, the tune "Silver Bells" was the blueprint for Halloween Carols. This type of exercise is worthwhile because students can still be creative, but they concentrate on writing certain parts of speech or the syntax of sentences. Also, these can be done in a short amount of computer time. And students get to practice two valuable word processing skills: inserting and deleting text.

Another novel use of the computer is to do a shape poem using words describing a particular concept or idea formed into a shape that echoes it. It helps to begin these ahead of time on paper and pencil because generating them on a computer can sometimes be tricky. This is especially true if the text is in a 40 column setup; often the printout fails to match the screen image.

Finally, I again like to tie writing at the computer to the grammar being taught in the classroom. By giving students short sentences to expand upon by using interesting adjectives, verbs, or prepositional phrases, you can provide them with a short writing assignment that piques their creativity and teaches a skill at the same time.

Editing

The editing stage incorporates someone's response to the writing, actual editing for mechanics, possible revision of the text or voice of a paper, and even some evaluation of what has been written. The teaching of this skill must not be taken too lightly. As teachers we must constantly model and teach editing to our students. Thankfully, the computer has made the task a bit easier. My experience with students has been that they become quite overwhelmed when faced with editing a whole screen of text, especially if it is the first time the editor has seen the writing. A few strategies to ensure editing is done on every assignment, that it doesn't take too long, and that it isn't too difficult a task for students to do help ease this strain.

I am a great advocate of editing the first draft (usually done on paper) before a student ever gets it on screen. This can be done by the writer, by peers, or by an adult. I like to use an evaluation sheet (see Figure 3.7.4) and to concentrate on checking for one or two criteria at a time. Even though this is only a proofreading mechanism for the first draft, it helps students bypass the time wasted in typing mixed up, unorganized text into the computer in the first place. There will be plenty of time to work on computer commands that edit, move, or replace text even if the students type into the computer what seems to be a pretty good draft. There are always typos, words stuck together, paragraphs to be separated, titles and names to be centered, and trite phrases to be replaced.

All these make for useful editing sessions later.

I like to have students edit in one of the following ways:

• First the writer must read through the text. If he or she cannot find any mistakes, a peer checks it over. If they both think they've got a pretty good draft, they are ready for me or another adult to sit with them and go over it.

• Sometimes editing is done for one item at a time by four students in a read-around group. The first reader will edit only for capitals, the second for punctuation, the third for spelling, and the fourth for usage. By the time I see the manuscript it's a breeze to go through. (I usually like to look at all of my student's text before it is printed, as I believe it's terrible public relations to send work riddled with errors home to parents.)

Of course, the key to this entire process is to give students practice at edit-

Figure 3.7.4

Creative Writing Evaluation Sheet							
Criteria Dates:							
Organization (makes sense in order)							
Lively, precise words							
Complete sentences							
Spelling							
Punctuation							
Capitals (Titles, important words)							
Neatness							
Creative ideas (Did you put much effort into this?)							
Mechanics grade							
Creative grade							
Other comments							
Title							
Name							

ing. It's not a bad idea to set up sentences or short paragraphs at the computer which focus in on specific grammar areas as well as the specific commands used to fix the errors. The teachers at my school do a lot of whole-group editing on the overhead, giving students hard copies of the text the teacher is presenting. Again, the class will read through the text and edit for only one item at a time, first on paper and later at the computer.

Publishing

It often seems that, by the time students get to the publishing stage of the writing process, it's time to move on to a new

Figure 3.7.5

How to Make a Book Using the Computer

1. PREWRITING
How will you do it?
Clustering
Brainstorming
Diagramming
Visualization
In/Out Charts
Sentence Strips
Will you do this prewriting on the computer?
Will you use pencil and paper?

2. WRITING
Which word processing program will you use? (Or will they do pencil and paper first?)
Magic Slate?
Bankstreet Writer?
AppleWorks?
Kidwriter?
Print Shop?
StoryMaker?
Newsroom?
Mousepaint?
Will it be a joint or a single effort?

3. EDITING
Will peers do it or will the teacher or will the individual writer? Will you print out the copy or edit on the computer?
Will you edit for specifics or expect the students to do the entire page?

4. PRINTING
Will students be allowed to print their work or will you or other adults do it?
Do you want to enlarge the print?

assignment. However, this is the most fun part of the experience for most students and it should never be left out. The published paper may be hung somewhere for others to see. Perhaps it is read to a PTA or senior citizens group, or just to classmates. Or it may be incorporated into an art project which is set out for Parent Night, displayed in a local bank for the community to see, or placed in the school library for others to enjoy.

One popular option is for students to publish a book (see Figure 3.7.5). When a writing is to be published as a book, there are a few decisions that will need to be made:

• *Which* word processing program will work best?

Don't forget titles, credits or title pages.
Some may want to include an "About the Author."

5. ILLUSTRATING
How will you do it?
Paint
Crayon
Chalk (Messy unless you laminate the page)
Magazine or discarded book pictures
Their own photos

6. BOOK COVERS
How will they be done?
Cardboard covered with paper, wrapping paper, contact paper, fabric, or artwork
Rings
Tagboard
Laminated construction paper

7. PUTTING IT TOGETHER (Directions for a tied book)
Cover the outer cardboard or other bookcover first.
Use a smaller piece of paper to cover the inside of the bookcover.
Lay the two covers flat on the table, leaving about 1/8 inch between them. (This will allow the jacket to close all the way.) Use packaging tape to bind them together.
Punch holes in the pages. (You may want to use the gummed hole reinforcers over each of the holes to prevent tearing.)
String yarn or string through the pages first.
Mark where the yarn is and punch holes through the covers at those points. A point from a compass works well.
Pull the string through first the front cover and then the back cover.
Tie the yarn ends together while the book is open on its face. This prevents tying the pages too tight and subsequent difficult page turning.

• What typestyle would you like?

• Does the program generate graphics that might add to the students' writing?

• Will the book be a joint or individual effort?

• Will students print their own work or does an adult need to do it?

• Will another program be needed to do title pages, credits, or an "About the Author" page?

• What about illustrations? Will you use crayon, paint, or photos?

• Will you laminate the pages?

• Will students cover the cardboard covers with fabric, colorful butcher paper, or contact paper?

If you can anticipate these choices ahead of time, there's only fun to be had! Some of my favorite publishing activities include the following:

• Enlarging and illustrating reports about community workers and combining them into a class book on the subject.

• Printing each line in a paragraph of a *fortunately / unfortunately* or *horrible day* paragraph separately so that each sentence becomes the text for a page in an illustrated book.

• Using a program such as *Print Shop* to print lists beginning with the letters of the alphabet for an "ABC Book of Things That Are Small" or "An ABC Book of Things That Make Us Laugh."

Places That Accept Children's Writing

Gifted Children Newsletter appeals to Grades 7-12 and accepts games, riddles, creative puzzles, nonfiction. Submissions: "Spin Off," Gifted and Talented Publications, Inc., Route 1, Box 115, Sewell, NJ 08080.

Highlights for Children prints all forms of the original work in "Our Own Page" section. Must be 150 words or less and must have a note from parents or teacher stating that work is original (ages up to 16). Submissions: *Highlights for Children,* 803 Church St., Honesdale, PA 18431.

Jack and Jill prints articles, letters, artwork, poetry, and stories (ages 8-12). Submissions: *Jack and Jill,* 1100 Water Way Blvd., Indianapolis, IN 46206.

Maggie Drawers Literary Magazine (Grades 7-college) accepts poems, es-

says, plays, short stories. Submissions: Bryan Lindsey, Editor, USC-S, Spartenburg, SC 29303.

Ranger Rick's Nature Magazine prints poetry, jokes, riddles, games, and letters (ages 7-12). Submissions: *Ranger Rick's Nature Magazine,* 1412 16th St., N.W., Washington, DC 30026.

Seventeen is a slick magazine that welcomes manuscripts, especially opinion pieces. It is receptive to different ideas. Submissions: Cathy Rindner, 850 Third Ave., New York, NY 10022.

Stone Soup accepts stories of up to 2,500 words. The entire magazine is written by children: fiction, poetry, artwork, and photography (ages up to 13). Submission: *Stone Soup,* Box 83, Santa Cruz, CA 95063.

- Printing text written about spiders only 15 characters wide, then folding the text accordion-style and using these strips as spider's legs, attached to construction paper bodies.
- Printing "What Is Peace?" essays in small text so that they may be glued to small doves and hung on mobiles.
- Reading radio shows and plays into a tape recorder to be played back for audiences.
- Saving personal collections of writing to display on a large *me* banner for hanging during Back to School Night.

Not to be forgotten are publications that accept children's writing. Many children's magazines are always looking for original manuscripts and might never get to see the wonderful pieces that pass our desks. We need to be advocates for children in this way. (See the sidebar for a list of such publications.)

Word processing and the writing process *can* become a natural part of the one-computer classroom without becoming yet another task for a teacher to do. Moreover, the teacher who does decide to take students through these steps will probably find students enjoying their writing tasks and improving their writing quality and fluency.

Article #8
A Writing Class Taps
Into a World of Knowledge

STUDENTS IN A ROCKLAND COUNTY, N.Y., HIGH SCHOOL ENGLISH CLASS USE THE
BREADNET ON-LINE NETWORK TO REACH STUDENTS IN SOUTH AMERICA AND AROUND THE U.S.

By
Gwen
Solomon

"In some parts of the United States, when you mention South America, people think that we live out in the jungle or on a mountain somewhere. It's like, 'yeah, yesterday we went out hunting on our llamas and caught us some dinner.' Actually, it's quite nice; I mean, Lima is like any other city in the world."

Thus an electronic relationship developed last fall between two students separated by two continents: one was in New York state, the other in Peru, South America.

What started as an on-line writing exchange program between two classes turned into something more akin to a cultural exchange program. The students are Joy Macari, a senior at Clarkstown South High School in Rockland County, New York, and Larry Schneider at Colegio Roosevelt High School in Lima, Peru. Joy and Larry are participants in BreadNet, an electronic network of students who use computers and telecommunications as tools to help them develop as writers. Teachers also use BreadNet as an on-line forum for communicating ideas on writing instruction.

Joy's English teacher, Ken Holvig, is a graduate of Middlebury College's Bread Loaf School of Writing. At Bread Loaf, Holvig and many English teachers from around the U.S. and abroad have become committed to using technology for improving students' writing skills.

The Peru Connection

Holvig's class has communicated with numerous schools, but his students seem to have learned most from their exchange with the students in Lima. First, students wrote about themselves so they could get to know each other as individuals. Then they learned about each other's cultures through discussions on topics such as sports, personal freedom, and corruption.

Holvig's students were amazed to discover, for example, that police in Peru can be bribed easily. Questioned on the effects of this, one Peruvian student responded: "I don't want to scare you into thinking this place is so horrible, cause it's not at all...it's just a different way of life. It all balances out."

Another Peruvian student wrote: "since drinking is so accepted as a part of the culture, you don't find the same abuse of alcohol as in the United States." Here in the U.S., where there are strict laws regulating the consumption of alcohol by minors, teenagers invariably test those laws. Peruvians, in turn, asked: "do you go to New York City much? Do you really get mugged and all near Central Park?" "Have you ever seen a real street gang?" "Is it true that kids just have candy bars for lunch?"

Some of the initial misconceptions aside, students found they had more in common than they had differences—

140

music, schoolwork, dating, and skiing, for example.

Students eventually shared their writing with, and responded to writing from, students on the other end of the line. They also posted their work on the on-line "Electronic Writers' Workshop" for all BreadNet participants to read and evaluate. Peer evaluation, in this instance, worked. As one student said, "Today over the wires I received an excellent example of constructive criticism...that's what this project is all about."

Writing for an Audience

With the support of Clarkstown South High School's English department chairman, Ray Roswell, Holvig acquired a computer writing lab with 25 Apple IIGS computers and six ImageWriter II printers. Thanks to grants from Apple Computer Inc. and from a private foundation, Holvig and the other teachers purchased modems and connect-time.

Holvig finds a difference in student writing when they write for an audience rather than for the teacher alone. He has always encouraged students to submit work for publication; in fact, he teaches an elective course called "Writing To Be Published." With the addition of BreadNet, his students have "a wider audience, another vehicle in which to be published."

Department chairman Roswell agrees: "the more students see publication of their work, the more pride they feel, and the better off they are. It's part of the writing process."

And students are enthusiastic about BreadNet. "BreadNet gives you another point of view on your writing rather than just from people who live in your area," says Clarkstown South senior Ethan Rosch. "It has improved my writing. I get different ideas and learn about different cultures."

Holvig noticed that his students seemed more willing to criticize writing from students who attended schools other than Clarkstown. In one instance, a friendly exchange that began over a baseball story became a heated debate. Students in Clarkstown, along with others in Wilsall, Mont. and Cook, Minn., learned about baseball and on-line etiquette from one another.

Other Clarkstown classes have begun to use BreadNet. "We encourage students in other classes to benefit from exchanging ideas across the wires too," says Roswell. For example, "When our literature elective on the American West got on-line with a Navajo reservation, they discovered that the number of ponies determines status there much the same as the make of car does in Clarkstown."

As an outgrowth of these exchanges of student writing, BreadNetters produce "Voices Across The Wires," a compilation of their electronic efforts, twice a year. The fall issue is edited by Clarkstown students, the spring issue by students at the Sewickley Academy in Sewickley, Pa.

Insight into Cultures

Perhaps the greatest effect on students is the knowledge of faraway places gained through personal (albeit "on-line") relationships. The stories exchanged often offer insights into the different cultures in which the writers live. For example, Warren Wesoja at Kearsarge Regional High School in North Sutton, N.H., wrote about hunting racoons. Maxine Last Horse at the Little Wound School in Kyle, South Dakota, described a tribal dancer. And students in Sewickley related family histories in the steel mills of Pittsburgh.

Says Clarkstown student Mike Schneider in "Voices Across The Wires," "I learned a lot about Latin America, quite a lot more than I could pick up from the news. I learned just as much about my own country. I wasn't aware of the gross injustices going on in the U.S. and the exchange made me focus on such problems."

Says BreadNet director William Wright, who runs the service from his home office in Washington, D.C., "linking to a different culture makes you aware of that place, tunes your senses in a way that lets ideas cut through the information glut. An example is our link with the school in Lima. Now every story in The *New York Times* about Peru jumps out."

A Resource for Teachers

In addition to student exchanges, BreadNet teachers discuss ideas and hold conferences on-line. Their goal is to improve the teaching of writing. A Recent BreadNet conference, for example, focused on the pros and cons of electronic pen-pal exchanges versus group writing.

BreadNet is a relatively small network, but it has big plans for the future. Some of these priorities, Wright says, are a conference of teachers of Native Americans, a conference of Midwestern teachers, the addition of more overseas schools, more collaborative writing projects, and a new interactive workshop called "World Trade" to allow students to share essays about where they are and what life is like there.

The key element in the success of BreadNet is the involvement of dedicated teachers. "All the projects work

because they're initiated by teachers," Wright says.

On the local level, the Clarkstown School District also encourages student and faculty exchanges over ClarkNet, a district-wide telecommunications network for writing. Two high school students operate this bulletin board from the English department office at Clarkstown South.

Through ClarkNet, Gwen Simerol's students at Link Elementary School, for example, receive advice on their writing from high school students at Clarkstown South.

Ken Holvig feels that his work with students on BreadNet and ClarkNet pays off. Students come into the lab eager to work, and they beg him to stay after school. Student attitudes and achievement are positive, perhaps, because someone's listening to the voices across the wires.

For information about BreadNet, contact the Bread Loaf School of English, Middlebury College, Middlebury, Vt. 05753; (802) 388-3711.

Article #9
Observations on Electronic Networks: Appropriate Activities for Learning

By
James A.
Levin,
Al Rogers,
Michael
Waugh,
and
Kathleen
Smith

The use of long-distance computer networks is becoming increasingly attractive for educators as the prices of modems and communication decrease and as communication software slowly becomes easier to use. Once we have purchased modems and interface cards and mastered complex communication programs, the question remains: what are appropriate network-based activities?

In the several years that we have been using the networks, we have formed some ideas about the role networks can play in classroom activities and the kinds of activities that are successful on them. These activities focus on electronic networks as a means of communication rather than as a means of accessing information.

We have been using FrEdMail, an informal grassroots educational telecommunications network. Each participating area has a microcomputer running the FrEdMail electronic bulletin board, accessible by a local phone call. Each of these FrEdMail computers serves as a "node" linked to one or more micros running FrEdMail and forming a national network with a few non-U.S. nodes. System operators or Sysops for each board are volunteers. Its primary function is to serve as an environment for student projects, providing real audiences and purposes for learning.

Electronic Pen Pals

One activity that occurs to many new users is some form of "electronic pen pals." Electronic pen pals seems like a productive way to start out a network interaction: students are motivated, they can write for a distant audience, and they may learn about different cultures through interaction with their electronic pen pals. However, there are a number of problems with this activity, especially when used as a whole-class introduction to the use of electronic networks. Too often the following scenario happens with electronic pen palling:

Your students work hard to write pen pal letters on a word processor. There is a lot of excitement and motivation, and this seems like a productive activity. Finally, you send off the pen pal letters to another site. The next day your students ask if responses have come back yet. (They know their messages have been sent electronically, and therefore were delivered "instantly," or at least overnight). There are no responses. The next day they ask again, and the next, and the next. . .

Finally, weeks later, responses come back, but only for some of your students. Those who got responses are excited, but the others are disappointed. You try to get them to send more messages, but it's difficult to motivate those who didn't get responses to write again. You want rapid turn-around, but school assemblies are scheduled, Johnny misses his turn at the computer because he's sick, Mary misses hers because of a field trip, and so forth. Weeks later you send out responses, but only from *some* of your students (*most* of your students that got

143

responses). Now you understand why only some of your students got replies. You also understand why they didn't get instant responses. It takes weeks to get your students organized and scheduled on the computer, and all the while students at the other school are asking their teacher every day if their responses have arrived yet.

Since only a dwindling fraction of the students at each school get responses, this activity rapidly dies away, leaving everyone feeling vaguely frustrated and unfulfilled.

A better initial activity than computer pals is to create and post a "class directory," in which students write a short description of themselves and what they are interested in. You can post this directory on the bulletin board ($KIDWIRE in FrEdMail), and then students elsewhere who read it and who have matching interests can establish contact with your students. If a cluster of common interests appears in the directory, then someone (you, one of your students, or someone elsewhere on the network) can use that as a basis for organizing a new network activity centered on that interest.

If your network has project-oriented activities, it's much easier to start out by joining in with an on-going activity, and then once you've gotten a feel for how the networks operate, you can suggest new ideas for activities. The FrEdMail network has a bulletin board called $IDEAS for teachers to exchange ideas about network projects. When project-oriented messages arrive, all students will be interested in them, and many will read them several times in the process of carrying out the project. When a "computer pal" message arrives addressed to one student, other students are much less interested in reading it, and none of the students are very interested in reading it in much depth.

This discussion is not to say that electronic networks should never be used for electronic pen pal exchanges, but our experience strongly suggests that electronic pen pals is not the best way to start out interacting on an established network. Instead, we suggest joining in a project-oriented network activity, such as the Noon Observation Project.

The Noon Observation Project

This project involved students in various locations in measuring the length of a shadow at noontime on a specified day in order to determine the circumference of the Earth. The project is a replication of the Eratosthenes of Cyrene experiment of over 2,000 years ago in ancient Egypt. Al Rogers, originator of the project, posted a message on $IDEAS describing the project. (See sidebar)

He invited teachers to participate, and set up a private conference for developing the project. The deadline to respond was April 22 giving everybody plenty of time to have spring vacations. Observations were to be conducted the week of May 2 and final results shared the week of May 9.

Responses came from schools in California, Montana, Illinois, Alaska, and Japan, providing the geographical distances needed for the project. Jim Levin volunteered to set up an *AppleWorks* spreadsheet for storing the data and for computing the earth's circumference from two sets of shadow measurements. He also supplied a simple method for calculating local noon given the participant's longitude.

Finally, the first week of May arrived, and shortly thereafter, messages reporting the data were sent.

There were then a set of messages discussing the analysis of the data. Although data came in from four sites, various problems arose that in the end only allowed the project to use the data from Champaign, Illinois and La Mesa, California. The data reported from Montana was collected on a different day from the other data, so it couldn't be used directly. Finally, the data collected from one California site deviated quite substantially from what was expected and would have predicted a negative circumference when combined with the La Mesa data. An exchange of messages revealed that this site collected their data an hour before local noon, having failed to take into account Daylight Savings Time, which had gone into effect shortly before the week of the data collection.

Despite all this, the estimated circumference of the Earth derived from the measurements at Champaign and La Mesa was within one percent of the current best measures. This is a surprisingly good estimate.

The students in Champaign sent out a summary of the project:

"Let us tell you a little about how we arrived at our reading. Well, on Tuesday, May 3rd we broke the class up into 10 groups of 3 each and with meter sticks taped to book ends we went out to the black top playground. We all split up and using computer paper taped to the ground we tried to measure the shadow our meter sticks cast. We measured every minute for 10 minutes. It was very windy so one person held the book end, one steadied the meter stick, and the third measured. We had a rough idea of what pattern the shadows should have— a lot of them didn't fit the pattern.

"On Wednesday our teacher showed us all the data and we decided we hadn't been very accurate. There was more than a 10 centimeter difference between the longest & shortest shadows in some minutes, and no two groups agreed on what minute (actual noon) had the shortest shadow: also there was some question as to whether we had missed absolute noon. So we decided to try again with a bit more organization and experience.

"On Thursday May 5th, armed with our meter sticks taped to book ends, we went out again. This time we had 11 groups, and we lined ourselves up on the painted end line of the basketball court (in an area we thought looked most level). We took 12-60 second interval readings. The wind was not as bad, and we were much better at keeping the stick still and marking an accurate shadow (where the dark edge started).

"When the data was displayed on the overhead on Friday we were delighted. There was only a 3 centimeter difference between the longest & shortest shadows over the entire 12 minutes, and 9 of the eleven groups reached their shortest shadow in minutes 6, 7, or 8.

We decided then to use only those 9 readings. We then threw out the longest & shortest of those and took the average of the remaining 7. This is how we got the length for the shadow we used to compute our angle.

"Our teacher then told us about how to find an angle in a right triangle using the tangent ratio and we came up with our angle.

"After we sent it off we couldn't wait to get the results. When we found out how accurate we were with the California reading, we were proud of our effort.

"Aside from getting two class periods on the playground, we also learned a lot from the experiment.

"It was interesting to learn about what

Eratosthenes figured out so long ago, and to do it ourselves in 1988. We also learned about the solstice, the Tropics of Cancer & Capricorn, the way the sun shines at an angle, the pattern the shadows made, and how careful you have to be to be accurate. We also felt the concept of circumference became clearer and we could almost visualize the curve of the Earth between here and California.

"So again, thank you to all the other sites, and we hope you enjoyed this Noon Project as much as we did."

    The Pre-Alg Class
    at Columbia Middle School
    Champaign, Illinois

As indicated by this message, students learned a variety of things from this project, many of which bridge the content areas in the conventional curriculum. They learned mathematics in a meaningful context, got a better feel for geography, learned first hand the importance of careful measurement, participated directly in dealing with the issues of data analysis and reduction, and learned some of the values of working jointly with others.

Providing Support: The Network's Role

In order to learn about the role that the network played in this project, let us consider whether such a project could have been done without an electronic network. In terms of conducting a project which provides a practical context for mathematics skills, the class could have gone out and used their meter stick shadows and the shadow of the school's flagpole to determine the height of the flagpole, as mathematics teachers have done for generations.

However, the network seemed to provide a highly motivating context for learning both for the students and for the teachers involved. More specifically, it provided:

- a source of ideas,
- a supplier of tools,
- a source of diverse data, and
- a diverse audience.

The network serves as a source of ideas suggested by students, teachers, or other adults elsewhere. Ideas for projects are posted on a bulletin board and those of interest can be picked up easily. Unlike source books of teaching ideas, the network provides an interactive environment, with which ideas can evolve.

The network provides a means for distributing various diverse tools for carrying out the project. Instructions, background information, and also computer-based tools (such as the spreadsheet developed by Jim Levin) can be posted and shared.

The network provides access to a diverse range of data beyond that available at any one location. In this project, the diversity was the different shadow lengths measured at each site. Phenomena that are common to different sites, but that differ in some specific way are good candidates for successful network-based activities.

Perhaps most importantly, the network provides a wider and more diverse audience for the learning activity. Student data collection, analyses, and project write-ups are aimed not just for the teacher (the usual audience) but also for a wider range of students, teachers, and other adults across the country or even around the world. Students' writing has been shown to improve when aimed at a wider audience provided by a network (Cohen & Riel, 1988). Our observation is that the same holds for students engaged in other sorts of network activities.

Providing Support:
The Role of the Class

We also learned that it's important to have data collection take place during class. In an earlier project called the Moon Observation Project (Waugh & Levin, 1988), students went home on the night of a first quarter moon and measured the angle that the points of the crescent moon made to the horizon. This angle varies from place to place as a function of latitude, just like the length of the noon shadow.

Some students failed to bring in an observation, others were not very careful about drawing the angle, and probably some students were not careful about making the observation at the specified time. The data reflected this by showing a large amount of variability, large enough to wash out small differences between sites that didn't have a very large deviation in latitudes.

We plan to switch to observing the last quarter moon instead (which appears in the early morning sky rather than the early evening sky), so that the observation can occur during school time as part of a class activity. It will be harder for students to forget to make the observation, they will have peer models and teacher help in making the observations, and the class as a whole will have a shared context to make the analysis meaningful. It will also make it easier for the teacher to integrate the whole process into the ongoing curriculum.

Improved Observations on Educational Electronic Networks

While we consider the Noon Observation Project a successful network-based project, we still feel there are aspects that need to be modified. These changes point to general properties of network projects as well. A strength of this project was illustrated by the summary message sent by the Columbia Middle School classroom. We would like to increase this sort of post-data collection student involvement. One problem for this project was the lateness in the school year that the data was collected. But we also think more emphasis and planning should go into the post-observational phase. Students should be encouraged to look in detail at the overall data, try to identify patterns, and interact with the other sites to clarify any problems or issues that arise.

Students should be encouraged to work jointly with other students to develop presentations of the project which could be a project for a school's science fair, or even a project for a *TeleScience Fair* (Levin, Waugh, & Kolopanis, 1988). This is a science fair activity conducted on an electronic network with project descriptions submitted electronically, posted and judged by distributed judges, and then "visited" by students, teachers, and other adults electronically.

Another post-observational activity is to write up the project reports for publication in a network-based newspaper or journal. In the area of science, we have explored the notion of *TeleScience Chronicles* (Levin, Waugh, & Kolopanis, 1988), an electronic journal with sections for student reports of network projects, as well as sections for review articles, discussion forums, book reviews, and so forth.

The main point of these suggestions is that networks can allow us to engage students in the full range of activities of adult scientists (conference presentations, paper submission, review and publication, scientific debate, etc.) not just as data collectors for some distant expert.

Finally, we would suggest opening up these activities so that students can acquire the expertise to transcend the "known answer" aspect of the project and tackle extensions that would challenge even adult experts. One extension for the Noon Observation Project was suggested in a message pointing out that an alterative to the round earth with distant sun hypothesis that Eratosthenes formulated is the hypothesis of a flat earth with a fairly nearby sun. The differing shadow length data fits both hypotheses. The challenge to the students and adults involved is to find other directly measurable evidence that the earth is round. It turns out to be surprisingly difficult to gather such first-hand evidence.

These observations on educational electronic networks can guide the exploration of their use in education. It is already clear that electronic networks are very good for conducting certain kinds of educational activities that would be very difficult in a conventional classroom. It is also clear that they are not suitable for all possible activities. Discovering appropriate network-based activities is the most important challenge to those exploring education on the electronic frontier.

References

Cohen, M., & Riel, M. (1988). "The effect of distant audiences on students' writing." *American Educational Research Journal*, in press.

Levin, J.A., Waugh, M., & Kolopanis, G. (1988) "Science instruction on global electronic networks." *Spectrum: The Journal of the Illinois Science Teachers Association*, 13, 19-23.

Waugh, M., & Levin, J.A. (1988). "TeleScience activities: Educational uses of electronic networks." *Journal of Computers in Mathematics and Science Teaching*, 8, 29-33.

Acknowledgments

We want to thank everyone who helped make the networking activities described in this paper possible. The communication was supported by the State of California, the University of Illinois, San Diego State University, and by over 70 elementary, middle, and high schools across the United States, each one with one or more truly dedicated teachers pioneering this new instructional frontier. We especially want to thank those teachers and students who participated in this project: Chris Martin and D. Starshi from Helena, Montana; Leigh Zeitz from Bell Gardens, California; Marsha Korobkin and the students of Helix High School, La Mesa, California; George Kolopanis and the students from Columbia Middle School, Champaign, Illinois; Naomi Miyaki from Aoyama Gakuin Woman's College, Tokyo, Japan; Dick Riedl, University of Alaska, Fairbanks, and David McMullen, Peoria, Illinois.

The Noon Observation Project

Project Name: ERATOSTHENES OF CYRENE EXPERIMENT

Purpose: Use simple measurements and trigonometric calculations to determine the north-south circumference of the earth

Content Area: Math trigonometry

Grade Level: Gifted 8th, 9th, or higher math trigonometry classes

Background: Background information below describes how over 2,000 years ago Eratosthenes made a remarkably accurate measurement of the earth's north-south circumference. This project requires collaboration of students in the northern and southern latitudes of the U.S. to make some simple measurements, share data, problem solve the algorithms required, and then replicate and share their results.

General Procedures:

1. At least two sites must collaborate whose latitudes are different enough to give a significant difference in measurement.
2. When at least two sites have signed up, a date will be set to conduct measurements.
3. On the given date (or within a day or two on either side, depending on weather conditions) students will conduct their measurements outdoors at high noon, local time. Local time must be used as with standard time the sun varies in altitude depending on location within your time zone. You can use this observation to discuss the whole concept of time zones looking at their locations on the map, etc.
4. Using a standard meter stick at precisely high noon local time, each team

of students (probably two per team) will:
   a. hold the meter stick perfectly vertical
   b. use another meter stick to measure the length of the shadow cast by the vertical meter stick to the nearest centimeter.
   c. Several measurements should be made by several different students or teams of students...the more the better.
   d. The longest length and the shortest length should he discarded. All others should be averaged.
5. This averaged shadow length, along with the standard time at which local high noon was observed, will be modemed to the other sites involved in the project.
6. This data, along with the precise latitude and longitude measurements for each site, should be enough information to use trigonometry to make a fairly accurate calculation of the earth's circumference.

Additional Details:

Additional details need to be worked out. I will work with you in developing the remaining details.

1. I am not a mathematician myself and thus don't have the actual algorithms required. However, it strikes me that this could be the basis for some really good problem solving for your class. Using your own "secret" algorithm, this could be a "contest" to see who, using this data, gets the closest results.
2. Or, this could lend itself to some

interesting discussions between the students at the cooperating schools to come up with a joint algorithm.

3. Preparation could include the drawing of pictures to illustrate the original Eratosthenes solution. Also of value would be pictures illustrating this experiment. You could mail these drawings to me. I will write up the results derived by participating schools and include samples of the best of these drawings, print them, and publish them for every participant in the project.

4. Plotting of each site on maps using latitude and longitude to the nearest second will enable each site to calculate exact north-south distance, east-west distance, and then exact straight line distance between sites. North-south distance is essential to know to solve this problem.

Manipulatives and the Computer:
A Powerful Partnership for Learners of All Ages

By
Teri
Perl

Children are sitting on the floor in small groups. In the middle of each group is a set of brightly colored geometric shapes called attribute blocks. Look carefully and you see four shapes, each in three different colors and two different sizes.

The game the children are playing involves building a "train" of blocks that differ from each other by only one characteristic at a time. A child stares at a large blue triangle, the last piece in the train. Several pieces can be placed next: a large blue square, small blue triangle, large yellow triangle, and so on—but not a yellow circle or red square, because they differ in more than one way.

The children are engrossed in their games. The teacher walks around and notices that some students are building trains that don't follow the rules. They are happily building their trains, but some of the adjacent shapes are different in more than one way.

Tomorrow the teacher will introduce these games on the computer using *Gertrude's Secrets* (from The Learning Company). It won't be necessary to monitor the students so closely; the computer will do that. This is one of the advantages of using manipulatives and computers together. We will be describing others in the pages that follow.

What Are Manipulatives and Why Do We Need Them?

Manipulatives are physical objects that can be picked up, turned, rearranged, and collected. They leave no messy trail as a pen does when an answer is changed or alternate solutions are explored.

Manipulatives are useful for modeling ideas. For some time now they have been used in math labs to help children understand abstract concepts. For example, base-10 blocks are used to teach our number system, and how it is possible to name any number—no matter how large—using only ten digits.

Support for the use of manipulatives comes from Piagetian theory, in which cognitive development is described as moving from concrete to abstract, through a series of developmental stages that are roughly age-related. A concrete-operational child cannot handle abstract concepts before arriving at the appropriate stage. However, with manipulatives it is possible for such a student to take the first steps towards exploring the concepts; manipulatives are concrete introductions to abstract ideas.

Much research supports the value of manipulatives in learning mathematics. And, contrary to the belief that manipulatives are useful only for little kids, these results hold up for older students as well. In a summary article *(Research on Instructional Materials for Mathematics,* ERIC/SMEAC Special Digest No. 3, 1985), Marilyn Suydam reports, "The use of manipulative materials in mathematics instruction results in increased achievement across a variety of topics at every grade level from kindergarten through grade 8, at every achievement level, and at every ability level."

151

Manipulatives and Software— Another Link in the Chain

As the evidence supporting the educational value of manipulatives continues to build, more and more educators are incorporating manipulatives into the math curriculum. At the same time, computers are finding their way into classrooms in increasing numbers. This raises questions about how computers and manipulatives relate. As we introduce computer-based learning, are we in danger of giving up the power of manipulatives? Is there anything that computer software can add to the process?

The National Council of Teachers of Mathematics, the main professional organization of math teachers, identifies an important role for computers "as tools to assist students with the exploration and discovery of concepts, with the transition from concrete experiences to abstract mathematical ideas." Computers can provide an important link in the chain, a connection between the concrete manipulatives and the abstract, symbolic, paper-and-pencil representation of the mathematical idea.

Researchers have substantiated the value of using manipulatives and computers together. For example, in a paper delivered at the International Congress of Mathematics Education in Budapest in 1988, Judith Olson reported on research with third-graders who used classification materials such as attribute blocks followed by software featuring similar activities. Her conclusion: Students who used both manipulatives and computer software demonstrated much greater sophistication in classification and logical thinking than did a control group working only with manipulatives.

Another more informal study, conducted in 1988 for Sunburst Communications by M. Bieck and M. Wilson, also concluded that software and manipulatives together can be more effective than either used alone. Third- and fourth-graders at Park Dale Lane Elementary School in Encinitas, CA, were divided into two groups, one using *Puzzle Tanks,* the other using water and containers to solve the same problems. The report states, "Students pouring real water gained a better understanding of the step-by-step processes involved through enforced record keeping, while students using the software concentrated on finding ways to solve the problems and solved the problems faster."

Support for the view that manipulatives and software can be a powerful combination also comes from constructivism, an approach to the study of how learning takes place. As summarized by Carol Maher, a leading thinker in the field, "The constructivist perspective on learning suggests that knowledge is not received passively; it has to be built up. Learning is an act of construction. It is important for learners to have the opportunity to build up a number of representations or models (both concrete and imagistic) and then to make the connection between the different modes of representation." By offering students the opportunity to work with manipulatives, pencil and paper, *and* software, we enable them to build a greater number of models and to begin making such connections.

> "The constructivist perspective on learning suggests that knowledge is not received passively; it has to be built up. . ."

If we are convinced that both software and manipulatives have a role in improving math learning and that the two together are more powerful than either alone, it's time to look at some of the products on the market that make such a combined approach possible. In attempting to pair manipulatives with complementary software, there are at least four different models to think about. Let's call these *mirroring, modeling, manipulating,* and *managing.*

Software as Mirror

Mirroring is one of the most straightforward ways in which software can complement manipulatives. In this model, the software displays objects that look like corresponding manipulatives and are used in exactly the same way.

The scenario presented earlier, in which students used attribute blocks and then *Gertrude's Secrets,* is an example of mirroring. The screen objects in *Gertrude's Secrets* are easily matched with the attribute blocks children hold in their hands. Both on screen and off, children engage in virtually identical activities, "picking up" the shapes and moving them around. Similarly, *Moptown Parade* and *Moptown Hotel* mirror activities students can engage in away from the computer with "people pieces" (blocks similar to attribute blocks, but in the shape of people).

Other examples of mirroring software include *ElasticLines* (designed by Education Development and published by Sunburst), which allows students to perform geoboard activities at the computer; *Puzzle Tanks* (an older Sunburst program created by Dr. Thomas C. O'Brien), which challenges students to identify a specific quantity of liquid by "filling and emptying" two on-screen containers of different sizes as many times as desired;

and *Algebra Concepts* (from Ventura Educational Systems), which includes activities based on algebra tiles to help junior high and high school students understand operations with polynomials.

In addition, there are programs such as Warren Crown's *Math Concepts* and EDC's *Exploring Measurement, Time, and Money* (both published by IBM); and *Hands-On Math* (from Ventura) that take a more comprehensive approach, mirroring a large number of manipulatives commonly found in the math classroom.

Advantages of Mirroring

Since mirroring software allows students to perform virtually the same tasks on and off the computer, one might wonder what the software adds to the process. In the mirroring model, software enhances the manipulatives in several important ways.

• *Software bridges levels of abstraction.* No matter how effectively software mirrors actual manipulatives, the screen representation is more abstract than three-dimensional models. As noted above, many educators believe that this extra level of abstraction provides an important bridge between the concrete manipulatives and the more symbolic mathematical constructs. For example, Barbara Bayha, former lead teacher in Apple's Classroom of Tomorrow's Cupertino site, finds it useful when teaching about grouping and patterns to allow primary students to progress from the people pieces manipulative to *Moptown* software to letter and number patterns on paper.

• *Software automatically monitors the activities.* Most good problem-solving activities, like the attribute games described earlier, allow a range of "correct" answers. This latitude makes the activities difficult to monitor, particularly by one teacher with a class of standard size. The computer, on the other hand, makes certain that the children's moves follow the rules. It can provide feedback in other ways, too. For example, in *Measurement, Time, and Money,* the user can drag coin combinations on the screen and hear, through digitized speech, the total sum of the set created. With the computer's help, children are less likely to build inaccurate conceptions. And at the same time, the software provides the "pat on the back" that encourages children to go on.

• *Software provides an "endless" and flexible supply of materials.* In certain situations, software plays an important role by giving students access to many more manipulative pieces than would be feasible without the computer. For example, *Math Concepts* offers an unlimited supply of unit cubes, ten-cube long rods, and 100-unit flats, making it possible for a student to build a representation of a very large number without worrying whether there will be enough cubes to go around.

Other times, the computer helps by providing a vast number of *choices.* For example, in *Puzzle Tanks* the computer generates a broad assortment of container sizes for students to use when "pouring" liquid back and forth; and with *Elastic Lines* students can create a geoboard with dimensions ranging from five to 15 pins across, in a square, triangular, or circular pattern. While it is possible for a teacher to purchase or scrounge actual containers and geoboards to represent such a vast range of choices, it is certainly not easy.

• *Software can extend the capabilities of the manipulative.* In a number of cases, the software goes beyond exact mirroring, adding an extra level of interaction. In *Elastic Lines,* for example, students can copy shapes they've created on the geoboard to a special drawing area and use computerized tools to flip and manipulate the shapes in ways not possible with a geoboard alone.

In *Gertrude's Secrets* we see another example of software extending the range of manipulatives. Here users can transform the standard geometric shapes into new shapes, or design their own. Playing the same games with different shapes significantly refreshes and enriches the activities.

• *Software is easier to manage and to clean up.* There are times when a teacher might prefer software to the equivalent manipulative because of the setup and cleanup time saved. For example, using the *Puzzle Tanks* program is easier and less messy than locating a sink, filling containers with water, carrying them back to the classroom, and pouring the water from one container to another. Even with manipulatives that create less of a mess, the software can save valuable time. Turn off the computer and the manipulatives vanish; turn it on again and they reappear in seconds. This is a clear benefit with materials that have many pieces, such as attribute blocks or base-10 blocks.

• *Software (with a projection device) makes it easier to demonstrate concepts to a large group.* Many teachers find it useful to teach large-group lessons with the help of manipulatives. For this reason, a number of manipulative providers sell two-dimensional representations

---

Software provides the "pat on the back" that encourages children to go on.

---

that can be placed on an overhead projector and used for demonstrations. With the computer and an LCD panel such as the PC Viewer, this process becomes easier and more powerful. For example, with *Algebra Concepts,* a teacher can quickly produce an arrangement of algebra tiles during a whole-class presentation without having to count out each tile and arrange it in place on the overhead projector.

The Drawbacks of Mirroring

Of course, there are also disadvantages to using the computer. Some mirroring programs on the market can be more bothersome than enlightening. It is not clear, for example, that online tutorials on the use of manipulatives offer much advantage over printed instructions. While the computer can enhance the use of manipulatives, something is generally sacrificed as well in the transfer from table-top to screen. Even in the best examples of mirroring, computer users must invest time in learning how to manipulate objects that require no explanation away from the computer. (For example, remembering which key to press to lift or place a rubber band on the geoboard in *ElasticLines is* far more confusing than the same task off-line.)

Further, when graphics (or hardware) are not state-of-the-art, the speed at which manipulatives are drawn, erased, and redrawn can be agonizingly slow. Fortunately, however, in many of the software products on the market, the limitations are more than offset by the advantages the computer offers.

The Manipulative as Model

A second way in which software and manipulatives work together can be referred to as "modeling." In this approach, the software plays the central role and the manipulative serves as an aid to visualizing the concepts developed at the computer.

For example, users of *The Factory* (designed by Marge Kosel and Mike Fish of Sunburst) are challenged to create a "product" by designating rotations, punches, and stripes to duplicate a given object. The sequence in which the operations are performed is crucial and can be difficult to visualize without off-line help. A simple paper square can be most helpful. "When I introduce *The Factory* to my class," says Diane Resek of San Francisco State University, "I first hand out squares to each student. Then they can manipulate their squares to act out a sequence of moves to help them solve the problem on the screen."

Manipulatives are helpful for users of another Sunburst program as well. *Building Perspective* (designed by Thomas C. Bretl) asks students to identify the relative heights of a series of buildings, given a top-down view and access to front, back, and side views. I found the task close to impossible until I brought out my set of Cuisenaire rods to keep track of the information offered by the different views. While the goal is clearly to develop the spatial visualization skills needed to complete the puzzles *without* added help, the manipulatives serve as an important first step to understanding and visualizing the problem.

The Computer as Manipulative

A new class of software has emerged in which the software itself serves as a manipulative. In this approach (made possible by new, more advanced graphical interfaces), the online representation rather than an off-line model is what users "touch," stretch, move, etc.

As substantiated by a recent study

(reported by Cynthia Char at the 1989 AERA conference in San Francisco), "Software can provide a new manipulative environment for young children's mathematical exploration, offering comparable and sometimes increased user control and flexibility over real hands-on materials." Such observations hold for older users as well. In fact, the computer's role as a manipulative is particularly important when teaching higher-level topics difficult to simulate away from the computer. For example, with *Calculus* (developed by Sensei for Brøderbund), students drag a mouse along a curve and watch the slope-line appear at each point the mouse touches. Simultaneously, an algebraic expression in a window on screen changes to reflect the new curve. The old system of laboriously calculating and plotting points by hand is beautifully taken over by the computer. In *Geometry,* another program in the series, there are other opportunities for students to touch, stretch, and manipulate shapes and figures onscreen, making inferences and discoveries as they do.

Writing about his current research on the value of manipulatives to help students understand concepts in algebra (*The Situated Activities of Learning and Knowing Mathematics,* Stanford University and the Institute for Research on Learning, 1988), Jim Greeno states, "If situations can be found in which students reason easily and effectively about functions and variables, these situations could be used to anchor students' understanding of algebraic notation. We might say, then, that this research could result in identifying materials for algebra that

> Manipulatives and software are individually important for math teaching, and are particularly valuable when used together.

play the role that place-value blocks, Cuisenaire rods, and fraction pie diagrams play for more elementary mathematics."

Such products are on the way. In fact, Warren Robinett's *Snap & Click Math,* in the final stages of development when we went to press, should soon be available from Tom Snyder Productions. This program is a construction set for building animated mathematical machines that move and compute. Users are able to view operations or equations in several different forms (a tree diagram, a standard equation, etc.), take the model apart, explore its components, then put it back together and watch how values flow through it.

Another product that provides online manipulative experiences not possible without a computer is *Letterforms and Illusions* (by Scott Kim, published by W.H. Freeman). These unusual puzzles build spatial visualization skills and offer experience with flips, rotations, and other elements of transformational geometry. Players create and decode messages using a number of cleverly designed fonts. One, for example, allows each letter to be broken into straight and curved lines; another is made up of letters that stretch into sinewy patterns; and so on.

The Software as Manager

Managing refers to a model in which the software and the manipulative work together as a single product, with the software controlling the manipulative. *LEGO TC Logo* is a wonderful example of this sort of relationship. Here the manipulative, in the form of a machine or robot-like device, is managed, maneuvered, and manipulated under computer control.

With *LEGO TC Logo,* users build off-line machines; connect them with wires and an interface box to a computer that speaks a dialect of *LogoWriter;* and enter simple commands to turn motors on and off, reverse their direction, or respond to feedback from specially mounted touch sensors and light sensors. This relationship between manipulative and software is particularly relevant since it gives users an experience of a real-world situation where machine performance is controlled by computer software.

Looking Ahead

Manipulatives and software are individually important for math teaching, and are particularly valuable when used together. Researchers, publishers, and educators all have an important role to play in spreading the word about such a partnership. Researchers can continue to study the effects of the combined use of manipulatives and software on learning, and report their findings to the educational community. Publishers can continue to develop programs in which the software itself is the manipulative and can begin offering packages that bundle "matching" software and manipulatives, making it easier for schools to buy them together.

And finally, teachers can become more cognizant of the connections between manipulatives and computer software. Understanding how these two classes of educational tools work together will allow us to maximize the benefits of both, using them to improve the teaching of mathematics in elementary and secondary schools throughout the country.

Article #11
Software That Helps Develop
Critical And Analytical Math Skills

HERE ARE MATHEMATICS SOFTWARE PROGRAMS, FOR GRADES K-12, THAT CAN
BE USED IN NUMEROUS WAYS IN THE CLASSROOM TO HELP DEVELOP CRITICAL THINKING.

BY
ANN
CORCORAN

In response to the criticism of mathematics instruction today, math teachers are looking more and more to the computer as an instructional tool. The computer is uniquely qualified to perform a variety of instructional goals within the mathematics curriculum: It can perform calculations, provide a motivating format, individualize instruction, and model or teach concepts.

The National Council of Teachers of Mathematics (NCTM) stresses the teaching of analytical skills inherent in critical thinking. With that in mind, the NCTM has raised concerns regarding the availability of software, software's ability to reach instructional goals, and whether a particular format detracts from the mathematical concepts it proposes to teach and expand.

In response to those concerns I will focus on a number of software programs that I believe can partially fulfill the NCTM objectives. Of the programs discussed, some are new to the market and others have built a solid reputation over the years for the development of critical thinking skills.

Two All-Around Programs

One approach to mathematics is the "Math Their Way" curriculum, which has its roots in the developmental approach to mathematics instruction and relies on the use of manipulatives. Sunburst Communication's *Balancing Bear*

158

is keyed into this curriculum. *Balancing Bear* can be utilized with continued interest by most students in grades K-3. The program offers a variety of activities which stimulate and develop "number sense" as opposed to rote drill. *Balancing Bear* is a visual introduction to addition and inequalities. Students place boxes on one side of a balance beam to match the number displayed on the other side.

This program is effective with small groups or individual students. Students working with the program in small groups have an opportunity to share strategies and thinking as they place numbers on the balance beam. Off-line activities, such as using an actual balance scale for demonstration purposes, work well with this program. *Balancing Bear* develops a solid base for the conceptualization of equality in young students and fosters the communication of mathematical thinking.

There are some software programs that lend themselves to continued use throughout the year. Students can be encouraged to repeatedly view the software in a "new" context. One such piece of software is *The Factory* from Sunburst. This program is rich in activities that promote discovery in mathematical thinking. Students start with a square object, and over the course of the program use three simple machines to turn it into a geometric "product." One machine punches holes in the object, an-

---

other adds stripes of varying thickness, and another rotates the object.

One activity I conducted with this software was to have the students draw a "product" and describe it without any references to the machine that would create the product. Then other students, using only the written description of the product, tried to reproduce it using the software program. This activity demonstrated the need for sequential directions. In addition, students gained skills in rotations and angles that were transferred successfully to activities in geometry. My third grade students this past year used *The Factory* exclusively for one semester.

For Use with Manipulatives

The standards of the NCTM charge teachers to use a variety of models to teach mathematical patterns or geometry. A teacher using pattern blocks, geoboards, and cuisenaire rods (non-computer manipulatives) in conjunction with certain software programs allows students to gain an additional dimension of thought. There are a variety of fine programs of this type on the market, and they are designed to promote a variety of critical thinking skills that are inherent to solid mathematical growth.

Such programs include The Learning Co.'s *Moptown* and *Gertrude's* series. Sunburst has produced another in their fine series of software, *Building Perspective,* which can stimulate a variety of activities with cuisenaire rods. Students learn to generate and formulate excellent strategies for determining the height of buildings in a city block. My sixth grade students built actual models with rods, in conjunction with the software activities, to solve a variety of grid problems.

Analytical Approach

New from Davidson is *Math Blaster Mystery Math.* This software is designed to foster the development of strategies and analysis in both logic and problem solving skills. The package has four separate activities: *Follow the Steps*, which teaches the steps for solving word problems by breaking the problem into workable parts; *Weigh the Evidence,* which challenges students to stack numbers on scale (this is similar to the "Tower of Hanoi" classic logic puzzle); *Decipher the Code,* which challenges students to make inferences based on their knowledge of math facts; and *Search for Clues,* which encourages students to develop definitions and terminology for numbers.

The program has four levels of difficulty for each activity, and provides record keeping and scoring features. Students can progress through various levels of detective status, from Computation Cadet through Chief Problem Solver. A certificate may be printed to acknowledge achievement at each level.

Math Blaster Mystery Math is designed for use in grades 5-12. The program covers whole numbers, decimals, percents, fractions, positive and negative numbers, interest, and pre-algebra concepts. This software meets my criteria for software that challenges and extends students' thinking.

Other programs which aid students in problem solving or developing strategies for solving word problems are *The McGraw-Hill Mathematics Problem Solving Courseware,* created for McGraw-Hill by Tom Snyder. Through a set of mysteries, one for each grade level 5-8, the program provides a series of math problems which lead students to gain information that is used to solve a larger mystery. The NCTM has stressed the need to develop appropriate note-taking skills in mathematics; this program promotes such skills.

Real World Applications

In response to the business community's concern about "math-illiterate" employees, the NCTM has charged teachers to create the link between mathematics and daily living. Two excellent programs, *Math Shop* and *Algebra Shop* from Scholastic Software, encourage students to solve math problems in a simulated "real world" environment. The shopping mall format of these programs is particularly appealing to students, who can work their way through the various shops in the mall using their math skills to serve customers. These programs are effective with individuals or small groups.

Learning to verbalize thought processes in mathematics is a crucial step in preparing students for a growing technological society. MECC's *The Market Place,* which allows students to run their own lemonade, fruit, or vegetable stand, and Sunburst's *Hot Dog Stand* (which can be purchased alone or as part of Sunburst's *Survival Math* program) are exceptionally well designed to promote this type of learning. These simulation software programs can be combined with spreadsheets, allowing students to expand their thinking in a way that explores "what if" scenarios.

Visual Representation

Also new from MECC is a welcome package called *Conquering Ratios and Proportions.* This program contains two guided practice programs which, although they assume some familiarity with ratios and proportions, make an ideal vehicle for whole class instruction utilizing a liquid crystal display (LCD) projector. There are teacher options available with the program that allow the teacher to adjust the number and type of problems presented.

The program also has two content-related games. One of these, called *Construct a Flag,* promotes an understanding of proportions in a unique fashion. My students in grade seven, previewing this software with me, enthusiastically constructed family crest flags. Some students played and conjectured with the fill option, trying to predict an assortment of patterns for each proportion selected. For instance, students could choose dragons and shields as crest symbols, determine the proportion of dragons to shields, and try to guess how the crest will fill up with the symbols. The students had great fun. And the flags can be printed.

Software that has an instructional model—which allows you to put the program on an LCD and explain the problem step by step—is particularly effective for the junior high/high school level of mathematics. An LCD can help a teacher demonstrate and explain algebra concepts, for instance, in a manner not available in the traditional classroom. Software which has proven to be reliable for such whole class instruction are Sunburst's *Green Globs and Graphing Equations* as well as the entire *Geometric Supposer* series.

The power of the computer combined with these software packages allows teachers to demonstrate, and students to explore, properties of mathematics in a format which promotes solid thinking, conceptualization, and verbalization of ideas.

An exceptional package that utilizes the power of the computer to explore is IBM'S *Mathematics Exploration Toolkit.* This program, reviewed in the June 1989 issue of *Electronic Learning,* provides endless opportunity for demonstration and discovery of higher mathematics concepts in algebra, geometry, and trigonometry.

Some Software Tips

The software explored in this guide was a sampling of the programs used over the 1988-89 school year, both in the computer lab and by classroom teachers, at Nashoba Brooks School, Concord, Mass. The choice of software is only a small sample of the many excellent programs available that aid teachers in the creative use of technology in the classroom. I encourage teachers to attend area workshops and conferences which present "successful" classroom strategies utilizing math software.

Another source for finding software is the vendors, as most publishers offer a 30-day preview of software. I recommend purchasing programs that have a challenge upgrade (the program can be made more difficult or challenging), authoring component, and branching abilities because they provide the potential for on-going classroom use. And, if at all possible, buy the school versions of software programs. The additional cost is offset by the support materials, the suggested activities for lessons or extensions, and the backup disks that are provided.

Ann Corcoran is Computer Curriculum Specialist, Nashoba Brooks School, Concord, Mass.

A Mathematics Software Sampler

Objective	Program	System/Price	Grade Level	Publisher
Fosters critical thinking by utilizing manipulatives in conjunction with software	Building Perspective	Apple II, Commodore 64, IBM PC/PC Jr., IBM PS/2, Tandy 1000, $65. 10-disk lab pack $195	4-12	Sunburst Communications 39 Washington Ave. Pleasantville, NY 10570-2898
	Gertrude's Secrets	Apple II family, MS-DOS, $59.95	K-3	The Learning Co. 6493 Kaiser Dr. Fremont, CA 94555 (800) 852-2255
	Getrude's Puzzles	Apple II family, $59.95	4-7	
	Moptown Hotel	Apple II family, $59.95	4-7	
	Moptown Parade	Apple II family, $59.95	K-3	
Fosters an analytical approach to problem solving	Math Blaster Mystery Math	Apple II family. MS-DOS. $49.95	5-12	Davidson and Assoc. 3135 Kashiwa St. Torrance, CA 90505 (800) 556-6164
	McGraw-Hill Mathematics Problem Solving Courseware	Apple II family, $69.95; 5- disk lab pack, $115; 10-disk lab pack $180	5-8	Tom Snyder Productions 90 Sherman St. Cambridge, MA 02140 (800) 342-0236
Fosters understanding by visual representation of mathematical principles	Balancing Bear	Apple II family	K-4	Sunburst Communications
	The Factory	Apple II, Commodore 64, IBM PC/PC Jr., IBM PS/2, Tandy 1000, TRS 80; $65; 10-disk lab pack, $195. Network 4, $195	4-12	Sunburst Communications
	Conquering Ratios and Proportions	Apple II family, $59	5-8	MECC 3490 Lexington Ave. North Saint Paul, MN 55126-8097
	Green Globs and Graphing Equations	Apple II, Commodore 64, IBM PC/PC Jr., IBM PS/2, Tandy 1000, TRS 80; $65; 10-disk lab pack, $195.	9-12	Sunburst Communications
	Geometric Supposer Series	Apple II, Commodore 64, IBM PC/PC Jr., IBM PS/2, Tandy 1000, $99; 10-disk set, $297.	8-12	Sunburst Communications
	Mathematics Exploration Toolkit	MS-DOS	10-12	IBM Educational Systems 411 Northside Parkway Atlanta, GA 30327
Fosters an understanding of real world applications of mathematical skills and thinking	Math Shop	Apple II family, MS-DOS. $69.95	4-8	Scholastic Software 730 Broadway New York, NY 10003 (800) 541-5513 in MO. (800) 392-2179
	Algebra Shop	Apple II family, MS-DOS. $69.95	7-10	
	The Market Place	Apple II family, MS-DOS. $59.95	3-9	MECC
	Hot Dog Stand	IBM PC/PC jr., Tandy 1000, TSR 80, $65. 10-disk set. $195	6-12	Sunburst Communications

The term "technology" generally brings to mind the tangible products of scientific research such as answering machines and voice mail equipment, video equipment, calculators, computers, and satellites. The term should also bring to mind the new ways we work and play.

Think about "technique" when you hear the term "technology." Think of how the techniques of the activities you engage in have changed because of the products of technology we use. As educators, we are always looking for better techniques. Some of the products of technology enable us to develop new techniques and put them into practice.

Technology in Secondary Math

Like the steam, electric, and fuel engines that drove the development of technology for most of this century, the microprocessor, microelectronics, and alternate techniques of information storage and retrieval will be the engines and techniques that drive technology far into the twenty-first century.

For years, students have been able to use calculators to do most of the calculations required of students in elementary through high school. Freed from hours of tedious calculations, students can now practice their skills on more complex problems like those they will encounter in the real world.

Now, calculators (if they can be called that) with symbol manipulation and graphic capability are available. Many of the skills taught in algebra classes are built into these devices. This brings into question the value of spending many weeks learning the skills that can be done by calculators. What *are* the skills that should be taught in mathematics classes?

New Math Software

Researchers and educators at the Educational Technology Center (ETC) in Cambridge, Mass., are developing techniques and computer software to help teachers help students better understand mathematics.

From their Geometry Software Project has come the *Geometric Supposer* Series. This software allows students to learn about plane geometry by working with geometric objects such as triangles, quadrilaterals, and circles on the computer screen. The students can quickly make accurate constructions and measurements that can lead to conjectures, then use the software to test these conjectures.

In the Algebra Project, the products help students understand the relationship between two representations of algebraic functions—graphs and equations. These representations are "linked" by being displayed on the computer screen at the same time. When one representation is changed there is a corresponding change in the other representation.

By
GARY G. BITTER
AND
HAROLD FREDERICK

163

The Word Problem Project designed software that uses this technique of linked representations of ideas and problems. Four levels of presentation are graded in difficulty from concrete (using pictures) to formal (using algebraic equations) to provide a "learning ramp" to help students understand mathematical ideas for example, ratio and proportion and to solve problems that involve these ideas.

Other projects at ETC include developing techniques and computer software to help students learn about fractions, basic geometry, and modeling of dynamic systems (population and ecological systems).

Microtechnology is getting less expensive to produce. For the same amount of money schools spent on a microcomputer 10 years ago, they can now purchase one that is more than 10 times faster and has 100 times the internal memory of the older computer. The possibility of supercomputer power in an affordable school computer within 10 years now seems feasible and will permit students to consider very complex problems.

Another example of the kinds of tools that could become commonplace is *Mathematica*. *Mathematica* runs on many computers, including Macintosh and NeXT, and can do almost any kind of numerical, symbolic, and graphical mathematical manipulation. How should these new tools interact with and influence the mathematics curriculum? Besides helping students understand mathematics, software like *Mathematica* gives students experience in using the kinds of tools that they will use in university courses and on future jobs. Electronic spreadsheets also have this dual advantage. When students use spreadsheet software to do calculations it frees them to concentrate on the mathematical phenomena they are studying.

For example, students can learn about the effects of inflation and depreciation on the value of products and money and not be concerned about all the calculations involved. They can learn about budgets and how different elements affect personal and school club budgets. They can learn about the effect of interest rates on savings accounts and on loans. Did you ever wonder how much money you have to save each year to become a millionaire and how long it would take? Students can develop a mathematical model of this problem in a spreadsheet and let the computer do the calculations. The models can be very complex with several variables. The ability to model problems mathematically is a basic skill that can be improved greatly through the use of electronic spreadsheets in the classroom.

One of the topics studied in algebra is the relationship between functions and their graphs. Traditionally, this has required many calculations and time consuming plotting. Mastering the skill of plotting made the task easier, but the calculations and the plotting took valuable time that could be better used to analyze the relationship between functions as equations and as graphs. By using software that plots functions, students can try "What if..." exercises to predict and confirm what happens when a parameter such as the constant, the coefficient, or degree of an equation is changed.

During this exploration with a function plotting tool, students will gain a richer understanding of the relationship between functions and their graphs, find other methods of determining the general shape of the graph of a function, and go beyond the type of functions normally studied at their grade level.

The software tools mentioned can be thought of as sandboxes for the older learner. They can be used to build structures of mathematical ideas and to bridge these ideas. The metaphor of an intellectual sandbox can be useful when thinking about and developing software tools and instructional techniques that use technology to achieve educational goals.

There has been little exploration of robotics and control technology as a "sandbox" for learning. Students can gain much knowledge about the world of controlled devices such as microwave ovens, traffic lights, and other programmed objects. Geometry is one area of the curriculum that can be integrated with the robotics topic when studying the motion of devices. For example, LEGO logo materials can fit into the middle school curriculum with more sophisticated ideas for learners to solve. Developing a curriculum that encourages more students to study further mathematics and an applications-based curriculum centered on robotics and control might encourage some at-risk students to continue their education in high school.

Another approach to learning mathematics is the Microcomputer-Based Math Fitness Project developed by researchers of microcomputer-based learning and research at Arizona State University. This project is a management system for pre-calculus mathematics, the focus of which is to offer students a self-paced alternative to traditional mathematics instruction. The project includes basic math, algebra, geometry, probability, statistics, and finite math. This approach enables learners to evaluate and improve their math competencies in a low stress, self-paced environment.

What Will Be Taught?

Besides looking at the effect of technology on how mathematics is taught, it is worthwhile to consider how technological advances will affect what mathematics will be taught. Earlier we mentioned the use of symbolic manipulation software in mathematics. With this tool available, educators and curriculum designers must consider the value of teaching some of the manipulative skills currently taught in the mathematics classroom and what other skills should displace those considered outdated by the symbolic manipulators.

The second pressure on what mathematics should be taught in high school (and elementary school) focuses on the needs of students entering fields in which they will use and develop new technology devices. Students will need skills that will help them to develop the algorithms to use on these devices, will need to understand topics in discrete mathematics to develop and understand the functioning of these devices, and will need to be able to apply problem solving techniques to solve the problems with the assistance of computers and newer technologies. Curricular changes are occurring at the post-secondary level; we can imagine these changes being felt at earlier levels, soon.

Videodisk Instruction and Resources

The use of videodisk hardware in the mathematics classroom has been slow to evolve because of the lack of mathematics-oriented disks to run on it. Several companies have now developed disks. Videodisk has the advantage over film and videotape of allowing the teacher full control of the material being presented. In conjunction with the computer, the material can be used interactively by students.

Mathematics training can be cost effective when using interactive videodisk stations. With disks such as *Adventures in Mathematics* (Mindscape), *Trigland* (MECC), and *The Mastering Math* series (Systems Impact, Inc.), the videodisk can become a useful resource for mathematics teachers. As new topics are introduced into the mathematics curriculum, the teacher may be able to look to videodisk materials on new topics as a valuable resource. We expect to see an increase in the range of mathematics-oriented videodisks.

Telecommunications, distance learning, video conferencing, and artificial intelligence, including expert systems, will all play a role in the future of mathematics education.

Telecommunications

The application of telecommunications will make data available worldwide, allowing for conjecturing and theorizing about mathematical concepts. For example, the Technical Education Research Center (TERC) Star Schools Project provides an application in one model to collect data on a unit entitled "iteration." The students can share this information with mathematics students throughout the world and can explore the mathematical theories on the basis of the collected data.

Many schools cannot provide the range of courses they would like for their students due to limited resources, lack of teachers skilled in particular areas, or small numbers of students. Video telecommunication courses can boost course offerings in these cases. This technology could also be used to deliver interactive in-service to help teachers get a "handle" on the new demands of the National

Council of Teachers of Mathematics Standards, and other changes that will be occurring.

Expert Systems

Expert systems will be available in the future classroom, and are being developed and tested in high school geometry and algebra classrooms. These expert system computers store all the information currently available about one particular subject and knowledge about learners' needs. As the user questions the computer, the expert system is able to search through its memory bank for the answer concerning that particular subject.

Expert systems access varied knowledge stored in their memory to make expert judgments and decisions (expert systems). An example that could be available soon is a giant educational computer that teachers can query, gaining curriculum advice for the students. The computer responds with questions the teacher answers. The computer searches its research data bank and presents a list of recommendations that teachers can use to enhance their teaching. This resource can help the teacher with ideas about how to help a student overcome difficulty or to develop ideas in depth.

In the future, students will have computerized work stations that can "learn" the students' strengths and learning needs as well as styles of learning. These computers can query, receive answers, evaluate student needs, branch the students to their level, and tutor the students as they study. The systems can also help students to understand their own thinking and learning styles and needs.

The Future

The National Council of Teachers of Mathematics has taken an active role in formulating curriculum changes for the 1990s. The preparation of the *Curriculum and Evaluation Standards for School Mathematics* recommends the following for the secondary mathematics curriculum:

1. Mathematics as problem solving
2. Mathematics as communication
3. Mathematics as reasoning
4. Algebra
5. Functions
6. Geometry from a synthetic perspective
7. Geometry from an algebraic perspective
8. Trigonometry
9. Statistics
10. Probability
11. Discrete mathematics
12. Conceptual underpinnings of calculus
13. Mathematical structure
14. Mathematical connections

The recommendations for the math curriculum are based on the following assumptions relating to technology:

- Calculators are available to all students at all times.
- A computer is available in every classroom for demonstration purposes and every student has access to a computer for individual and group work.
- Students should learn to use the computer as a tool for processing information and performing calculations in order to investigate and solve problems.

The new technologies provide phenomenal tools for teachers' use to help students learn. Imagine having students view a holographic image representing Euclid or Pythagoras delivering his mathematical findings. This image could act as a tutor, explaining concepts of the portions of mathematics which those historical figures developed and interacting with the learner about these ideas. The teacher can concentrate more time and attention on the students most in need of help.

The difference between the classrooms of the future and present classrooms is that future students will be in charge of their own learning. They will draw on a number of resources in their learning and interaction with teachers in different ways. Teachers already are referring to themselves as facilitators. This will be more the case as the sources of students' knowledge become more diversified.

The classrooms and homes of the future potentially can include any or all of the following:

- Robots will teach sequential and logical thinking.
- Digital Video Interactive (DVI) will simulate actual events and experiments.
- Idea Processors will assist in organizing thoughts for problem solving.
- Tools for the production and use of hypertext and hypermedia will alter the way we present and access knowledge.
- Artificial intelligence (AI) computers will diagnose learning styles and problem areas and help the teacher develop remedies, as well as logical reasoning and cognitive capabilities.
- Satellite telecommunications will bring scientific and historical programs into the classroom via satellite.
- Abstract ideas can be manipulated on the computer screen like the blocks young children use to learn

ideas, making abstract ideas more concrete.

- Future classrooms will be linked to databases nationally. Lessons will be enhanced and broadened over and beyond the regular assignment as information is retrieved from data banks in medicine, science, and engineering.

Conclusion

Technology affects mathematics and the teachers of mathematics in many ways. In the report *Everybody Counts* (1989), mathematics is defined as the foundation of science and technology. The report further states that computers influence mathematics both directly—through stimulation of mathematical research—and indirectly—by their effect on scientific and engineering practice.

A mathematical model mediates between phenomena of science and simulation provided by the computer. The potential of technology in the teaching and learning of mathematics is unlimited. Obviously, technology is also increasing the importance of mathematical knowledge. With the pervasiveness of technological change and its effect on society, we as educators must continually reflect on the phenomena and examine the needs of students for the future. We must also investigate how we can use this technology that is driving us into the future to enhance teaching, learning, and understanding in our society.

References

Arganbright, D. E. *Mathematics Application of Electronic Spreadsheets*. Novato, Calif.: McGraw-Hill, 1984.

Bitter, Gary G. "Educational Technology and the Future of Mathematics." *School Science and Mathematics Journal 6* (1987).

——"Microcomputer-Based Mathematics Fitness." *T.H.E. Journal* (1987).

Bitter, Gary G., and Camuse, Ruth. *Using the Microcomputer in the Classroom*. Englewood Cliffs, N.J.: Prentice-Hall, 1988.

Bitter, Gary G., Hatfield, Mary M., and Edwards, Nancy. *Mathematics Methods for the Elementary and Middle School: A Comprehensive Approach*. Boston: Allyn & Bacon, 1989.

California State Department of Education *The 1988-89 Educational Software Preview Guide*. Sacramento, Calif.: 1988.

Capper, Joanne. *Computers in Mathematics Learning*. Washington, D.C.: Center for Research into Practice, 1986.

Commission Standards for School Mathematics of the National Council of Teachers of Mathematics. *Curriculum and Evaluation Standards for School Mathematics*. Reston, Va.: NCTM, 1987.

Educational Technology Center, Harvard Graduate School of Education. *Making Sense of the Future*. Cambridge Mass.: ETC, 1988.

Hansen, Viggo P., ed. *Computers in Mathematics Education*. Reston, Va. NCTM, 1984.

Mathematics (6-12): Curriculum Software Guide. Apple Computer, Inc. 1987.

National Research Council. *Everybody Counts: A Report to the Nation on the Future of Mathematics Education*. Washington, D.C.: National Academy Press, 1988.

Office of Technology Assessment. *OTA Report Brief: Power On! New Tools for Teaching and Learning*. Washington D.C.: OTA, 1988.

As microcomputers become more powerful and less expensive, software is appearing that will have a substantial impact on both the teaching and learning of mathematics. Programs are currently available that can do much of the algebra we currently teach at the secondary level: Plotters can plot most functions, symbolic manipulators can perform all the basic algebraic manipulations, dynamic tutorials can guide students in solving word problems, and computational programs such as spreadsheets can manipulate numbers with dazzling speed.

The capabilities of these new algebraic tools raise important pedagogical questions. For example, if programs exist that can simplify any rational expression or solve any equation, why should students spend countless hours performing these same tasks? This leads to a far larger question: To what extent should people devote time to activities that machines can do faster and more accurately? Also, to what extent and how should technologies be used to help students learn concepts rather than computation?

These questions are complex and will take many years to answer to everyone's satisfaction. However, the National Council of Teachers of Mathematics has taken a first step in its recently released standards (*NCTM Standards: An Agenda for Action*). The NCTM emphasizes the use of computers as a way of decreasing the need for pencil-and-paper algorithms and plotting. More specifically, the council recommends using computer graphing and other computer-based methods such as successive approximations to help students develop conceptual understanding. The NCTM standards also stress the importance of using real-world problems in the classroom to motivate and apply theory. While such an approach was possible long before computers entered schools, the new technology makes it easier for young people to solve realistic problems without being deterred by the inevitable complexity of "real-life" numbers and formulas.

In this article, we focus on the growing number of microcomputer-based algebraic tools now available for the secondary school algebra classroom. Other algebra programs in the form of courses on disk or drill-and-practice software have not been included, although there are a number available that algebra teachers may want to consider.

Graphic, Numeric, and Symbolic Manipulation

In sorting through the algebra tools, it is useful to think of them as programs that accept input in the form of algebraic or numeric expressions and manipulate that input in any of three ways: graphically, numerically, or symbolically. The graphic tools—commonly known as graphing programs or function plotters—have been around the longest. You may even recognize some of your old favorites in the adjacent chart. With these programs, it's possible for young people to compare graphs of different equa-

By
JONATHAN
CHOATE

169

tions, look for points of intersection, recognize patterns, etc., without having to perform the cumbersome task of plotting by hand.

In addition to graphic capabilities, a number of the function plotters offer numeric output as well. By producing tables of values, allowing the user to request a numeric solution to a graphed equation, or making it possible to zoom in on a particular point and request its value, such programs are manipulating equations numerically as well as graphically.

The newest type of algebra tool is the symbolic manipulator. When the NCTM standards were being drafted just one year ago, there were almost none of these programs available for microcomputer users. Now there are several on the market, and more are on the way. A symbolic manipulator helps users solve equations one step at a time. With such a program, for example, a student might type in an expression and ask the computer to factor, expand, or simplify it. A student can also type in an equation and ask the computer to solve it (all at once or in separate steps).

In addition to the algebra tools that specialize in a specific type of manipulation (for example, function plotters that translate all input into graphic form or symbolic manipulators with no graphing component at all), there are a growing number of programs that perform all three types of manipulation—graphic, numeric, and symbolic. These are referred to in the pages that follow as "integrated tools."

Watching Two Students at Work

What would studying algebra be like with the help of such an integrated tool? Here is a possible scenario.

Lab partners, Anne and Tim, meet in the computer lab during a study hall to work on their math homework. They open their notebooks to the problem sheet Ms. Lincoln gave them in class earlier and re-read it:

The Hit 'n Miss record company is planning to cut a record by their new group, V3. They hire Minnie Anne Max as a consultant and she collects the following information for them: a) the function to determine the cost of producing x records is $C(x) = 50000 + 20x$ where $C(x)$ is in units of $10 and x is measured in units of thousands of records.

b) the function for the revenues from the sale of x records is $R(x) = 500x - .5x[2]$. The consultant claims that she can use the two functions given to decide: (1) how many records to sell in order to make a profit and (2) how many records to sell in order to make the maximum possible profit. How did she do it and what answers did she get?

Anne and Tim boot up their favorite algebra tool and decide to use the graphing option to get a picture of the cost and revenue functions. They enter the functions but then are stumped by what scales to use for the graph. After a brief discussion, they decide that the domain probably won't go beyond one million because only big hits have sales that high.

Thinking out loud, Anne says, "Let's see, to make a profit they must make more than they spend, so we've got to find the point on the graph where revenues are greater than costs." Tim uses the mouse to point to a portion of the screen where the graph of revenues climbs above the graph of costs. The partners then use the program's zoom feature to produce an enlarged picture of the region of interest. It appears that the two graphs intersect between 118 and 119. Zooming in even further, they now see that the answer is between 118.84 and 118.94. To get the answer more precisely, they request a table of values with the domain between 118.84 and 118.94 and discover that when x= 118.9 revenues almost equal costs. They've arrived at an answer for question number one: The company must sell at least 118,900 records to make a profit.

Part two is harder for them. At first they theorize that profits will be at a maximum when revenues are highest but a closer look at the graphs reveals that costs are also higher at the point where the revenues peak. After a period of silence, Anne announces, "I've got it. We've got to find the *difference* between the revenues and the costs. Profits will be greatest when R(x)-C(x) is greatest." They define a new function $(P(x) = R(x)-C(x))$ and have the computer graph it. Using the zoom and table options once again, they easily narrow in on the point where the profit graph is highest.

Reviewing their work, they realize they could have used their new profit function and the program's symbolic manipulation capabilities to answer the first part of the question. Solving $P(x) = 0$ would have been another way of finding the point at which costs equaled revenues. They decide to check their answer. They enter $P(x) = 0$, select "solve" from the menu and hit return. The computer confirms that the answer $x = 118.9$ is correct but shows them that $x = 841.2$ is another correct answer.

"Hey, Anne, there are two answers. We got one of them, but where did the second one come from?" Tim looks again at the original graph and discovers that there are indeed two solutions—two points at which the graphs of cost and revenues cross. They print out their answers and place the computer printout in their notebooks just as the bell rings to end the period.

The preceding vignette, adapted from a talk given by Kathleen Heid of Pennsylvania State University at a 1988 NCTM regional meeting in Boston, is fictional but is based on observations of students with computer-based algebra tools. It shows that by freeing students from a lot of tedious computation, such a tool allows them to arrive at a better understanding and to apply what they know to a variety of problems. Students will still need to know a lot about mathematics, but they will have new and exciting ways to put this knowledge to use.

Picking a Software Package

The checklist on the next page shows how each of the programs mentioned in this article measures up. In addition to basic functions, you'll want to consider the quality of the user interface. In general, the tools that offer pull-down menus, windows, and mouse-driven operations such as highlighting, copying, cutting and pasting are easiest to use. Fortunately, these options, which originally were available only of the Macintosh, are now appearing on other machines as well.

As you survey the field, you should be aware that other exciting products are on their way as well. For example, S-man, an integrated Macintosh package under development by Allen Hoffer, promises to offer an extensive list of features with an interface so simple even elementary students will be able to use it. Another integrated package, more appropriate for college students and teachers who want to design interactive lessons, is being developed by James White at Kenyon College. And keep your eyes open for two new products being designed by John Richards and Ricky Carter for Bolt, Baranek and Newman:

How the Algebra Programs Stack Up

Title / Company	The Algebraic Proposer (True Basic)	Cactusplot (v. 5.0) (CactusPlot Company)	Curves (v. 3.0) (Bridge Software)	Function Analyzer (Sunburst)	Function Graphing (2.0) (E. Kamische)	Graffiti (Bates Publishing Company)	Green Globs and Graphing Equations (Sunburst)	Kemeny-Krutz Series: Algebra & Pre-Calculus (True Basic, Inc.)	Master Grapher (Addison-Wesley)
GENERAL									
Algebraic Notation				√	√		√		
f(x) notation				√	√	√		√	√
Implicit Functions							√		√
Parametric Functions		√	√			√			√
Polar Functions		√	√		√	√		√	√
Parametric Definitions	√	√	√	√					
Defining and Storing Functions	√	√	√	√	√			√	√
Combining Functions		√			√			√	
Transformations of Functions				√	√	√			√
Built-in Functions		√	√		√	√	√	√	√
GRAPHIC MANIPULATIONS									
Zooming			√	√	√				√
Grids		√				√	√		√
Differentiating w/ Colors/Patterns		√	√	√	√		√		
Print Capabilities	√	√	√		√	√			
Text Insertion	√	√	√		√				
Interrupting and Controling the Graphing Process	√	√	√		√				√
NUMERIC MANIPULATIONS									
Function evaluation for a Particular Value	√	√		√	√	√		√	√
Tables of Values	√	√		√		√		√	
Fractions									
Complex Numbers									
Numeric Solution of Equations	√	√			√	√		√	
Exact Solutions									
SYMBOLIC MANIPULATIONS									
Automatic Algebraic Manipulations									
Algebraic Manipulations Based On Axioms/Rules								√	
Problem Solving Assistance	√								
Incorporating Programming Language Routines									
Ability To Learn Rules									
Interactive Scripting Capabilities								√	

MCP Plotter	The Homework Series: Algebra I /Simplify	muMath-80	CALC	MILD
Microcomputer Curriculum Project	Missing Link	University of South Carolina	IBM	Para-comp
√	√		√	√
√			√	
				√
				√
			√	
√			√	√
√			√	√
			√	√
√			√	√
√			√	√
√			√	
√	√	√	√	√
√	√		√	√
			√	
√		√	√	√
		√	√	√
		√	√	√
		√	√	√
		√	√	√
	√	√	√	√
	√	√	√	√
	√			
			√	
				√
			√	

an easy-to-use symbolic manipulator and an entertaining program that allows young people to build "function machines."

No existing program has all the features on the checklist. Some come close but either are expensive or require a great deal of memory. In the not-too-distant future, when inexpensive, powerful computers will be commonplace, programs will, we hope, be available with all the features listed, and the curriculum will have changed so that these powerful tools will become a central part of the algebra teaching and learning process.

Article #14
Dinosaur Roundup

By
Leslie
Eiser

Integrated curriculum units play an important role in many of today's elementary school classrooms. The idea of selecting one central topic as the focus for all reading, writing, science, math, and art activities is appealing. The challenge, however, is to find a theme that fascinates all of your students and, at the same time, offers interesting learning opportunities in a variety of content areas. One of the best themes of all times is one that has been around for millions of years—dinosaurs!

Take a stroll through any teacher supply house or children's book store and you'll encounter a bewildering array of dinosaur tools. There will be a selection of easy reading books, a collection of plastic blow-up models, and an eclectic group of dinosaur cut-outs. In recent years, the shelves displaying dinosaur paraphernalia have been expanded to make room for dinosaur related computer software as well.

If you've been teaching about dinosaurs for years, you already know that finding relevant material is not the problem; sorting through the piles of possible teaching tools is what takes so much time. And once you've found the books, models, and software you like, there's another challenge: designing activities that make best use of each available tool.

Let's look at some of the ways in which dinosaurs can enrich your computer-infused classroom.

Language Arts

Young authors can use any word processor to write dinosaur features—everything from scientific reports to fantasy stories involving imaginary dinosaurs and time-travel adventures. And now there are programs such as *Dinosaur Days Plus* (Learning Lab), *Once Upon a Time. . .II* (Compu-Teach), and the *Explore-a-Series* (William K. Bradford) that allow students to combine their simple stories and reports with dinosaur clip art and other prehistoric scenes in order to produce even more appealing work.

For pre-readers, *Dinosaur Discovery Kit* (First Byte) has a wonderful module that uses computer speech and a choice of pre-written phrases to help young students create a story which can then be printed out. Not only does this approach allow non-readers to become "authors," it also can be used with beginning readers to increase sight word vocabulary and porovide motivating reading material.

First Dinosaur Reader (Orange Cherry) takes a more traditional reading comprehension approach in an entertaining storybook format for primary-grade students. And if you're in search of a dinosaur program that helps older children practice their reading skills, you should take a look at *Return of the Dinosaurs* (AEC Software). While several of the other middle grade programs provide significant amounts of on-screen reading material, this is one of the few programs that actually require students to make use of what they've read. In order to succeed at the game, students must read paragraph-long clues and conduct searches in an extensive database.

Virtually all the available dinosaur programs offer some opportunity for

174

Reprinted by permission of: *Technology & Learning* (Formerly Classroom Computer Learning)
© Peter Li, Inc. 2169 East Francisco Blvd., Suite A4, San Rafael, CA 94901

vocabulary and spelling practice. (If you've ever needed proof of how well students learn when they're excited about a topic, just watch how quickly even the youngest children learn to spell "Tyrannosaurus" or to use the word "carnivore" correctly.) Particularly appealing is an activity in the *Dinosaur Blend* package (Math Learning Center) that encourages students to study a Greek reference sheet in order to figure out the meaning of dinosaur names.

Science Adventures

Of course, any unit on dinosaurs is bound to include a significant number of science-related activities. Many of the programs reviewed here teach students about dinosaur diet. Play "Walk-a-Dinosaur" in Designasaurus (Britannica Software) and you'll get to lead your Tyrannosaurus to a grazing Stegosaurus. Click the mouse and it's "Goodbye, Stegosaurus"—complete with animated effects. Other programs offer more traditional (and less gory) ways to teach such concepts. *Dyno-Quest* (Mindplay) sends students back in time to feed the dinosaurs little food packets, and *Dinosaur Blend* provides activity sheets that have students investigating the relationships between head structure and diet.

Dinosaur Blend not only explores dinosaur eating habits, it also offers a number of other science lessons, including one in which students learn how to classify dinosaurs by exploring the database and looking at various criteria for order and sub-order. This comprehensive package also provides detailed instructions for several hands-on science activities to be conducted away from the computer. (One, for example, has students searching for dinosaur "bones" in layers of gelatin.)

If you are interested in drilling students on dinosaur names and facts, you have a few choices. *Dinosaur Dig* (Mindscape) offers tutorials and games related to 40 different dinosaurs. *Who Am I? Animals of the Past* (Focus Media) focuses on a few dinosaurs at a time in a no-nonsense game that almost ensures the acquisition of facts. On a much more elementary level, *Talking Dinosaurs* (Orange Cherry) and *Dinosaurs* (Advanced Ideas) introduce very young students to some basic dinosaur facts while they work on "readiness" skills such as counting and matching.

Math and Computer Science

One of the things that fascinates students most about dinosaurs is their gigantic size. Calculating and comparing dinosaur dimensions are natural math activities for an integrated unit. *Dinosaur Blend* offers spreadsheet templates to help students arrive at average weights, heights, and lengths of various dinosaurs. Another spreadsheet activity has the students figuring out how much it would cost to feed a dinosaur if it were magically transported into today's world.

You might choose to design your own activities around an available spreadsheet program. For example, you can ask your students to enter formulas that allow them to compare dinosaur lengths to a known measurement such as the length of a car or the size of your classroom. Using a spreadsheet or database to rank dinosaurs by size also allows you to look for patterns. For example, can your students find any correlation between diet and average weight? Conducting such on-line activities using tools you already own, or investing in one of the dinosaur programs that offer extensive exposure to spreadsheets and databases, has the added benefit of teaching students how to use computer-based tools.

Your students might be surprised to learn that not all dinosaurs were big. To illustrate the great size differences that existed, you can use any computer graphing program to create bar graphs representing dinosaur heights, weights, or lengths. Or how about a dinosaur height line? The *TimeLiner* program and the *Dinosaurs and Other Big Things* database (both from Tom Snyder Productions) allow you to print out horizontal "time lines" that actually show the relative lengths of various dinosaurs. (Unfortunately, the program does not allow you to change from units of time to units of length, so you'll have to cover up the "year" or "month" labels that appear at the bottom of the printout.)

If you want to include drill on math facts and computation as part of your dinosaur unit, check with your favorite publisher of drill-and-practice software. Chances are, they'll have a program that uses a dinosaur motif. Such programs don't generally teach about dinosaurs (the graphics simply serve as a background or reward), but they should be of interest if your goal is to drill on basic math skills without departing from the dinosaur theme.

Dinosaur Arts and Crafts

While none of the dinosaur graphics tools we saw leaves much room for free artistic expression (they mostly allow students to piece together clip art or fill in electronic coloring books), your students will enjoy using them to create attractive room decorations. Several of the programs enable students to produce computer-generated banners and posters to announce the dinosaur unit.

It's also possible to print dinosaur calendars with *Dinosaurs Are Forever* (Merit Software); create dinosaur t-shirts with *Designasaurus;* produce a "big book" with *Dinosaur Days Plus* (Learning Lab Software); or design a prehistoric scene (realistic or fantasy-based) for a shoebox theater using your choice of programs.

Graphics activities can be used to reinforce scientific concepts covered during the dinosaur unit. For example, each student or group of students might be assigned the task of creating a mobile on a particular theme. One group might focus on flying dinosaurs; a second on plant eaters; and still others on dinosaurs from the Triassic, Jurassic, or Cretaceous period. Have the students use any of the dinosaur graphics programs to generate the appropriate printouts and then color and cut out the pictures to assemble the mobiles.

You and your class can also use *TimeLiner* to create huge wall charts showing the relative dates of various dinosaur families. Ask students to add colorful pictures of the dinosaurs (drawn by hand or generated by the computer) to make the time line more dramatic. How about juxtaposing several different timelines? Each one might focus on dinosaurs within a certain size range or in a particular geographic location.

Or you can set up a mystery corner in your classroom. Use *Designasaurus* to print a variety of different dinosaur skeletons and challenge students to match the skeletons with painted or photocopied pictures of dinosaurs—or to figure out which part of a pieced together skeleton doesn't belong. Cut up the dinosaur printouts and let students play "paleontologist" by reconstructing the dinosaurs from their bones. (*Tyrannosaurus Rex* from William K. Bradford provides an on-line version of this activity, and it's also possible to print out the Tyrannosaurus bones for use in your mystery corner.) You can control the difficulty of this activity by varying the number of skeleton pieces available.

Cave Dwellers and Dinosaurs— How Did They Get Along?

Even though fossil records tell us that over 45 million years separate the earliest human beings from the last of the dinosaurs, cartoon programs such as *The Flintstones* have managed to convince many young people (and lots of not-so-young people) that dinosaurs and cave dwellers existed at the same time. You may be wondering how the available dinosaur software deals with this issue. Several of the programs classified as *fantasy* on the adjacent chart do indeed show human beings and dinosaurs sharing the same space. Of course, these programs tend to include other elements that students should recognize as fantasy (dinosaurs wearing clothes or sitting in chairs, for example). Nevertheless, you might want to take this opportunity to discuss with your students the difference between fantasy (fiction) and nonfiction, and to reinforce the idea that pictures or stories that show dinosaurs living at the same time as human beings are purely "make believe."

Two of the more scientifically oriented programs use a format that has dinosaurs and human beings interacting. Both deal with this by presenting a scenario in which the human being or the dinosaur travels in time. *As long as the time travel premise is clear to your students,* this should do nothing to reinforce misconceptions. For this reason, and because the programs were scientific in other ways, we chose *not* to classify them as fantasy.

It's not just the obvious misconceptions about time that frustrate scien-tists. Other misinformation (and *contradictory* information) crops up in books and software because of the enormous changes that have taken place in paleontology in the past 25 years. In contrast to what was taught in schools during the 1950s, dinosaurs are no longer considered to have been over-sized reptiles, slow moving, cold blooded, and antisocial. Instead, work by paleontologists such as John Ostrom and Robert Bakker has demonstrated that dinosaurs may have been warm-blooded, agile creatures who held their tails high and were capable of running at speeds of up to 30 miles per hour. There is also new evidence of social behavior—of dinosaur herds and nesting grounds. Like modern birds, some dinosaurs may even have fed their nesting young.

Of the dinosaur programs we've seen, *Dinosaur Blend* does by far the best job of presenting the newest research. It is also the only program that touches on the possible reasons for dinosaur extinction.

Finally, if you're concerned about scientific accuracy, you should be aware that, because of the limitations of computer graphics, some of the programs take liberties with relative scaling. In *Designasaurus,* for instance, pictures of a Tyrannosaurus Rex and a Stegosaurus show them to be exactly the same size, when in reality one dinosaur was over twice as large as the other. Once again, you may need to do some extra work to counteract misconceptions if you decide to use such programs.

Whether your goal is to foster creative expression, convey scientific information, improve upon other basic skills, or combine all of these objectives in an integrated unit, you won't have to look far to find computer software that meets your needs.

Dinosaur Directory

Here is some software to consider if you're planning an integrated unit on dinosaurs. Each program was tested by the author and at least two students in the suggested age group. When software is available for more than one computer, the version tested is indicated with an asterisk (*). (Keep in mind that features and copyright dates may differ from one computer version to another.) In case your budget permits you to buy only one or two programs, we've indicated our favorites with a

Instructional Software

Dinosaur Blend (© 1989)

Published by the Math Learning Center and distributed by Portland State University, this incredibly thorough package was designed to be used with commercially available Apple II tools. Files provided (in *AppleWorks, FrEdWriter, FrEdBase,* and ASCII formats) include dinosaur databases, some word processing starter files, and a variety of spreadsheet templates.

The 270 pages of documentation include reference materials and suggestions for 75 student activities, both on and off the computer. Curriculum areas covered include mathematics, problem solving, writing, social studies, and art. Each lesson idea is presented at three levels of difficulty, ranging from primary-grade levels through junior high. In addition, the package contains a set of 40 dinosaur data cards (with pictures, scale drawings, and textual informa-

tion) and a large time line.

If you are looking for lots of detailed information about dinosaurs, presented in a manner that promotes thinking and reinforces the use of the computer as a tool, *Dinosaur Blend* is a great buy.

Hardware/Price: Apple II family (64K): $175.

Order from: Portland State University, Continuing Education, PO Box 1394, Portland, OR 97207, (800) 547-8887 ext. 4891 or (800) 452-4909 ext. 4891 in OR.

Dinosaur Dig (©1984)

This program has been around for a while, but it's still worth considering. The first of the two disks is an extensive tutorial on dinosaurs with simple but attractive graphics and animation. Although lessons are primarily of the "read and press return" variety, the information is up-to-date and presented in an interesting manner.

The second disk offers five drill-and-practice games focusing on dinosaur names, sizes, weights, and facts. Students testing the program found the game that focused on dinosaur comparisons particularly interesting. The program includes a keyboard overlay with special buttons that students press to make their choices. It doesn't quite fit a IIGS, but it works well with older Apple IIe's.

Hardware/Price: Apple II family (64K)*; IBM PC (128K): both versions $49.95.

Order from: Mindscape Educational Software/a division of SVE, 1345 Diversey Parkway, Chicago, IL 60614-1299; (800) 999-2242 or (312) 480-7667.

Dinosaur Discovery Kit (© 1988)

This is a wonderful program for pre-school and primary-grade students. In the storybook section, each sentence of a dinosaur tale is recited by the computer, with a phrase missing. The user picks from several possible phrases (also read aloud) and the story graphic is changed to reflect the addition. After the story is completed in this manner, the entire tale can be read back by the computer or printed out for the student to keep. The program also offers a Concentration-style game in which students are asked to match six to nine dinosaurs, and an on-line coloring book with several dinosaur scenes to complete. (Students receive factual information about dinosaurs as they complete the pictures.) The program makes excellent use of speech and graphics to create an appealing, age-appropriate program that young students can use independently.

Hardware/Price: IBM, Tandy (512K)*; Macintosh Plus, SE (512K)*; Amiga (512K): all versions $39.95. (Site licenses are available.)

Order from: First Byte, Clauset Centre, 3100 S. Harbor Blvd., Suite 150, Santa Ana, CA 92704; (800) 523-8070 or (800) 245-4524 in CA.

Dinosaurs (© 1984)

Designed for the youngest computer users, this five-part program emphasizes matching games. Absolutely no reading is required. The games build in sophistication and include shape matching, classification games in which students group dinosaurs based on their eating habits or habitat, and a final activity in which students match dinosaur shapes with names.

While the dinosaurs are not drawn to scale and the graphics are unsophisticated, young kids found the program very enjoyable to use. It kept one three-year-old occupied for over an hour. How well it will work in your school's kindergarten classroom depends on the sophistication level of the students and the role of the teacher. (Without a teacher's input, it's possible for students to learn to group the dinosaurs through trial and error and visual memory, without learning any of the science content involved.)

Hardware/Price: Apple II family (64K)*; IBM PC (256K); Commodore 64, 128 (64K): all versions $39.95.

Order from: Advanced Ideas, Inc., 2902 San Pablo Avenue, Berkeley, CA 94702; (510) 526-9100.

Dynoquest (© 1984)

This is a drill-and-practice game that sends players on voyages into the past, challenging them to feed the dinosaurs they encounter. The "challenge upgrade" feature makes it possible to increase the difficulty level of the game. Given the age of the program, the graphics are relatively attractive as well as historically accurate. Unfortunately, however, dinosaurs aren't drawn to scale and the educational scope of this program is relatively narrow—mostly dietary information. While students do obtain additional facts about their choice of dinosaur as a "reward" for feeding all of them correctly, there's little motivation for them to read or use these facts.

Hardware/Price: Apple II family (48K)*; IBM, Tandy 1000 (128K): all versions $49.99; $129 for a lab pack of six.

Order from: Mindplay (Methods & Solutions, Inc.), 3130 North Dodge Blvd., Tucson, AZ 85716 (800) 221-7911.

First Dinosaur Reader (© 1988)

Young readers hone their language skills

as they read four short stories presented using oversized text, attractive graphics and animation. The program pauses at several points during each tale and asks students to respond to multiple choice comprehension questions or to type in a word displayed on the computer screen (an activity probably most valuable as an opportunity for students to locate letters on the keyboard and to practice typing).

While the interactivity level is limited to these workbook-style activities, student testers loved the program's entertaining stories. From the Triceratops who plants a garden only to discover a thief in the night, to the Apatosaurus who rescues a friend from a tar pit, each story can be used as a springboard for class discussion or a focus for student writing. And while the stories are clearly fantasy tales, scientific facts are not ignored. Dinosaurs hatch from eggs, plant eaters must flee the large meat eaters and the danger of the tar pits is convincingly portrayed.

Hardware/Price: Apple II family (64K); Commodore 64: both versions $78.

Order from: Orange Cherry Software, Box 390, Westchester Avenue, Pound Ridge, NY 10576; (800) 672-6002 or (914) 764-4104.

Return of the Dinosaurs (© 1988)

In this program, students chase a dinosaur that has escaped from the past through a "crack in time." Reading clues about the creature's identity, searching a built-in database, and answering questions for the "DinoNews" paper keep students involved while they acquire information about dinosaurs. When they're not playing the game, students can also use the program as a regular database, accessing information on the 70 dinosaurs covered.

Return of the Dinosaurs is an excellent program despite an awkward interface. There are numerous "control" or "function" keys to be learned, many of them without obvious mnemonic connections. Occasionally the same key produces different results in different sections of the program. The graphics—even on capable MS-DOS machines—are fairly basic. Nevertheless, this is a challenging and entertaining way to practice reading skills and to learn about dinosaurs and databases.

Hardware/Price: Apple II family (256K)*; IBM, Tandy 1000 (256K)*: school versions $49.95; $89.95 for a lab pack of five.

Order from: AEC Software, 7506 N. Broadway Ext., Suite 505, Oklahoma City, OK 73116; (405) 996-1010.

Talking Dinosaurs (© 1989)

This program consists of six activities, including a counting game, a coloring book, an activity in which the computer reads aloud the names of several dinosaurs, and two games that require students to find dinosaurs in an outdoor scene or a lineup that includes modern animals. While several of the games are appealing at first try, student testers quickly tired of them because of their predictability and lack of scope. In the names activity, for example, only six dinosaurs are named. In the hidden dinosaurs game, there is a single graphic background with the same dinosaurs located in the same place each time. (Students were also confused by the word "hidden" since all the dinosaurs were in plain view.) In fact, each of the six activities takes a relatively short time, and once completed, offers little more in the way of challenges or rewards.

One of the greatest strengths of *Talking Dinosaurs* is its realistic speech. Unfortunately, this speech is not used for the main menu—which is text-based— making it difficult for young students to work with the program independently.

Hardware/Price: Apple IIGS (512K): $49 ($10 extra for backup disk); $118 for school site license; (network version also available).

Order from: Orange Cherry Software, Box 390, Westchester Avenue, Pound Ridge, NY 10576; (800) 672-6002 or (914) 764-4104.

Who Am I: Animals of the Past (©1989) This is a new addition to a series that uses simple deduction games to teach scientific facts. In this game, students must correctly identify one of four prehistoric animals (randomly selected from a database of possibilities) based on several clues and a picture. Points are awarded for correct guesses, and deducted for each clue required and for incorrect guesses. The program offers two levels of difficulty, an honor roll, a teacher editor that makes it easy to customize the questions, and student workbook with some crossword puzzles and at-desk activities.

Hardware/Price: Apple II family (48K): $55; $165 for a lab pack of 12.

Order from: Focus Media, 839 Steward Avenue, PO Box 865, Garden City, NY 11530; (800) 645-8989 or (516) 794-8900.

Tools

Dinosaur Days Plus (© 1989) This graphics package offers superior printing routines and a variety of dinosaur clip art. Printing options include a standard page (graphics and text on one 8.5 by 11 inch page) and a "big book" (graphics and text on four standard pages). The word processor is limited to one screen page and one font at a time but it is easy to use and offers a cute "rock" font to fit the prehistoric theme.

In addition to the main program disk, which contains the writing and art program (much of it with a fantasy focus), the package contains a disk with dinosaur pictures and facts. While this disk can be viewed as a pictorial database on dinosaurs and prehistoric life, it does not offer the searching and sorting capabilities that make a standard database so useful. Also, since the publisher provides few suggestions for using the database, it will take some ingenuity to give students reason to read the information provided.

Hardware/Price: Apple II family (128K): $49.95; $99.95 for a lab pack of five.

Order from: Learning Lab Publishing, Inc., 21000 Nordhoff Blvd. Chatsworth, CA 91311; (800) 247-4641 or (800) 222-7026 in CA.

Dinosaurs Are Forever (© 1988) This is essentially an electronic coloring book with a variety of printing options, including banners and calendars. (The Amiga version also includes sound.) If students choose, the program prints out a message or a description of the dinosaur to go with each picture.

Dinosaurs Are Forever is particularly useful for introducing young children to computer art. While users can do little more than fill in the lines, the vast number of colors, attractive pictures, and high-quality printing capabilities lead to very satisfying results—on screen and in print.

Hardware/Price: Amiga (512K)*; Apple II family (128K); IBM, Tandy 1000

(256K); Commodore 64, 128: all versions, $29.95.

Order from: Merit Software, 13635 Gamma Road, Dallas, TX 75244; (800) 238-4277, (214) 385-2353.

Explore-a-Story: What Makes a Dinosaur Sore (© 1987)

This is an animated storybook that students can customize in a variety of ways. The program design encourages open-ended play. It's possible to drag clip art on and off the screen, choose from a variety of background scenes, select from a number of existing labels, or type in text anywhere on the screen. (Unfortunately, editing features are limited, the text that can be entered is limited to one line at a time, and the only way to make corrections is to erase what you've written.)

The colorful graphics with their animated effects are more attractive than most found in Apple IIe programs, though not up to IIGS standards. Preschoolers and first-graders enjoyed labeling the objects, but the lack of specific directions and goals was frustrating for slightly older students. The program works best with teacher involvement.

Hardware/Price: Apple II family: (128K): $75. (Network versions and site licenses available.)

Order from: William K. Bradford Publishing Company, PO Box 1355, Concord, MA 01742; (800) 421-2009.

Once Upon a Time...II (©1989)

This combined graphics and writing program offers a dinosaur file with three graphic backgrounds and a variety of clip art which can be flipped, resized, and painted. (Unfortunately, there is no way to paint only part of an object; you'll have to decide whether you want your

trees to be totally green or totally brown.) Clip art is selected in an unusual manner: instead of picking from a menu, the user enters the object's name by copying from a list of what's available. While this takes time and may frustrate some students, it does reinforce typing and spelling skills. In the Apple IIGS and MS-DOS versions, early readers get extra help from a digitized human voice that reads aloud any word they select. The dinosaur printouts you can create with this program are quite attractive (nicely detailed and perfect for coloring when printed in black and white). However, they are in a single size only and the printing routine is relatively slow. The text editor is fairly easy to use and allows students to place up to four lines of writing below a picture or to create any number of additional pages of text.

Educators who want to incorporate this program into a dinosaur unit should be aware that two of the three files provided (showing underwater and forest scenes) have nothing to do with dinosaurs. More problematic is the fact that several of the items included in the dinosaur file—a number of cave people and a woolly mammoth—are unusable if pictures are to reflect scientific fact.

Hardware/Price: Apple II family (64K); Apple IIGS (512K)*; IBM, Tandy 1000 (256K); Macintosh (512K): Apple IIGS version $59; all other versions $49.

Order from: Compu-Teach Educational Software, 78 Olive St., New Haven, CT 06511; (800) 44-TEACH.

TimeLiner with *Dinosaurs* and *Other Big Things* database (©1988)

The *TimeLiner program* provides an interactive way of creating individualized time lines that can be expanded and compressed in various ways. The basic package is sold with only a few sample files, leaving users to create their own time lines. For those who want help, Tom Snyder Productions has created a number of data disks which can be purchased separately. Among the 17 files on the *Dinosaurs and Other Big Things* data disk are four on dinosaurs. Data provided include eras, sizes, and diet. In the right hands, *TimeLiner* can be a very powerful teaching tool.

Hardware/Price: Apple II family (64K)*; IBM, Tandy 1000 (256K): *TimeLiner,* $59.95; data disk, $19.95.

Order from: Tom Snyder Productions, 90 Sherman St., Cambridge, MA 02140; (800) 342-0236 or (617) 876-4433.

Hybrids

Designasaurus (© 1987, 1988)
This program has some appealing features, although by attempting to be both a tool and an instructional program, it does neither in great depth. The most educationally oriented of the three activities is Walk-a-Dinosaur, an ecology/ diet simulation. The sound effects and graphics on the Apple IIGS and MS-DOS versions are very entertaining, but a teacher hoping to cover dinosaur diet in any depth will be disappointed that only three dinosaurs are included.

Build-a-Dinosaur allows users to combine fossils of dinosaurs to form a variety of imaginary creatures. (This makes Designasaurus one of the only programs that provides dinosaur fossil printouts.) The results can be printed out in poster size, standard size, or as t-shirt transfers.

Print-a-Dinosaur provides black-and-white printouts of 12 dinosaurs using the same format options as Build-a-Dinosaur. Unfortunately, it does not allow the user to customize the picture before printing it. The lack of consistent scal-ing throughout the program is a problem as well.

Hardware/Price: Apple II family (128K)*: $39.95; Apple IIGS (768K)*: $49.95; IBM, Tandy 1000 (512K): $39.95; Commodore 64, 128 (64K): $29.95; Amiga (512K): $49.95

Order from: Britannica Software, 345 Fourth St., San Francisco, CA 94107, (800) 572-2272 or (415) 546-1866.

Explore-a-Science: Tyrannosaurus Rex (© 1987)
This program uses the same interface and tools offered by *What Makes a Dinosaur Sore,* but the content covered is more scientific. In one section of the story, students are asked to simulate the work of paleontologists as they unearth bones hidden in the ground. They can then put the bones together to form the skeleton of a Tyrannosaurus Rex. There is also a lab notebook in which the students can record observations (using the program's limited word processor), make copies of clip art, add scientific labels, and so on. Since the computer provides no feedback when a student completes an activity (or, for that matter, if the student skips the activity completely), teacher involvement is very important to help users see what to do with the program and how it fits into the science curriculum.

Hardware/Price: Apple II family (128K): $75. (Site license and network versions available.)

Order from: William K. Bradford Publishing Company, PO Box 1355, Concord, MA 01742; (800) 421-2009.

For more information on these programs, see the chart on the following page.

Dinosaur Programs At A Glance

	Program	Publisher	Suggested Grade Level	Approach	Shows humans and dinosaurs coexisting	# of different dinosaurs/ animals	Dinosaurs drawn to scale	Print Capabilities
Instructional	Dinosaur Blend	Math Learning Center	2 to 8	Scientific	No	40	In Documentation	Yes
	Dinosaur Dig	Mindscape	3 to 8	Scientific	No	32	No	No
	Dinosaur Discovery Kit	First Byte	Pre-K to 3	Fantasy	No	9	No	Yes
	Dinosaurs	Advanced Ideas	Pre-K-K	Scientific	No	6	No	No
	Dyno-Quest	MindPlay	3 to 7	Scientific	Yes (through time travel)	18	No	Yes
	First Dinosaur Reader	Orange Cherry Software	1 to 4	Fantasy	No	8	No	No
	Return of the Dinosaurs	AEC	5 and Up	Scientific	Yes (through time travel)	70	Yes	No
	Talking Dinosaurs	Orange Cherry Software	K to 4	Scientific	No	6	Yes	Yes
	Who Am I: Animals of the Past	Focus Media	5 to 8	Scientific	No	40	No	No
	Dinosaur Days Plus	Learning Lab, Inc.	K to 8	Fantasy	Yes	35	Yes	Yes
Tools	Dinosaurs are forever	Merit Software	Pre-K and Up	Scientific	No	26	Yes	Yes
	Explore-a-story: What Makes a Dinosaur Sore	William K. Bradford	K to 2	Fantasy	Yes	7	No	Yes
	Once Upon A Time... II	Compu-Teach	1 to 7	Fantasy	Yes	16	Partially	Yes
	TimeLiner & Big Things database	Tom Snyder Productions	K to 5	Scientifc	No	39	N/A	Yes
Both	Designasaurus	Britannica Software	K and Up	Fantasy	No	12	No	Yes
	Explore-a-Science: Tyrannosaurus Rex	William K. Bradford	4 to 6	Scientific	No	1	Yes	Yes

Article #15
Technology and the Science Class:
Going Beyond the Walls of the Disk Drive

SCIENCE SOFTWARE, AS WELL AS OTHER TECHNOLOGIES SUCH AS ON-LINE
NETWORKS AND VIDEODISCS, CAN MAKE CLASS SCIENCE EXPERIMENTS COME ALIVE.

BY
JEFF
HOLTE

Most adults looking back at science class in school probably do not remember monitoring, graphing, and analyzing the precise number of footcandles of light coming from the sun in a 24-hour period. Or collecting data from an experiment and electronically sharing it with students and experts from around the world. Such experiences are no longer uncommon in many K-12 science classrooms. The tools that make this possible are the microcomputer and software, and various technologies such as on-line telecommunications services and interactive videodiscs. These tools are beginning to change the way some teachers are teaching science.

Science technology tools, which also include various multimedia applications, laboratory probes, and simulations are often difficult to select. Some criteria might be helpful before starting the selection process:

Good science software and tools should:
- promote thinking;
- be simple to use; teachers or students should not have to spend a lot of time learning how to use them;
- be truly useful in helping students understand concepts or see relationships in ways that could not be done better, or more efficiently, another way;
- promote process science;
- allow for a more investigative and interactive classroom where students use various resources to investigate real or realistic problems.

The following overview of products is meant to represent a cross section of what I would consider excellent building blocks for a science program. Some of the items I list are new, some are old standards, and some are not even specifically designed for science, but all exemplify the criteria listed above.

Multimedia

Increasingly, science software is expanding "beyond the walls of the disk drive" by combining software with other media. This includes allowing the computer to manipulate a videodisc player or to interface with VCRs or video editors.

A videodisc player connected to a computer is the most recent trend in science classrooms, and for good reason. Many currently available science videodiscs can be used without computers and software, but the addition of computer software (interfaced with a videodisc player) allows science teachers or students to combine computer data bases, graphics, searching capabilities, video clips, and still pictures.

185

Technology Tools For Science

Program	Price/System	Grade	Publisher
MULTIMEDIA			
THE VOYAGER VIDEOSTACK	$99.95/Macintosh	7-12	The Voyager Company 1351 Pacific Coast Hwy Santa Monica, CA 90401 (800) 446-2001 (outside CA) (800) 446-2002 (CA only)
THE PRESENTER	$59/Apple 128K	K-12	MECC 3490 Lexington Avenue N. St Paul, Minn 55126 (800) 228-3504
BIO SCI LESSONS (HYPERCARD)	$125/Macintosh	K-12	Videodiscovery 1515 Dexter Ave. N. Suite 400 Seattle, WA 98109 (800) 548-3472
BIOSCI LESSONS VIDEODISC	$549		
PAINTWORKS PLUS	$49.95/Apple IIGS	K-12	Activision Presentation Tools 3885 Bohannon Drive Menlo Park, CA 94025 (415) 329-0500
INTERACTIVE NOVA: ANIMAL PATHFINDERS	Available late '89		WGBH Boston, MA Call (617) 492-2777 ext. 3810 for further information
TELECOMMUNICATIONS			
IRIS	Call for Price/ MS-DOS, Apple IIs, Macintosh	K-12	MECC (see above)
STAR SCHOOLS PROJECT	Call for Information		Technical Education Research Centers 1696 Mass. Ave. Cambridge, Mass 02138 (617) 547-0430
KIDS NETWORK	$232 (till Jan.) /Apple IIGS	4-6	National Geographic Society 17th and M Streets NW Washington, DC 20036 (800) 368-2728
THE WEATHER MACHINE	$159.95/Apple II Family	7-12	
COMPUSERVE	On-line service (call for information)		Compuserve 5000 Arlington Centre Blvd. P.O. Box 20212 Colombus, OH 43220 (614) 457-8600
POINT TO POINT	$99.95/Apple IIe & IIGS	7-12	Beagle Brothers, Inc. 6215 Ferris Square Suite 1000 San Diego, CA 92121 (800) 345-1750 (outside CA) (800) 992-4022 (CA only)

Program	Price/System	Grade	Publisher
LABORATORY PROBES			
SCIENCE TOOLKIT PLUS	$209.95/Apple II Family	4-12	Broderbund Software Inc. 17 Paul Drive San Rafael, CA 94903-2101 (800) 521-6263
FREQUENCY METER III	$39.95/Apple & MS-DOS	7-12	Vernier Software 2920 SW 89th Street Portland, OR 97225 (503) 297-5317
VOLTAGE PLOTTER III			
PLAYING WITH SCIENCE: TEMPERATURE	$129/Apple II Family	7-12	Sunburst Communications 38 Washington Avenue Pleasantville, NY 10570-2898 (800) 431-1934
EXPLORING SCIENCE: TEMPERATURE			
LEGO TECHNIC CONTROL STARTER PACK	$485/Apple & MS-DOS	3-12	LEGO Dacta 555 Taylor Road Enfield, CT 06082 (203) 749-2291
VOYAGER OF THE MIMI CURRICULUM PACKAGE	$1300/Apple 64K	4-8	Sunburst (see above)
SIMULATIONS AND OTHER SOFTWARE FOR SCIENCE			
LUNAR GREENHOUSE	$59/Apple IIe & IIGS	3-9	MECC (see above)
INVISIBLE BUGS			
GEOWORLD	$79.95/Apple IIe & IIGS	5-12	Tom Snyder Productions 900 Sherman Street Cambridge, MA 02140 (800) 342-0236
ANIMAL TRACKERS	$65/Apple II family	4-10	Sunburst (see above)

Some of these computer software interfaces are generic such as MECC's *The Presenter* or The Voyager Company's *The Voyager Video Stack*. These allow you to "repurpose" or alter any science videodisc to show particular stills or video clips in a sequence that is appropriate to your science lesson.

Other computer interfaces, such as *Bio Sci* by Videodiscovery Inc., are preprogrammed to access particular materials on science videodiscs. One exciting new project is from WGBH-TV (Boston) and Peace River Films called *Interactive NOVA Animal Pathfinders,* which is scheduled to be available sometime this year. The project uses a videodisc containing many short documentary films, still pictures, and written text about the natural world. The videodisc is controlled by a *HyperCard* stack on a Macintosh.

In a section devoted to bees, for example, users can act like a bee and "fly" in different directions—simply by pressing various buttons on the Macintosh screen that control which film clip of a bee flight will show on the videodisc. It seems as if the user is the bee. "Migration," "Metamorphosis," and "Human Threats to Animals" can be studied by accessing data from over 600 cards; on the *HyperCard* stacks, which in turn are correlated to the film clips and stills on the videodisc.

A less dramatic yet useful example of combining media is the common use by our students of ordinary graphics packages such as *Paintworks* by Activision Inc. After creating titles and other graphics with the software, we connect the computer to our videotape recorder and record these images into our student science videos. We also use graphics programs for creating science concept maps and science-fact posters.

Telecommunications

One of the most exciting new tools in science is the on-line network. Science students can now "move" electronically outside the classroom walls and communicate with people and resources around the world. Using a computer to access one of several telecommunications networks, teachers can conduct classroom projects ranging from science writing projects to on-line experiments.

Telecommunications is a technological tool that makes discussions, experiments, and data real. Students, sometimes for the first time, feel true ownership of their work.

A modem, phone line, and telecommunications software package are needed to get started. Some software, such as *Point to Point* by Beagle Brothers, can access any network. Other "front end" software works only with specific networks and automates many of the on-line functions, which simplifies the some-

times difficult task of using a network.

The National Geographic Society (NGS) and Technical Educational Research Centers (TERC) have developed on-line science experiments called *Acid Rain, Hello,* and *Weather,* which run on NGS's Kids Network and will be available several times during the 1989-90 school year. Students in my science classes have field tested these units over the past three years. The students collected acid rain samples and weather data, and conducted surveys. This information was shared and discussed with students around the world, as well as with on-line geographers and meteorologists.

My district is also involved with a similar project called the *Star Schools Project* developed by TERC and designed for secondary (7-12) science and math students. Some of the modules developed include *Radon, Weather, Design,* and *Polling.* Students in this project design experiments, then collect and share data with other students and experts via a telecommunications network.

Some electronic networks host discussions on science topics, issues, and curricula. *Compuserve* offers a variety of science forums for students, teachers, and the general public. There are also some projects in which classes can access networks to receive data. Currently, the most novel example is NGS's *The Weather Machine.* This multimedia package explores basic weather concepts by having students behave like real meteorologists. Using a computer and modem, students have daily access to real weather data from the National Weather Service.

Other student science projects, such as a national student plant-growing contest, are available on the new IRIS network, which is available from MECC.

Laboratory Probes

Microcomputer-based lab projects using software and probes are quickly becoming an important component in science classrooms from elementary to senior high. Classes use a computer, probe software, and attached probes to collect data easily, accurately, and over long time periods. An example of a probe: a thermistor to monitor temperature.

The use of probes with software allows students to concentrate more on observation and analysis rather than tedious and sometimes impractical data gathering. These easy-to-use instruments allow for investigative research that may involve temperature, light, sound, and more. Data from probes are graphically displayed on the screen during or after experiments.

The *Science Toolkit Plus Classroom Pack* by Brøderbund (which contains modules on temperature and light, motion, earthquakes, and the human body—all of which can be purchased separately), and *Exploring Science: Temperature* and *Playing with Science: Temperature* by Sunburst Communications are excellent examples of probe software kits, especially for elementary and middle-school science. Both are durable, and have multiple probe capabilities and a variety of experiments included that would enhance any class.

For the study of sound, Vernier Inc. offers its updated *Frequency Meter III* interface and *Voltage Plotter III* for analyzing voltage from up to four different sources. Sunburst's *Voyage of the Mimi,* although not new, is still an excellent example incorporating laboratory interfaces within a multi-disciplinary, multimedia curriculum.

A unique use of computer interfaces for elementary science is with the Lego/Logo activities by LEGO Dacta (the education division of LEGO Systems Inc.). LEGO Technic Starter Control Pack allows students to control Lego blocks containing motors, gears, and sensors using *LEGO* TC software, a special version of *Logo*.

Simulations, Etc.

While the recent trend in science education may be toward electronic tools such as lab interfaces and telecommunications networks, let's not forget there are many excellent science products developed for all levels and areas of science.

Some are well established: Tom Snyder's *Geoworld,* for example, is a classic geology simulation. Exciting new products that promote the "process" of science are now appearing with more frequency. Some examples include Sunburst's *Animal Trackers,* which lets students try to identify animals using clues. Or MECC's plant-growing simulation, *Lunar Greenhouse,* and its truly useful *The Invisible Bug,* which covers genetics.

Selecting software and other technology tools for science classrooms is obviously not as simple as it used to be. I have only scratched the surface of what is available today. I encourage science teachers to start with a small, simple project.

Finally, experimentation and patience are critical: both are prerequisites to integrating new technology into the classroom.

Jeff Holte, a science teacher at Central Middle School in Eden Prairie, Minn., was a 1988 Christa McAuliffe Educator.

Article #16
Ideas for Integrating Videodisc Technology Into the Curriculum

HERE ARE EXAMPLES OF HOW TWO TEACHERS BROUGHT VIDEODISC
PLAYERS INTO THE CLASSROOM TO ENHANCE SCIENCE, SPACE, AND OTHER PROJECTS.

BY
JOHN
PHILLIPO
AND
SANDY
MARTIN
MCCARTY

Perhaps the most serious challenge to educators in the years ahead will be the task of linking appropriate applications of new information and learning technologies with the school curriculum. These technologies, particularly videodisc technology, can help students to learn more effectively and productively, develop motivation and enthusiasm for learning, and prepare for future careers. To transform this vision into a reality requires considerable effort: developing conceptual frameworks, preparing curricula, and implementing programs, to name few.

The approach to technology education should be curriculum-based and focus on how the curriculum can be improved by the use of technology tools. This article illustrates for teachers and administrators how several videodisc applications were designed and implemented within an existing curriculum.

Strategy 1: John Phillipo

Videodisc technology arrived in my classroom at about the same time that I received a mandate from the assistant superintendent for curriculum and instruction. He said that the district was involved in a curriculum revitalization process that involved the integration of higher order process skills into all subject areas, as well as employing a more interdisciplinary approach to the core subject areas.

As I sat and *marveled* at *my* shiny, new videodisc, I recalled several of *my* own concerns regarding effective teaching. My greatest concern was that science education is considered by *most* students today to be a knowledge-based curriculum; in other words, students feel that the subject of science consists of a set of concepts and facts that have to be learned, memorized, and recalled.

Mitosis

Based upon these reflections, I set out to explore the videodisc's instructional archive on the topic of cell division, or mitosis. I was overwhelmed with the number and variety of visual materials available to me. However, I was most intrigued by a motion clip of an actual cell going through the cell division process.

In the past if I wanted to show my students this type of powerful video, it usually meant showing a 40- or 50-minute 16mm film that had already been used a thousand times. Due to the wear and tear, the finer details and intricacies of this phenomena were blurred and difficult for the students to see.

Traditionally, when I taught this concept, I required the students to write a

190

descriptive essay on mitosis. Although the idea of having a science teacher require written descriptive essays was quite novel, I was also aware of reality. The reality was and still is—students simply looked at the still frame images and descriptive text of the various stages of cell division within their textbook. Some of the more advanced students pursued a thorough description of the same phenomena using other resources, such as encyclopedias. However, after reading a hundred descriptive essays on mitosis, it was always quite apparent to me that I had 100 different versions of what the textbook had originally stated.

Durable

Early on in my work with videodisc technology, I recognized the durability of videodiscs as a medium. Through the use of videodisc, and aided by its durability, I decided to alter the mitosis lesson requirements. After completing the classroom unit on mitosis, I required the students to write a descriptive and analytic essay describing what they observed happening on the videodisc, starting at frame 6,409 and continuing through frame 74,710.

Unlike a 16mm film, I was not at all concerned with the number of students who would be handling the disk or the number of times the disk would be played, stopped, started, paused, and rewound. I arranged for the videodisc to be available in the reference section of the library for a specified number of periods during the week.

I spent very little time giving the students instruction on how to use the videodisc player, simply because the students in my class were "VCR literate," and as a result they readily understood how, when, where, and why one would use motion, fast forward, pause, etc. I

felt strongly that this approach (technology, content process) would give me the type of feedback I had always wanted. I had longed for the day when I could provide my students a motivating, learning framework in which they would describe a scientific phenomena in their own terms.

Success!

This approach to learning was an overwhelming success. However, I also observed that as the more creative students in the class struggled with this more demanding (and creative) assignment, other students were not to be fooled. They quickly realized that whatever happened on the videodisc filmclip (an actual cell going through the process of mitosis) must be identical to the print description described in the encyclopedias contained within the school library.

As a result of this, I explored further the potential of videodisc technology to assist me in short-circuiting my students' abilities to revert to the more traditional approach to science education. Once again, videodisc technology contained the modified solution that I was seeking. The next time I used the same assignment, I simply indicated to the students that for each event within the phenomena they were describing they must also "footnote" their description by using the frame numbers on the videodisc, indicating both the beginning and end of the phenomena.

In summary, I had effectively used videodisc technology to integrate the content of mitosis and creative and descriptive writing into the science education curriculum. But more importantly, I achieved this without significantly increasing the amount of time required to cover this aspect of the curriculum.

Strategy 2:
Sandy Martin McCarty

The videodisc player started out as a tool for the middle school teachers to enhance their classroom instruction and motivate young learners.

Early one morning an aspiring young astronaut (student) approached me for permission to look at a videodisc on outer space. After a few minutes, he recruited two crew members and set out to write a video story. The students developed an exciting adventure story about their trip to the moon. The story, complete with training films, lift off, moon walk, and splash down, was a huge success. The students took their video adventure to the N.H. 1st Christa McAuliffe Education Festival in Concord, N.H., and to a statewide Young Authors Conference where they received a glowing reception.

Interest Grows

As news of the young authors' success leaked out, it created a schoolwide enthusiasm for videodisc technology. Students at all grade levels flocked to the library for background information on various topics. With rough draft in hand, they signed up for time on the videodisc player. Students were working on their reports before school, during recess, and after school.

An entire fifth grade class created a slide presentation on primates. Each student selected and researched a primate. They previewed the disk for the best visuals and with the help of an authoring program added their stories. When the program was complete they presented it to other classes.

Eventually, the primary school got wind of the excitement brewing in the middle school and decided the laserdisc might be fun.

Honeybees

Three ambitious first graders began with a story they wrote on honeybees and asked to "put their story on the TV." With the help of their teachers, the students rewrote their story, selected pictures and recorded frame numbers. During the writing phase a young boy had his mother drive him to the public library one night. He claimed the school library didn't have enough information for his report.

The result was a dramatic story explaining the difference between queen, drone, and worker bees, and how honey is collected and stored.

Teachers were astonished at how quickly the students learned how to use the authoring program and create lessons. Conceptually the students were reading and comprehending at a high level.

Thanks to the latest in videodisc technology and some enthusiastic educators, students in New Hampshire found new ways to research and learn about their world and had a wonderful time doing it!

John Phillipo is director of Instructional Leadership and Technology for the Merrimack Education Center. Sandy McCarty is coordinator of the Technology Resource Center and training at the Merrimack Education.

National Geographic Kids Network: Real Science in the Elementary Classroom

BY
DR.
CANDACE L.
JULYAN

How would you define a pet? Is an ant farm a pet? How about a dog that you are hoarding indefinitely with relatives? Would you consider a pig a pet if it later became Sunday dinner? Thousands of fourth-, fifth-, and sixth-grade students recently discussed these questions and many like them with peers across the country and around the world. They were involved in field tests of an elementary science curriculum called the National Geographic Kids Network, developed by the Technical Education Research Centers (TERC) with funding from the National Science Foundation, and published by the National Geographic Society.

NGS Kids Network gives students the opportunity to collect and analyze data, and to share their findings with one another through extensive use of telecommunications. In effect, they actually *become* scientists doing real scientific work.

Hello! The Introductory Unit

In the introductory unit for the series, students examine information about the number and types of pets that they have. Cille Griffith's fourth-grade class in Walpole, Massachusetts, provides an illustration of the NGS Kids Network in action. As Griffith's students began to collect data about their pets, they found that agreeing on what is and what is not a pet required considerable discussion.

When one student, Shauna, wanted to count her ant farm as a pet, others took exception. Some felt that pet owners needed to "do things" with an animal for it to be counted as a pet. Others felt that feeding an animal made it a pet. Eventually, they reached an agreement.

At the same time, all across the country, other classes participating in the field test were having similar discussions. The next day, using the Kids Network telecommunications software, the classes communicated their conclusions to their research teams, pre-assigned groups of ten geographically dispersed classes.

Learning science is a richer experience when students pool their data and share their discoveries. Through the National Geographic Kids Network, fourth-, fifth-, and sixth-grade classes nationwide are going on-line to exchange data, compare observations, and test hypotheses on subjects they explore in common.

In addition to exchanging letters within their research teams, Griffith's students and the other field-test classes recorded their data on computer data entry forms and sent them to the NGS Kids Network staff and to geographer Dr. Barbara Winston, the Hello! unit scientist. (In each NGS Kids Network unit, a professional with expertise in the unit topic helps guide student scientists in making sense of the data.) The telecommunicated data were collated

193

and charted by the staff, and the results were reported to the participating classes within a week.

Information from hundreds of classes on the network was returned to Griffith's class in several forms: the actual data entry forms from research teammates at other schools, a compiled national chart, and maps displaying the distribution of specific pets across the country. In addition, all classes received a letter from Winston encouraging them to share their questions with research teammates and suggesting various ways to derive meaning from their data.

When the information yielded by the nationwide data was returned, Griffith's students began to compare their own findings with those of other research team classes. They wrote to each other for clarification, to share ideas, and to pursue the questions or theories their studies engendered. Some students wanted to know more about the logistics of pet ownership. Others had ideas about the differences between classes.

One student, Ben, was intrigued by the national data, and tried to find a way to understand what the numbers meant. He noted that the difference between the number of cats (7,713) and dogs (7,522) was small, while the difference between the number of cat owners (3,777) and dog owners (5,107) was large. So he decided to check the data from several research teams more closely, to see if they would reveal the same results. Griffith used his report to introduce mathematical data analysis techniques such as proportional samples. Were the data for their research team proportionally the same as the entire network data, or were there significant differences between their team and the whole? What might account for any differences? How could they test their ideas? While "pets" may not be a typical topic for study in elementary science curricula, the subject proved an effective vehicle for teaching scientific concepts. A group of fourth-graders in Kansas, for example, confused by the differences between their data and those of another class, finally determined that they had in fact collected different data. Although both data sets were about pets, the students could not compare them. They had collected only the *total number of pet owners* for each type of pet; the other class had collected only the *total pets* of each type. In a very meaningful way, these fourth-graders discovered the significance of comparable data, a difficult concept for many high school students.

Teachers in the field test found that *all* their students—not just those previously interested in science—were eager to participate. In a Maine school, for example, students were exploring why they had more than 120 pets, while a New Orleans school on their research team had only 25. Some thought that the difference was related to the hot weather in New Orleans, or a pet store strike. Then a student who rarely spoke in class and usually spent much of the school day in a special resource room became actively involved, hypothesizing that the school was situated in an area surrounded by government housing where pets were not allowed. This simple hypothesis from a fellow student,

> Teachers in the field test found that *all* their students—not just those previously interested in science—were eager to participate.

not the teacher or a textbook, made sense to his classmates, and they drafted a letter to the New Orleans school to find out if his theory was correct.

Acid Rain

After the preliminary work of the Hello! unit, Griffith's students were ready and eager to turn to more complex topics. Acid Rain, the second unit in the Kids Network series, addresses a more traditional science topic.

In this unit, students build a rain collector, learn to use pH paper, and record the pH reading for each rainfall over a period of several weeks. During that time, they explore acid rain through various other activities. For example, they run experiments to study the effects of different pH solutions on a variety of non-living objects and make calculations using a weekly log of odometer readings from their family cars to determine how much nitrogen oxide they themselves have introduced into the atmosphere.

Throughout the unit, students write and telecommunicate letters to their research teammates discussing the local significance of acid rain.

After several weeks (and finally some rain), Griffith's students sent their data to the Kids Network staff and to the unit's scientist, Dr. John Miller of the National Oceanic and Atmospheric Administration (NOAA). Within a week, they received "raw" data—as it was tallied on data collection forms—from their research team classes across the country, and a map file that provided a geographic overview of the national data. In addition, Miller sent a letter explaining how the students' data and NOAA data compare.

How, Where, and When to Sign Up

The NGS Kids Network curriculum is available from the National Geographic Society. Each unit includes program and tutorial disks, teacher's guide, activity sheets, 30 student handbooks, wall maps, materials for experiments, and a telecommunications subscription and software.

For information on cost, application deadlines, and materials, schools should contact the National Geographic Society, Department 5351, Washington, DC 20036; (202) 775-6734.

The students then compared their class readings with the readings of their research team classes as well as the national data, and looked for patterns. Again, a flurry of letters to fellow student-scientists ensued, asking for clarification about surprises or validation of theories. Having collected the data first themselves, they had more confidence in making sense of the data of others.

The Acid Rain unit ends with a look at the social significance of such research. Included in the unit materials are two "letters"—each written from the point of view of a hypothetical student participant—that argue for opposite courses of action. One considers the human problems of layoffs related to reducing acid rain. The other describes how acid rain has killed all the fish in a nearby pond and calls for immediate action as well as more research.

Classes discuss these opposing positions, vote to support one or the other, and share the results with their research team using the telecommunications network.

Kids Network units are blends of classroom activities, network exchanges, and software tools. The various components of the curriculum allow students to collect data, question their findings, make predictions, collaborate with peers across the country, formulate meaningful questions, and learn how to find answers to those questions.

Teachers and students who took part in the field tests indicate that the concept works well. Teachers have particularly welcomed the opportunity to teach science, math, language arts, and social studies in an interdisciplinary fashion, and they report that linking their students with experts and with a student-scientist community across the country provides them with some strong incentives to learning.

BY
GWEN
SOLOMON

Jeff Holte's students at the Central Middle School in Eden Prairie, Minn., are practicing science instead of studying it these days—and they're using a computer and telecommunications to help them.

Holte's five classes of sixth graders grow corn, track geese, measure acid rain, monitor weather patterns, and compare their findings with those of students across the U.S.

Holte uses MIX, the McGraw-Hill Information Exchange, an on-line network, to help him conduct the science projects. He also uses the National Geographic Society's Kids Network and local bulletin boards as well. With telecommunications, Holte's students perform real experiments, use real data, and have a real community of other young scientists with whom to share information.

Growing Corn

This past January, for example, Holte's students grew corn from seeds (indoors, of course—Minnesota winters are fierce) as part of a national corn growing contest. MIX sent them and other participating schools the seeds, maps of the U.S., and charts to monitor growth.

Students researched soil types in preparation and carefully planted, watered, and fertilized their crop. Then they watched the seedlings grow and recorded the amounts of water, fertilizer, light and location. Most important, they charted the size of the corn. They posted this data regularly on the MIX "Plant" electronic conference.

Each class used reports from all of the other sites. They monitored and compared seedling growth around the country, plotted and interpreted maps, produced charts and graphs, and wrote to one another on-line to compare notes. Says Holte, "this shared ownership of data with students all over the U.S. and the interaction made the experiment real."

Their corn wasn't the tallest, so Holte's students didn't win the contest. But, he says, "the students learned things they will always remember because they did true comparisons of real live information."

Weather, Etc.

Another on-line experiment had students all over the country measuring the outside temperature at 9:00 a.m. local time every day. When Holte's youngsters saw the posted data, they questioned some results. "Why," they asked, "is it consistently warmer in British Columbia, Canada, than it is here in Eden Prairie, when [British Columbia] is farther north?" Then they learned about the warming effect of the ocean on land mass.

They also downloaded weather data provided by the U.S. National Weather

197

Service through the local UPI newswire. With this information, they composed the daily weather report and forecast for a student television news show.

Another on-line experiment on MIX called "Twisted Science" began with a science teacher by the name of Ken Evans calling himself Captain Flathead and stating that the earth was flat. He presented good arguments to prove his point. Then he challenged students on-line to come up with arguments to prove that the earth is round.

Holte's students contributed their explanations and read the others. They were most impressed by the Canadian youngster who claimed that the earth must be round because when he was sailing, he saw only the top part of another boat's mast.

Holte's students noticed the honking of Canadian geese this fall as the birds travelled south for the winter. They tracked the migration of these geese as part of an on-line project with students from Canada to Florida. When they spotted geese in their area, they posted the information: how many birds they saw, where the birds were, and when the students saw them. As students in many areas spotted the birds and posted their data, Holte's classes used the national data to plot points on a map and keep track of the route.

Talk to the Experts

Students also connect with leading experts on the MIX "Nature Center" conference that Holte also coordinates. Last year, Jim Gerhart, a reptile specialist, answered questions; he'll be back this year by popular demand. Also this year, Karen Sharnberg from the Springbrook Nature Center in Spring Lake Park, Minn. discussed animal life with youngsters on-line. Questions included, "Where

do frogs go in the winter?" Other experts from the fields of astronomy, weather, and zoology customize answers to the age group asking each question.

Holte was also involved in "Agripals," an on-line project to compare life and conditions in different environments. Holte's suburban students learned about farm life from students in rural Ohio. "We're connected," says Holte, "with a whole world we never knew anything about—farming." His students eagerly asked about fertilizing and growing crops and found out where their food really comes from. Then the high school students from Amanda Clearcreek School District in Ohio visited Holte's classes for "a face-to-face follow up."

An outgrowth of exchanging data line is a new exchange of science videotapes. Holte's students are filming a documentary on how ice forms on a lake, and they're sending it to Bonnie Price's students in Whittier, Calif. Price's students are filming life in a tidal pool in return. Harris Thomas' students in Juneau, Alaska, will see those videos as well as create their own on Alaskan geograpy. After viewing the videos, students get back on-line to ask questions of one another.

Kids Network

For the past three years, Holte's students also have used National Geographic Kids Network, a scientific telecommunications project developed by TERC (Technical Education Research Center), located in Cambridge, Mass., and sponsored by the National Science Foundation and the National Geographic Society.

Kids Network distributes software and curricular materials and provides access to the on-line network for each project. Fourth through sixth graders around the country conduct experiments, upload their data to a central computer and then read, interpret, and analyze the maps and charts that come back.

According to Dorothy Perreca, manager of Kids Network, "all of the units involve hands-on science. Kids are the scientists collecting their data, analyzing it, and telecommunicating." Experts also participate by commenting on results and corresponding with children on-line. In fact, Dr. John Miller, deputy director of the National Oceanographic and Atmospheric Association's Air Resources Laboratory, presented some of the student's findings to a research committee.

Rain and Air

With the "Acid Rain" unit, Holte's students build rain collectors, use pH paper to test the acidity of pond, tap, and rain water collected, and make predictions about the effects of acids on various materials. They post their findings on the Kid's Network and watch the data come back as different colored dots on a national map.

"They are captivated looking at the dots—one of those dots is theirs," says Holte. They compare the levels of acid rain water to findings from different parts of the United States, Canada, and overseas. Then they analyze trends and patterns for their own region and others. They also compare their data with pH levels found by the Federal Acid Rain Network.

Another unit is "Our Air, Its Temperature and Its Motion," a weather study in which Holte's students and others all over the country collect information on temperature and wind direction over a period of six weeks. Using a variety of tools, from thermometers to compasses, students record daily statistics

and use special software to display the changing data visually on their computers and make predictions about weather patterns.

They also send their information on-line to a central computer at TERC and get back results from all over the network. These results are in the form of computer maps of national temperature data. Meteorologists are on-line to help the students explore the connections between wind and temperature and look for national weather patterns.

The Benefits

In all of these on-line experiments, students mimic the efforts of real scientists to establish national and international trends. Also, like adult scientists, they are investigating new areas and discovering things for themselves. According to Robert Tinker, director of TERC's Technology Center, "technology can engage kids in their own learning and thereby give them power over that learning."

"Science has the potential to be different now," Holte says. "Students participate, interact, collect data, and continually experiment. All of these things are exciting." and promote more scientific curiosity than dry textbook lessons, and they are more relevant than contrived laboratory experiments.

And, Holte adds, "Using telecommunications is cost effective for what it can do for a class. You need a modem and access to a telephone line, but a little on-line connect-time goes a long way. Kids combine everything and send all of their work in two or three minutes. At $6 to $10 an hour for connect charges, you can do a lot." Holte estimates that a typical school would have to spend only about $200 a year for on-line services.

Article #19
Learning to Save the Environment

By
Leslie
Eiser

There are hot topics, and there are hot topics, and right now one of the hottest is our environment. Global issues like ozone depletion and acid rain are being debated on television. Local problems like overflowing landfills and polluted lakes are being written up in newspapers and talked about at dinner tables.

A Comparison of Environmental Software

Program	Pollution Control	SimCity	ECODISC	Decisions, Decisions: The Environment	Audubon Adventure Series : Whales
Publisher	Focus Media	Broderbund	Educorp	Tom Snyder Productions	Top Ten Software
Computers	MS-DOS Apple II	MS-DOS, Macintosh, Amiga	Macintosh with CD drive	MS-DOS	MS-DOS, Apple II, Apple IIGS
Primary Focus	Local	Local	Local	Local	Local
Suggested Grade Level	7 to 9	5 and up	7 and up	5 to 12	4 and up
Issues, Subjects Addressed					
Fossil fuels		√			
Nuclear fuels		√			
Alternative energy sources					
Recycling	√			√	
Air pollution/green house effect global warming	√			√	
Water pollution	√		√	√	√
Land pollution/waste management	√			√	
Land use/conservation/green space/deforestation		√	√	√	√
Endangered species			√	√	√
Economics of environmental action	√	√	√	√	
The role of government in finding solutions	√	√		√	√
The role of individuals in finding solutions	√		√	√	√

200

As teachers, we are expected to help our students come to terms with such problems. But it's not always easy to decide how best to tackle the issues, and where to start the discussions.

Where Does the Computer Fit In?

The computer can't offer us a cure for our environmental problems, but it *can* provide us with a way to sensitize students to the issues. Educational software developers have taken an active role in developing materials for environmental education, and we've gathered together a group of their latest efforts. Some of these programs are computerized lectures with environmental morals, others are full-fledged simulations with an environmental twist, while still others are collections of data that can be

Water Pollution	EARTHQUEST	Balance of the Planet	SimEarth	Save the Planet	Global Recall
EME Corp.	Earthquest, Inc.	Chris Crawford Games	Broderbund	Save the Planet Software	The World Game Institute
MS-DOS, Apple II	Macintosh	MS-DOS, Macintosh	Macintosh	MS-DOS, Macintosh	Macintosh
Local	Global	Global	Global	Global	Global
7 to 12	3 and up	8 and up	7 and up	6 and up	7 and up
	√	√	√	√	(Global Recall does not directly address specific environmental issues. The program is a database of world statistics that can be used to study global environmental problems.)
		√	√	√	
	√	√	√	√	
	√	√		√	
	√	√	√	√	
√	√	√			
√	√	√			
	√	√		√	
√	√	√	√		
		√		√	
		√	√	√	
√	√			√	

searched in various ways. What they have in common is a distinctly pro-environment orientation and an eye toward the complexity of issues involved.

Starting Small

Before your students try to tackle environmental problems on a global level, they may find it helpful to grapple with the issues at the local level. After all, just understanding the importance of recycling efforts in our own communities and recognizing the impact that increased population can have on local areas are critical steps in the students' learning process.

Of course, issues that may be relevant in your region may be less so somewhere else. Luckily, there's a good range of issues to choose among here. If your school is near the coast, or if endangered species are of major interest, you'll find *Audubon Wildlife Adventures: Whales* to be of interest. Is there a lake or river nearby that needs cleaning up? *Water Pollution* and *Decisions, Decisions: The Environment* address the issue directly. Big-city problems need big-city answers, and *Pollution Control* does its best to identify many of the difficulties endemic to large metropolitan areas. *SimCity* offers the most complex simulation of the locally focused software. Not only are pollution and green space identified as issues, there are traffic problems to control; taxes to raise and administer; and trade-offs among industrial, residential, and commercial development to consider. The most open-ended of the programs with a local focus are *Decisions, Decisions: The*

Before your students try to tackle environmental problems on a global level, they may find it helpful to grapple with the issues at the local level.

Environment and *ECODISC*. Neither presumes to direct you toward a particular outcome. In fact, the buck stops with you in these simulations. If you don't do well you may lose your position as mayor of the environmentally threatened town in *Decisions, Decisions: The Environment,* or you may cause irreparable damage to the nature reserve you manage in *ECODISC.* The programs won't tell you which of your decisions was wrong, just that the impact was negative. It's up to you to use different tactics and try again.

Thinking Big

Once your students have discussed local problems, and perhaps even tried out some solutions, they will be ready to tackle global issues. Expect greater complexity and increased abstraction when they do. After all, you can show your students a landfill to demonstrate the importance of recycling. But it is much harder to convince them of the existence, let alone the significance, of a hole in the atmospheric ozone, or the devastation of forests in distant places.

Simulations like *SimEarth* and *Balance of the Planet* attempt to inform through game-like interfaces. Not only fun to play, both of these programs have distinct "agendas"—strong environmental orientations. Of the two, *Balance of the Planet* is most directly educational in approach. Issues like the economic impact of environmental protection, the importance and cost of research, and the interrelationship between increased taxes and decreased consumption are clearly demonstrated as students manipulate funds in an attempt to prevent worldwide starvation and flooding. In *SimEarth,* as in *SimCity,* you can create and manage a "system" from scratch—in this case an entire planet!

EarthQuest, Save the Planet, and *Global Recall* are not games as such, but interactive information sources with distinctly pro-environmental-protection orientations. *EarthQuest* is the most visual, featuring interactive graphics and entertaining "movies." *Save the Planet* is a remarkable value at $20 per disk, providing a wealth of information that's easy to access and use. *Global Recall* is not strictly an environmental program, but an immense database of information that can be used to look at a wide range of world issues.

Taking a Stand

While your students steep themselves in local and global environmental affairs through software packages such as these, you'll want them to engage in discussions, and probably even some good arguments, all of which will help bring the concepts home. Then, sooner or later, they'll likely be ready to move from class discussion to informed class action.

And act they should. According to American Demographics (April 1990), an incredible 76 percent of us (including our President) say that we are environmentalists. But if that's true, just who is throwing away those 16 billion disposable diapers, 1.6 billion pens, and 220 million tires a year? That's an astounding amount of waste, and the effect of not recycling it is equally mind boggling. Just this week, for example, 500,000 trees will have to be cut down to meet our need for newsprint. We teachers need to guarantee that our students are exposed to these problems, and we need to help them generate constructive solutions. So if you've been thinking about getting your classroom involved, do it now, while we still have an environment to save.

Article #20
The Computer-Infused Social Studies Classroom

By
Robert
Vlahakis

Erich pored over his Macintosh, using *The Comic Strip Factory* (Foundation Publishing, Inc.) to create a character who would represent the Colonists' viewpoint during the Boston Massacre. On another Mac, Annaliese and Charlotte were working on their newspaper layout for *The Green Mountain Boys Gazette.* Meanwhile, Hiro was slowly and carefully drawing a detailed map of Colonial Boston and its vicinity using *Deluxe Paint II* (Electronic Arts) on the Apple IIGS.

On the Apple IIe computers, Tara was compiling a comprehensive calendar of the important events of the Revolutionary War from 1775-1783, Deanna was constructing a timeline of George Washington's life, and Ken was working on a one-page newsletter about the Boston Tea Party.

The rest of the seventh-grade class were working on similar history-related projects, using a variety of software packages. All this was going on in what the Shoreham-Wading River School District in Shoreham, NY, calls a "computer-infused classroom."

After five years of experimenting and building upon past experiences, I have finally reached a point at which I integrate computer use into the social studies curriculum over the entire school year. While many of the teaching ideas are not new, the involvement of the computer throughout the year adds new and rewarding elements. What's more, the ideas that work with my American history course could be easily adapted to fit any other social studies curriculum.

There are three main components to my year-long program: simulations, telecommunication activities, and individual projects that require the use of utility programs.

With large-group simulations such as Tom Snyder's *Decisions, Decisions* series, students in my class apply their knowledge of history and social science, practice higher-level thinking skills, and become intensely involved in discussions of important issues that they may face later in their own lives. Participation in *The Other Side,* a Tom Snyder simulation in which players are called upon to negotiate a "peace bridge" between two nations, remains one of the highlights of each year for my students and for me. (For details on how I use this simulation, see "The Other Side: Snapshot of a Social Studies Simulation in Action," *CCL,* May 1987, pp. 4245.)

The telecommunications component of my curriculum involves the students in several projects that enable them to access current news information via modem (see "From TASS to Tallahassee: In Search of Today's News," *CCL,* May 1988, pp. 82-87) and to communicate with other students around the world in a variety of ways. Telecommunications projects involving letter writing, creative story writing, and on-line simulations with students as far away as Australia have led to exchanges of videotapes and friendships that never would have come about otherwise.

Tools, Tools, and More Tools

The third component of my computer-infused social studies curriculum, and the one that I'll focus on for the remainder of this article, is the use of "utility" software to enhance student projects. During the first few months of school, I set aside time to introduce certain utilities that I feel will be particularly useful throughout the year. For example, to introduce *Timeliner* (Tom Snydor Productions) I first work with the entire class to create a "birthdays" timeline. In one class period we create and print out a timeline showing when each student was born. Kids begin to see what the program can do.

The next step is to have students work individually on an autobiographical project. For homework have them come up with a list of 20 events or milestones in their lives. Then each student uses *Timeliner* individually to enter and edit these events. In doing this, students develop a better feeling for the software's capabilities, and each has a unique keepsake to take home. Students are now prepared for the final stage of the project: relating the tool to a specific historical curriculum. We divide the American history curriculum into ten-year segments, and each student researches a number of historical events in one of the decades. The end product is a huge timeline, covering several hundred years, which can be used as a reference and historical overview throughout the year.

By now everyone in the class feels comfortable using *Timeliner* as a tool. As the year progresses, different students will use this utility program to enrich their study of various time periods.

I try to work through a similar sequence with other utilities my students will use: first presenting a whole-class project, then assigning a personal project, then working through a curriculum application, and finally turning the utility over to students to use at any time during the year. But since there isn't time to complete these steps with all utilities, I sometimes use an alternative approach: I teach certain students how to use a program, then make them responsible for teaching other students. Much of this teaching takes place outside the classroom during free periods, lunchtime, or after school. The students' natural motivation to learn new programs keeps the enthusiasm high, while saving critical class time.

Historical Newsletters

Once students become comfortable with certain word processing and desktop publishing tools, we move on to a major project that involves working in groups to create historical newsletters or newspapers. The assignment is as follows: "select one of the 13 colonies and create a Colonial Age newspaper for that colony. Divide your group to cover a variety of issues that pertain to your specific colony. Pick a date for your publication, and make sure all articles are true to that date. Then select a title for the newspaper, and add pictures that can be scanned or copied into your paper."

These projects allow students to look at history from a more personal point of view, getting behind the scenes and expressing personal opinions and anecdotes from a particular era. In order to write about the past, students have to understand it, which requires serious research and analysis of the time period.

To create the newspapers, we use desktop publishing software, scanners, and a digitizer. (See "Equipping the Computer-Infused Social Studies Classroom" below.) We insert newspaper or magazine pictures, as well as a group picture of each newspaper's creators. Some students learn how to scan pictures, some capture video images, some enter text into the word processor, and others work with the desktop publishing program to develop a professional layout. Each group comes up with its own unique layout and design.

This year, we ended up with *The Jamestown Memo, The Pennsylvania*

Equipping the Computer-Infused
Social Studies Classroom

I am fortunate enough to have access to 15 computers to use with my class: two Macintoshes, three Apple IIGS's and ten Apple IIe's. Few of the activities described in this article are dependent on a particular computer. However, I do find it useful to work with several different computer models, because it increases the number of software titles that we can use. Some MS-DOS machines would broaden our choices even further.

How do I decide which utilities to use with the students? There are several categories of hardware and software that I have found useful:

• **Scanners** allow us to capture pictures from books and other print media. We use ThunderScan (ThunderWare, Orinda, CA). And a *digitizer*—Macvision (Koala Technologies, Santa Clara, CA) or ComputerEyes (Digital Vision, Dedham, MA) allows us to input real-life scenes, including "photos" of students themselves.

• **Integrated packages** offer us access to several tools at once. We use both *AppleWorks* (Claris Corp., Mountain View, CA), which includes word processing, database management, and spreadsheets; and *MicroSoft Works* (Microsoft Corp., Redmond, WA), which gives us all of the above plus telecommunications.

• A **graphing** utility such as *TimeOut Graph* (Beagle Bros., San Diego, CA) is very helpful.

• **Timeline** programs such as *Timeliner* (Tom Snyder Productions, Cambridge, MA) are especially critical for history presentations.

• **Graphics programs** are essential for creating a variety of illustrations. I use a number of different packages with my students, including *Dazzle Draw* (Brøderbund Software, San Rafael, CA), *Paintworks Gold* from Activision (Mediagenic, Menlo Park, CA) and *Deluxe Paint II* (Electronic Arts, San Mateo, CA).

• **Animation programs** (e.g., *Animate* and *Fantavision*, both from Brøderbund Software) are great for the creation of on-screen lessons and shows.

• **A slide show program** such as the new *Slide Shop* (Scholastic, New York, NY) and a comic strip program, such as *Comic Strip Factory* (Foundation Publishing, Inc., Minneapolis, MN), round out our graphics options.

• Finally, a **desktop publishing program**, such as *PageMaker* (Aldus, Seattle, WA) or *Newsroom* (Springboard, Minneapolis, MN), and at least one high-quality printer are needed for creating newsletters, newspapers, and other professional looking documents.

Journal and Weekly Advisor, The Savannah Speaker, The Boston Times, The Plymouth Bay Sun, and *The Charleston Tribune,* all with "publication dates" between 1608 and 1753.

Going it Alone

Once students are comfortable using the computer to conduct research and present information to their classmates and have had the opportunity to work together in groups to create a historically accurate newspaper, they're ready to take on independent computer projects of their own choosing. This is the culminating activity of the year. It allows students to take the expertise they've acquired throughout the year and apply it to a detailed and specific computer project. It also allows for individualization to a degree that I have never been able to achieve without the computer.

Each student is asked to select a historical topic to review (e.g., the Boston Tea Party, Paul Revere's ride, or the role of women in the American Revolution). Then I meet with every class member for a brainstorming and planning session, during which we devise specific computer projects for the topics. Students with similar interests can choose to work with a partner or in a small group. While I try to make few restrictions, I do find it necessary to monitor the number of projects for each computer, making sure that we never have too many projects that require the scarcer Macintosh computers.

After that, it's simple. The students all start out in the library researching their topics, and as the days go by, they begin to translate their research into computer projects. Not everyone progresses at the same pace. Some kids are in the library while others are on the computers and still others are at their desks working.

Such a scenario might sound like a management nightmare, but actually things tend to go smoothly because the students assume tremendous responsibility for organizing themselves. The library research is assisted by the school librarians, who are familiar with students' specific projects. And the students are familiar enough with the software to work on the computers independently, freeing me to help out with ideas and concepts on an individual basis. Since class members move back and forth between the computers and the library (even after they're well into the computer phase of their projects they often run down to the library to check out further information), there are always computers free to work on.

Each year, the management issues become easier, as I become more familiar with the software and learn what kinds of projects are most likely to be successful. While I have discovered that I must be familiar with all the software to some extent, I can count on the kids to explore and learn a lot as they go along. Very quickly student "experts" appear, who then take on the responsibility of teaching other students (and sometimes me). I've also learned that it isn't necessary for every student to learn every piece of software. As long as they have their own nucleus of applications, they are able to produce interesting projects.

The energy and excitement during these projects are tremendous. And as kids observe others working, they begin to see parts of history from different perspectives. At the end of the unit, we have a diverse range of projects that can be shared by all. Last year one student taught himself to use *TimeOut Graph* (Beagle Bros.) to analyze and look at population trends, growth patterns, and military troop increases during the Revolutionary War. Another group of students put together a slide show of Colonial times with illustrations of historical places, events, and clothing worn by Native Americans and Colonists, accompanied by a historically accurate soundtrack with music and narration. Additional projects included a series of maps showing the areas of influence of the British, French, and Spanish; a historical journal of the "Swamp Fox;" and a timeline of Paul Revere's midnight ride.

For me, computers have added another dimension to the teaching style that I have always employed—an experiential, problem-solving approach that encourages students to question, discuss, and analyze history. The computer has made it more efficient for me to focus on the individual needs of my students in a more diversified learning environment. What more can I ask?

Theme or Topic	Software	Computer	Actual Project
French & Indian War	Macatlas	Macintosh	Maps + mini-report
Boston Tea Party	Dazzle Draw	Apple IIe	Slide show with sound and narration
Ben Franklin	Paintworks +/Appleworks	Apple IIGS	Drawings and explanations
Boston Massacre	Dazzle Draw	Apple IIe	Slide show with sound and narration
Women's Role in the War	Appleworks	Apple IIe	Historical journal
Boston Tea Party	Dazzle Draw	Apple IIe	Slide show with sound and narration
The Green Mt. Boys	Pagemaker	Macintosh	Underground newspaper
Political Satire	Comic Strip Factory	Macintosh	Political cartoon strip
Paul Revere	Timeliner	Apple IIe	Timeline of night ride + journal
Boston Massacre	Dazzle Draw	Apple IIe	Slide show with sound and narration
Francis Marion "Swamp Fox"	Appleworks	Apple IIe	Map + historical journal
John Paul Jones	Timeliner	Apple IIe	Timeline of his life + map
Battle of Lexington	Paintworks+	Apple IIGS	Several drawings + mini-report
Revolutionary War on Long Island	Timeliner	Apple IIe	Timeline of events + map
Articles of Confederation	Appleworks	Apple IIe	Journal as delegate to convention
Revolutionary War on Long Island	Appleworks/Dazzle Draw	Apple IIe	Colonial journal + several pictures
Political Satire	Newsroom	Apple IIe	Political cartoons
Valley Forge	Newsroom	Apple IIe	Mini-newspaper
Colonial Armies/Statistics	TimeOut Graph	Apple IIe	Make graphs & maps of war
Paul Revere	Newsroom	Apple IIe	Mini-newspaper
Townsend Acts	Appleworks	Apple IIe	Colonial journal + several pictures
Revolutionary War Overview	Printshop Companion	Apple IIe	Daily calendar of events
British maneuvers	Paintworks Plus	Apple IIGS	Drawings + mini-report
Boston Tea Party	Crossword Magic	Apple IIe	Crossword puzzle

By
Carol
Holzberg

Courses in American history, government, and civics take on special meaning in an election year. There are real candidates and issues to examine and political platforms are given plenty of press coverage. It's a perfect opportunity to introduce your students to the office of the presidency, to review the accomplishments of past presidents and to follow the strategies of the current candidates as they campaign for votes. You can encourage research projects on topics such as the electoral college system, the three branches of government, and the impact of personalities on election outcome. Or you can simulate a presidential election in your classroom.

The computer is a handy device to get students actively involved in the political process. There are several good software programs available to supplement traditional classroom instruction about one of America's most important democratic achievements—the national election.

Simulating the Campaign

A number of the programs worth looking at are political simulations that encourage students to think dynamically about the election process, campaign strategies, and political leadership. These take a "what if..." approach, letting students make decisions about political platforms, fund-raising, advertising, courting special-interest groups, and directing the fate of a nation. All choices affect the outcome of the "election."

One of the most appealing simulations of the impact of presidential decision-making on leadership performance comes from Focus Media. In the program *And If Re-elected...* the student assumes the role of an incumbent president who is seeking re-election. In order to win, players must resolve 12 political crises (stated in the form of multiple choice questions) in ways that are favorable to 21 special-interest groups. Popularity polls, reported with the help of colorful graphs, gauge the public's reaction to the president's policy-making. After the votes are tallied, the incumbent president is either returned to office or defeated. A historical verdict is presented to the student, in which the candidate's abilities to handle foreign affairs, the economy, health, education, welfare, war and peace, and administrative affairs are assessed.

And if Re-elected... is open-ended enough to stimulate discussions on a number of different political topics. Students become involved first-hand as participants, making decisions about the political direction their government will take. They learn about the workings of the electoral college, the effects of public opinion on executive leadership, the importance of stroking key voter blocs, and the difficult decisions faced by politicians in the areas of foreign policy, economics, social concerns, and the environment.

Another outstanding simulation that focuses on simular issues but places greater emphasis on group discussion

209

and offline reading is *On the Campaign Trail: Issues and Image in a Presidential Election*. This program is one of the most recent additions to Tom Snyder Productions' *Decisions, Decisions* series. In this simulation students work in groups, playing the role of a third-party candidate running for president of the United States. With the help of on-line "advisors" who provide written advice on everything from party ideologies to budget deficits to national defense, students gain a clearer understanding of the political issues facing the nation and the strategies involved in winning an election.

The student candidates quickly learn that electioneering is no easy task. Success in *On the Campaign Trail* is measured by how well the candidates meet their political goals. The presidential hopefuls begin by setting campaign priorities. Are they out to win the election, build a reputation for the future, achieve bargaining leverage with the winning candidate, or keep campaign debts from piling up? Their goals defined, the students must then decide on effective strategies. Should they hold a press conference to discuss their views, meet with liberals and conservatives to win public backing and financial support, or hit the campaign trail for the final big push into the White House? Decisions, decisions. Actions taken by the players stimulate class discussions about the politics of electioneering and the major issues confronting the nation.

Added Ingredients: History and Math

If you're searching for a simulation that focuses more directly on specific candidates and elections past and present, you might want to take a look at *President Elect* (developed by Strategic Simulations, Inc., and distributed by Electronic Arts). With this program, students can predict the outcome of the 1988 election or replay the elections of 1960 through 1984. It's possible to set the computer to play the role of any of the candidates or to sit back and watch a demo of the 1960 election. Students can also cast their own candidates in contests of their choice, changing the historical facts to permit a "what if…" scenario. Imagine JFK running against Ronald Reagan in 1984!

If they choose to campaign actively, players decide where and how to concentrate their efforts—nationally, regionally, or at the level of individual states. Weekly polls post information about the popular vote. On election night the students view a color-coded map on which state-by-state returns are reported.

The limited use of graphics in most other sections of *President Elect* is disappointing and the historical demo is less effective than it could be were it to involve more interaction. (As it stands now, the computer even controls the length of time text remains on the screen). Nevertheless, this simulation offers students the chance to replay historical events and get a feeling for what's involved in running for office. For those following the 1988 election campaign, Strategic Simulations offers a map in the instruction manual showing electoral votes per state. The company is also sponsoring a contest to see how closely program owners can predict the outcome in November.

Geared toward younger students and taking a much lighter approach than the three programs described above, *Campaign Math* from Mindplay is an enjoyable package with a dual purpose. It's as much a math program as a social studies one, building on the excitement surrounding the American elections to drill students on fractions, ratios, and percentages. Elementary school teachers interested in an integrated approach to learning will particularly appreciate the first of the three activities offered by the program. In "Platform," students are presented with ten election issues and an appealing graphical interface that allows them to select different media sources for help in finding out where popular opinion lies. The numerical information gathered (in the form of percentages or fractions) from telephone calls, newspapers, radio, or TV aids the students in deciding whether they are for or against the issues.

The other two activities offer less in the way of social studies content. "Fundraising" is an arcade-like challenge in which the player runs through a fundraising maze to solicit as much money as possible from individuals, special-interest groups, and club banquets. As students answer math questions they must exercise care to avoid coming into contact with "scandal bugs." The object of "Race" is to buy the most effective advertising in order to cross the finish line first and win the election. If the math option is turned on, correct answers increase popularity and yield additional campaign funds.

It's certainly not an in-depth examination of the American electoral system, but *Campaign Math's* highly interactive format, colorful graphics, and sound will appeal to many students. The program offers challenging math practice while increasing general political awareness.

Name That President

As we focus attention on the current presidential race, it's only natural to think back on previous races and previous presidents. If you're interested in giving your students the "basic facts"

about the 39 men who've occupied the office of president of the United States, there are several programs to assist you.

The Medalists Series: Presidents from Hartley offers a straightforward, no-frills approach to learning the facts. The program randomly selects a mystery president and offers clues to help students identify the figure in question. Students choose whether to compete individually or against others.

This program has been around since 1982 and, compared to many other programs produced at that time, it permits a high degree of content flexibility. Students can study the clues (facts about the presidents) before playing the game and teachers can delete presidents from the list, modify the clues presented, and keep performance records on 50 students. However, the editing options are not up to 1988 standards. If you plan to delete clues or categories, it's best to print out a hard copy of what's available before making any changes since, once deleted, the data are gone for good. It also may be hard to maintain student interest in *The Presidents* since rewards are limited and the text-only screens do little to spice up the drill.

Facts and Faces of the U.S. Presidents from Visatex uses a graphics approach in its study of American presidents, although it too sticks to memorization of the facts. This is an "Edu-stack" for the Macintosh, providing a game-like format with both historical and contemporary information about the presidents. Students first answer multiple choice questions and win points for correct answers. When enough points have been accumulated, players move to the second part of the program. Here they view a screen which holds a picture of a president, hidden by "tiles." The students spend the points they have accumulated to remove tiles, attempting to identify the mystery president before running out of points.

This game is fun, but the version I tested made it difficult to get a high score. Visatex promises an update that will let the user have more chances to answer the multiple choice questions. Changing the scoring format will greatly improve the educational value of this presidential stack.

Presidential Profiles from Mindscape is another program that presents interesting facts about the backgrounds and accomplishments of the men who have served as president of the United States. To use the program, students place an "EasyKey" vinyl overlay on the computer keyboard, turning individual keys into "buttons" that can be pressed to select a specific president or activity.

In addition to a general database in which students can browse for information, the program offers three structured activities. In "Ask the Presidents," students try to guess the identity of five mystery presidents from clues provided in interviews with other presidents. "Pinpoint the President" challenges students to identify the years in which a particular president held office. "President Linkin" is a variation on the game of dominoes in which the object is to match pairs of presidents by picking a trait (e.g. place of birth, occupation, political party affiliation) that both of them shared.

Presidential Profiles is probably the most appealing and versatile of the three drill programs described here, but it is not without its flaws. Sometimes the EasyKey overlay doesn't work as planned (e.g., it misidentifies the location of the keyboard's shift key) and an incorrect key is pressed by mistake. Younger students tend to get very frustrated when this happens. It's also hard to predict which traits the computer will accept as

valid links in "President Linkin," and since students have no opportunity to explain their choices, the task can easily degenerate to one of trial and error.

A Database Approach

Two of the programs I reviewed encouraged students to manipulate available facts about the presidents in order to look for patterns and test hypotheses. *MECC Dataquest: The Presidents* and *The American Presidency: Hail to the Chief* combine information on America's presidents (their backgrounds, personal lives, ideologies, goals, decisions, and historical events taking place during their years in office) with practice in using a database. When students work with these programs, they learn to appreciate the value of electronic information storage. They also gain experience retrieving and classifying information in ways that facilitate data gathering and report writing.

The Presidents is part of MECC's *Accessing Information* series. It begins with an on-line introduction showing students how information is classified in the database and suggesting strategies for data retrieval. There are graphic illustrations as well as step-by-step instructions explaining how to look up information on all the presidents (e.g., to find out how old every president was at inauguration); *specific presidents* (e.g., by name); or presidents selected by *category* (e.g., only those presidents who were in office during certain years).

The tutorial complete, students are left on their own to explore the database with its 23 fields of information on each president. The program's manual helps out by providing some interesting suggestions for research topics.

Hail to the Chief is also part of an educational software series—

Mindscape's *Quest for Files*. Its 24 fields are quite similar to those used in the MECC database. There's information on age at inauguration, party affiliation, occupation before election, percentage of popular vote, Supreme Court appointments, vetoes during term, and more.

Once students complete an introduction that familiarizes them with the information available in the database, they are presented with three "lessons." Each lesson has a specific focus (historical facts, ways in which the presidents have used their authority, or the American political party system). A lesson includes six questions to stimulate curiosity followed by three hypotheses to be tested. (Students are able to select which of the questions and hypotheses to work on.) Hints on using the database to answer the questions are available.

Like *The Presidents, Hail to the Chief* presents an attractive, easy-to-use interface into the database and leads the student through the selection process with helpful prompts. Compared to the MECC program, however, *Hail to the Chief* provides more in the way of database options. For example, the user can construct complex search criteria, sort the information into a desired order or request that certain fields be totalled—options that are not possible with *The Presidents*.

Other Approaches

Looking for a tutorial on the presidency as an office? I found only one—*The Presidency Series* from Focus Media. This five-disk package does not have the appeal and high level of interactivity offered by *And If Re-elected . . .* from the same publisher. Yet it is the only program I came across that combines role-playing simulations and memorization

of historical facts with tutorials on the role of the president.

In the first lesson, students travel back in time to the Philadelphia Constitutional Convention of 1787. Here they learn about the proposals submitted by the 55 delegates regarding the creation of the presidential office and the powers of the president. The students evaluate the debate taking place and indicate whether they agree or disagree with the proposals.

In subsequent lessons, students learn about the evolution of the presidency, the constitutional requirements for the presidency, the American system of checks and balances, the powers of the president, and the evolving role of the cabinet. The final activity in the series asks students to analyze and evaluate the performance of past presidents with regard to such criteria as leadership, domestic achievements, foreign achievements, political appointments, integrity, influence on history, administrative skill, and charisma.

The Presidency Series is thorough but somewhat dry. If the program succeeds in holding your students' attention for long enough, it will certainly introduce them to some important facts and concepts.

The Classroom as Polling Place

It's not too late to hold a mock election in your classroom—complete with nominations, campaign literature, and speeches. And here again the computer can play a role.

With *The Voting Machine* from Career Publishing, students can create ballots, conduct an election, vote at the computer polling station, and tabulate the returns. Unfortunately, the program does not model itself on the electoral college system. It is a useful tool, however, for tallying the votes of individual students participating in classroom, school, or club elections.

The first task when working with *The Voting Machine* is to create a ballot. There's room for 50 different offices with up to nine candidates for each office. On election day, the students get to sign in and vote for the candidates on the ballot. After the last student has voted and the polls are closed, the computer tabulates the votes and prints out the results.

Secure a site license from Career Publishing and you can make multiple copies of the program for use in a single site. Then use several computers as voting machines. The program is able to combine the results from multiple computers to come up with the total number of votes received by each candidate for each office. The Voting Machine comes with colorful posters and other campaign artifacts to add a dash of sparkle and pizzazz to the election activity.

Perhaps you'd prefer to stage an election more closely modeled on the one your students will be following in November of this year. I haven't come across a commercial program that can be used to tally electoral votes, but that's certainly a task well suited to a spreadsheet. Of course, the focus need not be solely on 1988. You might choose to replay the great political campaigns of the 19th century instead.

Whatever era you choose, the computer can play an important role in the campaign process. You might make use of any one of the current crop of graphics and desktop publishing products to print out handbills, posters, political banners, and information about the candidates. If you have access to a Macintosh, your students can spruce up those mock election newspapers with realistic pictures of their favorite candidate. Visatex's U.S. Presidents ClipArt program sports a collection of easy-to-modify presidential portraits perfect for insertion in historical newspapers. And Visatex also offers a package with 27 portraits of the nine presidential hopefuls who first competed for the brass ring in the 1988 election—two serious shots and a caricature of each candidate.

So take the plunge and let your students electronically simulate the wonderful world of politics—its history, institutions, personalities, party ideologies, campaign adventures, election activities, and political processes. With any luck, the classroom activities will be so motivating that one of your students will grow up to become the president!

Information About the Products Mentioned in This Article

The American Presidency: Hail to the Chief (1987)
  Hardware: Appl11e II series (64K); IBM PC, Tandy 1000, and compatibles.
  Grade levels: 9-12.
  Package modules: Program disk with backup, teacher's manual with student handouts. Price: $49.95.

  Publisher: Mindscape, 3444 Dundee Road, Northbrook, IL 60062; (312) 480-7667.
And If Re-elected . . . (1986)
  Hardware: Apple II series; IBM PC, Tandy 1000, and compatibles.
  Grade levels: 7-12.
  Package includes: Double-sided program disk and backup, teacher's

lesson planner, student workbook.
Price: $89.00.
Publisher: Focus Media, Inc., 839 Stewart Ave., Garden City, NY 11530; (800) 645-8989 or (516) 794-8900 (collect in NY, AK, HI).

Facts and Faces of U.S. Presidents (1988)
Hardware: Macintosh Plus or SE with Hypercard version 1.2.
Grade levels: 9-12.
Package includes: Single 800K disk. Price: $49.50.
Publisher: Visatex Corporation, 1745 Dell Ave., Campbell, CA 95008; (800) 722-3729 or (408) 866-6596 in CA.

On the Campaign Trail: Issues and Image in a Presidential Election (1987)
Hardware: Apple II series (64K); IBM PC, Tandy 1000, and compatibles (with color graphics card).
Grade levels: 7-12.
Package includes: Double-sided program disk with backup, teacher's guide with lesson plans and student worksheets, 30 student reference books.
Price: $119.95.
Publisher: Tom Snyder Publishing, 90 Sherman St., Cambridge, MA 02140; (800) 342-0236 or (617) 876-4433 (in MA).

President Elect (1987)
Hardware: Apple II series (except Apple IIGS); IBM PC, Tandy 1000, and compatibles; Commodore 64/128; Atari ST.
Grade levels: 7-12.
Package includes: Program disk with instruction manual.
Price: $24.95 (Atari ST); $14.95 (other computers). Shipping/handling extra.
Publisher: Distributed by Electronic Arts, PO Box 7530, San Mateo, CA 94403; (800) 245-4525.

Presidential Profiles (1986)
Hardware: Apple II series.
Grade levels: 5-12.
Package includes: Program disk with backup, teacher's guide, program guide, and vinyl keyboard overlay.
Price: $49.95.
Publisher: Mindscape (see address above).

U.S. Presidents Clip Art and 1988 U.S. Presidential Candidates (1988)
Hardware: Macintosh family (512K).
Grade levels: Grade 5 and up.
Package includes: Single 400K disk.
Price: $25.00 for U.S. Presidents; $15.00 for 1988 Candidates.
Publisher: Visatex Corporation (see address above).

The Voting Machine (1987)
Hardware: Apple II family, TRS-80 Models III, 4; IBM PC, PC jr, Tandy 1000, and compatibles.
Grade levels: 7-12.
Package includes: Program disk, documentation, 300 "I voted today" labels, 3 wall posters, convention hat.
Price: $69.50; an additional $30 for site license.
Publisher: Career Publishing, Inc., PO Box 5486, Orange, CA 92613-5486; (800) 854-4014 or (800) 821-0543.

Publisher's Note: This product list has been abridged.

Article #22
Microsoft at Work

BY
ALICE
JAGGER
AND
BOB
VEECK

Works in the Classroom

The great advantage of Microsoft *Works* is that it is both an effective administrative tool for the teacher and an effective learning tool for the student. Microsoft *Works* has the capability and flexibility to assist many different types or learners in many different types of learning situations. Its capacity to produce a combination of wordprocessing documents, databases, and spreadsheets offers the teacher a great opportunity to enhance and enrich classroom activities.

We believe that Microsoft *Works* can influence and transform classroom learning on three different levels. Level One relates to providing students with large amounts of data. Level Two is directed at allowing students to use that data to develop higher level thinking skills. Level Three describes computer functions that make it easy for students to manipulate and organize data into significantly different forms and patterns and to create new sets of questions, hypotheses, and conclusions. The following article focuses on Level One.

The first and most basic use of Microsoft *Works* at Level One is to provide the student and ourselves with a vast amount of data in one easy-to-access place. When we first encountered databases, we were excited by the thought that teachers could take printouts from the computer, xerox them, and give copies of meaningfully arranged data to each student in class. It was our assumption that computers could make the classroom situation more dynamic and profitable for students by providing them with many facts organized in a way which would be meaningful to our lesson plans. Our imaginations were relatively restricted at this time in terms of the actual power of Microsoft *Works*. Later, we would learn how *Works* could enable students to participate in exciting classroom activities that give them a clearer understanding of the United States and the world within the context of this new composite of data. As time has passed, we have discovered that almost everyone initially regards the computer as we first did—as simply a convenient storage place for data. We would like to share some or the more significant things we have learned as we gained experience in using computers and Microsoft *Works* in the classroom.

We have used many methods at Level One for making our databases, spreadsheets, and word-processing documents available to students. These methods have changed, and continue to change as hardware and software configurations at our school continue to change. As noted above, we have printed out the information that students need for a day's lecture/discussion. It was easy to provide students with enough data that they could understand the concepts being discussed. As time passed and we became more confident in our use of Microsoft *Works*, we displayed the data on an overhead projection device so that the entire class could see the data being manipulated "live." This allowed us to be more responsive to students who wanted to ask questions and access in-

216

formation on topics we had not anticipated. We were able to share with the students the "let's-see-what-we-can-discover-together" experience while working with data that were easy to manipulate. Finally, we were able to have students manipulate the data themselves while working in a small group discussion mode, thus using computers to their best potential. Each of these Level One methods was highly successful, and we still utilize each style in our classrooms today.

The Power of Nation States

We have constructed several large databases, two of which have become commercial products. Our first database is called *The Power of Nation States*. It consists of 47 fields for each of the 167 countries in the world. The second database is called *State Data*. Each deserve a word or two of explanation about their place in the classroom and their influence on student learning.

Initially, *The Power of Nation States* was simply a database containing information on such topics as population, area GNP, GNP per capita, PQLI (Physical Quality of Life Index), military spending, and the size of each country's army, navy and air force. We believe that in the future databases similar to *The Power of Nation States* will de-emphasize the need for students to spend large amounts of time gathering basic information. It is not reasonable to expect students to compile as much data as goes into a comprehensive database of this type. We believe student research in the library should focus on projects and activities that make better use of students' time.

A comprehensive database such as *The Power of Nation States* can free students from the tedium of days of research and quickly give them a global perspective on critical contemporary issues. Once they gain this overview students eagerly return to the library and reference materials for a more complete understanding of the global phenomena the database has opened to them. For example, if the lesson is on world poverty it is highly desirable for students to have available a list of the names of all the countries in the world along with data on each country's gross national product per capita income and other key economic data that would indicate that country's level of wealth. After exploring the information in many different fields in the database, students can rank order the data, thus providing a stimulating and interesting approach to exploring what can otherwise be seen by the student as very dry information. Screen dumps from a specific country or from several countries provide instant information that normally takes the students hours to locate. Data to be used in lessons on military strength, trade and trade partners, ethnic groups, religions, type of government, colonial history and many other topics are almost instantly available.

The Concept of Power

Of course databases are very useful but they are only one way that Microsoft *Works* can be used in supplying students with basic facts. Most of the information in the *The Power of Nation States* database and many of the activities in class seemed to be oriented toward the concept of "power." We thought it would be productive to have a "text" that students could use to help in discussing the characteristics of different countries and the image of power the various countries projected. The word-processing capabilities of Microsoft *Works* allowed us to include in *The Power of Nation States* a 50-page text on the concept of power and its use and misuse in the contemporary world. The computer gives both the teacher and the students the opportunity to copy, amend, delete, or edit the text before, during, or after the lessons. There is a certain magic that occurs in the educational process as students change information they have been given in class based upon the learning that has been taking place. To make our resource easier to use we added a glossary that explains all of the terms in the database and many of the words in the text. For ourselves as teachers we added a database of 100 multiple-choice questions that can be selected according to concept and chapter.

> There is a certain magic that occurs in the educational process as students change information they have been given in class based upon the learning that has been taking place.

Microsoft *Works* enabled us to assemble a large amount of information not otherwise available in one convenient package.

We now have a database with over 7,500 items of information, a 50-page text that students and teachers can use in many different ways, a glossary that explains the major concepts we are studying, and a set of multiple-choice questions that measures student progress. As *The Power of Nation States* kept expanding we began to think of many other concepts and content areas that could be taught by using similar packages assembled with the help of Microsoft *Works*.

However Microsoft *Works* can do more than store information. Using its capability to sort information and create reports, *The Power of Nation States* was converted into a program that asks students to consider a definition of the concept of power, identify the components of power, and analyze which countries and alliance systems possess the most power. Six lessons and a teacher guide were added to *The Power of Nation States* and these lessons focused on higher level thinking skills and the use of Microsoft *Works* as a processor of information as well as a storer of information.

The Fifty States: An Analysis

Out of this realization grew *The Fifty States: An Analysis,* a database containing 117 different types of information on each of the 50 states. Categories such as number of national forests, federal expenditures per capita, acres of forested land, number of cities with population over 100,000, and percentage of population graduating from high school allow students to gain a statistical picture of any state.

The Fifty States: An Analysis contains 17 lessons addressed to all three levels of computer use. Level One lessons are designed to familiarize students with basic information about all the states in the United States. The methods we use to introduce and examine this data in our classrooms are very similar to those we use with *The Power of Nation States: An Analysis*. The focus of *The Fifty States: An Analysis* is on synthesizing and analyzing information. Microsoft *Works* tends to lead on in this direction; the data is interesting in itself, but the real advantage lies in manipulating the data and seeing the world in a different way.

When using computers at Level One, students are exposed to much more current information about a certain subject than they can obtain in most textbooks. The data can be used in such a way as to raise questions, generate new data, catalog key facts, and provide a statistical picture of the particular focus of study. Broad topics can be introduced quickly, and valuable classroom time does not have to be spent gathering information from many different sources. The challenge to teachers in the future is to discover how to utilize access to so much data. Textual materials can be added to the learning package, which both the instructor and the student can modify in a number of ways.

Over time, using much trial and error, we have learned that the really exciting application of Microsoft *Works* in the classroom comes when students move beyond the acquisition of basic facts to higher levels of thinking and when they begin to use computers to transform raw data that does not exist in any standard reference work. In future issues of Microsoft *Works* in Education we will discuss the second and third levels of using Microsoft *Works* in social studies classrooms.

Article #23
Women in the News

By
Beth
White

Three years ago, Congress established March as National Women's History Month. Celebrate women's achievements with a class newspaper, written and designed by your students with a desktop publishing program. The newspaper will act as an invaluable hands-on social studies project that you may share with your entire school.

Materials Needed: Have on hand an easy-to-use desktop publishing program such as *The Children's Writing and Publishing Center* (The Learning Co.), *The Newsroom* or *Springboard Publisher* (Springboard), or *Publish It!* (Timeworks). You'll also need resource materials about women's history, including encyclopedias, books, videos, and pamphlets (see Resources box). For use as models, bring into class several issues of local and regional newspapers.

Discussion: Challenge your students to write down five names of men who have made significant contributions to U.S. history. Have them add an adjective next to each name that tells something about the man in relation to his contribution. For example: "Neil Armstrong—brave." Discuss as a class the names that your students came up with. Make a list of them on the chalkboard. Why were certain men chosen?

Now repeat this process naming significant women in U.S. history. Was it harder to come up with women's names? Why? Were the criteria for men and women the same or different? Were the objectives similar or different?

Tell your students that, to help fill the information gap about important women in history, they will be responsible for producing a newspaper for Women's History Month. The newspaper should focus on women, past and present, who have made contributions to U.S. history.

Activity: Hand out your newspaper samples, and talk to your students about how a newspaper is organized. Explain that there are different sections that

---

Women of Note

This list of prominent women may help students get started thinking about subject matter for their newspaper.

Women of the Present: Barbara Bush, Margaret Chas Smith, Julia Child, Gloria Steinem, Sally Ride, Connie Chung, Sandra Day O'Connor, Shirley Chisholm

Women in History: Susan B. Anthony, Abigail Adams, Elizabeth Blackwell, Dolly Madison, Margaret Mead, Grandma Moses, Sacagawea, Harriet Tubman, Martha Washington, Amelia Earhart, Eleanor Roosevelt, Harriet Beecher Stowe

Women in the Arts: Beverly Sills, Louisa May Alcott, Diana Ross, Georgia O'Keeffe, Martha Graham, Barbara Streisand, Grandma Moses, Madeline L'Engle, Katherine Patterson, Maxine Hong Kingston

Women in Sports: Chris Evert Lloyd, Martina Navratilova, Jackie Joyner-Kersee, Florence Griffith Joyner, Joan Benoit, Billy Jean King.

220

will need to be researched and written. For example, students will need to research information for news articles, sports pieces, editorials, and classified ads, as well as comics and political cartoons. Their newspaper can also cover the gamut of history including the arts, politics, science, mathematics, social sciences, and business. Too often we think of history as just the political vein of life, but all areas of our daily living make up our history.

Activity: As a group, brainstorm a name for the women's history newspaper. Then review the following list of possible newspaper sections to decide which areas might be most interesting: national news, historical news, local news, the arts, sports, opinion and editorial page, classified ads, comics and political cartoons. Once the sections have been determined, decide who will be in charge of the different sections, as well as who wants to work mainly as writers, editors, or artists and designers.

Before they begin researching and writing, remind students that the newspaper's focus is on American women from all walks of life. You can help your students discover information about women from a variety of cultures—such as Native American, Hispanic, African-American, and Asian-American—by using your school and local libraries.

Activity: Have students working on the national and historical news sections develop a list of prominent women and important events that they wish to research and write about. (You might refer to the "Women of Note" below to get

---

Resources On Women's History

Two organizations that can be helpful in providing information are the National Women's History Project and the National Women's Hall of Fame. The Women's Hall of Fame (Box 335, Seneca Falls, NY 13148) has some information available and each year sponsors a poster and essay contest for students in grades 4-12. The National Women's History Project (Box 3716, Santa Rosa, CA 95402) can provide a list of resources for curriculum and project ideas.

---

them started.) Once students have selected and researched their subjects, they should write about them in news style (following your sample newspapers as a model). First drafts can be written by hand or with a word processor, then circulated among classmates for editing. Final drafts can then be prepared for assembling with the desktop publishing program. Remind students to write headlines and select graphics to accompany their stories.

> You can help your students discover information about women from a variety of cultures—such as Native American, Hispanic, African-American, and Asian-American—by using your school and local libraries.

Activity: Students covering sports and the arts can follow the procedures described for the news sections, above.

Activity: Every community has women who are active in local business or politics, run large charitable organizations, do volunteer work, appear on local radio and TV shows, or make significant contributions to the community every day, but never get the recognition they deserve. For the paper's local news section, have a team of students make arrangements to interview several of these women to find out what they are doing and how it influences their own lives and the lives of others.

Activity: For the opinion or editorial page, students may write essays expressing any of their opinions about women they've researched or issues of importance to women, such as child care and equal pay. Be sure to leave room for dissenting opinions. You may also want to have students research and develop editorial pieces on the woman they feel has made the most significant contribution to American history.

Activity: No newspaper would be complete without classified ads. For this newspaper, students could have fun developing some ads that tie in with women throughout history. For example: "Wanted: Black female to run underground railroad." or "Lost: Single-engine airplane with female pilot," or "Wanted: First woman to be honored by having her picture on a U.S.-circulated coin."

Activity: Someone in your class with an artistic talent may wish to research and develop a series of comics portraying women in history, or a political cartoon that depicts an important event in women's history.

Activity: When all of the sections have been completed, allow plenty of time for your class to pull the newspaper together on the computer using your desktop publishing program. Encourage them to add catchy graphics and type for the newspaper's name banner. After a final version of the newspaper has been printed out, photocopy it for distribution around the school, to students' families, and throughout the community.

Using *Carmen Sandiego* to Teach Reference Skills

BY
LYNN
MYERS

It's always exciting to find that an interesting and enjoyable piece of software can accomplish curricular objectives. The *Carmen Sandiego* series by Brøderbund Software has been used in social studies and computer literacy classes to teach a variety of topics from specific facts to problem solving. As a library media specialist, I have found *Where in the U.S.A. is Carmen Sandiego* useful in teaching reference skills to fifth and sixth graders. I do this as a group activity, requiring only one computer and a large screen monitor or LCD screen display.

The software presents the user with a theft committed by one of a gang of criminals. Clues to the thief's movement from city to city are provided through geographical facts about the United States. Students consult reference books enthusiastically to help them solve the crime. For example, if a clue states that the thief is seeking information about early English settlements on the Kennebec River, the students look up the Kennebec River to determine that they must travel to the state of Maine. I chose geographical and biographical dictionaries as the reference books to use for this lesson because they provide the information needed, and because of their similarity in format. Students also find a regular dictionary helpful when they encounter words such as "fugue" or "titian-haired" in the program. The lesson presented here could be adapted for other reference sources, such as the almanac or atlas. Students can use their experiences to evaluate the usefulness of particular books for meeting different needs. The lesson has also been used successfully with students beyond the sixth grade in understanding clues to the identity of the thief.

Several qualities of the software help to make it a very useful instructional tool. Essential among these qualities was that it fit instructional objectives already present in our curriculum. These include notetaking skills, the use of reference sources, and such thinking skills as identifying appropriate sources of information, distinguishing relevant from irrelevant information, and discriminating between supposition and fact. These thinking skills require students to function at the analysis and evaluation levels of Bloom's taxonomy of the cognitive domain (Bloom, 1956). The analysis level is used as students distinguish the relevancy of information and determine inconsistencies in reasoning. The evaluation level is needed as students determine if data supports conclusions they are making. Furthermore, the software was easy enough for students to begin their "playing" (and learning) after only a brief introduction, and it was not repetitious during the instructional time allotted. Finally, it created what students perceived to be a genuine need, thus enthusiasm, for the use of reference books.

I try to introduce these reference materials just before their use is actually required for a class assignment. Such opportunities arise when students are seeking information for social stud-

223

ies projects or reports, or when they need to learn about the historical importance of individuals.

Lesson Design

Where in the U.S.A. Is Carmen Sandiego?

Ideally, prior to the students' arrival, the instructor starts the program and plays it to the point where the theft is described. The monitor can then be turned off until the modeling part of the lesson. The lesson is designed for use with a single computer and large screen monitor or LCD screen display operated by the instructor with students working in pairs using reference books.

Instructional Objectives:

The learner will:

1) be able to state that entries in the geographical dictionary and biographical dictionary are arranged alphabetically.

2) name at least two geographical fea-

Clues Worksheet

Identity Clues:

Sex	Hair	Food	Sport	Hobby	Music

Destination Clues:

tures included in the geographical dictionary.

3) be able to state that entries in the biographical dictionary are by last name.
4) practice looking for information in sources and make notes.

Set:

We will be using computer software to help you learn how to use geographical and biographical dictionaries. Knowing how to do this will help you when you need information for assignments or for your own use. (Reference to a specific assignment is appropriate here.)

Input:

1) Show students a standard dictionary and remind them that words are arranged in it in alphabetical order.
2) Ask them to look in their geographical dictionaries to determine arrangement of words. (Elicit correct response.)
3) Ask them to look in their geographical dictionaries to see what kinds of information are there. Examples should include cities, rivers, lakes, mountains, and others.
4) Repeat numbers 2 and 3 with biographical dictionary.
5) Elicit the response that the key word to an entry in the biographical dictionary is the individual's last name.
6) Have students look at their "Clues Worksheet" and tell them that clues about these traits of the thief they will be tracking will be provided during the program. They will need to make notes about these traits as well as about where they should go next to try to find the thief. The objective of their search is to both

follow the thief and discover the clues they can enter into the computer to identify the thief allowing them to make an arrest.

Modeling:

Turn the monitor on and continue the game from the point at which you set it. Model, entering the thief's sex into the crime computer, looking for clues in different places by having students look up needed information, and writing notes that you would make (or using a transparency of the "Clues Worksheet" and an overhead projector).

Check for Understanding:

Use signaling method.
1) T or F—The geographical dictionary is arranged alphabetically.
2) T or F—The biographical dictionary is arranged by country where the individual was born.
3) T or F—Use the individual's last name when looking in the biographical dictionary.

Guided Practice:

Play the game for 20-30 minutes. At the conclusion ask students to write on their clue sheets:
1) How the names of people and places are put in order in the biographical and geographical dictionaries.
2) Which of a person's names is used as the key word in the biographical dictionary.
3) The kinds of places included in the geographical dictionary.

Independent Practice:

This will occur as students use these reference books.

Article #25
Lego Meets Logo

By
Marian
Rosen

The idea of LEGO TC Logo is simple and elegant. Build machines with LEGO blocks, gears, and motors. Connect those machines with wires and an interface box to an Apple computer that speaks a dialect of LogoWriter. Use a few simple commands to turn the motors on and off and to reverse their direction. Mount specially created touch and light sensors on the machines. Use other commands to monitor these sensors. And use feedback from the sensors to program the machines' next moves. The early results of working with children have been far from simple, but they can still be called elegant.

In the Ladue school district in St. Louis, Missouri, a group of us have been working on LEGO TC Logo projects with children in the first through eighth grades. On the first day we introduce the students to LEGO building blocks and challenge them to build a car that will roll down an inclined plane and continue traveling as far as it possibly can. Inventors compete against their own record, marking each run with masking tape and then rebuilding their cars to make them go farther.

After one group of 24 first graders had built 12 cars, we stopped to analyze the situation. We decided to roll all the cars down the ramp and compare how far they went. The students immediately entered into a spirited debate over the "rules of rolling" and how many trials each car should have. They finally agreed that the back wheels had to be placed at the top of the ramp, that the cars should be *released* rather than *shoved off,* that the teacher should be in charge of all releases, that each car would receive three chances, and that a trial in which a car turned over or around would still count as a turn. I kept reminding them that what they were doing was developing standards and testing for reliability. The kids listened politely, but in their language they knew what they were doing—they were making it fair.

One by one we let the cars go down the ramp, marking their finishing points with tape. At the end of the event we lined the cars back up on their tape marks. The 12 cars sitting in front of us represented raw data. The students were asked in what ways the leaders were alike and in what ways they were different. Since all the children had been making cars at the same time, there had been a shortage of "official" wheels and the class had been quite creative about using anything that was round. Cars were equipped with large and small rubber wheels; large and small gears with exposed teeth; pulleys, some covered with rubber O-rings and some not; and large cylinders meant to serve as the central drum of a washing machine.

The first thing the students noticed was that machines with bigger wheels went farther. We measured the circumference of each wheel and talked about how the same number of revolutions would make larger wheels go farther. We also discussed friction, both the friction caused by the gear-wheels getting snagged in the carpet and that caused

226

by putting the wheels on the axles too tightly. The students were also curious about how the weight of the cars affected their performance. It turned out that cars that were top-heavy toppled over or didn't go very far, but that low-slung cars with a moderate amount of weight went farther than lighter low-slung cars. As we made comparisons we inevitably found ourselves discussing the importance of comparing cars that were different in one way only—or in scientific terms, the importance of changing only one variable at a time.

The first graders had used five of their seven hours on building and rebuilding the cars, and although they had been completely engrossed with this LEGO part of the project, it was clear that they wanted to use the computers. So we hurriedly demonstrated how to hook up a motor and simple pulley to turn one of the car's axles and how to plug the wires into the interface. We then introduced the students to some simple commands for controlling the motor. To the surprise of those students who'd had some experience with LogoWriter, this new version of the language didn't use commands such as FD and RT to control the LEGO machines. Instead it used primitives such as ON, OFF, and RD (reverse direction)—commands appropriate to motors and machinery and ones that are so clear that the six-year-olds had no trouble using them. Within two hours every car had been hooked up to the computer and put through its paces—running around the lab forwards and backwards according to the whim of its designer.

For example, when we introduced a class to the light sensors for the first time and explained how an object passing between a beam of light and the sensor would break the beam and cause a reaction, I watched as the idea dawned on several children simultaneously: "Hey, that's just like the door at the supermarket!" Similar revelations occur as students debate whether to hook motors up to the front or rear axles of their LEGO cars. Sooner or later one child will suggest, "Let's make one with four-wheel drive like my family's Jeep."

For all of us—students and teachers alike—our work with LEGO TC Logo led to a new interest in machinery and industrial robots. One of my colleagues found herself unable to walk past a construction site without stopping to study the machines at work. And I spent an entire day on a Mississippi paddle steamer watching the engine instead of the scenery.

With the LEGO blocks, students start by building cars and robots, but soon they're thinking of scores of other real things they might build. We've had children create elevators, toasters, ski lifts, conveyor belts, mechanical houses with Murphy beds that retract into the walls, bingo spinners, and much more.

Like the real world, however, LEGO TC Logo can be frustrating. There just never seems to be enough time! Since we have a limited amount of equipment and many classes want to use it, we've had to restrict each group of students to ten hours of building time, after which they must break down their machines and pass the blocks on to the next class. This seriously restricts what each student can accomplish. The ideal situation would be to have a LEGO TC Logo setup for each classroom, with enough space to build whole cities and enough time throughout the year for kids to work on projects that grow ever larger and more creative.

In such an environment, technology-shy students would be able to begin by building and programming machines according to the "blueprints" that come with the LEGO TC Logo documentation.

Then, as they became more comfortable, they'd begin to apply the concepts in their own personal ways. Young children would have the opportunity to experiment freely with the LEGO blocks, developing their building skills before moving on to the computer. (Since the LEGO machines are quite complicated for primary-grade students to build, it would also be wonderful if the simpler Duplo LEGO blocks were incorporated in LEGO TC Logo.) And technologically advanced students would not have to worry about running out of time before having a chance to solve the wonderful problems they pose for themselves. Like a giant high-tech sandbox, the equipment would be readily available so that as issues arose in math and science, students would naturally use this environment to look for solutions.

In the meantime, however, there are some things to be learned from scarcity. Kids understand that they need to share precious resources and the level of cooperative learning is high. They also learn that careful planning pays off. We ask older students working on more complex projects to submit "grant proposals" if they want more than their fair share of motors and sensors. This fits in nicely with the fact that they are keeping inventors' notebooks in which they draw plans of their machines, make and test hypotheses about how they can improve them, and keep track of trial runs.

And there's plenty to be learned from LEGO TC Logo—even if time is limited. First of all, students encounter numerous problems in math and physics that need to be solved. For example, in an attempt to discover how to make their motorized cars strong enough to go *up* a ramp, fifth-grade students become engaged in a discussion of the relative strengths of pulleys and gears and of different gear ratios. Other groups encounter the classic gear problem concerning the relationship between speed and strength when they enter a contest to build machines that will pull as much weight as possible as fast as possible. Often it's necessary to translate the motor's energy from a vertical to a horizontal plane. There are a number of ways to do this, and the children try to solve the problem using crown gears, worm gears, and so on.

Students also become involved with the scientific method as they invent.

Students also become involved with the scientific method as they invent. When a machine doesn't work, the problem can be mechanical (a helicopter refuses to "go" because the pulley's too tight); electrical (a motor burns out or is improperly connected); or the result of a bug in the programming. The young inventors have to develop strategies for isolating the cause. Hypotheses are proposed and tested and it's often necessary to keep notes and to brainstorm solutions.

Finally, as the students design programs to control their LEGO machines, they are acquiring skills that fit in with curriculum units on logic, robotics, and interactive programming. For example, an eighth grader with experience in Logo worked for days on a Morse code machine that was mechanically simple, but required sophisticated programming skills. The machine itself consisted of nothing more than a pair of tunnels with lights at one end and light sensors at the other. But it was connected to two computers, one of which flashed the lights and the other of which "read" (decoded) the sensors and printed out the messages.

Another eighth grader with a particular interest in programming took Seybot and turned it into a machine he called Learnerbot. The program he wrote allows a user to take the car manually through a series of moves and then watch as the computer learns and duplicates the pattern. He placed a light sensor on the vehicle opposite a counting wheel mounted on an axle. (Counting wheels are small disks made up of white and black pie-shaped segments so that a light sensor can tell how far they have turned.) He then programmed the computer to count the number of changes from light to dark and store it in memory as a record of how far forward the car should go. Finally, he used touch sensors to communicate whether the car was to turn right or left and wrote a program that would store all this information and use it to run Learnerbot through its paces.

It worked . . . except for the fact that the student who developed it was more interested in programming than in mechanical accuracy. The turns were imprecise and although it was clearly trying, Learnerbot sometimes made turns of 120 degrees or 80 degrees rather than 90. An interesting thing happened at this point. The developer declared the project finished and a success. But other members of the class were dissatisfied and insisted on tinkering with the gearing of the machine until it made accurate turns.

This illustrates a point that we often see. Some students are programmers, some are engineers, some are dreamers, some are artists. The collaborative effort when they work together is wonderful. The products are beautiful to look at, functional, and well programmed. The students learn to respect each other's contributions and learning styles.

Of course, what young people learn from LEGO TC Logo is affected by their *teacher's* style as well. My own physics background has been limited to one introductory non-lab course, and although I knew a lot of Logo before I began working with this project, I had never even put two LEGO blocks together and couldn't remember whether "gearing up" involved going from big to little or vice versa. I compensated by reading and experimenting on my own and by putting my faith in the scientific method and the value of shared learning. I figured that the very worst that could happen would be that I wouldn't know *the answer,* that the kids would have a chance to see an adult commit the act of learning, and that we would all learn from each other. Based on my own background and goals, I steered the students I worked with in a particular direction: towards activities that involved scientific methodology, creativity, interactive Logo programming, and cooperative learning.

Clearly, the LEGO TC Logo environment can be used successfully by teachers with styles and objectives very different from mine. A physics or auto mechanics instructor, for example, might give assignments

> Some students are programmers, some are engineers, some are dreamers, some are artists. The collaborative effort when they work together is wonderful.

that required students to apply specific content and principles to the creation of machines. And a math teacher might hand students a pre-built machine such as a merry-go-round and use it to simulate problems related to speed, time, and distance.

The plastic building blocks called LEGO and the programming language called Logo have more in common than their names. Both are based on the powerful idea that you can take a handful of simple forms (in LEGO the blocks and in Logo the primitives) and combine them to build ever larger and more complex forms. Both are so carefully crafted that they are reliable paths to learning in the real world. Apparently some European automobile companies use LEGO as part of their design and mechanics courses. (Logo is a grandchild of LISP, a language that is currently used for artificial intelligence research.) Both allow students of all ages to become involved with projects that are meaningful to them and that encourage different learning styles. Both are fun. Both present a challenge to educators—they are so versatile and so rich in promise that we must find time for them in our schools.

Marian Rosen is a sixth-grade teacher for the Ladue Schools in St. Louis, MO. She also conducts LogoWriter and LEGO TC Logo workshops.

By
Beth
Smith

Curriculum Objective: Learning about nutrition and good eating habits.

Computer Skill: Creating and using a data base, writing with a word processor.

A good way for students to gain a better understanding and awareness of their nutritional habits is by having them monitor what they eat on a daily basis. This lesson plan lets students review the basic food groups and their components, and provides a means for them to analyze their own diets for nutritional value.

Materials Needed: You will need a data base, a word processing program, and a printer. If you decide to create a wall chart of the basic nutritional information in the FOOD FACTS box you will also need art supplies.

Preparation: Create a word processing handout or a wall chart of the basic nutritional information in the FOOD FACTS box.

Discussion: Using your wall chart or handout, review with your students the names and recommended daily servings of the four basic food groups. Point out that the four food groups supply the body with the necessary vitamins and minerals needed for it to be healthy and strong. Next, show how the food groups have been broken down into three essential "fuels." Tell students that they will be using the computer to examine their own eating habits.

Activity: In this first activity, students use a data base as a food diary for recording everything they eat each day.

Food Facts

Food Groups

(With Recommended Daily Servings)

Meat Group—2 servings
Milk Group—3 servings
Vegetable/Fruit Group—2 servings
Bread & Cereal Group—2 servings

Body Fuels

Carbohydrates: Foods like potatoes, corn, bread, cereal, and dried and fresh fruits are carbohydrates. Carbohydrates give the body energy. In order to have a steady flow of energy, you must eat the proper serving each day of carbohydrates.

Fats: Another important source of energy is supplied by fats. Most of the fats we need, we get without trying because they are in many foods we eat, such as: milk, eggs, nuts, cheese, and meat.

Proteins: Proteins are necessary for growing. No plant or animal can live without them. Protein is important in building, maintaining, and repairing body tissue. It makes up three-fourths of the solid matter in the body, such as hair, muscle, brain, bones, teeth, and fingernails.

231

Have students set up a data base file as follows:

DAY OF WEEK:
BREAD/CEREAL:
MEAT:
DAIRY:
VEG/FRUIT:

Print out and photocopy enough blank data records so that each student can record his or her eating habits at home as well as during the school day. Each day, students should be given time to input information into their diary. (As an added reminder post your nutrition information handout or wall chart near the computer.)

Activity: After everyone has finished collecting data for a week, students should begin the task of analyzing their own week's worth of dietary data. They can sort their data file by food group, for example, and compare their daily balance against what is recommended. They should also be able to pinpoint areas where a greater variety of foods might be called for. Using a word processor, have each student write a report on the analysis of his or her diet. Have each student include suggestions for improving his or her eating habits—like what type of foods he or she should eat more or less of to stay healthy.

Activity: Next, have students bring printouts of their data diary and their word processing report to a class discussion on eating habits. What similarities and differences are there in eating habits among classmates? Can students draw any overall conclusions or make any general recommendations to improve the class dietary balance?

Extension Activity: Ask students to collect recipes or create meal menus that would help balance their weekly diets. Have students add their recipes or menus to their word processing analysis reports, and circulate these (with names deleted) for class comparison and discussion.

Extension Activity: A month or so after this lesson is completed, have your students monitor themselves again for another week to see if they have made any lasting improvements with their diets.

TECHNOLOGY USE ISSUES FOR THE TEACHER

Chapter 4

1. "Technology as a Tool for Restructuring the Curriculum." Karin M. Wiburg. *CUE NewsLetter*. May/June 1989. pg. 7.
2. "Making the Future Work: The Road to Curriculum Integration." Robert McCarthy. *Electronic Learning*. Sept. 1988. pg. 42.
3. "Moving Your District Toward Technology." LeRoy Finkel. *School Administrator Special Issue*. 1990. pg. 35.
4. "Staff Development: How To Build Your Winning Team." Daniel E. Kinnaman. *Technology and Learning*. Oct. 1990. pg. 24.
5. "The Advantages Of Using a Network." Robert McCarthy. *Electronic Learning*. Sept. 1989.
6. "Integrated Learning Systems: A Primer." Judy Wilson. *Classroom Computer Learning*. Feb. 1990. pg. 22.
7. "Integrated Learning Systems/Instructional Networks: Current Uses and Trends." Charles L. Blaschke. *Educational Technology*. November, 1990. pg. 20
8. "Integrated Teaching Systems: Guidelines for Evaluation." Richard Alan Smith and Susan Sclafani. *The Computing Teacher*, November, 1989. pg. 36
9. "Alternatives to Integrated Instructional Systems." Peter Kelman. *Proceedings from the National Educational Computing Conference. 1990*. pg. 169.
10. "Classroom or Lab: How to Decide Which is Best." Michael N. Milone, Jr. *Classroom Computer Learning*. Sept. 1989. pg. 34.
11. "Examining Computer Configurations: Mini-labs." Robertta H. Barba. *The Computing Teacher*. May 1990. pg. 8
12. "On a Need-to-Know Basis: Keyboarding Instruction for Elementary Students." William J. Hunter, Gordon Benedict, Bohdan Bilan. *The Writing Notebook*. Nov./Dec. 1989. pg. 23.
13. "Touch Typing for Young Children: Help or Hindrance?" Jessica Kahn and Pamela Freyd. *Educational Technology*. Feb. 1990. pg. 41.
14. "LEP Students in the Basic Skills Lab." Evelyn Fella. *The Computing Teacher*. Dec./Jan. 1990-91. pg. 19.
15. "Writing Partnerships: Teaching ESL Composition through Letter Exchanges." Nancy L. Hadaway. *The Writing Notebook*. Sept./Oct. 1990. pg. 10
16. "Yes, We Can!" Linda Davis. *Teaching and Computers*, Nov./Dec. 1989. pg. 18.

You would think with all the wonderful information that you have read so far, that implementing technology in the classroom would be a clearcut, fairly easy, non-controversial thing to do. Not so! And not by a long shot.

For reasons that are not entirely clear, the subject of technology has created (or attracted) an enormous amount of controversy from "Should we at all" to "What's the *right* way to do it." You would expect that after 20 years of experience, there would be some definitive "right way" answers. But, alas, there are not. There just seem to be more questions and more controversy.

This chapter focuses on some of those issues that seem to elicit visceral responses from practitioners in the field. In some cases the articles are presenting hard-core, basic information included to bring you up-to-date on the topic. In others, they are presenting sides of the issue, usually with no conclusive single answer.

Restructuring is on the minds and tongues of all educators today, though the term means different things to different people. Is there a role for technology in the restructuring of schools and/or in the restructured school? Wiburg feels it is as she explains in her article, "Technology as a Tool for Restructuring the Curriculum." Technology has a role to play in defining new content in the curriculum; in changing the role of teachers; in changing the way we evaluate student performance; and in changing the way we train teachers—all basic ingredients in the restructuring movement.

McCarthy focuses attention on technology and the new curriculum. He describes many of the problems teachers are having integrating technology into the curriculum. This article, too, deals with restructuring.

After all these years, you would think we could benefit from the mistakes made by others. This is the thesis of the article, "Moving Your District Toward Technology" wherein Finkel (the *same* Finkel) describes some Do's and Don'ts based on 20 years of experience by others.

One of the great mysteries of instructional technology observers is that schools are hell-bent on spending money on the technology, but reluctant to spend dollars to train teachers to use it (let alone to buy materials to run on it!). But even when they spend money on staff development, *how* that training is done is filled with controversy. Kinnaman's article discusses the right ways to handle staff development for technology, again based on years of experience by others.

Because the subject of networking is so complex and so ripe for discussion, we included still another article on the subject—"The Advantages of Using a Network." We selected this particular article for a variety of reasons, the biggest of which is that it contains very solid information on a topic about which there is lots of debate.

Secondly, and just as important, this article focuses on only *one* use of the term networking, the LAN, or Local Area Network. Most articles we read confuse LANs with Integrated Learning Systems (see following articles) and/or use the term networking to mean LAN in one paragraph and telecommunications system in the next paragraph, totally confusing the novice reader. In other words, the Kinnaman article focuses on the computer hardware network as a hardware/software combination to aid instruction without confusing it with all the other abuses of the term.

And then we follow with the "fun stuff." The fastest growing segment of the computers-in-education business (from an annual dollar-sales standpoint) is that called integrated learning systems, integrated *teaching* systems, or integrated *instructional* systems—the choice of terms depends on whom you are talking to and their opinion of such systems. The "primer" article by Judy Wilson will lead you through the basics of these systems: the philosophy, the management, the players, and a chart showing who offers what.

We've hinted that ILS provoke controversy and we found a single article that "lets it all hang out" in plain, understandable, language. Peter Kelman is a software publisher who competes with ILS companies—he's very up front about where he comes from. His article, presented at NECC 1990, and many other times throughout the country, covers all the controversial territory about these systems, and does so in no uncertain terms. Kelman goes one step further than most writers and includes a full section of what he believes to be the appropriate uses of computers and technology. This is one of the most informative and entertaining readings on the subject—a must-read article regardless of your stand on the topic.

Should you place your computers in a lab, or in classrooms, or in mini-labs? Again, after 20 years, you would expect that this question would no longer be at issue. But it is! Milone's article, "Classroom or Lab: How to Decide Which is Best" is one of the best articles on the subject, so we included it here. Wondering what the answer is? It all depends on *what* you are using your technology to do! Doesn't that sound obvious? Read the article to find out more. There really is no simple answer to these questions.

As one of us is a former Business Educator, the issue of teaching keyboarding to kids seems a ridiculous thing to debate. But there is a debate and it goes on and on and on. Should keyboarding be taught in elementary grades? By whom? At what expense? (Taking time from what curriculum area? For how long?) In what depth? and on and on. Since one purpose of this book is to familiarize you with all the issues, we have included two articles on this subject. They cover the gamut of issues and answers and discuss the research as well.

Questions for Discussion

1. Why do you think that "technology does not seem to be a priority for many educational decision makers" as described by Wiburg in her article?
2. What impact should technology have on teacher training? What should be taught to prospective teachers and how?
3. With all the hoopla for so many years, why do you think that only "15% of all teachers in the U.S. actually use computers in their teaching?"
4. What's wrong with the comment, "If I can do it with chalk and talk, why do I need the machine?"
5. If you were to have the opportunity to install a computer on every teacher's desktop, what types of software would you include for all teachers and how would you suggest training them to use their new tool?
6. Discuss the comment, "It's been a truism that computer technology will never replace the teacher, but I question that truism if the technology is used to its full capacity."
7. Why is it important for teacher training activities that focus on curriculum to include technology as part of their program?
8. Why is a network not an ILS? What are the differences, really?

9. What does Kelman see as the more promising uses of computers, and why does he think they are important?
10. What does Kelman mean by the "dangers of the kind of quick-fix technological solutions for complex educational problems?"
11. Why do you think there is so much controversy surrounding the issue of when and how to teach keyboarding?

Questions from the Readings

1. How does Wiburg think the teacher's role will change?
2. How can we evaluate technology-delivered curriculum, according to Wiburg?
3. What are the reasons why the computer revolution has fallen short of educators' original visions, according to the McCarthy article?
4. In the McCarthy article, what is meant by "concentrate on problem areas?"
5. Why is making technology "simple" so important to teachers?
6. How do you "show" teachers how computers can help?
7. What did Bosco mean in the McCarthy article when he said, "Computers in K-12 are now at a crossroad?"
8. What are the lessons learned about teacher training in the Finkel article?
9. What are the five leadership points for administrators raised in the Finkel article?
10. According to Kinnaman, do we need a new beginning in training teachers to use technology? Why is this necessary?
11. Why does Kinnaman feel a technology coordinator is so important to the success of a school or district technology program?
12. What are the "three Rs" of staff development?
13. What are the advantages of using a network according to the McCarthy article?
14. According to Kelman, what is wrong with the research studies about the effectiveness of ILS?
15. What are the advantages of placing computers in the classroom?
16. What are the disadvantages of placing computers in labs?

Article #1
Technology as a Tool for Restructuring the Curriculum

By
KARIN M.
WIBURG

This paper addresses the question of what it means to develop educational uses of technology, offers a framework for increasing the educational impact of computers and other educational media in schools, and presents and analyzes a computer-based lesson developed by a student teacher operating within the proposed framework. The position taken in this paper is that educational use of technology must be developed within the larger question of the purpose of education in an information age.

The focus on technology as it relates to curriculum suggests the importance of asking more questions about the educational value of computers and technology and less about how to operate hardware and software. By using technology, we have the potential to provide students with the sort of interactive and individualized learning environments that educators in the past could only dream about. Computers can be powerful tools for learning in all academic areas and can provide exploratory activities that allow us to integrate content areas across the curriculum. In addition, computers are essential for managing the information explosion occurring in today's global society. Yet, the use of computers and other media in education has by and large been quite disappointing, particularly in terms of tapping their potential as creative and problem solving tools. Why?

The Need for Instructional Models

Limited access to computer hardware and software, which once prevented us from developing innovative educational computer-based programs, is no longer our biggest problem. Currently we lack a shared vision of how technology might be used to assist teaching and learning. There are few educational models that suggest the power of technology when integrated with new information about learning, exemplary instruction, and school-based management, all factors in what has become known as a movement for "restructuring" schools. There are even fewer guides on how to begin to implement such models. In fact, currently, there seems to be little agreement between computer educators, curriculum developers, principals, subject matter specialists, and parents about how to integrate technology with the curriculum and what an optimal model might look like.

Of even more concern is the fact that technology does not seem to be a priority for many educational decision-makers. A recent issue of the Association for Supervision and Curriculum

> Of even more concern is the fact that technology does not seem to be a priority for many educational decision-makers.

237

Development's (ASCD) UPDATE (1988) contained a list of 13 special interest groups with over 3500 members. Not one of these current groups focused specifically on issues involved in integrating technology and curriculum. Nor did it appear that any of them even considered technology integration as something of interest to them.

Recently as part of an effort to develop a new graduate program in curriculum and instruction, I interviewed administrators, curriculum coordinators, and teachers about their views on the changes needed in the curriculum. These leaders were interested in new models of teaching and learning and in restructuring schools to increase their effectiveness. However, they had very little concept of the potential of computers and other instructional media for assisting them in this work.

More important than discussions about what computers to buy, how to schedule classes in labs, and which word processor is best, is discussion about the adequacy of the current curriculum and the current structure of schools to meet the needs of today's students. It is only by adopting a perspective that considers technology as one of a variety of tools available for improving teaching, learning and school management, rather than an end in itself, that we can begin to tap the potential of technology to assist us in improving the instructional process. Technology is a key for upgrading the curriculum but this ideal will only be used if we have the courage to face large questions about the purpose of education today.

The Need for New Content in the Curriculum

Since the 1900s, educators in this country have by and large considered the purpose of education in very similar ways, stressing the acquisition of basic skills for all students. This has meant reading and writing, in a print medium, arithmetic computation, memorization of selected facts and concepts, and recall of this knowledge for examinations. However, to paraphrase Bob Dylan, "the times they are a' changing...." We no longer live in an age where it is possible to know all the facts, even just the "important" ones. In fact, we, and especially our future students, face an information explosion that is so extensive that the most valuable skill in the future will involve managing, not memorizing that information.

Not only will the volume of information increase but so will the variety of forms in which it is represented. Educators will need to teach students not only how to become critical users of print materials, but also how to analyze, synthesize, evaluate and create materials represented by graphic and video images, natural and synthesized sound, and new symbolic tools (graphing and outlining programs, hypermedia). Some of this could be very good news in terms of what we now know about human learning (Dede, 1988; Eisner, 1985, 1982). Increased understanding occurs when concepts are presented and manipulated using a variety of modalities. However, whether we are able to tap the potential of technology to increase learning by utilizing multiple media depends largely on our abilities to reconceptualize education in light of these new tools and to share our conceptions with other educators and the public.

The Changing Role of Teachers

Not only must we be prepared to rethink the content of the curriculum, but also the context in which it might best occur.

Teachers, for many years have been placed in the role of workers asked to deliver material designed for them by others (Drucker, 1987). The teacher has been the source of information delivered during a limited time period to a single large group of students, presumed to be more or less homogenous. Technology now supplies us with other options. By interacting with a video program and a computer, an individual student might learn more deeply and meaningfully about a subject from a source other than teacher lectures.

For example, imagine for a moment the child studying Egypt and choosing from a variety of learning options. The student has been given time in class during this morning to explore the variety of multi-media materials available on Egypt. She sits at a friendly computer that asks her to choose among the various options: does she wish to explore the pyramids, see a relief map of the Nile valley, or find out more about the form of government? During this same morning, other children in our imaginary classroom might be using computers attached to laboratory tools for measuring and graphing different heat values they had obtained while doing science experiments. Often during the day, the students will turn to their electronic notebooks (word processing space provided for writing and responding). While writing or sketching (of course a draw and graphing function are available at any time, as well as a calculator) the students might be responding to their teacher's questions, asking for clarification or help on something they are studying, answer mail from around the world, enter data into a study of television viewing habits being carried on by a local university, or complete their article for this week's CLASS NEWS. Teachers will need to develop entirely

new skills in order to manage and facilitate learning in such an environment and administrators will need to provide a different sort of support. Both will need to become developers, managers, and facilitators of rich, individualized learning environments rather than primarily givers of information to be learned and measurers of student knowledge of facts (National Technology Task Force, 1986).

The Need for New Forms of Evaluation

In addition to new teacher roles and new ways of studying content, we will have to rethink our methods for managing and evaluating students. Our current evaluation process has been limited by a focus on time. Classes have been structured in terms of periods, semesters, and year-long segments. Teachers are asked to cover specific amounts of material/time period. At the end of each unit of time, students are compared and graded in terms of the material learned. Students who have been told to work at their own rate using a mastery learning approach suddenly must be compared at the end of the school year. This amounts to comparing children in terms of the speed with which they learn rather than what they know. Computer-managed instruction could help us to continue to assess student's knowledge but on an individualized basis.

In addition, there is little in our current evaluation methods that allow us to evaluate the developing thinking skills of students. These thinking skills are most likely to be impacted in a well-designed computer-based learning environment. Available standardized tests give us a measure of the facts students remember, they don't tell us anything about how students can solve problems or what kinds of products they might be able to produce. These process skills are the new basic skills required in an information age. The use of technology in the curriculum will require that we develop methods for evaluating student problem solving strategies as well as the facts and concepts they remember. Learning how and when to use concepts in an age of information overload will become increasingly important.

We must face the fact that schools are and will continue to be largely test-driven. If our course objectives continue to stress only the recall of information, students will continue to excel at memorizing facts. If we change our objectives and our tests and begin to evaluate problem-solving skills, teachers will develop strategies for teaching problem solving, and students will become better problem solvers. New evaluative tools like the California Writing Assessment Test that suggests criteria for judgment of student products are a step in the right direction. Imagine the impact on the curriculum if an adopted standardized test asked only questions that required higher-level thinking!

A Framework for Teacher Training

Given the need for restructuring the curriculum and the availability of technological tools to assist this process, what is the best approach to implementing needed changes? If we have learned anything from the low success rate of movements for educational innovation (new math, language labs, open schools), it is that changes cannot be dictated from the top. Effective schools research reinforces the idea that the largest unit of real change is the individual school site, and within that site it is the teacher who can make or break any new pro-

gram. Therefore, it seems most useful to look to teacher education and supervision, both pre- and in-service, for a means of developing and implementing a restructured curriculum.

One area where I have been working with teachers is on the use of computers combined with exemplary instruction. This training involves collaborative efforts between our university and the local school district and includes a focus on what the masters student or teacher-in-training can do at the school site, not just in the theoretical university classroom. Also crucial to this approach to teacher education is the presence of professors in classrooms as active instructional leaders.

In terms of content of the teacher education curriculum, I'm convinced that integrating technology requires blending everything we know about teaching and learning with what we know about the potential of computers and other media to assist that process, and then putting all that in the context of the educational needs of students in a global information age. Our program begins with the sharing of new insights into human learning. We now have 10 years of recent brain and mind research that support some of our intuitions about affective-cognitive connections in learning, the existence of cognitive styles and preferred modalities, and the ways in which students can be assisted in making meaning out of the information around them. A second component, our "methods" course, involves empowering teachers to use a variety of successful teaching strategies, including developing skills in facilitating cooperative learning and peer tutoring. I particularly stress teaching techniques which help students to develop problem solving and higher-level thinking skills as well as creativity and flexibility in the face of rapid change. After teachers have gained a strong foundation in the principles of learning and teaching and have considered this content in the context of an information rich age, we then introduce the computer as a tool that can help them teach in a way that will be required if schools are to succeed in the future.

Finally, I suggest that as teachers begin to integrate computers into their teaching and planning they allow themselves to be guided by a fundamental question: "What can I do better with computers than without them?"

Within the framework of using computers in the content areas, the computer education component of our teacher training helps teachers find specific answers to this question.

Computers can help students to organize information, to ask, "what if" questions to provide concrete examples of abstract concepts, and to allow students to try out divergent solutions and get rapid feedback. In addition, working in a computer environment, in which a variety of information can be easily combined by the student in new ways, allows learning to become a process of creating knowledge and insights in contrast to merely receiving information. The value of learning by making seems extremely important. None of us would forget about the pioneers if we were allowed to make covered wagons and "cross the west" on our own homemade maps.

In addition to the value of computers for helping students learn, computer software applications can help teachers to keep records, individualize instruction, and develop their own teacher-made lessons. In addition to learning and practicing skills in the university classroom involving the use of computers for both student learning and teacher management, teachers are required to integrate technology and teaching at the school site.

Observation at the School Site

Recently, I observed a computer-based lesson created by a student teacher, Erin Federico. The final step in our teacher education program is a two-unit course titled "Professional Competencies." Teachers must be evaluated on a number of teaching competencies before they can graduate from the program. One of these competencies requires that future teachers be evaluated on their ability to develop and implement a computer-based lesson with students at the school site.

The following is a description of the lesson I observed and some reflections on this observation. It serves as both a model for a new type of instruction and a suggested format for qualitative evaluation of new educational environments.

The teacher, who did the following lesson, did not have access to the latest computers or interactive video disks. We all know such tools will allow us to do much more. Yet this teacher did very well with a room full of Apple IIe computers, some strong skills in teaching, and an understanding of motivation and how to teach problem solving. Perhaps doing a good job of using current tech-

> The value of learning by making seems extremely important. None of us would forget about the pioneers if we were allowed to make covered wagons and "cross the west" on our own homemade maps.

nology should be our first step.

The teacher did have access to specific guidelines and strategies to use in developing computer-based lessons. These suggestions are given below:

Guidelines for Developing Computer-Based Lessons

1. The computer use must be integrated with material taught at other times in the classroom.
2. The principles of lesson presentation learned in methods class must be utilized (essentially clinical teaching, see actual lesson).
3. New methods of classroom organization that enhance learning, such as cooperative learning and peer tutoring, should be utilized whenever possible.
4. Opportunities to go beyond recall, to use synthesis, analysis, and evaluative thinking skills should be provided.
5. The lesson should be presented using multiple modalities.
6. The teacher should model whatever she wants the students to do, including specific problem solving strategies.

The Lesson

Erin, the student teacher I observed, presented a lesson to a group of Fourth Grade Students that reflected an activity done earlier that week on masks (this was Halloween week). Her objective was to teach the students problem-solving using the content of an earlier art lesson. Erin began the lesson by holding up a mask and asking students how they would make the eyes and mouth in the mask (Anticipatory Set). The students responded that the holes could be made by cutting or punching out the paper. Erin then told the students that today they would be learning how to use a program called The Factory (Sunburst) on the Apple computers to make masks. She then made a simple mask on the monitor in front of the room while the students watched. After that the eleven students were asked to go to one of the twelve computers sitting around the room on which the software had already been loaded. The students were then led through making the same mask she had demonstrated on the computer.

After completing the mask, the children were asked to tell her the steps they had gone through in making the mask. She was careful that everyone understood the attributes of the factory program, i.e. that the factory could punch round or square holes, rotate an object by increments of 45 degrees, and add thick or thin stripes to the surface of the product. She then asked each student to make a mask and CHALLENGE another student to duplicate it (an option available on the screen). The students did this by changing places at the computers, at which point some confusion occurred since they had not been given a procedure for changing places. The students were able in the time allowed to each create one or two products and then challenge another student.

After this Erin asked the children to tell her what problem-solving strategy they used to make the same mask. She told me later she intended that the students develop a strategy that required them to think backwards to solve a problem, but found instead she got suggestions that involved trial and error approaches.

Finally, as a closure activity, Erin loaded a representation of a mask she had previously designed on the monitor and challenged the students to duplicate it. It was somewhat difficult and only two of the students were able to complete this task before the bell rang. (If given time and some guidance more could have completed this.)

This was a very good lesson for a beginning teacher. As is typical for someone learning to teach, Erin forgot to think about all the variables that might occur. I suggested that if children were to change places in the challenge activity she should tell them each to move to the left or the right. Better yet, she might have assigned children to pairs who could both challenge and help one another with the problem-solving process. Ironically, 24 children using twelve computers as partners might have more positive educational consequences than assigning one student per computer.

We talked again about the need to teach problem-solving strategies. The students were unable to come up with the strategy of working backwards to solve a problem. However, since the students had not had a lot of experience solving problems (see notes on the need to change the curriculum) it was likely that trial and error was a good first strategy. More talk about the process of trial and error, and how to create and then test solutions, might have been useful. When the students seemed ready to try thinking backwards as a way to solve a problem, Erin knew she would have to model this for the children.

The closure activity was especially enlightening. It occurred to me while watching the end of the lesson, how useful a computer activity was for understanding what students had learned. The student teacher was able to watch each student as they tried to make the mask, observe their strategies for learning, how they handled frustration, and

the kinds of questions they asked other students or the teacher. If students had been working in pairs, observing their interactions, and the kinds of questions they asked each other might have provided additional insight into the learning process. Closure in classrooms in which the teacher is the only source of information and direction must often be done with the teacher on the spot, unable to really observe the students' learning.

I was pleased with this lesson and the learning I observed in many of the children. These were children who were not highly motivated when observed earlier in the classroom, but when working with the computer they remained on task and interested. They could have benefited from additional problem-solving time. The real tragedy was that this lesson would probably never have taken place— I never would have seen the little girl who solved the teacher's puzzle light up with pride—if we had not built a required computer-based lesson and observation into our program.

The benefits of sitting and observing this learning environment, as opposed to evaluating education on the basis of standardized test score gains, also seem really important. As educators begin to implement aspects of a restructured curriculum, the use of observation and other qualitative evaluative methods seems crucial. Jeff Moonen (1988) has suggested such an approach to research in educational technology: (1) Do research in direct relation to school practice; (2) use teams (teachers, administrators, teacher trainers, and researchers) much as engineers do in research and development; (3) design approaches and try them out. Document what you see, and only after the model is successful should you worry about doing traditional comparative research.

This paper has suggested reasons for the lack of educational use of microcomputers and some suggestions for how technology can assist in the improvement of schools. The viewpoint was taken that this effort should not be limited to integration within the current curriculum, but that technology may assist us in shaping the future of teaching and schooling as well as being shaped by it. It was suggested that we must reexamine the purpose of schools today and how computers and other media might enhance that purpose. Such an examination should not be confined to those who are currently involved in educational computing. Educators who understand the potential of technology to assist teaching and learning must reach out to other leaders who may not be aware of how computer use might enhance the new educational strategies they are advocating.

Finally, a lesson which represented a simple first step for utilizing computers in a classroom was reported and discussed. The use of observation for evaluating teaching and learning in a computer-rich learning environment seems especially promising and certainly provides more information than a student score on a paper and pencil test. The ideas presented in this paper are offered in the hope that we will see more partnerships between those who understand technology and its potential and those who are working to improve teaching and learning environments.

The process of both school restructuring and optimal use of educational technology is a slow one. However, I believe that a significant contribution can be made by trying these new educational strategies in a small way and then reporting and expanding those practices that seem to be successful.

Bibliography

ASCD, 1988. "Network News," *Update*, Volume 30, No. 8, Association for Supervision and Curriculum Development.

Dede, Christopher. 1988. "Empowering Environments, Hypermedia and Microworlds." *The Computing Teacher, Vol. 15*, No. 3.

Eisner, Elliot. 1982. "Cognition and Curriculum: A Basis for Deciding What to Teach." Longman.

——— 1985. The Educational Imagination, "On the Design and Evaluation of School Programs," Second Edition. New York: Macmillan; London: Collier.

Moonen, Jeff. 1988. "Evaluation of Local and Regional Technology Programs and Policies," Proceedings of the National Educational Computing Conference, NECC. (*Jeff Moonen is at the University of Twente, The Netherlands.*)

National Task force on Education Technology, 1986. "Transforming American Education: Reducing the Risk to the Nation," *T.H.E. Journal,* August issue.

Perlman, Lewis, 1987. "Technology and the Transformation of Schools." Write the National Task Force on Educational Technology, United States Department of Education, Washington, D.C.

White, Mary-Alice, 1987. "What Curriculum for the Information Age?" Erlbaum Associates, Publishers.

The Lesson Plan

Date: Nov. 4, 1988
Content: Computers and Design
Grade Level: 3rd/4th
Concept: Factories use an assembly line process to make products
Materials: Samples of masks made in class
Software: The Factory (by Sunburst)
Hardware: 12 Apple IIe computers, Large teacher station with monitor

Anticipatory Set:

Look at any object—chances are it was made in a factory. It was probably made on an assembly line. Assembly lines may use a different machine to make each part of a product. For example, these computers were made this way. One machine made the monitor, one made the keyboard, another the disk drive, and another the chips inside. Remember when we made these masks in class? If you had a machines for making masks what would each machine have to do? (Get input from kids, talk about punching out eyes, nose, and mouth, adding stripes or lines, and rotating the shape to get different designs.)

Objective:

By the end of the lesson, students will be able to use the strategy of working backwards to create a mask from a teacher sample.

Presentation:

Today we are going to work with a program called, "The Factory." You will get to experiment with three machines that work on an assembly line. You will send a flat square-shaped piece of material through the assembly line in order to make an object. The first machine can PUNCH one, two, or three holes in your material; a second machine ROTATES the square 45, 90, 135, or 180 degrees; and the third machine paints the object with thin, medium, or wide STRIPES.

Guided Practice:

The students will watch me create a simple mask-like design on the large monitor. Then they will each go to the computers and I will walk them through the same design. After this the students will get to experiment with the program as the teacher observes. When students seem to get the idea, I will ask each to make a product that you want to challenge another student to duplicate. (After they have done this I will lead them to the CHALLENGE option in the software.)

Independent Practice:

Students will be able to make several designs and challenge their neighbor to do the design they created.

Closure:

I will call the students back together and ask them how they were able to make another person's design. I hope to lead them to talking about the need to work backwards to solve this type of problem. Then I will put a mask that I designed on the large monitor and ask each student to return to the computer and make the same design with their program.

Article #2
Making the Future Work:
The Road to Curriculum Integration

By
Robert
McCarthy

Ninety-seven percent of all schools in this country have at least one computer, and by now most educators know that technology is extremely powerful and can make a major contribution to many areas of education.

Just look at the facts:

• Funding, research and implementation are taking place from the federal level all the way to the school building level;

• Many schools of education offer computer education degrees; most require students to take at least one computer course; and many require some demonstration of computer competency for certification;

• Most industrialized nations are making major pushes into educational technology, and efforts are under way to bring technology into developing nations.

Yet, despite these major in-roads over the past decade, computers are still not universally integrated into the curriculum. In fact, by some estimates, fewer than 15 percent of all teachers in the U.S. actually use computers in their teaching, and the nation is starting to notice. A recent *New York Times* headline observes: "Computers are in the classroom, but no one is paying much attention to them." Another headline in the *Wall Street Journal* reads: "Computers Failing as Teaching Aids."

While there is abundant evidence that refutes such broadsweeping claims, it is true that the computer revolution has fallen short of educators' original vi-

sions. There are a number of reasons why.

First, the computer revolution has been interrupted by another revolution: the one attempting to improve the quality of the teachers, and to pay the teachers based on merit and competence instead of seniority. When this revolution sorts itself out, educators will be able to return full attention to integrating computers into the curriculum.

Another reason computer use has not proliferated is scarcity of school computers. Despite steady increases in numbers of hardware and software units purchased, computer distribution rarely matches the need. A recent study from Talmis, a New York City-based research firm, predicts that the K-12 hardware saturation point will be reached by 1992, at which time the child-to-computer ratio will stand at 10 to 1. Some school districts have yet to introduce the technology; in others, computers constitute a token presence at best. And if the optimum arrangement is a computer on each pupil's desk, then even those districts farthest along have a ways to go.

Inadequate teacher training also contributes to the lack of computer use. Certainly, more (and more comprehensive) teacher training would help drive the revolution forward, as would better, if not necessarily more, software.

Also, many teachers still find the technology difficult to use. As one computer advocate points out: "frustrating first time experiences have been a big turn-off for many teachers."

And finally many educators have the perception that computers aren't really all that helpful. "If I can do it with chalk and talk, why do I need the machine?" asks one teacher.

Does this mean the K-12 computer revolution is kaput? Far from it. The computer is too powerful an educational tool to be so cavalierly consigned to the educational broom closet. Yes, it's true that other powerful technologies—language labs, closed-circuit TV—are currently gathering dust there, but the computer is different. Not only does it convey information (like TV and educational films) but through its interactive capability, the computer can actually teach learning skills, thinking strategies, and logical concepts. Armed with a keyboard, students can participate in, shape, and change what the computer gives them. They can problem-solve. They call assay answers to questions and find out immediately whether they're right or wrong and even why they're right or wrong. Of no other educational technology is all that so completely true.

Yet, one must be wary of the dazzling effects of the computers power and potential. As one computer coordinator puts it: "many of us were so totally bedazzled by the computer when it first came out that we assumed the revolution would occur of itself almost by magic, as soon as the computers got through the classroom door."

Integration:
What Must Be Done

But if it won't happen by magic, what needs to be done to help educators fulfill the promise and potential that computers offer?

Concentrate on problem areas

Perhaps one answer is to concentrate on those areas where the computer may have a more positive impact than traditional education methods

Use of computers in K-12 seems to be proceeding down two distinct paths, says Henry Becker, principal research scientist at Johns Hopkins University's Center for Research on Elementary and Middle Schools. "One is the area of enrichment activities and kid-stimulation—drills, games, neat computer experiences, all of which remain tangential to traditional curricula and traditional pedagogy. On the other hand is computer use triggered by concerns about the test performances of the bottom 25th percentile of students. With the so-called 'slow learner' there may be more of a willingness to develop new pedagogical strategies, i.e., [strategies using] the computer, if only because there is a perception that the old strategies really haven't worked. It may be here that the integration of computers as fully-fledged curriculum components will begin to happen."

The application of computer technology to specific educational problem areas is, as a strategy, a vast improvement over wheeling the computers in and waiting for the magic to happen. Moreover, it's a strategy whose range is not limited to the slow learner.

Forward-thinking school districts like Monterey Peninsula Unified in Monterey, Calif. have already determined that the first step in the computer revolution is to isolate areas where teachers have traditionally had trouble teaching.

"It's logical to think if it ain't broke, why fix it?" says Gerry Montgomery, project coordinator of the district's five-year plan to study the use of technology.

"However, if it is broke. . ."

Montgomery advises careful analysis of the curriculum to pinpoint places where the application of computer technology makes sense. "Every teacher knows," she says, "of places in the curriculum where pupils always have trouble grasping the material as it's traditionally been presented."

"There are undoubtedly some lessons that can best be presented by hardware and software," says Montgomery. "And that's where you introduce the computer into the curriculum—with the teacher perhaps becoming the facilitator and the computer doing the teaching."

Robert Tart, computer coordinator of the Duplin County Schools, Kenansville, N.C., agrees. "You must pick your spots," he says. "A good example might be those science programs that allow for the simulation of laboratory experiments which might be too dangerous or messy or expensive to attempt with the actual materials. That's an excellent use of computer-assisted learning and a perfect entry for the computer into the curriculum."

Ask teachers what they want

In order to find these weak spots in the curriculum—spots where traditional chalk and talk pedagogy hasn't performed so well—you must talk with the teachers, and that's something else which has to happen before the computer revolution will arrive—more teacher input. Administrators, and software and hardware developers, are going to have to canvass the opinions and accommodate the wants and needs of the people behind the desks.

"After you find out all about the technology and its capabilities," says Doris Ray, director of Maine's Computer Consortium, "then you must find out what the teachers think. Teachers are the bottom line, the keystone of this whole revolution. We must find out what teachers want, and then determine if the computer can provide a solution. Throwing technology at educators hasn't worked, obviously; though it has informed us that computers aren't self-evidently pedagogical devices."

Okay, then what do the teachers want?

Make the technology simple

"I'll tell you one thing they're saying," says Brian Page, assistant superintendent of instructional services, Alpine School District, American Fork, Utah, "They're saying they are sick and tired of hearing about 'newer', 'faster', 'more powerful' technological innovations that do nothing to increase ease of use. In fact, innovation almost always means great complexity of operation. What teachers want to hear about is simplification, and I am talking radical simplification. Simplified instruction—no unreadable manuals and long in-service training. Extreme ease of use and lots of fail-safes in case the wrong button is pushed. Teachers can't take the time in a classroom to just stop teaching and spend minutes and minutes getting something up on the terminal. It's got to be bang, bang, point, click. The problem is that computer vendors know a lot about the mechanics of hardware and software, but nothing about the mechanics of teaching."

Vendor, take heed of that important message. For imagine yourself a teacher, facing 30 or 40 little bodies. They're all staring back at you, your students, waiting for you to tell them something. Some, of course, would be delighted if you made a mistake or messed up. Nothing is funnier to students than a teacher messing up.

Now, given the givens of such a job, is it any wonder teachers become uncomfortable if they have anything less than total control? If their omniscience is anything other than perfect? Consequently, teachers are often leery about anything that might make them appear awkward, fallible, clumsy or, God forbid, stupid. Fumbling around with a computer can and often does make them feel all of these things and it can happen even to those teachers who know about computers, who use them at home.

User-friendly technology is fine in the home and the office, where you're not on a stage, where you don't have to perform. But teaching is a performance; one which teachers strive to make smooth and effortless and elegant. But it can be none of these when, as Page says, teachers actually become physically ill at the prospect of having to operate a computer during a class.

If the object is to integrate the computer into the curriculum, user-friendly may not be enough. What we need is *teacher*-friendly.

Better software is also needed

In addition to friendlier hardware we need software that is not, as Tom Snyder says, "just more dinky little games." Snyder, who is the head of Tom Snyder Productions, the Cambridge, Mass.-based software house, professes constant amazement whenever, "I hear my fellow software designers shout about the launching of each new product: 'We're Ready Now! On With The Revolution!' And all they've got is some dinky little game, which perhaps teaches a little geography. With that we're ready to restructure schooling? Not really."

Jim Dezel VP and general manager of IBM's educational systems division, also says that full integration of the com-

puter will only occur when courseware adequate to the delivery of the curriculum becomes widely available.

"When the courseware is able to deliver the information," he says, "then the teacher becomes able to deliver a lot of individualized instruction. And that is what will change the face of teaching. The secret is lots more, significant, better, courseware. We need to get to the point where the computer can do what it does best and the teacher can do what he or she does best."

More talk between vendor and teacher

Other vendors, not unexpectedly, argue that there is plenty of good software available. The reason teachers haven't widely embraced the computer, they say, is the daunting amount of software on the market, and the difficult task in finding the right software for their needs.

"I could rattle off a lot of the standard explanations as to why the computer revolution in the school hasn't gotten on track," says MECC VP Don Rawitsch. "But I think the most important impediment to the use of some very good curriculum-based software is simply that communication between supplier and teacher has not been good. There is a daunting amount of product out there; it's an enormous task to sift through it and evaluate it. We need some ways to expedite this task for the teacher. Right now there are software curriculum guides and evaluations and compendia, etc., but they tend not to provide enough information so as to give the teacher the confidence that he or she is making an informed choice."

So let's add that to the list. If computers are ever to be integral to the curriculum, teachers need better information explaining the capabilities of software products. And as the numbers of such products grow, of course, this need will become more acute.

Better teacher training

But knowing what the software can do is not the same thing as knowing what to do with it in the classroom setting. Maybe what's needed is better teacher training on how to teach with the computer.

Trudie Mishler, instructional technology specialist with the Portland, Ore. schools, says that her district is offering classes in computer/curriculum integration.

"Teachers who have experience using the computer to help teach the curriculum are teaching other teachers how to," Mishler says. "What's more, because we're following guidelines established by the local University, we can offer these computer courses to our teachers for continuing education credits."

Courses at teachers' colleges

What would be even better is teachers' colleges and schools of education offering applied instruction in, say, How to Use the Computer in Teaching Eighth Grade Curricula.

"That's already happening in some schools of education," says Betsy Pace, U.S. sales and marketing manager for Apple Computer. "Eventually, there will be education school curricula dedicated to teaching teachers how to teach with computers.

Pace's view of the current status of the K-12 computer revolution is interesting for its *deus ex machina* kind of twist. Just wait until the first generation of computer-literate kids enters the teaching ranks, says Pace. These are kids who have grown up using computers, who've gone to school with them,

who couldn't imagine being without them. Once this group starts teaching, you won't be able to stop them from using computers to teach the curriculum. There'll be a grassroots upsurge of new strategies and methodologies for K-12 computer use.

Give computers to the teachers

A variant on that "just you wait" theory is the currently popular idea of getting the technology into the teacher's hands first.

"We all made a serious mistake in giving the computers to the kids first," says Tom Snyder. "We ignored the teachers, cut them out of the loop, and that's precisely the way to kill a promising educational technology. What we did was put computers in a lab and say to teachers, 'Here, use them.' What we should have done is given the computers to the teachers and said, 'Here, take them home and learn to use them.' Once teachers have learned what a computer can do, they can take something like *Carmen Sandiego* and understand, comfortably and intuitively, how to make it fit into a lesson or a curriculum."

A number of vendors and school districts are beginning to follow Snyder's suggestion. Apple has a program which grants educators special discounts on computer purchases; that program, says Pace, has grown more than 150 percent over last year.

The Lake Washington school district, in Kirkland, Wash., has begun giving Apple IIGSes free to every teacher willing to take some computer training workshops. "Last year," says Dr. William Lehman, director of planning evaluation and technology at Lake Washington, "we did a re-evaluation of technology. We found that over the past five years we had been training the same

100 teachers, out of a total of 1,100, on computer applications. Clearly, we had a few who were really excited by computers, and many who, I think, were hoping the computer would go away."

Since giving away the computers (which Lake Washington teachers can take home and use any way they see fit—including borrowing software from the district's software library), computer instruction in the schools has increased dramatically. According to Lehman, computer lab scheduling is wall-to-wall, and he has had more requests for software in one week, subsequent to the giveaway, than in the whole of the previous year.

Show teachers how computers can help

Putting the technology in the teacher's hands is unquestionably a better strategy than ignoring teachers, or bypassing them, or telling them to get in there and use the darn things because the kids need what the computer can give them. But giving computers to teachers will not automatically make the computer revolution happen. What is also necessary, says Tom Snyder, is convincing the teacher that the computer will enhance not only the student's learning experience, but also the teacher's teaching experience. "There used to be an educational technology called the 'language lab'," says Snyder. "Studies showed that it was both pedagogically effective and cost effective. Administrators loved it; students didn't mind it. And yet it has largely disappeared. A good portion of the reason why the language lab failed is that teachers were, by and large, cut out of that particular learning experience.

"If you've ever taught—and I have—you know that there are certain teachable moments in every class or lesson and with every student. It's these mo-ments the teacher lives for and wants to be there for. Teachable moments are the sources of enormous satisfaction. But if the student is staring at his terminal, is the teacher going to have to put her face in front of the screen in order to get to one of these moments?

"The lesson," Snyder continues. "is that if you bring into the school a technology that ignores the complex social and pedagogical environment that exists there—an environment that involves the student and the teacher and their various interactions—that technology won't be able to live. Teachers will kill it by simply ignoring it."

Is this going to be the death knell of the computer in the K-12 curriculum? Probably not.

The computer has already had an impact upon schooling orders-of-magnitude greater than the language lab; it won't be so easily ignored, but the image of a teacher thrusting her face between a plugged-in kid and his terminal is a good one to hold in balance against the blithe descriptions of the techno-classroom of the future, a classroom bristling with computers, workstations, VCRs, subgrouped students, multiple simultaneous projects, and a teacher whose task it will be to monitor all these activities, centrally intervening if necessary.

Is that teaching, or is it middle-management? Maybe teaching will have to become a little more like middle-management.

The structure of education may have to change

"The computer in education may well be a structure-changer," says Doris Ray, "a technology that can redefine teaching. But then we have to ask if that is, what we want it to do. Do we want technology-centered, as opposed to teacher-centered, classrooms? Or can we use the computer as a kind of super-glue, designed to hold the old system together?"

There are other questions, as well. How much, for example, will traditional pedagogy have to change if the computer becomes central to curriculum teaching? Not at all? A little? Totally?

Theorists and vendors casually speak of the technological transformation of teachers into "monitors," "facilitators," and "guides." How do teachers feel about such transformations? Will the computer intervene between the teacher and the traditional joys of teaching? Or, instead, will the computer open up new possibilities for teacherly satisfaction—such as the prospect of more one-on-one instruction?

Those questions, and others, concern James Bosco, director of the Tate Center for Research & Information Processing, Western Michigan University.

"What hasn't been clearly understood," says Professor Bosco, "is that when you talk about such matters as seeking to embed the computer more centrally into the curriculum, you are

Ten Steps To Curriculum Integration

The integration of computers into the curriculum won't just magically occur. Here are some ideas—opinions from educators and vendors interviewed for this article—that must be considered if integration is going to occur.

1. Concentrate on integrating computers in areas where traditional teaching strategies aren't working or in areas where computers have already helped.
2. Find out what the teachers want and then determine if the computer can provide a solution. Don't just throw technology at teachers.
3. The technology must become much simpler—some say "radically" simpler—than it is today.
4. The proper software to teach curriculum courses must be developed; software that allows the "computer to do what it does best, and the teacher to do what he or she does best."
5. There must be better communication between software vendors and teachers to help teachers sift through the enormous amount of software on the market.
6. More and better teacher training—at the in-service and pre-service levels.
7. Teachers colleges and schools of education should offer courses in integrating computers into the curriculum.
8. Give computers first to the teachers, then to the students. Let teachers learn how to use them first.
9. The teacher must be convinced or shown that the computer will enhance the student's learning experience and also the teacher's teaching experience.
10. The role of the teacher—and traditional pedagogy—may have to change if computers are to be successfully introduced into every aspect of the curriculum.

talking about, by implication, funda-mental, pedagogical changes.

"Let's say that the computer becomes the vehicle of curriculum transmittal—and that's what computer integration really means. Will not such a change manifestly lessen, for the teacher, the kinds of 'kicks' he or she is used to getting on the job? The primary thing about teaching that appeals to most prac-titioners is the direct contact with stu-dents that results in a genuine, perceptible learning experience for the student. When that happens the emo-tional rewards for the teacher are very great. But who gets those rewards now? The terminal?

"It's been a truism that computer tech-nology will never replace the teacher," he continues. "But I question that tru-ism if the technology is used to its full capacity. There are already many cases where a computer and software can be said to be performing a teaching func-tion. Since it's unlikely the technology will cease to improve, teaching function-ality will undoubtedly increase."

But does this mean that the teacher's transformation into facilitator is inevi-table, and that, in the future, a teacher's managerial skills will be more impor-tant than pedagogical ones? Or does it mean that teachers will resist (are re-sisting) the computerization of the cur-riculum precisely because such a change provides no place for them as teachers.

If the latter possibility is true, says Bosco, then computers in the curricu-lum are doomed.

"I'm a technology proponent," he says. "Yet, when I look at computers in schools I see a round-peg-in-a-square-hole prob-lem. There is a fundamental dysfunc-tion between how learning in schools is structured and the optimum use of tech-nology in schools."

Bosco is saying that over the course of 150 years some organizational and peda-gogical structures have developed and become deeply embedded in American schooling. One of these structures, of course, is that the teacher-with-text-book is the primary transmitter of the curriculum. The history of schooling is littered with miraculous new technolo-gies which were supposed to supple-ment/replace the teacher-with-textbook, and which didn't.

"It seems to me that computers in K-12 are now at a crossroads," says Bosco. "They may lapse to the marginal status of older miracle technologies like the radio and closed-circuit TV. Or they may move toward a real fusion with more traditional pedagogical forms. But fusion will only happen if we think delib-erately and consciously about our peda-gogical structures.

"I'm convinced there is a role for the teacher in the technologized classroom, that falls somewhere between being the sole source of information and being nothing but a functionary who sees to it the kids stay on their computer tasks. But what we have to do is think these new roles into being; experiment with structures until we find them."

Jim Dezell of IBM agrees: "I think it's far from an either/or type situation. It may be that in some courses the teacher will be delivering 90 percent of the cur-riculum, and the computer 10 percent. In other courses these ratios will shift, depending upon ages of students and subject matter. Over the next five to 10 years we will see, I think, an evolution-ary process of finding the right mix of instructional modes. What those mixes are is impossible right now to know. We are going to have to develop them em-pirically, through trial and error. That's the only way we'll know."

Article #3
Moving Your District Toward Technology

IT'S A BIT EASIER NOW THAT WE KNOW MANY OF THE DON'TS!

By
LeRoy
Finkel

What works and doesn't work in today's schools that use technology?

For the past 20 years or so, we technology educators have been sorting out the answers to exactly that question as we progress through the "experimental phase" of technology in schools.

Here are some do's and don'ts that we have learned which might make your district's move toward technology a bit easier.

Training Teachers

Years ago, we thought teachers should be trained in programming and technical operations. We now know they should learn in the classroom how to use the technology.

In the past, teachers were trained months, maybe years before the computers arrived at the school. Any interest stimulated in the teachers was lost, and they had forgotten nearly everything they learned by the time the hardware arrived.

Obviously, we learned that we should wait to train teachers until the computers arrived at the school and, during the teacher training period, reserve the computers for teachers' use.

Finally, we approached our training believing everyone would love computers, so we became disappointed when many teachers were turned away by our training.

If I had it to do over again, I would only train those who were interested because not every teacher will ever want to use computer technology in a classroom.

We also learned that teaching style has a lot to do with whether a teacher will want to use technology or not, so training should either match the teacher's style or enlarge that style tactfully.

Access to Computers

We have spent big dollars acquiring computers to be used by students while spending pennies providing computers for classroom teachers. As a result, the integration of computers into regular classrooms has been inhibited.

It takes time with a computer for a teacher to prepare lessons that include computer technology. If all the school computers are to be used by students, when does the teacher find the time to use the computer for classroom preparation?

If you want teachers to use computers, they need to have access to computers at convenient times, more than when students are not in the building.

Location of Computers

To teach computer programming and literacy, we grouped all of our computers in one or two rooms.

This was a natural thing to do since it allowed students and teachers to all be in the same location as the hardware they were learning about. It made life

254

easier from the standpoint of repairing faulty equipment as well as security against theft or vandalism.

In addition, the principal could place one person in charge of everything and that one person was stationed in the computer lab at all times.

This practice is fine for teaching about computers, but is having 30 computers in one room the best way to use computers to deliver instruction in science? Likewise, is it smart to ask inexperienced, somewhat reluctant teachers to take 30 students to a lab full of computers when those teachers are barely comfortable themselves?

I advocate placing computers in classrooms for use by teachers and students when they are being used as part of regular instruction. I believe having one to four computers located in the classroom is a more comfortable setting for both teacher and student and is a more natural way to integrate their use.

Yes, it means that the computers may not be used each minute of every day, but we should stop looking at computers as scarce resources. It also means having software libraries in each classroom.

More importantly, it means that teachers and students will use the computers when it is appropriate to use them. They will use them much more in the comfort of their own classroom than if they must trek to computer labs.

Administrators Are Crucial

I have observed that when an administrator wants technology to be part of the education program, it happens. Obviously, teachers play a vital role in implementing the program, but the leadership and money need to come from a supportive administration.

The supportive administrator encourages teachers to get involved with technology, provides them with opportunities for training and opportunities to train others at school sites, arranges for time to sift through the morass of new materials, and recognizes those who do good work.

These facts appear so obvious, yet it seems necessary to repeat them here. Simply, administrators are key to the success of schools' long-range technology programs.

Here are a few additional leadership ideas that may appear equally obvious, but we have seen many districts neglect them.

• Think technology, not just computers.

• If you as an administrator want technology to happen, make your desires public. Tell everyone that you do—don't keep it a secret. You will be amazed at how many people will do things "to keep on the good side of the boss!"

• Insist that your curriculum leadership include technology in their training activities. In the long run, integrating technology into the regular curriculum is the best approach.

• Encourage your personnel staff to seek new staff members with classroom technology experience. Focus on the *experience* the candidate has had, not what courses he or she has taken. Don't assume that teacher training institutions are adequately preparing future teachers to use technology.

• Create the infrastructure that is needed to support the implementation of technology. Nobody says it is easy to add technology to the schools' agenda. We now know that it takes a substantial mechanism of support people to make a successful technology program.

Plans and Planning

Most schools and districts have "approved" technology plans, but was your plan approved with dollar commitments and implementation timelines? A plan without these two elements is just another piece of paper in the files.

A five-year plan should be reviewed thoroughly at the end of three years since educational technology changes very fast. When you next change your plan, add a revised implementation timeline and dollar commitment so your school board will understand exactly what they are approving.

Once a plan with implementation timeline is approved, you should stick with it for a couple of years and not deviate from the plan. However, some flexibility can be built in.

Grants and gifts (even loans) of computers and other technologies should be evaluated in the context of the long-range plan. You should evaluate a potential gift with the same care that you evaluate something you plan to purchase. Just because it's free (or inexpensive) does not make it acceptable or desirable.

So What Does Work?

Understand that there are no simple solutions. If they existed, this article would be full of them.

Some of us who follow the industry are alarmed at the growing number of technology purchase decisions being made without teacher input and in contradiction to district planning guidelines.

School districts are regarding technology as a simple solution to large problems. Such is not the case. Those that have been experimenting for years feel technology can help, but it is not a solution.

Researchers Jack McManus and Terry Cannings describe "critical success factors" that made model technology school programs work effectively:

• A full-time lab assistant was present. This is the support infrastructure mentioned earlier.

• The principal strongly supported the effort.

• All department heads who were considered important to the effort were trained in-depth on the hardware, software, and applications.

• There was at least one key mover and shaker who has schoolwide credibility.

• A critical mass of 15 to 40 computers was maintained in a single location.

• There was a policy of open access that allowed teachers and students to sign up for scheduled classes. Drop-in times were planned before and after school and during lunch time.

• Schools identified and used other external funding sources.

• Schools made a multi-year commitment to permit their programs to become part of the school culture.

• Teachers had access to their own microcomputers at home.

• Mini-labs of four to six computers were established in each department.

Sharing Successes

We've learned a lot in the past 20 years, but quality research on the effectiveness of using technology to teach is still limited.

You can do all of us a favor by including some good research in your technology planning, and then sharing your results with the rest of us! By sharing our successes and failures, perhaps we will accelerate the progress of integrating technology into the mainstream of American education.

To share your experiences and request more information, contact LeRoy Finkel at the San Mateo County Office of Education, 333 Main Street, Redwood City, CA 94063; (415) 363-5459.

By
Daniel E.
Kinnaman

Why don't teachers know more about computers? Why have they failed to "get up to speed" with technology? Are they responsible for holding back the computer revolution in education?

Before placing blame, we need to remember that the majority of teachers in classrooms today have been teaching for more than 15 years; they had developed teaching practices well before the advent of the microcomputer. Computers weren't part of their experience as learners, either in their K-12 schooling or in their collegiate pre-service education.

Moreover, even for the thousands of veteran teachers who *have* given computers a try, the pace of technology development has been so rapid that it's been nearly impossible to get comfortable with a given computer or application before a new one is announced. Consider, for example, the fact that none of the hardware or software items listed below even existed just five years ago:

- Apple's Macintosh Plus computer
- IBM's PS/2 family of computers
- The Apple IIGS;
- LogoWriter
- HyperCard

Go back just three more years and none of the following was yet commercially available:

- AppleWorks
- Bank Street Writer
- Writing to Read
- The Apple IIc
- The original Macintosh
- IBM's PCjr

- The Tandy 1000
  (no deskmate either)
- The Commodore Amiga

Understandably, such major technological changes in a relatively short time have been overwhelming to many teachers. But the teacher-as-computer-novice problem isn't simply the result of lack of confidence or lack of interest on the part of educators. Many teachers were victimized by their own curiosity when microcomputers were introduced. Eager to participate in the educational computing revolution, they made every computer-related staff development program a sellout.

Unfortunately, many initial enthusiasts found their expectations went unrealized. Why? A key problem was that, because of machine limitations and the immaturity of the industry, there were few pedagogically sound software packages. This left many schools with the unrealistic expectation that teachers should produce their own courseware. To make matters worse, the majority of in-service programs were conducted by people who knew more about computers than education.

Thus, thousands of teachers ended up frustrated rather than fulfilled. Instead of discovering an educational panacea, they found themselves struggling through computer programming courses. Scores of teachers left their first experiences with computers convinced that the new technology made their lives harder rather than easier and that it

257

had little relevance to the real needs of teachers or students.

A New Beginning

Despite these difficulties, many teachers have persevered and the industry has matured. As we enter the 90s, there are more than two million computers in K-12 education. Powerful graphics-based computers are now priced low enough for purchase by schools. There are hundreds of first-rate educational software packages available. And technologies such as telecommunications, interactive video, CD-ROM, desktop publishing, and real-time simulations have emerged that make the types of classroom applications teachers were expecting ten years ago a present-day reality.

We are still faced with a huge problem. If we want teachers to feel comfortable using these tools in the classroom, if we hope to give educational technology the chance to fulfill its potential, we need to invest in staff development. While much lip service is paid to staff development, more often than not, professional improvement in the use of technology is still being left to enthusiasts willing to learn at their own expense. This needs to change.

The First Step: Developing In-House Expertise

What can your district do to ensure that staff development becomes a top priority? School districts must take an aggressive role in seeing that the staff development needs of their teachers are met.

There is no better way to do this than to invest time, effort, and money to build in-house expertise in educational technology. The cornerstone is the addition to the faculty of a computer education coordinator who is experienced in both technology and curriculum. This is not a frivolity; it is a crucial, cost-effective way of helping the majority of teachers in the district learn to make effective use of technology.

The coordinator can be a valuable asset to a district's instructional program in a number of ways. First, a good coordinator can be the key to creating, implementing, and directing a district-wide vision for educational use of technology. The coordinator can steer the district's acquisition and use of technology, aligning it with instructional goals and objectives, and ensuing equity and consistency among school buildings and across grade levels.

An equally important role for the coordinator is as the district's primary staff developer. One of the most successful approaches is for the coordinator initially to work with a core group of teachers comprising a cross section of the district's subject areas and grade levels. In addition to improving the skills of the core group, this strategy is a cost-effective way to build a high-quality staff development team for the rest of the district. As the members of the core group mature in their understanding and use of technology, they can conduct staff development activities for other teachers in the district. In this manner, a competent coordinator can build a team that is in tune with the district's needs and goals, and that can effectively (and relatively inexpensively) provide one-to-one support for every teacher in the district.

Focusing resources on the development of in-house expertise gives teachers ownership in and accountability for professional growth. It enhances collegiality and instills a sense of unity and pride in the district's efforts. It doesn't mean that the district will never bring in anyone from outside to do staff development, or that teachers will never be sent out of the district for professional growth. It does mean that the district need not depend on outside sources, which can never hope to provide the customized on-going staff development the district can get from its own in-house experts.

Breaking Old Habits

We need to be prepared to rethink the ways in which staff development has traditionally been conducted. Here are some old habits we need to break:

• **We have to do away with the notion of "teacher training."** Training implies an emphasis on teachers producing products by performing a set of tasks with a computer. Teachers don't need to be "trained." They need activities that engage them with the process of teaching—activities that encourage them to explore, create, and reflect upon the benefits and limitations of teaching with technology.

• **We need to avoid the "one-shot" approach to staff development.** It isn't fair to send a teacher to a one-day workshop "to learn computers." Seasoned staff developers report that there is a learning cycle most teachers go through. Usually, curiosity initiates teachers' involvement. This is generally followed by *high anxiety* and *frustration* as they experience an almost unavoidable information overload.

However, as the learner digests new information and has time to practice new skills, frustration and anxiety turn to *enthusiasm* and *excitement*. For teachers to complete the learning cycle, computer-related professional growth opportunities must be on-going and systematic.

• **Staff development activities should not be limited to large group workshops and classes.** A major benefit of using in-house experts for staff development is that large group sessions can be supplemented by coaching and modeling. Coaching involves one-to-one follow-up to a workshop. Generally, to be effective, large group sessions (conducted by the district staff development team) should be followed by coaching sessions with each participant.

Modeling is closely related, but isn't linked to a specific large group session. "I can show you better than I can tell you" is the theory behind modeling. The most effective modeling occurs in two phases. In the first, the staff developer works with a teacher's class while the teacher observes. In the second, the staff developer and teacher conduct the class together.

• **We must stop isolating educational technology as a separate discipline.** This means that teachers should not have to go to a separate computer conference to learn how to use computers to improve teaching in language arts, math, science, or any other area. The leadership in each discipline needs to help define appropriate roles for the use of computers within their content domains. School districts and individual teachers can make this happen by actively encouraging the professional organizations they're associ-

> It isn't fair to send a teacher to a one-day workshop "to learn computers."

ated with to make educational technology a more significant and visible part of their conferences.

When planning on a local level, it is important to link computer-related staff development with proven and emerging learning strategies and techniques. If, for example, cooperative learning is a priority for your district, give teachers opportunities to examine technology in that context. It is not enough to discuss cooperative learning or to conduct non-technology based staff development activities and point out, "by the way, the following software packages can promote cooperative learning." Teachers need to experience the software and the learning strategy in conjunction with each other and have opportunities to make links for themselves.

• *We need to remember that teachers, like students, need hands-on experiences.* Too often, staff development sessions consist of lectures and demonstrations. Putting teachers in the role of learners means more than telling them how technology contributes to instructional improvement. It means allowing them to experience the process.

Suppose, for example, that you are conducting sessions in the uses of technology to improve problem solving. It is essential to allow time for the teachers to use a variety of problem solving software—to encounter problems that have multiple solutions and to become engaged in using technology to investigate, conjecture, and experiment. Inviting teachers to be learners as they explore the potential of technology leads to more fruitful reflection when they put their teacher hats back on.

Investing in the "Three Rs"

Does staff development cost money? Yes. When budgeting for technology, we need to recognize that there's more to the equation than hardware and software: staff development is a vital component and requires funding. However, it's encouraging to note that, with sensible planning and an open mind about the incentives your district is willing to offer, a moderate staff development budget can go a long way.

The "three Rs" of staff development are release time, renumeration, and recognition. Release time—whether we approach it through the use of substitute teachers, creative scheduling, or redistribution of non-teaching responsibilities—is an essential way of freeing core group members to work with other teachers in the school or district. In addition, the core group and others who play a leadership role deserve some form of remuneration—at the very least a minimal stipend as a "token" of the district's appreciation.

Equally important are other forms of recognition. One of these is inherent to the core group approach: By encouraging teachers to become staff developers, we provide them with opportunities to develop skills and materials that can be presented outside the district (at conferences, in magazine articles, and so on). Such exposure can serve as an important incentive for the teacher at the same time that it provides publicity for the district.

Other forms of recognition being used effectively in school districts around the country include getting the word out to school boards, parents' organizations, and other community members about contributions of staff members; sending motivated teachers to national conferences at the district's expense; giving teachers who've emerged as leaders a major say in administrative decision about technology use; and allocating access to scarce and expensive equipment in part based on a teacher's willingness to take a leadership role in exploring how technology can be used to improve education.

Incentives and rewards are also important to teachers who are just getting started with technology. If we want them to attend workshops after school, on weekends, or during vacation, we need to think about ways of paying them for their time.

In some districts, this is done in the form of *per diem* payments: in other districts administrators are using continuing education units (eventually reflected in higher salaries or continued certification) or are working with nearby colleges and universities to arrange for teachers involved in staff development activities to earn college credit.

Realizing that daily access to computers is an important way of ensuring comfort with the technology, a number of districts are employing incentives that help teachers obtain computers for use at home.

In one part of Washington state, for example, every teacher who voluntarily attended a two-week in-service program was given a new computer as "payment." This approach was greeted with great enthusiasm by potential participants— and it saved more than $700 per teacher when compared with the cost of paying the same number of teachers a *per diem* rate to attend the staff development program. Other districts have set up programs that allow teachers to borrow school equipment for use at home and have set up special payroll deduction plans that assist staff members in purchasing their own computers at discounted high-quantity rates awarded to the district.

The point is not to coax, bribe, or beg teachers to learn more about technology. As we've seen over the years, there are always teachers who choose to learn, to grow, and to experiment without any support from administrators. However, if we want others in the district to benefit from these pioneers, if we want teachers to feel good about taking time from their already crowded schedules to acquire new skills, we need to provide incentives, rather than roadblocks.

Preparing for Change

Whether we like it or not, change has become a highly visible constant in today's world. We can't avoid it, we can't prevent it, and we shouldn't always embrace it. Teachers, however, are in a unique position to direct change and to give it meaning. In a very important way they are the key to the future of education.

Without regular participation in high-quality professional growth activities, educators will not be able to function effectively as leaders in a rapidly changing information society. And change it will. During the next few years we can expect dramatic changes in the very structure of schooling. We can also expect continued demographic changes in the school population. And, of course, we can expect further changes in the technology that becomes available to schools. There's one thing that won't change, though. A strong commitment to staff development will be found in every district that succeeds in using educational technology to improve teaching and learning.

Article #5
The Advantages Of Using A Network

NETWORKS OFFER EDUCATORS NUMEROUS BENEFITS — IN INSTRUCTION AND MANAGEMENT.
HERE'S A ROUNDUP OF WAYS NETWORKS ARE BEING USED IN SCHOOLS TODAY.

BY
ROBERT
McCARTHY

Networking has become one of the hottest growth segments in the computer industry. Worldwide sales of network hardware and software products jumped 85 percent in 1988 to $4.8 billion. The K-12 market is partially responsible for this growth.

According to QED, the Denver-based education information company, 1,567 school districts are using networks in some 24,829 schools. "Last year," says Jeanne Hayes, QED's president, "65 percent of the larger school districts were using some networking; this year, that figure is 71 percent."

Networks, which make communication and the sharing of software possible between numerous computers in a lab, school, or district, are becoming easier to use: that's one reason more schools are buying them. But the real forces behind their growth are the advantages they offer educators: networks assist in both instruction and management. From offering students in a class the ability to study or research as a group, to helping teachers assess or diagnose the progress of students, to saving money because they reduce the need for numerous expensive peripherals, networks help educators, and education in general, in many ways.

Easier To Use

Networks, say the vendors and some end-users, have become easier to install and operate, and there is much more networkable software available now than there was even two years ago.

"Yes, LANs [local area networks] have become easier to use," says Marvin Koontz, director of technology at Centerville High School, Fairfax County, Va. "However, to say they've become completely turnkey would be an exaggeration. There are some hidden problems, and the technology is still a bit leading-edge in some respects. But the front-end interface with the user is dramatically easier now, especially with the icon-based software that is used, for instance, in Apple Computer Inc.'s AppleTalk network.

"Over on the MS-DOS side." Koontz continues, "there are still some difficulties. You really need someone who knows about the system to be able to operate it and keep it operating."

Lloyd Meskimen, instructional computing specialist for the Portland, Ore. school district, agrees that there are significant differences among types of networks. "In terms of start-up time and training time," he says, "I find that Apple-based networks have a considerable advantage over MS-DOS networks. It's more difficult to install an MS-DOS system, both in terms of the wiring and in terms of getting the software into the system."

"Hooking Macs onto AppleShare [the network system software used with the AppleTalk network] is relatively easy," says Rick Nelson, systems engineer with Education Alliance, a Highland Park,

262

Ill.-based educational computer dealer. "All you need to do is lay the cable and plug everything into the server. It's also easy to use; each Mac on the network looks just like a standalone. The file server acts like a hard drive and each networked Mac simply pulls data from it." Networking Apple IIes is a little bit more complicated because network cards need to be installed.

In addition to Apple's AppleTalk, other manufacturers of education networks that connect Apple computers include companies such as Corvus and Lan-Tech.

Although some MS-DOS-based networks are more complicated than Apple-based ones, they are easier to use than in previous years, according to many educators. Manufacturers of MS-DOS education network systems include Corvus, IBM, and Tandy.

For example, Tandy's SchoolMate network system, according to Howard Elias, Tandy's vice president of computer merchandising, "is a sophisticated network, based on 3COM's 3PLUS operating system which, in fact, doesn't look like a sophisticated system. All the techie management chores have been hidden or done away with, from the end-user point of view. Being on the SchoolMate network feels just like being on a desktop. It's also easy to install and get up and running."

All right. Networks have become easier to install and more user-friendly. Networkable application software is becoming more plentiful. And networks have also become less costly—although *how much* less costly is difficult to say, since cost depends upon the numbers of machines to be networked, whether or not network cards are necessary, and numerous other variables.

But the bottom line, of course, is just how useful are networks? What impact do they have upon the computer lab, the classroom, and instruction in general? What can you do on a network that you can't do, or can't easily do, on a group of standalones?

Electronic Learning talked to a number of educators around the country who have network experience, and discovered a wide range of positive answers to these questions.

Educational Advantages

Networks, say many educators, facilitate group work, with students at different workstations able to work on different aspects of a problem and share their work or data base with partners. Sometimes, says Tim Taylor, math teacher and computer lab coordinator at Strasburg Middle School, Strasburg, Va., group work can be more of a fun project. Taylor's lab consists of 24 Apple IIGSes, a Macintosh file server, and a DigiCard network.

"We have a little activity called *Hot Dog Stand* from Sunburst," says Taylor. "A couple of kids together run a hot dog stand at a football stadium. There are eight games per season, and the students get pre-game weather reports and other types of information to help them estimate potential attendance. Then, using the attendance, they estimate needed supplies of hot dogs, buns, etc. The goal is to make a profit of $2,000. The students can work together on separate computers on various parts of the solution and then pool their data."

A more serious example of networked group work, in a real-life lab simulation, is Doug Ludwig's applied physics lab in Baltimore (Md.) County's Southeastern Vocational-Technical Center. Ludwig, who is the science and technology instructor, has a lab consisting of 15 Mac Plus computers networked to a Mac file server.

"I've tried to use the lab to create a high-tech environment wherein 11th- and 12th-graders, who might be bored in strictly academic courses and who don't consider themselves engineering material, can learn something about applied physics," says Ludwig.

In addition to the networked computers, Ludwig's lab contains electronic testing equipment, a model-making shop, and a machine tools shop.

"What we've done," says Ludwig, "is create a lab environment very similar to what exists in the workplace."

Ludwig's applied physics students work in groups. Tasks are assigned and broken down into components handled by individual students. Data is collected and analyzed; information is shared; reports generated; computer models are sketched; and then, using the machine shop, real machine parts are designed and built.

"Everybody has his task and the group helps those who need it," says Ludwig. "Students learn what skills they have and don't have. And that's a big help in preparing them for a technical career."

The ABCs of A Network

Just what is a network?

When it comes to technology, sometimes not even computer-using educators know the answers. Or at least that's what Peter Kelman, vice president and publisher of New York City-based Scholastic Software, discovered at a recent educational technology conference. Kelman also is a member of a Software Publisher's Association sub-committee created to study computer networking.

"Especially when it comes to networks," says Kelman, "I was rather surprised at the depth of misunderstanding that exists—even in the minds of computer coordinators at some larger school districts. At one point they were asked what kinds of networks they had installed in their districts. Here are some of the answers they gave: 'Two Education System Corp. (now Jostens Learning Corp.) labs, five Wasatch labs, three *Writing to Read* labs, five AppleShare labs.' etc. But a Wasatch lab, of course, isn't a network [it is an integrated learning system, or ILS], although it is undoubtedly networked. And as for *Writing to Read,* well, it's an IBM integrated learning system, and so it's probably running on a Novell network.

"But clearly," Kelman says, "the point is that these computer coordinators had failed to distinguish between integrated learning systems and networks." (For a comparison of networks and ILSes, see the sidebar, p. 271.)

So just what is a network, or of what does a network consist? Well, first you have to have computers to network. These can be IBMs, Apple IIes, Macintoshes, IBM-compatibles, Tandys, Commodores, and so forth.

Then you need a file server, which is nothing more than a high-powered desktop computer with a hard-disk drive, or in some cases a self-contained hard disk server. The file server functions as the network's information repository; hence, it needs large storage capacity. It also directs and monitors the flow of information to and from other computers (the workstations) on the network. Typically, any computer can act as the file server if it is attached to a big enough hard drive and has network-controlling capability built-in or plugged-in.

The final pieces of hardware are the networking cards that must be pur-

Ludwig does not believe his lab could function without the Macs on a network. "Logistically," he says, "it would be very difficult. You would lose that instant ability to share common files and data bases. But what I like best about the network is that it allows the students to add to a data base, so that they all can see it grow. And the network facilitates group accomplishment of tasks, and social interactions, which are also characteristic of how applied physics labs work in the real world."

For Brad Waggoner, coordinator of computer learning at the Maine Township school district, Park Ridge, Ill., one of the best uses of networking involves collaborative writing projects for students who don't like to write or who find writing intimidating.

"We have a software product called *RealTime Writer* (from RealTime Learning Systems, Washington. D.C.) that we run on our Corvus network," says Waggoner. "And what it does is allow students to 'chat' together about a writ-

chased if the computers to be networked do not have built-in networking capacity, and the cabling and wiring that physically hooks the system up.

Software is next, and the first component is called the network operating system software. Produced by such venders as Corvus, Novell, Apple, DigiCard, Lan-Tech, 3-COM, and others, the operating system software provides basic network linkage and controls all access to the file server. Which means that users wishing access to a particular program on the file server actually first pass the request to the network operating software, which then opens the file.

"At the next level, and sitting on top of the network operating software, comes what I would call the network management system software," says Kelman. "These are products like Apple's *Aristotle*, IBM's *Classroom Local Area Network (ICLAS)*, or Tandy's *SchoolMate*, all of which create a user-interface between the operating system and the applications software." *SchoolMate*, for example, provides users with pulldown menus and pop-up dialog boxes designed to eliminate confusing start-up procedures

and the technical aspects of a network. It also has such classroom management applications as *Roster*, *Grade Book*, and *Lesson Scheduler*.

An optional software level—which can be added at this point—is the instructional management software package.

"Curriculum-type or educational applications software come next," says Kelman. "And this would include integrated learning systems as well as individual network-compatible programs from publishers like Scholastic. Now, within this category of network-compatible software I would distinguish between what I would call 'networked products,' which have features like electronic mail, for instance, which don't make sense unless used on a network, and those products where the publishers have designed options allowing you to save locally to your [single] machine or to the file server, or to print locally or to join a networked printing queue."

Finally, there is software that ipso facto will run on a network as well as on standalone computers, and for which one is obliged to buy a networking license if one is legally to use it on a network.

ing assignment via windows which appear on-screen. Actually, the program allows for three such windows: in one, the writing assignment is downloaded from the teacher's workstation; in the second window, the students can chat concerning the assignment and exchange suggestions about how to attack it; in the third window, the teacher, who can monitor all the on-screen activity, can add comments to the student suggestions. Then, after this chatting activity has gone on for a while—in effect, giving the students a boost into the assignment—the kids can go ahead and begin to write on their own."

Waggoner is also high on another network product called *Close-up LAN*.

"*Close-up LAN*," he says, "is especially useful for teaching computer applications. What it does is allow the teacher to go through demonstrations of, say, word processing activities or data base activities—but these demonstrations are, via the network, totally transparent to all the computers hooked up to the network. So each student can watch his terminal and see the teacher go through the actual operation and see what happens on the computer when the operation is correctly completed. I think it's one of the most elegant and efficient ways to teach computing skills—and it's a way that absolutely requires networking if it's to function."

At Fidlago Elementary, Anacorda, Wash., principal Chris Borgen believes in stimulating all the various learning styles: the visual, the audile, and the hands-on. And for that there is no better means, he says, than a computer-based networked system.

"We have Apple Macintoshes in each of our classrooms," he says, "plus some in our special education room, in the staff rooms, and in some of the offices. All the Macs are networked to a file server and into this whole network we have integrated CD-ROM capacity. The result is a technology that provides a multiplicity of learning inputs to numerous students.

"Let's take, as an example, a student in a fifth-grade history class who wants some information on Lewis and Clark," Borgen continues. "He inputs the request and up pops the Grolier Encyclopedia article on Lewis and Clark—the whole encyclopedia having been inscribed on CD-ROM disks. But suppose the student wants more than words; suppose he wants to, kinesthetically, as it were, follow the route of Lewis and Clark. Well, by touching the correct icon on the computer screen, up comes a graphic in which a little pioneer figure makes his way across the continental U.S.

"Suppose, now, he wants audile input. By choosing the audile icon, up come not only the words to songs circa 1805, but simulated music and voices played by the Mac. Students learn in a whole variety of ways. By stimulating as many of these ways as we can, we hope that we'll be reinforcing each and every lesson."

Enhancing Journalism

John Wolverton, supervisor of instructional computing in the Wichita, Kansas School District, has already accomplished a sort of interdisciplinary networking.

"In one of our schools," he explains, "we've networked eight Macintoshes in a journalism class, two Macs in an art class, and three Macs in an industrial arts class. Moreover, all three classroom networks are networked. So, because of the journalism connection, we can combine language arts and graphic arts and page make-up over the networks to help produce the student newspaper."

Student publications are also a network application at schools in the Princeton Regional School District, Princeton, N.J. "We have in the high school a lab of eight Macs and two laser writers hooked up to a 50MB file server," says Peter Thompson, district technical coordinator, "and that network has been especially useful for student publications: the school newspaper, the yearbook, and the student literary magazine.

"In the past, students would type out the work and we would send it to the printer," Thompson says. "Now we use the Macs to process text, *PageMaker* software to do layouts, and the lasers to print galleys. So now what goes out to the printer is camera-ready copy. The network has helped to facilitate this, because, in the past, working with floppies on standalones, the students would lose articles—simply fail to store them on the disks or forget which disks they were on, or, students would work on earlier versions of a text, not knowing that later revisions existed. That's impossible on a network because of the hierarchical storage function."

Student Management

Student management functions are among the most impressive of network applications. Using certain software programs, schools and school districts can track student attendance, gather and collate grade information, track disciplinary infractions, and generate student schedules.

Arvid Nelson, superintendent of the Indian Springs School District, Indian Springs, Ill., has had an IBM student management network in place since the early 1980s. "What the computerization and networking of student management means," says Nelson, "is that teachers, principals, and superintendents now have instantaneous access to up-to-date, accurate information on students, whenever such information is required. This information then can be and is being used to assess and diagnose the learning program of every individual student."

To give a flavor of what automated and networked student management might mean to the classroom teacher, Nelson describes what the start of a typical day in a fully networked school might be like.

"The first thing the teacher does," says Nelson, "is go to the computer on his/her desk, and plug in a personal diskette. The system recognizes the teacher's ID number and immediately brings the teacher on-line with the mainframe in the district office. Which means, of course, that records of her students kept at district offices are available to the teacher.

"Next, the teacher takes attendance by calling up the attendance package. A screen appears containing the complete roster of students for that particular class. The teacher keyboards in absences and then, by executing one command, downloads the attendance information to a terminal in the principal's office.

"The teacher can also access the attendance record of any student in the class to see, for example, whether a student absent in that class was present for any earlier classes. After taking attendance, the teacher may want to access any electronic mail that's accumulated. Or, the teacher can access any number of modules containing various sorts of student data: grades, demographics, or schedules. And down the hall, the student counselor can access a student's disciplinary file and graduation requirements."

The networked student data can also be collated and abstracted in any number of ways to produce reports and comparisons.

In addition to such elaborate student management functions, networked classrooms can be useful in simplifying more mundane problems.

"Take something as simple as classroom seating," says Walter Ziko, seventh- and eighth-grade technology teacher at Shaw Junior High School, Corham, Maine. "If students change their seats in an un-networked lab or classroom, or even if you want to change a student's seat, you've got to shut down and transfer all the system disks and applications disks and data disks that the student is working on. But if you're networked, a student's work and programs are equally accessible from any workstation." Ziko runs a lab that contains 16 Macintosh workstations, networked via AppleTalk to a 20MB file server.

But a more important function, says Ziko, is file-sharing among teachers. "One of our goals," he says. "is to have computers in classrooms and on teachers' desks hooked into file servers located at various points throughout the school. In that way, not only can you share data bases and peripherals, but teachers can also share student files. For instance, if I have a student in 6th period and another teacher has him 5th period, working together we can have our common student producing projects

---

Why a network is not an ILS

When asked what kind of network they use, many educators respond by naming integrated learning systems (ILS), which are manufactured by companies such as Education Systems Corp. (now called Jostens Learning Corp.), Wicat Systems, Computer Curriculum Corp., and others. While ILSes are indeed networked, they are much different from a lab of networked computers.

Some definitions are in order.

Integrated learning systems are comprehensive packages of computer-based instruction that focus on basic skills. The components include hardware, courseware, and an instructional management system. Some systems use minicomputers to control the network, with the student stations being simply dumb terminals; in other cases student micros are cabled to a hard disk file server.

ILS courseware, which primarily focuses on K-8 math, reading, and language arts, is made up of tutorials, drill and practice, problem solving software, tests, and more. The instructional management system records how many of the lessons a student has attempted, how many he completed, etc.

A defining feature of the ILS network is its closed architecture: most often, the only thing that will run on the network is the ILS courseware. A true network's defining characteristic, on the other hand, is its open architecture: it will run any program compatible with the file server, provided that program has been written in a networkable form.

that combine the disciplines. On a network this becomes much easier to expedite and oversee."

Ziko also hopes to use his network to organize student work into what he calls "portfolios." Such portfolios, consisting of past and present samples of the student's abilities in math, writing, art, and other classes, would be stored on the network and accessible to appropriate teachers. "This application," Ziko explains, "will help teachers to whom the student is new obtain a quick sense of what kind of student he is and what sorts of work he is capable of—it is much more concrete and revealing than a series of grade marks."

Networks Can Save Money

Using networks to control software costs is an advantage cited by almost all network advocates.

"With a network," says Frank Windsor, assistant state superintendent for instructional technology, Maryland State School System, "instead of buying 30 pieces of software for 30 standalone workstations, you buy one piece of software and a site license—at a significant cost reduction."

Networks also save money by cutting down the need for peripherals. Educators in labs with standalone computers who found they could hardly cope with only one printer for every two workstations, now find that, networked, a single printer is often enough. "We have 14 IBM PS's Model 25 computers networked by Novell [a network company] to an IBM PS/2 Model 60 file server," says Janet Louthan, business teacher at Charleston High School, Charleston, Ill. "And when the IBM man told me we could get along with a single printer, I frankly didn't believe him. Before, with 14 standalones seven printers weren't

enough. But the IBM man was right: one printer can serve the entire network."

Everett McCassey, administrator of data processing for Medford Public Schools, Medford, Mass., agrees with Louthan. "Networks are ideal for allowing you to get optimum use out of expensive peripherals like laser printers." McCassey operates a number of Apple and IBM labs for such applications as English, math, and writing.

Other cost savings result from decreased need for blank floppies, the cost of wear-and-tear on floppy disk drives and the cost (and headache) of damaged or accidentally erased program disks.

"No matter how careful you try to be," says Evelyn Watson, computer instructor at Central Vocational-Technical School, Lexington, Ky., "students are always powering-down at the wrong time and erasing diskettes. With a network and a hard drive file server, both your software and your work files are safer." Watson teaches computer literacy on a Tandy network made up of Tandy 1000 workstations, a Tandy 1000 file server, and the Tandy SchoolMate network.

Dwayne Schneider, computer coordinator for the Mancado School District in Mancado, Kan., agrees, and points out that while it's almost impossible to lose things off the network, "with standalones you can have static electricity problems that can result in files being lost off the floppies."

More Efficient

Greater efficiency is an oft-mentioned networking advantage.

Time management and disk management are primary benefits for Taylor of Strasburg, Va., who has 24 Apple IIGSes networked together. "Instead of 24 separate program disks we have one program stored in the hard drive; an added bonus is that everything boots up quicker on the network."

"Data sharing is much more conveniently handled on the network," says Tim Loughlin, computer coordinator for the Saco Middle School, Saco, Maine. "With a standalone system, you'd have to print out umpteen copies of a file in order to have enough to give each student one. But if the file's on the network, each student can access it whenever he needs it."

Commodore Enters Race

The major computer vendors in education—Apple, IBM, and Tandy—are all marketing networks. Commodore, not willing to be left behind, recently announced its own network.

"We have, for the Amiga, a good, low-cost RS-232 network," says Gail Wellington, Commodore's general manager for world-wide software and product development. "It's not fast but it's very inexpensive. And it's easy to install. The network allows for the transfer of information and the sharing of peripherals; teachers can also access student files.

"Also, it doesn't need a network server; what happens is the network shares a hard drive. It's a distributed processing system. A typical set-up would probably be an Amiga 2000 with a hard drive attached to a number of Amiga 500s and assorted peripherals."

The Amiga network is being beta-tested in Israel and the U.K., and should be available for the American market in the fall.

"Ease of data access, which is already very good, will become even better," adds McCassey from Medford, Mass. "When we inter-network and connect the lab to the library and the media center, students can then start their work in the writing lab and, as needed, pull in data from all over the school."

There is one final thing that networking allows you to do, according to Ludwig, of Baltimore County, Md., and that is to get some additional use out of technology that may be considered obsolete.

"Apple IIes," he explains, "are kind of technologically passe. But by hooking a bunch of them to a Mac using AppleShare and network cards, and the *Aristotle* software to create a user-interface, you have a network in which the IIes essentially become dumb terminals for programs downloaded from the Mac file server. Whereas standing alone, the IIes are kind of technologically backward, networked to the Mac via *Aristotle* the IIes have access to the Mac's power and capacity. Consequently, the IIes, we feel, have some additional product life for us."

Admittedly, networks still lack a high degree of user-friendliness. And many educators are still scared to use a computer; to them, a local area network is the equivalent of Hydra, the mythological many-headed water serpent. But to many technology-using educators, networks help provide better instruction and management. And undoubtedly, today networks are on the way to becoming an integral part of education in the U.S.

Networks: What's Available to Schools

Networks can be confusing to the uninitiated. It's a fairly young industry, and seems to still lack a standardized system of names. For example, each network vendor may call a single component of a network something different. In an attempt to simplify networks as much as possible, *Electronic Learning* has come up with the following categories and definitions to help you understand the accompanying list of network vendors.

Network System: The network operating and/or management system that provides basic communication between the file server and workstations, and creates a user-interface between the operating system and the applications software.

File Server: Usually a powerful computer that acts as the network's information repository. It directs and monitors the information to and from the workstations (Note: Some companies offer their own self-contained hard disk server and are noted accordingly.)

Workstations: The computers where students and other educators work.

Company	Network System	File Server	Workstation Options
Velan Inc. 849 Independence Ave. Mountain View, CA 94043 (415) 960-3388	VNET	AT Compatible or Tandy 4000 with a 20MB to 115MB internal hard drive	Any combination of Apple II, Macintosh, IBM PS/2, IBM PC and compatibles, IBM PCjr, Tandy 1000
Control Data/Corvus 8800 Queen Ave. So. Bloomington, Minn 55431 (800) 451-2186	Omninet Constellation	OmniDrive (a hard disk server)	Apple II+, Apple IIe, Apple IIGS, Macintosh, IBM PCs and compatibles
Tandy 1700 One Tandy Center Fort Worth, TX 76102 (800) 321-3133	SchoolMate Education Network	Tandy 3000/4000/5000 server with at least 640K or a Tandy TX/TL with 768K, MS-DOS 3.2 or greater, a 20MB hard disk drive and a Tandylink or EtherLink Network Card	Tandy 1000 series with at least 640K, MS-DOS 3.3 or greater
IBM 101 Paragon Drive Montvale, NJ 07645 (800) 321-3133	ICLAS (IBM Classroom LAN Administration System)	IBM PC/AT, PC/XT (except 370 model), PS/2 Models 50 through 80	IBM PC AT (except 370 model), IBM PC/XT, PCjr, and IBM PS/2 Models 25 through 70
Apple Computer, Inc. 20525 Mariani Avenue Cupertino, CA 95014-6299 (408) 966-1010	Appletalk	Macintosh	Any of the Macintosh family, Apple IIe family and MS-DOS computers
Major Educational Resources 10153 York Road Suite 107 Hunt Valley, MD 21030 (301) 628-1527	Digicard D-Net	Shared Resource Controller (a hard disk server)	Macintosh, Apple II family and MS-DOS computers
Lantech 1181 N. Tatum Blvd. Suite P150 Phoenix, AZ 85028 (602) 953-6300	ELAN (Educational Local Area Network)	Any Apple IIe, II+, or IIGS	Any member of the Apple II family
3COM Corporation 3165 Kifer Road Santa Clara, CA 95052-8145 (800) Net-Com	3 + Open LAN Manager	286 or 386 based IBM PC/AT and compatibles; IBM PS/2 Models 50,60,70, and 80 and compatibles, and 3Com's 3S/400 hard disk server	IBM PC, PC/XT, PC/AT, PS/2 and compatibles and Apple Macintosh supported with 3Com 3+ for Macintosh
Digital Communications Associates, Inc. 7887 Washington Village Drive Dayton, OH 45459-3957 (513) 433-2238	10NET Lan	Any MS-DOS PC	Any MS-DOS compatible or IBM PS/2 compatible
Compulynx 9236 Deering Avenue Chatsworth, CA 91311 (818) 407-1985	Compulynx Server III Software and Printing Network	Compulynx Server III (a hard disk server)	Apple IIe, II, and IIGS
Novell Inc. 122 E. South Provo, UT 84606 (800) 453-1267	Novell Netware	IBM PS/2, IBM PCs, and compatibles	IBM PS/2, IBM PCs and compatibles and supports operating environment of DOS, OS/2, and Macintosh

Article #6
Integrated Learning Systems: A Primer

IF YOU ARE EXPECTED TO MAKE MAJOR DECISIONS ABOUT THE USES OF ILSs IN YOUR DISTRICT OR SCHOOL, YOU NEED SOME CLEARLY DEFINED STANDARDS BY WHICH TO ANALYZE AND COMPARE THESE PRODUCTS. HERE'S HELP IN MAKING SENSE OF THE VARIOUS SYSTEMS ON THE MARKET TODAY.

BY
JUDY
WILSON

The way the term "integrated learning system" (ILS) is currently used by educators, computer industry representatives, and the media can easily lead one to believe that there is a standard category of products for which the term applies. However, a closer look at the articles, brochures, and press releases covering these systems reveals that the products known as "integrated learning systems" vary greatly in philosophy, design, and content.

Perhaps the best definition of the term ILS comes from *Power On! New Tools for Technology and Learning,* the 1988 report produced by the U.S. Congress's Office of Technology Assessment. In that report, an ILS is defined as a system that includes both courseware and management software running on networked hardware. The courseware covers one or more curriculum areas in targeted grade ranges, and the management program generally provides tracking and reporting capabilities

In this article, we have identified 12 companies marketing products that come close to fitting this description. (Interestingly, very few of the 12 companies actually use the term "integrated learning system" in marketing their products.) While the systems have many features in common, each offers a different curriculum set and philosophical approach to the learning process. The

following information should help you sort out the options available to your school or district.

An Overview of the ILS Market

To begin, you'll want to consider some of the features that differentiate one system from another. They include the following:

Philosophical Approach. The philosophical approaches of the various companies profiled in this article cover a wide spectrum. Some of the systems are designed to be used for remediation, others for comprehensive instruction, and still others for development of higher-order thinking skills. Moreover, the approaches to the development of lessons also vary but can be generally categorized as either skills-based or concept-based. Skills-based programs are designed primarily to provide diagnostic/prescriptive intervention for remediation of precise skills (such as proper decoding of digraphs as a reading skill). Concept-based programs pay more attention to problem solving and higher-order thinking skills.

Curriculum Areas. The curriculum area most commonly covered by ILSs is mathematics, followed by reading or a combination of reading and language arts. Science, computer skills, tool skills,

272

social studies, and foreign language are also commonly covered. As noted in the *Power On!* report, the size and age of a parent company seems to correspond to the grade span and scope of the courseware offerings, with bigger and older companies offering greater coverage, and newer and smaller companies targeting fewer subject areas and smaller grade ranges. Although many companies listed claim that their systems support the use of third-party software, most do not actively promote such software as a part of the systems.

Management System. The management programs of the ILSs listed vary greatly ranging from simple tracking of a student's time spent on a given program to a complete evaluation and recording of a student's progress each time the "Enter" key is pressed. As a rule, the systems offer sufficient capability to manage a student's program and measure the achievement of objectives.

Costs. Costs of the systems listed here vary greatly depending on the size of the installation, the hardware included, and the scope of the courseware and management systems. Generally, estimated prices for a full-featured ILS running on 30 workstations range from $60,000 to well over $100,000. The *Power On!* report estimates the cost of a lab of 30 networked computers, courseware, and management system at about $110,000.

Company Stability. The companies providing ILSs are as varied as the systems themselves. The ages of the companies range from less than one year to 40 years. Sales figures range from estimates of $2 million to $85 million.

Who's Who

Each of the companies listed in this article offers a slightly different approach to learning through the use of technology. The short profiles below give you some idea of the particular "personality" of each company.

Computer Curriculum Corporation. Computer Curriculum Corporation was established some 23 years ago by Dr. Patrick Suppes, Stanford University professor and pioneer in the development of technology-based learning systems. In addition to the curriculum areas noted in the chart, the company offers material appropriate for the development of higher-order thinking skills and problem solving. Digitized speech is provided in a large number of courses in primary and adult literacy modules.

CCC's management system monitors virtually every student keypress and adjusts the content of the material presented based on the student's mastery of objectives. Detailed diagnostic reports of student performance in individual skill areas are provided. The system can also project a student's rate of gain over the school year, so that intervention techniques required for the student to achieve a certain performance level can be devised early in the year.

Computer Networking Specialists, Inc. CNS relies entirely on third-party software to deliver curriculum content. Currently, the CNS system offers software from 35 different publishers and includes several new writing modules. The company offers maximum flexibility by customizing course offerings according to the objectives and budgets of each school district.

CNS modifies all third-party software so that it will run with the company's management system. Once the software has been modified, the system tests for placement in the curriculum, tracks students' time on task and mastery of objectives, and branches for remediation and advancement.

Computer Systems Research, Inc. CSR specializes in providing remediation in basic skills through a diagnostic/prescriptive approach. The courseware, which is correlated to standardized basic skills tests, includes digitized speech at the primary level.

The company's management system offers extensive wrong-answer analysis and prescribes CSR courses to address those weaknesses. It can also manage IBM-compatible software developed by third parties.

Ideal Learning Systems. Ideal offers a comprehensive range of basic skills courses for elementary and high schools.

Ideal's system is totally modular, allowing schools to choose only those strands that meet their needs. Third-party software can be added to the AppleTalk system.

Ideal's management system monitors individual student progress, scores tests, gives immediate feedback, and provides mastery by objective for individuals or groups of students.

Innovative Technologies in Education. ITE is a relatively small company with strong roots in Israel. In fact, the company claims that over 45 percent of elementary school children in Israel currently use the system. Courseware is

What Kind of Schools Buy ILSs?

According to a recent Software Publishers Association (SPA) study, users of Integrated Learning Systems (with overall management systems) are quite different from users of computer networks that run third-party educational software with no overall management system. Among the study's findings:

Integrated Learning Systems:
- are used primarily at the elementary school level;
- are used primarily to teach math and language arts;
- are adopted by districts that emphasize central decision-making, accountability, and uniform coverage of mandated curricula.

Computer Networks:
- are used equally in elementary and secondary schools;
- are used to reach a wider range of content areas, including math, language arts, science, social studies, and adult literacy;
- are adopted by districts that stress decentralized decision-making and teacher professionalism;
- are adopted by districts that have central office technical capabilities to support network configurations.

The SPA report, which was conducted by Education TURNKEY Systems is available for $5 from Ann Stephens Research Director, Software Publishers Association, 1101 Connecticut Ave. N.W., Suite 901, Washington, DC 20036; (202) 452-1600.

primarily tutorial, with drill and practice in basic skills. Some curriculum software is available in versions that present the material in the Spanish, German, Portuguese, and Hebrew languages.

The management system provides testing, practice, tracking, and progress reports for individual students as well as for classes.

Jostens Learning Corporation. Jostens Learning was formed last year from a merger of the relatively young ILS developer Educational Systems Corporation and the 18-year-old Prescription Learning Centers. Jostens Learning currently offers a new line of products that combines the curriculum of the two companies. (Jostens continues to support ESC and PLC customers, allowing them to purchase additional products for their systems.)

The new line provides a developmentally sequenced series of lessons covering the basic curriculum areas, plus problem solving and higher-order thinking skills. The company prides itself on the use of high-quality graphics, voice, music, and animation. Its management system diagnoses student weaknesses, prescribes a plan of attack, tracks student progress, and redirects learning based on performance.

Jostens Learning is the only company currently using CD-ROMs as storage devices for the large amount of data necessary in an ILS. This has allowed the company to make its ILS curriculum available to home-bound students and their families. In addition, the company has pioneered the development of a multimedia encyclopedia for its system, one that also includes a writing tool allowing students to research and compose papers on-line.

MECC. Although MECC has been one of the key players in the field of educational technology for many years, the company's MECC Management Master (MMM) is only a year old. MECC is quick to point out that MMM is not a traditional ILS: it is a networked instructional management system for certain MECC software titles. Specifically, MMM tailors the content of and tracks student progress in the MECC Reading Collection and the Mastering Math Series of Software. (Both of these series are correlated to a variety of popular textbooks that are currently used in schools nationwide.)

Using MMM, teachers can customize lesson sequences and difficulty to fit the needs of individual students. The management system tracks student mastery of each discrete skill and moves students to more difficult material only after they have demonstrated a level of proficiency set by the teacher. Student progress records are generated for the teacher, parents, and administrators.

New Century Education Corporation. In addition to its reading, writing and math skills curriculum, New Century's system offers a special reasoning skills module for grades three through nine. Content area is made more accessible by a natural-voice speech component.

The management system, which is correlated to tests such as CAT and CTBS, diagnoses skill levels of each student and prescribes a sequence of lessons to achieve mastery of new skills. As students work, they receive immediate feedback on their answers, and the program branches students to new lesson sequences based on mastery of current concepts. The program provides performance records for all students each day they participate in the program. Individual data can also be graphed to show gains clearly.

The Roach Organization, Inc. (Control Data Corporation). In September of last year, The Roach Organization acquired Control Data Corp., one of the pioneers in ILS development. CDC once delivered its curriculum via mainframe computers, but now also offers its ILS on networked PCs. The company's PLATO courseware, which has been upgraded to reflect current educational strategies, focuses primarily on remedial basic skills curriculum across grade levels, with emphasis on high school basic skills courses. Additional courseware includes modules that teach job search strategies, life coping skills, and parenting skills. A special module allows teachers to design, print, and score customized tests.

The management component of the system currently offers an array of reports, including individual and class tracking systems. It also provides standardized test and state objectives that can be used to customize the curriculum.

Unisys Corporation. The Unisys ICON system, which is well respected and widely used in Canada, delivers third-party software only. Titles that will run on the system are quite diverse, ranging from kindergarten through adult education. In addition to covering the basic skills, titles include courses in French, business education, and other curriculum areas. Most were developed for the Canadian market.

The Unisys management system is designed primarily to deliver the correct program to the correct workstation on the network. Any tracking of skills learned, problems missed, or mastery level reached is left up to the developers of the third party software packages.

Wasatch Education Systems. Wasatch's courseware is based on the company philosophy of helping students learn to think. The materials emphasize integrated problem solving and higher-order thinking skills, and employ high quality graphics and simulations to help students develop these skills. Open-ended student responses are encouraged. Students have access to an on-line spelling checker, calculator, graphing function, Logo language, glossary, database, and word processor in their work. The reading curriculum encourages off-line reading of classic children's books.

The company's management system includes administrative functions (creating class rosters, generating administrative reports for enrollment information); teacher functions (monitoring student progress, scoring, repositioning students); and student functions (choosing course, unit, lesson, activity).

WICAT. WICAT's strongly graphics-based courseware is designed and keyed to complement major textbooks and national and statewide tests used in schools today. The system also includes a special test construction module for teacher use. The company's strong management system offers a variety of testing options, including a Reading Abilities Profile, Skills Assessment Test, WICAT Learner Profile, and Test of Basic Skills. The staff development program offered on-line as part of the system provides college credit through Utah State University.

For More Information...

Computer Curriculum Corporation
1287 Lawrence Station Rd.
PO Box 3711
Sunnyvale, CA 94088-3711
(800) 227-8324; in CA,
(800) 982-5851

Computer Networking Specialists, Inc.
61 E. Main St.
PO Box 2075
Walla Walla, WA 99362
(800) 372-3277; (509) 529-3070

Computer Systems Research, Inc.
Avon Park South
PO Box 45
Avon, CT 06001
(800) 922-1190; (203) 678-1212

Ideal Learning Systems
8505 Freeport Pkwy., Suite 360
Irving, TX 75063
(800) 999-3234; (214) 929-4201

Innovative Technologies in Education (ITE)
6220 S. Orange Blossom Trail, Suite 316
Orlando, FL 32809
(407) 859-8525

Jostens Learning Corporation
6170 Cornerstone Court East
San Diego, CA 92121-3710
(800) 521-8538; (619) 587-0087

MECC
3490 Lexington Ave. North
St. Paul, MN 55126-8097
(800) 228-3504; in MN, (800) 782-0032;
(612) 481-3500

New Century Education Corporation
220 Old New Brunswick Rd.
Piscataway, NJ 08854
(201) 981-0820

The Roach Organization
8800 Queen Ave. South
Minneapolis, MN 55440
(800) 328-1109

Unisys Corporation
PO Box 500, MS: B360
Blue Bell, PA 19424-0001
(215) 542-3998; (800) 547-8362

Wasatch Education Systems
5250 South 300 West, Suite 350
Salt Lake City, UT 84107
(800) 877-2848; (801) 261-1001;

WICAT Education
1875 South State St.
Orem, UT 84058
(800) 759-4228; (801) 224-6400

How the ILSs Stack Up

Company	Age of Company or ILS Division	ILS Approx. Annual Sales	Fileserver	Network	Workstation	Math	Reading
Computer Curriculum Corporation	23 years	n/a	IBM PS/2 model 80, Tandy 4000 or proprietary hardware	Novell	IBM PS/2 model 30/286 , Tandy 1000, Zenith, Atari ST	K-adult	K-adult
Computer Networking Specialist, Inc.	8 years	$4-5 million	IBM PS/2 model 70 or 80, Macintosh, or Network proprietary hardware	Novell, Appletalk, Digicard, LanTECH, Velan, Corvus	Apple IIe, IIGS, IBM PS/2 model 25, Tandy 1000, or compatibles	K-adult	K-adult
Computer Systems Research, Inc.	15 years	$6 million	IBM PS/2 model 60 or 80	Novell or ICLAS	IBM PS/2 model 25	K-12	K-12
Ideal Learning Systems	8 years	$2-3 million	Macintosh, IBM PC AT, or networks proprietary hardware	Appletalk, Digicard, LanTECH Velan, Corvus	Apple IIe, IIGS	1-12	1-adult
Innovative Technologies in Education	2 years	$3-5 million	proprietary hardware	proprietary network	MS-DOS, dumb terminal, or proprietary terminal	1-8	2-10
Jostens Learning Corp.	1 year (merger of 2 older companies	$85 million	MS-DOS or Macintosh-based CD-ROM	Novell, Appletalk	IBM PS/2 model 25, Tandy 1000SL or Apple IIGS	1-8	1-9
MECC	15 years (ILS products are less than 1 year)	n/a ($10 million company-wide)	Macintosh or network's proprietary hardware	Appletalk, Digicard, Velan, Corvus	Apple IIe, IIGS	1-6	K-6
New Century Education Corp.	17 years	n/a	IBM PS/2 model 30/286, Tandy, or compatibles	Novell	IBM PS/2 model 25, Tandy, or compatibles	1-8	K-10
The Roach Organization	1 year	$12-20 million	MS-DOS 386	Novell	MS-DOS	3-14	3-12
Unisys Corp.	40 years (ILS division 8 years)	$33 million	Unisys PW2-800	proprietary network	ICON II	K-adult	K-9
Wasatch Education Systems	10 years	$7-10 million	MS-DOS 286	Novell	MS-DOS	K-adult	K-adult
WICAT Education	10 years	$41 million	WICAT 1250, 2255, and 2275	ICLAS, ARCNET	IBM PC, PS/2 model 25, or Apple IIe (monochrome only)	K-adult	K-adult

Language Arts & Writing	Science	Social Studies	Foriegn Language	Computer Skills	Tool Skills	Special Population Served
3-adult	3-8			BASIC and other languages	word processing	AL, ESL, EC, SP, AR, CHP1, JTPA, GED
K-adult & process writing module	6-12	6-12	Spanish (6-12)		word processing	AR,SP, CHP1, AL, JPTA
K-12 & process writing module				Literacy, BASIC, and other languages	word processing	AL, AR, SP,ESL, CHP1, GED, JPTA
process writing module	4-6, H.S. physics		Spanish, German			JPTA, ESL, AL, AR, CHP1
3-10	9-12			Literacy, Pascal, BASIC, Logo	word processing, database	AL, EC, SP, AR, CHP1, JPTA
1-9 & research and process writing module (4-adult)	6-9					EC, SP, AR, CHP1
						AR, EC, AL, CHP1, JTPA
3-8					word processing	AL,AR, JTPA, GED, CHP1
3-12	9-14	9-12		Literacy, Pascal, and other languages		AL, AR, JTPA, GED, CHP1
K-adult & process writing module	K-adult	K-adult	French (K-adult)	BASIC, Logo, Pascal, and other languages	word processing, database, spreadsheet	AR, AL, ESL, CHP1, JTPA
K-adult				Literacy, Logo	wordprocessing, database	CHP1, AR, AL, ESC, GED, JTPA
K-adult	9-12	9-12	French (6-12)	Literacy (6-12)	word processing	AR, CHP1, GED, SP, AL, ESL, JPTA

Key for "special populations served" column

AL= adult literacy
ESL= English as a second languag
EC=Early childhood
SP= special education
AR= at risk
CHP1= Chapter 1 students
GED= General equivalency degree cources
JTPA= Job Training Partnership Act

Article # 7
Integrated Learning Systems/Instructional Networks: Current Uses and Trends

By
CHARLES L.
BLASCHKE

In 1989, Education TURNKEY Systems, Inc. (TURNKEY), conducted a study of the current and projected use of integrated learning systems (ILSs) and instructional local area networks for the Education Committee of the Software Publishers Association. The study sample included 22 school districts, of which 4/5ths had enrollments greater than 25,000 students; all were experienced users of ILSs and/or networks. Many districts are considered trend-setters and early adopters in the use of technology in education. Many findings from this study were generally corroborated by other, more recent studies of ILSs by TURNKEY for other private clients.

For purposes of this survey, an integrated learning system was defined as a local area network using a comprehensive instructional management system with more than half of the curriculum courseware published and sold by the ILS vendor. ILSs used by districts in the survey included Computer Curriculum Corporation (CCC), Education Systems Corporation (ESC), ICON, PLATO, Wasatch, and WICAT, among others; networks included Corvus, DigiCard, Lan-Tech, and Novell; and network vendors and VARs included CNS, Ideal Learning, and Prescription Learning. Nine districts were heavy networks users; six districts used both networks and ILSs; and seven were primarily ILS users.

Findings

The number of network installations has grown faster over the last year than the number of ILS installations; network expansion has been more *steady* within districts than ILS growth, even though the number of work stations with a typical ILS configuration has increased. The large increase in ILS installations in 1988, as reported in the education press, was somewhat misleading in that many installations were *pilot demonstrations,* some of which were discontinued after districts made their final selections.

While generalizations from this small study must be made with caution, there are a number of *school district characteristics* which appear to be associated with ILS versus network use. Districts that select ILSs tend to have one or more of the following characteristics:

- emphasis on centralized decision making where board members or superintendents exert great influence and
- a policy which emphasizes quality control, accountability for student performance, and assurance that mandated curricula will be covered uniformly.

Districts that are more likely to select networks:

- emphasize decentralized decision making and site management;

280

- promote teacher "professionalism"; and
- have central office or school-based technical capabilities to install, customize, and support a network configuration.

The *major reasons* for districts selecting networks or a mix of networks and ILSs include:
- improving student performance and achievement;
- reducing disk management problems;
- improving instructional management, monitoring, and reporting; and
- providing flexibility to modify the configuration (add or delete instructional courseware) and otherwise customize the configuration to school or classroom needs.

The primary reasons for selecting ILSs include improving student achievement and providing increased quality control over the instructional process. Generally, districts do *not* perceive networks or ILSs as a means of *saving software costs*. Nor do they feel that networks or ILSs will allow them to use existing hardware, thus "reducing" purchase costs.

The *current use* of networks differs in important respects from the use of ILSs. For example, districts with large numbers of networks and some ILSs (mixed districts):
- use network configurations to teach primarily math, reading, and writing, followed mostly by a number of other content areas and other tool applications; and
- typically have 20 to 25 work stations in a laboratory.

The vast majority of ILS use is at the elementary level, with more than 80 percent of ILS usage in reading/language arts and mathematics—usually in Chapter 1 or related programs.

The *selection process* of ILSs is generally more lengthy and complex than for networks. ILS selection usually involves the following steps:
- The District Superintendent or Assistant Superintendent for Curriculum/Instruction creates a central office committee, which reviews existing research studies and literature on various ILSs.
- Site visits to demonstration sites may be conducted.
- Selected vendors are invited to install pilot demonstrations in one school for between one week and six months.
- An evaluation committee, usually including teachers and subject area specialists, evaluates the different pilot demonstrations, applying a detailed checklist of criteria which focus primarily on curriculum fit and quality.
- The evaluation committee recommends one or more of the configurations.
- A big specification is sent to all recommended vendors or the district initiates negotiations with the selected vendor.

The *selection process* for network configuration usually is much shorter, with the primary focus on: (a) technical considerations (e.g., will selected third-party publishers' software execute on the network?); and (b) customization issues (e.g., is the network configuration capable of meeting building or classroom needs?). In many instances, the bid specifications include a requirement that specific software from various publishers be delivered on the file server.

Selection criteria for both ILSs and networks focus primarily on software, including:
- the extent to which the proposed courseware matches district curriculum objectives, frameworks, and inte-

gration of critical thinking skills into content areas;

- the technical soundness of the proposed configuration (e.g., access speed);
- the quality and capacity of the proposed instructional management system; and
- the degree to which the proposed configuration meets teaching staff needs.

The *key decision makers* for selecting ILSs include the superintendent, director of appropriate subject area, district technology coordinator, and director of elementary/secondary programs. The primary individual influencing the selection of networks is the technology coordinator who narrows the choices, with the final selection usually being made by the technology coordinator and a school-based committee, usually including teachers.

The *funding sources* for purchases of ILSs and networks by districts in our sample vary considerably. In ILS-using districts, the primary source is Chapter 1 (approximately one-third of ILS funding), followed by JTPA and special funds (e.g., business partnership grants, desegregation funds). In mixed districts, almost two-thirds of funding comes from the regular operating budget, followed by Chapter 11 and Chapter 1 funding. In network districts, primary funding sources include the regular operating budget (40 percent) and special funds (40 percent), followed by Chapter 1. We estimate that more than half of the ILS-using districts across the country use some of their regular operating budget for ILS purchases. While the number of network installations has increased steadily from year to year, purchases of ILSs are more sporadic—usually with large purchases occurring one year and expansion of work stations for existing configurations for two to three subsequent years.

In addition to purchasing hardware, courseware, and network software, about half of the districts also purchased *hardware maintenance, staff training, and software support* services from a vendor for the initial one or two years. Network or mixed districts are much more likely than ILS districts to have district staff select network software, reformat instructional software where necessary, and provide hardware maintenance, staff training, and software support.

The *implementation* problems reported by districts also varied. Network-using districts noted the following: (a) lack of availability of desired software to execute on the selected network; (b) time, effort, and technical problems associated with reformatting instructional software; (c) time and effort in negotiating with publishers/vendors and after installation getting sound technical assistance; and (d) inadequate teacher training. A variety of problems (e.g., pricing, flexibility, annual software support fee) were uniquely associated with specific ILS vendors.

Software *purchasing/licensing practices* vary significantly among the districts and among the vendors and publishers whose software products are used on ILSs or networks. Approximately half of the respondents indicated that software was licensed on an individual school basis. Approximately one-third reported district-wide licenses (particularly with MECC), with some districts reporting licenses per work station or file server. Network license prices per school or file server were two to five times the retail price of a single package.

Perceptions and Trends

The *philosophy* of school district Superintendents and other key decision makers will continue to be critical in the selection of ILSs and networks. Districts with a philosophical bent toward centralized decision making, quality control, and uniformity of curriculum with strong accountability policies focusing on student achievement will tend to select ILSs. Districts that have decentralized decision making and budgeting to the school building level, emphasize teacher professionalism, and wish to ensure flexibility will gravitate toward networks.

While both ILSs and networks will continue their current rates of *growth* over the next two to three years, the growth of network configurations will be steady and increase at all levels in a variety of content areas, including math, science, and tool applications. ILS growth will continue sporadically within a given district with the primary focus on Chapter 1 programs, basic skills, adult literacy, and school-operated JTPA programs.

The average number of work stations per network *configuration* will grow from 20 to approximately 30 over the next two years, while a typical ILS configuration of 15 will increase to approximately 25 over the same time period. District officials believe laboratory configurations will increasingly give way to "pod" configurations, where four to eight computer stations are placed in individual classrooms because: (a) pods are educationally sound and assist in integrating technology, particularly tool applications, across curriculum areas; (b) school buildings have limited space for laboratories; (c) costs for aides/lab managers will be prohibitive; (d) advances in networking technology will provide increased capacity for pod configurations; and (e) new regulations for Chapter 1 and special education encourage pod rather than pullout laboratory configurations.

School districts will increasingly de-

mand *district-wide licenses* from publishers for use of their software in network configurations and will negotiate school-based licenses with ILS vendors. Most district officials believe that the software cost per user will remain about the same or be reduced slightly through district-wide licenses. However, they also believe such licenses will reduce administration and monitoring problems and provide greater flexibility.

Over the next two years, districts with a technology office—with strong technical capabilities—will continue to do initial network customization, including software reformatting, installation, and follow-up maintenance for network configurations. Those without such capabilities will rely on the network vendors. On the other hand, districts will continue to purchase from ILS vendors (as part of the initial contract): customization, installation, training, and (to a lesser extent) hardware maintenance support. Software support contracts will increasingly be limited to those areas in which software upgrades are likely to occur (e.g., word processing).

Over the next two years, districts will also increasingly demand flexibility and openness (e.g., the use of popular tool applications), particularly in ILS configurations. Both network and ILS vendors will be required to either do curriculum correlations or demonstrate how their product meets mandated curriculum objectives; where gaps exist, ILS vendors will be required to include appropriate third-party instructional software or other media formats.

Districts will increasingly seek ILS programs and/or third-party networkable software which develops world-of-work and critical thinking skills, operates in a HyperText/LinkWay environment with CD-ROM or other optical media, and is discovery—as well as remedial-based.

Most district respondents believe that two or three networks will evolve as *industry standards* in education over the next two years. The network systems mentioned most frequently included Novell, Corvus, AppleTalk, and DigiCard—in that order. Responding district officials identified barriers to the expanded use of ILSs and/or networks, including:

- high recurring costs in the form of annual software support fees and salaries for laboratory managers to operate ILSs;
- the lack of teacher "ownership," particularly in ILS installations, where top-down marketing occurred;
- the lack of independent, objective research demonstrating improved student performance through the use of ILSs or networks;
- the perceived lack of a common management system which allows different instructional software from different publishers to be used;
- time and effort to prepare (e.g., reformatting) and install (e.g., cabling) networks;
- high initial funding outlays and inflexible pricing arrangements for ILSs and, to some extent, networks;
- the lack of software designed for networks; and
- the general lack of standards regarding networks and software licensing policies.

Industry Trends

In response to market pressures and other factors, a number of important trends appear to be surfacing within the industry.

First, a number of ILS vendors (e.g., Wasatch) are actively seeking quality third-party software that can be integrated into ILS courseware offerings to make them more comprehensive and complete. Some network vendors (e.g., CNS) are developing proprietary software to meet the needs of specific niche markets. In reality, the distinction between ILS vendors and network vendors will become increasingly blurred over the next two years.

Second, most ILS vendors are exploring and/or planning the use of multimedia and CD-ROM technology as part of their systems. The potential for multimedia in job counseling, ESL programs, work place literacy, and related programs is extremely high. In addition, several leading ILS vendors are considering on-line access to data bases (e.g., weather reports) tied to existing lesson plans through telecommunications networks.

Third, market analysts have projected increased sales for ILSs/networks over the next three years, to increase from approximately $175 million to over $300 million in the K-12 regular education market. While most sales will remain in Chapter 1 remedial programs, growth is also expected in regular mainstream programs, with a particular focus on math and science. The above projection for the regular K-12 market depends on important assumptions about the degree to which ILSs, in fact, will demonstrate significant student gains.

Recent market research conducted by TURNKEY projects even greater rates of growth in such emerging growth markets as JTPA remediation programs, correctional education/GED and education programs, community college remediation programs, and parent-child literacy programs. While these programs are heavily dependent upon Federal funding, the likelihood that such funding will become available is high, even if the economy takes a downturn; the prospects for ILSs and networks in these markets remain very bright indeed.

By
Richard
Alan
Smith
and
Susan
Sclafani

The hot new topic in the school computer world is the use of integrated teaching systems (ITS). Simply defined, these are turnkey computer systems that provide for instruction in several subject areas and include the production of reports on student progress.

The instruction offered by these systems is usually distributed to a class of students via computer terminals or through a network of microcomputers. Integrated teaching systems are generally characterized by providing what is considered "individualized instruction."

Incidentally, until recently, these systems have generally been identified as integrated learning systems. However, since integrated learning systems do not actually learn anything themselves, but rather participate in the teaching process, they are more accurately referred to as integrated teaching systems. After all, does the system learn students, or does it *teach* students?

Lately it seems that a superintendent or computer coordinator can hardly get through the day without being deluged with information from its vendors about the benefits of their system. It is also a common phenomenon to find that teachers who are loaned integrated teaching systems "for evaluation purposes" fall immediately in love with them and are loath to give them up (no matter whose product they are using).

For instance, we have found that integrated teaching systems generally tend to be very well accepted by the teacher-users and by the administrators of the various schools in which the systems are placed. The popularity of the various systems persists even though some of them have suffered serious hardware and/or software failures. In fact, at evaluation sites, some folks are ready to purchase even before the evaluations of their systems are complete.

It is obvious that felt needs on the part of teachers and administrators are being met by the ITSs. Most likely, it is the need to have some of the work load reduced and the satisfaction of seeing the students' attention fixed for the length of a class period on the instruction they receive.

However, the purchase of an integrated teaching system is a "big ticket item." Therefore the decision to buy or not to buy cannot be made solely on "gut feeling." Since each of the integrated teaching systems presently in our district differs in the content presentation of the instruction offered, we have found that any meaningful ITS comparison should consider a number of factors. The following list, derived from those factors, will be helpful to you if you are ever placed on a committee formed to consider the purchase of an instructional teaching system:

Did you clearly identify the problem that the ITS is supposed to solve?

An integrated teaching system is a solution to a problem in your school system. However, without defining the problem (low achieving students, low achieving teachers, inadequate curricu-

285

lum, and so on) these is no reason to believe that the solution that you are purchasing will actually address the specific problem troubling your district.

Do you have an understanding of the instructional theory upon which the ITS is based?

If we do not consider the theory behind the instruction that we offer our students we do our students, and ourselves, a disservice. After all, it is entirely possible that teaching the same subject according to two conflicting theories of education (for example discovery learning used by the teacher, and direct instruction used by the ITS) may be actually counterproductive. In effect, the possibility exists that such a course of action may reduce or negate the intended instruction or even contribute to a negative learning effect on the part of the students.

> If we do not consider the theory behind the instruction that we offer our students we do our students, and ourselves, a disservice.

However, instructional theory is rarely stated by the various producers of the integrated teaching systems. In place of a detailed explanation of instructional theory are such phrases as, "meets individual needs," "taught in a developing sequence based on prerequisite mastery," "designed by educators," "offers performance-based instruction," and so on.

The bottom line that you must carefully question the ITS vendor as to what instructional theory the curriculum offered is built upon. A determination of the instructional theory should be your starting point as to whether or not a particular system should even be considered.

Are the systems you are considering open or closed?

This point is related to the question of instructional theory used. We identify closed integrated teaching systems as those that provide direct instruction for 80% or more of the curriculum of a given course. The WICAT System is a good example of a closed system.

Other ITS systems have a different format. We call these open systems. Open integrated teaching systems provide a shell for the organization of the curriculum material already available in a school, be it software, books, films, or other resources.

In open systems, rather than receiving a large amount of direct instruction from the system students are directed to a variety of resources available in the school. The Prescription Learning System is a good example of an open system. Open systems range from those that direct students to a variety of software products, to those that direct students to a variety of resources in general.

Is the scope and sequence of the curriculum offered adequate for your needs?

Most of the ITS vendors sell systems that support mathematics, reading, writing, and language arts. The differences come at the grade levels for which the software is offered and in the order of the objectives selected for teaching.

One vendor may offer support in a subject area from K-12, while another may offer it only for 9-12. Even within one company's offerings there may be differences in the grade levels of software available.

In addition, many of the ITS companies have offerings in areas such as basic skills, General Education Diploma, and life skills. These too differ in scope, emphasis, and sequence, and it should not be accepted on faith that they will cover all of your instructional needs.

Are you targeting the ITS for the correct students?

Some systems are designed for use with general student populations. Other systems have specifically been designed for remediation, while others are aimed at advanced students. It is reasonable to assume that you would get the greatest amount of benefit from a system used with the student population for which it was designed. Another way of saying this is that no one system can meet all the needs of all your students.

Keep in mind that, in general, the kind of instruction offered by any one particular system (its instructional theory) does not vary. Only the pace and level of instruction varies. If, for example, you buy into the theory of learning styles, you might want to consider how your students' learning styles will interact with the kind of instruction offered by the ITS under consideration.

Is the management and reporting system adequate?

Virtually every ITS offers a system of testing students, placing students at their appropriate academic levels, and reporting their progress after receiving instruction. The part of the ITS that accomplishes these functions is known as the management and reporting system.

However, management and reporting systems vary in the way that students are tested and placed, and in the kinds of reports offered regarding students' progress. For example, some systems place students and track their progress through the use of off-line tests, while others test students completely on-line, automatically placing students at what is determined to be their proper levels. Several ITSs feature a great deal of teacher intervention in the sequence of lessons offered, and the students' placement in that sequence.

Can you afford the hardware and associated costs?

Hardware needs vary with the system under consideration. In general, most of these systems will allow you to use their software on networks of MS-DOS computers (such as IBM or Tandy), one of the family of Apple II computers, or the Atari family of computers.

It is also possible to have the option of using a system with terminals linked to a host computer, all offered under the brand name of the company selling the ITS. That makes the system all very neat and clean. However, if the company selling the system goes out of business, you will be locked into a system that is difficult to upgrade or to use with new software.

Be sure to add to the costs for the terminals or computer stations the price of the hard disk drive to store the software, a backup system, printers, cabling, new electrical installation (networks have special requirements), teacher training, and hardware maintenance. Also, many of the integrated instructional systems work best with a teacher aide to manage the system (some schools simply identify a teacher to take over this function).

In addition to software costs that can be as high as $60,000 or more above the hardware costs, most integrated instructional systems also require a yearly licensing fee that can range from $5,000 to $30,000 for a laboratory with 30 stations. These last two items, the aide and the licensing fee, are very good examples of "hidden costs." These kinds of unanticipated costs can destroy otherwise carefully planned budgets.

The bottom line is that the initial price for an ITS laboratory of 30 stations can range from about $60,000 to the area of $170,000 (hardware and software only), with yearly costs in the area of $20,000 to $45,000 (licensing fee and salary for a laboratory aide). It makes you stop and think, doesn't it?

What educational benefits do you hope to gain?

By far, the indicator of educational benefits most often cited by the vendors of integrated instructional systems are gains on standardized tests made by students already using the system. In general, after reading the ITS ads one would think that students' scores would increase uniformly after study with any of the systems. However, it ain't necessarily so.

A recently released study (Swann et al., 1989) done for the New York City Board of Education concerned the effect of ITSs with disadvantaged students. The researchers found that any positive effects of these systems as a measured by two tests, the Metropolitan Achievement Test (MAT) for math performance and the Degrees of Reading Power (DRP) for reading achievement, varied with the system used, the kinds of students, and the grade level of students using the system. There were also differences within the same systems between the reading and mathematics scores.

In this study it was also found that some systems for particular groups of students in certain subject areas actually produced negative results. The kids learned less than they would have using just the teacher in the classroom. Interestingly, some of the strongest effects were found for an open system that involved teachers to a great extent in the integrated instruction.

Accordingly, when considering the amount of gain on standardized tests implied by the vendors, double check and see how much academic gain the vendor actually guarantees that your students will demonstrate after using the system for a trial period. Then see if you get your money back if your students fail to achieve at the level promised!

In Conclusion

When considering the use of an integrated teaching system, be sure to define the instructional problem you are trying to solve. Also, identify the level of involvement with the system required of the teachers. The level of involvement will be a reflection of the amount of preparation and training for teachers that will be required.

You should, of course, note in advance how much are you willing to pay for the benefits promised and the kind of alternative solutions to the problem that may also be available to your district at an equal or lower cost. Alternative computer-based solutions can include computer laboratories dedicated to developing writing ability, laboratories with tool software such as databases, spreadsheets, word processors, and statistical programs, and computers integrated directly into classroom teaching.

In any event, take nothing for granted. Know your instructional needs and the solutions available to satisfy those needs. Integrated teaching systems can be of

> In any event, take nothing for granted. Know your instructional needs and the solutions available to satisfy those needs.

benefit if intelligently applied to a particular problem. Otherwise they will be an expensive solution in search of a problem.

Reference

Swann, K., Guerrero, F., Mitrani, M., & Schoener, J. (1989, March). *Honing in on the target: Who among the educationally disadvantaged benefits most from what CDI?* American Educational Research Association Annual Conference, San Francisco.

Dr. Richard Alan Smith, Director of Computer Curriculum, and Dr. Susan Sclafani, Assistant Superintendent of Educational Program Planning, Houston Independent School District, 3830 Richmond Ave., Houston, TX 77027; 713/892-6150.

Companies Offering Integrated Teaching Systems and Related Products

Autoskills, **Unisys Corporation**
P.O. Box 500, MS B330
Blue Bell, PA 19424
215/542-4583

CCC Microhost, **Computer Curriculum Corporation**
700 Hansen Way
P.O. Box 10080
Palo Alto, CA 94303-0812
800/227-8324

CNS, **Computer Networking Specialists, Inc.**
Route 1, Box 286-C
Walla Walla, WA 99362
509/529-3070

DEGEM CAI Systems, **DEGEM Ltd.**
Two Park Avenue
New York, NY 10016-5635
212/561-7200

Dolphin Curricula, **Houghton Mifflin Company**
Mount Support Road
Lebanon, NH 03766
603/448-3838

ESC's Integrated Learning System **Jostens Learning Corporation***
6170 Cornerstone Court East
Suite 300
San Diego, CA 92121-3710
800/548-8372

ICON Series, **Unisys Corporation**
P.O. Box 500, MS B330
Blue Bell, PA 19424
215/542-4583

Ideal Learning Systems, **Ideal Learning Inc.**
5005 Royal Lane
Irving, TX 75063
214/929-4201

Local Plato Delivery, **Control Data Corporation**
BCLW3A
PLATO Education Services
8800 Quenn Avenue South
Bloomington, MN 55126
800/228-3504

MECC Management Master, **MECC**
3490 Lexington Avenue, N.
St. Paul, MN 55126
800/228-3504

Prescription Learning Laboratory **Jostens Learning Corporation***
6150 N. 16th Street
Phoenix, AZ 85016
602/230-7030

WASATCH Education System
5250 South 300 West
Suite 350
Salt Lake City, UT 84107
801/261-1001

WICAT System
P.O. Box 539
Orem, UT 84057
801/224-6400

*The Integrated Learning System and the Prescription Learning Laboratory were formerly offered by two separate companies, ESC and the Jostens Company. Jostens purchased ESC, and the name of the resulting company is Jostens Learning Corporation.

Alternatives to Integrated Instructional Systems

Introduction

At the core of the recent popularity of Integrated Instructional Systems (IISs) is the conviction among politicians, business leaders, various commissions and educators that our present educational strategies are not working for that considerable segment of the school population regarded as "at-risk." However, while there is little disagreement that our educational system is facing problems of unprecedented proportions, many of us are not convinced that offering so-called "at-risk" students a steady diet of IIS no fail, "instant education bytes" will either whet their appetites for learning or develop their minds in ways that will assure them, or our nation, of future success.

This paper will strongly criticize Integrated Instructional Systems as being an inappropriate use of computers with students at risk, as well as being wasteful of limited computer resources in schools. It will further criticize the top-down manner in which these systems are being implemented in many school districts. It will then propose alternative models of computer-facilitated education for all students, including those at risk.

The IIS Phenomenon

A careful analysis of confidential sales figures from the educational computing industry suggests that school spending on computer software and hardware has more than doubled over the past two years. Moreover, these figures show that this increase is due primarily to the purchase by cities and large school districts of comprehensive computer managed instructional systems, commonly known as Integrated Learning Systems.* This analysis also reveals the fact that the funding for these purchases often comes from a variety of federal programs aimed at so-called "children at risk."

Led by the Jostens Learning Corporation (the combination of Prescription Learning and Educational Systems Corporation), more than a dozen IIS companies** are estimated to have sold in excess of two hundred million dollars in software alone in 1989. This amount equals the amount spent on non-IIS software from all other sources. Add to this a nearly equal amount spent on hardware to support the IIS software. For 1990, if we also add annual maintenance fees and a rapidly increasing number of these installations, it would appear that IIS-related purchases this year will exceed half a billion dollars.

Although there is considerable variation in curriculum focus, pedagogy, and age-range served among the various IISs, it is clear from private discussions with both buyers and sellers of IISs that their fundamental appeal to school administrators is the provision, in most cases, of: a computer-managed comprehensive basic skills training program for at-risk students that is run largely as a pull-out program in which every child spends 45

By Peter Kelman, Ed.D.

291

minutes to an hour every day; a plethora of accountability-oriented computer generated reports for each child, class, school, etc.; a single vendor for purchasing, technical support and staff training; and, in the case of Jostens, even assistance with funding the purchase through arranged financing and/or help in drawing up politically attractive bond proposals.

While representatives of the various IIS companies will undoubtedly claim that one or another of the characteristics just cited does not apply to their product, this overall description of their appeal to district administrators remains accurate. This can be ascertained by analyzing where the majority of IIS installations are (elementary schools in districts that emphasize central decision-making, accountability, and uniform coverage of mandated curricula) and observing how they are used (primarily to teach basic math and language arts skills). (Software Publishers Association, 1990.)

Some lessons from the history of Integrated Instructional Systems

Many of us who have been involved in educational reform efforts over the past 25 years and in educational computing for the past ten years, are painfully aware of the dangers of the kind of quick-fix technological solutions for complex education problems represented by the current generation of Integrated Instructional Systems and their forerunners, mainframe-based CAI. We are particularly wary of such technological fixes being applied to those children who most need a quality education. Thus, we are troubled by the rate at which many big city and large district administra-

tors appear to be rushing to spend enormous amounts of money on IISs, despite these systems' narrow focus on rudimentary basic skills, which in isolation are unlikely to prepare students for real success in life.

Further, many of us who are advocates of educational computing worry that the current enthusiasm for IISs will soon turn to disillusionment, to the detriment of all educational computing. This is precisely what occurred in the late 1960s and early 1970s. In 1972, the Educational Testing Service carried out a study to determine why educators at that time had not been particularly enthusiastic about the use of computers in education. (Anastasio et al., 1972) The study concluded that the principal reasons were: their high cost, the unreliability of the technology, and the inadequacy of teacher training. Also mentioned as factors in the study were educators' skepticism about results and negative feelings about computers dehumanizing education.

That study was based on educator reaction to the only use of computers in education at that time, which were IIS-like CAI systems, yet the conclusion drawn by many educators, politicians and the media for years to come was that computers, in general, were not effective or appropriate for use in schools. As a result, throughout the 1970s there was very little administrative support or funding for computer use in schools despite the availability of a number of mainframe and later minicomputer based CAI programs, including CCC, PLATO, and Time Share Corporation's (later acquired by Houghton-Mifflin) Dolphin System. Those systems, the progenitors of today's IISs, were bought in small numbers almost exclusively with federal funding targeted for the "disadvantaged."

Fortunately, the advent of stand-alone microcomputers in 1979 revealed and stimulated interest in a whole range of possible uses of computers in education beyond CAI, including motivational learning games, student and teacher productivity tools such as word processors, spreadsheets, etc., database activities, simulations, telecommunications, creativity and publishing tools, and much more. And, although, as with all use of computers in schools, there are really no reliable studies showing conclusively that any of those computer applications have a long-term ameliorative effect on test scores, there is little doubt in the minds of millions of teachers, students, and parents that such uses of computers enrich their learning and their lives.

Recently, however, with the increasing technical reliability of local area networking (LAN), many schools are linking their stand-alone microcomputers, primarily to achieve certain managerial and administrative goals. In itself, such use of networking can have positive effects on education, in particular more cost-effective limited hardware and software resources. Nevertheless, some of us worry that in too many schools networking is being used to turn back the clock, to reduce stand-alone microcomputer use and functionality to that of a terminal on a mainframe computer.

This is precisely the mode in which most IISs use computers. In the typical Jostens IIS installation, for example, short, focused student lessons are slowly downloaded from a central CDROM to a microcomputer workstation in advance of the student's arrival in the computer lab. The student completes the lesson in isolation and the "results" (e.g. time on task, progress through the lesson, items answered correctly/incorrectly, number of tries, etc.) are sent to an instructional management system and stored in a student file on a hard disk.

This is fundamentally the way the early mainframe-based CAI programs worked, except that all processing, as well as storage, was handled by the mainframe. In fact, some of today's IISs, such as CCC and PLATO are merely microcomputer versions of the original mainframe programs developed in the 1960s and 1970s. Others, such as WICAT and Wasatch, were originally developed for minicomputers or proprietary microcomputer hardware, but have recently been adapted for use with today's popular microcomputers. And even the Jostens IIS, although developed from the outset as a network-based system that would run on low-end Apple and MS-DOS machines, owes more philosophically to its mainframe progenitors than to the educational applications of computers that have driven educational computing throughout the 1980s.

Indeed, IISs use computers in exactly the same way that the ETS study found to be unpopular with educators in the early 1970s, and it is our fear that when educators determine that today's IISs are similarly ineffective and inappropriate, there will one again be a backlash against all computer use in education. Already, some administrators are beginning to realize that the on-going high costs of these systems may not be justified by the modest short-term score gains they appear to engender.

A Brief Critique of Studies of IIS Effectiveness

In making their sales presentations, some IIS companies contend that "the research" has shown their systems to be effective in, among other things, raising test scores. However, according to EPIE:

EPIE would have liked to have been able to include results of independently conducted, longitudinal, quantitative studies of IISs. Unfortunately, EPIE was unable to identify a body of such studies. This finding is confirmed by Dr. Henry J. Baker of Johns Hopkins University, an expert in research and evaluation methodology, who has investigated several studies to see if any meet the requirements of scientific design. To date, he has not identified any that meet this criterion (p.i.3, Sherry, 1990).

Similarly, this author has read and analyzed virtually every study cited by IISs to bolster their sales argument and has found them all to be unpersuasive.

First, a large number of the studies cited were commissioned by, or done in close cooperation with one or another of the IIS companies, and hence are suspect from the outset. Second, the claims made by representatives of some of the IIS companies regarding the results of such studies are, for the most part, not even supported by the studies themselves; this is especially true where results are too weak to be considered statistically significant or where the experimental design does not permit drawing the conclusion claimed.

Indeed, few of these studies were carried out under an experimental design that could validly determine the effectiveness of the IIS treatment. Thus, even those few studies that detected short-term test score gains cannot prove that the IIS treatment was responsible for these gains. For example, many of the studies were carried out on children in the primary grades, a period when test score gains would be expected to result from ordinary cognitive development.

Further, in most of these studies, no attempt was made to control for other treatments, including the rest of the school program, which for many of the students undoubtedly included other "at-risk" interventions.

Moreover, the design of those studies in which gains might be attributable to IIS treatment fails to isolate variables within the IIS (e.g. computer use, instructional design, time on task, frequency of exposure, teacher involvement, etc.), so that it could just as easily be concluded, for example, that any daily systematic program of instruction could have yielded comparable gains.

Finally, given the relatively short period during which the current generation of IISs has been used, none of the studies can measure such long-term gains. Yet such gains are by far the most important, most desirable, and most elusive result of any "at risk" intervention.

In light of the criticisms offered above, it is unfortunate that representatives from many of the IIS companies insist upon citing these various studies to support their sales efforts, particularly for IIS use in at-risk programs. Ultimately, this tactic is likely to backfire, when post-IIS test results in these districts fail to meet expectations.

A Critique of IIS Philosophy of Educational Computing

In addition to doubts about costs and effectiveness, an increasing number of concerned educators, including this author, are expressing their doubts about the educational philosophy of most IISs. To us, IISs represent a step backwards, a retreat from the great process educational computing has made since the days of mainframe-based CAI. Moreover, they embody a model of education and educational decision-making that has persistently failed to attract the support of teachers and other educators since the late 1960s. As such, these systems are likely to fail once again. Our hope is that this failure will not adversely affect all of educational computing.

It is thus important to distinguish the underlying philosophy of educational computing of most IISs from that of the majority of computer-using educators, who have long since progressed beyond mere CAI. Let us begin this by contrasting certain basic assumptions of more progressive educational computing with those of most IISs.

1. Despite our enthusiasm for computer use in schools, most computer-using educators believe that education is, at base, a human endeavor. It is first and foremost an interaction between people (student-teacher and student-student). Machines can be useful as tools, but not as stand-in teachers.

Although IISs theoretically can be used to facilitate student-teacher interaction, in the vast majority of IISs, that is not the case. In most IIS installations, the students work at a remote lab, their IIS lessons are not connected with the on-going classroom instruction, and the classroom teacher has little or no contact with the student, except, perhaps, to receive a report of progress every few weeks. Indeed, many IIS sales representatives position their system as a constantly on-task, tireless instructor "who" will carry out instructional tasks that teachers can't or won't or don't. This is an offensive rationale for IIS use that most computer-using educators find to be both demeaning to teachers and antithetical to a view of education as fundamentally an interaction between people.

2. Most computer-using educators also believe that teachers and students should control computers, not be controlled by them. Computers can be powerful tools of productivity, creativity, and empowerment. All students and all teachers should be provided with access to and training in the use of such tools.

In contrast, most IISs consist of computer-assisted instruction (CAI) that is little more than an efficient and controlling way to train children to master low-level reading and arithmetic skills. Virtually all thoughtful critiques of the use of computers in education over the past 15 years have pointed to CAI as, at best, a marginally useful and largely trivial use of computing power. To that critique, we might add "irresponsible," even "dangerous."

Numerous educators over the past ten years have suggested that there is a clear danger that computers in education will exacerbate the already widening gulf between the advantaged and the disadvantaged (Papert, 1980; Coburn et al., 1985). Nowhere is that danger more evident than in the unfortunate attempt to train the disprivileged in low-level skills through CAI, while middle class children are encouraged to use computers in school and at home primarily as tools of creative expression, personal productivity and intellectual empowerment. This contrast is an indictment of our society, and should be a warning to well-meaning educators considering the use of IISs with their disadvantaged students.

3. Most computer-using educators believe that when decisions are made concerning computer use in schools, extreme care must be exercised so

that educational value is not sacrificed for bureaucratic convenience. Otherwise the children may suffer.

While it is true that networked environments are often easier to manage than labs filled with hundreds of floppy disks and numerous stand-alone computers that require individual booting of programs, there are many ways other than IISs in which to use such networks. (More on that below.) Further, although it may be an administrative dream to deal with one vendor who can supply all your needs: hardware, software, service, training, etc., it may turn out to be an educational nightmare when the curriculum is shallow, the pedagogy inappropriate, the student outcomes disappointing and the financial costs astronomical—with some IISs the cost can be up to $150,000 per 32 student installation.

> All too often IIS adoption is a knee-jerk reaction by an administrator under tremendous pressure.

4. Most computer-using educators have learned from painful experience that unless teachers are involved at all levels of decision making concerning computer use in schools, implementation of the computer program will likely fail. (Coburn et al., 1984) Moreover, in light of the recent move toward "school restructuring," it would appear to be politically unwise for district level administrators to impose major curriculum programs on their schools.

Yet this top-down decision making process is precisely how most IISs are being brought into schools. Despite the fact that such a process flies in the face of "site-based decision-making" and "teacher empowerment," in IIS adoption after adoption, teacher involvement is minimal and their decision-making role nil.

Based on even a cursory knowledge of the history of educational reform, it is difficult to imagine curricular programs of the magnitude and cost of IISs being accepted by teachers after being imposed on them from above. This is likely to be especially true of the very teachers who are already disposed toward using computers in schools. These are the technology leaders in the school, yet in most cases the IIS purchase decision-making process ignores their interests and expertise. Moreover, in all likelihood, the pedagogy of the IIS runs counter to their educational computing philosophy. And, perhaps, worst of all in their eyes, after the IIS purchase has been made, there will be very little money left for technology purchases for some time to come. Yet without teacher support, especially from the school technology leaders, it is inconceivable that IISs will succeed in achieving the goals for which they have been purchased.

Ten Dubious Reasons Why IISs are Being Bought: A Summary

If IISs represent as dismal a prospect as indicated so far, why are they being bought in such large numbers by large school districts? Below are briefly critiqued ten major reasons, some of which are laudable in intent, but all of which are flawed in practice:

1. The pressure on large district administrators to do something (!) about their at-risk students.

Critique: All too often IIS adoption is a knee-jerk reaction by an administrator under tremendous pressure. Technology solutions to problems happen to be particularly popular at this time. Unfortunately, ultimate disappointment in technology is often proportionate to initially unrealistic expectations for it.

2. The somewhat illusory appeal of one-stop shopping for all the district's computer-based instructional needs, including hardware, software, technical support and training.

Critique: Most schools with IISs find that, in addition to the high annual charges for IIS maintenance, they still must deal with other vendors for their non-IIS computer needs.

3. The misguided attempt to use local area networks to attain both instructional goals and various administrative goals such as reducing the burden of floppy disk maintenance, dealing with one hardware service contract, and eliminating illegal disk copying.

Critique: Buying an IIS to justify the purchase of a LAN to simplify computer management is a situation in which the tail will end up wagging the dog; there are plenty of legitimate, instructional uses of LANS other than IISs and at far lower costs, as will be detailed later (Gevirtz and Kelman, 1990).

4. The dubious prospect of a "teacher proof," computer-managed curriculum solution, implemented in computer labs run by low paid teaching assistants.

Critique: In IIS sites in which the classroom teacher is really not involved, the teacher's commitment to the IIS is virtually nil, and the value of the IIS to the students, beyond their fascination with any computer-based activity is questionable. Moreover, the use of teaching assistants, few of whom have any education training, often results in students spending time stuck on a lesson with no appropriate human help available.

5. The misleading claim by many IIS companies that theirs is a comprehensive, diagnostic-prescriptive system that will virtually guarantee significant test score gains.

Critique: Although some IISs do offer diagnosis and prescription, most do not, despite their claims. For example, in the most widely used system (Jostens), students are tested initially, and based on the test they are placed in a given lesson. However after that point, the student merely progresses through a fixed sequence of lessons. There is no on-going diagnosis and prescription; there is no branching or cycling back, based on problems encountered; there is no sophisticated error analysis; there is very little reteaching; indeed, if a student becomes stuck in a lesson, that fact may not be noticed until weeks later, when and if the report is perused by the classroom teacher. This is all very disturbing, particularly when one considers the price tag and the students served, those most at risk.

6. The appeal of federally funded "pull-out" programs that ease the burden of the classroom teacher, by reducing class size.

Critique: Pull-out programs are known to be of value when student learning in the program is reinforced in their regular classroom. If teachers are alienated by an IIS, this is unlikely to occur. Moreover, the children who are pulled out for computer time are also often the children who are pulled out for other "at risk" interventions. This has been known to disrupt the children's classroom learning and alienate them from their classmates and teacher.

7. A veritable cornucopia of reports to provide documentation for accountability from the classroom level through the district level.

Critique: In many IIS installations there are too many reports, many of which are difficult to understand or use, and most of which arrive too late to be really useful for the classroom teacher.

8. High powered, often misleading marketing and sales campaigns waged by the more well-heeled IIS companies, such as Jostens.

Critique: These campaigns often result in enormous district-wide purchases made at the top with virtually no site-based input or decision-making.

9. The siren call of any educational panacea, particularly a high tech solution, that will give the political appearance of a major commitment to education.

Critique: Historically, the administrator who has made the decision to buy into IISs is long gone by the time the disappointing results come in. When that occurs, the new administration is often stuck with throwing out the now useless software, and in the case of proprietary systems, the hardware as well.

10. Administrative decisions made in the absence of knowledge about viable alternative uses of computers in education.

Critique: Such decisions come about when knowledgeable computer-using educators at the school building level are not consulted, and when decisions are made by administrators who have not been immersed in educational computing over the years.

The remainder of this paper will address itself to this last point by briefly describing some of the more promising uses of computers in education that may be offered as alternatives to IISs. It is hoped that this section, in particular, will be read by district level administrators, who will view it as a starting point for a more careful and skeptical consideration of IIS adoption, one that will involve input and decision-making at all levels of the school district.

Computers as Facilitators of Higher Order Thinking Skills

Most thoughtful educators today recognize that unless children have the opportunity to develop the thinking structures necessary to process new information, all the basic skills training in the world will come to naught. Used creatively and appropriately, computers offer unique opportunities to provide children with interactive environments in which they can develop their higher-order thinking skills.

Numerous software publishers have

> Although some IIS companies claim to address higher-order thinking skills, in few of these cases do the claims stand up to scrutiny of their product.

for years published dozens of programs aimed at promoting student critical-thinking and problem-solving skills. These programs have been used by thousands of teachers with millions of children with great enthusiasm and success. Yet, almost without exception, the IISs eschew such approaches to facilitating higher-order thinking, in favor of CAI aimed at low-level basic skills. Although some IIS companies claim to address higher-order thinking skills, in few of these cases do the claims stand up to scrutiny of their product.

Today, schools wishing the administrative convenience of networking without buying into the narrow basic skill-focused IIS vision of education, can do so because most educational software publishers are making many of their stand-alone programs available in forms that will run on networks. This includes hundreds of programs aimed at facilitating student higher-order thinking skills. Even owners of most IISs can use (and indeed are using) such programs, either by installing them on the network alongside the IIS curriculum, or by booting stand-alone versions of these programs in the floppy disk drives at the student work station. It should be noted that in most cases, these IIS owners are doing so without the cooperation of the IIS companies, despite the fact that many of these companies advertise "third-party" compatibility.

One approach to using computers to promote higher-order thinking skills with at-risk students is particularly worth mentioning because it also emphasizes the importance of human interaction in a computer-mediated instructional setting. This approach is the Higher Order Thinking Skills (HOTS) Program developed by Dr. Stanley Pogrow of the University of Arizona (Pogrow, *Phi Delta Kappan*, 1990;

Pogrow, *Educational Leadership*, 1990; and numerous other papers and articles by Pogrow on HOTS). HOTS is not a software program; it is a method in which teachers use off-the-shelf software with children in particular ways that systematically build all-important critical-thinking skills.

HOTS uses computers and special teaching techniques, particularly Socratic dialogues between students and teachers, to develop student thinking and social skills, as well as to increase student self-esteem. The HOTS strategy is proactive, rather than remedial. Instead of reteaching an atomized series of out-of-context "basic skills" over and over again, HOTS provides students with the general conceptual skills that enable them then to learn and retain the complex ideas and information found in most curricula and to do so the first time they are taught—by their classroom teacher.

Implemented as a pull-out program with Chapter 1 and mildly impaired learning-disabled students in grades 4-6, HOTS has been validated by the National Diffusion Network. Among other documented successes, HOTS students are currently surpassing national averages for basic skills gains in reading and math, and some HOTS students have actually been rediagnosed as "gifted and talented." This is an especially remarkable result because HOTS does not explicitly teach basic reading and math skills; instead it teaches the underlying thinking skills that enable students to confidently handle new and unfamiliar educational and intellectual challenges they encounter in the classroom, on standardized tests, and in life. If there is any IIS program that has been able to match HOTS in terms of independently validated results that last over time, this author is unaware of it.

Computers as Vehicles for Creative Expression

Throughout society and in thousands of school across the country, computers are used as vehicles for creative expression. Computer-based paint, drawing, and printing programs are used by children to express themselves in the graphic arts. Computer-based music composition and performance programs enable students to explore their musical talents. Word processing, classroom publishing, and other writing-based programs provide students with power tools to express their thoughts and ideas in writing.

Yet, none of the IIS programs provide graphics or music programs, and only a few contain even a rudimentary text editor, let alone a child-appropriate word processing or publishing program. Worse, the use of most IISs to process children through endless sequences of CAI lessons chews up so much of a school's limited and precious computer time that there usually isn't room or time for the children to use creative computer tools in the relaxed and contemplative atmosphere such use requires. Thus, it is not enough that a school is able to buy stand-alone creativity programs to use alongside their IIS program, they must also re-prioritize so that students have the right kind of access and time to use these tools creatively.

Moreover, a school that wishes to supplement an IIS with computer-based creativity tools must reconfigure their computer workstations and on-line printers in such a way that individual students can save and print their products at or near their local workstations. In contrast, many IISs are set up so that all saving is to the file server (since all that is saved is records of student CAI activity) and all printing is to a remote and secure central printer (since all that is printed are reports of student CAI activity).

Computers as Tools of Personal and Professional Productivity

Our society, both in the work place and at home, has been transformed by the emergence in the last ten years of personal and professional productivity tools such as word processors, desktop publishing programs, database managers, and spreadsheets. This fact has been recognized by educators across the country for at least the past five years, as school after school has made these power tools available to their students in a variety of ways: many elementary school students learn the fundamentals of keyboarding and word processing, so they can write short stories and reports on the computer; many middle-school students add to their word-processing skills the experience of using content area databases to actually research interesting questions in social studies and science; at the secondary school level, many students also get the opportunity to use more quantitative productivity tools such as spreadsheets, statistical packages, and function plotters in their business, social studies and math courses; and desktop printing in schools has become so prevalent at all levels that it is often called "Classroom Publishing."

Yet, none of these tools is available on most IISs. Again, while it is possible with most IISs for a school to buy such programs, many of which are now available in network versions, and to use them side by side with the IIS, this is rarely done. Why? First, because the IIS chews up virtually all available computer time. And second, after investing sometimes hundreds of thousands of dollars in IISs, there is little money (or professional commitment) remaining for other software approaches. With that kind of investment, what administrator can afford to have the computers used for any other purpose, but the one aimed directly at improving test scores?

This may well be the most serious indictment of IISs, since it means that when computer resources are devoted to IIS training on traditional basic skills, the children, particularly those at risk, are being denied the opportunity to learn the productivity skills that they will need in their lives and in almost any line of work in the twenty-first century. This is not unlike the tragic situation in too many Vocational Educational programs in which the neediest students are taught outmoded vocational skills on outmoded equipment, thereby dooming them to the most menial, unskilled labor.

The Role of Computers in Cooperative Learning Environments

Collaborative learning is more than an educational buzzword. It is an educational reflection of the emerging work place of the 1990s. As a result of both technological advances and business practices, more and more offices and factories depend on their employees to work cooperatively on every aspect of a project. And, in the more forward-looking schools across the country, collaborative learning is both a means to and an end of many classroom activities.

Just as computers play a major role in collaborative activities in the work place, so too may they play such a role in collaborative education in the school. Two outstanding examples of this are The Kids Network, developed under a National Science Foundation grant by TERC in Cambridge, MA and Earth Lab, developed under various grants by the Bank Street College of Education in New York City.

The Kids Network, now published by National Geographic, has gotten so much press attention recently (e.g. White, 1989) that it will not be discussed here in detail. Suffice it to say that in this program students all across the country (and the world) collect real scientific data and send it via modem to real databases, where real scientists use it to study real phenomena. Talk about empowerment, collaborative learning, and developing real-world skills!

Earth Lab is still at the stage of being implemented at a single pilot site, the Ralph Bunche Intermediate School in West Harlem, N.Y. (Newman and Reece, in Sherry, 1990). There, both in two computer labs and in various classrooms, students, many of whom are severely at risk, work quietly and enthusiastically at Apple IIe and GS computers connected by either a Corvus or an AppleTalk network. On both network systems, teachers and students can communicate written materials, notes, assignments, etc. through an electronic mail feature built into *The Bank Street Writer III*. In addition, students work on science investigations in small groups and as a whole-school team, by pooling data they collect in "work spaces" that are specifically set up by project on the network to facilitate such collaborative learning activities. In this way, student learning and instruction emulate the workplace by organizing all activities around projects and problem solving, rather than as a sequence of disconnected skill lessons or individual software programs, selected from a network menu.

Students at Earth Lab can also play a real-time network-based simulation game with other students. Finally, they can access any one of the dozens of network-compatible educational programs or boot up stand-alone educational software on disk drives at the workstations. These selections may be student initiated or assigned by teachers, often by leaving an assignment in the student's mailbox, not as in many IISs by having a student locked into a lesson by the system.

Earth Lab is a dramatic example of how a network environment can be used to promote specific empowering educational objectives and at the same time be open enough to accommodate individual teacher priorities and individual student interest.

Computers as Multiple Modality Learning Environments

Beyond the rhetoric and marketing hype of educational "multimedia" is the important recognition that all children, especially today's MTV generation, learn through many different modalities. The technologies of interactive videodisc and CD-ROM, with other multimedia technologies to come, are now presenting educators with ways to provide multiple modality learning environments for their students. Nowhere is this opportunity more welcome than for students at risk.

This year, educators are being treated to a cornucopia of new multimedia products including: ABC Interactive's current events videodisc series with titles on Martin Luther King, the Holy Land, and Election 88; National Geographic's history videodisc product GTV, complete with a "map rap"; Scholastic Software's multimedia educational productivity tool *Point of View: The Scholastic History Professor*; and a number of multimedia

authoring systems like *Tutor Tech*, *HyperStudio*, and *HyperScreen*.

Even some of the IISs are getting in on the act, or at least they would like their prospective customers to think they are. Jostens co-funded the development of the Compton's Encyclopedia on CDROM and includes it on the network alongside their IIS. But, like Jostens' questionably appropriate use of CDROM to download their IIS lessonware, this use of technology is more marketing fluff than of educational value. At this time, only a few of the student stations can access the Compton's Encyclopedia. In fact, when you consider it, the cubicle-like environment of most networked labs is singularly inappropriate for most students to really use the Compton's Encyclopedia, given the priority of moving as many students as possible through their CAI lessons, en route to test score improvement for the largest possible number of students.

Moreover, the mere presence of the Compton's Encyclopedia on the network does not mean it will be used in any meaningful way. Unless it is built into the curriculum, unless teachers provide assignments for which students would need to use it, unless the publisher provides guidance for its use in varied settings, the Compton's Encyclopedia, as delivered by Jostens, will be little more than a marketing ploy.

In contrast, all the other multimedia products referred to earlier come complete with lesson plans, connections to the curriculum, and, most importantly, easy to use authoring tools that enable students and teachers to create their own multimedia reports, presentations, and lessons, using superb footage from these videodiscs and any others the school might own or acquire. Now that's empowerment!

Computers as a Means of Empowerment

Let us conclude by reaffirming the desirability of using computers in all schools in the ways they are used in society: to empower their users. This means that computers should be used as personal and educational productivity tools by teachers and students. A corollary to this goal is the view expressed in writing and in speeches by countless educational computing leaders, that it is a waste of computing power, financial resources, and human potential to use computers for endless lock-step atomistic CAI lessons.

Instead, computers should be used by teachers to write lesson plans, reports, handouts, notes to students and teachers, to comment on student written work and other forms of expression, to keep track of student progress in their classroom activities, to facilitate classroom presentations and demonstrations, to keep up with professional developments and share ideas with colleagues, etc.

Thus, teachers need a computer workstation, loaded with personal and professional productivity software, at their desks, linked via network, to student workstations in the classroom or lab. And they need a similar arrangement at home, linked to the school by modem. Is this vision too futuristic? Not if we regard it as a guiding vision that we can work toward gradually. Many of us prefer such a vision, even if it cannot be fully implemented today, to the spectre of IIS administrator-controlled, centralized, record-keeping systems with little or no direct access by teachers. Apparently, so do the major teachers' organizations, to judge from a number of Albert Shanker's recent speeches and the NEA's request for information from the hardware companies for an affordable teacher workstation, similar to that described above.

Like their teachers, students should have the opportunity to use computers to explore ideas, to analyze data, to write papers and stories, to receive and carry out written assignments, to research databases, to design, compose music, publish, plan, work with a team on projects, etc.

Thus, students should have almost constant access to a computer workstation in the classroom and the lab, linked via network, to a fileserver containing a vast array of productivity software, creativity software, wholesome recreational software, educational software, shared hardware resources, shared databases, telecommunications capabilities, and much more.

This vision is not futuristic in the least. All of this is possible and is in place today in schools that prefer this vision of education (and networking) to the narrow vision of computer labs filled with students working in 20 minute chunks of time on "byte-sized" lessonware, controlled by an impersonal lesson sequence, developed by a distant software publisher.

References

Anastasio, Ernest and Morgan, Judith; *Study of Factors that have Inhibited a More Widespread Use of Computers in the Instructional Process*; EduCom, Interuniversity Communications Council; 1972.

Coburn, et al.; *Practical Guide to Computers in Education*, Second Edition; Addison Wesley; 1985.

Gevirtz, Gila and Kelman, Peter; *The Scholastic Guide to Educational Computer Networks*; Scholastic; 1990.

Newman, Dennis, and Reece, Paul; *"Using a Local Area Network and Sharing Data,"* in Sherry; 1990.

Papert, Seymour; *Mindstorms: Children, Computers, and Powerful Ideas*; Basic Books; 1980.

Pogrow, Stanley; *"A Socratic Approach to Using Computers with At-Risk Students,"* in Educational Leadership; February 1990.

Pogrow, Stanley; *"Challenging At-Risk Students: Findings from the HOTS Program,"* in Phi Delta Kappan; January 1990.

Sherry, Mark; *EPIE Institute's Report on Computer-Based Integrated Instructional Systems*; 1990.

Software Publishers Association; *Education Vendors Survey On Present and Projected Use of Networkable Software and Integrated Learning Systems in Schools*; 1990.

White, Mary-Alice; *"Educators Must Ask Themselves Some Important Questions,"* in Electronic Learning; September 1989.

Wilson, Judy; *"Integrated Learning Systems: A Primer,"* in Classroom Computer Learning; February 1990.

Footnotes

* Integrated Learning System is a somewhat misleading term under which some of these systems are marketed in an attempt to focus the customer's attention on the learning that is supposed to occur when they are used. EPIE, in its study of these systems, argues persuasively that it is more accurate to call them Integrated Instructional Systems, since they do not possess the level of learner adaptiveness and other features that education's yet-to-be developed computer assisted *learning* systems will one day possess (p.i.l, Sherry, 1990). For the remainder of this paper, we will use the term Integrated Instructional Systems or IISs.

** The largest and/or oldest of these companies are Computer Curriculum Corporation (CCC), Computer Networking Specialists (CNC), Computer Systems Research (CSR), Ideal Learning Systems, Innovative Technologies in Education, New Century Education Corporation, The Roach Organization (formerly Control Data's PLATO system), Wasatch Education Systems, and WICAT Education (Wilson, 1990).

Classroom or Lab: How to Decide Which is Best

By
MICHAEL N.
MALONE, JR.

The microcomputer has been with us for ten years, and in that brief time, it has become a fixture in virtually every school in America. Most students receive at least some instruction with the aid of computers, and schools spend more than five dollars per student annually on educational software. Yet many of us who work with computers in education are aware that they have not been as widely accepted among our teaching colleagues as we might like, and that computers have not altogether lived up to their potential in the classroom.

Why is it so? In the past, the answers we heard most commonly were a lack of appropriate, high quality software, and the high level of effort necessary to help teachers become comfortable with new technology. But in recent years both of these situations seem to have been addressed extensively, and we are seeing signs of improvement in both software development and teacher training.

Perhaps the chief culprit blocking widespread use of technology in schools today is the manner in which computers are integrated into the curriculum. In effect, the "models of instructional computing" that have emerged are not necessarily meeting our students' instructional needs.

The Heart of the Problem

A model of instruction is a set of practices and procedures that defines the manner in which teaching is undertaken. For example, in the primary grades, the most prevalent model is the self-contained classroom with a single teacher instructing in all subject areas. In contrast, instruction at the secondary level is carried out almost exclusively by specialists in each subject area, and students move from one classroom to another.

Within each broad category, there are other instructional models that shape how a subject is taught. In the upper grades, for example, the sciences are generally explored through a combination of classroom and laboratory activities. Elementary reading instruction, in contrast, is often presented by the teacher to small groups of students who have similar academic needs, while the rest of the class completes seatwork that supplements small group instruction.

Although these traditional models of instruction are not without their critics, they work well for traditional subjects. They are flexible, efficient in terms of resource allocation, and at least moderately effective.

But what happens when computers are introduced into the equation?

That depends on how well the new technology complements the instructional models that are already in place. If, for example, we put two computers in the back of a classroom where the primary method of instruction is lecture followed by whole-class assignments, those computers are likely to go unused. Similarly, arranging computers in a lab setting makes sense only if the teaching styles of the teachers in the school make it easy for them to take advantage of the lab

305

(accompanying students there or sending them in small groups to work independently).

It's time, then, for us to take a more careful look at the decisions we have made about how to allocate computer resources within our schools. Three major models of computer use have emerged in recent years. The question we need to ask ourselves now is: how well do these models match the instructional styles of the teachers who are supposed to be benefiting from them?

The Classroom-Based Computer

In an increasing number of schools, at least one computer is available in each classroom. It may be a permanent fixture, or it may be wheeled in and set up as the need arises. A software library is readily available, and students are able to use the computer any time during the day at the teacher's discretion. Clearly, the classroom-based computer has the greatest potential for becoming an integral part of the curriculum. It is proximate, available, and easily supervised. With proper management, the classroom-based computer can become a tool that greatly enhances student learning.

Yet having a computer in a classroom is not without its pitfalls. It occupies space, goes unused whenever students leave the room for recess or other special activities, can be distracting, and is just one more activity the teacher must prepare for and supervise. Also, it's frustrating to have so few computers that several weeks might pass before a student gets to use one. In more than a few classrooms, the computer has assumed the dubious distinction of being the most expensive, least used piece of equipment.

In what sort of instructional environment does the classroom-based computer

model work best? One setting where it is likely to succeed is the classroom which is set up around the concept of "learning centers." In such a classroom, the computer serves as an additional workstation at which students can do their work independently.

For the teacher who does a great deal of large group instruction, the classroom-based model can also work, as long as the computer is available as a demonstration tool for the teacher's own presentation. A large monitor—or, better yet, an overhead projection device—can increase the effectiveness of this approach.

Finally, the presence of one or two computers in a classroom is useful in a setting where both computer software and traditional materials are essential components in the learning process. For example, a science unit that involves one computer simulation, one filmstrip, two off-line experiments, and a reading assignment is more likely to be successful in this classroom-based model than a writing unit for which each student is expected to create her own document using a word processor.

The Laboratory Model

Computer labs can be found in all levels of education, but in junior and senior high schools in particular they have become the model of choice. The chief reason for such widespread acceptance is that computer labs are easily managed. The hardware and software are located in one place, a single person is responsible for the lab, students usually come to the lab as a group for a common purpose, and computer use is not a distraction from other learning activities. Another advantage of the computer lab is that it makes efficient use of valuable resources. With careful scheduling, it is possible for the computers to be in use virtually every moment of the day.

But the laboratory model does have some serious shortcomings. Quite frequently, computer use in labs is unrelated to regular instruction. In fact, more often than not, lab-based instruction focuses on computing as an independent process rather than as a tool to assist in learning or to reinforce what has already been learned. For example, it is rare indeed for a teacher of English to accompany a class to the lab and conduct a lesson in writing using the word processor.

What determines success in a lab setting? Clearly, the computer lab lends itself well to use by entire classes that are focusing on skills such as programming, business applications, keyboarding, and the like. Other special classes or activities that might be scheduled to meet regularly in the computer lab include SAT preparation, advanced mathematics, and process writing.

The lab can also be valuable to teachers who encourage their students to complete projects independently or in small groups during designated class periods each week. In such a scenario, the lab might be used by students from several different classes at once with the lab coordinator providing general supervision. Or the subject area teacher might accompany the entire class to the lab for activity periods a few days a week.

The Mini-Lab Model

The third principal model of instructional computing in use today is the mini-lab, featuring one or a few computers in a central location such as a library. Mini-labs are often established when there are too few computers to stock a full-sized lab or when there are more computers available than lab space.

A mini-lab is inexpensive, flexible, unobtrusive, and easily managed. It is a good way to provide a large number of students with at least some exposure to computers. In small schools with tight budgets, it is an acceptable alternative to classroom- or lab-based computing. However, the drawbacks of using a mini-lab are substantial. Computing in a mini-lab is displaced from the rest of the curriculum, it requires almost as much effort to maintain as a full-sized lab, and students must leave the class group to use the computer. Perhaps the most significant limitation of the mini-lab is that it can put excessive demands upon the teacher and the person managing the lab. Preparing students, getting them to and from the mini-lab, and providing them with adequate support while they are computing can become so time-consuming that teachers may choose not to use the mini-lab.

In what schools do mini-labs work well? First, in ones where libraries and resource rooms are treated as extensions of the classroom. If students are accustomed to signing in and out of such a resource area and the librarian or resource person is comfortable with a management role, the mini-lab is more likely to be successful.

Other settings in which the mini-lab can succeed are classrooms with instructional aides or student teachers who can supervise a small group; and schools using integrated learning systems that are essentially self contained, require little supervision, and allow students a simple way to log on and off.

The Next Steps

The classroom-based computer, the computer lab, and the mini-lab are providing adequate service in schools where they give educators a feeling of familiarity. But perhaps it's time to look beyond those three computer models to newer models that capitalize more fully on the power of the new technologies.

In order to explore such possibilities, we need to become more disposed to accepting a reasonable level of risk. To borrow a phrase from skiing, "No guts, no glory." If we don't take chances and experiment with innovative approaches to education in general, it is unlikely that new or improved models of instructional computing will emerge. This is not to suggest that we should throw away what we have now and rush pell-mell into something new and untried. But we should be willing to take the chance to experiment with innovative educational practices that seem to hold potential.

For example, here are some new instructional models whose time may have come:

• The in-class lab, with enough computers for each student to work alone or with a peer.

• The "lap-lab," in which students begin activities they can finish at home or in the library. (In rural communities, students might even be allowed to go online at home for a day of schooling a week.)

• The co-lab, shared, supported, and maintained by several teachers for use by their students.

• A full day of intensive computer based instruction each week in all subject areas for which it is appropriate.

• A productivity center in which students have access to a wide range of productivity software and a support person to help them use it successfully.

• A math or science lab to which students report once or twice a week for computer-based instruction by a master teacher.

• Networked computers, managed by a computer coordinator but placed in classrooms throughout the school. Students can log onto the classroom computer and have access to any software package owned by the school, or request on line help from the computer coordinator.

As we experiment with these and other new models of instruction, we are likely to find it necessary to invest in new technology—an inclination many educators have avoided in recent years. Taking advantage of networking, laptop computing, speech and sound, new storage technology, faster microprocessing, and the like will provide the groundwork that is needed for the schools of tomorrow.

By being willing to take chances, we will no doubt contribute to the creation of exemplary models of instructional computing. These models, in turn, will help us become more productive teachers so that our students can become better learners.

Examining Computer Configurations: Mini-labs

What computer configuration is best? Are large computer labs better for instructional purposes than one computer in a classroom? What is the best computer configuration for integrating the microcomputer into the existing curricula?

In an effort to decide which computer configuration was best, computer teachers throughout the Albuquerque Public Schools district began an effort to evaluate computer configurations during the 1986-1987 school year. They compiled the following configurations:

- computer labs with 12-15 computers
- one computer in a classroom
- mini-labs with three or four computers mounted on carts.

The lab model had been the focal point of the district's computer literacy program. Would it provide a model for delivery of instruction in the content areas?

Advantages of
the Computer Lab

- Cooperative learning is facilitated with a computer lab. Students work with one or two partners and engage in peer teaching and learning. Two students on a computer is an efficient number and an optimum learning atmosphere (Webb, 1984).
- Computer labs significantly reduce the numbers of "target students." (Many teachers select three to seven students per period to interact with and direct most questions to—thus the name "target students.")

- The computer lab is highly effective. Large groups of students can be taught one skill, such as word processing, at the same time. Teachers don't need to repeat the same instructions each time a new user boots up the computer.
- The computer lab is cost-effective. Many programs can be legally booted on all the machines from a single diskette.
- Central storage in the large lab aids in security of hardware and software.
- Computer labs receive high usage by teachers and students in Albuquerque. Labs are used between 42% and 71% of the instructional day.

Disadvantages of
the Computer Lab

- Classes must be scheduled into the computer lab. A sign-up system is necessary to reserve the lab space.
- Large computer classrooms in Albuquerque don't meet fire code for science classes. When science teachers sign up for the labs and conduct laboratory activities using interfacing devices, chemicals, and burners in the large labs, fire code is violated.
- There are frequently conflicts between the classroom teachers and the teachers who run the computer lab. Who is responsible for clean-up? What rules should apply to teachers and students who visit the lab for instructional purposes? How should rules be enforced?

By
Robertta H.
Barba

309

The computer lab with 12 to 15 computers is an inflexible classroom. It is very difficult to rearrange furniture to meet the needs of one or two teachers who may want to conduct special activities while in the microcomputer room.

The one-computer-in-a-classroom configuration has been studied by many researchers during the past decade. The strengths and weaknesses of this computer configuration can be summarized as follows (Wainwright & Gennaro, 1984):

Advantages of one Computer in a Classroom

Figure 4.11.1

- One computer in a classroom is great for demonstrations.

- One computer in a classroom assures availability of the computer when the teacher requires it.
- Science classrooms already meet fire code, so using one computer to teach science eliminates code violations.
- Flexibility is a trademark of the one-computer classroom. The computer can be physically moved to any corner of the room that the teacher desires.
- When teachers have computers in their classrooms there is no conflict between the computer users and the computer custodian. Each teacher sets his or her own rules regarding use of the computer in the classroom.

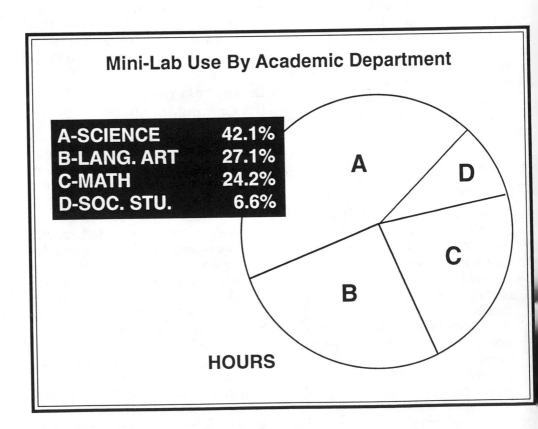

Mini-Lab Use By Academic Department

A-SCIENCE	42.1%
B-LANG. ART	27.1%
C-MATH	24.2%
D-SOC. STU.	6.6%

HOURS

Figure
4.11.2

Types of Computer Packages Used (Applications)

Types of Package	Hours of Instructional Usage (1 School Year)
CAI (Tutorials)	244 hours
Word Processing	260 hours
Graphing	108 hours
Interfacing	99 hours
Problem Solving	110 hours
Simulations	60 hours
Games	40 hours
Telecommunications	8 hours

Disadvantages of One Computer in a Classroom

- One computer in a classroom tends to become the teacher's personal tool. When software is damaged or students misuse the machine, the teacher becomes possessive of the tool and tends to restrict its usage. In Albuquerque, some teachers used the computer as little as 14% of the instructional day.
- There is little time for individual student use of the computer. In departmentalized school, students might receive as little as six to eight minutes per week of computer time.
- Teachers all need their own software; thus costs might be increased over a computer lab.
- More planning is required by the teacher in order to offer on-line and off-line activities at the same time.
- Computer hardware and software are not as secure when they are located in every room of the building.
- Cooperative learning rarely occurs in the one-computer classroom model.
- Target students are prevalent in classrooms where the one-computer model is used.

Is there an alternative? Neither the computer lab nor the one-computer-in-a-classroom model was suited for all computerization needs. The computer resource staff of the Albuquerque Public Schools decided to pilot a third computer configuration—the computer "mini-lab" (Valdez, 1987). Teachers could sign up for the mini-lab in the same manner they signed up for VCRs filmstrip projectors and movie projectors. The mini-lab was stored in the school media center and was subject to the same sign-up procedures as other audio-visual equipment.

Advantages of the Mini-lab

- The mini-lab is highly flexible. Teachers can arrange the computers any place in their rooms in order to suit their instructional program.
- Software sharing reduces the cost of computerization. Teachers in the same department or grade can share software.
- Demonstrations on the computer are possible with the mini-lab as with the one-computer-in-a-classroom model. The mini-lab is cost effective. During a two-year study in Albu-

querque Public Schools, the computer mini-lab was used between 90% and 100% of the time.

- Students receive adequate computer time. Two or three students per computer in a mini-lab receive far more instruction than they would in a one-computer classroom.
- The mini-lab eliminates conflicts between computer-using teachers and the custodians of the large computer labs.
- Numbers of "target students" are greatly reduced when mini-labs are used.
- Cooperative learning is facilitated in classrooms where computer mini-labs are used.

Disadvantages of the Mini-lab

- Sign-up is required for the mini-lab.
- The mini-lab requires that teachers plan on-line and off-line activities. Only half the class can fit on the mini-lab at one time.
- The mini-lab requires flexible classroom management.

How effective was the computer mini-lab? How much usage did the mini-lab receive? What types of activities did classroom teachers conduct on the computer lab?

We piloted the computer mini-lab at several sites in Albuquerque. During that piloting period, we observed several trends. First, the computer mini-lab was used 90% to 100% of the time. Second, all academic departments found

Figure 4.11.3

Computer Mini-Lab Usage by Subject

Department	Computer Usage	# of hours/year	Percent Dept. Use
SCIENCE	tutorials	103	26%
	interfacing	99	25%
	word processing	53	14%
	simulations	45	12%
	programming	20	5%
	games	20	5%
	telecommunications	8	2%
LANG. ARTS	word processing	182	72%
	tutorials	35	14%
	graphing	25	10%
	games	10	4%
MATH	problem solving	90	40%
	tutorials	70	31%
	graphing	40	18%
	simulations	15	6%
	games	10	5%
SOC. STUDIES	tutorials	36	59%
	word processing	25	41%

use for the mini-lab during the pilot period (Figure 4.11.1). Word processing was the most popular use of the mini-lab (Figure 4.11.2 and 4.11.3). Some departments, such as science and mathematics, used the computer more than others (Figure 4.11.1).

On a school-wide basis, word processing was the most popular use for the mini-lab (Figure 4.11.2). The second most popular use was for tutorial instruction or computer assisted instruction. Telecommunication applications and instrument interfacing seem to have found an audience only among science teachers in this population. Teachers in the pilot schools used the mini-lab for research papers, school newspapers, problem solving in mathematics, graphing tutorials, 11-sentence paragraphs, simulations, and mapping activities.

The computer mini-lab also proved to be an effective tool for addressing equity issues. During science fair time, students were allowed to use the mini-lab before and after school to work on their projects. The result was that students from disadvantaged homes were able to compete effectively against more affluent peers. The level of competition dramatically increased on the school level. Students who otherwise would compete from a handicapped economic position became competitive.

At the end of the mini-lab pilot period, computer resource teachers were concerned about the amount of time that classroom teachers spent using tutorial packages. It is the philosophy of the Albuquerque Public School that computers ought to allow teachers to emphasize higher order thinking skills and problem solving. When one science teacher was asked why she used the computers so much for tutorial work, she responded, "I use CAI packages because I can cover the same work in far less time."

By using the computer to handle drill and practice learning, this teacher created blocks of time that could be used for other activities, such as problem solving.

The Albuquerque Public Schools are not abandoning full-scale computer labs or one-computer classrooms. In fact, as new computers are acquired, they are being installed in the large labs. But whereas the old computers used to be traded in, they are now being kept for use in the growing number of mini-labs that offer an affordable, flexible, and viable alternative to other computer configurations.

References

Valdez, D., Einhorn, C., & Resta, P. (1987). *Computer configurations*. Paper presented at New Mexico Council of Computer Users in Education Conference, Albuquerque, NM.

Wainwright, C., & Gennaro, E. (1984). *The one-computer classroom*. The Science Teacher, 51(4), 59-63.

Webb, N.M. (1984) *Microcomputer learning in small groups: Cognitive requirements and group process*. Journal of Educational Psychology, 76, 1075-1088.

Robertta H. Barba, College of Education, The Pennsylvania State University, University Park, PA 16802

Article #12
On a Need-to-Know Basis:
Keyboarding Instruction for Elementary Students

By
William J.
Hunter,
Gordon
Benedict,
and
Bohdan
Bilan

Although a rich variety of computer input devices are available, at present, most of the work that students do on computers requires the use of the keyboard. This is particularly true in the case of language arts applications, where word processing has become an important feature of much instruction in writing. Consequently, there is increasing interest in the question of how to help students become more adept in the use of the keyboard. This question draws forth strong opinions, yet, unfortunately, has attracted scant research attention. This article attempts to summarize the research findings that are available and makes suggestions that may be useful to teachers and administrative decision-makers.

Method of Learning

Current thinking about teaching methodologies in language arts, mathematics, science, and social studies emphasizes the role of the learner in actively *constructing* meaning and developing personal organizations of knowledge. The methods supported by this thinking require the teacher to serve as a guide and an enabler who helps students to explore new areas, gather and interpret information, and express ideas in oral and written form. Consequently, teachers who have been influenced by this thinking tend to doubt the value of traditional keyboarding instruction, which has emphasized precisely the kind of drill and practice that many teachers are seeking to minimize in their own classrooms. In particular, elementary language arts teachers often argue that simply letting children use the keyboard should be sufficient instruction and that children will acquire speed and accuracy with time. Secondary typing teachers, on the other hand, argue that technique (proper fingering) is essential and must be taught and practiced. Furthermore, they claim (e.g., Britten, 1988; Rauch & Yanke, 1982; Stewart & Jones, 1983) that students who have learned "bad habits" pose particular difficulties when they later take typing courses: "...any typewriting instructor who has experienced the challenge of retraining a typist under such conditions will readily admit that the task is difficult if not impossible." (Stewart & Jones, 1983, p. 11) Although this concern has a long history, we were unable to find an empirical study that actually examined the keyboarding achievements of students who entered typing classes with or without "bad habits."

To resolve this dilemma, it is important to recognize that keyboarding is a psychomotor skill and to allow for the possibility that such skills may be learned in a manner different from that which we apply to the acquisition of cognitive information/organization. Specifically, the practice-with-feedback methods of behavioral training generally are acknowledged to be successful in helping individuals to develop more skilled *motor* performances. Granting this, it *seems* reasonable to suggest that

314

young children be encouraged to explore and use keyboards freely until such time as they begin to learn to use word processors. At that time it is reasonable to expect them to learn such fundamentals as "home row" and proper fingering for the letters of the alphabet. Having acquired these skills, meaningful practice with their own compositions should enable them to continue to develop both speed and accuracy. Since children are unlikely to have a sense of what constitutes reasonable proficiency in the use of a keyboard, it would also be desirable if they were given frequent opportunities to observe adult typists of varying levels of proficiency. This experience should help to motivate the child to set higher personal standards for speed and accuracy.

Age for Starting Instruction

There is limited but fairly consistent research related to this question with respect to children in the upper elementary grades. Although Cowles and Robinson (1983) demonstrated that children as young as five years can learn to use a keyboard correctly, Warwood, Hartman, Hauwiller, and Taylor (1985) question whether children younger than grade 4 are ready to learn this skill. Still, Jackson and Berg (1986) indicate that third grade children can learn to keyboard. Thus, while there is some question about the readiness of children in grades K-3, there is general agreement that by grade 4, children are ready for keyboarding instruction.

This may be a moot point, however, since both Ball (1985) and Warwood et al. (1985) point out that the software used in the early grades generally requires only single keystroke responses. (Teachers who use word processors, databases, and LOGO with young children

might well want to take issue with this observation.) Perhaps the most reasonable approach to the question is that taken by Byfield and LaBarre (1985). They suggest that the time to teach keyboarding is just before the introduction of word processing. If we take that stance, then the more important questions become: at what age should we begin to teach word processing? If word processing begins early enough, can we postpone or omit instruction in cursive writing? Although the benefits of writing with a word processor are still open to question (e.g., Hunter et al., 1988), enthusiasts would argue that children should be introduced to word processing as soon as possible. Until better data are available, it might be best to take the position described by Lockard, Abrams, and Many (1987): introduce word processing when it is appropriate to expect students to write at the length of at least a short paragraph (this will vary with the methods used to teach writing and the individual development of the children). It would then be reasonable to begin keyboarding instruction two or three weeks ahead of the introduction of word processing and to continue to teach keyboarding until established performance criteria have been met.

Performance Criteria

Since the rationale for teaching keyboarding to younger children is to enable them to achieve more in writing than they might otherwise, it would be sensible to develop keyboarding performance standards related to that objective. However, any set of standards also should be sensitive to the norms of children's keyboarding achievement at various ages. Unfortunately, such norms are not yet available. Reported figures range from the observation by Wetzel

(1985) of third, fourth, and fifth graders typing at 2.5 words per minute to Ray's observation (reported in Warwood et al., 1985) of fifth and sixth graders typing at 40 words per minute following one year of daily instruction (one hour per day). On the other hand, Wetzel (1985) reported that even when students were typing from copy as slowly as 7 words per minute, they did not scan the keyboard, did not become frustrated with use of the keyboard, and did not lose their place on either keyboard or paper. This indicates that, despite their speed, the students had begun to master keyboarding technique. In the long run, we can expect that speed (and accuracy) will improve with practice if appropriate technique is being used. To achieve the desired effects on writing, then, we should perhaps focus on individual children's comparative rates with pen and keyboard, rather than seeking normative guidelines. As long as a child is typing at a speed that equals or exceeds his or her own longhand speed, the potential for beneficial use of word processors exists. If, in addition, the child uses correct fingering, we may expect continued improvement over time.

Student Attitudes

To date, there have not been systematic studies of students' attitudes toward the use of keyboards or to instruction in keyboarding. However, researchers and writers in the area have reported informal observations. In general, it can be said that students who learned to use a keyboard for the purpose of word processing do not seem more positive about the process than students who use word processors without having had keyboarding instruction (e.g., Gerlach, 1987; Palmer, Dowd, & James, 1984). How-

ever, Wetzel (1985) noted that students who lack keyboarding skills become more frustrated as a result of looking back and forth from notes to keyboard to screen, frequently losing their place in the process. It is perhaps unrealistic to expect students to be immediately enthusiastic about instruction that requires disciplined practice and repetition. If we are to find positive attitudes toward keyboarding, it is likely to be among students whose instruction is well behind them and who are now reaping the benefits of easier, more fluid word processing. More evidence on this matter will likely be forthcoming as more and more schools confront the issue of keyboarding instruction for elementary school students.

Other Issues

Any change in educational practice tends to require many practical adjustments to the way things are ordinarily done. In the case of teaching keyboarding to elementary children, one significant practical problem is: who will teach keyboarding at the elementary level? Naturally, business education teachers argue that they have special expertise in this area (e.g., Headley, 1983; Kisner, 1984), but Williams (1988) reported that elementary teachers who could type required only one day of instruction to be able to successfully teach keyboarding skills to their students. Those without typing skills required three weeks of instruction in order to teach keyboarding to their students. The use of computer-based keyboarding tutorials might serve to reduce this time even further. Given the age-appropriate training and experience of elementary teachers and the fact that they have chosen to work with young students, we believe it preferable to entrust elementary keyboarding instruction to elementary teachers willing to undertake the necessary additional instruction.

Another practical problem is the availability of keyboards with which to teach. Learning to use a keyboard requires a one-to-one person to machine ratio—it cannot be done vicariously. On the other hand, the instructional programs used in the research reported here generally involve 30 to 50 minutes per day for 40 to 60 days. Depending on the school's schedule and size of classes, this means a lab of 15 computers could serve from 7 to 45 keyboarding classes, with most elementary schools falling somewhere between these two extremes. It must be remembered, however, that the purpose of keyboarding instruction is to enable students to benefit from the use of word processors, so it is essential that sufficient hardware be available to also leave time for students' writing activities. Wetzel (1985) summed up the problem of hardware limitations by pointing out that if children's access to time on machines is limited by a shortage of hardware, "...there is no time—or need—to teach keyboarding" (p. 17).

Finally, we must also question the assumption behind our interest in teaching keyboarding; that is, that students will ultimately write better as a consequence of their more efficient use of the keyboard. There currently is no research to support this assumption. Gerlach (1987) assessed the quality of fourth graders' writing whether or not they used a keyboard properly. "Good" keyboarders did not write more words nor did they make more or different revisions than their classmates. However, Gerlach was looking for rather immediate effects (8-week keyboarding intervention, 3 months experience with a word processor), and we might more justifiably expect that any benefits of keyboarding instruction would not be seen in measures of the quality of students' writing until they had ample opportunity to apply their skill to many writing assignments. Furthermore, as Daiute (1986) and Macarthur (1988) point out, word processing simply makes revision easier. It does not help the writer to know what needs to be revised or how to go about making revisions. Increased efficiency in entering letters at the keyboard might result in students having more time available for revision, but it will not ensure either that they will, in fact, spend that time in revision or that they will be any more capable of productively revising their work.

Conclusion

It is far too soon to draw conclusions about the benefits of teaching children to use a keyboard, but it is not too soon to conclude that the increased use of word processors as part of writing instruction demands that we take keyboarding seriously. We should expect that today's elementary students will graduate into a world in which the ability to directly manipulate information will be an essential part of many occupations. It is certainly possible that advances in computing technology (voice recognition, handwriting analysis) will make other input options available, but it would be short-sighted of us to fail to provide students with the skills necessary to use keyboards as one way of working with information stored in computers. It would be equally short-sighted for us to pursue this course without gathering the information to address the many unanswered questions raised in this article.

References

Ball, S. (1985, September). *Valuable alternatives to keyboarding in grades K-3*. Austin, TX: Paper presented at the Fall conference on perspectives on the young child and the computer. (ERIC Document Reproduction Service No. ED 264-957).

Britten, R. M. (1988). "The effects of instructional keyboarding skills in grade 2." *Educational Technology, 28(4)*, 34-37.

Byfield, J. S., & LaBarre, J. (1985). "Integrating information processing into keyboarding typewriting." *Business Education Forum, 30* (Apr/May), 53-56.

Cowles, M., & Robinson, M. (1983). *An analysis of young children and learning keyboarding skills*. Nashville Tennessee State University, Center for Training and Technical Assistance. (ERIC Document Reproduction Service No. ED 275 394).

Daiute, C. (1986). "Physical and cognitive factors in revision: Insights from studies with computers." *Research in the Teaching of English, 20* (2), 141-159.

Gerlach. G. J. (1987). *The effect of typing skill on using a word processor for composition*. Washington, DC: Paper presented at the Annual Meeting of the American Educational Research Association, April 20, 1987 (ERIC Document Reproduction Service No. ED 286-465).

Headley P. L. (1983). "Keyboarding instruction in elementary school." *Business Education Forum. 38*(3), 18-19.

Hunter, W. J., Begoray, J., Benedict, G., Bilan, B. Jardine, G., Rilstone P. & Weisgerber, R. (1988) *Word processing and writing: A critical synthesis*. Alberta: University of Calgary, Education Technology Unit.

Jackson, T. H., & Berg, D. (1986). "Elementary keyboarding—Is it important?" *The Computing Teacher 13*(6), 10-11.

Kisner, E. (1984) "Keyboarding—a must in tomorrow's world." *The Computing Teacher 11*(6), 21-22.

Lockard, J., Abrams. P. & Many, W. A. (1987). *Microcomputers for educators*. Boston: Little Brown and Company.

Macarthur, C. (1988). "The impact of computers on the writing process." *Exceptional Children, 54*(6). 536-542.

Palmer, A., Dowd, T. & James, K. (1984). "Changing Teacher and student attitudes through word processing." *The Computing Teacher 11(9)*, 45-47.

Rauch, V. C., & Yanke, P. B. (1982). "Keyboarding in kindergarten: Is it elementary?" *Business Education Forum, 37*(3), 19-20.

Stewart, J., & Jones, B. W. (1983). "Keyboarding instruction: Elementary school options." *Business Education Forum, 37*(7), 11-12.

Warwood, B., Hartman, V., Hauwiller, J., & Taylor, S. (1985). *A research study to determine the effects of keyboard use upon student development in occupational keyboarding*. Bozeman, Montana State University. (ERIC Document Reproduction Service No. ED 265-367).

Wetzel, K. (1985). "Keyboarding skills: Elementary my teacher?" *The Computing Teacher, 12*(9), 15-19.

Williams, B. (1988). "Preparing teachers to teach keyboarding to elementary students." *Business Education Forum, 42* (Mar), 27-29.

Article #13
Touch Typing for Young Children: Help or Hindrance?

By
Jessica
Kahn and
Pamela
Freyd

Keyboards are not straightforward tools: the letters are oddly arranged, and spacing and capitalization require specific keystrokes. If children are to use word processing, they need to know how to use the keyboard. But what are the best ways to help children acquire that knowledge?

Many writers recommend the introduction of formal keyboarding skills, including the prescribed "reaches" and postures of touch typing (Balajthy, 1988; Suttles, 1983; Warwood, 1985). "Lack of keyboarding skills is the most often cited hindrance to effective use of word processing technology." (Balajthy, 1988) Is touch typing a prerequisite for using computers for writing? At various grade levels, exactly what keyboarding expertise do children lack, and how can they acquire that expertise? The current focus on keyboarding skills risks the danger of complicating rather than facilitating children's writing. How skillful do children need to be in order to use word processing to advantage, and what needs to be done to help them become skillful? Should kindergarten and first graders, or even fifth graders, learn correct fingering to avoid having to unlearn bad habits later (Balajthy, 1988; Schmidt, 1983) or is it sufficient to help children to locate the keys (Jackson and Berg, 1986)? "Presently there is more opinion than solid research to guide decisions on the when and why of teaching keyboarding." (Kroenke, 1987)

To address this issue we draw on data from two research studies: "Microcom-puters in Writing Development," which examined the word processing and writing experiences of ten classes of children from kindergarten to fourth grade over three years, and "Cooperative Writing in Computer Environments," a one-year study of fourth and sixth grade classrooms in a public school in downtown Philadelphia where word processing was taught without formal keyboarding instruction. Based on this work, we argue that insistence on teaching touch typing to young children as it has been taught in high schools and as a prerequisite to writing is an exaggerated response to children's unfamiliarity with keyboards and is developmentally inappropriate. We further argue that this issue is an artifact of an out-dated vision of keyboarding, one that fails to take into account the ways children in schools actually use computers for writing. A formidable investment of resources is recommended for children to master the techniques of touch typing. We question the merit of using elementary school time and resources for such training.

Concern has been voiced that children who develop "hunt and peck" strategies on computer keyboards will have a difficult time unlearning those bad habits. This is not a new problem. For as long as we can recall, children have been taught to print in the early grades and no one has considered it a "bad habit," even though a few years later it interferes with the introduction of cursive writing. Rather, it is considered an appropriate instructional response to

319

children's level of motor control. Touch typing skills have been taught successfully in public schools since 1915 (West, 1983), frequently to children who have already used keyboards and developed "hunt and peck" strategies. The issue is not *whether* touch typing is a useful skill, but rather, as computers become available in schools, *when and how* to teach touch typing. We do not suggest that poor typing habits should be encouraged but rather that the methods that have been used to teach touch typing at the high school level are inappropriate for elementary children.

In this article we consider for whom and under what circumstances "hunt and peck" fingering really is a bad habit— or, to put it another way, for whom and under what circumstances is touch typing a necessary skill? We take apart the issues, in order to avoid applying a solution (touch typing) where there is no problem.

What Our Research Indicates

Repeated observations of kindergarten and first grade children in the "Microcomputers and Writing Development" project shows that touch typing was not necessary for these children. It was surprising to the research team, as they observed children working at computer keyboards, to find that these children needed very little instruction to get started with word processing. Keyboarding was not an issue, since they took as long to decide what letter to type as they did to find it on a keyboard. Children in these classes reported that typing was easier than handwriting. When they began to use the computers to write their own stories, using invented spellings or copying spellings from other sources, the facilitating qualities of word processing (e.g., automatic left-to-right

and top-to-bottom progression, legible letters spaced evenly on the screen) were apparent. The research team observed that in many cases children's writing with word processing was more ambitious than their writing with pencil and paper. One child composed this sentence "Yns opn a tm dr ys a hse" (Once upon a time there was a house) with word processing in November of kindergarten. She made no such attempt with pencil and paper.

One argument against teaching touch typing to primary age children has to do with developmental issues. The prescribed reaches of touch typing were designed for adult hands. Young children (kindergarten and first graders) have enough to do to decide what to write, how it is spelled, and what the next letter looks like without worrying about which finger to use. Even if they know the associations for touch typing, their facility in composing will be more dependent on their ability to figure out spellings than on their ability to figure out the keys.

Our observations revealed that for older primary age children—second, third, and fourth graders—familiarity with the keyboard was a factor. In end-of-year interviews, second graders, who had used the computers to write at least three separate pieces, reported that they preferred writing with computers, while those who had less opportunity to use computers reported that they preferred to compose with pencil and paper because they had difficulty finding the letters on the keyboard. In other words, children became familiar with the keyboard *as they wrote* and the more they wrote, the more familiar they became.

Third and fourth graders all preferred to use word processing at some point in their writing. When asked what teachers should teach in order to help children use word processing, these students said that children needed to know where the keys were. Their teachers had considered teaching touch typing. In fact they began each year by introducing the notion of correct fingering. However, they abandoned this in favor of practice sessions with laminated printouts of the computer keyboard (Kahn, Avicolli and Lodise, 1987). Rather than stress the reaches of touch typing, they chose to familiarize the children with the locations of the keys, rightly assuming that this familiarity would be sufficient help. These practice sessions lasted five minutes each day for the first six weeks. (In contrast to elaborate requirements of whole-class instruction in touch typing, this activity could be done in any spare time between other activities.) In end-of-year interviews, almost every child commented on how helpful these practice sessions had been. Observations and interviews with teachers during the three-year study made it clear that instruction of this kind in addition to writing with word processing allowed children to work easily at the computers.

The argument has been made that this sort of practice fails to supply the kinesthetic experience of working at a keyboard, and is therefore not valuable. West (1983), addressing this same objection in relation to typing practice on different keyboards, makes the case that for older students mastering touch typing, the mental practice of finding the keys on any keyboard is valuable. It is precisely this activity that our students found helpful when they began to write with word processing.

The "Cooperative Writing in Computer Environments" study looked at handwriting speed and typing speed in fourth and sixth grade classes where word processing was introduced for writing. Because of limited access to comput-ers the teachers in the study had made the decision not to teach touch typing skills to the whole group. Instead they introduced the children to the idea of home keys and correct hand position, and showed them how to use a computer typing program that was available for use during students' free time. During the course of the year, we observed many children as they practiced typing. Sometimes they would work with the typing program, concentrating on speed. Sometimes they chose to practice with whatever they were composing, moving in and out of correct fingering. Children made trade-offs between writing and touch typing tasks. When the demands of the writing were great children paid less attention to correct fingering; when the demands were light, fingering was a concern.

In October, the mean typing speed of 34 sixth graders who had had previous computer instruction in Logo was 6.62 words per minute. Between October and May children received no formal typing instruction for speed or accuracy. Instead, they composed and revised in pairs at computers for approximately one hour each week. By May, the mean typing speed had risen to 10.12 words per minute, a figure not significantly different from the average handwriting speed of children of this age (8.8-12.5 words per minute—Groff, 1961), nor significantly different from these children's own handwriting speed (11.4 words per minute). The argument has been made that for children to use word processing successfully they need to be able to type at least as quickly as they handwrite (Fidanque, Smith, and Sullivan, 1986). Wetzel (1985) suggests that the ability to type ten words per minute allowed children to "make adequate use of the computer and word processing programs." The children in this study reached this speed. It would seem that keyboarding instruction lasting fifteen hours (Wetzel, 1985), sixteen to eighteen hours (Warwood, 1985), or thirty hours (Jackson and Berg, 1986) is not necessary. Our findings indicate that this goal can be achieved as children write. Because typing speed gains that are achieved after intensive training are often lost if there is not consistent practice (Warwood, 1985), perhaps time may be better spent in production typing with steady slow gains over several years.

A highly significant correlation between handwriting speed and typing speed (p > .001) was found in October. That is, children who were able to handwrite quickly tended to type quickly. They also showed a wide range of both handwriting and typing speeds (3 wpm- 21 wpm). Taken together, these findings suggest that it would be inappropriate and probably unproductive to demand that all children acquire some minimum typing speed, any more than we require a minimum handwriting speed. If children do not see their speed or lack of it as a problem, why should teachers?

Computers in Schools: Limited Resources

The argument against elaborate keyboarding instruction in elementary schools takes into consideration the environment in which teachers and children work and the resources of time, equipment, and expertise available to them. In elementary schools, where the student/computer ratio is still more than thirty to one (Office of Technology Assessment, 1988) it is difficult to provide adequate access to computers. The curriculum is full, and resources are scarce. Given this reality, teachers must decide how best to use computers.

All of the teachers in the "Microcomputers and Writing Development" study, given autonomy to make curricular decisions concerning the use of word processing, chose to focus on writing rather than typing skills. However, even with this commitment to computers in writing, the lack of equipment (two computers per room, twelve students per computer) and pressures of other curricular demands meant that some children only used the computers three times during the school year. If these teachers had felt compelled to teach touch typing, the children might never have used the computers for writing at all. The teachers in the "Cooperative Writing" study also felt that limited time was better spent teaching block movement commands to aid revision than teaching typing skills.

It will be noted that the teachers in the "Cooperative Writing" study worked with their classes in a lab setting (two children per computer) while the teachers in the "Microcomputers and Writing Development" study had two computers in each classroom. The location of computers in elementary schools is a central issue here. When asked for their recommendations concerning the distribution of computers in the school, the "Microcomputers" teachers unanimously opted for computers in their rooms, rather than a lab. They felt that they had greater flexibility in scheduling children at the computers, and the opportunity to use the computers for other activities, such as making banners and taking spelling tests. The teachers in the "Cooperative Writing" study initially had no choice concerning the distribution of computers, but have since successfully applied for grant money to obtain classroom computers. They also valued the increased flexibility in scheduling that is possible when there is a computer in the classroom.

But even when computers are not a limited resource, time always is. It is difficult to find thirty or forty-five minutes, three times a week for six weeks in the elementary school schedule, a time commitment that seems to be the minimum recommended for mastery of keyboarding skills. This intensive practice is only the beginning requirement of touch typing advocates. Balajthy (1988) admits that the gains in speed and accuracy attained with these sessions will be lost if children do not have continuous access to computers. In other words, setting out this block of time for keyboarding skills is not enough; children need to consolidate their typing skills by using them for writing tasks.

Our argument is that children can learn to type within meaningful writing activities rather than with concentrated practice on unrelated drills. Other researchers have found this to be true. "College students who learned the keyboard by composing simple business letters on themes set by the instructor did better at the end of the semester than those using nonsense drills for the first nine weeks to learn the keyboard." (Barton, 1926, as reported in West, 1983) West notes that "indeed, one of the truisms about formal schooling is that a quarter to half a century commonly elapses between the first appearance of a superior practice and its general adoption in the classroom." We are just about due.

The resource argument we make is that time, equipment, and expertise in elementary schools are better used to help children compose and revise on keyboards from kindergarten on. To wait until some preliminary level of keyboarding skill has been attained unnecessarily postpones the very real benefits of writing with word processing. No one suggests that children postpone writing by hand until they master cursive writing skills. Likewise, keyboarding skills should not be a prerequisite to writing with computers.

Keyboarding Skills: To What End?

Why are keyboarding skills an issue now? We believe that this issue is an artifact of an out-dated vision that has more to do with secretaries and typewriters than with computers and children. "It is a well-known observation that each new medium of communication begins its life by first adopting the contents and formats of the media it is likely to replace or modify." (Salomon and Gardner, 1986) Weizenbaum (1976) comments that it is rare for "a tool and an altogether original job it is to do, to be invented together." Such is the case for word processing in elementary schools. We have transferred the methodology that came with typewriters to computers when in fact the new technology is different from the old in important ways that make this methodology irrelevant. In addition, the ways children in elementary schools use word processing are different from the practices of secretaries in offices. What are the skills that keystroking exercises are designed to build? The ability to type with accuracy, speed and uniform pressure on the keys without looking at the keys. But are these skills relevant to the ways children use computers for writing?

Let us first consider the issue of accuracy. Both teaching methods and electronic media suggest that accuracy is not an issue when young children compose, particularly first drafts. The most recent research on children's composing points to the value of postponing concerns about correct spelling, grammar, and punctuation until meaning has been clarified. Furthermore, accuracy is an issue when it is difficult to make corrections, as it is on paper with pencil. Making corrections on a computer screen is literally child's play. Research has shown that children enthusiastically edit their work with word processing, attributing their enthusiasm to the ease of correcting on an electronic screen rather than on paper (Kahn, 1987).

Is speed a concern when composing with computers? Composing is not transcribing; it requires thought and reflection. And composing is what children in elementary schools do. Word processing is valuable precisely because it simplifies the production of text, freeing children to concentrate on creating meaning. Our research shows that children only need to type at least as quickly as they write—ten words a minute—in order to compose as comfortably at computers as they do on paper. We know, because we have asked the children, that when they can find the letters on the keyboard they all report that it is easier to push a button than write a letter.

Do children need to be trained not to look at the keys? Secretaries doing copy typing can look at the copy and at the keys simultaneously. But composing at keyboards is a different issue entirely. We have seen rooms full of professional programmers composing at keyboards. These programmers continuously watch the keys and have developed reasonably quick hunt-and-peck strategies. For beginners at keyboards at any age, West (p. 57) suggests that looking at the keys helps students to learn their locations.

In a related argument, teachers express concern that using keyboards without touch typing skills will reinforce "bad habits" that will be difficult to unlearn. West (in a personal communication) states that twelve hours of formal touch typing instruction is sufficient to undo any "bad habits" and that, as our own experience suggests, familiarity with the locations of the keys facilitates learning touch typing. We question the difficulty of unlearning these "bad habits" when we know that we ourselves like so many other students who successfully learned to touch type in high school, easily traded our hunt and peck strategies for the smoother flow of touch typing. Many students who have been hunting and pecking for years successfully learn touch typing in high school when they are motivated to do so and where it is easy to find time, equipment and a competent teacher.

Conclusion

We return to the questions with which we began this paper. What do children need to know in order to use word processing for writing? Children need to know where the keys are, including the space bar, return key and punctuation marks, and how to use cursor movement arrows or commands to insert and delete characters. With this information, children find word processing to be a "convivial tool." (Eisner, 1985)

Our article refutes the claim that intensive touch typing instruction modeled from traditional high school instruction is necessary for elementary school children. It is true that children are often frustratingly slow at the keyboards when they begin to use computers. However, instruction in touch typing is an exaggerated response to young children's unfamiliarity and lack of expertise about keyboarding. Our research shows that by the time children have used the computers for writing on three separate occasions, they have become sufficiently familiar with the locations of the keys to use word processing. Any further learning about the keyboard can take place as they do meaningful writing.

Research indicates that for very young children, physical production of text claims attention, and therefore interferes with the ability to compose (Scardamalia and Bereiter, 1982; Graves, 1982). Advocates of word processing in schools argue that computers for composing can circumvent such issues as the formation of letters, left-to-right and top-to-bottom progression, and motor ability (Smith, 1987). This may be so for primary age children, but considering the difficulties these children have with handwriting, in many cases, it takes very little exposure to a computer keyboard for a child to type more quickly (and more legibly) than he or she can write.

For middle school age children, however, composing at keyboards is not simply a matter of producing text quickly. Children of this age suffer less than younger children from the interference of production factors, and research tells us that removing the interference of production factors does not improve the quality of their work. Gerlach (1987) presents evidence that concentrated keyboarding instruction (fifteen lessons, each twenty-five minutes long) does not lead to either longer compositions or more extensive revisions. Word processing makes writing easier for these children, but that is all. Classroom instruction, response groups and regular publication of written work will have a greater impact on the length and quality of children's writing than the acquisition of keyboarding skills.

Our research (with children K-8) indicates that with brief introductions to the locations of the keys and encouragement to use both hands, children learn to manage computer keyboards as they do their writing. This ability to produce text easily allows children to concentrate on composition concerns. The introduction of touch typing, where students must type without looking at the keyboard, using correct fingering, substitutes new production difficulties for old. Furthermore, we risk losing sight of the objective. In elementary schools word processing should facilitate composing rather than introduce a new set of problems for children.

References

Balajthy, E. "Keyboarding, Language Arts, and the Elementary School Child." *The Computing Teacher,* February 1988, 40-43.

Becker, H. J. *Instructional Uses of School Computers: Report, from the 1986 National Survey.* Center for Social Organization of Schools, Johns Hopkins University, 1986.

Bereiter, C., and Scardamalia, M. *Psychology of Written Composition.* Hillsdale, NJ, Lawrence Erlbaum Associates, 1987.

Eisner, E. *The Educational Imagination.* NY: Macmillan, Inc., 1985.

Fidenque, A., Smith, M., and Sullivan, G. "Keyboarding: The Issues Today." *Proceedings of 5th Annual Extending the Human Mind Conference.* University of Oregon, 1986.

Gerlach, G. "The Effect of Typing Skill on Using a Word Processor for Composition." Paper presented at Annual Meeting of the American Educational Research Association (Washington, D.C.), 1987.

Graves, D. *A Researcher Learns to Write.* Exeter, NH: Heinemann Educational Books, Inc., 1984.

Jackson, T., and Berg, D. "Elementary Keyboarding—Is It Important?" *The Computing Teacher,* March 1986, *13,* 8-11 .

Kahn, J. "Emergent Writers Using Word Processing: Making it Easier and What that Means." Paper presented to the Eastern Educational Research Association, Miami Beach, FL, 1987.

Kahn, J., Avicolli, M., and Lodise, K. "Learning the Keyboard." *Interface,* January 1988, 4 (4).

Kroenke, K. "Keyboarding: Prelude to Composing at the Computer." *English Education,* December 1987, 224-249.

Lamon, W. "Using Microcomputers in the Elementary Schools: The 1987 Oregon Assessment." *SIG Bulletin for Teacher Educators* 1988, 4 (2). Eugene, OR: International Council for Computers in Education.

Milkes, J. *Teacher's Manual for Keyboarding Papers.* Bronx, NY: MPC Educational Publishers, 1985.

Power On! New Tools for Teaching and Learning. Congress of the United States Office of Technology Assessment. Washington, DC, 1988.

Salomon, G., and Gardner, H. "The Computer as Educator: Lessons from Television Research." *Educational Researcher,* January 1986, 13-19.

Scardamalia, M, and Bereiter, C. "The Role of Production Factors in Writing Ability." In M. Nystrand (Ed.) *What Writers Know. The Language, Process, and Structure of Written Discourse,* 1982, 173-210. Orlando, FL: Academic Press, Inc.

Schmidt, B. *Keyboarding: The State of the Art: Project Report.* Blacksburg, VA: Virginia Polytechnic Institute and State University. [ED 236-352] 1983.

Smith, F. *The Promise and Threat of Computers.* New York: Manor House, 1987.

Suttles, A. "Computers and Writing: Contemporary Research and Innovative Programs." *Computers in Reading and Language Arts,* Summer 1983, 1, 33-37.

Warwood, B., Hartman, V., Hauwiller, J., and Taylor, S. A. "Research Study to Determine the Effects of Early Keyboard Use Upon Student Development in Occupational Keyboarding." Bozeman, MT: Montana State University. [ED 265-367] 1985.

Weizenbaum, J. *Computer Power and Human Reason: From Judgment to Calculation.* San Francisco, CA: W.H. Freeman and Co., 1976.

West, L. *Acquisition of Typewriting Skills.* Indianapolis, IN: Bobbs-Merrill, Inc., 1983.

Wetzel, K. "Keyboarding Skills: Elementary, My Dear Teacher?" *The Computing Teacher,* June 1985, 12, 15-19.

LEP Students in the Basic Skills Lab

By
Evelyn
Fella

The population of Limited English Proficient (LEP) students in American schools is sizeable, with numbers expected to reach majority levels in some school districts in the next decade. Meeting the special language needs of these students presents a problem to many teachers and administrators. One means of addressing LEP needs and enhancing language instruction is using Chapter 1 basic skills computer labs.[1]

Many of the resources available for basic skills improvement in language are appropriate, or can easily be made appropriate for LEP students. However, LEP students, sadly, often remain in their ESL bungalows or trailers with little or no contact with other students or school facilities such as computer labs. According to the Office of Technology Assessment's 1988 report, *Power On!*, LEP students have the lowest access of all students to computers.

It seems that one of the greatest barriers to the utilization of computers by LEP students is teachers' unwillingness to use computers with them at all. The percentage of teachers who use computers with LEP students is consistently less than one-half the percentage of teachers who use computers with other students (office of Technology Assessment, 1987). ESL teachers who are unfamiliar and uncomfortable with the computer lab may not seek out the lab as a source of instructional enhancement for their students. The same can be said for lab teachers: uncomfortable and unfamiliar with the problems of second language learners, they may not make an effort to bring these students into the lab. Indeed, when hired to take on the coordination of a high school Language Arts Computer Center, I was advised to forget the ESL 1 and 2 students because they didn't speak enough English to use a computer.

My experience as a writing lab coordinator at a language school for international students had proven to me that beginning level students who speak very little English are in fact among the best and most avid computer users. The computer lab is a wonderful source of language development for even beginning LEP students. Though not a great deal of software has been written specifically for them, a sufficient amount of language arts software can be used by LEP students, often with only a minimal amount of editing by the teacher.

Students are willing and able, and software is available. The missing links—computer lab teachers and ESL teachers—must join forces to give their students the opportunity to use computers. However, simply giving LEP students computer access will not ensure success. Beyond signing up for lab time, ESL and basic skills lab teachers need to pool their insight and expertise about the students and the computer software in order to make computer time rewarding. I have developed some guidelines for taking the first step of bringing first- and second-year LEP students into a high school language arts lab. Special considerations for the needs of LEP students will influence how computer introduction and activities are planned, how time is structured, and which of the many available software programs will be used.

327

Starting Up

The first difference in high school LEP students that can affect lab lesson plans is their lack of prior computer/keyboard experience. Most students in high schools have received basic computer training, such as keyboarding or using a computer or a word processor. Students quickly pick up these skills anyway while working on their writing, so I had always considered teaching such skills a waste of time in a writing lab. Though I still believe this, I've had to make compromises when beginning ESL students come to the lab for the first time.

I started with ESL 2 students, naively assuming they had had prior computer exposure, especially at a school which was well-endowed with computer labs. Without going through all the embarrassing details, this first attempt at a "correct the error" exercise with a word processor was a flop. The students had no idea how to delete or how to use the arrow keys or even the spacebar. A quick survey revealed the reasons for this. Of 60 ESL 2 students, 41 reported having been in the U.S. between one and two years and had never touched a computer. Nineteen students reported having been in the U.S. between three and four years and to having had some experience (such as a game in one math class).

After this initial setback, I realized beginning LEP students would have to ease into using the word processor for grammar and writing assignments. Some kind of orientation would be necessary, but with some major differences to what might be done with a group of native speakers or even advanced LEP students. The language of standard "elementary" introductory programs, such as *Apple Introduces Apple* is still too difficult for low-level students. In ori-enting ESL students to using computers, one must remember their problems in understanding the language, especially directions. The following techniques used with beginning ESL students have resulted in successful first days in the computer lab. I still do not spend more than five or 10 minutes of the lab time in preparation for the computer work, but those 10 minutes result in 40 minutes of concentrated work or language tasks and virtually no struggles with the computer.

Techniques for Starting Up

1. Find out about prior computer skills

When bringing ESL classes into a computer lab, find out what experience the students have had. Take a survey or have the ESL teacher take a survey depending on the schools and teachers in your area, students may or may not have had prior computer exposure.

2. Don't start with word processing on the first day.

Keyboarding can be a problem for many students. There are many grammar, reading, or vocabulary programs available that give students the chance to get used to the keyboard by using arrow keys or the space bar or typing just one letter or one word. Choose programs that have a limited amount of on-screen instructions. I start with *Player's Choice or Mixed up Sentences*. This is not meant to discourage word processing. Even my ESL 1 students eventually do a lot of word processing, but it is overwhelming on the first day.

3. Have students sit away from the computers at first.

Most well-designed labs have desk or table space where instructions can be given. Oral instructions are important and when competing with a computer, fighting for students' attention is always a losing battle.

4. Give only instructions necessary for that day.

Don't overload students; if they're not doing word processing on that day, they don't need to know how to use the Delete key.

5. Introduce vocabulary.

Most beginning ESL students will tell you they know what "key" means. If you ask them to show you one, they will probably pull a locker or house key out of their pockets. Sometimes some unexpected words may present a problem. For example, in the phrase "Press Any Key," students might not know what "Any Key" means. They will sit staring at the keyboard, looking for the key marked ANY. Introduce vocabulary orally and by writing it on the board. Point to the words as you say them and, again, introduce only those words necessary for that day's work.

6. Demonstrate on the board or with an overhead.

You can point to the space bar and tell students what it's called and *write* the word on the board. But do they all know what the word "space" means? Have students show you what a space is in a sentence on the board. If you are doing word processing, use an eraser as your "cursor" to show students how to delete from the right. Go over the language exercise as well as the computer functions necessary to complete the exercise. I begin the year with the program *Mixed Up Sentences* in which students use the arrow keys and Return to put the words in a sentence in the correct order. With a sentence on the board, we practice putting the words in the correct order,

along with using the arrow keys and pressing Return to select. By doing this, novice computer users feel much more confident when at the computer. If ESL students are struggling with anything, it should be the linguistic task, not the computer.

7. Load disks to the easiest point of startup.

Often educational programs have many screens of credits or directions that ESL students will not understand and just waste time trying to read. So that students can concentrate on their language exercises for as much of the time as possible, load the disks in the lab before they arrive. If the program asks for a name, type in "Student" and then answer all other questions about sound or disk drives. When students become more comfortable and proficient in the lab, they can learn to load their own disks.

8. Give simple, clear, oral instructions for disk use.

Many lab teachers have developed thorough written instructional handouts for computer and disk use. Reading instructions, however, is not always as effective as listening to them because many high school LEP students have better aural comprehension skills than reading skills.

A sentence such as "Insert disk label-side up" could not be read by an ESL 1 student. However, all ESL 1 students will understand if the teacher shows and tells students in simple sentences how to insert a disk. This is also true for on-screen instructions. Go over them orally or just tell students what they must enter at certain points of the program.

9. Use lab assistants if available.

Verbal interaction is important in

making the time in the lab a total language learning experience for ESL students. If teacher assistants are not available, student monitors can be very beneficial in working with ESL students. Beginning ESL students spend most of their school day in classes together and have little contact with non-LEP students. The lab is a wonderful, non-threatening way for native speakers and LEP students to meet. Native-speaking students enjoy their role as tutors, and LEP students like getting help from peers. Student monitors in the lab can prove to be a rewarding learning experience for everyone.

Computer time that is not planned can be frustrating and unrewarding for LEP students, not to mention discouraging to teachers who, as a result, will conclude that LEP students cannot profit from computers. The ESL and computer lab teacher each have insights the other needs in order to make computer time a meaningful, effective source of language enrichment. These teachers are the key to LEP students' gaining access to computers in our schools. By working together, they can effect a change in the nation's lopsided statistics on computer access and provide LEP students with a highly motivating means of improving language skills.

References

Office of Technology Assessment. (1987, March). *Trends and status of computers in schools: Use in Chapter 1 programs and use with limited English proficient students*. Washington, DC; U.S. Government Printing Office.

Office of Technology Assessment. (1988). *Power on! New tools for teaching and learning*. Washington DC; U.S. Government Printing Office.

Software

Apple Presents Apple. Apple Computer, Inc., 20525 Mariani Avenue, Cupertino, CA 95014.

Mixed Up Sentences. Bilingual Instructional Technology Program, San Diego State University, San Diego, CA 92182. (This program was written for elementary students. ESL 1 high school students enjoy it, but older students might find it too childish.)

Player's Choice - ESL Patterns #1. CUE Softswap, P.O. Box 271704, Concord, CA 94527-1704.

Footnote

[1] Chapter 1 of the Education Consolidation Improvement Act (ECIA) provides compensatory educational and related services to educationally disadvantaged students who attend schools in low-income areas. Check district guidelines for LEP student eligibility.

Recent research provides us with a broadened vision of writing, with a focus on holistic and process approaches. As with native speakers, findings indicate that "second language acquisition is facilitated when the target language is used in a natural communicative context." (Diaz, 1986, p. 169) Writing instruction should be centered around students' backgrounds and needs, rather than around rules and structures.

Many teachers of limited English proficient (LEP) students assume that if these children cannot speak English, then writing instruction should be deferred and/or highly controlled. Recent findings do not support such teacher actions. Hudelson (1984, p. 221) notes that "child ESL learners, early in their development of English, can write English and can do so for various purposes." Practice and research are demonstrating that children at all ages and levels of schooling and language proficiency can and *should* write and that through writing they can expand their language base and other language skills, especially reading. In fact, a host of researchers have found that for both native speakers and second language learners, writing may very well precede formal reading (Bissex, 1980; Edelsky, 1982; Hansen, Newkirk, & Graves, 1985).

Thus, like native speakers and writers of English, LEP children need: opportunities to write, role models who demonstrate and value writing, room to experiment with language and make mistakes, and a safe and secure environment in which to practice and take risks in writing.

Letter writing proves to be an ideal activity for the second language learner. Through letters, children are provided a genuine audience, a real purpose for writing, and lots of nonconfrontational feedback about and response to their writing. The project described in this article involves a letter exchange linking university students preparing to become teachers with bilingual and English as a second language (ESL) students. The exchange, the results of the project, and implications for using letter writing to teach composition skills are discussed, along with applications of the computer in this process.

By
NANCY L.
HADAWAY

The Project

Over the course of a year, bilingual/ESL students in grades 2 through 12 were paired with university-level teacher preparation students for a letter exchange. Forty-eight students were involved during the fall semester and 85 in the spring, with 40 of the 85 carried over from the fall semester. Eight schools from four separate school districts participated in the project. Each member of the bilingual/ESL classes participated, so that all children, regardless of language proficiency, were writing and receiving letters. University students received their penpal assignments at the

331

beginning of each semester and then initiated the first piece of correspondence to their partner. Writers were given no instructions or assignments about their letters except to write, and each subsequent letter after the initial introductory one from the university students was a response to a previous letter. In addition to letters, pictures and small gifts such as pencils and stickers were also sent.

Project Results

Although the logistics of coordinating such a letter exchange were tremendous, the linguistic and emotional benefits made it all worthwhile. The penpals overcame language and cultural barriers to get acquainted and, in some cases, bonds of real friendship and support developed.

Topics covered in the letters included school, coursework and studying, family and home, hobbies and interests, language learning difficulties, and moving and adjusting to a new country and/or a new school.

Limited English proficient children and university students shared cultural aspects of their lives that included holiday celebrations, recreation, language, and foods. Embedded within the school year were several holidays, which offered many opportunities to share vocabulary, family traditions, and customs. These were familiar and important happenings that elicited much language from the children. At the same time, the LEP students gained insight into university life and activities through their penpals' letters. They read about football weekends, sororities, dorm life, and academic majors. Some became curious about how one studied to become a teacher and what it meant to attend college.

The letter exchange fostered growing self-confidence. A critical need for writers is "ownership over their topics, a chance to feel a sense of control over their own ideas." (Jochum, 1989, p. 1) With the exchange of letters, children experienced the freedom to choose topics of interest to them. Even though they were aware of their responsibilities to their writing partner, the LEP child could still initiate new topics or change the topic completely. These tactics helped the second language writer to manage the linguistic difficulty and interest level of communicating. Indeed, the letters often centered around juvenile concerns. However, such ownership in the writing process kept the lines of communication open and provided valuable practice in writing for the LEP child, along with opportunities to share their native language with their writing partners. This opportunity to teach was indeed validating.

Perhaps the most successful aspects of the exchange from a psychological and linguistic perspective were the support and role modeling. University students served as native speaker role models, and their language was authentic, including slang, college jargon, and informal syntax, rather than complete and formal sentences only.

In addition, every letter extended understanding and support. University students encouraged LEP children to study and to master English. The children followed suit and began to encourage their penpals through the tough academic moments of college life. One fourth grader wrote, "You will do good on those tests. You just have to believe in yourself." Support was offered on the personal side as well. When one university student broke up with her boyfriend, her bilingual penpal sent an original poem entitled "Don't Be Sad."

Homesickness and language difficulties were another topic that proved to bring out the best of both correspondents. University students shared recollections of moving to a new city or school in the hopes of helping bilingual/ESL students in their adjustments. One university student had recently come to the U.S. from Taiwan, so she had firsthand knowledge and suggestions to share with her penpal.

Classroom Applications

Letters involve reading as well as writing. Not only do LEP students reread as they compose, but their penpal letters must be read in order to frame an appropriate response. Peer conferencing can greatly enhance this process. When letters are received, pairs of students can work together reading letters aloud, confirming comprehension and brainstorming possibilities for replies. As a group, second language students can share more about their penpals and have the opportunity to talk more about what they may write in return. This whole class interaction can even evolve into group brainstorming or content mapping exercises that will help many students to further develop vocabulary and language structures.

The letters themselves also can serve as a basis for instruction. In the spirit of process writing and whole language, here the child's own interests and language provide the material for lessons. In communicating with a penpal, the LEP child will be using familiar and meaningful words and structures. With copies of their own letters and their penpal's responses, the second language learner can identify words that are difficult to spell or focus on areas where a lack of vocabulary may have inhibited communication. The teacher may then take several areas of concern that are thematically related and develop a spelling/vocabulary lesson on a recurring topic such as family or pastimes. Through the use of vocabulary/semantic webs, the whole class can expand their vocabulary. For more individual problem areas, students can develop personal word lists from their letters, which can provide more than enough input for spelling and vocabulary work.

Letters can be used also as a source of content in other subject areas such as social studies or math. With each letter providing a rich source of information about culture, family, traditions, holiday celebrations, geographic roots, and much more, children can take information about their penpals and chart it for the class as a whole. Bulletin boards can be developed to display maps that note each partner's birthplace and hometown. This data can then provide the input for a math lesson on computing distance or a social studies lesson on map skills. As the writing partners share information about their families, interests, recreational activities, and pets, it can be incorporated into graphic displays (pie, line, or bar graphs) on all correspondents. In all cases the content of the lessons has meaning and personal interest for students.

> In the spirit of process writing and whole language, here the child's own interests and language provide the material for lessons.

Using the Word Processor

If second language learners are using a word processor to compose and/or type their letters, the use of spell checkers and thesaurus/dictionary aids can help them to work independently. For younger children especially, using a word processor will make their writing easier to read. The computer is also a real confidence builder and motivator. One young second grade student who initially refused to participate in the letter exchange changed his mind after a brief introduction to word processing and subsequent composing via the computer. If school finances allow, networking via a modem also provides exciting possibilities for linking students in different parts of the country or world.

Summary

The more LEP children read and write, the easier those tasks will become. Letters are relevant and meaningful communication, and letter exchanges provide strong motivation to write as well as providing an emotional link with another individual who can serve as a role model of the target language. Students can choose and utilize realistic topics and language and will be encouraged to stretch their own language limits in order to communicate fully with their partner. Taking it one step further by using the LEP child's own words and interests to draw lesson content makes letter exchanges a teaching and learning opportunity not to be missed.

References

Bissex, G. (1980). *GYNS AT WK*. Cambridge, MA: Harvard University Press.

Diaz, D. M. (1986). "The writing process and the ESL writer: Reinforcement from second language research." *The Writing Instructor, 5, (4), 167-175*.

Edelsky, C. (1982). "Writing in a bilingual program: The relation of L1 and L2 texts." *TESOL Quarterly, 16, (2), 211-228*.

Hansen, J., Newkirk, T., & Graves, D. (Eds.). (1985). *Breaking ground. Teachers relate reading and writing in the elementary school*. Portsmouth, NH: Heinemann.

Hudelson, S. (1984). "Kan yu ret an rayt en ingles: Children become literate in English as a second language." *TESOL Quarterly, 18, (2), 221-238*.

Jochum, J. (1989). "Writing: The critical response." *Texas Reading Report, 12, (1), 1/10*.

Nancy Hadaway, Assistant Professor / Assistant Director of Field Experiences, The University of Texas at Arlington, Box 19227, Arlington, TX 76019.

Word Processing and Writing Instruction for Students with Special Needs: English as a Second Language (ESL)

Herrmann, A. W. (1985). *Word Processing in the ESL Class: Integrating Reading, Writing, Listening, and Speaking Skills.* Paper presented at the annual meeting of the Modern Language Association, 12p. [ED 274 980]

Discusses how creating a writing workshop atmosphere using computers in the ESL classroom improves opportunities for integrating all language skills: listening, speaking, reading, and writing. Argues that by using word processing, students become highly engaged in writing and learning language, gain new sensitivity to the flexibility of language, appear more receptive to feedback concerning the need for revision and editing, and improve their overall writing and language ability.

Huffman, D. T., & Goldberg, J. R. (1987). "Using word processing to teach ESL composition." System, 15(2), 169-175.

Reviews specific word processing programs to teach foreign students English language composition. Discusses advantages and disadvantages of features such as spell checkers, prompts, and formatting programs. Presents suggestions for enhancing students' writing skills both with and without word processing help.

Piper, A. (1987). *Helping learners to write: A role for the word processor.* ELT Journal, 41(2), 119-125.

Discusses the value of using a word processor to help ESL students improve their writing. Includes student assessment, teaching methods, and learning activities.

Wyatt, D. H. (1984). *Computers and ESL.* Language in Education: Theory and practice (No. 56). ERIC Clearinghouse on Languages and Linguistics, Washington, DC; Harcourt Brace Jovanovich [ED 246 694].

Examines state-of-the-art computer assisted language learning (CALL) in instruction of English as a second language. Discusses computer roles in language learning, computers and the standard curriculum, computer requirements for different types of CALL (instructional, collaborative, and facilitative), the promise of CALL in the ESL curriculum, and the benefits of computer assisted learning.

Article #16
Yes, We Can!

NEW TOOLS FOR COMMUNICATION, INFORMATION, MOTIVATION.

BY
LINDA
DAVIS

The scene could be unfolding in your school: Two students are working in the computer lab to create a spreadsheet that will calculate the school's basketball stats, fervently debating over which formulas to use.

The only difference here is that these students are profoundly deaf and communicating problem-solving tactics through sign language. They are students at the Missouri School for the Deaf (MSD) in Fulton, Missouri.

As IBM puts it, a personal computer can be "the window to much of the world for the blind" and a source of "new hope" for "the deaf, the voiceless, slow learners, the mentally retarded, people with brain injuries, and—most dramatically—those contending with severe mobility problems." But realizing the potential of technology for special needs learners has been a slowly accelerating process.

In The Beginning

Computers infiltrated American education quickly, usually without much advance planning. In regular classrooms, where the ratio of machines to students was usually 1:30, students were soon "fighting" for time on the computer. Special needs students were basically left out of this early computer mainstream. They rarely, if ever, saw any computer time at first. As computers then gradually made their way into special classrooms, it was often accompanied only by modifiable software—that is, software

manufactured for regular classroom use which could be slowed down or adjusted for different levels. Teachers in the special needs classrooms found this type of software insufficient for their specific needs. Learning disabled, behavior disabled, slow learners, mentally retarded, and other students needed special software suited to their specific abilities and interests. Physically disabled students also wanted a share of the computer time, but it was evident that many would require some type of adaptable software or hardware. Because of these inadequacies, the computer was soon being questioned in terms of its educational value for special needs students. Fortunately a few diligent individuals continued to press for more innovative ideas. They saw the unlimited resources of the computer and endeavored to pursue them.

A Case Study

At MSD we found ourselves within this prevailing trend. One of the first problems we encountered involved software reading levels. The average deaf high school student reads on a fourth- to fifth-grade level. If we ordered the correct reading level the program offered subject matter and feedback that a fourth or fifth grader would enjoy (trains, turtles, and so on) obviously not ideal for high school students. To help alleviate this we tried to focus our purchases on modifiable software programs and programs that were limited in graphics (at the risk of diminished general appeal). We also

336

came to depend heavily on the 30-day preview option to make sure software was really useful to us before we purchased it.

Finding appropriate text and classroom material to go with our computer curriculum was also difficult. For example, students in the Advanced Computer Class working comfortably with computer concepts at the secondary level had to struggle with computer skills textbooks that were beyond their reading level. The curriculum had to be revised and rewritten to accommodate these different competency levels.

Other challenges soon followed. We first attempted to set up our computer lab in rows but found that this arrangement made seeing the instructor difficult—a real problem for deaf students, for whom it is vital to have a clear view of the instructor during signed lectures. We rearranged the lab into a semi-circle, and added swivel chairs to make it easy for students to switch between facing the computer and facing the instructor.

Every aspect of the computer program was examined to insure all possible benefit to the student. We even salvaged an oversized old black and white television from the basement and connected it to a computer. Deaf students are very visual and the large monitor provided extra stimuli to help reinforce lectures.

New Hardware, Software, Support

While MSD and schools like it proceeded through trial and error, the technology continued to develop one step ahead of us. Today, I doubt any educator will dispute the fact that we've come a long way in a short time.

The awareness of computer possibilities for special needs students is defi-

nitely growing. Two recently formed research and support centers—INM's National Support Center for Persons with Disabilities and Apple Computer's National Special Education Alliance—have emerged as top industry resources in the area of special needs and computers. And there are many new and exciting technology developments already underway in special needs classrooms:

• For example, blind students can use adaptive tools such as Echo+ speech synthesizer and VersaBraille from Telesensory Systems, Inc. The Echo+ synthesizer is a plug-in board that converts ASCII text to speech. VersaBraille is a machine that connects a braille keyboard to an Apple IIe. It is currently in use by the Visually Handicapped Program in the Los Angeles Unified School District, where students also use a transition and translation software called BEX (Raised Dot Computing) to perform word processing. Braille 'n Speak, from Blazie Engineering, is a pocket-sized, battery-operated notetaker and speech output. IBM's Screen Reader allows blind or visually impaired users to hear text just as a sighted person would see it.

• Adaptive keyboards control devices, such as a headstick or mouthstick, may be used by persons with limited physical mobility. For example, *Light Talker* by Prentke Romich Co. is a device that uses an optical head-pointer, speech synthesis, and special software to allow the user to easily select function keys. To compensate for reduced fine motor control, students may use a keyguard—a keyboard overlay that stabilizes finger, hand, or stick movement for selecting specific keys without accidentally activating others—or keylatches, devices that toggle off and on to lock keys temporarily. A membrane keyboard can be used by those who can more easily press on a flat surface than on raised keys. For those who have trouble targeting standard-sized keys, there are expanded keyboards, while miniature keyboards aid those with a limited range of movement.

• There is even assistance for the special needs student who is limited only to head movement. A device similar to a light pen sits on the user's head like a headphone and registers head movement as he or she points to a word or character on the screen. For those people who can only use their breath, a "sip and puff" device or a mouth stick might be the answer. With the appropriate control device, such individuals can often use standard off-the-shelf software and hardware.

• For retarded students, personal computers can be effective skill development tools. The computer can present skills at the right level and pace, record progress, chart weaknesses, and offer remedial help in a patient, non-judgmental way. Not all of this is through drill and practice, either. For example, students at Miller School in Burbank, Calif., use Dr. Peet's Talk/Writer software from Hartley Courseware to write stories and record sight words, which Dr. Peet "reads" back, using synthesized speech. If students hear a word mispronounced, they know it's misspelled and ripe for editing.

• There's also been plenty of innovation for hearing impaired individuals. Students now have access to special fingerspelling practice software, which presents hands which form the letters of the alphabet in sign language. IBM has recently announced *SpeechViewer,* a vocalization system which allows a deaf or hearing impaired person to see his/her voice on the screen, then attempt to match proper sounds. Another language software package, Alpha Project from Dunamis Inc., displays actual signs from the American Sign Language.

New Features for Special Students

Today at MSD, computer labs are present in the elementary, junior high, vocational, and high school. The original purpose of the computer program at MSD was to help support concepts from the classrooms, but other objectives are now emerging from the computer room. We've developed a computer skills program that begins with introductory applications on the Apple and advances through five stages to desktop publishing advanced utilities, and data processing skills on an IBM. The program is helping prepare our students for jobs that once were limited to hearing individuals. People everywhere are communicating through computers linking ideas via local area networks and telecommunications. Communication is no longer limited to the spoken word and we want our students to seize the moment.

Computers are not only opening new career doors, but also allowing once suppressed thoughts, ideas, and dreams to finally emerge in a new form of communication. The child who was incapable of speaking—once trapped in her or his own mind—can now "talk" through the computer, and be heard.

What Lies Ahead

If we look at the future of computers for special needs students, it can only be described as exciting. The innovations seem endless, as software and hardware both become more finely adaptable and thus more universal.

I foresee an increase in software specially designed for learning and behavior disabled, mentally retarded, hyperactive and other students that require special instruction. Certainly, some of the present software can be tailored to meet their needs, but if students require special classroom instruction, specially trained teachers, and special materials, why not target special software that will also meet these specific needs?

Hopefully computers will continue to break down the misperception of physical disabilities as mental disabilities so that a greater understanding of the capabilities of every individual may emerge. As bumper stickers in the halls at MSD remind us "Deaf people can do anything—except hear."

The awareness and understanding of special student needs—and the use of computers to help meet them—will continue to increase. We have only touched the surface of the endless possibilities of this technology. Our dreams are restricted only by those limitations we allow ourselves and others to make.

Resources

NOTE: The array of special needs resources is extensive; this list is intended only to inform educators of some of the possibilities and encourage further exploration into specific areas of need.

IBM National Support Center for Persons With Disabilities
P.O. Box 2150
Atlanta, GA 30055

National Special Education Alliance
Apple Computer, Inc.
20525 Mariani Avenue
Cupertino, CA 95014

SpecialNet
National Association of State Directors of Special Education
GTE Education Services
2021 K St. NW, Suite 315
Washington, D.C. 20006

Closing the Gap
P.O. Box 68
Henderson, MN 56044

Center for Special Education Technology Council for Exceptional Children
1920 Association Dr.
Reston, VA 22091

HCCCP Newsletter of the Handicapped Children's Computer Cooperative Project
c/o Sherwood Center

7938 Chestnut
Kansas City, MO 64132

Handicapped User's Data Base CompuServe, Inc.
5000 Arlington Center Blvd.
Columbus, OH 43220

Technology Resources for Special People
Salina Technology Coalition
3023 Canterbury
Salina, KS 67401

Massachusetts Special Technology Access Center
c/o The Exceptional Parent Foundation
605 Commonwealth Ave.
Boston, MA 02215

Nevada Computer & Technology Center for the Disabled
819 Las Vegas Blvd. South
Las Vegas, NV 89101

Technology Center for Special Education
University of Missouri/Kansas City
School of Education
5100 Rockhill Rd.
Kansas City, MO 64110-2499

Chapter
5

Classroom Management Strategies and Teaching Techniques for the Technology Age Classroom

1. "Teachers vs. Students: In Whose Hands Should We Put the Computers?" Henry Olds, Jr. *Classroom Computer Learning,* April 1989. pg. 33.
2. "Today's Software, Tomorrow's Children's Workstation." B. Kurshan, B. Hunter and S. Bazak. *Teaching and Computers*, October 1989. pg. 20.
3. "Selecting Software—Who Me?" C. Fetner and K. Johnson. *Teaching and Computers*, March/April 1990. pg. 12.
4. "What Makes a Good Tutorial?" Leslie Eiser. *Classroom Computer Learning,* January 1988. pg. 44.
5. "Networking: How It Has Enhanced Science Classes in New York Schools." D. Brienne and S. Goldman. *Classroom Computer Learning*, April 1989. pg. 45
6. "The Truth about Cooperative Learning." Dr. David Dockterman. *CUE Newsletter*, May 1990. pg. 1.
7. "The Problem of Assessment." Holly Jobe. *CUE Newsletter*, May/June 1991 pg. 10.
8. "Worth A Second Look: Past Times, Future Times and Time for Planning." Gai Marshall. *CUE Newsletter*, June 1991. pg. 1.

This chapter highlights some issues and questions you will, and do, confront as a classroom teacher. Where should I locate the computers? Does a network system promote a more effective learning environment for my students? How do I select software? What kind of tests should I use that assess skill attainment in an information society?

Numerous articles could be placed in this chapter but we have selected just a few that raise many questions with some suggested solutions. For example, Holly Jobe asks "How do teachers decide what is important for children to learn?" and "How do children show us what they know?" These types of questions will generate much discussion—there is no one right answer. As you read these articles ask yourself what role technology should and will play as you attempt to resolve the issues.

What is a "Children's Workstation?" What software titles are appropriate for the workstation of the future? As you read the Kurshan, Hunter, and Bazak article you will be able to select the tool software for use in your classroom. Under each general software category area the authors state the features that are necessary for effective student use. They discovered many excellent "pieces" of software but found no single existing product that exemplified both the desired integration of functions and the suitability of interface.

Carolyn Fetner and Kay Johnson guide us through the basics for selecting software that is appropriate for classroom use. If you are an experienced technology user, you can write Part 2 of this article and list effective strategies to integrate the computer into your curriculum.

In similar vein, Leslie Eiser describes four high-quality science programs and gleans from them the features that make a "tutorial" effective. Not all educators are strong "tutorial" proponents while advocates press claims of cost-effectiveness for this type of software. Begin a list of pros and cons as you read the article, review some of the software listed and make your own decision on the viability of tutorial software.

Should you include a keyboarding class in your course? If you answered "Yes," Gerald Bracey examines five approaches to keyboarding instruction to determine the best way to learn this essential skill.

If networks are effective for administrative tasks, will they enhance the way children learn? According to Brienne and Goldman, Bank Street College researchers say "yes" and they've created the project to prove it. These developers created two science units, water/climate and plate tectonics to run on a network enabling science teams, not only to collect data but share a data pool to discover scientific principles. If students are to conduct real-world science activities, local and long-distance networks provide this opportunity to collect data from different sites enabling students to perform analyses as "real" scientists.

Cooperative learning has become a popular and powerful teaching strategy. Now the educational computing industry has attached the term to a number of its products and activities. Is it justified? Does technology support cooperative learning and vice versa? The article by David Dockterman illustrates the role of technology in a classroom that supports cooperative learning strategies. He lists particular pieces of software that support the notion of team members' gathering information and data from multiple sources. He suggests that kids learn better when they learn cooperatively. Are you convinced?

Are current methods of assessing student performance adequate in today's schools? Why is portfolio or authentic assessment a more effective technique for documenting student progress? Holly Jobe's article presents some important aspects of this approach to assessment. She gives some examples that incorporate technology tools and suggests that the use of technology in the classroom will force some teachers and schools to reexamine assessment practices. Do you agree?

You will implement many of the strategies outlined in this chapter as you create and promote an educational environment that enables a student to reach his or her potential in an information society. Classrooms of today cannot be the same as yesterday—today's workforce demands different skills from that of the second wave or industrial eras. It is your challenge to create that environment!

Questions for Discussion

1. Where would you locate 15 computers in an elementary school? Who would have first "call" on the computers? Why?
2. You have been hired by a software publishing company to produce an integrated piece of software for primary grade students. List the characteristics of this software and describe how a child would use it.

3. Is cooperative learning an easy strategy to implement? Why? What are its benefits? How do you promote this approach with technology?

4. List the methods and approaches today's schools use to assess student progress. In another column list the techniques that should be used in the Year 2000. How will schools move from column one to column two?

Questions from the Readings

1. Describe a "Children's Workstation."
2. What are the minimal characteristics of a word processing and desktop publishing piece of software?
3. What is an excellent example of a data base designed for data manipulation by students?
4. What is the difference between problem-solving software and "tool" software?
5. How can you spread the word about good software examples?
6. What are the characteristics of an ideal tutorial program? How would you use it?
7. Which approach to teaching keyboarding skills do you prefer? Why?
8. What are the advantages of students' accessing multiple data sources for scientific analysis?
9. How was this type of activity modeled on the work of scientists?
10. What is *Earth Lab*? How would you use it?
11. Define cooperative learning. How is it different from group learning?
12. Why is cooperative learning an important teaching/learning strategy?
13. What is portfolio assessment? What would you include in a portfolio for a math class? A science class? A primary grade class?

Article #1
Teachers vs. Students:
In Whose Hands Should We Put the Computers?

In an ideal scenario would you want to see a computer on every student's desk? Can the computer teach as well as a teacher? Better? Is it more important to ensure that every student has hands-on time at the computer or to get computers into the hands of teachers where they can be used as tools for large-group instruction?

These are some of the questions that computer-using educators tend to get pretty passionate about. And among the most eloquent speakers on such issues are two teachers-turned-software-developers, Art Bardige and Tom Snyder. There's a lot that the two agree about. They both care deeply about education and see the computer as a potentially valuable tool in schools. But, as you will soon discover, they have some sharp differences with regard to exactly how this tool should and should not be used in the nation's classrooms.

Art, a former physics and math teacher and curriculum coordinator, is now president of Learningways, Inc., a development group that has designed software for companies including D.C. Heath, Mindscape, Sunburst, and the Society for Visual Education (SVE). He takes great pride in Learningways' products such as the *Explore-a-Story* and *Explore-a-Science* series because he believes strongly in placing computers in the hands of students and providing them with graphically powerful toolkits for their imaginations.

Tom was for ten years a middle school teacher of science and social studies. Since the day he bought his first TRS-80 computer, he has been writing software to help teachers work with kids. With his current software company, Tom Snyder Productions, he is committed to producing software that writes the teacher "into the loop"—not as an optional participant but as an essential player.

The dialogue that follows has been excerpted from two discussions between Bardige and Snyder. The first took place at the Tenth Annual Lesley College Educational Computing Conference in Cambridge, Massachusetts, where the two participated in a panel discussion on the topic, "Whom do we make software for?" Several weeks later, the editors of *Classroom Computer Learning* met with Art and Tom to continue the dialogue.

CCL: *Even though the number of computers in schools continues to increase, we are nowhere close to having one computer for every teacher and student. If you were a superintendent today, how would you allocate your scarce computer resources?*

Tom: I would get them into the hands of the teachers first.

Art: Yes, and I'd get them into the hands of the teachers who are really going to do something with them. But then I'd make sure they were used with the kids.

Tom: Okay, but the teachers are key. The more I study the history of innovation in schools, and the more I go to

COMPILED AND EDITED BY HENRY F. OLDS, JR.

343

schools and talk to teachers, the more I realize the astounding political naivete in our industry. We think we can take a technology, even one that works, inject it into schools, and thereby revolutionize education. But when external groups develop wonderful things and try to put them in schools, they disappear. They never get replicated. History shows that you can't force this stuff into schools until it has a rightful place.

The Rand Corporation's study of innovations in education said that any innovation in schools will fail if it doesn't do two things: It must take into account the complex social structure of schools, and it must put the teacher in the dead center of the loop.

CCL: *So, if you had only enough computers to have one per classroom, you'd give them to the teachers even if it meant the students never used them individually?*

Tom: Absolutely. I'm not arguing against using good software with kids. I just think by giving it to the kids and expecting the teachers to catch up, we're going about it backwards. It's got to go to the teachers first.

Last year, Lake Washington School District near Seattle, Washington, bought an Apple IIGS for every teacher in the district who wanted one. In exchange, the teachers attended workshops and subsequently got hooked on word processing. This year, the teachers want modems. They want to send curriculum ideas back and forth. They're being professionalized by the computer. If you go there in a couple of years and try to take the computers out of that district, you'll have a tough time.

Art: Well, in school districts where computer resources are extremely scarce,

I'd have to agree with Tom and let the computer be more of a teaching tool to help the teacher. If you stick one computer in each classroom because you're trying to be egalitarian, then you don't give any student enough computer time to be of value. If a kid can only be at the computer for five minutes a day, that's crazy. But if I could arrange for multiple computers in the classroom, then I'd want the students to be using them.

Tom: One way in which I'd try to give students access to any extra computers is by modernizing our libraries. I think they are the perfect places for computers because they have always been research and media centers. Furthermore, they can absorb computers without disrupting the rest of the school.

CCL: *If you didn't have to worry about scarce resources, what would you imagine ideal schools and classrooms would look like?*

Tom: Even if I had all the resources in the world, I'm not sure I would give one computer to every kid. There are some good things that kids can do with computers—simulations and word processing, for example—and I've seen some fabulous examples of kids learning with computers. But no matter how great software is, no matter how great the individual program, I don't think schools will adopt a computer-intensive model for teaching kids. Even if you could prove that every piece of software out there is wonderful, given a choice, I think schools will opt for *teachers* teaching kids.

Art: I don't think we need one computer per student either. I certainly don't see students going to their computerized cubicles for instruction and coming out only for recess. But I do think com puters should be available to them, just like paper and pencils, both for serious instruction and for doodling. I think four to six computers per classroom would be about right. There needs to be enough computers so that a student can use one about an hour a day on the average.

I would certainly agree with Tom that students need lots of real human interaction. But I also think there are lots of good reasons for students to use computers—everything from CAI to creativity tools. The really exciting part is that we now have some ideas for using computers in ways we never thought of before. I think that when we can give students tools, images, and models to explore, these things will enhance students' imaginations and their abilities to express their ideas.

Tom: But I'm really concerned, Art, that if we make promises casually and not carefully about how computers can deliver instruction, people will start to believe us. I don't think we do know how to do it yet. I hear many people making a case that computers are smart enough to teach and that we can create marvelous instructional environments with them, but I don't know of any really convincing examples.

Art: I certainly agree that we mustn't pretend that computers are smart. And I'm distressed that most of the software that has been developed so far assumes that the student should sit in front of the computer pushing buttons and that the computer should respond by telling the student whether or not he or she has pushed the right buttons. The student gets the impression that the computer knows something, and that's crazy. But if we think of the computer in a different way, I believe we can use it to help kids understand ideas. Take math, for ex-

ample. I think that one of the biggest problems students have in learning math is that they can't visualize what's going on when they are asked to solve a problem. If they can't do that, all the computation skills in the world won't do them any good. And teachers frequently have a hard time breaking through the kids' inability to see the problem in a way that is solvable. The computer can help the teacher by providing students with tools for visualizing those problems.

Tom: I agree. As a matter of fact, we're developing a tool called a math visualizer that will let students do just that. If they have a division problem, they can create a visual model to see something being divided. But we're making the tool for the teacher, not the student. We're doing that because I believe that no matter how well you try to explain something to any student, even the simplest thing, they often don't get it, and they become frustrated and feel intimidated.

As a teacher, I know that I must be constantly looking at the student. I've got to have a relationship in order to work toward real understanding. What goes on in the learning process is so far beyond what the computer can handle that the model of computer as teacher just doesn't work. Teaching requires good eyes, a good heart, and all kinds of good intentions.

Art: Why can't students pick their own best way to learn? Why can't you give them a menu of options so they can pick their own way of visualizing something? We don't push kids' imaginations enough because we never give them enough alternative images to work with.

Let's look at math again. We know that students can't jump straight to the abstract, symbolic stuff in textbooks. Many teachers today accept that students should begin with manipulative materials and they provide materials like cuisinaire rods. But then, after the kids work with them, teachers expect the kids to make the leap directly from the manipulatives to the symbolic. But the transfer doesn't seem to work, and by the time the students are in fourth grade, they are learning the symbolic stuff by rote again and not understanding it.

Jerome Bruner has proposed three phases of concept development: concrete-manipulative, pictorial-iconic, and symbolic. I think in education we've paid no attention to the second step, the iconic. And the reason we haven't done it is that we've had no good tools to present dynamic images for students to work with. But now we have the computer, and the computer's the perfect tool for presenting that second step.

Tom: I do think the computer can help kids make that jump from concrete to abstract better, but I'm not sure it always works that neatly. David Perkins from Harvard has this concept of conceptual welding. Even if you take the most elaborate simulated games, sometimes when students leave the computer, they don't test that well. What they've learned is conceptually "welded" to that simulation environment. You have to pull it out in one way or another.

One of the best ways to pull it out is simply to have kids explain it to each other, thereby putting into their own words what they have learned. Getting students away from the computer, where they are in a relatively simple world of choice-making and problem-solving, and back out to the real world of confusion and excitement and disagreement is important. Teachers can do that very well.

Art: Tom, when you focus on group interactions and teachers leading discussions, I think you're postulating a classroom that doesn't exist today. About two-thirds of the on-task time in most classrooms is students sitting in their seats by themselves doing problems in textbooks or on worksheets.

I don't want to replace *teachers* with computers; I want to replace *textbooks* with computers. It's textbooks that are difficult for kids. We've been suffering for years with a curriculum delivery system that's doesn't meet the needs of teachers, students, and society. A textbook can be very dry, and it's often outdated and irrelevant.

I see computers as a wonderful solution to the textbook problem. I see them delivering fundamental curriculum in critical subject areas on a day-to-day basis. Computers can provide a broader and deeper curriculum than textbooks. With the computer we can give students much more interesting math problems to solve, with visual models to explore, with pictures to draw, and with interactive activities to do on the screen.

I'm not arguing against one-to-one interactions between teachers and students. I'm just saying that even if you could have wonderful discussions all the time, they're not enough. It's important for students to sit down alone and work through problems, and I think that is often best done with computers.

CCL: *We are all aware that a significant teacher shortage is being predicted. Is technology one answer for addressing this shortage?*

Art: I believe so. We face a *huge* teacher shortage. We will be about 100,000 teach ers short every year for as far as we can see. By 1992, that's half a million teachers short of a total teaching population of 2 to 2 1/2 million. We are likely to be 20 to 25 percent short of teachers. Average class sizes of 25 will go up to 32.

Tom: I'm not sure I agree with those statistics. But even if we do face a serious teacher shortage, the thing I don't understand is how you jump from the idea of the shortage to the conviction that computers will solve it. The answer to the teacher shortage is not more computers; the answer to the teacher shortage is more teachers.

Art: But the only way we will be able to get all the teachers we need is by bringing less fully trained professionals into the schools. We won't be able to get all the four-year college graduates we need, much less people with professional master's degrees. We'll have to use people with high school diplomas or with one or two years of college.

They will be trained para-professionals, they may be great with kids, but they will not have all the background and training needed to work with textbooks. If the curriculum passes to students through textbooks, you need a highly trained professional to make it work. Students can't learn from textbooks by themselves. Teachers have traditionally received training in how to use them. And they've had the chance to learn from experience. With less training and experience, a para-professional will need to work with a less demanding medium for conveying curriculum. I think the computer offers that medium.

Tom: But I think the problems in developing the software you imagine are much bigger than the problems in training more good teachers. Who is going to develop it? If you and I did nothing for the next year but develop some really good software, you might be able to do five or ten programs and I might be able to do the same. Even if all the good educational software developers combined their efforts, we wouldn't have time to develop a whole curriculum for the whole nation in all subject areas.

So far I think we've only been exploring what's possible. We have some nice theoretical models, and we've given some kids a couple of worthwhile experiences. But I don't see that we've done that much. I keep asking people to show me situations where software is really working. I've seen some kids using games or simulations that work well enough. But we are not talking about a few games here. We're talking about fundamental successes within the regular instructional program.

Art: You're right, I can't point to a lot of great software. What I can point to are some wonderful metaphors that we can now use to build good curriculum software or good teacher software. Tom, you've done a fabulous service to education by having taught us that the computer can be a mechanism to bring kids together to solve problems. Our *Explore-a-Story* series provides a metaphor that says that if kids can play with visual images, they will learn to use their imaginations in more creative ways.

I believe some of us have reached a fairly advanced level in developing software. We now have development systems that are capable of producing a lot of products in a reasonable time and at a reasonable cost. So we can concentrate our focus on the design of the curriculum, not on the design of the software. We don't have to produce the entire curriculum. We do have to produce the parts that are not now well served by the textbook. If we had stronger financial support, we could do it fairly quickly.

Tom: I really don't think it's that easy. Developing software is very different from writing books. If we are sitting in a design session and trying to figure out a nifty way to write a book to teach about adverbs, we can write that book fairly quickly and effectively. If we are designing software, it takes forever to come up with creative approaches because it's such an open-ended field. I just can't see enough rich stuff coming out of a development process like ours. What I do see happening is people trying to emulate the textbooks you're so critical of with big, powerful, integrated systems.

That's what happens if we keep promising that computers are going to be the answer to our problems. If there aren't enough teachers and someone is going to try to solve the problem with computers, it's not going to be done with stand-alone computers and individual titles. It will take a great big system, with thousands of software titles that we couldn't possibly write. And I'm really worried about that.

I'm worried about those situations where teachers don't have choices because a decision is made at the district level to adopt a technology. It's usually in very big school districts where there are strong fears that the schools are failing. Large corporations, backed by a lot of money, are out there selling integrated learning systems to big city school districts with the promise that they will solve the schools' problems. This approach could have very unfortunate consequences for the very kids who need the best teachers, not technology.

Art: Though I believe that we must have curriculum-based software, software that does the kinds of things that textbooks do, we must not do it like textbooks. I feel it's a shame to use the computer like a teaching machine, and unfortunately that's what a lot of the large systems have done so far. They fragment knowledge as if all the kid needs in order to understand something is a nice simple sequence of little knowledge molecules. I don't want to see technology used to perpetuate the vision that learning is memorizing little tidbits of knowledge. But I don't believe it has to be that way.

I see curriculum-based software offering *creativity* to kids. Kids learn to solve problems by actively trying things, and the computer can provide such experiences. I would argue that kids can't express things as well as they can imagine them. They can't draw as well as they can see pictures in their heads; they can't write as well as they can think about things. If we can get the computer to act as a toolbox, a writer's toolbox, an artist's toolbox, and a thinker's toolbox, then I think we've solved something.

Article #2
Today's Software,
Tomorrow's Children's Workstation

WE SEARCHED THROUGHOUT THE BEST OF TODAY'S APPLICATION PACKAGES
FOR ALL THE FEATURES WE'D LOVE TO SEE IN THE IDEAL ELEMENTARY SOFTWARE OF TOMORROW

What is a "Children's Workstation?" It's what we hope will be the elementary school computer of the future, with software that is fully-integrated, easy-to-use, and powerful enough to support learners not only in acquiring skills but also in solving problems, developing critical thinking skills, communicating ideas, and working collaboratively on multidisciplinary projects.

But since we live in the present, we examined nearly 50 existing software products to identify functions and features that come closest to our workstation of the future. The programs we looked at all are used in schools now and provide one or more of the following functions: word processing and desktop publishing; data base; spreadsheet; graphics (including both graphic arts and graphing/mapping); telecommunications and networking; and instructional management.

The software we examined was selected on the basis of popularity, current review, publisher reputation, and recommendations of experts. As part of the examination, small groups of elementary-aged children used the software in an after-school learning center. The programs we looked at are listed below. This article reports the highlights of our review; the existing packages which contain the features we sought are listed in italics throughout the text.

General Features
- **Friendly Interface**
- **Easy Integration**

Suitable user interface and integration of functions are important in any workstation, but are especially critical for young children. The interface features we looked for include iconic menus *(Explore-a-Story)*; input with keyboard, tablet, and/or mouse *(The Newsroom)*; simple screen layout with only a few choices provided on the screen *(Kidwriter)*; uniform screens, menu selection devices, and function access *(AppleWorks, Eight-in-One, The Children's Writing and Publishing Center)*; a filing system with student directories and subdirectories *(A+)*; and sound and voice output *(My Words, Talking Textwriter)*. In terms of integration, we looked for integration of tools accessed from a main menu *(Kid Talk);* messaging among users and functions *(Bank Street Writer III);* integration of guides to systematic thinking and problem solving *(SemCalc, Homework Helper Math* or *Writing);* and a built-in calculator across functions *(Math Problem Solving Courseware)*. In addition, to facilitate use of the Children's Workstation, some keyboarding activities should be included in the form of a "type" program to introduce the keyboard and other input devices at the workstation.

BY
DR.
BARBARA
KURSHAN,
BEVERLY
HUNTER,
AND
SUZANNE
BAZAK

349

In general, a Children's Workstation should be simple enough for children to use yet sophisticated enough to be used by the teacher for instructional design and classroom planning tasks. These characteristics were not completely found in any one existing package. In addition, teacher users will require an effective teacher-oriented management system: we could not find good examples of a management system for tool applications for the classroom.

Word Processing and Desktop Publishing

- Basic text entering and editing
- FIND and REPLACE feature
- Speech option
- Varied text sizes
- Integration with graphics
- Iconic menus
- Simple print layout selection
- Spell checker with word-addition option
- Teacher template option

Of all the existing word processing and desktop publishing software we reviewed, *Kid Talk, Kidwriter, Magic Slate, Talking Textwriter*, and *My Words* were some of the most appropriate word processing packages for grades K-3. *Kidwriter* is very simple to use and provides students with both word processing and the ability to illustrate with clip art, although it does not allow a story to be edited once it has been saved. *Magic Slate* does not include graphics, but it does use large text (a 20-column screen) and has many more word processing capabilities than *Kidwriter*. *My Words* and *Talking Textwriter* have the extra feature of voice output; *Kid Talk* has

both voice output and an excellent iconic interface. A new package called *FirstWriter* combines words, pictures, and voice output for children in grades K-2.

For elementary students of all ages, the *Explore-A-Story* series and *Bank Street Story Starters* combine word processing and graphics in unique ways. *Bank Street Story Starters* allow students to create story pages with personalized graphics using a mouse or a joystick. Pages can be flipped through like a book, text windows can be added, and illustrations can be animated. The *Explore-A-Story* series provides icon menus and simple mouse input for selecting from a bank of clip art characters, objects, text, and background scenes. By clicking the mouse anywhere on the screen, students are also able to enter their own text or add text from a data base of terms.

For grades 4-6, there are several good word processing packages. *Magic Slate* can be used in its 40-column or 80-column version, while *Bank Street Writer III* and *HomeWord* offer enhanced text, varied print options, and advanced editing. Of the three programs, *HomeWord* provides the easiest control components with its iconic menu selection; *Magic Slate* is controlled by single key stroke commands; and *Bank Street Writer III* has the menu at the top of the screen. All three provide students with a spell checker.

Special features for helping students organize information are provided in *Writer's Helper* and *Homework Helper Writing*. Both of these programs would usually be used in middle or upper grades, but have some appropriate applications for younger students. *Writer's Helper* allows the teacher to set up templates of questions to guide students through a particular writing project. *Homework Helper Writing* has a similar option, but the questions are generated by the program and not the teacher. *Writer's Helper* also provides several tools for evaluating student writing. One particular feature that could be adapted for elementary writing is the option for a teacher to specify up to 25 words that can be checked in a student's writing project.

Most of the software packages which adequately combined fundamental word processing features and graphics fell into the category of desktop publishing; these include *A+, AppleWorks IIGS, The Children's Writing and Publishing Center, Newsroom,* and *NewsMaster.* Created specifically for elementary school students, *The Children's Writing and Publishing Center* provides simple enough screens to be used by even those with limited reading ability. All of the other packages are too sophisticated for independent use in early primary grades, although they have features that could be easily simplified and adapted for elementary students. *A+* has an excellent filing system allowing students to organize their work in files which are displayed as three-ring binders on the screen. It is also driven by iconic menus, as is *Newsroom* and *AppleWorks IIGS.* These packages and *NewsMaster* all provide several different text fonts and the ability to integrate text and graphics on the same screen with text wrapping around or over pictures.

In our review of existing word processing and desktop publishing tools, we found several characteristics that would not be appropriate for a Children's Workstation. First, if speech is to be an option, it should be integrated into the writing process, not separated from it. Second, word processors that provided the standard 80-column format were not well received by younger children; those with larger text work better. Several programs allow students to create stories but give them very few, if any, options for editing those stories. The desktop publishing programs assumed a level of understanding of publishing that was not realistic for elementary age students. Finally, several programs have quite complicated commands for performing special functions, requiring students to memorize keystrokes rather than simply making a selection from a menu.

Data Bases

- Basic features for entering, editing, searching,
- and sorting data
- Ability to integrate pictorial data
- Integration with graphics and graphing tools
- Voice output option
- Ample storage
- Interface to laboratory equipment for data collection
- Networking capability for collaborative use

All of the traditional menu driven data base management programs we reviewed (*PC File, AppleWorks,* or *Computer Literacy Through Applications*) provide basic data entry, data editing, search, and sort features. All are adequate for grades K-6 when used by the teacher or curriculum developer to set up data base files which students can then manipulate.

An excellent example of a data base designed for data manipulation by students is the simple data base integrated into the *Where in Europe is Carmen Sandiego?* program. This data base is limited to information for a specific use, but for young learners it models appropriate search algorithms for problem solving. The *Explore-A-Science* programs come closest to providing data base features that would allow younger students to enter text, graphics, and numerals. These programs provide students with an internal pictorial data base, with which pictures and diagrams could be labeled with text and then stored on the disk. However, the data bases in the *Explore* series are limited and do not provide the functions necessary for searching and sorting data.

For older students and more sophisticated applications, the data base tool in *AppleWorks GS* allows graphic art to be stored as data. *Think Quick* comes with a graphing tool for editing pictograph symbols. Although the manipulation of the graphical data is limited, these features indicate an interesting development for elementary level data base applications. The *Science Toolkit* program provides a model of interfacing a data collection program with laboratory equipment such as probes and sensors. For a glimpse at the potential for collaboratively shared data, check out *Kids Network*.

Overall, we found that several otherwise useful data bases limited the search and sort features; these should be standard issue in the data base function of a Children's Workstation. Another disadvantage of many of the existing data base programs is their standard 80-column display format, in which data fields are simply listed one after the other on the screen. Information in a Children's Workstation data base program should be displayed using a more creative visual approach.

Spreadsheets

- One screen with row and
- column format
- Simple formatting features
- Algebraic equation format for calculations
- Teacher template option
- Access to on-screen calculator
- Integration with graphing tool

Very little is currently available in spreadsheet applications for primary school students. For older elementary students, *Computer Literacy Through Applications* provides the traditional spreadsheet format, but with limited spreadsheet functions (although it does offer formulae entry in the form of algebraic equations). Of the more sophisticated programs that integrate with other tools, *AppleWorks* allows the user to format whole rows or columns, while *Eight-In-One* provides access to graphing capability.

The *Semantic Calculator* (otherwise known as *Semcalc*) and *Homework Helper Math* combine the traditional spreadsheet row-column format with special features that promote the development of good problem solving skills. *Semcalc* forces students to think about the semantic meaning of the data they are entering and the units in which they expect their output to occur. *Homework Helper Math* provides on-screen instructions for a step-by-step heuristic approach to problem solving. Students can practice with problems that are already set up in the program or use the tool to solve their own problems. When solving problems that are already defined in the program, students are able to view on-screen diagrams depicting the problem to be solved.

An on-screen calculator as a built-in feature of an elementary workstation is available in varying forms in some tool packages for elementary school students. The calculator in *Homework Helper Math* is actually an equation solver and does not provide the traditional calculator features. *A+* offers a very nice built-in calculator that the student can access from a variety of places within the tools. An additional program that features a "pseudo" calculator is *Mathematics Courseware Problem Solving,* which uses the calculator to help students set up word problems in proper mathematical equations and do the calculations.

Graphics

- Graphing and Mapping
- Integration with data base
- Integration with spreadsheet
- Simple data entry
- Easy editing
- Teacher template option
- Multiple format options (including pictographs)
- Color
- Lab equipment interface with real time graphing
- Map display
- Graphic Arts
- Basic shape-creating functions
- Optional input devices
- Variable text fonts
- Ample available clip art
- Integration with graphing tool for pictographs

Graphics are a vital part of our Children's Workstation. Current graphic arts packages can be divided into three categories: those that use clip art only, those that allow students to generate their own art, and those that provide both clip art and free form drawing. Clip art-based graphic packages that are exceptionally good are *Print Shop* and *Super Print,* while *Draw-It, A+, Dazzle Draw, Paintworks,* and *Blazing Paddles* all provide students with features for creating their own graphics with tools for drawing circles, boxes, and straight lines. All five programs provide for text additions; *Dazzle Draw, Paintworks,* and *Blazing Paddles* have the extra advantage of allowing input from something other than the keyboard (such as mouse, graphics tablet, or joystick). *A+, Dazzle Draw,* and *Blazing Paddles* all have nice iconic menus which children find easy to understand and use; *Dazzle Draw* has additional pulldown menus for special filing and editing features.

The ability to integrate graphics with a word processing document increases the power of any drawing tool. *Multiscribe, A+,* and *AppleWorks IIGS* currently provide this integration.

Several drawing packages force students to draw pictures using the keyboard and plotting pixel by pixel. These packages are cumbersome and could not compare to those that provide input from some other source. Several packages also have very limited editing features: once a drawing is produced, it is very difficult to change. Flexibility when drawing and writing should be essential.

Graphing and mapping programs which allow students to display numeric data graphically are also an essential part of the Children's Workstation. Two existing programs which provide this capability are *Easy Graph II* and *Eight-In-One Graphing. Easy Graph II* is appropriately named in that it is very simple to learn. Although it limits the user to a small number of data items, it makes for simple creation of bar graphs, pie charts, and (especially nice for younger children) pictographs. *Eight-In-One Graphing* is a more sophisticated graphing package and can be integrated with the *Eight-In-One Data Base* and *Spreadsheet*.

Graphing is an added function to several excellent programs. *Think Quick,* a problem-solving game, provides many different on-screen symbols that can be edited by the user when creating original *Think Quick* games; a similar symbol editor would be appropriate for creating personalized pictographs. *Science Toolkit* provides a lab equipment interface which allows for "real time" graphing of data students collect.

There are two special elementary school programs that approach graphing, charts, and tables in a unique manner. *Kids Network* provides a special feature for displaying data on maps. *Project Zoo* teaches students about graphs and charts in the setting of a zoo, and even allows students to build a zoo by examining information about animals and visitors in graphs and "pseudo" data bases.

Communications

- **Both local area networking and telecommunications ability**
- **Structure for collaborative learning**
- **Shared data bases**

Local area networking and telecommunications support are essential to our Children's Workstation. In addition to the convenience and range both kinds of networking provide, they can support collaborative learning through messaging among students, teachers, and administrators and through use of shared databases. They also add power to instructional management.

Only one of the existing programs reviewed was designed to take this kind of advantage of local area networks. *Bank Street Writer III with E-Mail* has a built-in feature to be used with an Apple Talk Network, allowing students to write, send, and receive "mail" to and from other students and teachers.

There is also at least one existing program which makes good use of telecommunications for access to information networks and bulletin board systems. *Kids Network* provides for telecommunications among schools involved in its network, and has an easy-to-use communications interface for uploading and downloading messages and data base information. In addition, a new version of this front-end interface will provide other tool capabilities such as word processing and graphics.

Conclusion

As we looked for current software products that help point the way to a next generation Children's Workstation, we found many excellent "pieces" but no single existing product that exemplifies both the desired integration of functions and the suitability of interface we seek. While integrated software packages which include word processing, database, spreadsheet, graphing, pictures, and communications are found in many homes and offices, none of the current integrated products are designed for elementary age children or classroom environments. Providing such a workstation for children will require a more powerful hardware base than is currently found in schools. Current programs designed for children are constrained by the installed base of equipment. However, it is time to begin planning the Children's Workstation software for the next generation of computers that will become available in schools over the next few years.

Glossary

Interface: The "control panel" by which the computer user interacts with a software or hardware product or system; includes all facets of how you tell the computer what to do and how it asks you what to do. If using a program is as easy as ordering a pizza delivery by phone, the program is said to have a "friendly interface."

Integration: The ability of different programs to work together easily. Ideally integrated software tools would allow you to create a data base of the planets, transfer data into a spreadsheet to calculate travel time between planets, feed the spreadsheet figures into a graphing program, shift to a drawing program to create portraits of the planets, then pull it all together in a word processing or desktop publishing document—all without reentering a bit of data.

Voice output: The ability of software and hardware to "talk"—that is, to read aloud in a computer synthesized voice what appears on the screen. Voice output requires hardware with built-in or added-on speech synthesis capability, plus speech-equipped software.

Iconic menu: Lets you command your computer by selecting small, simplified pictures representing different functions, instead of typing in numbers, words, or codes.

Template: A reusable software tool "shell" into which the user can type specific data.

Publishers Addresses

Baudville
5380 52nd St. SE
Grand Rapids, MI 49508
616/698-0888

Britannica Software
(Designware/Eduware)
345 Fourth St.
San Francisco, CA 94107
800/572-2272; 415/546-1866

Brøderbund
17 Paul Dr.
San Rafael, CA 94913-2947
800/527-6263; 415/492-3500

Buttonware Inc.
PO Box 5786
Bellevue, WA 98006
800/528-8866; 206/746-4396

Claris
440 Clyde Ave.
Mountain View, CA 94043
415/960-1500

Conduit
Univ. of Iowa
Oakdale Campus
Iowa City, IA 52242
319/335-4100

D.C. Heath
125 Spring St.
Lexington, MA 02173
800/334-3284

DLM
One DLM Park
PO Box 4000
Allen, TX 75002
800/527-4747; 800/442-4711 in Texas

First Byte
2845 Temple Ave.
Long Beach, CA 90806
213/595-7006

Hartley Courseware
Box 149
Dimondale, MI 48821
800/247-1380; 517/646-6458

Houghton Mifflin
Educational Software Division
Dept. 39 Box 683
Hanover, NH 03755
800/258-9773

The Learning Co.
6493 Kaiser Dr.
Fremont, CA 94555
800/852-2255

McGraw-Hill
1200 NW 63rd
Oklahoma City, OK 73116
405/840-1444

Mediagenic (Activision)
3885 Bohannon Dr.
Menlo Park, CA 94025
415/329-0800

Mindplay
100 Conifer Hill Dr.
Building 3, Suite 301
Danvers, MA 01923
800/221-7911; 617/774-1760

Mindscape
3444 Dundee Rd.
Northbrook, IL 60062
800/221-9884

National Geographic
Society Educational Services
Department 88
Washington, D.C. 20036
800/368-2728; 301/921-1330

Paperback Software
2830 Ninth St.
Berkeley, CA 94710
800/443-0100; 415/644-2116

Savtek Corp.
PO Box 1077
Waltham, MA 02254
617/891-0638

Scholastic Software
PO Box 7502
2931 East McCarty St.
Jefferson City, MO 65102
800/541-5513

Sierra On-Line
40033 Sierra Way
Oakhurst, CA 93644
209/683-4468

Spinnaker
One Kendall Square
Cambridge, MA 02193
617/494-1200

Springboard
7808 Creekridge Circle
Minneapolis, MN 55435
800/654-6301; 612/944-3912

Sunburst Communications
39 Washington Ave.
Pleasantville, NY 10570-2898
800/431-1934; 914/769-5030

Unison World
1321 Harbor Bay Parkway
Alameda, CA 94501
510/748-5680

Software Summary

Key to headlines

A: MS-DOS
B: Apple
C: Word Processing
D: Desktop Publishing
E: Data Base
F: Spreadsheet
G: Graphing
H: Graphics/Drawing
I: Graphics Clip Art
J: Animation
K: Voice Output
L: Color
M: Mouse, Joystick, Tablet
N: Management
O: Communications
P: Teacher Tools

Title	A	B	C	D	E	F	G	H	I	J	K	L	M	N	O	P	Publisher
A+	√		√			√							√	√			Savtek
Appleworks		√	√		√	√	GS			GS	GS		GS				Claris
Bank Street Story Starters	√	√	√			√	√	√		√	√					√	Mindscape
Bank Street Writer	√	√	√													√	Scholastic
Bank Street with E-Mail		√	√									√	√	√	√	√	Scholastic
Beginning Keyboarding	√	√												√			Houghton Mifflin
Blazing Paddles		√				√	√					√	√				Baudville
Children's Writing & Publishing Center	√	√	√	√			√	√				√	√			√	Learning Co.
Computer Literacy Through Applications	√	√	√		√	√										√	Houghton Mifflin
Cotton Tales	√	√	√	√			√										Mindplay
Create with Garfield	√	√	√				√			√							DLM
Dazzle Draw		√	√			√	√			√	√						Broderbund
Designasaurus	√	√			√		√	√		√							Britannica
Dr. Pete's Talk Writer		√	√							√						√	Hartley
Draw-It	√					√	√			√							Paperback
Easy Graph II	√	√				√	√			√							Houghton Mifflin
Eight-in-One	√	√	√		√	√	√							√			Spinnaker
Explore-a-Science		√	√	√	√		√	√		√	√					√	DC Heath
Explore-a-Story		√	√	√	√		√	√		√	√					√	DC Heath
Fantavision		√				√	√	√		√	√						Broderbund
Firstwriter		√	√	√			√			√	√	√				√	Houghton Mifflin
Homeword Plus	√	√	√														Sierra
Homework Helper Math	√	√				√							√				Spinnaker
Homework Helper Writing	√	√	√										√				Spinnaker
Kids Network		√	√		√		√					√	√	√	√	√	Nat'l Geographic
Kidwriter	√	√	√			√							√				Spinnaker
Magic Slate		√	√										√			√	Sunburst
Mathematics Courseware Problem Solving		√			√			√		√			√			√	McGraw Hill
Math Talk & Kid Talk & Fraction Talk		√	Kid							√	√	√					First Byte
Multiscribe		√	√			√	√			√	√						Scholastic
Muppet Slate		√	√				√			√							Sunburst
My Words		√	√								√						Hartley
Newsmaster	√		√	√		√	√										Unison
Newsroom	√	√	√	√		√	√			√	√						Springboard
Paintworks		√	√			√	√			√	√						Mediagenic
PC File	√				√												Buttonware
Print Shop	√	√		√		√	√			√	√					√	Broderbund
Project Zoo		√		√		√		√		√						√	Nat'l Geographic
Semcalc		√			√											√	Sunburst
Science Toolkit	√	√		√		√					√					√	Broderbund
Story Tree	√	√	√														Scholastic
Super Print	√	√		√		√	√			√	√						Scholastic
Talking Textwriter	√	√	√							√		√				√	Scholastic
Think Quick	√	√				√	√	√		√	√						Learning Company
Type!	√	√														√	Broderbund
Where in Europe is Carmen Sandiego	√	√			√			√		√	√					√	Broderbund
Writer's Helper	√	√	√													√	Conduit

Article #3
Selecting Software . . . Who, Me?

By
Carol
Fetner
and
Kay
Johnson

Teachers at Gung Ho Elementary are "up" on what's "in" in educational software. When computers first began invading the educational scene, Gung Ho teachers began experimenting with software, in search of a wide variety of skills and approaches to ensure success for all students. Once they learned what type of software was available, the characteristics of quality programs, and ways to match software to their classroom needs, they found selecting software to be a snap!

What am I Looking For?

The first thing Gung Ho teachers learned was how to ask themselves certain key questions about what they needed and wanted in terms of classroom computing. For example, into what subject area do I want to incorporate the computer? Will I be using it to practice basic concepts, provide remedial help, provide enrichment, or all three? Will I be using the computer with the whole class, with small groups, or with individual students? Given all of the other material I plan to use for this subject area, how much time will my students have to work with this software?

Software Species

The next thing Gung Ho teachers wanted to learn was how to sort software into types.

• Drill and practice is the kind of software they found surfacing most often—and with good reason. Kids have historically learned facts using this method, a method consisting of one person calling out questions and one answering. The computer eliminates the need for such a duo. Not only do good drill and practice programs provide the questions, but instant feedback as well. This feedback, often in the form of exciting graphics displays, offers the student the opportunity of a second chance to achieve the objective, and failing this, the answer itself—privately!—thus avoiding any embarrassment.

Another type of software Gung Ho teachers encountered was the *tutorial,* which teaches a concept from scratch. Gung Ho teachers are somewhat hesitant to rely on a computer program to teach content for which a student will be held accountable. They prefer to use the tutorial as reinforcement—except in the case of keyboarding tutorials, which are especially valuable because of their direct connection to computer skills.

• *Simulation* programs are a "turn-on" for Gung Ho students—not to mention their teachers and parents. These programs, while presenting life-like situations, also require decision-making, calculating, and long-term planning. What a perfect way to relate education to the real world.

• *Problem solving* software fits right in with an increasing emphasis on problem solving as an educational objective in the elementary school. Students love a challenge, and the intrigue intensifies when they can meet these challenges using a computer.

• Also gaining popularity among Gung Ho teachers is *"tool"* software, such as

358

graphics programs, word processors, data bases, spreadsheets, and more.

When planning an in-service on software selection, build in time to demonstrate one or more programs from each of these categories, and help teachers brainstorm ways that each might be used in real classroom settings.

Reviews and Previews

Once teachers have a sense of their software needs and a general idea about the kinds of packages available, they can move to the "fact-finding" stage of their software search. They'll need to learn several methods of identifying possible packages.

• *Reviews.* Your school or district probably has on-hand a variety of sources of software reviews, including computer magazines (like this one), books such as *Only the Best* (R.R. Bowker, New York, N.Y.) or *TESS* (EPIE, Water Mill, N.Y.), or your own evaluation reports. Show teachers how to use these resources by modeling a search for a particular kind of program—for example, a science simulation program for independent study use by kids in grade 5. Emphasize the key types of information teachers should look for in reviews, beyond the overall quality of the program—such as its ease of use by students, its pedagogical approach, and its price. Encourage teachers to cull a list of one to three programs that are potential "winners."

• *Word-of-mouth.* Don't let teachers overlook their colleagues as useful sources of information about software. Encourage them to ask each other for leads about what works and doesn't work in a classroom. This "word of mouth" kind of research may well go beyond your building to other schools in the district—or even to state and regional educational computing groups.

• *Previews.* Once teachers have a short list of possible packages, encourage them to try before they buy (or borrow, if you're operating a central software library). More and more, companies are providing the opportunity to preview software before actually purchasing. This provides teachers with an opportunity to run through their own checklist of "winning ways" (see next section) as well as to submit the software to its true test: how well it works when actually used with students.

Winning Ways

Suppose a program fits a teacher's curriculum objectives and classroom setup. What else should he or she look for before saying yes to this software?

• *User friendliness.* Just as we seek out friendly people with whom to spend our time, the computer "experts" at Gung Ho Elementary select computer software that is "user friendly." Software that provides easy-to-follow directions and simple documentation is a must. Educators just don't have time to spend trying to "make a program work" over and over. User friendly software is in great demand by teachers and students.

• *Individualization.* Once the program works, teachers demand much more than just "friendliness." A program that allows for individualization (one that allows for different students to work at different levels of ability) is a true teacher aid. The ability of the teacher to prescribe and manage the computer efforts of the students is invaluable—a perfect example of incorporating the computer into the teaching curriculum.

• *Record keeping.* Teachers want the computer to help them keep track of how students are performing on the tasks the software presents. Programs that keep student records and help analyze errors are favored among teachers.

• *Student reaction.* Students demand even more than their teachers, if they are to stay involved in the activity. Programs that give immediate feedback, reward correct answers, correct wrong answers, and eventually provide a right answer become true friends to the student. What's more, the computer should offer students a means of interacting with a program to input the right answer or make a decision. Teachers at Gung Ho Elementary know that this active involvement, combined with high quality graphics, will hook a student every time. Each student gets a nonjudgmental, private tutor—a dream come true.

Spreading the Word

Once a teacher has found a piece of software that works, encourage her or him to toot its horn, in one or more of the following venues:

• At a grade level or subject specific in-service session. Who better to tell a teacher what works than another teacher? When teachers leave, they are equipped with a new tool for their classroom. In-services held on a regular basis provide teachers with the opportunity to acquire many such tools in a short amount of time.

• Faculty meetings! Just two minutes is enough time to tell of a new program and what it will "do for you." *Teachers will beat a path to your door before the meeting is over.* Be sure you always have documentation (directions) available to accompany the software as teachers "try it out."

• In the school newsletter. "Extra! Extra! Read all about it! New software at Gung Ho Elementary . . ." Such a proclamation in the newsletter is certain to promote interest in any new program.

• On the walls, in the halls . . . . Encourage teachers to use graphics programs to print eye-catching posters or banners for the teachers' workroom, the mailbox area, even the restrooms (what better place for reading material?). It's a sure sell for good programs—and their colleagues will thank them!

What Makes a Good Tutorial?

A LONG TIME EDUCATOR LOOKS AT FOUR HIGH-QUALITY SCIENCE PROGRAMS AND GLEANS FROM THEM THE FEATURES THAT MAKE A TUTORIAL EFFECTIVE

BY
LESLIE
EISER

Depending on where you sit, tutorial software is either the potential saving grace of computer education or a bugaboo to be avoided at all costs. People who hate tutorial software frequently justify their position by pointing to programs that follow a strictly linear presentation, that feature irrelevant graphics, that consider "interaction" to be pressing the space bar, and that treat all learners in exactly the same way. At the same time, proponents of tutorial software cite the tremendous growth in the number of tutorial programs throughout the business sector and point to industries that have transferred much of their new employee training to this kind of technology, based on cost effectiveness.

Obviously, some middle ground must exist. While there is no question that many early tutorials were actually computerized textbooks with the return key substituting for physical page turning, newer tutorials are more likely to take advantage of the computer's ability to present models in dynamic ways. Because of their improved flexibility and power, tutorials are again becoming popular, and rightfully so. Used properly, they can only make our jobs easier and more fun.

If you have been considering using tutorial software in your classroom, this article will point out some of the newer capabilities to check against your own selections. Moreover, if you are a science teacher, then you will be particularly interested in the specific programs highlighted: All are science tutorials chosen because they illustrate some of the newer possibilities. And if you have decided that tutorials will never work in your classroom, you may want to reconsider. Interesting tutorials can currently be found for all curriculum areas.

The Power of Interactive Graphics

Graphics are unquestionably one of the main reasons that computerized tutorials score points with students. High-quality graphics and animation that amplify and explain content should be a requirement—not an option—in any tutorial you consider.

Unfortunately, inappropriate graphics abound in much of today's tutorial software. Some programs, for example, allow enthusiasm for pretty pictures—animated aliens or cutesy professors that dash across the screen, "you won!" messages, etc.—to overcome common sense. In other programs, a simulation that looks real enough may in fact be inflexible and very much under the control of the computer: only certain actions or choices turn out to be acceptable to the computer program, whereas in real life many more options are available. And still other programs, in attempting to simplify complex concepts and represent them graphically, manage to present misleading information about those concepts.

361

But graphics need not be inane, misleading, or oversimplified. In both Brøderbund's *Physics* and IBM's *Scientific Reasoning* series, for example, the graphics and animated sequences are consistently relevant. In Brøderbund's section on velocity and acceleration, for instance, acceleration-time, velocity-

A Sampling of High-Quality Science Tutorials

Don't look for any tutorial program to embody all the characteristics mentioned in the accompanying article. However, each of the programs mentioned in the article does offer some special strengths. Here's an overview of those programs.

Physics
from Brøderbund Software

This package presents with amazing effectiveness a textbook-oriented physics course on the Macintosh. Graphics are spectacular, not so much in novelty as in variety and quality of interactivity. However, lack of structure within the program may make the graphics difficult for beginning physics students to use without some help from the teacher. This problem is the weakest part of an otherwise fabulous program for the senior high school and first-year university student.

Package contains: 2 disks with backup, manual
Hardware: Macintosh, Mac Plus, Mac SE (512K)
Grade level: 9 and above
Price: $99.95
Ordering information: Broderbund Software, 17 Paul Dr., San Rafael, CA 94903; (415) 492-3500

Physical Science Series and Earth Science Series
from Educational Activities, Inc.
Physical Science Series:
    Sound

    Machines, Work and Energy*
    The Structure of Matter
    Heat and Light*
    Electricity and Magnetism*
Earth Science Series:
    Earth: The Inside Story
    The Earth Through Time and Space*
    Weather

These programs offer good pedagogy in a highly structured and linear set of tutorials. Lovely color graphics add appeal; recordkeeping helps the teacher monitor access. Material is up-to-date and includes some very current information. Some interaction with the graphics is provided, but always within limits set by the program. Fairly standard evaluation material is provided at the end of each section.

Each package contains: 1 disk with backup, teacher's manual, reproducible activity masters
Hardware: Apple II series
Grade level: 4-8 for Physical Science series; 5-9 for Earth Science series
Price per title: $59
Ordering information: Educational Activities, Inc., PO Box 392, Freeport, NY 11520; (800) 645-3739

Scientific Reasoning Series
from IBM
Series includes:
    Concept Development: Heat, Temperature and Graphs
    Measurement Process: Distance and Area*

time, and distance-time graphs are shown side by side on the screen. Slope, curvature, and starting position of one of the graphs can be manipulated by the student, and the other two graphs change instantly. This kind of interactivity is impossible to demonstrate effectively without a computer. Similarly, in the

Ratio Reasoning: Crystals and Speed*
Scientific Models: Batteries, Bulbs and Families
Theory Formation: Reflections and Patterns

This series offers excellent pedagogy presented in a structured manner and focusing on concepts rather than formulas. The graphics are interesting, but the limitations on interaction with the models presented can become frustrating to better students. An excellent choice for students confused by basic scientific concepts. No recordkeeping is provided.

Each package contains: 2 disks, instruction card
Hardware: IBM PC, PCjr, XT, AT, PS/2 family (128K)
Grade level: 7 and up
Price per title: $75
Ordering information: See your local IBM dealer. For dealer information, call (800) IBM-2468.

Physical Science Series and Earth Science Series
from Prentice Hall
Physical Science Series:
  Newton's First Law
  Newton's Second Law
  Newton's Third Law
  Velocity and Acceleration
  Voltage, Current and Resistance*
  Electromagnetism
  The Lever
  Physical and Chemical Properties
  Kinetic and Potential Energy

  Atomic Nucleus*
Earth Science Series:
  Plate Tectonics
  Continental Drift
  Weather Forecasting Station Earthquakes*
  Volcanos
  Ocean Floor Hurricanes
  Life Cycle of Stars
  Interplanetary Travel*

These are menu-driven, but still linear, tutorials that cover the appropriate content in great detail. Nice use of color makes them attractive to young students. Models seem to be chosen for impact and are in agreement with materials published by the same authors. While each instructional unit contains questions that must be answered by the student, the primary evaluation tool is available separately on the main menu, and records are kept only on the results from this section. The use of multiple-choice questions that require drawing inferences as well as strict recall is a welcome touch.

Each package contains: 2 disks with backup, teacher's manual
Hardware: Apple II series (64K), IBM and Tandy 1000 (128K)
Grade level: 6-12
Price per title: $69
Ordering information: Prentice Hall, Sylvan Ave., Englewood Cliffs, NJ 07632; (800) 848-9500

(*reviewed in depth)

IBM program that covers the same content, the student is able to shoot balls at differing velocities by pulling back variable spring-loaded "guns." By trying to match their results with those of the computer (shown in slow motion so that differences are easy to see), students can effectively investigate what happens to the moving balls under varying conditions. Again, such a demonstration is difficult to recreate in the classroom, but easy and attractive on the computer screen.

Programs that force students to wait out each animated sequence before continuing can be very annoying, especially when the animation is irrelevant to the content. Far preferable are programs that permit either teacher or student control over timing. Educational Activities' *Physical Science* and *Earth Science* series often directly ask the student if he or she wishes to see the animation again. And Brøderbund's *Physics* takes this feature one step further by placing all control over the graphics in the user's hands.

Which Concepts . . . And In What Order?

Who should control the flow of information as it is presented to the students: an unfeeling, unsympathetic machine; a harassed teacher; or a lost and confused student? None of these, you say? Well, how about an intelligent, multi-directional tutorial program; a knowledgeable teacher/tutor; or a student aware of what he or she doesn't know and keen to fill in those gaps?

The ideal tutorial should be flexible enough to permit the latter three to control the flow of information, while limiting the control of the first three. Totally linear presentations—screen 1 followed by screens 2, 3 and 4—are ex-

amples of machine-dominated control. The pace and content will always be wrong—either too fast or too slow, too complex or too simple. While absolutely linear programs are rare these days, even good tutorials such as the Prentice Hall, IBM, and Educational Activities series described here are still primarily linear in design: One screen follows another and students are expected to begin at one end and work their way to the other. The problem with many linear programs becomes apparent when student interaction is required: Too often the program does no more than label answers "correct" or "incorrect" before continuing on through the tutorial. In the IBM materials, however, a more sophisticated branching in response to errors occurs: in some of the units some of the time, students who answer incorrectly are guided through a step-by-step solution that is not offered to students who get the right answer on the first try.

Relying on the teacher to determine the flow of the tutorial is good only in theory. In practice, few of us have the time to write customized sequences for each of the 100 or so students we might teach. And relying totally on the student for control is often inappropriate. It is a rare student who knows exactly what he or she should be spending time studying. Most want and need at least some structure and guidance.

The ideal tutorial, then, should permit but not require teacher modifications for the program to function. It should support an interface that allows students to move around with ease, while preserving a structured approach to the content for those who need it.

But wouldn't it be nice if the program were intelligent, too? The ideal interface would be capable of monitoring a student's progress as a human tutor might. If the student seems to be floundering, either by continuing to give incorrect answers or by frequently requesting repetition of a certain section, then the program would unobtrusively branch to another path that presents the same content in a different way. Proven teaching strategies such as breaking down problems into smaller steps, highlighting difficult sections or guiding the student through more detailed interpretations of the material might be available. On the other hand, if it becomes obvious that the student is capable of skipping ahead, that too should happen.

How close do the current science tutorials come to this ideal? None of the programs I looked at really offered the kind of multi-layered branching that in theory is possible. After receiving a series of wrong answers, most programs give up, either continuing on with new material or suggesting the student ask his or her teacher for help. In some cases, the student is simply directed to review the same material—not the ideal solution. In terms of offering alternate paths through the tutorial material, Brøderbund's *Physics* comes closest to the ideal by providing advanced materials that can be selected by the interested student. In addition, an index card motif allows access to content by key word, and a table of contents permits selection by chapter (major concept area).

On-line Evaluation

Evaluation, like it or not, still forms an important part of teaching, and most tutorials include quizzes or problem sections. The Prentice Hall series offers strong evaluation sequences, selectable by the student from the main menu and stressing not only recall, but also drawing inferences. In the program called *Atomic Nucleus,* for example, students are shown data from two experiments

similar to Rutherford's classic experiment using alpha particles and gold foil to predict the existence of the nucleus. Then they are asked to draw a conclusion. The exercise is nicely done, particularly considering that the intended audience is middle school students.

In the ideal tutorial, questions would probably vary from straight recall to inferring and extrapolating knowledge. The computer's reaction to the responses would also be crucial. In one mode, incorrect answers would be analyzed and students would be routed to appropriate review material. More important, records would be kept so that the next time a student used the program, a review sequence would be initiated that covered only the appropriate material. In another mode, the computer might respond to an incorrect answer by walking the student through the solution, step by step. And in a third mode, the student might be asked to enter every step of a solution separately so that the computer could evaluate not only the answer, but also the procedures used to obtain it.

Recordkeeping

Recordkeeping is an essential part of any tutorial intended for use in the classroom. Even though keeping manual records is always possible, it seems wasteful not to take advantage of the computer's power to maintain detailed records of student performance. (To satisfy those who would prefer not to see tutorials keep scores, it should be possible to turn off this option.)

In addition, students must be able to save their places, and upon returning to the computer they must be offered a choice of reviewing current material or jumping directly to where they left off. Some tutorials still support no place saving at all, forcing all students through the material in an identical fashion, with no ability to interrupt except by turning off the computer. More common (and almost as irritating) are programs that legislate when interruptions can occur—conceptually appropriate perhaps, but these points rarely fit exactly into a class period, forcing students to work past the period or to experience idle time toward the end of class.

Brøderbund's *Physics* permits students to interrupt at any time and to jump back to the same place the next time the program is used (unfortunately, this feature is available only to one user at a time). The science tutorials from Educational Activities support a large number of students (75) and records the quiz scores of each student at the end of each section (however, the program permits interruption only at the end of a complete section). The Prentice Hall materials, which support up to 100 students, provide access to the evaluation sequence on the main menu so that quizzes can be taken at any time. The scores of these "tests" are recorded, along with a tally of which questions were missed. The IBM series offers no recordkeeping at all, but does permit students to exit at any time.

In my opinion, none of the programs listed here offers sufficient information on student progress. While it is nice to know which students finish a unit, just knowing their results on a 5-10 question quiz is hardly sufficient to make one confident that they have learned the material. Since all of the packages offer multiple opportunities for student input through answering questions or making judgments, it seems a shame that more extensive records are not made available to either the teacher or the student.

Conclusion

Is there a perfect tutorial out there? Perhaps, but that is not the point. A better question is: are you willing to live with what is available in your subject area right now? As far as general science courses go, I was quite impressed with the overall quality of both the Prentice Hall and Educational Activities programs and would very confidently recommend them to middle school teachers. As for high school, the material from IBM, while very structured, does a fine job of tutoring in basic scientific concepts. And the Brøderbund program is a classic. It is not perfect, but it is oh-so-close. It's superb for delivering individual tutorials on any of an enormous variety of physics concepts covered. And what's more, the graphic images make it an excellent lecture tool. The worst problem with it? It's on the Macintosh, and that means projecting the images is difficult at best. (Macintoshes have no video output ports to which you can hook a large screen projector.) However, according to the people at Sensei Software who wrote the program for Brøderbund, an Apple IIGS version will be available soon.

Even more exciting are the changes that tutorial programs have undergone in recent years. Just like much of the rest of the industry, they are coming of age. Who knows where the next major change will take place!

Leslie Eiser is a lecturer in the faculty of education at McGill University in Montreal, and has master's degrees in both education and computer science.

Networking: How It Has Enhanced Science Classes in New York Schools... And How It Can Enhance Classes In Your School, Too

Could a change in the way we structure science education inside our school—by creating a simulation of the way real scientists work—make a difference in the attitudes children have about becoming scientists or using science in their everyday world? Some aspects of real scientific work, such as collaborative research driven by inquiry, have been successfully replicated in school science programs. Would it be possible to add to this model the power of computer networks and telecommunications so that elementary school children could communicate data and share hypotheses not only within their classes, but also between classes in their school and with others beyond the school building? These question and others were among those addressed during the past two years in a research project at Bank Street College called *Earth Lab: A Network for Young Scientists*.

Earth Lab, directed by Denis Newman and funded by the National Science Foundation, is a computer-based project designed to promote students' and teachers' collaboration in science investigations. The project, which was field-tested with sixth graders in two New York City schools, featured at its foundation a local-area network that linked microcomputers in classrooms and labs throughout each school site. In addition, a modem provided a link to computers and telecommunications networks beyond.

In part, we were hoping to explore how the use of a local-area network might alter the academic environment in which students work. We wanted to know whether access to networks would encourage teachers to assign more collaborative projects that would better mirror real-world science activities. We also wanted to know whether using a network could help to break down the artificial boundaries that generally separate science from other academic disciplines. And we wanted to find out whether direct access to real-world data via any computer on a school-wide network would better empower students to take control of their own learning.

The science curriculum that we and the teachers in each field-test school designed to run on the network included two units: one on weather and climate and the other on plate tectonics. These units consisted of database and writing activities as well as hands-on science experiments. Once students chose a project to work on, the network supplied the tools appropriate to the kind of science work to be accomplished. If students were recording observations, keeping journals, writing reports, or corresponding with others, they chose a networked version of the word processor *Bank Street Writer* that also offered electronic mail capabilities. (This version of *Bank Street Writer* is now available commercially from Scholastic Software, New

By
Deborah
Brienne
and
Shelley
Goldman

367

York.) If they were working on entering data into their own database or analyzing variables from a pre-existing database, they chose a networked version of *Bank Street Filer*.

Let's take a closer look at some of the real-world science activities our students were able to perform using our networked computer environment.

Student Databases— Weather Data & Forecasting

Twice a day in the blustery cold of a New York winter, Paul Reese, the computer coordinator at P.S. 125 in central Harlem, bundled up and led small groups of sixth graders up two flights of stairs, through the gymnasium, and onto the roof of the school. Their destination was a weather station where students could collect data on temperature, air pressure, wind speed, wind direction, clouds, precipitation, and general weather conditions using instruments and charts and by making their own observations. Back in the computer lab, each group of students entered data onto a shared weather database. The observations of each team eventually led to a large collective pool of data assembled on the network.

Once the database was well-stocked (three to four weeks of consistent data collection were sufficient), students used the capabilities of *Bank Street Filer* to come up with a set of "rules" about weather to use in forecasting. For example, when students printed a report that compared the air pressure tendency and precipitation fields, they were able to see patterns that led them to determine that falling air pressure signals rain or snow, while rising air pressure is correlated with clearing and sunny weather.

Other "weather rules" the *Filer* helped students discover included the relation-

ships between wind direction and temperature; wind direction and humidity; and cloud patterns and the approach of cold and warm fronts. As students continued taking their weather readings from the instruments at the weather station, they compared that information with the weather rules. By adding information about the west-to-east movement of frontal systems from newspaper weather maps, they were able to make large-scale forecasts.

This activity gave students the opportunity to model the work of scientists in several ways. First, each science team gathered data that were contributed to a collective pool; second, students used this data pool to discover scientific principles; and finally, students used their "discovered principles" to predict real-world events. The local-area network was important not only because it served as a shared database—a repository for all the data collected by individual groups—but also because it allowed each group a fresh opportunity to analyze the data and deduce from it scientific principles about the weather.

Teacher-Made Databases— Earthquakes, Volcanos, and Continental Drift

While student-constructed databases offer hands-on experience in collecting and analyzing *raw* data, teacher-made databases can be a valuable way of presenting students with a set of *controlled* data that can also be manipulated and analyzed to discover certain scientific principles. (This technique is most successful in teaching principles that do not lend themselves well to science lab investigations and therefore might otherwise have to be presented in a more expository manner.) In one such project, the Earth Lab staff created a database listing the locations, by latitude and longitude, of over 300 earthquakes and volcanos. Pairs of young scientists were then given an assignment to use these data to decide if the location of the disasters yielded any patterns that could help them draw conclusions about the relationship between earthquakes and volcanos. Each pair drew from the network a different list of 30 earthquakes or volcanos within specified longitudinal boundaries. They then took this printout to a large world map covered with a sheet of acetate, and marked with an "x" the location of each earthquake or eruption. (Having each pair of students responsible for covering a different longitudinal area of the map kept them from bumping into each other while doing the plotting.) The activity provided clear evidence to our young scientists that the earth was shaking and moving around some very distinct boundaries. And of course, it modeled the way scientists actually discovered the "Ring of Fire."

In another project, students used a teacher-made database on fossils to discover the theory of continental drift. One large piece of evidence supporting the theory is the discrepancy between climates at the locations where fossil remains have been found and the type of climate that the fossilized creatures could actually have lived in. Our database contained general information on fossils (kind of fossil, scientific name, common name, age); on where each fossil was found (latitude, longitude, continent); and on the kind of climate each creature could survive in.

Each student science team was assigned a continent and told to find all the fossil records in the database that were discovered on that continent. The teams then went through each record, and created a picture of the fossil (photocopied or hand-drawn, labeled and glued onto a sticky "post-it" note), and placed it on a map titled "Where the Fossil Was Found." Next they took a reproduction of the picture of the fossil, and going to a second map titled "Where the Fossil Could Live Now," placed that picture on a continent of their choosing that was within a climate region appropriate for the fossil's survival.

When this activity was completed, a discussion ensued. Students began to see the discrepant information that the two maps yielded. For example, they observed that the New York state fossil Eurypterids (a sea scorpion that looked like a nine-foot lobster and lived 400 million years ago) could have lived only in a tropical climate. From this observation, they began to generate theories about how these fossils ended up in hostile climates. Students were eventually led to suggest the theory of continental drift.

Presenting such teacher-made databases via a network, in which all the information is stored on one central hard disk, makes it much easier for students to log on, retrieve files, and analyze data.

On-line Databases— Weather Forecasting

10:00 AM: Heavy rains are delaying flights at Detroit's airport. Skies are beginning to cloud over in Buffalo, New York. 2:00 PM: Detroit's weather is clearing and rain is starting to fall in Buffalo. Barbara, one member of a team of young scientists, is excited because she accurately predicted the movement of the cold front. A lucky guess? Not at all.

Using weather data gathered via a modem from airports in the northeastern section of the United States (available through the commercial databases CompuServe and Accu-Data), groups of students at P.S. 125 were able to plot weather conditions on large weather maps several times a day and observe the movements of frontal systems. From this, they were able to make fairly accurate predictions about where and when a storm system would arrive.

The excitement that the groups of young scientists felt at using the same data that meteorologists were using to construct their weather reports in this project was virtually tangible. And while use of the local-area network was minimal, the activity reinforced the students' sense of empowerment in gaining access to real-world data via the wide-area network of telecommunications.

Local-Area Electronic Mail— Researching Hurricanes

Local-area networks also make possible electronic mail systems that allow students and teachers to communicate with one another via "mailboxes" on the network. Interestingly, we found that not only does such a system facilitate communication between students and teachers, it also helps to "break down the barriers" between academic subjects within the school setting.

In one instance, the electronic mail system that we set up facilitated the connection between the investigation of weather occurring in science class and topics more often explored in social studies or language arts classes. Specifically, students researching hurricanes at one point began focusing on how these weather disasters affect people's lives. Each team of children came up with a list of topics to research, among them: What kind of damage do hurricanes do? Where is the best place to hide from a hurricane? Who invented the word hurricane? Why are hurricanes named after people?

Sixth-grade teacher Mona Monroe encouraged her students to send their questions and researched answers to each other via electronic mail. An interesting outcome of this type of sharing was that students were able to become content critics for each other's work. Groups were then able to incorporate each other's suggestions and to revise their work. Electronic mail provided a vehicle for new audiences and new sources of information for students' writing.

Long Distance Electronic Mail—Sharing Weather Experiences

Long-distance electronic mail gave young scientists access to the resources of experts in the outside world and provided students with wider audiences for their scientific observations and their findings.

In one case, our students shared New York weather data with children in Boston and Hawaii. In the following example, Valerie, empowered by the expertise her class's weather data provided, contradicts information sent from Caroline in Boston. The message was followed by a printout of the weather database readings for March third and fourth.

Dear Caroline,

Hi my name is Valerie. Do you remember the other day when you sent my computer teacher a message on what your weather is and then you said that you got information from The Globe, the newspaper, etc., well I'm sorry to say but the readings you send us are wrong because on March 3, 1987 it was not sunny. On March 4, 1987 it was sunny but it was somewhere in the 30s, down at the bottom of this note you will find the weather temperature for March 3, 1987 and March 4, 1987. But we would like to thank you for trying to give us the right information for those dates, we really appreciate it.

To keep telecommunications costs low, students in our project stored long-distance messages in a specified mail box on the local-area network; then, at the end of the day, when phone calls were less expensive, a teacher would send all the messages at one time. Once again, the local-area network proved useful in facilitating a computer environment rich in information resources.

The young scientists in the Earth Lab Project used the network to model the activities of real-world scientists in a variety of ways. They collected data in teams, contributing to a shared pool of information that allowed the whole group to draw conclusions about scientific principles. They used raw, on-line data to make predictions. They modeled the process of scientific discovery using data to generate scientific theories. And, finally, they shared their data, hypotheses, and conclusions with other teams and communicated their findings to wider audiences. By facilitating and supporting these processes, the Earth Lab network helped bring the real world of science into these elementary school science programs.

Earth Lab was supported by National Science Foundation grant No. MDR 8550449. Any opinions, findings, conclusions, or recommendations expressed in this paper are those of the authors and do not necessarily reflect the views of the Foundation. For more information on the project, contact the authors at Bank Street College, 610 W. 112th St., New York, NY 10025; or Denis Newman at BBN Laboratories, 10 Moulton St., Cambridge, MA 02238.

Deborah Brienne, now a teacher at the Fieldston School, was curriculum coordinator for Earth Lab. Shelley Goldman, a research scientist at Bank Street College of Education, was director of research and curriculum.

Article #6
The Truth about Cooperative Learning

By
Dr. David
Dockterman

In the last year or so, cooperative learning has become a hot educational topic. You see articles in journals, workshops at conferences, and claims on packages. And, as it has done with most educational buzz phrases—like critical thinking, individualized instruction, and problem solving—the educational computing industry has attached the term to a number of its products and activities.

But is this attachment justified? What is cooperative learning anyway? And what do computers have to do with it, if anything? Cooperative learning is more than just pairing kids at the machine and letting them take turns at the keyboard. Maybe we should start with a little background.

What is Cooperative Learning?

The notion of kids working together in groups is not new. Most activities that occur on the playground are group-oriented, and most classrooms are organized around groups, usually large ones. Group learning, however, is not necessarily synonymous with cooperative learning. After all, the bulk of school activities are competitive, not cooperative. The class may be taught as a group, but the participants, the students, often compete with one another for grades or other academic rewards.

Even most small group activities that traditionally take place in the classroom are not really cooperative. The turn-taking that occurs when students are forced to share a limited resource, like a computer or a book, involves a degree of cooperation. Although a better term might be "agreement." The kids agree to abide by the rules of sharing, but the actual activity is focused on the individual.

The same is true of small group, expert activities. You know the kind. A team of four students is given the task of preparing a report on Egypt, and each student becomes an expert. One kid builds a model pyramid, a second writes a report about religion and daily life, a third charts the progression of Pharaohs and dynasties, and the fourth prepares a menu of ancient Egyptian delicacies for the rest of the class to sample. Their results are pooled into a final presentation. Now the pooling process might be somewhat cooperative, but the bulk of the effort is done independently.

The key to cooperative learning is interdependence. The members of the group must interactively need each other and have a stake in each other's understanding and success. Creating this type of cooperative environment in your classroom is not at all easy, and it is something with which few teachers (and few students) have had any experience.

Even some of the "cooperative learning" techniques offered by its supporters can easily dissolve when both the teachers and students are confused about their roles. For example, a beginning cooperative learning strategy is to divide your class into small groups of four students each. Each member of the group should take a number from 1 to 4. Assign some questions to the class (whatever is

372

appropriate for what you're teaching). Then randomly pick a number from 1 to 4, and that person from each group will be the one to present the answer to the question. Everyone in the group gets the same grade.

In essence, this creates an incentive for the group to make sure that every one of its members knows the answers to the questions. They are forced to share ideas and information. It sounds cooperative. Interdependency, however, can quickly shift to dependency if, as so often happens in group work, the "smart" kid does all the work and then simply gives the answers to his or her teammates. For this technique to work, the kids must be prepared to accept a variety of leadership and facilitator roles. Not surprisingly, they need to be liberated from some rather restrictive patterns of traditional schooling.

Of course, before you attempt to transform your classroom into one that supports cooperative learning, you should be convinced that it is worthwhile. I think it is.

Why is Cooperative Learning Important?

As an end in itself, cooperative learning does have value in the curriculum. After all, teamwork and the ability to communicate successfully and constructively are essential parts of the social world in which we live and work. Recent research by folks like Robert Slavin at Johns Hopkins, Spencer Kagan at the University of California, and David and Richard Johnson at the University of Minnesota, however, suggests that co-operative learning does much more than teach students how to work in groups. The process of learning cooperatively actually improves the acquisition and retention of content and skills throughout the curriculum. Kids learn better when they learn cooperatively.

That shouldn't be surprising. When you are forced to articulate your ideas to another person or group, you have to process the information in a new way. Think about your own experiences as a teacher preparing to teach material new to you. You not only have to learn the material yourself, you must strive to understand how others will learn it as well. You organize and reorganize to an extent well beyond what you would do as an independent learner. This process can be a very potent learning mechanism.

> When you are forced to articulate your ideas to another person or group, you have to process the information in a new way.

This doesn't mean that all instruction should take the form of cooperative learning. It does suggest, though, that teachers should work to add cooperative learning strategies to their array of classroom teaching methods and strive to apply those strategies appropriately as they proceed through their curricula. And in fact, the computer can help.

Cooperative Software

One of the greatest obstacles to applying cooperative learning techniques in the classroom is management—management of information, responsibilities, and student behavior. The computer can help in all three areas. By controlling the flow of information, like the scrolling messages in *The Other Side* or the timed displays of *Decisions, Decisions,* the software can force students to delegate responsibilities. No one member of the team can gather all the necessary data, so each student has something essential to contribute to the group. *National Inspirer* and the new *International Inspirer* go so far as to come with sets of different materials. Every member of the group gets a unique resource and the computer makes sure that more than one resource is always required.

In each of these programs, timers force the students to plan carefully at their seats within their groups. The software helps manage the rotation of the teams (up to 6 small groups with only one computer) through their turns with as little "down time" as possible. The pacing has been devised to prevent the logjam of students waiting for their chance at the machine, a situation which can easily lead to disruptive behavior. Most of the action, by far, takes place where it should: among the students, within their groups. It is a true interdependent learning situation.

Most of us may not be ready to dive head first into the ocean of cooperative learning, but it is time we at least tested the waters.

By
Holly M.
Jobe

One of the problems in educational re-structuring is how to effectively assess student progress. As we change our paradigms about education and plan for more learner-directed educational experiences, problem-and inquiry-based curriculum, and a process-oriented learning environment, it becomes increasingly difficult to rely on old assessment tools such as standardized multiple choice tests. Richard Mills, Vermont Commissioner of Education, quoted a teacher as saying: "how confusing it is to coach students in good writing, and then test them by asking them to fill in a multiple choice test! How perverse to insist they write and rewrite and edit over days, and then test them with a 40-minute writing sample!" How can we effectively measure a student's "thinking skill?" "Product" is easier to measure than "process."

How do children show us what they know?

The last few months I've continued my "wanderings" to schools and agencies that are actively involved in creating effective schools and tackling the complex problems of student assessment. As some technology-infused curriculum projects such as the use of multimedia, the *National Geographic Kids Network,* or TERC's *Global Laboratory* are challenging us to re-examine current testing practices, technology itself can contribute to alternative assessment strategies.

Teachers and administrators at the Narragansett Elementary School in Gorham, Maine, asked the following questions as they thought about their current assessment practices: how do children show us what they know? How do children recognize themselves as learners? How do teachers decide what is important for children to learn? How do teachers assess what students have learned?

The teachers then examined closely how they assess students. They found that in addition to standardized tests (some of which they scored and analyzed themselves so they could discuss the mistakes with the children), they used many other types of assessment.

How do teachers decide what is important for children to learn?

Alternative types of assessment include **observation and documentation** which in addition to teacher observation, and student and parent interviews, may include audio, video, and photographic documentation. **Portfolios** are samples of student work selected by students and teachers that represent significant performance by the learner and provide a good sense of their personal academic history and growth. **Performances and exhibitions** are usually representative of work completed over time. This may include a report, project, play, video, multimedia project, or artifact. **Competency-based assessment** includes open-ended tests where the students perform real tasks within time bounds, such as the New York state fourth grade science test which was

375

trialed in May 1990. All 200,000 fourth graders took the hands-on test by rotating through five stations where they had seven minutes to solve given problems.

As mentioned, technology can be an asset when thinking about alternative assessment. For example, at the Key School in Indianapolis, each student has a video portfolio of his or her work. The students choose what they would like to tape (reading a story or report they wrote, a performance, etc.) and it remains as part of the permanent record that they can take with them when they leave the school.

The Narragansett teachers are looking at other forms of technology for storing student portfolios. They plan to store portfolios digitally including multimedia work samples, text, graphics, writing, read aloud, music, etc. With a "portable studio" shared by several teachers that includes a Macintosh, scanner, laser printer, handscanner, MacRecorder, and *Computer Eyes,* teachers will store student work on a large networked file server. Each year students and teachers will determine what work should be left in the portfolio to be "passed-on" to the next year's teacher. At graduation or transfer to another school, students will be handed a CD-ROM portfolio of their work. The faculty is working very closely with the community to design an assessment system that meets the communication needs of parents, students, and teachers. They feel current technology will enable them to efficiently and effectively provide an accurate portrait of student work that could also be provided to prospective employers.

Many educators, such as the Narragansett team, view assessment as another avenue into the restructuring problem. By changing how we measure student progress we precipitate change. Project Zero, the Harvard-based research project run by Howard Gardner *(Frames of Mind)* is looking at the Narragansett and other projects that are restructuring through assessment.

At the Shaw Jr. High School, also in Gorham, I observed an example of a competency-based assessment structure heavily involving technology. Wally Ziko's technology class is required by all seventh and eighth grade students. He has developed a curriculum that is project-based and interdisciplinary where students are involved in authentic work. Using a Macintosh lab where each student has a station, students receive a standard form that is designed to hold a personalized solution to a problem. Students have several days to work on each project, such as designing a map of how to get from their home to the local shopping mall, including written directions. Another project is to create a product packaging box complete with UPC code, ingredients and logo that must fit together when printed and cut out. Students are assessed on their performance. The emphasis in this class is on problem solving. The students use computers and tool software as a means to an end, not as the end itself.

Vermont is the first state in the nation to adopt a statewide portfolio assessment for writing and math. The project is in the pilot year with sample and volunteer schools. The schools are developing portfolios for writing and math students in grades four and eight. Assessment will include a writing sample or uniform test for math, three pieces of student work for the portfolio, and a sample of the student's "best work." I was privileged to attend one of the regional math training sessions where teachers met to discuss what exactly to include in a portfolio. Discussion was lively and suggestions focused on including teacher comments about the work and skills expected as well as a commentary by the students. The focus of the math portfolios appears to be not on collecting evidence of the student's computational ability, but on how he or she solves problems. Students are asked to include a narrative of their process.

One of the sub goals of the Vermont assessment project is to effect change in classroom teaching strategies. Much of the meeting included a lively discussion about teaching problem solving versus computation. Teachers are actively involved in designing the state standards for portfolios. Plans are to expand portfolio assessment to other subject areas, to all grades and all schools throughout the state.

Evaluation of student work is a major consideration for school restructuring. In some cases, the use of technology in the classroom is forcing teachers and schools to reexamine assessment practices. We also need to consider how technology can play a part in providing real and authentic assessment of students. We may finally have tools available that help us show not only what students can do, but also why he or she can or cannot do it.

Article #8
Worth a Second Look: Past Times, Future Times and Time for Planning

By
Gail
Marshall

The Educational Testing Service, creator and marketer of the SATs, among other tests, has announced several changes in their time-honored college entrance exams. Students may be able to write, on the spot, a brief essay, which will be scored by holistic scoring procedures. Equally revolutionary, students will be allowed to bring calculators into the exams and use the calculators to solve numerical problems. Since the announcement, pros and cons have been debated in the press. Many commentators have said the use of calculators will widen an already wide gap—poor students, who can't afford breakfast before school and seldom face the prospect of a square meal after school, can't be expected to buy calculators for the SAT. So the more prosperous students gain another edge. Other commentators complain that calculator use debases computation skills and that under no circumstances, especially in the hallowed precincts of ETS, should calculator use be encouraged.

Where are the voices that question the fundamental assumptions of the SATs as they are currently written? Who asks if multiple-choice questions about vocabulary and basic computation are necessary and sufficient for a society that worries about an urban underclass on the one hand and the future of supercomputers on the other hand? Tinkering with the SATs reflects the post-baseball season pastime of many Americans—tinkering with education. Instead of arguing whether calculator use is appropriate or inappropriate, or whether essay reviewers will be fair and consistent, we ought to be asking whether or not today's SAT tests reflect the changes introduced by a technology-using society.

From our perspective, half a century after the SATs gained wide-spread acceptance, and a century after the development of the first child-centered intelligence tests, we think human skills are immutable. Socrates and Plato would have gotten combined scores of 1590, but Einstein probably would have scored about 1000, we say. But historical evidence suggests that human thinking changes as cultural conditions change. Daniel Henry Calhoun, in *The Intelligence of a People* (Princeton University Press, Princeton, NJ, 1973), a historian with an interest in American education, wondered if there was a significant change in American intelligence from 1750-1870. To answer the question he studied the history of the testing movement, newspapers, pamphlets, economic data and, uniquely but significantly, products of the American mind of the period—sermons, ships, and bridges. Starting out as an examination of New York State schools from 1750-1870 when the state was spending large amounts of money on schools, Calhoun asked, "did educational modernization actually improve the ability of people to think about their world and perform in it...?"

Calhoun started out by noting that as children grow up their scores on intelligence tests often rise. To Calhoun, as to

378

many psychometricians, an individual's experiences, family life, societal demands, formal schooling, interact with the individual's ability to learn. Now suppose, thought Calhoun, societal demands and/or formal schooling or other factors change over time. He suggested that changes in the level of intelligence result from the training people receive in order "... to participate in the desired kinds of relations between communicating individuals." In other words, if the community emphasizes sermons, as the communities of the Northeast did during the late sixteenth century, one aspect of intelligence, verbal facility, will be emphasized and prized. Later, when trade is a fact of life for the economic well-being of the Northeast, the good ship builder will be prized so spatial analytical skills will take precedence over verbal skills. While Calhoun says the changes aren't planned (a society doesn't always sit down and lay out an agenda), he does say that changes can occur only through a process of "mutual adjustment."

Discussing Northeastern Americans' ability levels in 1750, Calhoun says there were at least two acceptable levels of expertise. In 1750, the church dominated life in the villages of the Northeast. Sermons were designed to be listened to, understood, acted on, debated and repeated. The "technology" of the sermon was surprisingly more complex than our current level of discourse. According to Calhoun, elaborate analogies, word play, imagery derived from medieval days, even the style of a mounting series of repetitious, gripping themes, were part of the complex verbal discourse of the typical sermon. And people listened, and they remembered, and they repeated the sermons—over and over.

Then, as economic necessities plagued the citizens of the Northeast, a shift occurred. Speedy ships, with large capacities and stability, and which were easy to build, were demanded by merchants. America had to compete with Europe for goods. So American talents at ship building were supported financially. The new hero was not the

---

Here are a few questions to ask your colleagues, both computer users and computer phobics:

- Do existing tests adequately tell me all I need to know about my students?
- Do some students, who seem especially gifted with computers and other technology devices, score well below other students? And, if so, are the higher scoring students truly more advanced?
- What skills do students exhibit that are not described in current tests?
- How often do we teachers limit ourselves (and our students) to the acquisition of skills measured by popular standardized tests?
- What kind of a society do we envision in the Year 2500, and how successfully are today's educational activities preparing students?
- What's holding each of us back from achieving our full potential—fear of failing the task or the test?
- What two (three, four, five or six) key skills have we acquired as a result of using technology, and what positive difference have those skills made in our lives?

preacher, but the ship builder, or his partner, the sailing captain. Ship building depends not on verbal ability, but on visual intuition. Ship building called for analytical gifts. Says Calhoun, "the builders worked out characteristic methods for solving problems, methods that amounted to cultural versions of 'learning strategies' that in some psychological theories are crucial in the growth of intelligence." They worked alone, they looked over one another's solutions, and collaboratively they produced faster ships that carried heavier loads.

Suppose all the ship builders and bridge builders had to take the SATs! Suppose their verbal ability—the skill of finding three, four or five meanings for a single phrase—wasn't as well developed as the other villagers.

Suppose they were made to sit in the back row, lost interest, wandered into the towns, and passed their days sitting around playing mumblety-peg. Who knows what course history would have taken!

Today, with many Americans concerned about the selling of American assets to foreign interests (which economists tell us is no bad thing) and with Americans concerned about students gaining skills for the 21st century, we need to think again about the shifts in cognitive skills required by a society that is becoming more and more technologically oriented. This doesn't mean we stop teaching reading or computation. It doesn't mean we focus exclusively on instrumental goals—teaching students how to format blank disks or how to install computer hardware, for example. It doesn't mean we throw out Shakespeare and emphasize skills needed for reading a software manual. We'll always want to keep our links with the classics, be they sonnets or square roots. But we must begin to ask our-

selves if what we're teaching and how our students are learning matches our goals for the next few decades.

If we emphasize (or over-emphasize) computation, will our students be able to do little more than compute? If, on the other hand, we weave together number knowledge and geometry and logic and probability, won't our students be more skilled, more varied, more flexible? If we teach reading as critical thinking, and not as word naming, won't we reap the benefits of an analytical work force? But that means a shift in our measurement strategies, and in our national priorities. Because although we say we prize individual thinking and analysis and fluency, our tests don't always reflect those priorities. We should be asking, in these first few months of 1991, and throughout the rest of the decade, what direction we, as a people, will take from the year 2000 A.D. on. Do we want to manufacture machines—designed by us or by others? Do we want to use the existing machines to their fullest capacity? Or do we want to turn away entirely from manufacturing, from controlling equipment, and emphasize services or the arts, or space? Whatever choices we make, computers are going to play a role. Sorting out the promises and priorities means we get to make the choices instead of having alternatives imposed on us. Given the bifurcation in personal economic productivity, with the "haves" getting proportionally more spending power than the "have-nots" these days, computer-using educators ought to be thinking about the implication of slow growth or no growth in educational computing.

Technology and Students with Special Needs

Chapter 6

1. "Comp. Ed. Kids *Can!*" Patricia Blevins. *CUE Newsletter*, September/October 1989. pg. 15.
2. "Technology and the At-Risk Student." J. Roberts. *Electronic Learning*, February 1989. pg. 15.
3. "Using Technology to Reach At-Risk Students." Gwen Solomon. *Electronic Learning*, March 1990. pg. 14.
4. "Computers and At-Risk Youth: Software and Hardware That Can Help." E.R. Bialo and J.P. Sivin. *Classroom Computer Learning*, February 1989. pg. 48.
5. "Tykes and Bytes." B. Levine. *Los Angeles Times*, July 1, 1990. pg. E1.
6. "Questions and Answers About Computer-Assisted Instruction for Children with Learning Disabilities." William W. Lee. *Educational Technology*, August 1989. pg. 29.
7. "A Guide to Special Education Resources." Bill Morgan. *Electronic Learning*, February 1990. pg. 26.
8. "Adapting Computer Applications for Multicultural Teaching." Jo Lynn Autry Digranes and Swen H. Digranes. *The Computing Teacher*, November 1989. pg. 20.
9. "Tools For Teaching ESL and Foreign Languages." David Hoffman. *Technology and Learning*, May/June, 1991. pg. 12
10. "Computers in the Early Childhood Classroom." Linda Kostner. *The Computing Teacher*, May 1989. pg. 54.
11. "Appropriate Uses of Computers With Young Children." Kevin J. Swick. *Educational Technology*, January 1989. pg. 7.
12. "Who Can Draw With a Macintosh?" Bonnie Meltzer. *The Computing Teacher*, April 1990. pg. 21.

All children are learners. However, some children learn faster and in more depth while others require additional assistance with completing learning activities due to special physical, language, emotional or intellectual needs. It is our desire as educators to meet the needs of children who require additional resources, assistance and support. What can technology do?

Technology is one tool that can help both teacher and students promote a learning environment that focuses on every child reaching his or her potential. In this chapter we have included a variety of articles illustrating the many learning needs that confront a teacher on a daily basis. Articles cover topics ranging from the "At-Risk" student to multicultural teaching and early childhood education. You will read about the atrocious dropout rate in some schools and how technology can be a motivating force that pulls many of these students back to the classroom.

However, technology cannot do it alone. Simply plugging students into a computer will not cause a dramatic decrease in the dropout rate—it takes a combined effort from all members of the school and the larger community. In addition, beware of claims that all disadvantaged, at-risk, or low-achieving students require a heavily-structured learning environment. Some educators propose, we feel quite erroneously, that this type of student requires an approach to learning that includes much drill and practice software. Often, these programs contain skill development strategies that are broken down into their smallest components for the computer to record attainment or non-attainment of these skills.

While these students may require a structured environment for part of their education experience, it is not necessary to label these students so that they become constantly bombarded with programs that are no more than tutorial in function and approach. All students need tool software; all students can create with technology; all students will be motivated through a multisensory approach to learning in a technology age classroom.

The first article in this chapter by Patricia Blevins explores these thoughts further. She is puzzled as to why publishers suggest that Compensatory Education programs require drill and practice software while Gifted and Accelerated programs require simulation and problem-solving software. She asks a very important question: "Why wouldn't the slower learners benefit from the same kinds of thinking exercises that the gifted learners receive, only at a slower pace, or with more introduction?" What is her answer? More importantly, what is your reply?

Jack Roberts, the founder of "Electronic Learning," convened a national panel that addressed "Technology and the At-Risk Student." Some of the discussions, comments and recommendations from the panel are included as the next article. Compile a list of ways to use technology with the "at-risk" student as you read the panelists' comments. Read the types of software recommended by the panel members. Do you agree with their suggestions? Why?

The next two articles also focus on the needs of "At-Risk" students. Gwen Solomon describes students at a North Carolina junior high school as the "light-trained" generation. She found that the computer was the switch to turn on their creative minds for the students in this program. The computer became a tool that matched their learning styles. As you read the article, list three things: software used, impact of the technology, and the interdisciplinary nature of the program and comment on their applicability as effective learning strategies.

With a boost from computers, kids with disabilities find the world is filled with possibilities, suggests Bettijane Levine in an article from the *Los Angeles Times*. Throughout the story, Levine shows how technology provides tools for the physically handicapped child—tools that were not available six years ago.

The ethnic diversity in our schools demands software to meet varying needs of our student population. However, finding instructional software and materials specifically designed for various cultural groups is difficult—it is very limited or non-existent. The Digranes's article illustrates how word processing, data base, and spreadsheet programs can be easily adapted to meet special cultural needs. Obviously, the same techniques are used for other cultural groups.

We have included some articles on the use of technology with young children as some teachers are reluctant, or hesitate, or use technology tools with four- and five-year olds. The authors of the articles encourage the use of this type of tool provided they present developmentally appropriate experiences for young learners. Linda Kostner suggests that computers can be used with a large screen monitor for the whole class and at the "computer center." She suggests that like finger paints, wooden blocks, and playdough, technology and computers can be used as another tool to facilitate learning through discovery and experimentation.

Similarly, Kevin Swick suggests that the effective utilization of computers in early childhood education must be based on an understanding of how children learn. He suggests several appropriate uses of computers with young children such as opening up a new world language development and language creation. If oral language is the child's most natural medium for integrating symbols into their experiences in a meaningful way then the computer environment is ideal for promoting children's oral language. Software programs can stimulate the use of new words and the construction of new stories to accompany computer and child-generated graphics.

Bonnie Meltzer suggests that using a computer for creative self-expression will enhance their self-confidence, improve their visual skills, enrich their language skills and add loads of fun to the process. As you read the article "Who Can Draw With a Macintosh?" keep a record of the developmental processes experienced by the children. Can you add to the list of skills developed as children draw with technology? What is the advantage, or disadvantage, of young children drawing on the computer as compared to paper and crayon?

The articles in this section reflect the uses of technology with students who possess special needs. As you read each article keep a list of how you would use different types of technology with the variety of learning needs you will find in a regular classroom. The trend to keep all children in regular classrooms suggests that the material in this chapter will become even more important as time progresses.

Questions for Discussion

1. Do you agree with Blevin's question, "Why shouldn't the slower learners benefit from the same kinds of thinking exercises that the gifted learners receive, only at a slower pace, or with more introduction?" Why?
2. Is it important for teachers to select tool or problem-solving software that can be used across traditional curriculum boundaries and for different ability groups? Select three pieces of software that fit this description and discuss how you would use them across subject boundaries and with students who have special needs?
3. How can you use tutorial and some drill and practice software with underachieving students? Why do standardized tests reflect increases in basic skills attainment following use of drill and practice software? Should we continue to use this type of software for some students?
4. Watch some young children use a Muppet Keyboard or similar equipment. Watch the same children use manipulatives. Now list software functions, elements, or characteristics that you would like to see in software that is suitable for 4-5 year olds.
5. Do we provide sufficient opportunities for creative development in our classroom? Discuss several strategies that use technology to provide a creative environment for children 5-12 years old.

Questions from the Readings

1. List the software recommended for Compensatory Education programs by Patricia Blevins. Can you add to her list?
2. What was the impact of Blevins' program on her students? How did she measure "effectiveness"? Can you suggest some alternatives?
3. What is your definition of the "At-Risk" student?
4. Who is responsible for educating these students? Why?
5. If businesses spend an additional $40 annually on remedial education, how should we form school/business partnerships? What is the role of the business partner?
6. Distinguish between the terms "light-trained" and "paper trained."
7. Why is an interdisciplinary or project approach to learning an important teaching strategy for at-risk students?
8. Describe some of the devices and peripherals used by special education students in the Levine article.
9. How can you use a database in a multicultural classroom?
10. How would you use a computer at a learning center with young children?
11. What are some important concepts for four-year olds to learn?
12. What do Papert and Beaty/Tucker mean when they state that young children must learn to develop self-confidence in "controlling technology?"
13. What aspects of the environment are essential to integrating computers?
14. List the skills that young children can learn through creating expression on the computer.

BY
PATRICIA
BLEVINS

A catalogue crossed my desk the other day, extolling the virtues of some new software written specifically for Compensatory Education programs. Anticipating some wonderful and innovative software, I eagerly opened to the first page. I was greeted with a detailed description of drill and practice software, guaranteed to drill those facts into their heads. Each screen contained only one math problem, so as not to confuse the student with too much information at one time. An explanation of the proper steps needed to solve the problem is available, if the student misses it on the first try.

In the same batch of mail, I received a catalog for software for Gifted and Accelerated programs. This software included simulations and problem-solving activities in exciting formats with colorful graphics. These were the kinds of programs I would like to try myself. All of this made me wonder why there should be a difference in the type of software programs that gifted students can benefit from, as opposed to the software programs for Comp. Ed. students. Why wouldn't the slower learners benefit from the same kinds of thinking exercises that the gifted learners receive, only at a slower pace, or with more introduction?

When I first accepted the position of Compensatory Education/Math instructor at my school, I visited similar programs to get ideas on how to set up a new program. The majority of these programs were based on three elements: ditto drill and practice, manipulatives, and assisting the student with the classroom assignment. While I agreed with using the manipulatives, I felt these students needed an approach to mathematics instruction that differed from the standard textbook methods.

The majority of the students who qualify for a Comp. Ed. program have already experienced two or more years of drill and practice and textbook work in the classroom, but it wasn't working for them. Many of these students are kinesthetic learners, and have difficulty with the usual modes of delivery in the classroom. These students are often easily distracted in a large group setting. To have an effective program, I felt I had to try a different approach for delivery of their math instruction.

Mathematics encompasses more than just computation and application. It also involves problem solving, estimation, categorizing and critical thinking. While these skills are covered in many textbooks, they are often listed as additional or enrichment activities. The students who finish their assignments quickly have time to get to these sections. Frequently, Comp. Ed. students operate slowly. There are many reasons for this. Problem behavior can get in their way, or their organizational skills aren't well developed. They waste time getting the pencil and paper ready before focusing their attention on the task at hand. Often they don't finish the assignment, much less additional activities. These students miss out on the whole picture of mathematics. I decided to base my program on problem solving activities,

385

improving questioning and listening skills, building their self esteem, and increasing their computer proficiency.

I set up a lab of six Apple IIe's with color monitors, Koala Pads and an assortment of software. After giving each student an initial diagnostic test, I separate them into ability groups of six students each. I schedule these groups for 1/2 hour a day, four days each week. The students are told they are coming to Computer Lab—this avoids any negative feelings they might have about Comp. Ed. math. Each student receives two hours of individual computer time per week.

The software I have chosen to use is: *Gertrude's Secrets, Gertrude's Puzzles* and *Moptown Parade* from the Learning Company, to explore attributes, logic, patterns and Venn diagrams. I use *Number Stumper,* also from the Learning Company, for younger students and *Teaser's by Tobbs,* from Sunburst for older students to explore number families. *The Factory* from Sunburst, gives all students experiences in visualizing, reverse problem solving and degrees of rotation. *The Incredible Laboratory* from Sunburst, allows 4th through 6th graders to explore the scientific method of discovery through a group process. Younger students use the Koala Pad to reinforce number concepts and the Boehm concepts (above, below, under, around, etc.). Older students learn how to create equivalent fractions on the Koala Pad.

The students are first introduced to each piece of software with a concrete experience. Before the students go to the computer, each activity in Gertrude's Secrets is practiced on the floor, with plastic attribute blocks. The *Moptown Parade is* introduced with activities such as "People Sorting" and "Guess My Rule" from "Math for Girls and Other Problem Solvers." *Number Stumper* is introduced by playing the game with dice and number cards and *The Factory* is preceded by manipulating cardboard products and describing how they would be created. I structured the *Incredible Laboratory* activities by providing chart paper for the students to record the body part produced from the various chemicals. Each group works as a research team, trying the different chemicals, and recording the results. Describing the body parts so that other "scientists" can verify their findings, is a language lesson in itself! The Koala Pad combines kinesthetic experiences on the tablet with the abstract symbols on the screen. My job is to provide lots of reinforcement, both verbal and physical, in the form of a pat on the back or a handshake, given during all the activities.

In addition to the computer software, I use a variety of supporting activities, such as the Mystery Stories from "Math for Girls and Other Problem Solvers" and activities from "Family Math." Both books are from EQUALS at the Lawrence Hall of Science, Berkeley, CA. I also use math facts games, one minute timed tests and manipulatives for place value and fractions.

Another facet of this program has been computer literacy training. Each student is trained to identify the parts of the computer and how they hook together. They are trained to load, re-boot and execute a program. I occasionally sabotage the lab by disconnecting monitor cables, power cables or placing unformatted diskettes in the drives. The students are then trained in what to do when the computer doesn't work. After we have finished a particular software program, I send it to the classroom teacher and ask him/her to use my students as tutors for the rest of the class. I also ask them to rely on my students for help with their computers. Most teachers welcome another helper where the computer is concerned and it gives a real boost to the self-esteem of my students.

Computers have helped to shape the basis of my program. They intrinsically have high interest for students. The computer allows the student to feel in control. A student can proceed at his/her own pace. It is non-judgemental. It doesn't react to the amount of time a student takes to answer a question. It gives immediate feedback, and doesn't let an error perseverate. The software I use has many different levels of difficulty. This allows all students to work on the same program, but at different levels. The students can be challenged to move at their own pace and there is no stigma attached to being in an easier part of the program. The roll I play with my students has changed. I have become the advisor, the co-explorer, not the giver of information. When asked questions, I give very few answers. Most often I ask, "What have you tried? What do you think will work? What could you try next?" Then we explore the student's ideas together. Discipline problems are practically non-existent.

My program is now in its fourth year. The results have been very satisfying. Attendance has vastly improved. The students are eagerly waiting at the door for their turns. Students not in the program have asked how they can qualify. The attitude of most of the students has really improved. I often hear "wow, I'm good at this!" and "I can do math!" Teachers report that my students are actually volunteering to answer questions in class and getting the answers right. Test scores have improved. Most of my students either migrate or graduate out of the program by scoring above the 25% on the Comprehensive Test of Basic Skills. Out of 60 students in the program this year, only 18 were in the program last year. Of the 20 students (out of 120 students) that I have had for two years in a row, 90% showed increased scores on the C.T.B.S. My reward, however, is when I see a student who had a very difficult time with a software program last year, tell a fellow student, "don't worry. It may seem hard at first, but you'll get it. I did!" Compensatory Education students can master programs aimed at gifted students. They can benefit from software involving the higher level thinking skills and it can improve their overall performance in other academic areas, as well. Comp. Ed. kids can!

Resources:

Cossey, Ruth; Stenmark, Jean Kerr; Thompson, Virginia; "Family Math," Equals Lawrence Hall of Science, Berkeley, CA, 1986.

Downie, Diana; Slesnick, Twila; Stenmark, Jean Kerr, "Math for Girls and Other Problem Solvers," Equals Lawrence Hall of Science, Berkeley, CA, 1982.

The Learning Company
6493 Kaiser Drive
Fremont, CA 94555

Sunburst Communications
39 Washington Avenue
Pleasantville, NY 10570

Article #2
Technology and the At-Risk Student

EDITED BY
JACK
ROBERTS

Thirty-five percent to forty percent of American students in K-12 are classified as at-risk. For public high schools, the dropout rate hovers at around 25 percent; in some urban schools the rate is more than 50 percent. Those statistics are startling and lead to the dismal conclusion that our present education system is not properly preparing all Americans to lead happy, productive lives, and that America itself may soon be considered at-risk if our future workers continue to drop by the wayside.

Certainly our present system of education can't be made the only scapegoat for at-risk students. It's a massive problem that is compounded by language barriers, the circle of poverty, and the sheer magnitude of those labeled at-risk. The National School Boards Association reports that of the more than 3.6 million children who began their formal schooling in September 1986, 25 percent were from families who live in poverty, 15 percent were physically or mentally handicapped, 15 percent were immigrants who speak a language other than English, and 14 percent were children of unmarried parents.

Combatting the at-risk dilemma will require help from all areas of school and community.

Technology can play an important role in reducing the number of at-risk students by providing an extremely effective learning environment for dropouts and potential dropouts. To understand just how effective technology can be in this area, *Electronic Learning* convened its first annual Technology Leadership Conference, with the theme Technology and the At-Risk Student.

On August 19, 1988, nine esteemed educators and national policy makers—and one former dropout—met at *EL's* New York City offices to help provide leadership for educators working with technology and at-risk populations.

Led by *EL* editorial director and founder Jack Roberts, the panelists helped define the problem, examples of where technology is working as an intervention tool (and what kinds of technologies are working), suggested what the technology industry can do to help address the problems of students at-risk, and provided policy recommendations.

Sitting in the audience were members of the industry, representing hardware, software, videodisc, and other technology companies. These industry members participated in the dialogue, providing a balanced vision and offering insightful suggestions.

Below is a transcript of the conference, edited for clarity and length.

Defining the Problem

Who is at-risk? And what are the problems we face in meeting the needs of those who are at-risk?

Marilyn Gardner. From an urban perspective, there is a wide group of at-risk students, including black, Hispanic, bilingual, special-need, poor students and unwed mothers, to name just a few. And I am sure we're going to get a broad spectrum of definitions today of an at-

388

risk student. So I thought I'd focus on one piece of interesting research by Signithia Fordham and John Ogbu in which the authors talk about a tremendous social pressure, among minority students, against striving for academic success.

There are certain behaviors, certain characteristics, certain activities, events, symbols, that are seen by a large group of minority students as not appropriate, and those behaviors, meanings, events are characteristic of white Americans. Peers often construe such behavior, including academic success, as trying to join the enemy.

I think many of us can relate, from our high school days, to not wanting to succeed in front of our peers. Recently, in Boston schools, for example, a student received first prize in a city-wide contest for science, and he took so much razzing from his peers that he actually destroyed the trophy as a symbol of not succeeding.

The point I am trying to make is that what we have found in Boston schools, and what we have found in urban education, is that technology offers an opportunity for at-risk students to succeed privately. They do not have to go forth with that peer pressure.

And continually we hear from teachers who say, "My goodness, Johnny does terribly in math; but now he's doing his math through the use and help of technology, and he's forging ahead." We're all aware that with the use of computers students' peers do not know where they are on the whole spectrum of their instruction, and we have found tremendous success with many of these at-risk students.

Antonia Stone: I guess my own personal definition of an at-risk student would be someone whose needs are not being met by society and who is in danger, or at-risk, of not being able to lead a productive life.

I also look at this question of technology and the at-risk student from the point of view of someone who has seen enormous change in at-risk individuals. I've seen people who have rebelled physically against the system, who have thrown things, attacked teachers, people who have then given up, turned away from their families, from authority, from anyone. They've then come to a computer, used a computer, and discovered the enabling characteristics of working with a computer.

It is easier to learn how to use a computer than to learn mathematics or how to read, and many of these other things that people are called upon to learn in school. But the computer is more important to a lot of at-risk students than reading or writing or being academically successful.

So by giving them an opportunity to achieve a recognizable success with something that they think is important, you're giving them empowerment. I realize that empowerment is almost a dirty word these days because so many people use it. But it's real, and that's what's happening.

Shelley Goldman: Here is one definition of at-risk students that I found in The RBS At-Risk Project Brief: "As students, they are generally low achievers. They also differ from their more successful peers in development of self-esteem, task performance, cultural aspirations and life experience. It is estimated that two-thirds of these students are from families at the poverty level, and that many are Black and Hispanic. Many are the victims of family trauma, physical, emotional, alcohol or drug abuse. Nationally, these students number 4.5 million." [*The RBS At-Risk Project Brief,*

Number 5; Research for Better Schools, Philadelphia, Pa.]

Without sounding like I am making light of this definition, I personally take the view, however, that everybody is at-risk. Because, in fact, everyone is at-risk, except for maybe the top 5 percent or 10 percent of kids in the population who are very wealthy and get to have the best quality educations available.

I think the answer for at-risk is a general improvement in the quality of education in the country for all students, and maybe taking some of the things that have worked in our highest quality schools and somehow finding ways to make them available to everyone.

Thelma Scott: I consider at-risk children those who are not achieving for some reason. It's not their fault usually. Very seldom do you have a child who doesn't learn because he doesn't want to learn.

Frank Withrow: We've had at-risk children for a long time now. Several decades ago when I was first a classroom teacher, I remember my principal said, "Frank, we have a challenging class for you." And we called them challenges at that time, rather than at-risk. But they had many of the same characteristics that we're talking about now: handicapped, poor, single parents. But I do

An After School Center that Empowers People

Playing to Win, Inc. began its crusade against computer inequity by offering computer education in correctional facilities. The idea was that computers could serve as a bridge to society for inmates.

Since then, Playing to Win has opened two computer centers—in East Harlem, N.Y., and Somerville, Mass.—to expand opportunities for disadvantaged people there.

"My own definition of an at-risk student is someone whose needs are not being met by society and who is in danger of not being able to lead a productive life," says Antonia Stone, president and founder.

Helping others to lead a productive life is the theme of such Playing to Win projects as: establishing computer education programs in correctional institutions in six states, developing and helping others to develop educational software, and providing technical assistance to organiza-

tions and individuals seeking to expand computer opportunities for disadvantaged people in their communities.

Playing to Win's East Harlem Center consists of 40 computers, three teachers, an assistant, and a staff of volunteers—all in the basement of a housing project. About 500 people, ages three to 93, visit the center each week, and 99 percent of them have never seen a computer before.

My experience with at-risk youth is not in the schools, obviously. It is after they have dropped out, after they've gotten into trouble, after they have, in fact, failed to be served by the school system and by the technology."

Why concentrate on technology? "Because it is easier to learn how to use a computer than to learn how to read, and many of these other things that people are called upon to learn in the school system," says Stone, former chairperson of the think that things are somewhat different today. If we look at some of the demographic data we have more bilingual children in our schools today. We have more children who come from poor families. We have more who come from families where the parents themselves are children.

One of the most staggering facts in the U.S. is that we have the highest rate of teenage pregnancy of any developed nation in the world. This very day, for example, there will be 50 teenage girls under the age of 15 who will have had their third child delivered. Now that is an incredibly astounding statistic—think of that first child, or the second or third. How much nurturing, how much family, how much community background is that child going to have? Those people are truly at-risk.

Now our statistics show that we have somewhere between 35 percent to 40 percent of our children in schools today that are classified as at-risk. That's more than we've ever had before. And that changes the whole complex of what's happening in our schools and how we address them and how we can apply technology to the problem.

Carol Edwards: I believe the others have given a very good definition of at-risk, but one of those factors doesn't

mathematics department at Columbia Grammar and Prep School, New York.

"So by giving students an opportunity to achieve success with something that they think is important—a computer—you're giving them empowerment."

The impact of this empowerment is real and far-reaching, says Stone. "Our teenagers, dropouts, the people that come from adjudicated group homes, they often have really big problems manipulating a pencil or a pen. So word processing is just a boom. Kids are encouraged to write letters. The computer opens communications.

"There was a kid from a group home who was writing a letter and I was walking around the computer room with a visitor. We were looking over his shoulder, and he blocked the screen with his arms. We said, 'that's all right; we don't need to see what you're writing about.' It turned out he was writing about girls, but realized that what he was saying was not something he should show in a computer center. But he had the freedom to do that, and he wrote something he wanted to talk about."

Technology reaches into so many interdisciplinary areas, says Stone, "it represents practical ways to stretch ourselves as human beings, and as students, to do things we have never been able to do before. But I think industries, schools, non-profits, communities and parents have to get together. Parents are really important. The students from illiterate homes do not get the support that children from literate homes get—they can't.

"I think we have an opportunity and technology is part of that opportunity, and the at-risk student is one of the motivations to take advantage of that opportunity to change the current model of education."

necessarily put you at-risk. Usually it takes multiple factors. If you're both minority and poor, for example, that will put you at-risk. Of course, there are—some single factors that can put people at-risk, and of course the thing that comes to mind is AIDS. We have to think about the growing number of children now who have AIDS. They are immediately at-risk, with no other factor involved. Even if they come from the wealthiest families in the world, they're still at-risk.

I think what hasn't been focused on is what the problem is for us, who are not at-risk. I look around here and see that we are pretty much the same age. And when we retire, who are we going to have to retire on—from a purely selfish point of view—and who can we rely on for the productivity of this country, for our future productivity?

I think we also have to look at being at-risk as a failure on our part to serve children who have a need. We have to look at ourselves: educators, software developers, hardware vendors. What is it that we are not doing to serve all of society? And particularly, those who are hard to serve. We have not been successful at that, and I don't think we need to blame the victim of that. We need to blame ourselves, and then we can move on and ask the right questions to get the solution.

Karen Golden: Well, first of all I am honored to be here. I dropped out of

One High School's About-Face

"At-risk, from our small-town perspective, are those students who are not achieving academically, are potential dropouts, are not being accepted socially, are having family problems, personal problems or for whatever reason are not being successful—and I mean successful in life," says Melvin Smoak, assistant superintendent of schools in semirural Orangeburg, S.C.

The Orangeburg district supports 11 schools. One of those, Orangeburg-Wilkinson High School, was featured on the May 2 cover of Newsweek because of its revitalization at the hands of Smoak, then principal. Now Smoak is tackling the district, where 80 percent of the 7,000 students are minorities, and 78 percent of those students qualify for free or reduced lunches.

As part of the effort to help these at-risk students, comprehensive remediation programs in language arts, reading and math are required of K-12 students who do not meet state standards.

The remediation program is part of the regular school day, in time slots created by restructuring the curriculum (without lengthening the school day) and by "cutting out some of the fringes," Smoak says, "like homeroom."

The remediation program may be the saving grace of some of these students, because as of 1990 all the state's high school students will be required to pass an exit exam.

Technology is a large part of the remediation program (with one computer for every 20 students in Orangeburg-Wilkinson), and all students can work on computers in a number of places: the remediation labs, the library, or the general computer labs; and they can work during scheduled times, through lunch period or after school hours (the school is open until midnight each day).

school 15 years ago, at the age of 15. I was pregnant, my parents had separated, and I just felt like my world was just crumbling down. And I couldn't handle it. So I got to thinking one day, and I said, "Well I have to take my life into my own hands." I felt pressured and unhappy and alone. So I moved out.

After I had my son, things just started falling in place, and I became a full-time mother. One day I was sitting talking with him, and I was telling him how important it was to get an education. And I had to stop and think for myself, you know, because how could I tell him how important it was for him to get an education, when I didn't have one? So I made up my mind that I had to go back and get this for me, and set an example for him.

And so I did. And, by the way I have a daughter now, and my son is 14, and my daughter is 11, and they're proud of me and I am proud of myself. Because I did prove to them that it could be done; it wasn't too late, even after 15 years.

Nick Vasquez: First of all, I want to echo what Carol was saying about all of us being at-risk. Because of the changing demographics in the Southwest, with the minority becoming the majority, it's clear that you don't have a trained, young workforce to take up where the traditional segment of our society has been involved.

The added problem is that we need to introduce computer technology to our students, so that when they do come to

---

"We've seen great success out of the remediation program," says Smoak. The dropout rate went from 8.6 percent to 2.5 percent; 30 percent more students meet the standards; 62 percent of the students go to college.

Technology is working for the teachers and administrators as well, especially where attendance is concerned.

"With the computer, we can now track our students' attendance. And a computer-generated calling device will call the home [from 5 PM to 9:30 PM] of those students who are absent from one or more class each day.

"So this has had an impact, along with other things, to reduce the absenteeism at our school," says Smoak, who in his career has taught mathematics, coached basketball, was in-school suspension coordinator, assistant principal in charge of discipline for Orangeburg-Wilkinson, and then its principal. "We also require

parents to come in during the year to meet with the teachers."

To eliminate paperwork for teachers and administrators, testing and grade reporting are also on-line. Future plans include linking all the schools in the district to the main office via a network.

Smoak is also working to set up a system so that students gain credit for partial completion of coursework. Other innovative programs are already in place.

"This [past] summer we required all students who participate in extra-curricular activities and come on-campus for weight training or conditioning, to also set aside time to prepare for the SAT.

"Our students, when they leave the school system, whether they're gifted or whether they're low achievers, they will be computer literate, because everything you do in life now has to do with computers," says Smoak.

the university they won't be further behind. When they do get there they compete with students from the San Fernando Valley, Beverly Hills, who have 4.1, 4.2 GPAs, and the facilities and the teaching in these districts in many ways are just a lot better.

And access is definitely a big problem. We want to make sure that there is some way we can arrange for students to go and have access to computers.

Where technology is working

What are some examples of how technology is making a difference as an intervention tool for students at-risk?

Sara Sieland-Bucy: I believe the key word in this question is "tool." A computer is a machine. It's a wonderful machine, because it enables me to do things.

And I try to get the students in my computer lab to reach the point where they see the computer as a tool to help them, like a screwdriver or a wrench or a car.

I asked my students to tell me how the computer helps them learn, and I found three major points where computers were impacting on their lives.

One was their self-efficacy. You know we talked about how empowerment is almost a nasty word because it's been bounced around so much, but students in adult education have never felt in charge of their own lives. Learning traditionally *happened* to them.

But the computer sits and looks at you. If you get the wrong answer, it's not the computer's fault, because the computer has an answer that was programmed in. And computers are neutral. They don't know if you've had a bad day, purple hair or are mean. They just know what answer you put in.

One day I kept hearing a machine reboot, and I asked the student why he was doing that. The student said, "every time I make a mistake, I re-boot so it forgets what my score is." I thought that was wonderful. He wanted to beat it. When he got done he wanted it to give him a score of 100. And it took him all day. And he was just learning and learning.

I have had non-readers, general education graduates and others, and one of the largest impacts was on their thinking skills. One of my students told me while we were discussing coming here [to the At-Risk conference], that the computer forces you to think because it won't think for you. Teachers tend to fill in. Teachers ask a question, wait just so long for the answer, and finally teachers give them the answer. Computers don't. They'll wait for a half-hour, and if the student hasn't come up with that answer at least she'll ask somebody, and the computer's still sitting there when she comes back.

And they like that. The pressure is off. They don't have to come up with the answer in 30 seconds, or a minute and a half or whatever.

Elbert is a student in the reading lab who doesn't read and who's 45 years old. I asked him how he felt about computers, and he hemmed and hawed, and he came up with the greatest line I ever thought about computers. He said: "it's wakening my train of thought. I look at it and I realize it's waiting for my answer. And I'm important, because if I don't answer, it can't go anywhere."

I feel that technology can be an opening wedge into the adult education student's mind that says you are not stupid, and you are not a failure.

Golden: I feel that if it wasn't for the computer program class at Urban Adult a lot of people wouldn't get that first-hand basic experience about how much you can learn from computers, and how computers can help you in the future. A lot of low-income people wouldn't have that opportunity if it weren't for programs like the one I was in.

When I first sat down in front of a computer I was afraid because I thought it had control over me. When I found out that it didn't, it was fun. And there were so many different programs to work with, and it actually makes you stop and use your mind and think about things. The experience was great.

I plan to continue working with computers. And my daughter has had a computer class, also. I would mess up on the terms, different words, pronunciations, and she would correct me. That made me feel good, because she was paying attention to what I was doing. And that was just a great feeling.

Scott: Two years ago we became an official ACOT classroom. [ACOT stands for Apple Classroom of Tomorrow. Each student in the class has a computer on his desk and another at home.] And we haven't had time to stop and really evaluate what we've done since then, because we have been running as fast as we could for at least 20 hours a day.

People say, "but just what have you gained?" Well how can you put your finger on that? It's difficult to evaluate. What do you want me to evaluate? What is your opinion of evaluation? Do you want it on some standardized test, which I don't give, and don't think has anything to do with evaluating the student. Or are you interested in the whole student? I think you must evaluate the whole student.

And that's hard to do. We have seen complete transformation in these students. Now when I started teaching,

those students sat in a row, quietly, they didn't move unless they raised their hand and I gave them permission. When we walked down the hall, we walked in a straight row.

Those classrooms with computers in them are not that way. It's an entirely different classroom. One where the student is very much in control.

Do computers make it easier on teachers? Don't kid yourself. It's the hardest thing in the world to try to work the computer into a curriculum. We must change that curriculum. We failed children for years and years. Not just these children that we've identified as at-risk children. We failed all children throughout the time we've taught.

We have to develop a curriculum that meets the needs of society.

There were two things that set the Memphis ACOT site apart from the other four throughout the nation. One was telecommunications, where each child had his own modem at home, and is hooked up with a tutor, so that the tutor can help him with his subject. And the other [difference] was that we were at-risk.

[The modem also allows the school to] interact with the parents. You see, parents of at-risk students, they have not been successful themselves. So why should they interact with the school? I couldn't get them to talk to me on the phone. Many, many times I'd call, and they'd say, "ain't nobody by that name lives here."

Now I can call any home, I can talk to everyone I want to talk to there, and the children are interacting, and it's been a marvelous experience.

Melvin Smoak: We restructured our curriculum; we went from six to seven academic periods without lengthening the school day, so we just cut out some of the fringes—homerooms, for example. We also revised our lunch program. Now we require all students to enroll in this [computerized remediation] program who are not meeting standards set by South Carolina.

And we've seen great success out of it. Our drop-out rate which was at 8.6 percent, went down to 2.5 percent. At one time we had only around 40 percent of our students meeting standards. Now we have 68 percent to 70 percent who are meeting standards on the two skills tests developed by the state. We have a lot of work to do in our area as it relates to at-risk students. However, we are seeing a lot of success as it relates to the technology that we have incorporated into our program.

Technology is also working for the teachers and administrators. If you walk in any time of day, you'll see our superintendent on his computer. With my transition to the district office, the first thing I moved was the computer.

Technology helps eliminate a lot of the paper work for the principal at the high school. With the computer I can immediately look at grade distribution for whole classes. If a parent is calling me because she's upset about what's happening at the school as it relates to her child, I can look at the student's history right there at my desk.

As far as improvement of attendance is concerned, we can now track our students. If they're not in school there's a [computerized] calling device that will call the home.

The students can go to the library, take a disk and work on their own. They can go to the remediation lab, where they compete, not with the class, but with themselves. The computers are recording and checking their work, and telling them where they need to go back, and what they need to do.

As I said before, a lot of our academic success has been definitely linked to technology. At this point, with that population that I told you about, we have 62 percent of our students attending college after graduation. This past year, with a graduating class of 377, we had scholarships awarded in the amount of $1.1 million.

And it's even working with those younger kids as well as the ones at the high school. We start our four-year-olds with computers. You should see some of the things that those four-year-olds are developing on the computers.

The success again was not just because of technology, but it was because of the staff having the caring attitude. They do not mind going the extra mile.

Withrow: I am going to give you one example of something that worked in the metropolitan Washington, D.C., area, where we are consumed with teenage pregnancies. This past spring and early summer, with money from the Women's Leadership Group and the Metropolitan D.C. Boys and Girls clubs, kids in a club that is right in the heart of the drug world in D.C. were given technology tools—cam recorders, computers, desktop publishing, what-have-you.

They came up with a teenage video and supplemental materials published on computers. It was called *Stop Having Babies*. [The kids came up with the title.] They developed a rap song, and a great deal of role playing. One would take the role of the father of the girl who was pregnant. And he certainly was going to go out and find Johnny boy, and find out what Johnny boy was going to do about this pregnancy.

They also used the computer to create the graphics on the TV program. They made 40 copies of the video and print material, and some 50,000 of the boys and girls from the athletic programs in the district are going to see the video this fall.

I am terribly impressed by how much creativity the young people can come up with in using these things as tools. And while I think it's important for us to think of computers, it's also important for us to think of the total array of communication technologies that we have available to us today.

What Kind of Software is Working

Stone: Our teenagers, the dropouts, the people that come from adjudicated group homes, often have problems with manipulating a pencil or a pen. So word processing is just a boom. Kids are encouraged to write letters. The computer opens up communication for them.

We had a kid who wanted to use *Print Shop*. He saw a greeting card on the wall that another kid had done. He didn't know how to write, so he made his greeting card exactly the same way. He used the same words to say the same thing. It said, "Terry loves Ivan" because those were the coeds that were on that other one. But a couple of weeks later, he's writing his own, and that's the important thing, to get that desire to move ahead, that desire to learn.

I think that the tools, the kinds of software that enable you to create, enable you to put something of yourself into that machine, and to come out with something that you can see, that's palpable—that's one class of software.

Is there a place for drill-and-practice programs? Sure there is. A drill-and-practice program or a tutorial program is absolutely ideal on the computer when what you want to learn is to bypass your mind. When you want to learn to go from looking at a letter "A" to having your finger type it, you don't want to think. You want to take that necessity of thought away from the process. So drill and practice on a computer is ideal for that.

Edwards: I think there's a lot of misuse of drill-and-practice software, and confusing drill-and-practice with the role of direct instruction and tutorial.

Unfortunately, I think lots of times drill-and-practice software gets misused because the diagnostic problem of the learner has not been correctly identified. And the child is having procedural problems, not declarative problems. And they're given the wrong software.

You will notice, for example, [with drill and practice software] that they will start at one level, and if they get that level right, they go to the next level, etc. Well, what happens is they finally get to a level were they don't know the procedure, they don't get anything right, and if it's one of those branching programs that automatically kicks them down to a lower level, then they practice something that they know already, that they have the declarative knowledge for, and they're bored.

Another example of a program that works is *Where in the World is Carmen Sandiego?* which, it seems, all kids love. What this program really requires is for you to know how to use an atlas, to have some map skills, and to know how to use reference materials.

Librarians will tell you that when trying to teach kids reference skills, it sort of goes in one ear and out the other, because they've got all of these artificial things to teach these skills with. If you use that particular program as a vehicle for teaching reference skills, they've got a purpose for using that atlas. They learn in five minutes what a teacher could not teach them in six months in terms of reference skills.

I think it's the problem-solving type of software that is motivating to students because it gives them complex enough and challenging enough situations for them to want to then go back and get all that dull stuff that they had to get through in the past.

What the Industry Can Do

What are some of the ways the educational technology industry can help educators with the problems facing at-risk students?

Withrow: I think one of the greatest barriers to putting technology into the schools is the way we finance it. We're faced now with schools that 10 years ago bought the generation of computers then. They're not worn out, but they're obsolete.

And of course, our public school systems have absolutely no tax break for any capitalization that they do. As a matter of fact, it's a liability, and they've got to go to the taxpayer to get the money to do it.

And then they have no way of insuring it, other than self-insurance. And if tomorrow morning the school where Melvin put his 120 computers burns down, those computers are gone, and there's no recovery. The schools are mostly self-insured.

Technology Sheds Light on Bright Minds in Memphis

"I consider at-risk children those who are not achieving for some reason. It's not their fault, usually. Very seldom do you have a child who doesn't learn because he doesn't want to learn," says Thelma Scott, consultant to Apple's ACOT project and, until this year, coordinator of the Lester Demonstration School, Memphis, Tenn.

"When we got computers into the [Lester] classrooms, those at-risk children were able to work with the computers; they were empowered by the computers."

Like the other four ACOTs (Apple Classroom of Tomorrow) nationwide, every student at Lester (which comprises grades 4-6) has an Apple IIe at school and an Apple IIc at home. But Lester—the only ACOT where all (75) students are considered at-risk—also gave every child a modem at home as part of a telecommunications project, and set up an electronic bulletin board.

"Now, I was thoroughly convinced that we'd put the computers in the home and when we'd ask for them back, the computers would not come back," Scott says. "That was my idea, because it's the highest crime rate area in our city. But every computer came back that first year.

"We have two stories there, though, that I think are unique. One of them is that we had to de-bug the computers, and I'm not talking about computer language."

The other one is that there was one little boy that we had no way of getting on the modem. I mean excuses, excuses, you name it, we got it. I knew the modem wasn't in the home. But the modem came back still in the box that we sent it home in. So, you see we had at-risk children who did not use the technology at home."

Scott realized early on both the importance and the difficulty of interact

So there's no basis or incentive for anyone there, and there's still the problem of obsolescence that we started out with. So what I am suggesting is that there might be somebody that is a third-party, private-sector person between the hardware/software and school people, that might be called something like an "educational technology general contractor," that you might go to, just as you might go to an architect, and say I have a need for at-risk programs. [The third party will] figure out the whole plan for the school, finance the whole plan for the school. And there are tax incentives.

We need to have a way to take care of technology's obsolescence. And I think that a user-fee, lease arrangement with a third-party contractor is one that schools should at least take a very close look at.

Stone: We need the developers in the publishing worlds to take some risks along with us.

There is a great deal of development work being done. There is an enormous amount of government money being spent on innovative practices, on creative, innovative ways of using software in the schools—for science, social studies, mathematics, English, writing, you name it. The National Science Foundation, for example, has sponsored millions and millions of dollars worth of projects—which we pay for out of our own pockets—which

ing with the students' parents.

"You see, parents of the at-risk students in the inner-city schools have not been successful themselves. So why should they interact with the school? I couldn't get them to talk to me on the phone. Many times I'd call, and they'd say, 'Ain't nobody by that name lives here.' But I knew I was talking to the right person. So we couldn't get the interaction." Now modems nearly guarantee that interaction.

Technology helps children to build self-confidence, says Scott, "to develop the attitude that they can do it. And we, as teachers, are marveling at what we're able to do.

"It's the hardest thing in the world to try to work the computer into a curriculum. We must change that curriculum. We failed children for years and years. Not just children that we've identified as at-risk; we've failed all children."

Even with vast improvements in its four-year history, the Lester School still has the lowest achievement scores of any school in Memphis, says Scott.

"And, you know, classroom control in a technological environment is difficult. Computers make it necessary for those children to move around. Discipline doesn't mean a towering approach. But it means one where there is a relaxed atmosphere, where discipline is really a part of mutual respect, honesty between the teacher and the student, kindness and understanding.

"There are more questions than there are answers, but there are solutions that are emerging as we work with these children. We have seen complete transformations in [some of] these students. These are students from low-income, usually single-parent homes that have never seen the Mississippi River six miles away, and now they are going all over the world, talking to people [as ACOT students]."

get finished, labeled, and put on the shelf.

The industry isn't listening to the research, and it isn't pushing it and supporting it in the schools. It's still reacting and saying, "what do you want? We'll give you what you want." There has to be the willingness [on the part of the industry] to take a little bit of a leadership role.

Goldman: I work in a research and development laboratory in a college, where we spend two or three years developing and researching prototypes of software technology that can be used in schools. And then at the end of a project (and I've just had this happen to me) where we've gotten incredibly good results we said, "well, is there any interest in publishing this software?" The response [from the software publishing industry] was, "no market. I don't think there's going to be a real big market for that, or if there is a market, it's not coming for 10 years."

And it's very frustrating. I can talk about four or five incredible projects that have been done in our lab alone, for which there is no market to publish them. And they've had incredibly good results with kids, and they've done a full range of things, using a full range of different types of technology. And that's very frustrating. So we said, "okay, we'll just keep researching and trying to find out, using our best ways to get things out."

I would like to see the industry put a little bit more charity behind getting

Revitalizing Adult Education Students in Detroit

There are 45,000 adult education students in Detroit, says Sara Sieland-Bucy, a computer lab teacher at the Urban Adult Education Institute there, "and every single one is at-risk because they've failed already, or they wouldn't be an adult-ed student."

Not quite a year ago, in January, Sieland-Bucy (who's been teaching at the Institute for 15 years) began using computers to teach reading. Her students (age 17 to 70) read at a semi-literate level, but their enthusiasm is immeasurable.

"I have to stand at the power switch and say, 'thirty seconds to finish up or I'm turning off the power to the machines.' I never get out of the building on time; I hardly ever get lunch. It's glorious. It's so wonderful to see a student drill five basic beginning sounds for an hour and 10 minutes and, when I say it's time to go he'll say 'I'm going to beat these, I'm going to learn these.'

"Technology can be the opening wedge into the adult education student's mind that says you are not stupid, and you are not a failure. You just didn't happen to learn something that's essential when you were five or 12 or 82; now you can learn it."

The make-up of students in Sieland-Bucy's program ranges from young women who left school to have children, to parolees, to people in drug rehabilitation. "But they're just people that need to know that the system hasn't forgotten them," she says.

Sieland-Bucy describes her students' reactions to the computer as "a feeling of wonder, because they can learn, and it doesn't have to be horrible, it doesn't have to be painful. And some of them almost feel angry that learning is fun and they had never known that."

Educators, says Sieland-Bucy, have to have "at least enough courage to let some products out to schools. Because there are excellent products that have been developed in eight or ten research labs in this country that are just sitting in those research labs because there's no market.

Linda Tsantis (IBM): You mentioned before that industry should also take an active role in research, and that's really a very complex issue. Because it depends on how the research is conducted. If it's internal, than it's tainted because it's internal research. If you pay for groups to do it, it's considered solicited. So it's very difficult to get plain research when you do it yourself as a vendor.

So we depend on the schools to conduct research and help us with those kinds of results. What's happened, however, concerns how schools have to respond to the type of measurement that goes on. Because whenever you're looking at gain scores and standardized tests for the measurement [of technology's impact] we're sort of dead.

We're having a tremendous problem trying to demonstrate the impact of empowerment without the hard data. The hard data does not match the phenomenon that we're seeing with technology. So we need some guidance as to what we can do to influence that. We can talk about the empowerment issue, we all know it's there. We can do all those things, but until we have some way to measure the change that school boards and admin-

students in on the joy of learning. Technology helps tremendously. But you can't get students excited about technology if teachers aren't excited."

Sieland-Bucy says her philosophy "has always been contrary to the American educational system, which seems, to think that teachers have to know everything before they can teach anything."

Case in point, she says, is the diving coach, "usually a pot-bellied man with a whistle who couldn't swim a hundred yards if his life depended on it. He will get a person to dive off that board in splendor, and nobody says, 'how can you be the coach when you can't do that?' Well, I can teach. That's my job; not to be the expert in the subject."

When Sieland-Bucy asked students how they feel about the computer, she recognized an impact in several areas of their lives. One was self-efficacy.

"You know, students in adult-ed have never felt in charge of their own lives. And a lot of them don't learn the first time they hear or see something, and they've been hustled through [school]. In 4th grade you have to learn this; in 8th grade you have to learn this. There is no 'have to' in my computer lab. If you want to go over that drill on consonant sounds for an hour and 10 minutes, I'm not going to say, 'you should have learned it by now' The computer never says, 'you should have learned it by now.' They love that."

Sieland-Bucy also found that computers impact on self-esteem. One middle-aged student, who does not read, commented that the computer was "wakening my train of thought." Sieland-Bucy said she found the computer "woke up everything the students hadn't used before, and they love it with patience."

istrations can buy into, we can't do it.

Goldman: I think that technology offers a great opportunity for getting beyond our current assessment tests in education. Assessment is a huge problem, but everywhere that I go now, to conferences, or to meet people to talk about technology, everybody is very aware that something's wrong with the way we assess kids' achievement in school. And basically we're set up wrong, because in American education we're set up assessment-wise for half the kids to always fail. We've got a bell-curve mentality which means 50 percent of the kids in this country are going to fail no matter what.

Edwards: The fact of the matter is, gain scales are always going to be important, as long as two things are true: that scores are the criteria for getting into college, which is, in fact, the ticket to a higher degree and a better earning power; and as long as the public thinks that that's the important thing. So I think we have to begin to change those things.

Dale Richmond (Pioneer): We do need to communicate quantitative and qualitative information. I think that it's incumbent upon you to ask us [the industry] for what you need. I know, speaking for Pioneer, that when anybody asks us for anything we certainly try to meet that need and exceed it.

Sieland-Bucy: My biggest concern is for all of us in school districts who have bought computers that are now obsolete, or almost obsolete. Great things are coming out that I can't use, and that makes me mad.

If software manufacturers could get together with hardware manufacturers, to make upgrades economically feasible, it would help all the small schools that bought lower-memory computers.

If I have to put 80-column cards on a

hardware requisition and *MECC Dataquest Composer* on a software requisition, I don't know which one would ever come in first. But if they were hooked together and it looked like a nice deal, I think more school systems would begin to look into upgrading their computers.

Mattie Lesnick (Tandy/Radio Shack): Let's look at the federal monies which are targeted toward the at-risk population, the (Chapter 1) monies, and how they're allocated. It appears to me in my reading of the reforms and the legislation that has passed now, that they're going to encourage technology be used in the next few years.

We'd like to work with you so that you can be more flexible in the use of that funding, and not just target it for programs or at-risk students, but allow your children maybe to co-mingle, if that's what you think is best for your students. As I am sure everyone here today knows, we must determine where we need to go in this educational reform, and as a major vendor, we'd be happy to help do that.

Policy Recommendations

Vasquez: There needs to be one place, perhaps *Electronic Learning* magazine, where this information can be found, to help us keep in touch, to help all of us pursue our goals, and carry on from here in different areas of the country.

Sieland-Bucy: The line of communication must be opened up between the industry and teachers. During teacher in-service days, for example, industry could come in and impart a great deal of information to a whole bunch of teachers at once, instead of trying to do it a little bit at a time.

Edwards: Teachers have to be trained:

they have to feel comfortable using computers, and they have to know how to use your product well. That's expensive, and we've got to work on a solution to that together.

How about good state-of-the-art $100 computers, and good state-of-the-art $15 software? This is something to work toward. And we've got to be creative and flexible in how we can do that, so that everybody has the state-of-the-art. We don't need the bells and whistles.

Finally, I would encourage you to at least take a portion of your budget to do something that will help out in the long-term, but may not realize immediate gain.

Withrow: I would like to recommend that from a policy standpoint we think of alternative ways to finance both the capitalization, and the maintenance and operation of the technology that we want in our schools. I think we have to be expansive, look at some radical ways of doing that. I would personally opt for a third-party vendor, which would finance, maintain, and operate those programs.

Scott: I have two recommendations: first, let's develop some way of evaluating what we're doing, not by the standardized test that we've used before, but by evaluating the whole impact that technology is having on the child.

And secondly, let's develop a curriculum that fits the needs of the student.

Education is an investment; it's not an expense. Yesterday is the cancelled check; tomorrow is the promissory note. Today is the only cash you have so we better spend it wisely. So let's all work together to find the funds for technology and for education. Let's give these at-risk students the opportunity to develop confidence, to develop marketable skills, and let's believe in the student, and help the student to believe in himself and to have the atti-

tude, "I can do it."

Goldman: One thing universities can do is provide good research and also better ways to disseminate that research.

The second is teacher-training. Our universities are the place where our teachers are trained and prepared for entering the classrooms, and as an ex-teacher, I know I didn't learn anything in college that prepared me for my first day of teaching.

I think if technology has the capability to be the new shot in the arm to improve education in this country, I would like to see technology developed that doesn't fit exactly into how we think about education today, that it's something different, but not so different that no one can hitch onto it in any kind of way. But that it continues to keep a healthy tension in education.

I really see technology as having the potential to do things differently. A lot of my research shows that in certain uses of technology, failure is gone. It is absent. It is not an issue. Well that would be a real nice, refreshing thing, to have your kid go to school, and not have to worry all the time about whether or not he's going to fail.

Stone: I think we have an opportunity, and I think technology is part of that opportunity, and the at-risk student is one of the motivations to take advantage of the opportunity to change the current model of education.

The school, as Shelley has said, is not a model of the way people work anymore. They don't do that. And the more that the school can be a model of the way people work, the more people who go to school will be prepared to work in the world, and the more they will be able to recognize that they are getting something valuable in education.

I support collaborations. I think it's the only way, because the problems are so big, we can't do it separately. And we have to forget a lot of the things that bother us, like, "I don't want to tell anybody who funds me, because maybe they'll get the money the next time." And that's a very real issue, very real for non-profits, and for universities, and so on.

But I think industries, schools, non-profits, communities and parents have to get together. I don't think we've said enough about parents today. Parents are really important The students from illiterate homes do not get the support that children from literate homes get. I think we need to do something about bringing parents into the situation.

I think that the schools can help by keeping computers available after school hours. Somehow there's got to be a way around the cost to keep the schools open. There's got to be a way to get the community in there to let the students teach the parents, to get the parents to use the computers and to spread the knowledge that exists, or the potential for knowledge that exists, about that technology.

Smoak: We all talk about the product that's being produced by our schools, and I would just like to see the industry continue to enhance their commitment to form partnerships with the educational industry, so that we're all working in the same direction.

I think with this partnership, we will not be on one side, saying this is what's happening, and you on the other side saying well this is the product that we are producing. And with that kind of effort we can go forward.

Gardner: Many crucial decisions are being made far from urban schools, and I would like to suggest that those who are actually shaping technology in education right now need to seek the guidance from those school districts who have the most to gain, and those are the urban school districts.

I also suggest that equity and at-risk be on every conference and meeting agenda, and not as a separate compartment but a part of the whole. It should be in everything we do, whether we're developing software or hardware or whatever.

I think federal, state, and local policymakers must insist that technological resources be equitably distributed around all schools. Policy makers must demand that technological resources are accompanied by funding for skilled teachers, for staff development, and for administrative staff.

We have to build the expertise within school systems. I can't believe how many school districts keep relying on the experts to help them. Principals are actually giving computer instructors the run of their programs, because they're afraid of technology. We have to bring the principals along so people that shouldn't be making curriculum decisions aren't.

There's a lot of federal money available from the National Science Foundation, Department of Education and others, and what is the first thing they say? "You cannot buy equipment with these funds." That is totally absurd. I am tired of trying to write proposals for professional development to buy software. I can't buy equipment. They have to start thinking about letting us buy equipment, or forget it.

And I think NSF and the Department of Education have to stop giving so many grants to universities. I know some universities get upset about this, but we just received an NSF grant of $600,000, and they told us, 'you are the first public school system we have ever given an NSF grant to. We're nervous, but we're going to try you out."

I think with limited resources, we have to identify where technology is most successful. Special needs is one example. We know it's successful there. The National School Board Association. with which I agree, says, "excellence and elitism are not synonymous." We have to re-affirm our commitment to full opportunity and achievement. We can't do what we're doing without that, and then, hopefully, everyone will get the message.

A CHARLOTTE, N.C., JUNIOR HIGH SCHOOL "LIGHT-TRAINS" MEMBERS OF
THE "VIDEO-GAME GENERATION" WHO ARE IN DANGER OF NOT COMPLETING THEIR EDUCATION.

BY
GWEN
SOLOMON

If you're reading this, you are probably what Gail Morse calls "paper trained." Her students and yours are more likely to be part of the "light-trained" generation. According to Morse, a science teacher at J.M. Alexander Junior High School in Charlotte, N.C., and former national Christa McAuliffe Educator, "These youngsters are a television, VCR, and video-game generation. Although they've been labeled otherwise, they are bright, creative kids who respond to visual stimuli; they are 'light-trained' while most of us are 'paper-trained' learners."

A Technology Center

Morse and teacher Pam Schillinglaw started MATEC, the Media and Technology Enrichment Center as an alternative approach to educating students who are in danger of not completing their education. They work with 54 seventh graders selected from the 800 students enrolled at the junior high. The learning tools they use, which are housed in two classrooms, include an Apple IIe computer, two Apple IIGSes, three Macintosh SEes, three Pioneer laserdisc players, and the school's satellite dish.

At the beginning of the school year, Morse's students take a learning-styles inventory, which assists in determining what teaching methods will best help a student learn. In addition, the two teachers, a guidance counselor, the student, and parents meet to develop a personal growth plan. They look at factors such as attendance, disciplinary records, grades, and standardized test scores as well. They continue to meet regularly during the year to measure student efforts and accomplishments against this plan.

MATEC students spend their mornings in the center and take regular school electives in regular classrooms in the afternoon. Morse finds that their desire to learn carries over into these traditional classes.

Morse developed her theories at home. Four of her own seven children, she says, did very well in school. The youngest three didn't respond to traditional education in the same way because they grew up with PacMan, Nintendo, and VCRs. Like the students Morse teaches, somewhere in the early grades they got turned off to traditional learning.

"For youngsters like these," Morse says, "the computer is the switch to turn on their creative minds, and I find that they are very creative and talented. You just have to tap into that talent with the right tools. Then they're able to analyze information, synthesize it, solve problems, accept challenges, and apply their creativity in real-life situations. The computer is a tool that matches their learning styles."

In addition to using applications software such as *AppleWorks* and *Microsoft Works* for word processing, data bases, and spreadsheets, Morse's students use

405

laser videodiscs and probeware to study science, public-domain software to practice mathematics, video cameras to record experiments, satellite communications to get news broadcasts and television channels from foreign countries, and telecommunications services to reach people and places around the globe.

Morse's students learn skills that they had ignored earlier in their education. "They want to learn skills [that help them conduct] a project," Morse says. "They ask for math skills to calculate their experiments and writing skills to write an explanation. These are kids who were reluctant students. Now I can't teach them fast enough."

"When they received their first report card this year," Morse says, "some students cried. Seventy-two percent of the MATEC students made the school's A or B honor roll. They hadn't seen such good marks since first or second grade. In fact, the grandparents of one student had to renegotiate their offer of $50 for every A. They hadn't ever paid out before; this time they found themselves in debt." In addition, there were no disciplinary referrals, and attendance went up.

What is Taught

Much of the students' learning is interdisciplinary, and does not always include technology. When they studied environments in science recently, for example, they conducted decalcification experiments on eggs. In order to calculate density and weight loss of the eggs, they learned fractions and decimals in math. In social studies they studied how climatic conditions determine life-styles around the globe. And in English class they wrote descriptive essays on specific environmental problems.

Students often work in small groups to plan and investigate a topic of mutual interest. One group measured acid rain. They grew their own plants, collected water samples, tested them, and charted the results; then they used magazine articles and other reference materials to put their findings into perspective. When they felt they knew enough, they wrote a report for the class using a word processor.

A second group studied bubbles (Morse calls it, jokingly, bubbleology). They conducted laboratory experiments to research how to make solutions and measured the effect of various agents on water. They videotaped their experiments, added audio voiceover for explanations, and showed the tape to the class.

A third group studied natural disasters that involve water. They used segments of Optical Data's videodisc *Earth Science* to prepare a multimedia presentation.

The fourth group studied frogs and used desktop publishing to create a magazine called, appropriately enough, *Frogs*. It included editorials, news about frogs, recipes for frogs' legs and frog brains, a section on frog sports, and original cartoons and stories. College students enrolled in a pre-teacher program at the University of North Carolina in Charlotte serve as mentors and group members for this project and others.

The Tools

In science, the course content actually comes from videodiscs; textbooks are used only as a source for review. For example, they use videodiscs such as Systems Impact's *Chemistry and Energy* to study atomic structure and *Earth Science* for static pressure, land forms, and natural disasters. They use Optical

Data's *Windows on Earth Science* and *Earth Science* for environments and communities, and Videodiscovery's *BioSci* for invertebrates. "Sometimes my whole class watches," says Morse. "Sometimes both classes watch together, and very often individuals or groups use the laser discs. How we teach dictates how we use it."

Science probeware, such as Brøderbund's *Science Toolkit,* is used to test endothermic and exothermic reactions, and to measure the reflective quality of the colors in the students' clothing. When there were complaints this past winter about the temperature in classrooms throughout the building, students placed probes in various parts of each room to gauge the temperature. They determined that there was too much heat lost through the windows and made some recommendations for improvement to the school administration.

For social studies and English topics, they use the 40-videodisc set of *The Video Encyclopedia of the 20th Century* from CEL Educational Resources. "Every significant piece of video is there," Morse says. "The world wars, John Kennedy's assassination, Martin Luther King Jr.'s funeral, Mother Theresa's acceptance of the Nobel Peace Prize."

They also use the school's computer lab, which has 15 IBM PCjrs, to run traditional educational software.

MATEC's satellite dish is turned to the world of news and language. Students get a boost with their French by tuning into programs broadcast by a French television station. They watch news broadcasts that originate in Japan and Israel and contrast the presentations with American television news broadcasts. The crumbling of the Berlin Wall became a social studies lesson, and the San Francisco earthquake was integrated into math and science. NASA's satellite channel gives students detailed information on space science before a launch. Students also use the dish to participate in tele-conferences.

Television by satellite changed the way some students think about the medium at home. One father called to find out what MATEC was doing because his son was watching news in the morning instead of cartoons.

Morse's students also use several on-line networks, such as National Geographic's Kids Network (to study acid rain) and MECC's Iris network (for on-line writing projects).

The students also provide special services for the staff. They run a laminating service, make the school's morning announcements, produce cards and fliers with computer graphics, and are in charge of recycling for the school. MATEC is a resource for teachers. Students help create videodisc lessons, videos of experiments, and HyperCard stacks to store reference information. And they serve as mentors when teachers bring other students to use the equipment.

This is the first year that MATEC exists as a formal entity but Morse has applied elements of this type of restructured environment in her science classes for the last several years. In fact, some of her graduates formed a science club at the high school to help influence the kind of learning that happens there.

"MATEC is a change agent to help people look at restructuring," Morse says. "It's a subtle, gradual model for change that's very positive, very upbeat. Teacher reaction has been overwhelming. We've had lots of offers of help to expand the program."

Article #4
Computers and At-Risk Youth:
Software and Hardware That Can Help

By
Ellen R.
Bialo
and
Jay P.
Smith

What kind of software is most likely to be effective with at-risk youth? Which of the new technologies can help students who are disillusioned with school or having trouble keeping up? What computer-based tools are important for teachers and administrators who are working with these students?

All around the country, teachers and administrators are creating their own answers to these questions. Many are choosing from the full range of educational software titles on the market, attempting to identify for themselves those programs that will work best with at-risk students. Others are focusing on a small but growing number of software programs designed specifically with the at-risk population in mind. Both approaches seem to be yielding positive results.

Let's begin with a look at the different types of general-purpose software being adapted by educators for use with at-risk students.

Basic Skills Software

Since at-risk students frequently have serious deficiencies in basic reading, writing, and math skills, many educators place a heavy emphasis on remediation in these areas. These educators are gravitating toward basic skills software, available in several formats.

Some of these teachers focus on *microcomputer-based* drill and tutorial programs. If their students are adolescents or adults, the challenge these educators face is to find packages that cover extremely basic skills (ones usually introduced in elementary school) without talking down to the older students or insulting them with "cute" reward sequences and childish graphics. The programs they generally select are the more text-based basic skills packages—ones that have been stripped of most graphics and sound other than those needed to illustrate particular concepts. But, since most at-risk students need more motivation than that provided by such "plain vanilla" packages, many educators find it necessary to supplement these packages with classroom projects, career search programs, and other activities that help students see a *need* for the knowledge and skills covered.

Other educators in search of basic skills software to use with at-risk students adopt programs such as CCP (included in the directory at the end of this article), which offers remedial lessons primarily built around existing workbooks, audiovisual aids, and computer software.

Still other educators find basic skills software in the integrated learning systems (ILSs) that link a powerful microcomputer or minicomputer "host" to a number of microcomputer workstations. ILS programs, often designed originally with a broader audience in mind, are being used successfully with large numbers of at-risk youth. Virtually all ILS publishers can tell you of sites where their basic program is making a difference to dropouts, adolescents in trouble,

408

adults in need of remediation, elementary students in Chapter 1 programs, or others who have been identified as being at-risk.

ILSs are popular among educators working with at-risk students in part because they often include extensive management systems that provide detailed diagnostic information on students. What's more, ILSs seem to be particularly effective with students who respond to a consistent and individualized approach.

While most educators who turn to ILSs look to them for drill and instruction in basic skills, it should be noted that many ILS publishers are adding new components to their systems that broaden the approach taken. For example, several ILSs now offer word processors, outliners, and other tools that encourage students to explore topics such as process writing.

Creativity and Thinking Skills

Although software that focuses on basic skills is important for many at-risk students, it is not the only approach educators are considering. Antonia Stone, executive director of the community-based Playing to Win program, is an eloquent spokesperson for the use of tools, simulations, and other software that fosters creative thinking: "in school, at-risk kids are usually the ones who are singled out for remediation while the other students are given 'enrichment.' I believe that it's enormously important for at-risk students to have enrichment opportunities as well. They've been remediated out of their minds."

In a more traditional setting, Aileen Clifford, a special education teacher at Truman High School in the Bronx, is using tool and simulation software to provide her students with such enrich-

ment opportunities. Clifford believes that it is important for special education students to learn how to gather and compare data, and to test hypotheses—so that they can challenge their own preset opinions. To support this goal, her classes engage in a variety of database activities. Clifford's students also use the computer to produce political newsletters and print materials for a mock presidential election—activities that help them understand the need for organization, planning, and compromise in maintaining a democracy. Finally, to help her students identify with history as the story of real people with understandable feelings, she encourages her classes to use word processing software to write about historical events from the point of view of the people of the times.

Involving Videodiscs and Other Media

Still other educators are finding that a multi-media approach is effective with at-risk students. The realistic graphics and sound offered by videodiscs and videotapes can be important aids for students who lack basic reading skills. And in this day of television, rock videos, and movies, video-based lessons are one way of gaining the interest and attention of young people who have been turned off to school.

In addition to using video as an instructional tool, some teachers are providing at-risk students with the opportunity to develop their own multimedia presentations. For example, in Gail Morse's junior high school classes in Mooresville, North Carolina, a diverse group of students (including many who have been identified as at-risk) use commercially produced videodiscs to learn about a variety of science topics, and then share what they have learned with parents, teachers, and fellow students by producing their own videotapes. The student response to this use of technology has been tremendous. In fact, Morse reports that many former discipline problems, physically disabled learners, and other potentially at-risk students now line up for the chance to spend their lunches, recesses, and after-school times taking part in the "computer connection" group she has organized.

Administrative Packages

School administrators seeking to lower their dropout rates are getting still another type of help from computers, peripherals, and software. At many school sites, administrative packages are being used to track student achievement and identify those who need remediation. Used in conjunction with such packages, software and hardware for scanning test responses into the computer save a lot of scoring time and make it easy to keep records updated.

Administrative software is also being used to improve the attendance records of chronic "cutters," another group at risk of dropping out. Attendance tracking software helps identify students with consistently poor attendance records; some packages even automatically telephone the homes of chronic absentees.

The Los Angeles Unified School District is an example of a school system that uses computers extensively for administrative purposes. The district's Dropout Prevention and Recovery Program, which combines system-wide and school-based efforts at dropout prevention, uses a school-based computerized student accounting system for grades 7-12 that tracks attendance and achievement. Preliminary results show overall improvement in student retention, attendance, and achievement.

Customized At-Risk Software

In addition to producing "general" software that sells to both regular and at-risk classrooms, some software developers have turned their efforts to developing products tailored specifically to at-risk youth. These programs tend to use a high interest/low reading level approach to cover topics such as "life skills" (applying reading, writing, and math to everyday living), GED test preparation, occupational preparation for the non-college-bound, and substance abuse. The directory that follows includes information on a number of these products.

A Directory of Products Designed
Specifically for At-Risk Students

Integrated Learning Systems

(specialized modules that supplement the basic systems)

• Computer Curriculum Corporation (CCC) has a GED preparation course and a survival skills course which develop math and reading skills in the context of everyday life. They are also developing a high interest/low readability reading course for junior and senior high students.

Computer Curriculum Corporation, 700 Hanson Way, PO Box 10080, Palo Alto, CA 94304; (800) 227-8324 or (800) 982-5851 (in CA)

• Control Data's PLATO education system has two components especially geared for at-risk students: a life coping skills course that focuses on understanding oneself and others, overcoming self-defeating behavior, and developing communications skills; and a job search course that helps students learn how to market themselves to employers and maintain a job once they get one. The program connects students with lessons from PLATO's basic skills program when they are appropriate. (For example, the students are motivated to complete a lesson in letter writing in order to learn how to write a cover letter to a potential employer.)

Control Data BLC W3A, PLATO Education Services, 8800 Queen Ave. South, Bloomington, MN 55431; (800) 328-1109

• Prescription Learning Corporation offers an adult literacy course; a series of courses that combine reading, writing, language arts, and mathematics with life skills; a newly revised GED preparation program; and a vocational awareness course. Prescription Learning also has a program in which students are loaned software and a computer for study at home.

Prescription Learning, 6150 North 16th St., Phoenix, AZ 85016; (800) 422-4339 or (602) 230-7030

• Wasatch offers a Life Skills Course, in which students help several characters solve problems in their day-to-day lives. The practice items on screen require students to read and interpret the material in accompanying activity booklets. The software provides hints and corrective feedback for students experiencing difficulty.

Wasatch Education Systems, 5250 South 300 West, Suite 350, Salt Lake City, UT 84107; (800) 288-2848

• Wicat Systems, Inc., has developed an alternative education program. It includes remedial reading, writing, and mathematics lessons that were designed especially for junior and senior high school students at risk, as well as students preparing for the GED exam.

WICAT Systems, 1876 South State St., Orem, UT 84058; (800) 453-1145

Microcomputer Software

• *Alcohol: 4 Interactive Programs,* by Student Awareness Software (SAS), offers tutorials and simulations to provide comprehensive instruction on the physiological, social, economic, and legal consequences of using alcohol.

Apple II family; IBM PC and compatibles (256K): $89.95; Student Awareness Software, PO Box 18134, Portland, OR 97218; (503) 287-3530

• *How to Read for Everyday Living, How to Write for Everyday Living,* and *Math for Everyday Living* are three programs designed by Educational Activities for secondary school students and adults reading at a fourth- or fifth-grade reading level. *How to Read for Everyday Living* presents tutorials and game-format practice activities to teach reading labels, reading menus, buying from ads, reading classified ads, completing applications, managing money, and interpreting maps and schedules. *How to Write for Everyday Living* focuses on the writing, communication, and reference skills needed in real-life survival tasks. And *Math for Everyday Living* teaches real-life math and business skills through tutorials and simple simulations.

Apple II family; TRS-80; IBM PCs and compatibles: Reading *$139;* Writing *$159;* Math *$119; Educational Activities, PO Box 392, Freeport, NY 11520; (800) 645-3739 or (516) 223-4666 (in NY)*

• *Jobs in Today's World,* the *Job Readiness Series,* the *Job Success Series,* and *Improving Your Self-Concept* are all programs from MCE, a company that specializes in software for at-risk students. *Jobs in Today's World* is an occupation inventory for non-college-bound students. It matches each student's interests with the characteristics of almost 100 jobs. The *Job Readiness Series* and *Job Success Series* each consist of four separate programs focusing on such topics as job attitudes, interviewing and applying for jobs, resumes, and appropriate personal and work habits. *Improving Your Self-Concept* provides students with interactive assessments of their strengths, weaknesses, likes, and dislikes, in order to encourage them to see their own self-worth. Students also receive suggestions on how to become more honest with themselves and others.

Apple II family; IBM PCs and compatibles: Jobs in Today's World, *$79.95; other titles, $69.95; MCE, Inc., 157 South Kalamazoo Mall, Suite 250, Kalamazoo, MI 49007; (800) 421-4157 or (616) 345-8681 (in MI)*

• *Math on the Job, English on the Job,* and *Career and Social Skills Training* are three packages designed to help at-risk students make the connection between what they are learning in school and what they actually need to function in the "real world." The first two packages help students explore different careers and practice basic skills related to those careers. Each of them includes numerous (one for each career area) double-sided program disks, 31 student guides, and a teacher management system. The *Career and Social Skills Training* (CAST) series includes videotapes, software, and print materials focusing on the social skills necessary to be successful in a wide variety of occupational areas.

Apple II family: $1,695 per package; $59.95 for each individual career area; The Connover Company, PO Box 155, Omro, WI 54963; (414) 685-5707

• *Project Star,* designed as a comprehensive, sequential literacy program for adults, is also useful with nonreading adolescents. The program includes several levels of basic instruction (reading levels 0 through 3), each with approximately 90 lessons focusing on sight words, vocabulary development, spelling, and reading comprehension.

Speech is incorporated using either cassette tapes or computer synthesis. A number of language experience activities help students expand their reading vocabularies and express their own ideas and experiences in writing.

Apple II family (64K); Echo or Ufonics speech cards optional (Echo requires 128K): $655 per level; Hartley Courseware, PO Box 419, Dimondale, MI 48821; (800) 247-1380 or (517) 646-6458 (in MI and Canada)

• *Reading Realities,* by Teacher Support Software, offers reading comprehension practice and prompted writing activities (using a built-in word processor) based on high interest/low readability material. The directed reading/thinking activities focus on dilemmas teenagers typically face, court cases students must decide, and career choices. The program can take advantage of the Slotbuster and Echo speech synthesizer, and has a built-in dictionary for difficult words appearing in each passage.

Apple II family (64K): $449.95 for entire package ($159.95 for guided stories only, without court cases and careers); Teacher Support Software, PO Box 7130, Gainesville, FL 32605; (800) 228-2871 or (904) 371-3802 (collect)

• *The Right Job* is a job search program for special education students and others who do not plan to go to college. The program helps students define their interests and skills and match them with specific jobs.

Apple II family: $189; Sunburst Communications, 39 Washington Ave., Pleasantville, NY 10570; (800) 431-1934 or (800) 247-6756 (in Canada) or (914) 769-5030 (in NY)

• *A Week in the Life* is a simulation that allows students to interact with fictional adolescents as they face decisions about smoking, alcohol, drugs, eating habits, sex, friendship, and many other issues. The program includes a dictionary students can consult to acquire detailed information about the problems the simulated characters face. There is also a bulletin board for sharing ideas with other students. Originally developed for use on the ICON networked computer, there is now a microcomputer version available as well.

IBM PC and compatibles (256K): $249; $895 for a network version; Interactive Image Technologies, Ltd., 49 Bathurst St., Suite 400, Toronto, Ontario M5V 2P2; (416) 361-0333; or Alpha Resource Center, 910 Independence Ave. SE, Washington, DC 20003; (202) 546-2269.

Videodisc Applications

• *PALS* is a comprehensive program from IBM designed to teach adults and adolescents to read. The program uses a lab of four InfoWindow units which include computers, touch-screens, videodisc players, printers, and typewriters.

Hardware and software costs total between $70,000 and $75,000 before discounts; contact your local IBM education representative for ordering information.

• TARGET Interactive Project (TIP), another program developed with support from IBM, is distributed by the National Federation of State High Schools Association. It uses an InfoWindow system configured with a computer, a touch screen, and two videodiscs to teach students about "chemical health." Aimed at "average" students who are non-users or experimental users of drugs and alcohol (*not* at those who are addicted or hard-core users), the program is useful for a wide audience, including junior high school students who are at-risk of becoming involved in substance abuse and dropping out. The program involves students in a simulated party at which they "meet" various characters, help them make decisions, and view the consequences of their choices.

InfoWindow system included in the package price of $14,250; National Federation of State High Schools Association, 11724 Plaza Circle, PO Box 20626, Kansas City, MO 64195; (816) 464-5400.

• *What's Next* is an interactive videodisc program that uses a level-two videodisc player (one with a built-in microprocessor) to present a realistic simulation concerning a high school student's decision about whether to drop out of school. The program comes with 100 student workbooks and ten teacher/counselor guides.

Pioneer 6000/6010 videodisc player and monitor (no computer necessary); $3500 with hardware; $1500 without hardware. Interactive, Inc., 440 Riverside Dr. #117, New York, NY 10027; (212) 663-6415.

Other Applications

• *Comprehensive Competency Program* (CCP) is an extensive basic skills educational system that uses workbooks, audiovisual materials, software, and one-on-one instruction by teachers to present individualized, self-paced instruction to students in need of remedial skills work. Developed with grants from the Ford Foundation and the Charles Stewart Mott Foundation, the lessons are based on a large selection of third-party materials. Sites adopting the program have many choices about which components to adopt. CCP can be implemented using stand-alone or networked computers.

Apple II; IBM PCs and compatibles: Prices vary according to the components purchased; U.S. Basics, 1521 16th St. NW, Washington, DC 20036; (202) 667-6091.

• The Higher Order Thinking Skills (HOTS) program also consists of a collection of third-party software and lessons, but its focus is quite different. The HOTS program, developed for Chapter 1 and learning disabled students in grades 4-6, combines Socratic dialogue with computer software to help students develop four types of higher-order thinking skills. Each lesson consists of a "learning drama" led by the teacher in which the software is used as a part of the scenario. The program's developer, Dr. Stan Pogrow of the University of Arizona, is in the process of publishing data that show significant gains on standardized tests by students using HOTS regularly for one to two years—greater gains than those made by a control group using a drill-and-practice approach.

Apple II family: $550 for a set of lessons for one year and a one-week training session (software must be purchased separately from the publisher); Thinking With Computers, PO Box 22801, Tucson, AZ 85706; (602) 575-1599.

Article #5
Tykes and Bytes

WITH A BOOST FROM COMPUTERS, KIDS WITH
DISABILITIES FIND THE WORLD'S FILLED WITH POSSIBILITIES.

By
BETTIJANE
LEVINE

The first thing to know about the bright-eyed toddlers who zoom, lurch, plop, play, sing, and go potty at UCLA's Intervention Program is that they are the advance guard of an army yet to mobilize.

Mostly they act just like toddlers everywhere—but they're not.

With varying degrees of disability due to cerebral palsy, Down's Syndrome and an array of what program director Dr. Judy Howard calls "fancy diagnoses," they are among the world's youngest computer whizzes.

Sure some have poor motor skills and muscle tone, little or no speech, minimal vision—all sorts of knotty physical or mental problems. But at ages 18 months to 3 years these toddlers technocrats are already equipped with PCs, power pads, switches, speech synthesizers and other electronic gear designed to even the playing field between them and so-called normal children.

They are part of the first toddler generation whose disabilities can be mitigated by technology, who can be judged by their potential rather than by their limitations. They are the first to prepare from babyhood for a life that will be computer-friendly in the extreme, and, as a result, productive.

Jay Horrell, 2, has used his computer since he was 18 months old. "I don't know where we'd be without it," says his father, Michael, who explains that some Down's syndrome children, such as his son, are "able to receive a lot more information than they can give back. They know the answers and they know what's going on, but can't respond" as they'd like to.

The computer allows Jay to display and improve various skills. It talks to him and waits patiently for answers; it puts him on more even footing with classmates at the Intervention Program and with his brother in their North Hollywood home, where Jay's setup includes an Apple PC, an electronic touch pad (in place of a keyboard), a speech synthesizer that gives voice to the letters and pictures he calls up on screen—and as many software programs as his parents can find.

Jay will attend a regular preschool in September. Down the line, Horrell adds, "I believe the computer will allow him to be a productive member of society."

Gabriela Cellini was 17 months old, had cerebral palsy and lacked certain motor skills when her parents took her to the Computer Access Center in Santa Monica. There, a staff member explained what the toddler could do with a computer and special accessories suited to her needs.

"Gabriela took one look and was riveted to the screen," her mother, Harriet, recalls. "Her muscle tone increased. She was so motivated to play with it that she sat up straight all by herself for about a half-hour. She quickly understood the cause-and-effect principle of hitting the switch and activating games."

415

Now 2 1/2 and a student at the UCLA Intervention Program, Gabriela uses computers at her Pacific Palisades home and in class. "It's delightful to watch," her mother says. "This strange computer voice says 'Gabriela, stack the blocks.' Or 'Gabriela, build a face.' Or she shoots airplanes off a carrier, increasing her speed each time she scores a hit." Gabriela still needs some assistance in other areas, Cellini says, but she's her own person in front of the computer.

UCLA's Howard, a pediatrician who has headed the Intervention Program since 1974, began teaming disabled toddlers with computers in 1981. She found children of the age are "automatically computer friendly, which immediately sets up a positive response in adults. Suddenly, you see they have abilities, and you start to set expectations for them that you weren't able to set before. When you have children who cannot talk, who are visually handicapped, who for any reason cannot pick up a crayon and draw or play with dolls, puzzles and toys to show you what they can do," it is difficult to know what they are capable of, she explains.

The first step is to find a way for each child to access the computer. In the early 1980s, there were few devices commercially available to provide that access. Now there are dozens: large switches, oversized alternative keyboards, touch windows with built-in sensors that attach with Velcro to a computer screen. And there is a growing body of knowledge about how to rig the devices so a child can work the computer by using whatever part of his body he controls best. Says Howard: "every child can work one, even if he can only use one finger, his ear or a toe. With appropriate software, they can solve puzzles, build with blocks, dress dolls. They can even play all the traditional favorite toddler games—two kids at the computer together—so they learn sharing, success and winning.

"Toddlers soon start to visually track on the screen because they're so highly motivated. They hold their little heads up and you see all the things that eventually lead to reading. That's the purpose of all this."

Kit Kehr, executive director of the UCLA program, says: "the younger you help these children, the better they'll do down the road. A kid who can't build with blocks or push cars around the way other kids can is missing essential play experiences." He also falls behind in language development and social skills, she says.

Rev Korman, a computer consultant in special education for the Los Angeles Unified school district, remembers such a child, named Kim. "She'd had a stroke before she was born. It affected her vocal cords, so she had no speech and the doctors told her parents she'd always be a vegetable. She was 3 when they rolled her into my office in her wheelchair. I set up a communication board, a speech synthesizer and the computer, so that it would speak to her. She took about 10 minutes to learn to push the pictures that communicated her needs and wants. 'I don't want to go to bed. I want a red balloon.'

"We then moved to a 24-picture board, which she mastered quickly. By using this setup, she able to communicate for the first time in her life so that people could hear her. She spent 45 minutes using the Muppet keyboard, and by the end of her visit she was teaching herself the alphabet.

"Kim's parents went right out and bought the computer, the speech synthesizer, the electronic board. Now she's reading and the whole bit."

(Computer setups for children like

Kim cost about $2,000, Korman says.)

Dr. Phillip Callison, head of special education for the Los Angeles Unified School District, has participated in the UCLA project from its beginning, and is credited with providing assistance and inspiration. He says he believes in computers for all children, especially those with disabilities. Right now, the school district can provide such equipment for severely handicapped students, he says.

(Six hundred toddlers with a variety of disabilities are using Palsy Assn. nursery school programs across the country. The projects are run by a coalition of the association, UCLA and Apple Computers.)

Many adults still know little about home computers and next to nothing about the rest of the exotic equipment needed to adapt it for use by children with disabilities. In fact, UCLA's Kehr says that even the salespeople in most computer stores "won't know what you're talking about" if you walk in and ask for a power pad, a speech synthesizer and a special switch to help you adapt a PC for your child.

Jackie and Steve Brand of Albany, Calif., found little help in 1983, when they realized their 6-year-old daughter, Shoshana, "needed technology in her life." Shoshana has multiple disabilities, including cerebral palsy and poor vision. "The standard teaching tools just weren't working," Jackie Brand says. Her husband took a one-year sabbatical from his teaching job, went to computer school and eventually put together a system Shoshana could use. It has a touch-sensitive keyboard with large keys and a synthesizer that gave voice to whatever she typed, so she could hear what she was doing rather than having to see it on the monitor.

"My daughter played for the first time in her life," when she got her computer, Brand says. "By that time she was 9, and we realized we needed to establish a program so others don't have to sacrifice years of their kid's lives."

The couple started the Alliance for Technology Access, which now has 43 chapters in 32 states. Each is a resource center where anyone with any disability—or parents of disabled children—can learn in informal, friendly surroundings what technology is available and how to customize it for their needs.

> "The bottom line is that each family knows their child's potential. They need to find out what their options are and try out different hardware and software to see what works best for the child."

Nothing is sold at the centers, but they house an array of computers, access devices and information on companies that manufacture accessories not available in local stores but essential for those with special needs. The goal, Brand says, is simply to show people what they can do for themselves or their children, without making them go through "the usual hoops."

"Typically, you go to a doctor, evaluation center or clinic where they do an extensive evaluation of a child and prescribe what they think the right technology might be. In some situations that's needed." But doctors and clinics are not always on target when it come to decisions about recreation and education for kids with handicaps, she says.

Sometimes they tell parents a child won't benefit from technology, Brand says. "But the bottom line is that each family knows their child's potential. They need to find out what their options are and try out different hardware and software to see what works best for the child. They need to be empowered to make their own decisions. That is what the Alliance helps them do.

"To people who say we must have realistic expectations for our children, I say I hope every family [of a handicapped child] has unrealistic expectations. That's the only way you will find your child's potential, so that your child can show you who he is and what he can do."

Brand's daughter will go into ninth grade in a regular public school in the fall. She uses a wheelchair, a computer for writing and a tape recorder with special levers for recording her notes, which she listens to at night. "This is a kid who nobody would have thought could function in a regular school program, and without technology, she couldn't. Yet she is doing phenomenally well. And she's not unique, she is typical," Brand says.

The Computer Access Center, which rents space from the John Adams Middle School in Santa Monica, is one of three Southern California chapters of the Alliance. The volunteer staff helps each visitor (by appointment) to understand how life for a disabled person can be enhanced through the magic of technology. And they are very up-to-date.

Last week, for example, the staff arranged a demonstration by Daniel Fortune and John Ortiz of Zofcam, a Palo Alto-based firm.

The two men have designed a device called the TongueTouch Keypad, which looks like an ordinary orthodontic retainer worn by most kids after their braces are off.

But this retainer is a wireless transmitter with built-in sensors. By touching different sensors with one's tongue, a user unable to move any other part of his body can gain almost total control of his environment.

To the astonishment of onlookers, Fortune answered the phone when it rang without seeming to move a muscle. He turned on and off the VCR, the TV, the fan. He used the computer and explained that there is an almost "unlimited array" of equipment that can be operated (including a page-turner) with the new device, which will probably be marketed at the end of the year.

Mary Ann Glicksman, a staff member at the center, was intrigued. Her son, John Duganne, just graduated from Santa Monica High School and starts college in the fall. He intends to make animated films and already works part time, creating computer graphics for a software firm.

Duganne drives his power wheelchair with his chin, she says, but that's about the extent of what his body can do. (He has cerebral palsy.) To work the computer on which he does his schoolwork and art, he uses a headset with an ultrasonic device and a bite switch in his mouth. If the TongueTouch could work for him, it would be an improvement, she said. The designers cautioned that it is meant primarily for people with spinal cord injuries, and that those with cerebral palsy might not have enough tongue control. But with optimism typical of Alliance members, Glickman said she'd rather give her son a chance to find out if it works than take the inventor's word that it won't.

Two other Southern California branches of the Alliance for Technology Access, funded by Apple Computers, are: The Special Awareness Computer Center in Simi Valley and Team of Advocates for Special Kids in Anaheim.

Questions and Answers About Computer-Assisted Instruction for Children with Learning Disabilities

By
WILLIAM
W. LEE

Introduction

The prospect of computer applications for children with learning disabilities is an exciting area with great potential, but it is an area of research just beginning to be explored. It is a concept that should not be oversold at this time. The following questions and answers may help the learning disability teacher decide which students will best benefit from computer-assisted instruction (CAI) and help parents decide if they should buy a home computer for their child who has a learning disability. The information in this article is an outgrowth of research I have conducted to determine those components of computer courseware that learning disability teachers felt were essential for optimum learning by their students (Lee, 1986, 1987, 1987a). These answers should enable teachers and parents to make more informed decisions about the purchase and use of a computer for learning disabled (LD) children.

Question 1: What can computers do for LD children that traditional instruction cannot?

The motivation or excitement to learn generated by a computer is, indeed, a big "plus." LD children become discouraged with the pencil-and-paper practice that must take place for them to completely learn a skill. The computer can serve two purposes here. First, the computer will wait as long as necessary for children to grasp a concept. They will soon perceive the computer as a non-threatening medium where they can risk being wrong. If children lose patience with the computer, they can turn it off and come back later.

Second, using a computer for drill-and-practice can eliminate the need to copy problem after problem on paper—a task that is difficult for LD students. The computer will also immediately let the child know if his or her answer is right or wrong and will keep track of how many answers are correct. Since the students can get more problems completed in less time, the extra practice they need is accounted for in a fraction of the time required by pencil-and-paper practice.

Third, parents of LD students are very conscientious and want to do whatever can be done to help their children. I'm sure a familiar scene involves the parent and child sitting at the kitchen table struggling together over the homework assignments that are due the next day. The computer will not replace these times together, but it may change them from frustrating to enjoyable experiences. Don't forget that learning can be accomplished through games. The computer has great capability here. Learning can be interesting and competitive, and the parent and child can engage in it together.

Fourth, the true value of the computer to the LD child will be overlooked if the computer is only used for drill-

419

and-practice. One of the other great needs of the LD student is to communicate in writing. Getting past the frustration of repeated erasing and rewriting until the paper is unreadable is an area where the computer can be very useful. As a word processor, the computer allows students to put their ideas on the screen and then go back and make corrections. The product that later comes off the printer is clean and readable, allowing the student to take pride in what he or she has accomplished. A number of word processing systems are published that are easy for elementary and secondary students to use.

The only requirement for effective word processing is that the student possess adequate typing skills. This is also handled by the computer. Several very good CAI typing tutors, i.e., *Mastertype* and *Typing Tutor*, have been published that help students learn the necessary typing skills through interesting games.

Fifth, the computer can also provide the child opportunities to communicate with others in writing. For an extra $150, a modem can be purchased that, when attached to the computer and the telephone, becomes a telecommunications device. Two or more people can communicate over the phone using the computer to write messages back and forth. The communication capabilities provided by the modem can motivate students to make writing clear and effective. The letters they receive from other members of the "users group" provide good models of clear communication.

It is even possible for the computer to communicate verbally with the student. This is a big advantage to students who have severe reading problems. Computer hard cards and software can be purchased that have the capability of using software that synthesizes speech and reads what is on the computer screen to the student so he or she can answer the questions. Tape recorders can also be attached to the computer so that verbal directions can be taped to accompany the lessons.

Question 2: What type of computer should students use?

The most critical thing to keep in mind when choosing a computer is the type of software that is available to meet the needs of the child. Some computers are very inexpensive, but they may also have very little software that can be used with them. The more limited the software, the less chance there is of finding materials that will benefit the child.

The second consideration is to buy a computer with enough memory storage to allow students to use software that is high powered enough to benefit them. The software must be able to respond in many different ways depending on the child's answer. The more user friendly the software, the simpler the program will be for the child to operate. A computer with at least 128K of memory should be sufficient to handle the storage needs. Most new software being produced today requires at least 64K, but the more high-powered software requires at least 128K.

If the school has computers available to the child, the teacher will have to use those computers. It is probably wise for parents to buy the same computer so that work begun at school can be completed at home. Software made for one type of computer will often not work on another computer.

A survey of sixty-five learning disability teachers in the State of Pennsylvania (Lee, 1986) found that over 95% of the computers in these LD classes were Apple II, Apple II Plus, and Apple IIe types. Presently, Apple Computer seems to have the most software targeted for the elementary and secondary school content areas.

Question 3: What part can teachers and parents play in the use of the computer?

Although the excitement of using a computer is important, other factors must be considered. One of these factors for parents is the child's access to a computer in school in the regular or special class. If the school is not using microcomputers in its learning disability class, the parent may become the teacher where the computer is concerned. Most parents do not have the knowledge of computers to help their children if they encounter problems.

Lack of knowledge should not discourage parents. An introductory course is usually included with the purchase of the computer. The parent can attend these sessions with the child. A few hours of instruction will show what a simple machine the computer is. In those cases where school computers are not available, parents must make a commitment to become somewhat knowledgeable of computer operation. Later, the parent will probably learn from the child as he or she experiments and tests the computer's capabilities.

For teachers, their involvement with the computer will be in several roles (1) to review, select, and order computer materials that will best meet the needs of the majority of their students; (2) to help parents choose appropriate software for home that matches the learning goals for the child, and (3) to relegate drill-and-practice exercises to the computer while concentrating on developing higher level thinking skills in students during direct instruction.

Question 4: What types of computer materials will be needed to accompany the computer?

After the computer—what then? Software materials can be very expensive to buy, and most software is not of high enough quality to meet the needs of LD students (Lee, 1987). The school that uses computers can be very helpful with this problem. Schools can join organizations such as the Minnesota Educational Computer Corporation (MECC) that produces and distributes computer materials to member organizations. Students with home computers can borrow the disks and bring their assignments home.

If the school does not have computers or does not subscribe to MECC, then parents will have to make a commitment to purchase materials. Many sources of software evaluation are available. The *Journal of Learning Disabilities* publishes courseware reviews as a part of its monthly issue. The *Educational Products Information Exchange (EPIE)* is another source available to parents by subscription and is also found in many libraries. Teachers can assist parents by reading courseware reviews and making recommendations regarding the suitability of the content for its match with the educational goals found in the child's Individual Educational Program (IEP).

An excellent book to recommend to parents and teachers of LD children is Delores Hagan's *Microcomputer Resource Book for Special Education* (1984). Hagan's book describes the potential uses of the computer for disabled children, reviews software, and provides addresses of publishing companies that produce and sell computer software.

Question 5: How long will the computer hold the LD child's interest?

Teachers can play an important role here. If the child is showing an interest in the computer in school, it indicates that purchasing a home computer might be a good idea. If the child is not showing an interest, teachers might recommend that parents wait to buy a computer until the student's interest in the school computer is sustained for a reasonable length of time. Six months should be an adequate period of time to judge if the student has a sustained interest in the computer. To encourage interest in CAI, the teacher can help motivate the student by selecting software that is exciting and interesting while at the same time helps the student learn.

Even though there may be no computers in school, there are other indicators of students' potential interest or aptitude for using the computer. Many classrooms have other types of mechanical learning devices. If students show interest in these machines, it is highly likely that a computer, with its interactive capabilities and interesting graphics, will hold their attention even longer.

Summary

This article has presented those questions most frequently asked by teachers and parents regarding LD students and computers. If used properly, the computer can be a very effective tool in a child's education, but it is not the solution to all of his or her needs. The computer has great potential for helping LD individuals cope with their disability. The computer may actually open up new career and job opportunities to the learning disabled because it allows them to deal more effectively with many of their communication problems.

The computer is not a passing fad—it is here to stay. If handled correctly, it will greatly benefit children with learning disabilities. Through the cooperation of the school helping the student increasingly understand and use the capabilities of the computer, and with the commitment of parents to also understand the computer and work with their child, the expense involved will be minimal over the twelve to sixteen years that the child spends in elementary, secondary, and higher education.

References

Hagan, D. *Microcomputer Resource Book for Special Education,* Reston, VA: Reston Publishing Co., Inc., 1984.

Lee, W. *Microcomputer Courseware for the Learning Disabled: Production and Evaluation Guidelines,* doctoral dissertation, The Pennsylvania State University, University Park, Pennsylvania, 1986.

Lee, W. "Microcomputer Courseware Production and Evaluation Guidelines for Students with Learning Disabilities." *Journal of Learning Disabilities,* 1987, 20 (7), 436438.

Lee, W. "Microcomputer Courseware Production and Evaluation Guidelines for Students with Learning Disabilities; Two Studies." Paper presented at the Ninth Annual International Convention of the Association for Children With Learning Disabilities (ACLD), San Diego, October 1987.

Article #7
A Guide to Special Education Resources

HERE IS A LIST OF RESOURCE GUIDES AND CONFERENCES FOR TEACHERS AND ADMINISTRATORS WHO USE TECHNOLOGY IN SPECIAL EDUCATION CLASSES, PLUS, TIPS FOR SELECTING SOFTWARE.

BY
BILL
MORGAN

With the increase in special education applications and methodology comes an increase in resource guides and conferences intended to keep teachers and administrators in the field up to date. Listed on these pages are some of the major guides and national conferences that cover technology and special education products, services, and organizations.

The guides, which cover numerous aspects of special education—learning disabled, handicapped, and gifted students—are listed alphabetically.

Also included is a section on important factors to consider when choosing software for learning disabled students.

Special Education Resources Guides

Apple Computer Resources In Special Education and Rehabilitation

This 400-page volume, published by DLM Teaching Resources, details special education hardware and software compatible with Apple computers. Developed by the Office of Special Education Programs at Apple Computer Inc. in association with the Trace Research and Development Center at the University of Wisconsin-Madison, the guide has a thorough list of special education organizations. Another chapter of the book lists more than 125 publications (books, magazines, and newsletters) aimed at special education teachers and administrators. There are also extensive listings of product catalogs, special education networks, and publications that contain information on hardware and software products. Cost: $19.95 plus shipping and handling. Order through Apple Computer at:

- Office of Special Education Programs/MS 43F
  Apple Computer Inc.
  20525 Mariani Ave.
  Cupertino, Calif. 95014

The Catalyst

This quarterly newspaper, published by the Western Center for Microcomputers in Special Education Inc., features 20 pages of useful information on special education. *The Catalyst* includes its own special education resource guide, hardware and software reviews, and articles ranging from first-person, hands-on experiences to reporting on special education conferences and conventions. Subscriptions are $15 for schools or organizations and $10 for individuals. For more information, write to:

- Western Center for Microcomputers In Special Education
  1259 El Camino Real, Suite 275
  Menlo Park, Calif. 94025

423

Closing the Gap 1989 Resource Directory

An annual resource guide to special education technologies published each February by Closing the Gap. The 1989 edition contains 1,814 listings, an increase of 18 percent from the 1988 edition. Hardware and software sections match products with applications and disabilities.

The back of the directory alphabetically lists all companies, addresses, phone numbers, and a complete list of their special education products. An eight-page directory of organizations completes the guide.

This 140-page resource guide contains a wealth of information, especially in the short descriptions of the products.

The 1989 edition of the guide is $12.95 plus $2 postage and handling. The price for the 1990 edition, due in February or March, was not set at press time. The bimonthly newspaper, *Closing the Gap, is* $26 for a one year subscription (six issues) or $42 for two years (12 issues). To order the guide or newspaper, write:

- Closing the Gap
  P.O. Box 68,
  Henderson, Minn. 56044
  or telephone (612) 248-3294

Computer Access in Higher Education for Students with Disabilities

Elementary and secondary educators should not be put off by the title. This book, financed through a grant from the Fund for the Improvement of Post-Secondary Education, is an invaluable resource guide for those in the special education field.

Computer Access in Higher Education for Students with Disabilities was written by Carl Brown and colleagues from the High Tech Center for the Disabled, California Community Colleges Chancellor's Office, Sacramento, Calif. *Computer Access* serves as both a resource of special education products and as a guide to proven techniques for teaching students of all types of learning disabilities.

Additional chapters profile a high tech center director, detail how to fund a center, discuss computer access, disability and the law, and future trends in adapted computer technology. A guide to adapted computer hardware and software lists products by disability.

Computer Access in Higher Education for Students with Disabilities is free and can be obtained by making a written request to the following address:

- High Tech Center for the Disabled
  California Community College
  Chancellor's Office
  1109 Ninth St.
  Sacramento, Calif. 95814

Because of a limited supply of copies, requests must be made in writing by a district superintendent, computer coordinator, or other administrator instrumental in making technology-related purchases.

Computer Disability News

Published by the National Easter Seal Society, *Computer Disability News* is a quarterly newspaper full of timely information. In addition to relevant news articles for special education teachers and administrators, the newspaper reviews current books, interviews leaders in technology for special education, and features a regular conferences column. The "Soft-Talk" column contains lists of public domain software and reviews of new products. *Computer Disability News* costs $15 per year. Write to:

- Computer Disability News
  The National Easter Seal Society
  70 East Lake St.
  Chicago, Ill. 60601

IBM National Support Center for Persons with Disabilities Resource Guide

IBM, through its National Support Center for Persons with Disabilities, offers five different resource guides covering mobility, hearing, speech and/or language, learning, and vision. More than 800 MS-DOS products from more than 600 companies are featured in the five guides. Each guide gives an extensive listing of hardware and software products specific to that disability, along with detailed product descriptions. Manufacturer's name, address, and phone number are included with each product entry. Another section lists support agencies and associations in each state. The resource guides are free. Write to:

- IBM National Support Center for Persons with Disabilities
  P.O. Box 2150
  Atlanta, Ga. 30055

Trace Resourcebook

Subtitled *Assistive Technologies for Communication, Control and Computer Access,* this 800-page book is published by the Trace Research and Development Center at the University of Wisconsin-Madison.

The *Trace Resourcebook* has 22 chapters of special education hardware and software products listed by function rather than by disability. Each hardware entry is accompanied by either a photograph or drawing of the product.

Appendixes include additional product information, other resources, and a list of associations. The current edition of the *Trace Resourcebook* was published in early 1989 and costs $49. For copies write:

- Trace R&D Center
  Information Project
  S-151 Walsman Center
  University of Wisconsin-Madison
  1500 Highland Ave.
  Madison, Wis. 53705
  or call (608) 262-4966

Article #8
Adapting Computer Applications for Multicultural Teaching

By
Jo Lynn
Autry
Digranes
AND
Swen H.
Digranes

Schools reflect cultural diversity and as one of their special functions attempt to recognize and to address the diverse needs of different cultures (Banks, 1975). Multicultural education in the school is generally a task assigned to the classroom teacher. In performing this task the teacher must act as an instructional designer who chooses instructional materials appropriate for the content and learners (Briggs, 1977). Locating instructional materials specifically designed for various cultural groups is difficult because such materials are typically limited or non-existent. The teacher's options are to create new instructional materials or to adapt other available materials to the special cultural needs. Creating new instructional materials is a labor and time-intensive process. Teachers will often choose to adapt existing instructional materials. Computer software applications, such as word processing, databases, and graphics programs, are commercially available instructional materials that can be easily adapted by teachers to meet special cultural needs.

We have worked primarily with American Indian populations and have developed some examples of computer application adaptations for teachers working with these students in both elementary and secondary schools. The examples can be easily modified for other cultural groups.

Word Processing

Word processing is a commonly used software application. There are even programs available for the Spanish language. However, other languages are not readily available in American software catalogs. Although a teacher may not be able to address a culture's language (the youngster may not know the language anyway) the teacher can still adapt word processing to recognize cultural differences. Methods include:

1. Use word processing for story or myth writing. Students can document oral histories, myths, or their own stories/poems with word processing (Jacobi, 1985).

2. Use word processing to simulate cultural business environments. In a summer camp for gifted/talented American Indian students ("Explanations in Creativity." American Indian Research and Development. Inc., Norman, OK) one of the authors (Digranes, 1987) had students write business letters to simulate letters originating from tribal offices. Examples included CDIB (Certificate of Degree of Indian Blood), voter registrations, and housing notifications (see figure 6.8.1).

Databases

Databases can be particularly helpful in the social sciences and in business edu-

426

cation classes for multicultural teaching. Examples include:

1. Use databases to simulate cultural business environments. Have students create and input databases to be used in an office, such as a tribal roll office. Students decide what type of information is necessary, design the database, input the information, and then create reports used in the office (Digranes, 1987).

2. Have students design databases that contain historical information for various cultures. Pon (1984) suggested that databases be set up for social science or science classes. She used a database management activity in which her elementary students constructed and manipulated/searched a database with information about California Indians. The use of database management was directed at inquiry learning for the stu-

---

Figure 6.8.1

Sample letter created in the Word Star Word Processor

Tribal Headquarters
Election Board Office
100 Canyon Way
Canyon City, State 88111

Ms. Rebecca Harjo
Rt. 1, Box 80
Canyon City, State 88111

Dear Ms. Harjo:

We recently received your request for a new voting identification card with your new address. We have completed the address change and are enclosing your card.

Your tribal polling place will be the Community Center, 1 South Main, Canyon City. Our next general election for council members will be October 21, 1989.

If you have questions or need further corrections, please contact the Election Board office, 333-9987. Thank you for notifying us of your address change.

Respectfully,

Eddie Scott
Election Board Chairman

Enclosure

dents. The use of databases for the development of higher order thinking skills (Watson & Strudler, 1988; Pon, 1984) is beneficial for all students and can be easily adapted to teaching about different cultures.

Spreadsheets

Spreadsheets can be customized to your needs. Simulations of cultural business accounting as well as documentation and projections of cultural populations can be used in multicultural classrooms. A teacher could:

1. Simulate a tribal business that must keep accounts for various offices, such as housing, health services, tribal land, and tribal rolls. Students design spreadsheets, input information, and print reports.

2. Have students document cultural populations over a period of history. Future population projections can be made from the existing data (see figure 6.8.2). Students can then discuss what factors may influence the projections.

Graphics Programs

There are a variety of graphics programs, ranging from simple, easy-to-use printing programs to very sophisticated design and drafting programs. These programs are very easy to adapt for multicultural settings. Some ideas are:

1. Have students print cards, signs, banners, and letterheads with prepackaged graphics. The students can easily write whatever text they wish. Our gifted/talented Indian students used graphics programs to make covers for the anthologies written by the creative writing students. Often there are some cultural designs included within the graphics for the print programs.

2. Computer art programs can allow students to duplicate their culture's designs or to create their own interpretations of cultural art. Logo can be used

Figure 6.8.2

Population projections developed in a Super Calc spreadsheet

	A	B	C	D	E	F	G	H
1				Indian Population Statistics*				
2			1940-1980 (with projections for 1990 and 2000)					
3								
4	***							
5		1940	1950	1960	1970	1980	1990	2000
6	***							
7	Total	334000	343000	524000	793000	1479000		
8								
9	Increase		9000	181000	269000	686000		
10								
11	Percent		.03	.53	.51	.87		
12	Increase							
13								
14	Average				.48	2188920	3239602	
15	Increase	(and projections based on average)						
16								
17	Mode	(and projections based on mode)			.52	22332190	3372268	
18								
19	***							
20	*Based upon U.S. Bureau of the Census Figures							
	FOR EDUCATIONAL USE ONLY							

very effectively for this type of student activity (see figure 6.8.3). In the summer camp for gifted/talented American Indian students, some of the computer students duplicated traditional designs and created some unique cultural design modifications (Digranes, 1988). In the Rapid City, South Dakota, schools (Jacobi, 1985) the turtle's playground was displayed Indian-style, interpreting the spatial directions as Indian attributes such as wisdom and respect.

Storybook Programs

There are several storybook or storymaker programs available commercially. Unlike word processing software, many of the storybook/storymaker programs allow branching capabilities. Some programs allow the author to create graphics for the story. Ideas for adapting storybook/storymaker programs are:

1. Students can document the oral history of their tribe or culture with these programs. Many historical facts and stories are lost if not documented.

2. Students can write stories based upon their own lives growing up in a multicultural environment. These stories might provide insights for both the student and teacher.

Crossword Puzzle Programs

Crossword puzzle programs are fun both for students and for the teacher. You can create your own crossword puzzles using English terms that apply to various cultures, or you can create crossword puzzles that contain words and/or clues from various languages to provide language practice for students. Teachers can:

1. Create a crossword puzzle that contains English clues but cultural language words. Students will work on language skills while solving the puzzle.

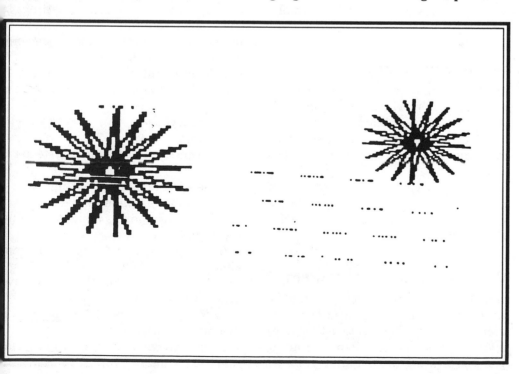

Figure 6.8.3

Design created in Apple Logo

2. Have students create their own crossword puzzles with words that describe their culture. If there are students from many cultures in the class, have students try to guess which culture is being described in the puzzle.

Music Programs

Music programs are also fun for both teacher and students. These programs have music already programmed in, but allow computer users to create their own music and even print out the music. The authors haven't seen any music programs with songs from various cultures already included in the software, but the teacher or students can input their own music. Try these ideas:

1. The teacher can (or have a musician friend) input songs from various cultures. Have the students identify the cultures and the songs.

2. The students can input their own culture's songs or create their own melodies.

Spelling Programs

Most spelling programs allow teachers to input their own lists of spelling words for the students. A teacher can:

1. Input a list of words in the students' language if working on bilingual education.

2. Input special English word lists for students who are bilingual for make-up work if they are having problems with the English language.

Desktop Publishing Programs

Desktop publishing programs can be used for a variety of applications. Students can write and create art for their own cultural stories (often combining word processing or computer graphics programs with the desktop publishing software). Students can publish newsletters/newspapers with cultural emphasis. Examples of applications include:

1. Creating a cultural newsletter. In the gifted/talented Indian student summer camp, students created a newsletter for the camp using American Indian designs and information. Students can even pinpoint a certain time period in history and create a newspaper that highlights the tribal or cultural history of that period. They can also "modernize" an older tribal newspaper, reprinting it with the computer sophistication we have today.

2. Writing anthologies using a combination of word processing and desktop publishing programs. Students can document their culture or create their own stories.

Conclusion

The first benefit of adapting computer applications to multicultural settings is the recognition and encouragement of multicultural education in the classroom. According to Shepherd and Ragan (1977 p. 285) multicultural education contributes to the development of individuals who:

1. Respect themselves and have self confidence.

2. Respect others and are courteous to them.

3. Defend the rights of self and others

4. Assume responsibility.

5. Have an inquiring mind concerning social problems.

6. Identify with and project personal effort into situations.

7. Show growth in ability to solve problems.

8. Make decisions after considering available information.

9. Acquire meaningful human relations vocabulary.

10. Show growth in understanding basic human relations concepts.

11. Understand that problems are best solved through the use of intelligence and pertinent information.

12. Practice self-evaluation.

Another benefit is that students either develop or enhance their computer skills while also developing or enhancing other academic skills, such as problem solving or writing. The use of these types of teaching activities also helps teachers to integrate computer education into the classroom.

To adapt computer applications to the multicultural classroom, first be open to using the computer in the classroom. Second, learn how to use the computer and the software. (The students typically are very quick to learn how to use the software and may go beyond the teacher's expertise.) Third, integrate some of the examples in appropriate lessons. Fourth, evaluate the computer integration in planning for future use of computer applications. Finally, always remember that the computer is a method of delivering or reinforcing instruction. The teacher is the expert who must plan and guide that delivery or implement that reinforcement.

Computer software application programs offer many possibilities for teachers in multicultural settings. Those presented here provide a sampling of possible teaching exercises. Once you try one of these examples you may get "hooked" and develop new applications for your multicultural classroom.

References

Banks, J. A. with Clegg, A. J., Jr. (1985). *Teaching strategies for the social studies: inquiry, valuing, and decision-making* (3rd ed.), New York. Longman.

Briggs, A. J. (1977). *Instructional design, principles, and applications* (3rd ed.). Englewood Cliffs, NJ: Educational Technology Publications.

Digranes. J. L. (1988). *Applications for computers directed toward minority programs*. Project presentation. Equal Access to Technology Conference, Oklahoma State Department of Education. Oklahoma City, OK.

Digranes, J. L. (1987). "Development of an individualized computer curriculum for gifted/talented American Indian students." [Summary]. *Proceedings. National Educational Computing Conference* (p. 233). Eugene, OR: International Society for Technology in Education.

Jacobi, C. (1985). "Project DISC: Developing Indian software curriculum." *The Computing Teacher*. 12(7), 12-16.

Pon, K. (1984). "Databasing in the elementary (and secondary) classroom." *The Computing Teacher*. 12(3), 28-30.

Shepherd, G. & Ragan, W. (1977). *Modern elementary curriculum* (Sixth edition). New York: Holt, Rinehart, and Winston.

Watson, J. & Strudler, N. (1988). "Teaching higher order thinking skills with databases." *The Computing Teacher*, 16(4), 47-50.

Article #9
Tools for Teaching ESL and Foreign Languages

By
DAVID
HOFFMAN

Educators are devoting much attention these days to teaching English as a second language (ESL) in part because of the astonishing increase in American schoolchildren whose native tongue is not English. Simultaneously, interest in teaching foreign languages in American schools is rising as we realize the implications of living in both a shrinking world and a global economy.

Software publishers have long been producing products for both ESL and foreign language classrooms, but until recently, forward-thinking teachers haven't been too impressed with what the mostly drill-and-practice software did for their language students. In the past year or two, though, software publishers have begun to build programs around language teaching methodologies that stress everyday communication skills over drill and practice. And perhaps more importantly, these same publishers have begun to incorporate more sophisticated technologies into their programs—technologies such as digitized speech output and input, the CD-ROM, and sometimes even interactive video that add both speech and cultural richness to classroom activities.

Over the past month, we surveyed a large number of programs that embrace these new teaching methods and technologies. We group them for you here— first for ESL teachers and then for foreign language teachers. Within each group, you'll find two categories: our "courseware" category includes programs that focus on developing grammar, vocabulary, listening, reading, writing, and speaking skills. Our "writing and reference tools" category covers tool software—including word processors, automatic grammar and style checkers, and grammar, vocabulary, and usage references—targeted at students learning a second language.

We've also added a couple of boxes that both ESL and foreign language teachers will want to look at. One is on lesson-making and authoring tools, and the other is, in effect, a grab-bag of popular software products you might not have known were available in any language but English.

Courseware for ESL Teachers

• *English Express,* a new program from Davidson and Associates for students in grades five and up, includes eight videodiscs, software, and supporting print materials.

The foundation of the program is the "natural approach" to language acquisition—an approach that focuses on creating a need for communication and then providing the tools to make communication possible. *English Express* provides these tools in large part through 1,400 images contained on the videodisc—images drawn from the well-known ESL resource *The Longman Photo Dictionary.* The images are organized into more than 60 "semantic categories," and enhanced by textual labels, audio pronunciations, and short dialogues that present the words in context. Illustrated "storyboard sequences" for each word category are

432

also provided via the video screen to prompt conversation in the classroom. And of course, Davidson provides loads of suggestions for structuring lessons.

The program also includes two other important modules. *Speech Master,* which works with a speech input/output device and microphone, lets students record their own voices and compare their pronunciation to a digitized model. And *Language Builder* offers games and activities enhanced with digitized speech.

For MS-DOS computers (512K) with a hard drive, IBM Speech Adapter or Creative Labs Sound Blaster speech input/output device (not required for the Tandy 2500 series computer), microphone, headset, videodisc player with barcode reader. (Software for Macintosh and Apple IIGS is being prepared for release soon, along with CD-ROM versions for both MS-DOS and Macintosh platforms. The CD-ROM versions will incorporate the contents of the current videodiscs and will add greater interactivity to the English Express *system.*

Pricing ranges from $7,000 to $10,000, depending on the number of student stations licensed. Contact Davidson for stand-alone site licenses, Jostens Learning Corporation for networked versions.

• *ESL Companion* from Creative Pursuits is for those who like the "natural approach" to language teaching, but aren't equipped with the hardware that *English Express* requires. Created by the designers of *The Children's Writing & Publishing Center* to be used with that program, *ESL* Companion consists of a set of graphics files and templates that provide a variety of teaching materials, including a series of illustrations with teacher cues to prompt conversation; an enormous, unlabeled U.S. map that can be printed out and assembled;

flashcards; patterns for puppets, gameboards, and a model city. Accompanying lesson plans suggest on- and off-screen activities corresponding to the levels of second-language acquisition (pre-production, production, speech emergence, and fluency). While the program is not technologically sexy, it is a rich resource.

For MS-DOS (384K) or Apple II (128K) computers, $119.95; (Children's Writing & Publishing *Center from The Learning Company required).*

• *Inform,* from Proficiency, is a CD-ROM-based set of 36 listening and reading comprehension lessons targeted to intermediate and advanced secondary and adult students. There's lots of high-quality sound here, as well as speech input capabilities through audio input devices such as Proficiency's Encore; Farallon's MacRecorder; or (in upcoming releases of the program) the built-in capabilities of the Mac LC and IIsi. Inform lessons are easy to run (mouse clicking only, no keyboard input), and presented in a magazine format. Each "issue" has six theme-related lessons built around subjects such as travel, sports and leisure, and daily living. Each lesson is composed of an illustrated article, a related dialogue, and two sets of review questions, all in text and audio form. On-screen controls include buttons that produce a reading of the story or dialogue, as well as others that display the English text while it's being read. In addition, there are "hot" links for individual words that provide both pronunciation help and dictionary definitions.

For Macintosh (2 meg) with hard drive, CD-ROM drive, and speech input/output capabilities; $495.

(For an additional program useful in ESL classrooms, see also Learn to Speak

English, *by Hyperglot, covered with* Learn to Speak Spanish *and* Learn to Speak French *in the foreign language section below.)*

Writing and Reference Tools for ESL Teachers

• *Dos Amigos* from Westcliff Software is a full-featured word processor with most of the capabilities of a business product. What sets it apart is that it has been created for use by both Spanish and English speakers; this feature also makes the program useful in Hispanic ESL and Spanish foreign language classes. The program allows toggling between Spanish and English interfaces (menus, help messages, etc.); spell checking against either a Spanish or an English dictionary; and use of an on-line bilingual dictionary. With the latter, ESL students can type a Spanish word into their English text, and with just a few keystrokes, have the computer search out and insert the English equivalent. The process can be reversed for students of Spanish.

For MS-DOS computers (512K) with hard drive, $99.

• Scholastic's *ESL Writer,* a word processor with spelling and grammar checking capabilities, is targeted to the growing population of intermediate-level ESL students, and particularly to those of Hispanic or Asian background. (The Asian language groups covered include Vietnamese, Cambodian, Filipino, Laotian, Chinese, Japanese, and Korean.) The program addresses language interference difficulties common to these groups. For example, when Hispanic students run spelling checks of their written English using Spanish Spell Help, the program will flag "bery" and offer as alternatives "very," "bury," or "berry." Asian Spell Help flags "lanch"

and offers "lunch," "launch," and "ranch."

The grammar checking part of the program catches structural errors, then identifies the nature of each error ("subject/verb agreement" or "helping verb problem"). There are 12 grammar help categories in all, and they're a boon to any ESL student trying to puzzle out how English speakers phrase questions (Why goes he home?), use articles (She is good friend of mine), and so forth.

One or two proofing passes of *ESL Writer* still won't produce flawless English, of course. As Scholastic points out, the program doesn't recognize semantic, or meaning-related, errors. But *ESL Writer* can provide students with powerful help in analyzing and correcting their own work.

For Apple II (128K) or MS-DOS computers (256K), $99.95.

• *European MacProof* and *Bilingual PC Proof* (functionally the same product for Macintosh and MS-DOS platforms, respectively) are grammar, spelling, style, and usage analysis programs from Lexpertise Linguistic Software. Lexpertise has taken its programs developed for native speakers/writers of English, and created separate Spanish, French, and German versions that look for language interference problems from speakers of those languages who are writing in English. The programs also watch for "false friends" (Spanish "actual" and English "actual" are not equivalents) and possible mistranslations. They suggest corrections for misused prepositions (a Spanish speaker might want to "marry with her," a German "speak from this"); unacceptable noun plurals (in French, "informations" is correct); and incorrect verb forms (typically irregular past tense and past participle). This is on top of the checks *MacProof* and *PCProof* perform in their "domestic" versions.

For Macintosh (1 meg) or MS-DOS (640K) computers (hard drive required for MS-DOS version); $249.

Courseware for Foreign Language Teachers

• The Athena Language Learning Project, an academic research project at MIT has produced *A la rencontre Philippe,* the first of several interactive videodisc-plus software programs in development. Although not yet commercially available, *Philippe* is being offered to educational institutions in a pre-release version.

Through an interactive videodisc simulation, intermediate and advanced French students are drawn into an engrossing story about a young Frenchman who has been kicked out of the apartment he shares with his girlfriend. Speaking directly to users, Philippe enlists their aid in helping him find new digs. Through the cleverly planned branching program, students are able to explore leads around town, make phone calls and pick up messages for Philippe, meet him at pre-arranged times and locations, and "do" a great deal more. Depending on the decisions users make (which are affected by how well they understand the conversational dialogues and the situations that come up on the video), Philippe's quest can end in seven different ways, each played out on the video monitor.

The program provides a broad range of tools to help students comprehend material that might otherwise overwhelm them. These include video controls that cause the last utterance on the videodisc to be repeated, or that switch to a second soundtrack where the same phrase is more clearly enunciated. At students' request, the program will also produce French subtitles for the video,

as well as additional cultural information and a glossary.

For Macintosh (2 meg) with hard drive, videodisc player. Pre-release version available to educational institutions, $100; a finalized version is expected to be commercially published later this year, and should cost approximately $100.

• *Learn to Speak Spanish, Learn to Speak French,* and *Learn to Speak English,* from Hyperglot, are beginning language courses based on a teaching model that includes situational dialogue, vocabulary lists, cultural notes, grammar lessons, and drills to hammer home each lesson's content. Traditional though this approach may be, many educators like and use it, and Hyperglot has adapted the advantages of computer technology to it very well. The lessons are highly interactive, delivered through *HyperCard* stacks, audio CD, and CD-ROM. The key strength of the programs is that all dialogues and many of the exercises are delivered in pristine-quality CD audio which can be controlled from the computer screen. (The audio CD can also be played on a regular CD player; the dialogues are also available on cassettes.)

The programs are essentially self-contained, single-user lessons, not designed for classroom use. But their ease of use, excellent sound, and interactivity make them helpful for students who want to do additional work on their own, or for teachers who want to assign supplementary work, perhaps in a lab setting.

For Macintosh (1 meg), with CD-ROM drive. Program on one CD-ROM and one CD audio disc, $249.95; on 15 floppies and one CD audio disc $249.95; on 15 floppies and an audio cassette tape, $149.95.

• *Granville,* published by Britain's Cambridge University Press and available through Gessler, is a charming computer simulation for intermediate to advanced French students. The program drops you off in a seaside village on the coast of Normandy with a hotel booking, a budget to get you through one week's vacation, and lots of authentic information in French about the town and vicinity. Actual local maps; promotional flyers for sight-seeing activities and excursions;

"I Didn't Know This Program Was in That Language"

There's a whole range of programs—and we can only scratch the surface here—that have been published in foreign language versions as well as in English or that use both English and a second language. With a little adaptation and imagination a foreign language or ESL teacher can put them to good use. Here's a sampling of such packages.

• **Writing tools.** IBM publishes its children's word processor *Primary Editor Plus* in a Spanish version *Mi Editor Primario* for Spanish-speaking kids who are learning to write in their native tongue. (The program is meant to be used in conjunction with IBM's *VALE,* the Spanish version of *Writing to Read.* Similarly William K. Brodford/D.C. Heath publishes *Leer, Escribir, y Publicar,* their Spanish version of *Read, Write and Publish.*

• **Videodisc packages with two language tracks.** Those programs with a cultural content are your best bets. In your French class try *Louvre* or *Salamandre: Chateaux of the Loire* [both interactive video programs] or *Musee d'Orsay* (a non-computer-based videodisc program). For German classes a good choice is *Vienna: The Spirit of the City* videodisc (stacks forthcoming). All four programs are from Voyager.

• **Word games, language arts, games, and storybook programs.** Sunburst publishes *1-2-3 Sequence Me* in French *(1-2-3 Ordonne-Moi),* and *M-ss-ng L-nks* in French German and Spanish. RDA's *Rhubarb,* a "text reconstruction" game and *Double-Up,* a "sentence reconstruction" game, are published in French as *Strumph* and *JuxtaMots,* respectively. Gessler's catalog is loaded with other popular titles—*Les Secrets de Gertrude* and *French Micro Scrabble,* for example. And Discis's CD-ROM talking storybooks have versions with at least some of the audio accessible in Spanish.

• **Other games.** Just as teachers can offer game software in English to reward ESL students with fun language-building experiences at the computer, teachers of foreign languages have the same option. For example, Lucasfilm Games publishes *Indiana Jones and the Temple of Doom* and several other titles in a variety of languages and students of French can track down Carmen Sandiego *en français* using Brøderbund's *A la Poursuite de Carmen Sandiego dans le Monde.*

bus, train, and boat schedules and fares; restaurant menus; and a great deal more are all reprinted in the manual for you to consult. The idea is to fill your seven days with fun—doing anything from shopping to touring Mont St. Michel to gambling at the local casino. All the activities are simulated in some simple fashion on screen—if you go skeet shooting, for example, you shoot at moving targets; at the casino, you place chips and bet on cards the dealer turns over, your winnings or losses reflected in your available cash. But you have to figure out how to get to each activity using local or regional transport, interact in French with locals, find restaurants and stores, order food or make purchases, pay your tab, change money, and do all the other things that go along with a vacation in a foreign land. The printed resources are authentic, rich, and fun, and while the straight forward on-screen simulation isn't flashy, it's very engaging.

For MS-DOS computers (256K) or Apple II Family (128K). $39.95.

Writing and Reference Tools for Foreign Language Teachers

• *Salsa: Writing Assistant for Spanish,* from Interlex, and *Systeme D: Writing Assistant for French* from Heinle and Heinle, are two programs by the same development team that provide fast and easy access to language information for students working on writing assignments. Each is equipped with a word processor that can handle all the necessary characters, and a "database" students can jump to when they're confused about a meaning, unsure about a structure, or stumped by a verb tense. There's a bilingual dictionary that offers not only word-for-word equivalents, but also comprehension-expanding definitions in the second language and examples of the word in context.

If students are struggling with a verb tense, they can jump to an extensive verb conjugator. There is also a grammar reference that can be searched, a vocabulary index that organizes words around a topic (e.g., money, morning activities, and natural catastrophes), and a collection of idiomatic phrases grouped by theme. The information is painless to get at while writing, so students will likely end up communicating more complex ideas.

Interlex has also prepared a customized "companion" to *Salsa,* called *Salsera,* that gives Spanish teachers the ability to develop and add their own input to the *Salsa* database, whether it be more grammar explanations, more dictionary entries, or word or phrase collections that suit the circumstances of the classes they're teaching.

For MS-DOS computers (512K) with hard drive. Salsa, $75, and Salsera, $175, available from Interlex. Systeme D, $89, available from Heinle & Heinle.

• MicroTac's *Language Assistant* packages for French, Spanish, German, or Italian are well-organized, useful references for students. In addition to a basic word processor, each features an electronic Random House Bilingual Dictionary (which can be edited or expanded) that provides target-language equivalents for an English word, or vice-versa; a verb conjugator that delivers all forms and tenses of any verb in the dictionary (and a noun declinator in the German version); and a grammar section with clear English explanations of important grammar points. There are hypertext links in the program, so relevant information from these sections can be accessed during the writing process. For example, you could be writing in German, type the English word "spend," bring up the bilingual dictionary to display the German infinitive, switch to the verb conjugator to check the verb's forms (all numbers and tenses), select one of the tenses, link to a discussion of its use (and branch, if you can keep from getting lost, to related grammatical topics), and finally insert the correct verb form into your document. You can also invoke the reference features of *Language Assistant* from within your favorite word processor.

In the latest version of these programs, MicroTac has included a "translation assistant," which the publisher points out is meant to *help* translate *simple* English. It's intriguing, but not surprisingly, its translations are more amusing than correct. This part of the program is probably more useful for the discussions it will prompt about the nature and complexity of human communication, the value of human interaction in language study, and the incredible difficulty of any sort of "machine" translation.

For MS-DOS computers (512K), $79.95.

• *GramR,* a French product available in North America through Schuller & Associates, finds and alerts users—in French—to errors in spelling, grammar, and syntax contained in French texts. As your intermediate or advanced students labor over their themes, *GramR* can help them spot and learn the nature of their errors. With that information they may recognize the "fix" immediately, or they can turn to you or their books to determine how to correct the error. In either case, because of their active involvement, they will be less likely to repeat the errors. There are complete verb conjugations available at a keystroke as well. A separate French keyboard conversion utility is included.

For MS-DOS computers (640K), $150. (Macintosh version to be published later this year.)

• *Grammatik Français* is the French language version of Reference Software's *Grammatik* package that analyzes English writing. Like its English "brother," *Grammatik Français* not only searches out spelling, grammar, and syntax errors, but also signals (in French) possible errors in style and usage. It's a very sophisticated program, most useful to advanced students who can benefit from features such as its ability to critique text in any of seven writing styles (including commercial, fiction, strict, and technical). *Grammatik Français* works with most of the well-known word processors on the market.

For MS-DOS computers (512K), $298. (Macintosh version to be published later this year.

(For another program useful in foreign language classrooms, see also Dos Amigos from Westcliff Software, in the ESL section above.)

David Hoffman is associate editor of Technology & Learning.

Lesson-Making/Authoring Tools
for Both ESL and Foreign Language Teachers

MacLang 4 available through several companies is a marvelously versatile program for creating language-learning exercises. The program can convert your keyboard to accommodate English and 11 other languages (including the major Western European languages, Russian, and even Japanese). Moreover it offers a wide range of lesson templates to which you add your own language material. You can create vocabulary drills, fill-ins, multiple choice questions, reading comprehension exercises, cloze questions, scrambled sentences, or multi-format exercises. In addition you can preface any exercise with introductions or explanatory material; choose the number of "tries" students get before the right answer is revealed and create helpful feedback and hints.

Your exercises can include text only or text and *MacPaint* graphics; they can even link to a segment on an audiocassette or videodisc. You can also create branching programs in which the next item to appear depends on the answer a student has just given. The options and flexibility in *MacLang 4* are many and they'll accommodate just about any lesson idea you can come up with.

For Macintosh (1 meg). *Available from Exceller Software ($95), Gessler ($79.95) Intellimation ($89.95) and RDA ($129).*

• ICD's *Versatext Authoring System* for the Macintosh is a great program for teachers who want to create reading comprehension lessons for their students. *Versatext lessons* and exercises start, of course, with a reading passage that has been typed or imported into the lesson file by the teacher. The passages can then be "enhanced" in a number of ways: you can cause important parts of the passage to appear highlighted; add original or imported graphics; append notes—which pop up at the click of a mouse—to any words in the passage; and even add digitized sound. You might, for example, input definitions for all new vocabulary words in a lesson with each definition including both a graphic illustration and a "sound bite." Graphics and sound bites can be gathered from clip art or clip sound programs; or they can be created using paint programs such as Claris's *MacPaint* and sound digitizers such as Farallon's MacRecorder and the sound input capabilities of the new Macintoshes.

Once you've completed your annotated reading passage you can easily create true/false multiple choice and fill-in questions all with a few mouse clicks and a little keyboarding. There is also a way to provide helpful feedback after a wrong answer and congratulations after a correct one.

Lessons made with the *Versatext Authoring System* are run by students using the companion *Versatext Instruction System*. This program not only provides access to all the reading, graphics, sounds, notes and questions you've packed into the lessons but keeps a record of what each student has worked on and how well he has done. ICD also has prepared sets of ready-made lessons, some of which could be useful to ESL teachers.

For Macintosh (512K); $195 includes

Versatext Authoring System software plus Instruction System *software with site license.*

• *Talk to Me,* from Educational Activities gives you the power to build simple on-screen interactive language lessons using text graphics and your own (or anybody else's) voice. It works with an Anivax (or other) voice input/output board and a microphone to digitize your words or sentences, enabling your students to hear as well as read your questions.

More than that, the program lets your students respond orally via a microphone (repeat after you, answer your dictated question, etc.). Students can listen to a question over and over again, re-record their responses until they're happy with them and then pass their lesson disks over to you as homework!

Once you've practiced, *Talk to Me* becomes quite easy to use although the interface seems a bit clunky. (There's a confusingly wide range of keystrokes required to get things done.) You can load the special character file if you'll be writing questions in a foreign language and there is a utility (available separately) that allows you to import additional graphics to supplement those provided. One important limitation to the program is the four-second maximum "sound bite" for any question or response. This limits you from including questions such as "What do you see in this picture?" Educational Activities says it chose to limit the duration of each sound bite so that a typical 20-question lesson would fit on a 320K floppy.

For MS-DOS computers (256K) with voice input/output capability. Software and manual, $169; software, manual, Anivox I/O board, microphone, headset $298.

• The "engine" used to create *Talk to Me,* called the *Anivax Voice-Animation Toolkit,* is itself a useful program for language teachers. Available from Animated Voice Corporation, it can produce language lessons with any of the features of *Talk to Me.* The program also allows you to do some interesting editing of your digitized voice input. For example you can alter the pitch and intonation of a stored utterance and "reuse" it in several places. With the help of a paint program you can also create simple animations and intriguingly *synchronize* them to sound clips, building animated scenes with sound.

Equally intriguing since the program can recognize and differentiate between a few simple pairs of words such as "yes/no" and "true/false" you can create questions that accept certain spoken responses from students (through the microphone). For example depending on a student's response the program might congratulate the student and advance her to the next question, prompt her to try again or provide her with a hint.

While there's no programming needed to use the *Voice Animation Toolkit,* creating lessons with speech output/input and animation is a complex task. But if you're the adventurous "techie" sort you'll find the program's powers intriguing.

For MS-DOS computers (256K) with voice input/output capability; $99.95.

ESL and Foreign Language Software Publishers

Here are the names, addresses, and phone numbers of the companies whose programs we've mentioned here. Keep in mind that many of them offer other ESL and foreign language products as well.

Animated Voice Corporation
PO Box 819
San Marcos, CA 92069
(800) 942-3699

Athena Language Learning Project
MIT Technology Licensing Office
28 Carleton St. 20C-130
Cambridge, MA 02139
(617) 253-6966

Brøderbund Software
PO Box 12947
San Rafael, CA 94913
(800) 521-6263

Creative Pursuits
12151 La Casa Lane
Los Angeles, CA 90049
(213) 472-1179

Davidson and Associates
PO Box 2961
Torrance, CA 90509
(800) 545-7677

Discis Books
45 Sheppard Ave. East
Suite 410
Toronto, Ont. M2N 5W9
Canada
(800) 567-4321

Educational Activities
1937 Grand Ave.
Baldwin, NY 11510
(800) 645-3739

Exceller Software
Cornell Research Park
223 Langmuir Lab
Ithaca, NY 14850
(800) 426-0444

Gessler Educational Software
55 W. 13th Street
New York, NY 10011
(212) 627-0099

Heinle and Heinle Publishers
20 Park Plaza
Boston, MA 02116
(800) 237-0053

Hyperglot Software
505 Forest Hills Blvd.
Knoxville, TN 37919
(615) 558-8270

IBM Direct PC Software
One Culver Rd.
Dayton, NJ 08810
(800) 426-2468

ICD
750 N. Freedom Blvd.
Suite 303B
Provo, UT 84601
(800) 658-8567

Intellimation
PO Box 1922
Santa Barbara, CA 93116
(800) 346-8355

Interlex
PO Box 252
Ithaca, NY 14851
(607) 387-9688

Jostens Learning Corporation
6170 Cornerstone Court
East San Diego, CA 92121
(800) 521-8538

Lexpertise
Linguistic Software
380 S. State St.
Suite 202
Salt Lake City, UT 84111
(801) 359-0059

Lucasfilm Games
PO Box 10307
San Rafael, CA 94912
(415) 721-3300

MicroTac
4655 Cass St. Suite 214
San Diego, CA 92109
(800) 366-4170

Proficiency
185 S. State St.
Suite 950
Salt Lake City, UT 84111
(800) 765-4375

RDA/Mind Builders
10 Boulevard Ave.
Greenlawn, NY 11740
(800) 654-8715

Reference Software
330 Townsend St.
Suite 123
San Francisco, CA 94107
(800) 872-9933

Scholastic Software
PO Box 7502
Jefferson City, MO 65102
(800) 541 -5513

Schuller & Associates
300 Brannan St.

Suite 307
San Francisco, CA 94107
(415) 882-4088

Sunburst Communications
101 Castleton St.
Pleasantville, NY 10570
(800) 628-8897

The Voyager Company
1351 Pacific Coast Hwy.
3rd Floor
Santa Monica, CA 90401
(213) 451-1383

Westcliff Software
200 Washington St.
Suite 207
Santa Cruz, CA 95060
(408) 459-8811

William K. Bradford Publishing
310 School St.
Acton, MA 01720
(800) 421-2009

Young children learn best through social interaction and exploration of materials. Preschool and kindergarten classrooms are visual representations of this type of learning. The rooms are bright, decorated, and packed with an amazing array of visual stimuli—a sandtable, a puppet stage, puzzles, paints, books, and blocks. Every inch of space encourages young children to discover, explore, and experiment with new concepts. But in many early childhood classrooms one very valuable learning tool is missing—the computer.

Some teachers hesitate to use computers with four and five year olds because they fear it will perpetuate the "Superbaby Syndrome." Others are reluctant because they are unsure of how to manage computers in such active settings. The computer is valid and viable for young children when it becomes an educational tool. Like a picture book or crayon, it provides children a unique way of dealing with information. With planning and sound instructional practice, computers provide developmentally appropriate experiences for young learners.

The National Association for Education of Young Children, presented a position statement on the education of young children. The NAEYC believes that the quality of an Early Childhood program is determined by the degree to which the program is developmentally appropriate. NAEYC states that developmentally appropriate programs are both age appropriate and individually appropriate; that is the program is de-signed for the age group served and implemented with attention to the needs and differences of the individual children involved. The computer, combined with the right software and a good teaching plan can be developmentally appropriate for students in preschool and kindergarten.

Introducing Students to the Computer

A lot of planning must precede introducing the students to the computer. Young children will be curious and eager to understand how the computer operates. They will want to see, touch, and try using the computer and the software. The teacher should spend time identifying and labeling the parts of the computer. Children need to understand that the computer is a machine that can only do what the user tells it to do.

A good introduction to the computer combines *Muppets on Stage* (Sunburst Communications), the *Muppet Learning Keys* and a large screen monitor. *Muppets on Stage* offers three programs, *Discovery, Letters,* and *Numbers.* All three choices present opportunities for students to experiment inputting numbers, letters, and colors. For example, a child can enter the letter and a picture of a lobster will appear. Another child can enter the numeral 6 and six lobsters will appear on the screen. And another can change the color of the lobsters by selecting a color from the paint palate on the keyboard. The *Muppet Learning Keys* uses an alphabetical keyboard, Muppet characters and other familiar symbols.

By
Linda
Kostner

443

The keyboard connects to the computer video with a long cable that makes it ideal for passing among a group of children.

Using the Computer With the Whole Class

The computer, when hooked to the large screen monitor, and facilitated by the teacher, becomes an effective medium for whole class interaction. Some software programs encourage student participation in discussion. *Choices, Choices: On the Playground* (Tom Snyder Productions) leads students through a real-life situation involving a new and different-looking child on the playground. The students must use their receptive and expressive language skills to evaluate situations and make decisions.

A teacher can also increase language development opportunities using a word processing program. With *Talking Text Writer* (Scholastic, Inc.) a teacher can record language experience stories. The software takes advantage of synthesized speech and will "read" the story back to the students. Other programs like *LogoWriter* (LCSI) and *Once Upon A Time* (Compu-Teach) assist teacher and students in generating simple story scenes and labels that promote collaboration and communication among students.

At the Computer Center

Once the students understand the guidelines and keystrokes to use the computer, they are ready to work with the computers at a Computer Center. Even if more than one computer is available, keep them together in the same center so they can share a printer or other peripherals. It is also easier for the teacher or aide to monitor the computers when they are grouped. The area should be arranged to facilitate interaction between children. Placing at least two chairs at each computer tells children that using a computer is a cooperative activity. Young children prefer social use of computers and many studies have found that computers encourage social interaction. Several other reports confirm that children spontaneously and effectively teach and help each other in computer environments.

Software at the computer learning center should be developmentally appropriate. *Patterns* (MECC) uses a cosmic space theme with spaceships, space creatures, and satellites to develop pattern recognition skills. The program encourages young children to work cooperatively to decode and create patterns and sequences. *Bumble Games* (The Learning Company) is a problem solving software program that allows students to explore numbers and number relationships. *Juggle's Rainbow* (The Learning Company) facilitates students' understanding of above, below, left, and right.

Other Learning Centers

Take advantage of the way children learn. Young children learn best through activities that encourage interaction and creativity. When students become more skillful with computers, place the machines in the existing learning centers. Here computers become a technological learning device that the students can select and use at their own pace. They become another instructional choice in the language center, math center, writing center, and art center. However, software for these centers must be selected with respect to instructional objectives and developmentally appropriate criteria. The following are some considerations for selecting software appropriate for early childhood learning centers:

- Age appropriate: Is the content and presentation of information relevant for the student's age level?
- Individually appropriate: Can the pace and sequence of the program be directed by students? Are they active participants in the learning process?
- Clear instructions: Are the directions given nonverbally through graphics, symbols, or speech synthesis? Are these symbols and graphics clear to the learner?
- Discovery approach: Children learn through discovery rather than drill on specific facts. Does the software allow the student to be in control of what happens? Is the child given opportunities to test alternative responses without fear of failing?
- Real world representation: Does the content deal with concrete representations? Is it clear, interesting, and not distracting from the learning?

Some programs appropriate for a math center include *Counters* (Sunburst), and *Math and Me* (Davidson & Associates). The language center could contain *Pictures, Letters, Sounds* (Hartley) and *Tigers' Tales* (Sunburst). Software for a writing center might include *Color Me* (D.C. Heath) and *Muppet Slate* (Sunburst).

Like finger paints, wooden blocks, and play dough, the computer is another tool to facilitate learning through discovery and experimentation. When preschoolers use computers they are constantly exploring new concepts and learning new skills. If the computer instruction is guided by the teacher and used in combination with other concrete experience, it can offer children a new and motivating way to learn.

References

Clements, D.H. 1987 (November). "Computers and young children: A review of research." *Young Children*. pp. 34-44.

Haugland, S., and Shade, D. 1988 (May). "Developmentally appropriate software for young children." *Young Children*. pp. 37-42.

National Association for the Education of Young Children. (1988). *Position statement on developmentally appropriate practice in programs for 4- and 5-year olds*. NAEYC, Washington, DC.

Software

Bumble Games, Juggle's Rainbow. The Learning Company, 6493 Kaiser Dr., Fremont, CA 94555.

Choices Choices: On the Playground. Tom Snyder Productions, Inc., 90 Sherman St., Cambridge, MA 01140.

Color Me. D.C. Heath and Co., 125 Spring St., Lexington, MA 02173.

LogoWriter, LCSI. 121 Mt. Vermont St., Boston, MA 02108.

Math and Me. Davidson & Associates, 3135 Kashiwa St., Torrance, CA 90505.

Muppets on Stage; Counters; Tigers' Tales. Sunburst Communications, 39 Washington Ave., Pleasantville, NY 10570.

Once Upon A Time. Compu-Teach. Inc. 78 Olive St., New Haven, CT 06510.

Patterns, MECC. 3490 Lexington Avenue North., St. Paul, MN 55126.

Pictures, Letters, Sound. Hartley Courseware. Inc., 133 Bridge St., Dimondale, MI 48821.

Talking Text Writer. Scholastic Software. Inc., 162 Madison Ave. New York, NY 10016.

Article #11
Appropriate Uses of Computers With Young Children

By
Kevin J.
Swick

The computer is not a toy or an isolation booth for reinforcement of nonsense symbols. The computer is another technological advance which enables people to extend their intellectual and creative powers. When the computer is used to foster these goals, it can be an important and useful addition to early childhood learning. (Steve Tipps, 1987, p. 159)

Many questions have been raised regarding the role of computers in programs for young children. Unfortunately, these questions are often asked by individuals who have not explored recent advancements in technology and early childhood education.

The questions that guide this presentation on computers in early childhood education are drawn from the most recent work in the field: how will or can computers influence the goals of a quality program? In the context of a good program, what is the place of computers? When acquiring a computer, what should be the major criteria considered? What are some appropriate and effective ways of introducing young children to computers? In integrating computers into early childhood programs, what are some major considerations to examine? What are some appropriate uses of computers with young children? The emphasis of these questions on the "appropriateness" of computers throughout this presentation is on utilizing computers in developmentally appropriate ways with young children.

Computers: Their Role And Place in a Quality Program

Computers, like other learning tools, have a natural and valuable place in quality programs. However, they are not and should not be a panacea that is used to solve basic program needs. Tipps (1987, p. 158) states it clearly:

The first priority is still building an environment of real experiences from which language, science, and math concepts arise. Blocks, books, puzzles, sand and water, house and dramatic play, wheeled toys, puppets, records, and many other traditional pieces of equipment are more essential. Also, money for cooking, art supplies, and field trips is needed continuously.

Not only are the "basic tools" of a quality program essential, but practices that promote an active, interesting curriculum should permeate the learning environment. Given the context of a quality program, computers can enrich and extend the goals and substance of the curriculum.

The effective utilization of computers in early childhood education must be *based on an understanding of how children learn.* Young children learn through many natural interactions in the environment. As Kamil (1985) notes, children acquire an understanding of the environment through experiences which they can then use to construct images of

446

the world around them. Swick (1987, p. 16) extends this point:

> The learning of any concepts requires the acquisition of "concepts of how to learn." While adults may find this to be a rather pedantic issue, it is critical to children's formation of a sound foundation for learning and development. It is counter-productive to try to teach a 4 year old to count when he has not acquired "how to learn" concepts. Children must acquire the concepts of "people, events, places, relationships" and then construct an image of how these elements fit together. To achieve this image-building process children need to develop and use the following skills: direct experiential learning, observational learning, and language learning.

With the nature of children's learning and development serving as the basis for utilizing computers, specific criteria have been identified as critical to their successful integration into the classroom. For example, Shade, Nida, Lipinski, and Watson (1986) identified two criteria in their study: (1) integrate the computer into the natural context of the classroom, and (2) utilize the computer as an "interactive" learning tool. Further, Tipps (1987) suggests that when computer content is related to children's experiences they grasp the utility of the computer as one of many learning tools in a meaningful way as opposed to simply using it for periodic activities.

Ultimately, *the computer must be related to the curriculum goals of early childhood programs.* When the impact of computers on early childhood programs is placed in a "developmentally appropriate framework" the following observations have emerged: computers provide an exciting, dynamic new learning tool; they can enrich existing instructional practices by providing a medium for extending learning to new visual and manipulative modes; they are potentially a self-confidence building experience for many children; and recent research indicates computers can serve to strengthen children's social skills, especially team planning and cooperative learning (Beaty and Tucker, 1987; Harlow, 1984). Additional benefits include the use of computers to meet special needs such as children with cerebral palsy or speech, hearing, or visual impairments. In essence, computers can broaden the learning arena of quality early childhood programs. In doing so the goal of autonomy for each child has a better chance of being achieved.

Once a decision has been made to integrate computers into the program two issues need close attention: *criteria to consider when acquiring a computer, and needed training for effective use of computers in early childhood programs.* In the early days of computer mania many schools and early childhood centers made the mistake of buying any computer that was popular at the time or that had a particularly attractive feature. Only later did they find that their acquisition was a poor investment. Four criteria should serve as guidelines when buying a computer for an early childhood program: *reliability, flexibility, compatibility, and durability.* Is the computer equipment reliable? Does it have a history of quality performance? That is, will it work on a continuing basis without constant maintenance? One way to answer this question is to inquire at centers that have used computers, study the information available on different computers in professional magazines, contact a neutral consultant, or use a combination of these information gathering modes. Beware of "cheap computers" that promise great results; you will get what you pay for. A second area to investigate is the flexibility of the computer in terms of usage. How many functions can the computer serve? Is it built for use with different input devices? Can the memory be expanded as the computer arena becomes more sophisticated? A computer that is limited in functions is not suitable for use with young children as they need equipment they can truly manipulate and experiment with. While more expensive, a comprehensive computer environment that allows for full use of children's motor, visual, social, and intellectual skills is the most desired tool for an effective learning arrangement.

The compatibility of the computer with the stated learning goals of the program is a third criterion. For example, a computer environment that allows for only drill type activities would not be compatible with the goals of developmentally appropriate programs. Another dimension of this criterion is the compatibility of the hardware with software that is available and desired for use with the children. A quality piece of hardware that is not compatible with software needs is a danger to avoid. Consult with various sources in other schools and universities to resolve this concern before making the investment. A fourth criterion to attend to is the durability of the computer. Buy a computer that can be used by children in an active way and will be usable for several years. While every computer will need regular cleaning and maintenance, the basic hardware should be able to experience heavy usage for an extended time period.

Along with the acquisition of a computer is the *needed teacher training* for effective utilization in the program. Swick (in press, p. 5) states:

> The starting point for teachers is to acquire a basic literacy in computer usage. While teachers of young children do not have to be experts, their skill and attitude in using the computer provide a role model for the children. Knowing the physical composition of the computer, how it works, and its many uses provides teachers with a foundation for carrying out basic classroom instruction and a basis for extending their own computer literacy.

Most universities, many computer stores, and some schools provide basic training as a part of the acquisition process. An important note to the training process is that continual growth in computer learning should be a goal of every teacher.

The selection, organization, and use of software is another part of the teacher's skill kit. Unfortunately, many software programs that claim to be especially designed for young children are of poor quality, and in some cases, totally inappropriate. Knight (1987) provides a review of critical features to examine when selecting software: does program content promote continuous student interaction? Does the program handle student errors in a constructive manner? Is the program designed so it can be adapted to individual needs? Is the material presented in an interesting, sequential, and logical manner? Are the sound and graphic features appealing to children? Finally, is the material designed for use in an instructional setting? Familiarity with software and creative ways to use the computer are not only helpful in designing appropriate settings for children but very useful for "educating" parents about appropriate ways to utilize it in the home. Teachers are also faced with many decisions regarding the design of the computer environment as related to the total classroom setting.

The overall structure of the program (including the basic philosophy about children), the unique needs of the children, and the specific objectives of the curriculum should serve as the framework for deciding the place of any technology in the program. In programs designed to meet developmentally appropriate educational needs of young children the following guidelines are especially pertinent:

1. Integrate the computer into the environment so that children use it as a natural medium for learning.
2. Provide extensions of the classroom computer environment in another part of the center where special projects and parent-child computer experiences can occur.
3. Use the computer as part of the total curriculum, relating its content to the context of other activities in the program.
4. Select software that promotes children's active exploration of the environment; programs such as Logo are excellent in promoting children's thinking and analytic skills.
5. Experiment with different uses of the computer so that the program avoids the "mechanical" flavor often associated with commercial learning tools (Swick, 1987).

Introduce Children to the Computer

A major consideration of any new learning experience in developmentally oriented programs is the intimate involvement of children in actively pursuing the total process. This is especially true of children's initial experiences with computers. In effect, whatever process is used to engage children in learning about computers, it must be based on a concrete, active-involvement philosophy.

Papert (1980) notes that the real value of computers for young children is that they learn to develop self-confidence in "controlling technology" for their uses. Beaty and Tucker's (1987, p. 19) statement provides a basis for orienting children to computers in a developmentally appropriate manner:

> The initial introduction between child and computer is crucial to the continuing relationship. Children need to be in control from the very beginning. If children are not allowed to touch the computer during the first session they may be reluctant to use it during future sessions.

Not only must children be able to manipulate the equipment, they need experiences with turning it on/off, loading and unloading the computer, and learning to understand the many dimensions of the computer. Are there proven methods of introducing children to the computer? Not really! However, research and practice have identified some useful approaches:

1. Locate the computer in a "low-traffic" area of the room; in a place where the sunlight will not hit it directly. Remember, temperature extremes can damage floppy disks and the computer chips.
2. The computer should be placed near a wall; a three-pronged outlet is needed and, if possible, cover the wires with a panel.
3. Use child-size furniture and provide flexible and usable chair arrangements; the physical arrangement should allow for children to use their skills in an effective manner.
4. Provide the children with some precomputer readiness experiences; many teachers have found floor size keyboard mats and typewriters good

tools for helping children understand how the computer operates. Another helpful strategy is to acquire an old computer the children can take apart and see its parts.

5. Use "pairs" or very small groups of children when introducing them to the computer. The computer is a social experience; no more than three children should be using it at one time unless the group is very mature.

It is important that children have a positive experience with computers and the many ways they can use it to enrich their lives. It is important to discuss with children the value, role, and place of computers in the classroom. Beaty and Tucker (1987) recommend the following as "positive rules" for children to understand and follow as they use computers: *no liquids near the computer, use one key at a time, and clean hands before using the computer.* Naturally, other issues will evolve as children use the computer: whose turn is it? Where to put the software? How do we keep it clean? These and other issues should be resolved through discussions with the children. In developmentally appropriate programs, the computer is used not only as a way of introducing children to technology but also as a means of strengthening their social skills, stimulating their inventiveness, and encouraging them to explore new ways of thinking (Papert, 1980; Tipps, 1984).

Appropriate Uses of Computers with Young Children

Computers should serve to function as unique parts of a quality early childhood education program. Beaty and Tucker (1987) point to the following as appropriate instructional functions the computer can meet: manipulation, mastery, and meaning. For example, from the very beginning of a computer experience, children *learn to use fine motor skills* to manipulate the keyboard, a joystick, or touch-screen in drawing, painting, printing, or puzzle activities. Also, as children "play" with even the simplest of programs they quickly master the pattern or mode of the concept presented. This allows them to acquire some *perspective on cause-effect relationships and to gain confidence in their program solving efforts.* Finally, as children master the rudiments of the "computer environment" they initiate their own ideas in relation to creating new and more exciting activities than might exist in the software itself.

Within the framework of the functions of manipulation, mastery, and meaning are various uses that computers can be activated to serve: meaningful play, word processing, oral language development, drawing and painting, and experiences in building environments.

Play is often referenced as the "child's work." Yet Brown (1987) notes that play is really a "mind set" that includes a sense of pretend, internal motivation, openness to new experiences, process oriented, and inherently enjoyable. Used in the proper manner, *the computer can become a medium for strengthening children's playful attributes.* The introduction of a computer into the learning environment "invites" many playful moments from children. Initially, they simply want to see what it does and how it works. Later, they want to explore the many different aspects of the computer. Some of the various forms of play that occur in computer environments are: language play, game play, motor activities, social play, and imaginative activities. While the emphasis is often on the cognitive power children can gain from the computer, recent research notes that social skills are actually the main benefit of this technology for young children (Sweetnam, 1982; Isenberg, 1984; Beaty and Tucker, 1987).

One program that is especially appropriate for stimulating children's "playful attributes" is *Jeepers Creepers* (Kangaroo Inc., 110 S. Michigan Avenue, Suite 469, Chicago, Illinois). It is a mix and-match animal game that shows a picture of an animal divided into three parts. Through keyboard manipulation the child can match the body parts and/or mix a series of combinations of parts. A critical point here is that, as Brown (1987) notes, in order for the experience to be "play," children need the freedom to explore *Jeepers Creepers* in their own way.

Recent advances in computer hardware and software have provided special opportunities for the very young child who is just beginning to explore literacy. For example, *Stickybear Opposites* (Weekly Reader Family Software, Optimum Resource, Inc., Norfolk, Connecticut) is designed so that with the use of three keys children can explore shapes and sizes as well as colors. It is, if used effectively, an excellent program for stimulating children's interests in many dimensions of the geometric world. The adult can help the child identify the way to work the program and then let them play with it. In most cases the children will master it in a short time and begin creating their own version of this program. Another tool for the preliterate child to use is the *Touch Screen* (Personal Touch Co., 4320 Stevens Creek Road, San Jose, California). It enables the child, through the use of motor/touch action, to make something happen on the monitor. Indeed there are options for games, painting, drawing, and printing.

Computers (along with the needed printer accessories) open up a *new world* of *"language development"* and *"language creation" for young children.* The "visual and auditory" world of the computer make it possible to: let children play with language (create their own symbols or words); use language to invent stories or describe experiences (language experiences through word processing); create "shared experiences" such as a group story; develop a "letter or word" bank; and use word processing experiences to promote discussions about the meaning of various words and phrases. The most difficult lesson for teachers to follow is to allow children maximum freedom to explore language through the manipulation of a responsive technology. Brown (1987, p. 59) provides teachers with an important reminder:

> It is the greatest arrogance for one human being to think they can dictate all of another human's experiences. Certainly children need our guidance, our suggestions, and a structure and pattern which we impose on their lives, but they also need freedom within the structure to direct themselves spontaneously, to challenge their growing abilities, and to make sense of their experiences through the natural process of play.

There are various word processing programs available. The use of these programs to promote both guided and unstructured learning should be in the minds of teachers as they implement them with young children. Two programs are particularly useful in early childhood education: *Bank Street Writer* (Brøderbund Software, 17 Paul Drive, San Rafael, California), and *Stickybear Printer* (Weekly Reader Family Software, Optimum Resource, Inc., Norfolk, Connecticut). Each of the software programs offers advantages to the early childhood professional. *Bank Street Writer* provides a comprehensive word processing package usable with children and as a professional tool for teachers' instructional planning and professional development needs. The main difference with the *Stickybear Printer* is that it offers more options for the children and fewer options for direct usage by teachers. It has pictures and graphic forms to go along with the printing so children can make stories with pictures, but it is not especially useful as a teacher tool.

Oral language development is the child's most natural medium for integrating symbols into their experiences in a meaningful way (Chukovsky, 1986). As Beaty and Tucker (1987, p. 145) point out, the computer environment is ideal for promoting children's oral language:

> Because children acquire language competence through interacting with people and things in their environment, the computer's interactive features make it a powerful language development tool. Certain programs can stimulate the use of new words, and the making up of stories to go along with computer pictures.

Sharing computer experiences at the language center is probably one of the most significant features of computer environments. Conversations about what is happening on the monitor, what it means, and related inquiries are rich content for children's language building. It is ironic that "computers" have gained the reputation of being "chatterboxes," as originally professionals worried that they might become isolation booths. What do children talk about while involved with computers? They give information, and directions, ask questions, answer questions, settle disputes on turn-taking, critique their work, make up games, and invent new ways to use language (Beaty and Tucker, 1987).

One of the "oral language" experiences children like to engage in is making up stories. An excellent program for preschoolers and K-primary children in this regard is *Facemaker* (Spinnaker Software Co., 215 First St., Cambridge, Massachusetts). While the preliterate child will initially need some assistance, this program not only engages the child in constructing faces but also in choice making and story invention activities. The program moves sequentially from building a face to making the face move and finally to describing what one's construction means. Very young children may not complete any of the three sequences fully but do elaborate fully on their incomplete designs. Again, the real value of this experience is that it involves the child in using technology in a creative, playful manner.

Two added dimensions to the computer have expanded options for facilitating children's language development: the addition of sound-responsive software and music software. Tipps (1987, p. 155) highlights the value of the *Talking Textwriter*:

The word processor (*Talking Textwriter*) also talks. Anything that is typed is read by a speech synthesizer. The speech synthesizer can read words or letters on an immediate or delayed basis. Without formal reading lessons, children learn about left to right progression, the important role of spaces and vowels in word formation, and the expression of ideas in writing. Many ideas which could only be told about can now be experienced.

Music programs also offer new avenues for encouraging children's "sound play" and "expressive skills." For example, *Stickybear Music* allows children to create sounds, match sounds to keyboard letters, and to invent rhythmic patterns. While this program does require adult assistance, many children enjoy controlling the sounds that result from their manipulations. *Talking Textwriter* is produced by Scholastic Software, 730 Broadway, New York.

Drawing and painting with the computer are yet other valuable uses of this technology. Children learn many skills through their creation of visual patterns: fine motor skills, geometric patterning, and expressive play skills. There are many programs that focus on supporting children's artistic development. Among the more appropriate programs: *Dazzle Draw* (Brøderbund Co.), *Touchwindow* (Personal Touch Co.), and *Mouse Paint* (Apple Computer Inc., Cupertino, California).

Autonomy is the ultimate goal of all educational strategies. Computer programs like *Logo* base their designs on the precept that children should use the computer environment to control and create the direction of their learning. For example, *Logo* allows children to gain maximum control of the computer ecology; they construct and direct the shape of the environment. In this way children not only learn about simple geometry but more importantly they can conceptualize and refine their ideas about the world of shapes, sizes, places, and directions. For preschool children, see *EZ Logo* (MECC, 3490 Lexington Avenue North, St. Paul, Minnesota). *Logo Writer* (Logo Computer Systems Inc., 555 W. 57th St., New York) is an appropriate program for primary grade children.

The appropriate use of computers in early childhood education programs is or should be premised on the construct that children are active, curious, and playful in their learning endeavors (Swick, 1987).

Integrating Computers into the Early Childhood Environment

The integration of computers into developmentally appropriate programs requires attention to criteria and practices that assure its place is a valid and dynamic one. Six criteria are briefly explored as follows.

The learner must be in control. In too many cases computer environments are too limited, forcing the child into a rigid relationship with the computer. Drawing, painting, writing, and problem solving are ways that children can "control and direct" the environment. Further, children can use computer learning to extend concepts learned in other modes.

The environment should be stimulating and responsive. Unfortunately, too many computer environment designs are lacking in needed accessories that make responsiveness possible. When acquiring hardware obtain items such as the printer, color graphics, speech synthesizer, and needed disk drives. In the same regard, select software that contains multiple and stimulating learning possibilities. Through responsive learning activities children learn how things work and how they can be manipulated and improved.

The environment should be flexible allowing for multiple uses of the child's senses. A real advantage of a well-designed computer environment is that children use all of their senses in creative ways. Tipps (1987) notes that programs such as *Talking Textwriter*, *LOGO*, and *Stickybear Opposites*, are examples of flexible environments for children.

The environment should be a true representation of reality. Programs that attempt to be overly academic often distort the symbolic nature of the content presented. For example, purely abstract material is "not real" to the child and therefore inappropriate. Realistic content is best portrayed through concrete symbols. *Jeepers Creepers,* for example, uses animal parts to represent part-whole relationships and sequencing concepts. In this way the child can visualize how the concept "part-whole" is actually represented. In a similar way, *Stickybear Opposites* uses the active movement of objects on the screen to visualize opposite modes in a concrete manner thus enabling the child to actually make "opposites" happen. Extensions of computer activities to the real world of the block corner or the role playing center can greatly enhance the "reality" of learning for young children.

The environment should be unique and add something special to the child's learning. To invest in a computer and then use it for tasks such as drill and counting is not only foolish but most inappropriate. On the other hand, word processing, drawing, Logo, and problem solving software offer the child an environment unique in learning opportunities. Consider the vantage point the child can acquire when seeing shapes take place on the screen as a result of simple logical moves on the keyboard, as occurs with the use of Logo. Or, in using *Touch Screen* the child can both visually and motorically create a shape or drawing to match a story dictated in the language center of the classroom or learning center environment.

The environment should be enjoyable and produce a sense of achievement in the child. Restrictive environments (only one way to do it) produce more failure than success. Computers offer new avenues for visual, language, motor, perceptual, and cognitive development and should be used in this light.

For additional information on the above criteria see Tipps (1984, 1987), Beaty and Tucker (1987), and Swick (1987). Practices that support the effective integration of computers into quality programs include: the deployment of the hardware in a natural context, relating software to the overall goals of the curriculum, integrating computer usage into other learning activities in the program, sequencing programs according to the developmental levels of the children, provisions for extending program concepts to other learning stations such as the block center, and the deployment of software that invites creative participation by the children. Buckleitner and Hohmann (1987, p. 340) synthesize the current picture as well as the challenges confronted in making computers a viable part of quality early childhood programs:

> In short, we have found the computer to be an educational asset when integrated into a developmental program in a way that supports the curriculum goals. Major effort needs to be directed toward identifying the contributions computers can make to children's learning and to early childhood educational work. Moreover, new materials and systems to aid children's learning need to be developed.

References

Beaty, J., and Tucker, W. *The Computer as a Paintbrush: Creative Uses for the Personal Computer in the Preschool Classroom.* Columbus, OH: Merrill Publishing, 1987.

Brown, M. "Play as a Learning Strategy for Acquiring the Symbolic Abilities Required in Mathematics and Literacy." In K. Swick (Ed.), *Math-Technology in Early Childhood Education: A Resource Guide.* Columbia, SC: College of Education, University of South Carolina, 1987, 48-62.

Buckleitner, W., and Hohmann, C. "Technological Priorities in the Education of Young Children." *Childhood Education,* 1987, 63(5), 337-340.

Chukovsky, K. *From Two to five.* Berkeley, CA: University of California Press.

Harlow, S. "The Computer: Humanistic Considerations." *Computers In the Schools,* 1984, 7(1), 43-51.

Isenberg, J. *Microcomputers in a Developmentally Based Program: Assets or Liabilities?* Paper presented at the National Association for the Education of Young Children Conference, Los Angeles, November 1984.

Kamil, C. *Young Children Reinvent Arithmetic: Implications of Piaget's Theory.* New York: Teachers College Press, 1985.

Knight, P. "Software Evaluation and Selection." In K. Swick, (Ed.), *Math-Technology in Early Childhood Education: A Resource Guide.* Columbia, SC: College of Education, University of South Carolina, 1987.

Papert, S. *Mindstorms: Children, Computers, and Powerful Ideas.* New York: Basic Books, 1980.

Sweetnam, G. "Computer Kids: The 21st Century Elite." *Science Digest,* November 1982, 85-88.

Swick, K. *Math-Technology in Early Childhood Education: A Resource Guide.* Columbia, SC: College of Education, University of South Carolina, 1987.

Swick, K. "Rural Teachers Integrate Technology into Their Early Childhood Education Programs." *Rural Schools,* in press.

Tipps, S. "Computers: A New Learning Environment for Young Children." *Dimensions,* 1984, 13(1), 15-18.

Tipps, S. "Early Childhood Learning in the Computer Age." In K. Swick, (Ed.), *MathTechnology in Early Childhood Education: A Resource Guide.* Columbia, SC: College of Education, University of South Carolina, 1987.

Ziajka, A. "Microcomputers in Early Childhood Education: A First Look." *Young Children,* 1985, 38(5), 61-67.

Kevin J. Swick is Professor of Early Childhood Education and Director, Math-Technology in Early Education Project, University of South Carolina, Columbia, South Carolina.

Article #12
Who Can Draw With a Macintosh?

BY
BONNIE
MELTZER

Five-year-old Nick goes over to the bookshelf in his classroom and pulls out a small bound book. Even though he has a copy of this book at home, he still likes to turn the pages and show his friends the drawings he has made. His teacher says he has gained confidence from the book project.

Shaun just didn't want to stop drawing. He even gave up going to outside recess so he could continue. Even though he just turned four years old, he drew for almost an hour. The ability to draw white on black made it easier for him to see the images.

With each shape that Bryan drew he had a story. It changed from Sister falling down, to Grandpa and Sister with their new hats by the Christmas tree.

All kids (and adults for that matter) can use a boost of self-esteem. But it is especially crucial for the children described above to feel more confident. All of them are hearing-impaired to some degree. Bryan and Nick are in total communication classrooms, while Shaun is in an oral/aural classroom.

As part of a special project with the Portland Public Schools, I was invited to bring my Macintosh computer to three primary classrooms of hearing-impaired children to teach drawing. Some of the students, including Shaun, were also vision-impaired. In addition, one child in the project had cerebral palsy, and one had been in a coma the previous summer. The book commanding Nick's attention was created by Nick and his classmates on the Macintosh. The finished pictures were laser printed, then photocopied and bound. It was a great challenge for the kids and for me. I think we all rose to meet it.

I spent the equivalent of one week at an elementary school in Portland, Oregon. Most of the time was spent with individual instruction, although the whole classroom came together for demonstrations. I was amazed how few words I needed to teach the students before they could use the Mac. Two classes used sign language, while the third was an oral class. Their initiation lesson consisted of my holding their hands over the mouse and making the various moves and selections with them.

I was reminded of learning to ride a bicycle: my mother held the bike and ran with it, and when I felt steady she let go. I tried to do the same thing with teaching the use of the mouse. When I sensed that the students were steady I would let go. On a fresh "page" they would just begin to draw by themselves. In the classes that used sign language, a translator was by my side for questions that either I or the children had. Most of the questions or statements were about drawing and not about using the Macintosh. Typical questions from me: "Where is the dog's nose?... Do you like your drawing?" Typical answers: "I want to draw a horse. Yes! Print! More!"

We concentrated on drawing with one brush shape. I started them with black, but soon moved on to the different patterns. The circles and the rectangles were next. The majority of the group stayed with these tools. As some became more comfortable with the new "crayon" I would introduce a new tool or idea. One little girl just loved the paint bucket.

456

"Undo" was a favorite, as was double clicking on the eraser to make the whole screen disappear. Magic tricks! A few children even learned to select and hold down the option key to get a duplicate. More magic. Each child got to type his or her name by hunting and pecking. Remember that these kids were from three- to seven-years old. Some were just beginning to read; most were not. If they had a comment to make, we would type it under the drawing. They all would have liked more time on the Macintosh, but most of them had three turns of about 20 minutes each. After 20 minutes or so I would pry one child off the computer and give the next eager one a chance.

I used *MacPaint 4.5* because of its uncluttered menu and its ease of use. More recent versions and other drawing programs have too many options, creating a visually more complicated menu. For instance, not having automatic scrolling becomes an advantage with small children. It confines them to drawings of screen size, which enables them to see the total image. *MacPaint 4.5* can no longer be purchased, but almost anyone with a Macintosh has the old program. It used to be the only paint program, and it came with the computer.

No adaptive hardware or software was needed for the visually-impaired students, although an enlargement program was available. As each drawing was finished I printed it immediately on the ImageWriter. With each pass of the printer head, the hovering children would follow its movement. After everyone had a turn, I printed all of the drawings, two to a page, on my LaserWriter. Printing with the LaserWriter made the drawings blacker and bolder. Making the book helped the students remember the experience, but more importantly, it gave value to what they were doing. Everyone got a book to take home. It looks terrific.

For all the children it was the first time that the computer was used as a creative tool. Some of the children had played games or used the classroom computer for drill. This time there were no templates to follow. They were free to create. A blank screen was before them, ready for their creativity. All the drawings were made completely by the children. I did not add or delete anything to make their pictures "look better."

The variety of skills learned by drawing on the Macintosh is extensive. The first is obvious to a computer class, while the rest are more subtle.

1. **Keyboarding and Mousing**
2. **Shape Identification:** Perfect squares, rectangles, and circles are easy to draw and recognize with a Macintosh.
3. **Object Identification:** Deciding what to draw and how to depict it is fundamental to making artwork.
4. **Eye/Hand Coordination:** Making the connection between what occurs on the screen and the movements of the mouse is especially consequential to the physically handicapped child. For one severely motor-impaired girl in the class it was her main accomplishment.
5. **Controlled Movements:** To move the mouse, hold down the button, and actually draw something was quite difficult for the children with motor problems. The more the children drew

> Each child got to type his or her name by hunting and pecking. Remember that these kids were from three- to seven-years old.

on the Macintosh, the more they were able to control the designs they were making. The printed page was tangible proof of the control they had accomplished.

6. **Visual Stimulation:** The Macintosh patterns create additional stimulation for visually-impaired children. They needed no prompting to try each pattern in the menu. The results were intricate and exciting drawings.

7. **Language Stimulation:** Many children, like Bryan, told me about their pictures. Sometimes they would have the idea first and try to draw it, but at other times the drawing stimulated their imaginations. The symbiotic relationship between words and images encourages children to communicate.

8. **Creative Expression:** This was the initial reason for doing the project—to bring an art program to the classes. All of the previous skills help toward encouraging creativity.

Computers will be a vital part of the adult lives of these three- to seven-year-old children. Deaf people are especially dependent on the written word. Modems will be used more and more to communicate information in the future for the hearing and the hearing-impaired. Becoming computer literate is a great equalizer. With the use of computers, disabled people can become independent. The earlier they become computer literate the better. This project certainly helped put the children on the road to computer literacy. In addition, they improved their self-confidence, enhanced their visual skills, enriched their language skills, encouraged their creativity, and most important, they had loads of fun in the process.

Bonnie Meltzer, 9124 N. McKenna, Portland, OR 97203.

EMERGING TECHNOLOGIES

Chapter 7

1. "Videodisc Software: Levels and Use." Gregory C. Sales. *Computing Teacher,* March 1989. pg. 35.
2. "Software's New Frontier: Laser-Disc Technology." Therese Mageau. *Electronic Learning*, March 1990. pg. 22.
3. HyperCard K-12: What's All The Commotion?" Ariella Lehrer. *Classroom Computer Learning*.
4. "The Multimedia Sandbox: Creating a Publishing Center for Students." Fred D'Ignazio. *Classroom Computer Learning*, October 1989. pg. 22.
5. "The Multimedia Classroom: Making It Work (Part 2of 2)." Fred D'Ignazio. *Classroom Computer Learning,* December 1989. pg. 36.
6. "Through the Looking Glass." Fred D'Ignazio. *Classroom Computer Learning*, December/January 1989/1990. pg. 25.
7. "Applications of Videodiscs in Education." Gregory Sales. *Computing Teacher*, May 1989. pg. 27.
8. "Multimedia Curriculum Development: A K-12 Campus Prepares for the Future." J.D. Couch and A.J. Peterson. *T.H.E. Journal*, February 1991. pg. 94.
9. "CD-ROM: A Technology that is Steadily Entering School Libraries and Classrooms." Roxanne Mendrinos. *Electronic Learning*, January 1990. pg. 34.
10. "Beyond Videodiscs: Compact Discs in the Multimedia Classroom." Judy Salpeter. *Technology and Learning*, February, 1991. pg. 33.
11. "The Rich Potential of Educational Television." Michael N. Milone, Jr. and Holly Brady. *Technology and Learning*, January 1991. pg. 21.
12. "Distance Education in U.S. Schools." Chris Clark. *Computing Teacher,* March 1989, pg. 7.
13. "Telecommunications in the Classroom." Therese Mageau. *Teaching and Computers,* June 1990. pg. 18.
14. "Distance Learning." Isabelle Bruder. *Electronic Learning*, April 1989.
15. "Breaking Down Classroom Walls: Distance Learning Comes of Age." Gregory Jordahl. *Technology and Learning*, February 1991. pg. 72.

Introduction

Our students are inundated by constantly changing images as they grow up in an MTV world. They are surrounded by videos and images that show the world at war; they view movies at a greater rate than ever before. They watch MTV before and after school for stimulus and relaxation and they view sports programs that are offered 24 hours a day. Have you ever counted the number of times the image changes in a 60 second MTV presentation? We have—it changes every 2-3 seconds. Compare that statistic with some classrooms where the image changes every 35-40 minutes! Obviously, these are two extremes but you can understand why our students are sometimes bored.

Take the impact of visual imagery to the classroom and use it as a motivation and instructional tool in the learning process. Research is now indicating that more of our students are visual learners than we first anticipated. The emerging technologies of laserdisc, CD-ROM, and distance learning provide the tools for using visuals in the learning and teaching process. The accompanying computer software allows students and teachers to have control of what they see, and in what order they view it. More recently developed computer software tools such as HyperCard, Linkway, and HyperStudio provide users with presentation tools. Students and teachers can create their own visual representations of world news, historical conflicts, science experiments or a simple narrative.

No longer is it necessary to show a 20 minute video or 16mm film to illustrate a concept that could be viewed in a 60 or 90 second video clip. The ability to store numerous stills and video segments on a laserdisc, for example, enables a teacher to access these images within seconds. The user can freeze-frame the image on a CAV laserdisc, and then continue with the segment, all at the touch of a mouse or a button on a remote control device.

The evolving technologies challenge the many current educational practices of "chalk and talk" but they complement and encourage individual expression and cooperative learning. These new tools allow us to give students the ability to generate non-linear, non-text formats that represent group decision-making. For example, a group of students could complete a video paper illustrating the feelings of children from both Israel and Palestine using ABC News' "In the Holy Land." Or groups within a class could be given the task of defining what "Hatred in the Holy Land" means from a historical perspective using the same ABC multimedia material.

As you read the articles, list strategies and methods that you can use to incorporate visuals into your classroom to make it exciting and exhilarating. What is more important, note the tools that are being developed for student and teachers to present their own visual compositions and reports.

The ability to reach the isolated learner and to connect students internationally has been a quest for many educators since the early 1980s. The increased use of satellite communication systems and telecommunication systems to connect people over long distances has become a reality in many schools as a result of decreased costs, equipment availability, and proficient use.

Students can now compare, for example, acid rain data they have collected across the country and hypothesize why the data are different. Teachers can interact with students in remote rural areas and provide course content that was previously unavailable. Several "distance learning" technologies are currently available for transmitting information and knowledge but, more importantly, it provides a means to implement the "global community" concept.

The first article by Greg Sales describes three levels of videodisc use by educators. Initially, many teachers will begin using this technology with a Level 1 application by holding a remote control. By pressing the appropriate buttons or a bar-code reader that reads a bar-code imprint on the instructional material package the user can access moving or still images.

Others will begin with the computer controlling the videodisc player through programs such as HyperCard and Linkway. The software programs give the user greater control of search functions and allow the teachers to organize their own presentations.

Therese Mageau raises some very interesting questions in her article on "Software's New Frontier: Laser-Disc Technology." For example, she asks: What are the pedagogical implications of using visual nonlinear instructional materials in the classroom? Are the new platforms as educationally valid as their proponents say? What is more important, she reflects on the larger question of: can publishers and educators be successful in implementing a technology based on new ideas about how children learn in a world that may still be linked to old metaphors of teaching and learning?

She also raises another important question related to the integration and alignment of this material with mandated curriculum frameworks: "Will laser-Disc technology be any different?" These evolving technologies must make the teacher's job easier, not more difficult. After you view a particular laserdisc or CD ask the publisher how the material is integrated into your curriculum or how you can adapt it to meet your district's instructional objectives.

With decreasing funds available for schools, not all superintendents can allocate sufficient moneys to purchase multimedia hardware and software. Fred D'Ignazio, in a series of articles, describes several different approaches to multimedia design and implementation. For those on a low-tech budget, the articles are full of ideas. Yes, your students can become multimedia scavengers—it will amaze you what they can find and deliver! These KISS (Keep it Simple to Survive) techniques will provide the foundation for more sophisticated approaches and tools you can implement when funds become available.

Educators have been using media for instructional purposes for decades: movies, slides, maps, charts, audio-cassettes, video-cassettes. But as Gregory Sales suggests, with the introduction of videodisc, students and teachers have more control over the material through content selection and presentation tools. The videodisc can be used for direct instruction and instructional support or for independent research. Some educators are even considering its use for testing students.

Other optical media are finding a place in the classroom. A CD-ROM disc can store vast amounts of texts, images, and sound, making it useful for data base searches. It is not possible to store large amounts of video (moving) images on CD-ROMs with existing technologies in schools. As this technology is developed to include video, and the cost is much lower, it may be an ideal technology for schools.

Judy Salpeter explains the acronyms DVI, CD-I, CDTV, and describes their application and potential in the education and home market. Will a CD-I player become the multimedia station in every home? Will CDTV become a reality for schools? She lists several cautions and several possibilities for using digitized text and video in the learning process. Beware of "vaporware" in some of these developments. Can you visualize a single machine with many of the above technologies included? What would it look like?

Television has been around for 40 years. Why is it beginning to have an impact on classrooms again? We are a nation of TV watchers and producers are re-packaging many TV programs for educational purposes. Training programs (whole language teaching, AP courses, veterinary surgical techniques) are becoming popular in all avenues of life.

Schools are also becoming television producers and consumers. Milone and Brady describe several ventures by schools as they use this medium to promote effective interaction and learning. Throughout the article note that students can be active learners with many educational television programs. CNN, for example, now invites students to submit original video programs for broadcast on CNN Newsroom.

Whittle Communications' Channel One has created some negative responses by leading educators, as to the role of commercials supporting educational TV in schools. What is your reaction to this response? How would you involve students in your classroom with Channel One?

Reaching the isolated learner through satellite and telecommunications systems can be very compelling. Chris Clark presents an overview of the different types of technology, and the issues involved as students and teachers are linked nationwide to share learning experiences. Many teachers believe that telecommunications can be used to teach the curriculum as it motivates children to learn by providing an expanded audience, breaks down the isolation of a single classroom, and helps children understand that they are part of a world community.

"Distance Learning" is easier said than done! While this technology presents enormous possibilities and avenues for learning, it has not achieved anywhere near its potential. Educators are effectively using the technology to reach remote learners. There are examples of audiographic teleconferencing and satellite connectivity technologies as tools to support the learning needs of rural students. Should these strategies and technologies find their way into the urban and city classrooms?

In Conclusion

New and evolving technologies will continue to bombard the education system. Some teachers are still trying to recover from or even acknowledge the introduction of the personal computer in the late 1970s. However, as your students will spend most of their adult life in the 21st century we must provide them with the skills they will need to survive in that age.

Our responsibility becomes enormous but we must continue to adapt these new and evolving technologies into our classrooms. Interactive multimedia provide some exciting tools for both teacher and student. Distance learning and telecommunications systems provide the opportunity for connectivity across state and national boundaries.

The challenge is before us: we must develop techniques and strategies that incorporate curriculum mandates, evolving technologies and continued staff development to meet the demands of the 90s.

Questions for Discussion

1. How can teachers provide access to the evolving technologies for all students? Will the gap between the haves and have-nots grow as new technologies are developed? What strategies can be implemented to prevent this trend?
2. Interactive multimedia promotes a different paradigm for learning. The non-linear approach may not be an appropriate strategy for all students. Conversely, the visual learners can access a plethora of images to create an exciting learning

environment for them. How do teachers construct appropriate environments for all students that incorporate the evolving technologies?

3. Telecommunications and distance learning environments have not reached their potential. How can educators promote the effective use of these technologies? What types of activities are relevant for this type of environment?

4. Educators do not agree on the educational value of television. Divide the class into two sections and debate the educational viability of television.

Questions from the Readings

1. What are the advantages of Level I videodisc use?
2. Why are few educational videodiscs created for Level II use?
3. Why would you use a Level I application?
4. What is an "idea" map? What is its function? Do you agree with the concept?
5. What are Walter Koetke's research findings on the use of interactive multimedia?
6. What is the function of ABC News' "documentary maker?"
7. What does Fred D'Ignazio mean with his term "KISS?"
8. How could you create a publishing center using D'Ignazio's ideas and suggestions?
9. What are D'Ignazio's seven layers of multimedia?
10. How would you use a videodisc for direct instruction?
11. Can you use a videodisc for testing purposes? How?
12. What resources can a school use to initiate and implement a multimedia lab?
13. List 5 advantages or uses of a CD-ROM disk in a classroom.
14. Where would you locate a CD-ROM player? Why?
15. What is the difference between videodiscs, DV-I, CD-I, and CDTV?
16. List 3 advantages of using CD-I and CDTV in the home.
17. How would you use TI-IN if you were teaching in Iowa?
18. Are the commercials on Channel One an unnecessary intrusion into your classroom?
19. How do you select appropriate educational television programs for classroom use?
20. What is audio-graphics? How would you use it in a rural setting? Urban setting? Why would you consider it?
21. What is "Kids Net" or "Kids Network?" Why would you use it?
22. How would you use telecommunications to expand your students' horizons?

Article #1
Videodisc Software: Levels and Use

By
Gregory C.
Sales

For years instructional videodisc software did not seem to exist outside of business-funded training programs, laboratories, and conference demonstrations. This was due, at least in part, to the prohibitively high costs associated with developing or acquiring software of commercial quality. Development costs commonly ran over $100,000 per disc. Purchase prices for commercial videodiscs ranged from $1,000 to $10,000.

The increased demand resulting from the growing installed base of hardware, advances in production techniques, and increasing interest in the technology have helped to bring costs down. Many interactive instructional discs are now selling in the $100 to $1000 price range. Other discs which can be used in support of instruction, such as documentaries and visual data bases, are available for as little as $30. Several different types of instructional videodiscs are available, each with its own advantages and disadvantages.

Instructional Videodisc Levels

To help standardize communications about videodisc software, several categories have been agreed upon. These categories are referred to as levels. Each level can be identified by characteristics of the software and hardware system required for its use. As the levels of software increase, the level of interactivity and the sophistication of the hardware required increase.

Level I: At this level the videodisc is used for teacher-mediated presentations. As the videodisc is played, the sequence of displays, pauses, and checks of student understanding are determined and controlled by a human instructor (no computer control is present). Student interaction is limited to viewing, listening, and discussing the presentation with the teacher and other students.

Advantages

- relatively inexpensive software
- needs only a player and monitor to operate
- easy to use for large group instruction

Disadvantages

✓ requires a teacher to design and deliver every lesson
- does not store performance data
- limits direct/active involvement of students

Level II: Videodiscs at this level contain a computer program on audio track II. The presentation of the instruction is mediated by this program after it is read into a microprocessor built into the videodisc player. Students interact with the instructional presentation via a keypad similar to a remote control for a television. Based on student input the computer program regulates displays, branches, pauses, and so forth.

Advantages

- lessons are preprogrammed
- lessons are interactive
- effective for small groups and individualized instruction

464

Disadvantages

- requires a player with a built-in microprocessor
- programming cannot be modified after the disc is pressed

Note: The program controlling a level II videodisc can be rendered ineffective by turning off the audio track II when booting the disc. This technique can be used to force level II discs to operate as if they were level I.

Level III: The videodisc presentation is computer-mediated. A videodisc and accompanying computer disk are required. The entire instructional presentation is controlled by the program contained on the computer disk. Lessons can be designed to allow students to interact with the presentation through any computer input device (e.g. keyboard, touch screen, mouse). Performance records can be stored on disk and maintained by the computer.

Advantages

- lessons are preprogrammed
- lessons can be very interactive
- performance data can be stored

Disadvantages

- requires a computer controlled system
- expensive software

In addition to these levels, several different definitions of level IV videodisc software have emerged. These definitions have tended to focus on technical features of the disc production and hardware requirements (see Phillipo, 1988; Circus, 1987). They do not reflect advances (beyond a level III system) in the mediation of the presentation or involvement of the student(s).

Teaching Uses by Level

A creative instructor, equipped with the appropriate tools and knowledge, can take any level of videodisc and create a wide variety of lessons. However, as you may have deduced from the preceding descriptions, different levels of videodisc software are better suited to different types of instruction.

Level I. Level I videodiscs are produced with instructor-mediated delivery in mind. The images and/or motion sequences on the disc focus on specific content such as mammals, a country, or the work of a particular artist. Often this material is selected with the idea that an instructor will be using it much as he or she would a collection of slides or videotape footage. For these reasons, level I videodiscs are often most appropriate for use with large groups where teachers can interact with students, leading discussions and directing students' attention to important details of the presentation.

Level II. With this level of software the need for a human instructor becomes optional. The instructional design for the content of the disc is programmed when the disc is produced. These discs teach specific content or provide students with specific experiences. An instructor may choose to serve as the keypad operator, inputting decisions at the directions of the students or elaborating on the instruction in large group settings. In small group settings several students may share the decision-making and keypad operation. Some level II discs have even been designed especially for small groups. These discs require each student to take an active role in the instruction. One problem with using level II discs for unsupervised instruction is that they are incapable of storing records of student performance.

Level III. The union of the videodisc player with the computer makes this level a particularly powerful instructional tool. The capability of complex program design makes computer-assisted management of students and detailed record keeping possible. Level III software can also take advantage of the wide variety of computer input devices. Lessons become highly interactive, requiring frequent input, delivering sophisticated feedback, and adapting to each student based on his or her performance. For these reasons, level III videodisc instruction is often most appropriate for use in individualized instruction.

The levels and uses described above provide a brief overview of videodisc software as it is today. Just as the attributes of the different disc formats (described in Part I of this series) result in the discs that are best used in different ways, the attributes of the different levels of software help to determine their most appropriate uses.

Summary

Increases in the number of videodisc systems available in educational settings and decreasing production costs have resulted in a wide range of instructional videodiscs. These discs represent three basic levels, each of which has specific capabilities and limitations. Lower level discs are less expensive and operate on less sophisticated hardware, but rely on the teacher to mediate the presentation. As the level of the disc increases it generally becomes more expensive, or becomes more technology dependent.

References

Circus, J. (Presenter). (1987). *Inter-act '87 Teleconference* [Videotape #1]. International Interactive Communications Society. San Diego. CA: UC Chico.

Phillipo, J. (1988). Videodisc players: A multi-purpose audiovisual tool. *Electronic Learning.* 8(3), 50-52.

[Gregory C. Sales, University of Minnesota Curriculum and Instructional Systems, College of Education ,130 Peik Hall, Minneapolis, MN 55455]

Software's New Frontier: Laser-Disc Technology

By
THERESE
MAGEAU

A new definition of educational software is emerging. No longer is software viewed simply as the little square disks that go into microcomputer slots. Software industry and education leaders now see software as any platform that can electronically deliver instructional materials, regardless of the kind of machine it runs on. And the newest platform at the frontier of the 1990s is laser-disc technology—specifically, videodisc and CD-ROM platforms.

But wait a minute! How can people be talking about laser-disc technology when classroom teachers are still struggling to integrate standard educational computing into the curriculum. While acknowledging that the metamorphosis is still a ways off, industry and education leaders believe that the emergence of this nonlinear, interactive software is a result of profound changes in the way we understand how children learn, and that it will have a more profound impact on the future of teaching.

"I think we're seeing a shift in the educational design elements of software," says Dr. Paul Resta, director of the University of New Mexico's Center for Technology and Education, "and these [new] kinds of software are in effect the result of a change in how we view the learning process."

The software that first made its way into classrooms and computer labs 10 years ago "really emerged out of one particular view of learning," Resta says. This view was deeply influenced by B. F. Skinner's theories about the stimulus-response nature of learning, and educa-

tional software, with its question-response-feedback format, reflected that model.

Because more recent research shows that children learn better actively, nonlinearly, visually, and cooperatively, the software publishing industry has made great attempts in the last decade to adapt software to these new models. But until the emergence of videodiscs, with their ability to give teachers and students random access to thousands of visuals, and CD-ROM, with its capacity to allow learners to explore enormous amounts of textual data in a nonlinear fashion, software developers were somewhat limited in how they could help students be proactive, visual learners. As Apple Multimedia Labs manager Kristina Hooper explains, "I now have the tools to show what I used to theorize about."

From a publishing industry standpoint, these new technologies mean new players on the software development scene. Who are they and where do they come from? Can these new players compete in the school market with the established educational software publishers? Are the established publishers themselves embracing the new platforms?

As these emerging technologies slowly make their way into schools, some questions worth considering include: Are the new platforms as educationally valid as their proponents say? What are the pedagogical implications of using visual, nonlinear instructional materials in the classroom? Is the new technology affordable, from budget and time perspectives?

467

And, perhaps most important, can anyone—publishers or educators—be successful in implementing a technology based on new ideas about how children learn in a world that is, in Resta's words, "still linked to our old metaphors of teaching and learning?"

The Technology

The two current major platforms in laser-disc technology are videodisc and CD-ROM. While both formats have their followings, "the established base out there is videodisc, and I see that for the next several years, says Richard Pollak. founder and president of the St. Paul-based Emerging Technology Consultants, an educational technology and marketing group.

This established base saw its beginnings in 1982 when Optical Data Corp. released the first commercially available educational videodisc. Getting teachers used to the idea of nonlinear video was one of the biggest obstacles encountered by Optical Data co-founder and president, Bill Clark. To *this* day it remains a challenge. "The idea of being able to randomly access visuals and control what and when and at what rate the visuals appear on the screen—that is a degree of control totally alien to people."

User control is key to laser-disc technology. Videodiscs' increasing popularity is to a large extent, a result of giving teachers control over the medium despite their hesitations. "Look at teachers' attitudes about instructional television and why it failed," says John Phillipo, director of instructional leadership and technology for the Merrimack Education Center in Chelmsford, Mass. It gave teachers increased access to instructional materials, but it limited their control in terms of when they could watch it, what the students would see, and whether or not it would correlate to their instructional design," says Phillipo. "Videodisc technology increases teachers' access to learning materials, but does not in any way restrict their control. Level one videodisc is the only technology in the last three decades that can make that statement."

Level-one videodisc gives the user access to any of the 54,000 frames on a videodisc via a simple remote control or bar-coding device. Punching in the number of a frame, or running an electronic "pen" over the bar code assigned to a particular frame, will bring the frame up on-screen, with no searching, fast forwarding, or rewinding required. Level-three videodisc (level-two videodisc, roughly equivalent to the electronic touch-screen kiosks commonly found in shopping malls, is, with the notable exception of IBM's InfoWindow system, rarely used in education) requires a computer hookup to the videodisc player that enables users to both access and order the visuals in any manner they wish.

While level three allows teachers more sophistication—they can go in and create their own video sequence, for instance—the degree and ease of control depends entirely on the interface, the software the computer uses to access the videodisc. To date, *HyperCard,* Apple Computer's icon-based authoring program, and other hypertext applications,

> "Videodisc technology increases teachers' access to learning materials, but does not in any way restrict their control."

like IBM's *Link Way,* are the most common videodisc interfaces in education.

Where is CD-ROM's established base in education? According to Pollak and other industry observers, CD-ROM has entered schools mostly through the libraries. "I see it more as a resource," says Pollak, "because what can you do with CD-ROM? You [can] put lots of data on it."

Lots of data, of course, is the particular province of the reference-book world, and so far most of the CD-ROM activity has been in the reference area. Several encyclopedia companies, including Groliers and Britannica, have put entire sets of encyclopedias on a single disc. Significantly, CD-ROM represents perhaps the best chance for textbook publishers—who have largely failed at developing microcomputer software—to successfully enter the educational technology market. There is much talk in the industry, however, that CD-ROM will not remain solely a text platform as technological advances will allow it to eventually handle moving images (see box below for related story).

The New Publishers

One of the more interesting market phenomena is the growing list of companies trying to establish themselves as educational publishers through the new laser-disc medium—notably, companies who have made their names and fortunes in entertainment such as Lucasfilm, filmmaker George Lucas' production company, and ABC News, both of which have made substantial inroads into the educational videodisc business. The entertainment industry clearly knows how to create a visually exciting product, but does it understand education? Can Indiana Jones teach our children geography?

"We're not trying to do this alone," acknowledges Craig Southard, director of Lucasfilm Learning Systems, an outgrowth of Lucasfilm's games division. "We're essentially working with partners who have the 'educational credibility' but maybe don't have the production skills, the creativity to turn that educational curriculum and pedagogy into something that is interesting or useful in the classroom."

Jane White, education director for ABC News Interactive, a new education division of ABC News, agrees. "We are not trying to be educators. We are trying to stay very close to what we can provide educators, to make their lives and their jobs more interesting, and the interaction between kids more exciting."

To that end, both Lucasfilm and ABC News Interactive have teamed up with established education companies, National Geographic and Optical Data respectively, to produce interactive videodisc programs. White feels that ABC has learned valuable lessons since their first program, *Vote 88,* which they produced independently (but which Optical Data is now distributing).

"We didn't know what the educational community needed," she concedes. "We knew how to put together documentaries, but those aren't designed for the curriculum, for use in the classroom." So ABC went to Optical Data and consulted directly with teachers and curriculum specialists. The result, White feels, is a product more responsive to "what happens in the classroom."

Competing With MTV?

But entertainment's presence in education is sparking another debate, at the heart of which is the question: how important is an "exciting" visual presentation—which everyone acknowledges is entertainment's forte—to the educational value of a product?

Southard believes it is crucial. "We are targeting a whole segment of the popula-tion in the classroom that is completely turned off to education," he says. "You've got to make the classroom interesting to them and you've got to make it meaning-ful. But first and foremost you've got to

Which Disc Is In Your Future?

You may have heard people pros-elytizing about various laser-disc technologies—videodiscs, CD-ROM, CD-I, DVI—and arguing over which platform is likely to be the platform of the future. If you're confused, you aren't alone. Some of the more respected people in the industry will confess, in a private moment, that they don't quite un-derstand what any of it means.

Essentially, the debate is over whether digital or analog signals are the best way to store and transmit data. Digital platforms, like CD-ROM, can store enormous amounts of text in very efficient ways, explaining its popularity with companies like the Library Corp., which puts all the Li-brary of Congress' English-language holdings on three 4.75-inch discs. Digi-tal platforms can also store small bytes of sound and RGB (red, green, blue) graphics. But digital signals don't handle moving images.

If this were all that were true, it would seem there would be no debate: why not put large amounts of text on CD-ROMs and motion pictures on vid-eodiscs, and call it a day? Ah, but nothing in technology comes that easy. The controversy centers around ex-pected—but as yet unseen—advance-ments in digital formats. The idea is that if motion can be digitized, such as in CD-I (compact disk interactive) and DVI (digital video interactive), users will have an unheard of amount of access to and control over the me-dium. CD-I, proponents claim, will be able to store tremendous amounts of moving images on a digitized platter, far more than the 54,000 currently stored on an analog videodisc. CD-I is not interactive in and of itself, but because the images are digitized they can be transferred to an interactive digitized format, such as DVI, to be manipulated. With DVI programs, viewers not only can call up a video sequence of, say, a room, but through simple commands can zoom in on and pan the room—manipulating images in the room and simultaneously do textual investigations, all on the same screen. When this technology is both possible and affordable, the argument goes, analog technology like video-discs will be a thing of the past.

Most people seem to agree that some form of digitized motion video will be in our future, but no one agrees when that future is. Some say the capabili-ties already exist and that it's a mat-ter of the technologists holding out for the market to catch up. Other will tell you it will be years—some even say 20 years, although most estimates are more liberal than that—before educa-tion will see anything in digitized video that will come close to the visual clar-ity of videodisc.

make it interesting because we're competing with MTV for the hearts and minds of the kids."

Tom Snyder, founder and chief designer of Tom Snyder Productions (TSP), believes, however, that "there are ways to intrigue kids that don't have to compete with MTV. The problems with educational software are not that the graphics aren't powerful enough," he says, "but that the structure of the software has nothing to do with a school environment."

Scholastic Software publisher Peter Kelman agrees, "You put these tools in the hands of some very talented filmmakers and people who are visually clever and know a lot about gimmicks," says Kelman, "but who really don't know a blessed thing about education or the content they're dealing with, and what you come out with is flashy, and to my mind, not very valuable. I worry about that because I don't want it to spoil the field."

But Marge Kosel, vice president of Sunburst Communications, which has recently opened up a new office in California to produce interactive multimedia products, isn't worried. "Entertainment people in the industry only stretch imaginations," she says. "They usually have more money than we do in educational development so they can help set standards and stretch imaginations about what can be done. And then we can apply it in our own little way," she adds laughing.

The Old Publishers

Sunburst's presence in the interactive multimedia market is in many ways an interesting phenomenon. While indisputably a successful and respected developer of microcomputer software,

Sunburst is considered one of the least flashy publishers in the industry. Why is a company whose emphasis has never been visual going into a highly visual medium?

"When you're in the market you have to stay up with the market," says Kosel. "Technology is always changing. Therefore we have to change."

CD-ROM is on the publishing agendas of four prominent microcomputer software publishers—Tom Snyder Productions, Scholastic Software, CompuTeach, and Microsoft Corp. "We're looking at CD-ROM as a way of getting enormous amounts of pictures, sound, and data into the classroom very cheaply," says Snyder. TSP plans to release a social-studies/problem-solving program this year—tentatively entitled *Idea Map*—that will run on MS-DOS machines and work with an as yet unnamed CD-ROM data disc.

Scholastic Software has its eye on CD-ROM, but is holding off on publishing for it and instead is executing what Kelman calls a "strategy to bridge from now to later." This May, Scholastic plans to release *Point of View*, a "history processor" that will give students a programmatic context in which they can explore all the U.S. census data for the past 200 years. The program and the data will all reside on several Macintosh disks. "I think in 1990-91 we're going to see Macintoshes being bought in very significant numbers," says Kelman, "and within a couple of years CD-ROMs are going to be part of [microcomputers] just as 800K floppy disks are now. Kelman's next step will be to put *Point of View* on CD-ROM in two to three years and add music, graphics, and more data.

CompuTeach president Dave Urban says that his company plans to introduce its first CD-ROM program within the next 18 months. "The only delay," says Urban is the cost of the hardware. We're waiting for it to come down in price.

Microsoft, which currently sells *Bookshelf,* a CD-ROM of writing reference texts, says that it has "between 81 and 100 people working on revising current titles and creating new titles for CD-ROM," according to product manager Craig Bartholomew.

And Optimum Resources Weekly Reader Software has announced that it has entered a partnership with American Interactive Media, a CD-I (compact disc interactive) development group. "We're looking at working together on a number of products," says Optimum Resource's Sally Carr Hannafin.

What about other established microcomputer software publishers? Are other companies moving in this direction? MECC has already produced two interactive videodiscs that focus on training teachers to use interactive multimedia. Ironically, even though MECC has beaten some of its competitors to the interactive punch, it is also the most circumspect about committing itself to a future in interactive media. "We're testing the waters with these discs," says Susan Shilling, MECC's vice president and creative director. "There are no set persons at MECC assigned to videodisc development. We're just looking right now."

MECC and Brøderbund both carry third-party laser-disc courseware in their catalog. But Brøderbund is making no public statements about their publishing directions. What many microcomputer software publishers, including Davidson & Associates have said echoes The Learning Company's Pat Walkington, who states, "We think these are outstanding technologies and we're definitely looking into them, but at this point we've made no commitment to

developing for CD-ROM, videodisc, or multimedia."

One reason why everyone is not jumping on the multimedia bandwagon is the enormous cost involved in production, particularly videodisc production. "We can't afford to create videodiscs," reports Scholastic's Kelman. "We don't own the footage."

The going rate for video and film footage is about $3,000 a minute. Still photographs can sell between $100-$500 per image, and considering that a videodisc has 54,000 frames, the cost of filling them at prices like these can be staggering, leading David Borhman, executive producer of ABC News Interactive, to comment: "Only a few people can do this. It's the people who have the archives who will succeed."

Sunburst's Kosel disagrees. "There's a lot of stock footage available," she says. "But a lot of it has to be reshot. There are certain parts of stock footage you can use, but if you're going to get a good application of videodisc, you're going to end up shooting."

Does It Fit the Curriculum?

A major criticism of much of microcomputer software—and perhaps one of the reasons it has not revolutionized teaching the way pundits thought it might a decade ago—is the difficulty teachers have integrating it into their curricula. Will laser-disc technology be any different?

According to Bill Clark, it has to be. "Teachers today are saturated, and if you're going to push something in the front door, something has to go out the backdoor. Whatever you're replacing you have to have a very compelling argument that it's going to make the job easier for the teacher or it is going to be more effective for the student."

How can publishers make teachers' jobs easier through interactive multimedia? To Merrimack's John Phillipo, the answer lies in tying the medium to the textbook. "There are probably 30,000 science teachers in America using D.C. Heath science books," he says, "and they are all being told, go get that filmstrip, or get that video, take students to this type of habitat. Good videodisc would be sensitive to the directions of the curriculum the teachers are trying to implement. The classroom is still driven by textbook publishers, whether we like it or not because students can put hooks under their arm and go home with them. You can't go home with multimedia."

Is interactive multimedia more effective for the student? Walter Koetke, director of Research and Development for Scholastic, vigorously supports the idea. "Because of research we've done, we've learned that sound and visuals, particularly when they're under the control of teachers and kids, are a very powerful learning device," says Koetke, who is working on a videodisc package under the sponsorship of Commodore. "What can you really do with learning when you're talking about motion video combined with music and sound? The answer is, according to research, virtually everything. I can impact people's emotions, and since emotions are how our memories are organized, I can clearly have a big impact on learning."

Large data storage capacity is another reason educators believe that laser-disc technology can play a key role in helping children learn better. Emerging Technology's Richard Pollak believes that the switched emphasis from access (getting to the information) to manipulation (what you do with it) "is going to change education." The question will be, says Pollak, "how can our kids in the future use all this information to their benefit?"

Tom Snyder has the same question. "One idea I'm not sold on that comes along with videodiscs," he says, "is that all you have to do is give kids access to enormous amounts of data that's indexed in delightful new ways and kids will spend all their time poring over this information. After a little bit of time it won't happen any more than it happens that kids pore over the encyclopedia." To that end, Snyder's design aim in *Idea Map* is to give kids programmatic "incentives to browse," which he believes are the cornerstone of discovery-based learning. "I don't think it's enough to say that the sexy new presentation is going to turn our kids into browsers."

How Much Does It Cost?

What about costs to educators? Can schools afford laser-disc technology? Right now, the price of a CD-ROM disc averages around $300, and a videodisc can range in price anywhere from $30 to $1900, but averages for educational discs (which usually include microcomputer software and teaching guides) are around $500. While admitting that prices appear steep, most videodisc publishers cite the enormous costs of production (including the costs of archival film and video footage), and the still relatively modest sales, as factors. "I think there's a problem with users looking at the price of a disc and not having a perspective on what's involved in making one," says Joe Clark, founder and president of Videodiscovery. When you start to build a data base that's information-dense, that's a lot of money."

John Phillipo agrees that educators have to look at product cost differently than they have in the past. "We need more prudent financial analysis," says Phillipo. We have to create an economy of scale."

Economy of scale, according to Phillipo, means that educators should look at a piece of software—any kind of software—and determine its "cost per objective." If a math videodisc costs $1,200 and covers grades 3-6 and meets 85 objectives, and if a piece of microcomputer software costs $85, and meets only three objects, what's the cost per objective for each?" he asks. "That's the kind of change [in the purchasing process] that has to go on in schools. Otherwise, at face value, it's too expensive."

Joe Clark also acknowledges that he had hoped "that the market would take off faster so that I could reduce the price because I'm interested in running a business that contributes to education and not exploiting a market. If we can get the number of orders up we can reduce the price, and we will."

The cost of hardware is the other half of the story. What's the best way to get more of the hardware into schools? "I think what changes education is price breaks," says Emerging Technology's Pollack. "What allows us to get that equipment into the classrooms? It's lowering costs."

Joe Clark takes it one step further. "Equipment producers are not very forthcoming in planting equipment." Clark cites the example of Apple Computer back in the early 1980s when they literally gave Apple IIs away with the idea that the value of the equipment would be perceived and that would lead to bigger orders. The videodisc companies are not at amenable to that [idea]."

Paul Zimmerman, Eastern zone sales director for Pioneer, a major supplier of videodisc players to education responds that "Pioneer has made significant concessions for lowering prices. For example, the LD-V 2000, the bottom of the line player, has dropped from a list price $735 to $595 because we recognized the need for a low cost player [in education]."

Zimmerman says that "our early sales just do not support giving away equipment. We're spending our marketing money trying to make the technology visible—to create an awareness." As part of that effort, last year Pioneer made a major commitment to help seed the conversions of over 200 Encyclopedia Britannica Education Corp. and AIMS Media titles from film and VHS format to videodisc.

What are hardware prices? Pioneer recently released the 2200 model videodisc player that list prices at $895. There are also widespread but unconfirmed rumors that Tandy will release a CD-ROM player that will sell for between $200 and $300. Tandy's currently available external drive costs $995. Are these prices budgetable? "I think schools can budget in the cost of a videodisc player," says Dori Bower, Videodiscovery's director of marketing, "especially with the new Pioneer 2200." Many industry observers also suggest that schools can enter laser technology into their computing budgets by designating the hardware and software as peripherals.

> One hears about other emerging technologies, like CD-I and DVI. Should educators wait to see what happens before they make an investment?

Making an Investment

Is it realistic that education can incorporate this technology and this approach into the school environment? John Phillipo points out that most schools have a librarian, a media specialist, and a computer coordinator. "In most cases these individuals are very independent and not interactive," says Phillipo. In a typical school if I wanted to create a multimedia lesson I might have to go to the library to get the videodisc, the computer coordinator to get the computer, and the multimedia specialist to get the videodisc player. We need better organizational structures to support the classroom teacher."

The issue of feasibility becomes even more complicated when the question of technological stability arises. How can decision-makers who want to take some first steps toward interactive multimedia be assured that the investments they make now in equipment and software won't become obsolete in five years? One hears about other emerging technologies, like CD-I and DVI. Should educators wait to see what happens before they make an investment?

This question concerns John Phillipo, whose job it is to advise schools about their technology purchases. "My fear, and I'm as guilty as anyone else is about this, is if I continue to encourage schools to keep on using videodiscs and *Hyper-Card*, at what point do I have to start advising differently? When is that zenith going to happen? When this industry switches over and decides that it has the capacity now to merge digitized image with digitized text, who is going to be left holding the bag? The guy who is developing the disc has the ability to go either way today."

One answer Phillipo has found is that schools "need to have a plan. Most schools just acquire the technology and use it. There's not a plan for the on-going development of the equipment, which includes obsolescence. The plan should include the fact that the technology will be replaced at some point. I refer to it as staging and phasing." As schools stage

in what they're going to buy, they have to phase some things out. "Something has to go," states Phillipo. We have to stop buying 16 millimeter projectors."

But the investment is emotional as well as financial. An admitted technophobe before she began working for ABC News Interactive, Jane White cautions teachers who have reservations about getting involved with technology. "If you are waiting for the river of technology to stop before you make a commitment, you're going to be waiting a long time. Because technology is not going to stop. And it's important to be able to understand how it can provide a really amazing experience."

For Apple's Kristina Hooper, laser-disc technology provides tools "that finally allow us to match how we teach with how children learn. The most important thing we've discovered about learning," Hooper says, "and it's something we've always instinctually known, is that it is an active process, a difficult and intense endeavor." Interactive multimedia technology, through its "rich visual, textual, and acoustic domains, can provide learners with unheard of opportunities to actively and efficiently gather new knowledge and create new ideas."

Hardware-Software Partnerships

Where do the major microcomputer hardware companies—Apple, Commodore, IBM, and Tandy—figure in to the interactive multimedia picture?

"One role of hardware companies is to show what's possible," says Kristina Hooper, manager of Apple Multimedia labs, who has co-developed many multimedia projects with software publishers and technology enterprises. Hardware companies must play a much more active role, Hooper says, because of the many diverse elements involved in multimedia products. "It's not simple software production any longer."

Other companies would agree. "I don't think any of these products can be done in a vacuum anymore," says Howard Diamond, director of education for Commodore. Commodore has been working with Walter Koetke, director of research and development at Scholastic, to co-develop a junior/ senior high social studies interactive videodisc. Koetke and his team (which is distinct from Scholastic's software division) are developing the programs to work with the Amiga—a microcomputer generally acknowledged to be highly suited to multimedia—using Commodore's as yet unnamed and unreleased icon-based authoring program. Commodore has made, says Koetke, "a very significant investment" underwriting the entire development costs of the project.

> "I'd have to be honest and say that we haven't been as aggressive as Apple or IBM in sponsoring and supporting projects. Suffice it to say we are becoming more aggressive."

IBM has funded similar projects, notably TLTC *Physical Science,* a ninth-grade interactive science program co-developed with the Texas School Board Association for the IBM InfoWindow system, an interactive touchscreen system housed in a computer kiosk. "It was very powerful and it was very expensive," reports IBM vice president Jim Dezell. "What we're going to do now is take those functions that reside on InfoWindow and make them available on standard IBM PS/2s" either through a card or other add-on devices.

IBM is currently working with National Geographic and the Smithsonian Institution. "What we hope to do is bring our technology and our technical expertise together with those people who own the data bases and have the subject-matter knowledge. Out of that we hope we can produce exemplary kinds of products as joint ventures."

Is IBM going to release a personal computer with a CD-ROM drive? "I can't announce unannounced products, but if we're not working on a CD-ROM product somebody ought to be fired," says Dezell.

This spring Radio Shack/Tandy will release a 5.2-inch internal CD-ROM drive that will fit into their computers. While Tandy won't sell computers equipped with the drive, Tandy owners can obtain it through special orders.

Jim McGrody, Radio Shack vice president for marketing and sales, acknowledges that Tandy has not nurtured the same kinds of partnerships with software companies as his competitors. "I'd have to be honest and say that we haven't been as aggressive as Apple or IBM in sponsoring and supporting projects. Suffice it to say we are becoming more aggressive."

But McGrody has reservations about multimedia that other hardware vendors don't seem to share, or at least, voice. While McGrody states, "there's no question that there is a market opportunity with multimedia and it "can help provide solutions, he does question its role in education.

"I don't know if multimedia will ever become a mainstream activity. It's a very expensive hobby. How many collections of hardware can you reasonably expect to have in a school district? We have some concerns that this may be more sizzle than reality."

Article #3
HyperCard K-12: What's All the Commotion?

By
ARIELLA
LEHRER

Since Gutenberg's invention of movable type, books and magazines have remained essentially unchanged. Text and pictures are organized sequentially with one topic following the another...this, despite the fact that our minds remember and store information in a manner more akin to a spider web than a straight line.

As long as 40 years ago cultural soothsayers such as the late Vannevar Bush, science advisor to President Roosevelt, foretold the ability to jump about electronically within large amounts of text, linking related ideas, following particular tangents that directly reflect our needs or interests and allow us to bypass irrelevant information. During the 1960s Ted Nelson, another computer visionary, coined the term "hypertext" to refer to such a powerful and flexible environment.

Since then the concept of hypertext has been expanded to encompass other media as well; the terms "hypermedia" and "Interactive multimedia" have both been used to refer to the ability to link not only words but still images, sound, and video. Today, hypertext and interactive multimedia are becoming a reality—through the development of products such as *HyperCard*.

Apple Computer introduced *HyperCard* in August 1987. While not the first product of its sort ever to be developed, *HyperCard* has attained broader distribution and acceptance than any of its competitors, in part because of Apple's marketing strategy: the company provides a free copy of *HyperCard* with every new Macintosh computer sold. (Macintosh owners who purchase their computers before August, 1987, and have the required configuration—one megabyte of memory and two 800K disk drives or one 800K drive and a hard disk—can purchase *HyperCard* from an authorized Apple dealer for $49.) The accessibility of *HyperCard* to so many Macintosh users has spawned an entire cottage industry of low-cost *HyperCard* applications, which have further contributed to *HyperCard's* popularity.

But What Exactly Does It Do?

HyperCard and other hypertext-based programs like it define a new genre of software that makes it possible to represent knowledge and information just as we do in our minds—nonsequentially, by association and context.

HyperCard programs are assembled in *cards,* much like a file box of index cards. Collections of cards form a *stack.* Each card contains one or more mouse-activated *buttons* which lead to related cards. Buttons can also perform calculations, trigger animated sequences, play sounds, and even control a peripheral such as a videodisc player or CD-ROM drive.

You can develop your own stacks by creating cards and then typing in text, designing illustrations using *HyperCard's* drawing tools, pasting in graphics from other applications, and placing buttons on the cards to link them. You can control any object (a button, field, card, or stack) by writing a script in *HyperCard's* English-like *HyperTalk* programming language to determine what that object does.

A Tool for Teachers?

"So what?" you might ask. "It sounds like just another authoring program." In the past we've seen numerous authoring systems that promised to make software design easy for teachers and other non-programmers. Yet such systems have languished in the hands of educators, primarily because most teachers simply do not have enough time to develop their own software applications.

Why then has *HyperCard* generated so much interest on the part of educators? In part, it's because the HyperTalk tools make it relatively simple for beginners to achieve dramatic results. While creating an original stack still takes considerable time and planning, the process is easier with *HyperCard* than with many other authoring systems. And modifying any of the growing number of commercial and teacher-authored stacks is easier still.

In addition, the structure of the *HyperCard* environment lends itself well to educational applications. In learning a new concept, we often compare one idea to the next, build analogies, make connections. *HyperCard* stacks mirror this process, allowing users to navigate easily through vast quantities of new information and to make many more such associations.

Finally, *HyperCard's* popularity is due in part to its value as a tool for interac-

---

In learning a new concept, we often compare one idea to the next, build analogies, make connections. *Hyper-Card* stacks mirror this process, allowing users to navigate easily through vast quantities of new information and to make many more such associations.

---

tive multimedia development. With *HyperCard* you can create programs that access a wide variety of computer peripherals.

The Teacher as Information Manager

In the world of business and government, a number of information providers have discovered the joys of *HyperCard*. For example, the U.S. Department of the Interior recently wowed the various watchdog agencies to which it reports with a *HyperCard*-based analysis of thousands of pages of budget documents. "Some people thought that somehow we had rigged the press conference," says Bob Lamb, director of the Division of Budget Operations. "Whenever Secretary Hodel would talk about a topic, we'd open up cards that addressed it. They couldn't believe we could access facts on so many random issues during the secretary's question-and-answer period."

Such a process can be equally powerful in the classroom. By building *HyperCard* stacks with information on a particular topic, a teacher creates a flexible tool that can be used for classroom presentations. Imagine, for example, that you are teaching a unit on medieval life to a class of high school students. You have created text-based cards relating to daily life, describing laws and government, and discussing the role of religion. You have scanned in pictures, maps, and diagrams illustrating the dress, architecture, and history of the period. And you have access to CD and videodisc players with relevant music and video enactments.

Midway in your explanation of the morality play *Everyman*, a student raises her hand and asks about the treatment of minorities during this period. Using the "find" or "keyword" feature in *HyperCard*, you locate linked cards under daily life ("serfs and slaves"), under laws and government ("law of exclusion"), and under religion ("forced conversion of Jews during the Crusades"). You later access video segments from the movie *Becket*. As you continue the lesson, you are able to improvise and go into more detail related to the questions being asked. And when the bell rings, you can freeze the day's discussion, so that next time you can pick up right where you left off.

Promising Projects in Development

While few teachers have the time or resources to create such an elaborate presentation tool from scratch, we are likely to see some dedicated groups of educators working together during summers and sabbaticals (often with the help of grants and hardware donations) to develop stackware for others to use.

One such project is underway in San Francisco. High school teacher Pat Hanlon and librarian Bob Campbell have been working for several years on an interactive multimedia tool to teach students about life in America in the 1930s. Known as *Grapevine*, this program began as a series of lessons related to John Steinbeck's *The Grapes of Wrath*, and with support from Apple's Multimedia Lab, grew from there. The current version is only a design example, but it provides educators with a glimpse of what's possible. The *Grapevine* project offers students a variety of resources, including a videodisc with newsreels and still images from the 1930s; folk music and oral interviews digitized and stored on disk; a "who's who" stack describing important people of the period; a bibliography annotated with information, pictures, and quotations; several interactive games and quizzes; guided tours of the period, following selected themes; and a "story maker" tool that makes it easy to design one's own tours or "newspaper reports."

Another stack under development at Pepperdine University is a curriculum planning tool for educators called *Learning Navigator*. When completed, this program should make it possible for a teacher to choose a curriculum topic and grade level; search through relevant state curriculum frameworks and district objectives; match these with approved textbooks, software, and video titles that teach the selected objectives; and then link up with daily weekly, and monthly lesson plans—all in a matter of minutes.

Still other promising products are being developed by commercial software and hardware producers as well as by institutions such as National Geographic, the Smithsonian, various television stations, and others who have access to large quantities of film footage and still images. One interesting example that will soon be available to educators is *Interactive Nova: Animal Pathfinders,* a joint project undertaken by WGBH television, Peace River Films, and Apple Computer. Based on an episode from the *Nova* television series, *Animal Pathfinders* focuses on several topics relevant to junior high and high school biology students: animal behavior, migration, ecology, and habitats. With a Macintosh computer hooked up to a videodisc player, users can view still frames and video sequences, create their own presentations, select from a set of pre-planned "guided explorations," or take part in game-like learning activities.

Existing Stacks

Animal Pathfinders is now available while *Grapevine* and *Learning Navigator* are currently design examples only. So what's out there for educators who want to obtain educational stacks today?

One of the most interesting new educational products on the market is *The '88 Vote* from ABC News Interactive and Optical Data Corporation. Based on the actual *HyperCard* stacks used by Peter Jennings to research and organize information for television coverage of the 1988 presidential election, the program offers text, graphics, and extensive video footage on the primaries, conventions, candidates, and key election-year issues. Teachers and students can browse or request video "help" from Jennings. They can view a transcript of any speech on the Macintosh screen as it is being delivered or print it out to be read later. (A notemaking tool allows them to add their own commentary before printing.) It's also possible to switch back and forth between the actual soundtrack and the videodisc's second sound channel with commentary by ABC's political director, Hal Bruno. And using the program's flexible "documentary maker," teachers and students can cut and paste video sequences to design their own custom presentations.

While multimedia products have particular appeal, there are many other useful stacks that require only *Hyper-Card* and a Macintosh computer. A number of these are instructional programs developed by educators and distributed by software exchanges set up to allow individuals to sell or swap stacks that they themselves have created. Others are commercially developed interactive stories for children. Still other *Hyper-Card* stacks of interest are general purpose tools that can be used by teachers and administrators to keep records and organize their time.

Students as Authors

Despite the number of commercial and teacher-authored stacks being developed, many educators believe that *HyperCard's* greatest value is as an authoring tool placed in the hands of students. Instead of pencil-and-paper reports, students using *HyperCard* can design original presentations or lessons for their classmates. Geography and science reports take on new life with the help of on-screen maps and diagrams that change scale at a user's request, animated sequences that illustrate a point, and several levels of detail available through the use of help buttons. And students take a new interest in the writing process when presented with the opportunity to design HyperCard-based interactive fiction.

HyperCard gives young people the chance to be information manipulators and disseminators, not only information gatherers. As they design their own

> HyperCard gives young people the chance to be information manipulators and disseminators, not only information gatherers.

stacks, they are forced to decide not only what information to represent, but how to represent it: a graph documenting polling results? Photographs of famous people? A video of a historical event? By focusing this sort of attention on a particular topic, they learn to view the topic in a new and more sophisticated way.

The Future

Judging from the enthusiasm of educators and students who have used *Hyper-Card,* it looks as though *HyperCard's* popularity in schools will grow in years to come. However, the process may be a slow one at first. While the number of Macintoshes in K-12 classrooms doubled between 1987 and 1988, there are still relatively few of the machines in high schools, and even fewer at the elementary and junior high levels.

In addition, although new educational stacks are appearing every month, many potential users are having difficulty finding out about them. As better resources are developed to provide teachers and administrators with information about available stackware and distribution channels, the use and acceptance of *HyperCard* will undoubtedly grow.

As it does, we are likely to see some significant changes in education and in the publishing and broadcasting industries. *HyperCard* is already sparking new Macintosh software development at a lower overall cost to customers and raising users' expectations as to how flexible and easy to customize programs should be. It may also be the catalyst that convinces many educators to invest in and use a variety of computer peripherals such as videodisc players, CD-ROM players, LCD projection devices, optical scanners, and audio digitizers. In response, we can expect program develop-

ers of all sorts to find new ways of combining the vividness of film and animation with the depth of print media and the flexibility of good software.

Ariella Lehrer is president of Lehrer Associates, an educational consulting firm in Los Angeles specializing in software design, evaluation, and marketing.

By
FRED
D'IGNAZIO

Imagine a classroom in which students take on the role of multimedia authors—creating radio shows, movies, books, magazines, advertisements, and slide shows about fractions, prefixes, Spanish verbs, Helen Keller, or any of a variety of other curriculum topics. Imagine productions so fresh and unusual that they are shown to the entire class, to other classes, to the PTA and the local school board; or displayed (and catalogued) in the school library and aired on local cable TV. And, if that doesn't move you, imagine a setting in which the technology involved in such productions—those finicky, malfunctioning machines that seem perversely designed to drive teachers into premature retirement—is managed primarily by students themselves.

Sound unreal? It's not. What you are imagining is a *multimedia classroom,* and teachers in Birmingham, Alabama; Oakland County, Michigan; Blue Earth, Minnesota; Cupertino, California; Nashville, Tennessee; Toms River, New Jersey; and elsewhere have already created such classrooms in their schools.

Multimedia has become a hot new topic in educational technology circles. But if all you think about when you hear the term "multimedia" are the new commercial programs that incorporate computer software with videodiscs (see "Interactive Multimedia: The Next Wave," *Classroom Computer Learning;* September 1989, pg. 56), you ought to think again. Some teachers are taking a differ-

ent approach to multimedia: they are placing the technology in the hands of the *students* and allowing *them* to take on the active role of multimedia producers.

The resulting sense of pride among student authors is amazing. It is one thing to "publish" for your teacher's work folder or your family's refrigerator door. It is something else again if your "publication" is an electronic slide show that the administration displays in the school office, or a book that the school librarian reads to young children, or a movie that the kindergarten teacher shows to incoming parents and children on orientation day.

Better Low-Tech Than No-Tech

"Sounds great," you may be thinking, "but we can't afford it." Perhaps you've had fantasies in the past about becoming a "cutting-edge teacher"—until you looked at the resources available in your school. You may be a daring soul who would love to experiment with the newest technologies (desktop publishing, desktop presentation tools, telecommunications, desktop video, hypermedia and so forth), but the only equipment at your disposal is a 64K computer, a printer, a cobwebby tape recorder, and a VCR and TV, which, from their Victorian styling, appear to be at least a hundred years old.

Take heart. Dozens of teachers are experiencing success with multimedia

483

technologies in schools with scarce resources and skimpy budgets. Their motto: "scavenge, improvise, and trust." Teachers and students scrounge multimedia resources from around the school, from members of the local business community, and from students' homes; and with it they assemble a publishing center—a sort of multimedia sandbox—where student authors and producers can create publications and presentations about topics they are studying in the curriculum.

Why not try using this *scavenged multimedia* approach to assemble a multimedia center for your school? After all, the secret to being a cutting-edge teacher is not in the megabucks of hardware you use in your classroom, but in the ingenious ways you use the hardware to get kids to learn.

Creating a Publishing Center

There is no blueprint for building a multimedia publishing center. Since each school creates the center from materials it scavenges, each center is different.

You can make your school's first publishing center a school-wide process. Other teachers can help you find a wheeled cart which was tucked away and forgotten. Students can take home notes ("published" on the computer) inviting their parents to contribute used equipment from around the home. (Many homes are littered with extra tape recorders, "boom boxes," keyboards, old VCRs, and TVs which parents would love to donate to their school—especially if persuaded that their donations would be used for educational purposes.)

Many teachers report that they began their multimedia publishing centers with fear and trepidation. They had barely mastered keyboarding on a Commodore 64 or Tandy 1000, and now, suddenly, they were leading a group of enthusiastic students who were talking about connecting up a computer, a video camera, a boom box, a VCR, and the classroom's record player. Initially the teachers figured they had to know in advance what to do each step of the way. But they were relieved to find out that this was not necessary—that the students were happy to pitch in and learn with them.

The best tack to use is to follow KISS rule—"Keep It Simple to Survive!" You don't need to assemble a full-fledged multimedia center at the beginning. Instead, start by focusing on one or two media and add others gradually as they seem necessary or important. For example, maybe you want to start your young authors with a simple audio project. You and your class can set up a "recording studio" with an old tape recorder or a boom box that a student brings in. Have students read their stories and poems into the recorder's built-in microphone, and voilà, you have "Literature on the Air," a weekly radio program in which budding young authors do readings from works in progress.

Or you can try a simple movie. First, track down your school's video camera. Have your class figure out how the camera works. Put in a blank videotape and let the students create a simple skit on "Fractions in Everyday Life" or "What

> You don't need to assemble a full-fledged multimedia center at the beginning. Instead, start by focusing on one or two media and add others gradually as they seem necessary or important.

Started the Civil War;" or send them to do a video documentary on "Fire Hazards in Our School," "What Happens if You Get Sick?" "Live Animals in School," or "Pollution on Our Playground."

Just remember, no matter what medium you choose to start with, keep it simple. Your goal is not to train the next generation of Steven Spielbergs and Stevie Wonders. You don't need to create elaborate props, costuming, or special effects: Such things take enormous amounts of time, and you will quickly find yourself overwhelmed and a candidate for *multimedia burnout*. Instead, look for ways to create simple "how-to" productions that will enrich your curriculum and improve students' process skills.

Making Connections

Once you and your students are comfortable with a single publishing medium, you will be ready to begin making the sorts of connections between diverse tools that add magic to multimedia production. For example, you can connect the computer to the VCR using a few inexpensive cables and create colorful titles and credit screens for student-produced videos. Or you can save to videotape computer-based slide shows and animated "shorts" for playback at home or over local cable television.

With the help of the microphone on your video camera or another sound source such as a tape or record player, you can add musical soundtracks and special sound effects to multimedia productions. And, if you eventually find yourself with a bit of money to invest in equipment, the purchase of a single extra tool—a video digitizer or an overlay card, for example—can open up a whole new world of possibilities.

Article #5
The Multimedia Classroom:
Making It Work (Part 2 of 2)

By
Fred
D'Ignazio

In the previous article, I introduced the idea of *scrounged multimedia*—creating a multimedia publishing center using hardware and software already available in your school and community. It takes no more than a few basic tools to get started on assembling a complete edit studio!

After you have gathered some equipment and software (computers, VCRs, graphics programs, music or animation software, tape recorders, and other local finds), you're ready to begin experimenting. You may want to start by exploring each medium—audio, video recording, and so forth—individually. However, eventually you'll want to make connections between the different media.

The key to such connections is a simple, inexpensive cable. If you're using an older composite monitor, you probably already have such a cable connecting the monitor to your computer. If not, the cable you need (referred to by a variety of names including "RCA cable," "dubbing cable," and "multimedia cable") can be purchased from your local Radio Shack or other electronics supply store for less than $10. While you're at the store, you'll probably want to buy several of these cables and a few inexpensive "adapters" designed to modify the cable ends to fit into the openings on the various machines you'll be using. (A 1/4-inch "phone" adapter, a 1/8-inch phone adapter, and a female-to-female adapter allowing you to connect two multimedia cables together for added length should be all you need.)

Marrying Computers and Video

One of the easiest and most magical connections you can make is the connection between the computer and the VCR.

First, unplug the monitor from the computer and run a multimedia cable from the monitor jack on the computer to the VIDEO IN jack on the back of your VCR. Set the VCR for "LINE INPUT" and press the TV/VCR button so that "VCR" is lit up. You will now see your computer image on the television attached to your VCR. If you then place a blank tape in the VCR and press the "RECORD" button (it may be necessary to press "PLAY" at the same time), you can record the computer graphics displayed on the TV screen directly onto videotape.

With the help of your favorite paint program or a specialized package such as Scholastic's *SlideShop*, Epyx's *Home Video Producer,* or Brøderbund's *VCR Companion,* you can use this same connection to add introductions, titles and credit screens to school-made videotapes. (Note: with most common hardware set-ups, this process involves *alternating* video and computer screens rather than *combining* them.)

To add narration to computer-generated videos, the simplest approach involves using another multimedia cable (with whichever phone adapter fits) to plug your school's video camera or camcorder into the AUDIO IN jack on the back of your VCR. The microphone on the camera is now directly wired to

486

the VCR. Your students then read their book reports, term papers, and stories aloud in front of the camera's mike at the same time that computer images are being sent to the VCR, and their voices are recorded onto the videotape to accompany any colorful computer graphics they may have created. They can also add a musical soundtrack by playing a keyboard, record player, or tape recorder in the background while a script is being read.

Multimedia Inventors

Once your students are familiar with these few basic multimedia connections, they are ready to start inventing their own. A little experimenting, for example, is likely to lead them to another way of creating musical soundtracks and special sound effects: by hooking a musical keyboard, a tape recorder, or a record player *directly* into the VCR. (In this case, one end of the familiar multimedia cable plugs into the audio output or PHONES jack on the sound source, and the other plugs into the audio input jack of the VCR.)

A basic understanding of the pathways between the different machines will help your students dream up logical connections. As they encounter each new device, encourage the students to examine the "jacks" (holes) in the back of the machine and identify which ones are INPUT jacks (bringing signals into a device), which are OUTPUT jacks (carrying signals out of the device), and what sort of signals (e.g., audio, video, etc.) each one accepts.

To reinforce these concepts, ask the students to draw "maps" showing how the information flows between the devices. For example, suggest that they draw diagrams with pathways to show how audio and video signals travel between the computer and the VCR when they are hooked up as suggested earlier.

Arrows or color-coding can be used to distinguish between input and output or to indicate the *media content* (e.g., music, voices, images, text) being sent along a particular pathway. With younger children, it's sometimes helpful to have them *act out* the connections, using pieces of colored yarn to represent the input and output cables.

After diagramming some connections that they know (from experience) will work, your students can move on to mapping some *potential* connections. Have them discuss the most promising ideas and then hook up the devices to test their hypotheses.

Not all of your students' experiments will work, but reassure them that they're not likely to harm the equipment or themselves as they explore. In particular, there is no danger of electrical shock from the multimedia cables that connect one device to another. The electrical signals carrying the images and sounds are quite small, and unlike the devices' power cords (which *do carry high voltages* and should not be experimented with!), the multimedia cables present no hazard to students' safety.

> A basic understanding of the pathways between the different machines will help your students dream up logical connections.

Freeze!

In addition to gathering scrounged materials for your multimedia center, you will want to be on the lookout for some newer products that can be obtained at bargain prices. One of the best bargains in the multimedia world—after the multimedia cables—is a simple video digitizer. This relatively inexpensive device makes a new connection possible: it allows the user to capture a live image (using a video camera as the input device) and output it to the computer screen, printer, or floppy disk.

Here's an example of how one digitizer, Digital Vision's *ComputerEyes,* works. After plugging the *ComputerEyes* circuit card into a slot inside your computer and attaching the digitizer's three cables to the school's video camera, computer, and VCR, student publishers boot up the *ComputerEyes* program disk. Pointing the video camera at an object— a guinea pig, for example—they press the RETURN or ENTER key on the computer. A few seconds later a "freeze-frame" image of the guinea pig appears on the computer monitor. *The guinea pig has just became part of multimedia history!* The students have transformed the little creature's live video image into a digital computer image which can be shrunk, enlarged, inverted, scrolled, colorized, and stored on a computer disk.

Once it's been captured, the digitized image can be sent to the VCR through the *ComputerEyes* cable and recorded onto blank videotape. In this way, students can add freeze frames to other video segments, creating dramatic effect. (Such freeze frames often appear at the end of movies or commercials: the action freezes just as a couple embraces or an athlete achieves an incredible feat; the image then remains on the screen as music is played or credits scroll upward.)

Still images captured with a digitizer can be used in other ways as well. With Scholastic's *Slide Shop,* for example, a *ComputerEyes* image can be "imported" as a graphics background for a single slide. *Slide Shop* then lets you "decorate"

the video image with a border and colorful clip art. You can also add captions, titles, and credits, and insert a music or sound effects clip to accompany the slide. Finally, you can link the slide with other slides into a presentation that features animation and special effects.

Once such a slide show is complete, student authors have various publishing options. They can publish *live* by giving an oral report backed up by their computerized slide show. They can publish on *paper* by printing out the slide show screens and pasting them into a book, which they assemble themselves. They can publish in *video* by sending the entire slide show from the computer to the VCR and recording it on a blank videotape. Or they can publish on *computer* by creating a self-booting "show disk" which runs unattended.

Video Overlay

As video overlay cards have started to appear for an increasing number of computers, a whole new world of possibilities has opened up for young multimedia producers. A video overlay card is a board that plugs into the motherboard of the computer and makes it possible to combine video input (from a video source such as a video camera, VCR, or videodisc player) with computer-generated graphics *on the same screen.* Essentially the video signal has two layers: the bottom layer is a video image; the top layer is computer text or graphics.

To understand video overlay better, imagine sitting in front of a TV set while you hold a piece of orange construction paper between you and the monitor. The TV picture represents the video layer the paper represents the computer graphics layer. You can't see the picture on the TV because of the paper. However, if you take a pair of scissors and cut a square hole in the middle of the paper, you can see the TV picture through the hole. What's more, the picture is nicely framed with an orange border.

When you look at a computer video overlay, the effect is the same. If you begin with a screen filled with orange, you cannot see the video picture underneath. However, you can designate another color (usually black) as the "video key color"—an "invisible" color that lets the underlying video picture show through. If you draw a box on the orange screen and fill it in with the key color, you can see the video image framed with an orange border.

Students can use such "windowing" effects in a variety of ways to enhance their video productions. Windows can be small or large; they can be square, oval, or any other shape the student chooses. The printed background or border need not be a single solid color; students can create detailed backdrops (with a graphics program, or by using a video digitizer to capture a video image and save it as a computer graphic) and insert small windows through which videotaped actors appear. (In this way, it's possible to place a student in a fictional setting—on the moon, in a fantasy land, and so on—without creating and filming elaborate sets and props.)

It's also possible to place several video windows on different parts of the screen or to start with the entire screen in the transparent key color and then use a paint or titling program to superimpose credits, labels, or other graphic elements in non-key colors.

> Many teachers manage multimedia by creating student teams that specialize in different parts of the multimedia process.

Next Steps

Depending on your school's resources and the types of computers you use, there may be other multimedia tools available to you as well. If your school owns Macintosh computers, for example, you will have access to *HyperCard;* if you have IBM computers, *LinkWay* is an appealing option. Similar multimedia/hypermedia authoring tools are becoming available for other machines as well and may be worth purchasing for your publishing center.

Other multimedia gadgets that are gaining popularity include audio digitizers (useful for computers that have sound playback capabilities and sufficient memory), videodisc players, scanners, frame grabbers (which can digitize individual frames from moving video or computer images), CD-ROM players, and a host of new MIDI musical devices. You will be reading more about these newer technologies and their applications in future issues of *Classroom Computer Learning*.

The People Connection

In a multimedia classroom, no one needs to know everything. And every person can make a contribution. Many teachers manage multimedia by creating student teams that specialize in different parts of the multimedia process. Here are some teams which teachers have created: brainstormers, researchers, writers, producers, reporters, musicians, camera whizzes, print magicians, and slide producers. The equipment in a multimedia center can be used together, but it is usually divided up for use by different specialist teams. For example, the musicians get the musical keyboard, the reporters get the video camera, and the print magicians get the computer and printer.

Good organization also helps deal with the problems of limited time and scarce resources. Many smart teachers have realized that much of the multimedia thinking, collaborating, writing, and researching can be done *before the multimedia equipment ever arrives.* The key is to view multimedia publishing as an *add-on* to current classroom activities and not as a replacement.

Multimedia offers great potential to educators at all grade levels. It can help bring even the driest areas of curriculum to life and turn the classroom into an exciting, studio-like arena. One technology expert referred to the 1990s as the "Multimedia Decade." That means that we have many years to learn and grow. But now is the time to get started!

Fred D'Ignazio is President of MultiMedia Classrooms, Inc. *4120 Okemos Rd. Suite 24, Okemos, MI 48864; (517) 337-1549. He conducts teacher workshops all over the U.S. and Canada, and is a national leader in the areas of multimedia, emerging technologies, and cooperative learning.*

Great Ideas For Multimedia Projects

Here are just a few of the exciting multimedia projects that students and teachers around the country have completed:

• A fourth-grade class at West Elementary School in Vestavia Hills, Alabama, produced a weekly "Science Radio" show. The program offered current-events tidbits, tutorials on the weather, math brain twisters, a listener "call-in" segment, and more. Although the resulting program was not actually broadcast over the air waves, it was a big hit within the classroom where it was "aired" with the help of a tape player. At the end of the year, the students took a field trip to a local radio station and had the opportunity to collaborate with the station's disc jockeys on a program that was broadcast to local radio listeners

• A kindergarten teacher at Cahaba Heights Community School in Birmingham, Alabama, took a small "mini-cam" crew of student producers to a pumpkin patch. The students shot a video of their Halloween pumpkin growing on the vine, being cut, and being hauled back to the classroom. The class then cut open the pumpkin, took out the seeds, and created a jack-o'-lantern, videotaping each step and showing how the pumpkin could be integrated into math activities, including counting, estimation, measuring, place value, and graphing. The students showed the video to other classes and the teacher showed it at inservice workshops.

• A sixth-grade class at the same school created a video yearbook out of segments shot by students at important events during the school year. The class sold dozens of tapes and made enough money to buy new multimedia equipment.

• Another project at Cahaba Heights Community School involved a class of sixth-graders who were studying the environment, toxic waste, and pollutants. The students hiked along a river bank near the school and gathered data. They published their findings in several media, including books, videotapes, and audio recordings, and mailed the resulting projects to local members of Congress and TV stations. The students also made presentations to their parents, to the school board, and to the PTA.

• Middle-school students at Royal Oak Schools in Royal Oak, Michigan, interviewed their classmates on video, asking them what they remembered about Dr. Martin Luther King. The students then developed a printed, video, and slide-show publication on King's accomplishments and his place in American history.

• In Gardendale, Alabama, a class at the Gardendale Elementary School sent a crew of student reporters around the state to research state history and geography. The student reporters were equipped with a tape recorder, a video camera, a Polaroid camera, notebooks, and pencils. The entire class then reviewed all the images, sounds, words, and pictures that had been collected and assembled them into lessons which they published and shared with other classes and the school PTA.

• A fifth-grade science class at Blue Earth Elementary School in Blue Earth, Minnesota, shot video segments about their community during different seasons in the year. Then they spliced the segments together to show the effect of weather and climate on plants, animals, buildings, and human beings.

• Third-graders at Hewitt Elementary School in Trussville, Alabama, created a video called "The Last Warriors" based on native American folk tales and myths. The class designed backdrops and props using a computerized paint program and then videotaped popsicle-stick characters acting out the story in front of the computer backgrounds.

• Other third-graders at Hewitt Elementary took a trip to the zoo, where they took notes about the animals they saw, videotaped them, and recorded animal sounds. When they returned, the students digitized the animal images on the computer and added descriptive captions and animal sounds. The young authors then created an electronic slideshow which categorized the animals by distinguishing characteristics (mammals, fish, large animals, small animals, plant eaters, etc.). They also published an "alphabet book" which was used by the kindergarten class to learn their letters.

• Sixth-graders at Shades Mountain Community School in Birmingham, Alabama, took on the role of political candidates and conducted campaigns for which they created TV and radio commercials promoting their candidacy. They also published promotional flyers, political newsletters, and booklets.

• A teacher at Hope Middle School in Holt, Michigan, created an animated slide show which served as an "electronic flyer" at the school's science fair. The slide show described the science

fair's rules, criteria for judging, and entry categories. It was exhibited just inside the front door of the school where everyone could see it.

• As part of a unit on critical thinking three middle school teachers at the same school created a videotape on decision making. They visited a fire station, interviewed a fire captain and several fire fighters, and added scenes from actual fire emergencies. They then used a graphics program to create several "question" screens which focused students' attention on the key decisions firefighters have to make when faced with a real fire. When the tape was shown to students, the teachers paused the tape frequently and engaged students in discussion relating to critical thinking strategies employed in fire fighting.

• A fifth-grader at Southminster Elementary School in Vestavia Hills, Alabama, created an animated movie of a black hole in outer space. The project earned her first place in the school's science fair. She wrote the script for the movie using a word processor, designed the animation with a computer-based graphics program, and filmed the results with a video camera while she was reading the script aloud and playing the sound track from the movie *Jaws* on a tape recorder.

• At ACOT (Apple Classroom of Tomorrow) sites in Memphis, Tennessee, and Blue Earth, Minnesota, students digitized images of themselves and sent them over the telephone line to other students in distant schools. Students then acted as "foreign correspondents" for the other schools covering news about their community, region, state, and country. They exchanged digitized photos and published them in student newspapers, term papers, and video documentaries.

• A popular multimedia project with the elementary and middle-grade students at the Toms River Regional Schools in Toms River, New Jersey has been the creation of "video storybooks." First, each student used a software program with graphics and text features to create a story. Additional computer graphics were generated to introduce the story using a graphics or video titling program. Then, with the help of a "genlock" device (also known as a video overlay card), a computer-generated byline was superimposed over a live camera shot of each student. This was followed by the student's story, read by the student, with background music dubbed in. The process was then repeated for each class member. The resulting 15-minute "storybook" was aired on the school's closed circuit TV and broadcast to the community on cable through the district's television studio.

• A fourth-grade student at Marble Elementary in East Lansing, Michigan, collected images of whales from videodiscs, videotapes, magazines, and books. He found whale sounds on a record from National Geographic, and stories about whales in "Reader's Digest," in a whale watchers handbook, and in the encyclopedia. The student then created and presented to his classmates an "electronic field trip" to the whales' habitat.

• To culminate a unit on business, special education students at Garfield Middle School in Albuquerque, New Mexico, produce videotapes for others in the school. The students apply for and are given jobs as film crew members, interviewers, researchers, graphic artists, script writers, technicians, editors, narrators, and ad writers. Each team then researches a particular business, visits relevant work sites, and produces a videotape to teach fellow students how the business works.

• Seniors in the world studies classes at Forest Hills Central High School in Grand Rapids, Michigan, have been using telecommunications programs, computer databases, and print resources from around the world to create multimedia presentations on global issues. The presentations take the form of videotapes, slide shows with (audio) taped soundtracks, and *HyperCard* stacks.

Article #6
Through the Looking Glass:
The Multiple Layers of Multimedia

By
Fred
D'Ignazio

Oh, Kitty, how nice it would be if we could only get through into Looking-glass House! I'm sure it's got, oh! Such beautiful things in it! Let's pretend there's a way of getting through into it, somehow, Kitty. Let's pretend the glass has got all soft like gauze, so that we can get through. Why, it's turning into a sort of mist now. I declare! It'll be easy enough to get through..."

—Alice, in Lewis Carroll's
Through the Looking Glass

And You'll Feel Just Like Alice

In a few short years when you look at the monitor screen on your computer, it will be like gazing into Alice's magic looking glass. You will see worlds within worlds, resizable windows into reality, layers of knowledge, images, symbols, animations, and 3D mathematical models.

Perhaps this "looking glass"—these worlds, layers, and windows—will be displayed on a tile-like mosaic of flat-screen monitors "pasted" on the wall behind your CPU, or perhaps they will be squeezed onto a single screen connected to several speaker systems so that multiple audio "windows" can be played and accessed simultaneously with multiple visual (text, diagrams, photos, full-motion video, and animation) windows.

And, there you'll be, Alice-like, perched on the chimney piece, gazing into this looking glass. All the while, running through your mind, will be the question: "what should be my first step?"

BOWs: Buttons, Overlays, and Windows

Before you panic, ask yourself, "what are the things I might do on a multimedia computer?"

It is likely you will be at the computer for one of the following purposes:

- Browsing
- Exploring
- Capturing
- Communicating
- Learning
- Investigating
- Composing

Regardless of your purpose or the make of your computer, you will be working with at least three kinds of basic constructs on the multimedia computer of the future: buttons, overlays, and windows.

Buttons represent "hot spots" or gateways from the information displayed in a single window (card, node, etc.) to information displayed in other windows. You can think of buttons as little jet cars that transport you from window to window.

Windows are the places that buttons take you to. Each window represents a multimedia "knowledge window" (e.g., the window could be an article on Thomas Jefferson from an encyclopedia stored on CD-ROM, a three-minute videodisc clip of the Vienna Philharmonic playing Beethoven's *"Emperor's Concerto,"* an audio database of Melanesian folk mu-

494

Reprinted by permission of: *Technology & Learning* (Formerly Classroom Computer Learning)
© Peter Li, Inc. 2169 East Francisco Blvd., Suite A4, San Rafael, CA 94901

sic, a live news report on an election in Soviet Armenia, or a computer animation of the Voyager 2 spacecraft doing a flyby of Neptune). The windows may be related thematically (e.g., audio, video, graphical, and text representations of "whales") in a single multimedia document (a "stack"), or they may be unrelated parts of different documents.

In a full-blown hypermedia system of the future, each window will be a looking glass of its own into a sort of *visual reality*. Users will have complete control over the representation of reality contained in the window. They will be able to rotate the images in the window, zoom in and zoom out, pause, go into fast forward and reverse, or step through events one step at a time. They will be able to add invisible acetate overlays (see below) to annotate existing windows with text, diagrams, and pictures. Each key word in the window will be automatically referenced to on-line encyclopedias, multimedia databases, dictionaries, and thesauri. A user can resize a window larger to take up dozens of virtual (imaginary, large) screens or smaller to the size of a postage stamp or less. All the while, the window stays active—movies keep playing, animations keep rolling, text scrolls by. The user can dive in at any moment, cut out a slice of reality (a "sound byte," "visual byte," or "thought byte"), and paste it somewhere else in the window or in a different window.

Overlays are layers of windows atop other windows and layers of buttons atop other buttons. The buttons and windows may be invisible, visible, or translucent. The effect of overlays is to make your computer screen into a real, three-dimensional pool of knowledge, much like Alice's looking glass.

Get the picture?

KISS—Keep It Simple to Survive

You won't have to worry about your students diving into this multimedia "looking glass." They will take to it like Alice.

But what's to become of adults who have been schooled for most of their lives in linear, print-based media? How are they to handle knowledge exploration that seems to be some kind of complex combination of *Nintendo, Wheel of Fortune,* and MTV?

In these columns we explored ways teachers can begin to play with multimedia by assembling "scavenged" multimedia centers equipped with desktop computers and old equipment scrounged from around the school. We looked at how such a center could be constructed and for what kinds of activities students might use such a center.

We've kept things simple so we wouldn't get lost. Now it's time to go deeper, to investigate multimedia at all levels. But we'll still follow the KISS rule—Keep It Simple to Survive! This month we'll separate multimedia into seven layers and take a brief look at each layer. Let's begin with the world of the present.

Layer #1: Databases, Publishing, and Telecommunications

This is the layer most computing teachers find themselves at now. Their students are building and accessing databases on science, social studies, etc. They are doing some word processing and perhaps some desktop publishing. And they are making their first attempt to hook up a computer modem and connect their computer to other students' computers across their country and across the world.

At this layer the computer is hooked

up to relatively few devices: a disk drive or two, a printer, a monitor, and perhaps a modem. Most data being processed in the computer is *textual data* (i.e., words and numbers). Databases are purely textual, publishing is mostly textual (with some illustrations to spice things up), and telecommunications is purely ASCII (limited to the 26 letters in the alphabet, punctuation, the blank space, the 10 digits 0 to 9, and one or two control characters such as a carriage return or line feed).

If you are already working in all three of these areas with your students, rejoice! In the world of the 1990s you will be doing these same computing activities—databases, publishing, and telecommunications—except you will add a multimedia dimension to each activity. But conceptually you will still be in the same ballpark!

Multimedia Databases. By attaching computer controlled, random-access devices to your computer such as a laserdisc player and a CD-ROM player, you can enter the world of multimedia databases. With a database program such as Optical Data's *LaserTalk,* IBM's *LinkWay,* or Apple's *HyperCard,* you can access your multimedia database. Your database may be *Billie Holiday's Greatest Hits* (on audio CD), Brøderbund's *Whole Earth Catalog* (on CD-ROM), or Optical Data's *Encyclopedia of Animals* (on laserdisc). With multimedia databases like these and with appropriate software, you can search and retrieve information in the form of text, still images, full-motion video, sound effects, high-fidelity music, audio recordings of famous speeches, and computer animations.

Multimedia Publishing. Major publishers such as Time-Warner, National Geographic, *The Wall Street Journal*, and others, are quickly diversifying beyond *print* publishing to *multimedia* publishing. In the future these publishers say that we should think of them as "information providers" or "content providers" rather than as publishers. In fact they will be multimedia publishers who publish nonprint media (audio tape, videotape, computer software, telecommunications services, etc.) as well as print media.

In the future, students and teachers will also be able to publish in multiple media. They will be able to create student movies, video yearbooks, radio documentaries, computer slide shows, hypermedia stacks, and more. Participating in such services as National Geographic's Kid's Network, they will be able to collaborate with other teachers and students in remote classrooms and *telepublish* original scientific findings on major environmental issues such as acid rain. Programs are now being tested that will enable students to compose *multimedia documents* by cutting and pasting segments from such sources as news programs, PBS documentaries, compact disc music, and on-line databases, and assembling them into a final multimedia file that can be stored on a computer disk.

Multimedia Telecommunications. Wire services such as AP and UPI, newspapers, and magazines use the phone system to transmit photographs and artwork *(infographics)* along with numbers and words around the globe. Television and radio broadcasters transmit moving images and sounds via satellite almost instantaneously across thousands of miles.

In the 1990s, satellites, faster modems, higher-speed desktop computers, and videocompression techniques will make it possible for students in widely dispersed classrooms to capture and share images and sounds as part of their multimedia publishing and multimedia databases. "Eyewitness" student reporters will be able to collaborate with fellow students across continents to assemble newspapers, hypermedia stacks, databases, and videos from original materials they have collected in their community. Multimedia pen pals will be able to exchange videos of their families, classmates, school sports, and extracurricular activities. Student scientists and researchers will have access to the image, voice, and words of famous experts and policy makers from all over the globe for use in student multimedia term papers and science projects.

Layer #2: The Computer-Video Connection

As we saw in the second column ("Multimedia on Wheels"), all layers of multimedia begin with one simple connection—between a VCR and a computer. On most computers all you have to do is take the monitor-cable out of the computer monitor and plug it into the VIDEO IN jack of a VCR. With a blank tape in the VCR and the VCR set to "Record," you can begin recording crisp, clear computer images directly onto videotape—without a video camera or expensive hardware or software!

Layer #3: Audio and Video Digitizing

Digitizing—converting electronic signals into digital (binary, "on-off") format—is also at the head of multimedia. Digital codes for words and numbers were devised at the dawn of the computer age in the 1940s, so most computer processing has been limited to numbers and words. Now new devices—audio digitizers and video digitizers—are becoming available that allow us to convert music, sound effects, voices, video images, artwork,

and photographs into computer files. Once these pictures and sounds are digitized they can be stored on a computer disk, recalled, and manipulated by any of a variety of computer music programs, paint programs, slidemaker programs, and desktop publishing programs.

Digitizing is accomplished by plugging a digitizer circuit card into the motherboard of a computer. The circuit card has cables or jacks that allow you to connect your computer to a video source such as a video camera or an audio source such as a record player. The digitizer card also comes with a software program stored on a computer disk. When you run the program you can activate the digitizer card to "capture," "grab," or "freeze" the sounds or pictures coming from the external source and convert them into a binary digital file inside the computer.

There are many different kinds of video digitizers. A *frame grabber* captures an incoming video frame in 1/30 of a second and transforms it into a computer graphic. Frame grabbers are expensive. Less expensive video digitizers may take up to six seconds (or 180 frames) to create a digitized image in the computer. In addition, there are *scanners* that scan pages with printed text, graphics, and photos and transform them into computer image files.

Audio digitizing is known as *sampling*. A sound wave is captured by a microphone or input jack and piped into a computer. Samples of the sound wave are made by the sampling program then recorded as digital codes inside the computer's memory—the higher the number of samples per second (typically 5K, 7K, 11K, or 22K), the more lifelike the digitized sound.

Sound waves that have been digitized can be displayed on the computer screen then cut, copied, pasted, and manipulated just like words in a word processor. A sampled sound can also be piped into a sampling keyboard that has MIDI (Musical Instrument Digital Interface) jacks. The sound becomes a "musical instrument" that can be played, at different pitches, on every key on the keyboard. This is remarkable, considering that the sound might be anything from a jazz saxophone to a water fountain, a fire alarm, a person's voice, or seagulls overheard outside the classroom window.

This ability to capture, manipulate, and control sound waves allows student producers to create *audio environments* that will greatly enrich their multimedia presentations.

Layer #4: Video Overlay

Another word for video overlay is *genlock*—locking the signal from an external video source underneath a picture being generated by the computer. The words "video overlay" come from the process of overlaying the graphics image from the computer atop the video image. To see video overlay in action, turn on your TV set, turn down the volume, and watch the screen. Pay special attention to news programs and commercials. Whenever you see graphic images appear on the screen atop video images, that's "video overlay."

When would you use video overlay in the classroom? For example, a student might interview the mayor for a videotape "term paper" on municipal efforts to counteract pollution. After shooting the interview of the mayor the student would rewind the videotape to the beginning of the segment, then cable the video camcorder to the INPUT jack of a video-overlay circuit card installed in the computer. This would feed the video signal into the computer, and the mayor's image would appear on the computer screen. Now the student could load a paint program into the computer, frame the mayor's image inside a bright blue graphics box, and type the mayor's name and title (as a *chyron)* across the mayor's chest. The final image (video plus graphics) can be quite snazzy!

Video overlay is accomplished by plugging a video overlay (or genlock) circuit card into the motherboard of the computer. The circuit card has cables or jacks that allow you to hook up a video source for INPUT and a video destination for OUTPUT. The input source can be a video camera, a VCR, a videodisc player, or a broadcast TV signal from an antenna, cable, or satellite. After the computer overlays a graphics layer onto the incoming video, the combined signal is output to a large-screen monitor, VCR, or video projector for presentation. Or the signal can be rebroadcast (e.g., over the "public access" channel on local cable).

How does video overlay differ from digitizing? The input source (VCR, video camera, videodisc player, etc.) can be the same in digitizing and video overlay. However, once the video enters the computer, different things happen. The *digitizer* circuit card converts a single frame or still image from the video into a computer graphic image. This image can then be saved as a computer (binary) file on the computer's disk. The *video overlay* circuit card, on the other hand, does not convert the video image into a computer graphic. Instead it *combines* the image with a computer graphic and outputs the combined signal as a standard (*composite* or NTSC) signal to a VCR or TV. Some video overlay cards also output an RGB signal as well.

You can manipulate digitized images (e.g., shrink them, invert them, copy them, expand them). You cannot manipulate video overlay images.

You can *print* digitized images. You cannot print video overlay images. (You can print the graphics layer, but not the video layer.)

Already these simple distinctions are beginning to dissolve. Expensive circuit cards are now available which combine overlay with digitizing. Full-motion video images can be piped into the computer then expanded, shrunk, rotated, and placed anywhere on the computer's screen. This is possible because the images are really digitized images. High-speed computer chips and video-compression techniques (e.g., DVI—Digital Video Interactive) make it possible for the computer to handle these images in color and at a rate of 30 frames per second.

Layer #5: Still-Image Video

Think of still-image video as "video slides." A still-image video camera is used to take a video slide, the slide consists of a single frame of video, stored on a small disk roughly two-thirds the size of a 3.5" disk. Up to 50 video slides can be stored on a single disk—sometimes with a couple seconds of audio attached to each slide.

If you have purchased one of the new still-image "camcorders" (e.g., the device from Canon advertised on television), you can plug video cables directly from the camcorder to your TV or VCR and play your video slides, one by one, on your television screen. If you like, you can save the images on a blank videotape in your VCR in the form of a video slide show and send the videotape home with your students, or mail the tape to "video pen pals" in the U.S. or abroad. On broadcast television; you see still-image video used as a dramatic "freeze frame" at the end of a movie or commer-

cial. For example, at the end of a news program the poignant still-image of a white child playing with a black child might appear while production credits scroll over the top of the image (an example of still-image *and* video overlay).

Still-image video is useful because it can be combined with digitizing and video overlay. You can digitize the still image, then manipulate it and add it as a graphic background in a large number of paint programs and computer slide-show programs. You can also send the still image into the computer as the video layer and add a graphics layer (titles, boxes, clip art, etc.) atop the image.

In the near future still-image video players may have an RS-232C jack similar to the jack on the back of videodisc players. This will allow teachers to connect their computer to their still-image player. The advantage that the still-image player offers over videodisc players is that teachers and students can capture their *own images* then play them back under computer control. The still-image player is also preferable to a VCR because the images on a still-image player can be accessed randomly and almost instantaneously by the computer. This makes the still-image player suitable for use as a device for interactive hypermedia (i.e., nonlinear database search, retrieval, navigation, and reporting).*

Layer #6: Videodisc and CD-ROM

Videodiscs and CD-ROM discs are laser-discs that can be accessed by a computer cabled to the appropriate videodisc player or CD-ROM player. Information is "read" from both kinds of discs by a laser beam being refracted off the disc's surface. A videodisc (in CAV, or computer-readable, format) can hold up to 54,000 still images or up to 30 minutes of live, full-motion video and sound on each of its two sides. A CD-ROM disc typically holds around 500 million bytes or characters of data on its lower side. A videodisc is either 12 inches or eight inches in diameter; a CD-ROM disc (or audio CD disc) is approximately 4.75 inches in diameter.

A videodisc player and a CD-ROM player are connected to the computer as *input-only* devices. Videodiscs and CD-ROM discs can be loaded into the players (one at a time) as multimedia databases (text, photos, full-motion video, sound, and animation) that can be accessed by a computer program running on the computer. The multimedia data on these databases can be accessed much more quickly than data on a VCR, but not quite as quickly as data on a computer's hard disk or internal (RAM) memory.

Until recently only text, diagrams, animations, and digitized pictures and sounds could be stored on CD-ROM discs. Now special purpose DSP (Digital Signal Processing) chips and video-compression techniques make it possible to store over an hour of full-motion video and high-fidelity digital sound on small (4.75" diameter) DVI discs. Audio compact discs can already be accessed interactively by computers (using the same CD-ROM players), and high-fidelity digital sound can be played out of amplified speakers cabled directly to the CD-ROM player.

It is possible to create your own laserdisc or CD-ROM disc for under $600 (as a one of-a-kind *check disc*). In the near future we will see *read-and-write* laserdiscs and CD-ROM discs. Users will be able to record their own multimedia data on these discs, then recall the data using customized database programs.

However, the need for computer speed and storage will become prodigious. A system currently on the market for professional video producers, for example, requires users to hook up seven 600-megabyte hard disk drives to their computers just to store a single hour of live, full-motion video. That's 4.2 *gigabytes* of on-line storage!

Layer # 7: Hypermedia

The definition of hypermedia can be very simple or very complex. At one level, hypermedia is merely a way to organize information *topically* as well as *linearly*. This is the same relationship you see between a book's index and its table of contents. In the table of contents the book's parts (chapters) are listed in order of their physical appearance in the book. In the index, the major topics in the book are listed in some non-physical (e.g., alphabetical) order. Under each topic are lists of pages on which references to the topic can be found. For example, under "reality" in Heinz Pagel's *Dreams of Reason* (Bantam, 1988) you see:

    computer simulations of, 89-90
    depictions of, 163
    differing views, 325-326
    dualistic views of, 11-12

and so on.

In a hypermedia system such as *HyperCard* from Apple Computer, linear and topical ways of organizing a subject can be overlaid, one atop the other. For example, if Heinz Pagel's book were created as a *HyperCard* stack (a sequence of related "cards," pages, windows, or screens), then it would be possible to create *HyperCard* buttons that would let a user navigate linearly or topically through the book. For example, left and right arrow buttons could be used to turn the pages (or "cards") in the book. In addition, key words in the book representing major topics (such as "reality") could be made into buttons. When the user pointed a screen-arrow at one of these words and clicked on the mouse button, *HyperCard* would send the user to the next page in the book on which that word appeared. By clicking on the word again the user would be transported to still the next page. This process would be equivalent to looking up the word in the index and turning to the pages on which the word appeared.

Hypermedia enables users to navigate linearly or topically through an on-line database. This becomes a powerful tool when the database is composed of *multimedia data,* such as text, photos, full-motion video, computer animations, spoken words, musical passages, and sound effects, and when the computer is hooked up to several input devices at the same time, such as a hard drive, a video camera, a videodisc player, a CD-ROM player, a VCR, broadcast television, a scanner, a microphone, and modem.

Hypermedia can be a text-only environment with only one layer of information being displayed to the user at a time. Or it can be gradually expanded into a full-scale multimedia environment that combines all the above layers.

At this expanded, full-blown level, each hypermedia "card" can be seen as a gateway to multiple, simultaneous representations of a given subject that are stored in a stack (the thematically linked group of cards). By pressing buttons on the card's surface, users can instantly call up "windows" and "overlays" featuring dramatic video clips, real-life photographs, colorful animations, recorded speeches, and sound effects. These windows can be called up separately and closed after they are viewed (or "listened

to"), or they can be arranged around the screen as simultaneous, multiple representations of a given subject. For example, in a "Whale Watch" stack of the future, a student team might have the following active windows on the screen at the same time:

- A video of a finback whale feeding on herring (with sound).
- A video of a mother humpback whale with her calf (with sound).
- A diagram of the humpback whale's internal anatomy.
- A map of major humpback whale feeding grounds in the North Atlantic.
- A page from Farley Mowat's book *A Whale for the Killing* (Bantam, 1972).
- An audio window with buttons keyed to different whale songs.
- A scratch-pad window half-filled with notes the student team is making based on their observations.
- A storyboard window with each tiny storyboard frame being a miniature, full-motion version of the other windows.
- A multimedia "document" window with text, buttons, and icons. (The document is the hypermedia stack—a multimedia term paper—that the student team will complete and submit to their teacher for a grade.)

In the past, multimedia and hypermedia were offered as frozen, prefabricated databases stored on laserdisc or CD-ROM. A student team could *navigate* through these databases, but could not use them as raw material to rearrange or *repurpose* for their own composition.

This view is changing quickly. Today's *hypermedia systems* (multimedia databases plus search and retrieval software) are viewed as combined *navigation* and *composition* tools. For example,

Apple's new *Visual Almanac is* a two-sided videodisc (that stores a total of 108,000 multimedia images—or over 7,000 multimedia "objects") accompanied by 14 megabytes of *HyperCard* stacks that offer three levels of user interaction:

- **Collections.** Explorer teams can "browse" through the collections of images, text, sounds, etc. just as they might browse through a regular printed almanac or through an art museum.

- **Activities.** Teams are encouraged to explore the almanac thematically and interact with different subject areas through dramatic story problems, by making experiments, forming questions, and testing hypotheses.

- **Compositions.** Teams can create their own multimedia "documents"—narrative text passages illustrated with full-motion video clips, colorful video slides, sound effects, music, etc.

Footnote

* The idea for connecting the still-image player to a computer comes from Dr. Carrie Heeter, Director, Communications Technology Laboratory, Michigan State University, East Lansing, Michigan. Dr. Heeter is doing some of the most advanced hypermedia research and development in the United States.

Videodiscs are found in many different environments. They are in homes, arcades, auto parts stores, car dealerships, department stores, tourist information centers, elementary schools, universities, and other locations. Even though these settings vary, the applications of the videodiscs within each of them can be placed into one of three categories: recreational, informational/marketing, or educational.

Recreational discs, as implied by the category name, are designed for entertainment only. Examples are *Mystery Disc,* an interactive problem solving game, and *Dragon's Lair,* an interactive video adventure game (Bluth, 1984). This category also includes a large library of feature length motion pictures that are available in videodisc formats.

Informational and marketing discs are found at many locations including kiosks (automated information stations) at stores and information centers. Discs in this category include *Greek Vases* (Circus, 1988-89), a disc available for use by visitors to the Getty Museum, and College USA discs, which are used to market colleges and universities to prospective students. Many of the discs in this category are not commercially available. They are produced for use in a limited number of settings and often have a short usable life.

Educational applications of videodiscs are just beginning to be explored. Four areas of application (direct instruction, instructional support, independent research, and testing) show promise and are worthy of elaboration (see Figure 7.7.1).

Direct Instruction

This is the most advanced form of videodisc instruction and is possible only with level II and III software. These levels of software have programmed lessons that are designed to present instructions directly to the student without intervention from a teacher. Direct instruction discs are available in surprisingly diverse areas. For example, videodiscs have been developed to teach CPR, welding, basic math, science, punctuation, foreign languages, word processing, and trigonometry.

Level III videodisc-based direct instruction often closely parallels traditional instructional techniques. Typically this type of instruction would include videodiscs, computer disks, and print materials for student use. The video presentation, managed by the computer, would deliver content, feedback and practice examples or questions, The computer would supplement the content presentation, check and record the student's performance, and adapt the presentation to accommodate specific needs that become apparent from response patterns. The print materials would be used by the student to prepare for an upcoming lesson, elaborate on the presentation, and provide off-line practice opportunities.

A trigonometry package. *Trigland,* produced by MECC, is an example of a level III direct instruction program designed for use in the schools. This package was developed specifically for use in schools where a small number of students were interested in an advanced

By
Gregory C. Sales

503

math course, One or two students at a time, under the supervision of a math teacher, work through the semester-long course. Using a videodisc player interfaced with an Apple IIe computer, the students view motivational videodisc presentations of concepts followed by computer mediated elaboration and practice. The students' instructional progress is monitored and recorded by the computer and occasionally checked through teacher administered paper and pencil tests.

Instructional Support

Teachers have been using media for instructional support for decades, They have used movies, slides, maps, charts, graphs, and audiotapes to help students better understand the content of a lesson.

When videodiscs are used as instructional support the teachers are responsible for the design of the lesson. Teachers must determine the portions of the disc they wish to use, how they will involve students, and to what degree students will be held accountable for the content presented.

Perhaps the most obvious instructional support application of videodisc is for the delivery of visual aids to illustrate points made during a lecture or to motivate students. This use of videodiscs as visual databases has resulted in development of a large number of discs of this type. Discs containing video images, artwork, plants, animals, historical events, geographic formations, human anatomy, and more serve as valuable resources to teachers at all grade levels and in all content areas.

Figure 7.7.1

Educational Applications of Videodiscs

✓

Application	Definition	Example
Direct Instruction	The presentation of a complete lesson or unit of instruction via a videodisc delivery system and supporting documentation.	A lesson designed to teach and provide practice on the use of quotation marks.
Instructional Support	The use of videodisc materials to supplement a component of the instruction.	Illustrating a lecture on Shakespeare's use of humor with vignettes from a videodisc
Independent Research	The use of videodiscs as resource or reference materials when investigating a topic.	Viewing a videodisc on whales in preparation for a lecture or report.
Testing	The integration of videodisc images into an instrument designed to assess student understanding	Presenting a series of paintings and requiring students to identify the artists.

An art teacher lecturing on the works of Vincent Van Gogh might find images from the disc *Vincent* to be ideal for contrasting the periods of his work and maintaining students' attention. As part of the lesson preparation students could read through the disc's chapter index to locate potentially useful material. After a quick visual review of the major works from the periods to be covered, students could identify frames and segments to be instantly accessed (by pressing a few buttons on a remote control) during the lecture.

Independent Research

Disc directories, paper documents similar to a table of contents, accompany many level I and level II discs. These directories are designed to help the user by providing information needed to access specific topics, thereby eliminating the need for the user to browse the entire video.

The ease with which these directories can be used has resulted in some schools placing videodiscs in the reference section of their libraries. Students conducting research for class reports have the option of using videodiscs in conjunction with traditional reference materials. One possible advantage of this type of research is that students will have an opportunity to see, hear, and read about a topic. This should reduce the likelihood that students will misunderstand the information.

A student preparing a report on life in a weightlessness environment might use the videodisc *Space Shuttle* as one of the references. This disc could help the student to see how microgravity effects such routine tasks as walking, exercising, eating, shaving, and sitting. In addition, the student would be able to hear astronauts discuss the sensations associated with "weightlessness." The insights gained from research conducted in this medium would be difficult for a student to glean from written materials and photographs.

There is another benefit to this type of research. Students can use the disc for instructional support when giving oral reports. They can illustrate or animate parts of their presentations with images located while researching a topic.

Testing

On-line testing is possible with level II and level III software. After the content for a lesson or course has been presented it is appropriate to check the students' understanding. On-line tests usually make effective use of the video and audio capabilities of the technology. Many different styles of questions are possible, but common forms ask the student to identify an image or to react to content of a short segment.

On a level II disc, such as Health EduTech's *Interactive Science-Plants,* testing is built into the program that controls the presentation. As students work, content is presented visually and aurally. They are instructed to take notes on off-line materials, given the opportunity to review, and quizzed. The on-line quizzes usually consist of a few multiple choice questions (remember level II input is limited to keypad presses). After each response the students receive immediate feedback and if necessary, remediation.

Teachers can also use the disc images of their choice in testing. Authoring tools, which are available for most systems, allow teachers to create level III computer-controlled tests that display questions, access the video, record student responses, and provide feedback (with or without video).

Video-augmented testing has great appeal. Several professional groups are considering the use of videodisc tests for their certification programs. One videodisc-based certification program is already being piloted. A five state region in the Midwest is using a videodisc-based test to certify farmers in the use of pesticides (Montgomery, 1988).

Summary

Videodisc technology is becoming an increasingly popular instructional tool. Instructional applications of the technology take advantage of its flexibility. It is being used for direct instruction with groups as well as individuals. The visual database design of some discs make them excellent for integration into instruction as support to teacher presentations. This design also makes them valuable as reference materials for students doing library research. A final instructional application is testing. In addition to the preprogrammed tests on level II and III discs, teachers can prepare videodisc-based tests using authoring tools.

References

Bluth, D. (1984). *Dragon's Lair: An animated interactive arcade game.* Airborne, 16- 18.

Circus, J. (1988-89). *Greek Vases:* The J. Paul Getty Museum. *Interact Journal,* 1(1). 8-9.

Montgomery, R. (1988, October) *Private pesticide applicator training.* Paper presented at a meeting of the Minnesota chapter of the International Interactive Communications Society. Minneapolis, MN.

Videodisc Software

College USA, $325/yr., Intro-Disc Corporation, 1 Professional Drive, Suite 134, Gaithersburg, MD 20879: 800/618-6422.

Trigland: An Interactive Videodisc Minicourse, $250, Minnesota Educational Computing Corporation (MECC), 3490 Lexington North St. Paul, MN 55112: 800/228-3504.

Vincent Van Gogh: A Portrait in Two Parts. $49.95, Pioneer Laserdisc Corporation: 800/255-2550.

Space Shuttle., $395/three-disc set. Optical Data Corporation, 30 Technology Dr., P.O. Box 4919, Warren, NJ 07060: 800/ 524-2481.

Interactive Science—Plants, $1,250 (entire series $4,995), Health EduTech, Inc., 7801 E. Bush Lake Rd., Minneapolis, MN 55435: 612/831-0445.

Gregory C. Sales, University of Minnesota, Curriculum and Instructional Systems, College of Education, 130 Peik Hall, Minneapolis, MN 55455.

By
JOHN D.
COUCH
AND
DR.
ANDREW J.
PETERSON

Obviously, new technologies hold great promise as facilitators of personal growth and formal education.[1] This article describes the evolution of computer-based tools on the campus of a K-12 private school of 525 students in San Diego county.

You will read a story of how a group of parents took the school from the edge of non-existence to becoming one of the premiere sites in the area for multimedia curriculum development with Macintosh computers and interactive videodiscs. The process was a grassroots movement and shows just what schools can accomplish with local community support. Hard work and the generous gifts of parents and charitable foundations made it all happen.

A Brief History

After years of financial struggle, the Santa Fe Christian School (SFCS) was closed down in 1985. A group of parents soon reopened the school, however, and they decided to try some unique strategies to ensure its continuation. One tactic was to develop a high-profile approach to educational technology.

There were some Apple IIs on campus, but they were not integrated into the curriculum. One day in 1986 a board member donated three Macs, put them on a table in the lunch room and stepped back to see what would happen. Immediately, students discovered these machines and were soon engaged in a variety of games, graphics and desktop publishing projects. This led to a new school newspaper, a yearbook, a brochure for the school and automated statistics for its sports teams.

Both the school's staff and the students preferred the Mac's [then] distinctive "user-friendly" graphic interface over other systems. The Mac was chosen for administration and training tasks. By 1988 office personnel were using it to do a host of administrative functions. And last year SFCS offered a payroll deduction plan for purchasing a computer; many teachers and support staff subscribed. The recent introduction of low-cost Macs has meant that more teachers are purchasing them for word processing, lesson preparation and test construction.

The Labs: Big Mac and Little Mac

The second phase of technological development at SFCS involved renovating one of the school buildings into a computer lab. Soon there were 24 Macintoshes networked to each other and to a laser printer in what became known as the Big Mac Lab. The instructor's computer system was connected to an LCD projection panel on an elevated overhead projector for group presentations. Programs also often include use of CD-ROM-based material from The Voyager Co. via a CD-ROM drive tied to the instructor's system.

Beginning in the third grade, Hyper-Card and MacPaint are taught to all

507

students by instructors Sue Pollard and Matt Evans. Word processing, desktop publishing, and animation are added as students advance.

The journalism program is stationed in a smaller room adjacent to the Big Mac Lab. Ten computers are in this Little Mac Lab and are dedicated to a student-produced newsletter, class meetings and faculty projects.

SFCS's lab complex is a boon to an active-learner approach as well as a real showcase for the school in terms of student and faculty recruitment, plus general public relations.

Evaluating Curriculum

All administration, planning and fund raising goes toward one thing—transmitting a curriculum to students. Computers have not been more successful in helping to turn back the tide of mediocrity in our schools, we believe, because too little attention has been paid to the *content* of the courseware. Regardless of "wicked" speed, vast memory or stunning graphics, the benefit of a computer-based delivery system is limited by the substance of its message.

In light of this, the school, in conjunction with the Santa Fe Educational Foundation (SFEF), has begun a long-term project of curriculum evaluation. Every teacher is building an academic portfolio for each class that include the following categories:
- general *aim* of the course;
- substantive *content* of the discipline;
- educational *objectives* for the student;
- daily *agenda* of classroom work;
- favorite teaching/learning *activities*;
- media *resources* for instruction;
- means of *evaluation* of student performance;
- record of class *handouts;* and

- Christian *perspectives* on the subject matter.

Academic portfolios have many advantages. While most classes tend to operate in isolation from one another, the curriculum developer can study these portfolios as a basis for designing an integrated and comprehensive program. They provide valuable transition material and continuity in case of teacher turnover. Staff and textbook evaluation is facilitated for parents and school supervisors. And finally, these records provide a wealth of material for lecture courseware development.

Sound Development Practices

Another important reason for the yet unrealistic potential of computer-based tools in education concerns instructional design. In any pedagogy there must be a balanced mix of drill, tutorial, simulation, games, and archival browsing. Instruction includes both authority and exploration. There must be a mastery of the basics and a drive to apply those tried-and-true principles to new situations. Telecommunications, computers, audio, video and print are proven media in the teaching/learning process—the trick is to design a curriculum using them that avoids the extremes of boredom and chaos.

Knowing the importance of these fundamentals, we set out to write a "white paper" on "MultiMedia Curriculum Development in the 1990s." Along with historical background about contemporary educational practices and results, we articulated areas of focus for our future work:
- Academic Content (Substance)
- Instructional Design (Style)
- Educational Evaluation (Assessment)
- Communication Technologies (Tools)
Preparing for a series of curriculum

projects, we made a preliminary study of the California state frameworks, standard textbooks in the field and Christian treatments for each discipline. The question of technology became a "window of opportunity" for us to examine the conventional content and design of available materials as well as the critiques of dissenters who would add or subtract from the common faire. What principles and perspectives should be included in the archive of knowledge in each field of study?

Educational evaluation is key to any effective curriculum. The computer offers new ways to provide more responsive feedback to students.[3] With colleague Ross Cooper, who is a computer consultant for test publishing firms, SFCS is looking for ways to combine the helpfulness of normative testing such as Stanford Achievement Tests, with the strengths of criterion-referenced assessment. Thus, in the course of an individualized mastery-learning approach, our curriculum remains accountable to national norms and comparisons.

Staying current with state-of-the-art educational technology is a full-time job. Maintaining personal contacts in the industry, consulting with leading companies, teaching at university departments of educational technology, attending trade shows and reviewing trade journals are among the variety of ways our team of associates remains aware of new developments in hardware and software. For example, the team recently visited MIT's Media Lab on the occasion of its fifth anniversary to see how they are "inventing the future."[2]

Multimedia Lab

In January of 1990 the MultiMedia Curriculum Development Lab (MMCDL), sponsored by the SFEF, was established on our campus. It has become a gathering place for sample texts, videodiscs and trade information. Our equipment includes a Macintosh II tied into the campus network, Pioneer videodisc players, a Toshiba large-screen monitor, an Apple CDSC CD-ROM drive, Mass Microsystems' 45MB removable-disk cartridge system and a video-capture board.

Video products and software packages are reviewed or developed in the Little Mac Lab regularly by staff, faculty or parents. Creating new stacks for *HyperCard* is a popular activity. For example, an animated lesson on the anatomy of the ear was produced by Bonnie Ferris, a third grader's parent, and tried out in the classroom immediately. It was a great success both academically and motivationally—the kids could hardly stay in their seats!

It does take a significant amount of money to use and develop these sorts of multimedia materials. While there is clear and obvious benefit, a school is unlikely to have much excess capital, especially if it has high-quality teachers who are paid sufficiently. Therefore, a good deal of grantsmanship has been required. In the beginning, local foundations (Santa Fe Educational Foundation; Charles and Ruth Billingsley Foundation) supplied the funds that helped get the curriculum development underway and the "white paper" written. In April of 1990, the school received a significant grant from a major foundation in southern California to support multimedia curriculum development in middle-school science.

The Science Project

For our science project, we are constructing two products. The first is a multimedia enhancement to an existing middle-school science program, which involves utilizing a computer-based videodisc system to improve large-group presentations and writing a well-organized agenda for life and earth science. The second project is creation of a sample videodisc that shows others the capabilities of videodisc/computer technology. A variety of media (text, graphics, slides, audio and video) and instructional format (drill, tutorial simulation, game and archival browsing) are demonstrated.

Setting Analyzed: The setting for the project is the seventh and eight grade classes at SFCS with approximately 25 students in each class. This will be the beta-test site. Attitude questionnaires and achievement pretests were administered in each class in order to assess the effective and cognitive characteristics of the learners. Instruction takes place in the middle-school science room, comprising six large lab tables and a set of traditional school desks. The teacher has a white board and an overhead projector.

Management Organized: Parents of students in the school have helped substantially with the project. Jonathan and Bonnie Ferris, owners of Interactive Presentation Technology, which does Mac-based animation for business clients, are providing computer-graphic art and animation for the demonstration videodisc. Video footage will be completed by another parent, Dan Leomer, owner of WRI Education Inc., which has produced award-winning educational videotapes and instructional packages used nationwide. Michael Carroll, multimedia producer-educator at Reuben H. Fleet Space Theater and Science Center and a freelance artist, is working with us on exciting visuals for the demo

disc. In short, there seem to be many professional media people interested in contributing to our project.

Objectives Specified: As we go through the academic year, learning objectives are being written for each unit and each lesson. With all the media options and an emphasis on discovery, objectives help the designer to keep in mind the scope and sequence of the domain of knowledge. At the same time, expectations of students are not limited to behavioral objectives. We have followed O.K. Moore and the Clarifying Environments Program, which lists principles to which the classroom should adhere rather than specific actions that students would take in a test situation. Moore's principles of perspective, productivity, personalization and autotelicity provide an environment in which a student can engage in creative problem-solving while still learning the basics.

Media Selected: Eventually we plan to produce interactive multimedia courseware in the digital format. However our strategy is to start with generic videodiscs available from Optical Data Corp. and Videodiscovery. Currently the MMCDL is a beta-test site for the BioSci II *HyperCard* stack. And in the course of using the videodiscs, teachers are culling ample ancillary materials and lab activities.

To run the multimedia components, we outfit our science classroom with a high-tech presentation system. A Pioneer videodisc player controlled by a Mac IIci displays images on a Mitsubishi large-screen TV. LCD products from Proxima/Computer Accessories Corp., a local firm, are also integrated. And demonstrations using a camera connected to the large-screen TV are planned for the second semester.

Prototype Constructed: The multimedia-enhancement project was implemented the first day of school. A custom-made *HyperCard* interface for the teacher is used daily in the earth- and life-science classes. Attitudinal and achievement tests were administered to students. Careful documentation is retained for each unit and lesson.

With the classroom component currently well underway, the design of the demonstration videodisc has begun in earnest. *SuperCard* is the software being used for designing the computer interface. Material will be selected to accomplish objectives and conform to general instructional principles of the MMCDL.

After all the material is recorded onto one-inch videotape, it will be taken to a videodisc-recording center where a check disc will be pressed. After formative evaluation, a master disc may be pressed: this is significantly more expensive but also provides the basis for having multiple copies made at a relatively low cost.

Project Evaluated: Formative evaluation will continue as the videodisc packages are used in the earth- and life-sciences classes. The teacher and the designer will select the best material for illustrations and evaluate student reaction and progress. In addition to attitude and achievement post-tests, student opinion will be measured via magnitude-scaling methods.

When the demonstration videodisc is produced in March of 1991, it will be used for classroom presentations and by individual students. Eventually we want to use erasable/rewritable optical-disc technology for individual exploration via an electronic notebook. This would enable a student, for instance, to cut and paste material into his or her notebook while the teacher makes the group presentation.

Next Steps

Most of the work on the Science Project will be completed in April, 1991. In association with the Santa Fe Educational Foundation, the MMCDL will then apply for grants to do multimedia curriculum development for U.S. history in grades 5, 8 and 11, and a Phase II science project including high-school biology. Following the pattern in the bio-tech industry, we hope to create tools and courseware that lead to commercial spin-offs. The royalties then come back to the foundation so that more basic research can be done.

It is the purpose of SFEF to sponsor and promote research and development in educational technology and new curricula. With the educational implications of the quantum leaps in communication systems becoming more apparent, SFEF wants to facilitate a network of users and developers who share our vision of ethical, intellectual and technological excellence.

Readers wanting more information should contact:

Santa Fe Educational Foundation
201 Lomas Santa Fe, Suite 360
Solana Beach, CA 92075

References

1. Ambron, S. and Hooper, K. *Learning With Interactive Multimedia: Developing and Using Multimedia Tools in Education*, Redmond, WA: Microsoft Press (1990).
2. Brand, S., *The Media Lab: Inventing the Future at MIT*. New York, NY: Viking (1987).

3. Moore, O.K., "About Talking Typewriters, Folk Models and Discontinuities: A Progress Report on 20 Years of Research, and Development, and Application," *Educational Technology* (1980), pp. 15-27.

Products and Companies Mentioned in this Article:

Apple CDSC CD-ROM drive: Apple Computer, Inc., Cupertino, CA

BioSci II: Videodiscovery, Seattle, WA

Flash: Beagle Bros., San Diego, CA

HyperCard, MacPaint: Claris Corp., Santa Clara, CA

Interactive Presentation Technology, Escondido, CA

MacroMind Director: MacroMind, Inc., San Francisco, CA

Mac School: Chancery Software, Ltd., Vancouver, BC

MASS Microsystems, Sunnyvale, CA

Mitsubishi Electric Sales America, Inc., Cypress, CA

Optical Data Corp., Warren, NJ

Pioneer Communications of America, Inc., Upper Saddle River, NJ

Pixel Paint: SuperMac Technologies, Sunnyvale, CA

Proxima/Computer Accessories Corp., San Diego, CA

SuperCard: Silicon Beach, San Diego (a division of Aldus Corp.)

Toshiba America Consumer Products, Inc., Wayne, NJ

The Voyager Co., Santa Monica, CA

WRI Education, San Diego, CA

John D. Couch is a member of the board of directors at Santa Fe Christian Schools and president of the Santa Fe Educational Foundation. He was vice president of software and development and director of new products at Apple Computer, Inc. from 1978 to 1984. He has also taught undergraduate courses at University of California, Berkeley and graduate courses at San Jose State University.

Andrew J. Peterson, director of the MultiMedia Curriculum Development Lab, is on the board of the Santa Fe Educational Foundation. He taught in the teacher training program at Grove City College from 1983 to 1988 and in the department of educational technology at University of Pittsburgh, PA

CD-ROM: A Technology that Is Steadily Entering School Libraries and Classrooms

A CD-ROM DISC CAN STORE VAST AMOUNTS OF TEXT, IMAGES, AND SOUND, MAKING IT AN IDEAL TECHNOLOGY FOR SCHOOLS. HERE'S AN OVERVIEW OF THIS TOOL, INCLUDING A LIST OF POPULAR DISCS.

By ROXANNE MENDRINOS

Compact Disc Read Only Memory's (CD-ROM) entry into society has been referred to as the silent revolution. Businesses and educational institutions have been quietly, but steadily, embracing this technology. General Motors and Ford use CD-ROM to store and access complete car service manuals. Businesses gain instant access to corporate annual reports and other important financial data. Secondary and elementary schools, as well as universities, have instantaneous access to magazines, newspapers, and academic journals.

Just what is this impressive technology? CD-ROM is a 4.75-inch laser disc capable of holding 250,000 pages of text, 2,000 high resolution pictures, or 74 minutes of high fidelity sound—or any combination of all three. The huge storage capacity of a CD-ROM disc makes it a leading medium for the electronic publication of large data bases such as reference data, library catalogs, and other data-oriented products.

In a school library, for example, a computer connected to a CD-ROM player can provide swift, efficient retrieval of sought-after information. A student or teacher looking for magazine or journal articles on a particular topic can simply type in a search term and the full-text article or its citation or abstract appears instantly on screen, saving hours of searching a variety of print indexes or leafing through individual periodicals.

Nonmagnetic and less susceptible to damage than a floppy, a CD-ROM disc has information stored in microscopic pits on its surface, making it less vulnerable to spilled beverages, dust, and scratches. Expect a disc to last at least 10 years.

CD-ROM players can be an internal drive alongside the disk drive in a computer, or an external peripheral. Standards for the software that acts as the interface between the player and computer have been emerging for several years. Concerned hardware and software companies formed what's known as the High Sierra group, which has proposed a set of minimum logical standards to the National Information Standards Organization (NISO). Those standards have been accepted by most CD-ROM laser disc producers.

Compatibility Is Key

The computer software is written specifically for, and shipped with, each CD-ROM laser disc product. The value of the optical disc will depend greatly on the quality of the indexing and search and retrieval software provided. It is the software interface that makes the CD-ROM laser disc user friendly. The software is written to activate a particular brand of player. In other words, the CD-ROM player is disc- and software-specific. Before you buy a CD-ROM laser

513

disc player, it is critical to identify the CD-ROM laser disc(s) you intend to purchase in order to assure compatibility.

For example, Grolier's *Academic American Encyclopedia* has an Apple or IBM version. Sony, Philips, Hitachi, NEC, Apple, and Amdek CD-ROM players are recommended depending on the computer used. However, if you want to also subscribe to Infotrac's *Magazine Index,* an MS-DOS computer is needed and only Sony and Hitachi players are compatible with the *Magazine Index* disc. If you want to begin inputting the school library catalog on disc and match it to Bibliofile's *Library of Congress* CD-ROM disc, MS-DOS or Hitachi drives are recommended.

A helpful tip: Identify the CD-ROM laser discs of interest, and then make sure the CD-ROM disc player, the computer, and memory requirements are compatible. Buying a CD-ROM player and computer without a purpose, to be technologically in the forefront, makes no sense educationally or financially. MS-DOS-based CD-ROM players range in price from $680-$1,000. CD-ROM players that operate with Apple computers range in price from $800-$1,200.

MS-DOS/Apple

Most CD-ROM discs today run under the MS-DOS operating environment, and are used for storing large electronic text data bases. But in the future you will see discs that are controlled by *Hypertext* programming and combine sound, graphics, and text. Some of today's more popular MS-DOS titles include *ERIC, Psych-Lit, Magazine Index, Reader's Guide Abstracts, Dissertation Abstracts, Newspaper Index, Science Helper K-8,* and *Microsoft Bookshelf.* Many of the newer MS-DOS-based CD-ROM products do or will require a hard disk drive and 640K

of RAM. A hard disk drive speeds access and retrieval.

Many discs that are controlled by Apple computers and compatible CD-ROM players utilize Apple's *HyperCard* software. Research toward a multimedia environment is being pursued by third-party developers. For example, *The Whole Earth Catalog,* distributed by Brøderbund, contains more than 2,500 entries covering a vast array of subjects. It utilizes sound, graphics, and text. Silver Platter CD-ROM data bases, which include *ERIC* and *Peterson's*

CD-ROM Player Companies

- **AMDEK CORP.** 3471 N. First St. San Jose, Calif. 95134; *(408) 436-8570*
- **APPLE COMPUTER** 20525 Mariani Ave. Cupertino, Calif. 95014; *(408) 996-1010*
- **DENON** 222 New Rd. Parsippany, N.J. 07054; *(201) 575 -7810*
- **HITACHI SALES CORP. OF AMERICA** 401 West Artesia Blvd. Compton, Calif. 90020; *(213) 537-8383*
- **NEC HOME ELECTRONICS (USA) INC.** 1255 Michael Dr. Wood Dale, Ill. 60191; *(312) 860-9500*
- **PHILIPS** Laser Magnetic Storage International Co. 4425 Arrows West Dr. Colorado Springs, Colo. 80907-3489; *(719) 593-7900*
- **SONY CORP.** 1 Sony Dr. Park Ridge, N.J. 07656; *(201) 930-6104*
- **TOSHIBA AMERICA INC.** Disk Products Division. 1737 North First St. #300 San Jose, Calif. 95112; *(408) 452-0860*

Gradline, are available for use with Macintosh as well as MS-DOS computers. Microsoft Corp. is even considering putting a number of software programs, such as *Excel, Word,* and *Mail,* as well as clip art, animation software, and Apple's *HyperCard* (to act as the user interface), on one disc. Users could then have access to all of those programs and files without having to handle multiple diskettes.

The Dynabook

An innovative product now on the market is the first MS-DOS laptop computer that includes a built-in CD-ROM, but the twist is that there is no keyboard or mouse. Dynabook (Dynavision Inc., Boston, Mass.) is specifically designed for CD-ROM applications. All commands are entered via a touch screen. The goal is to combine vast amounts of data with simplicity and portability. Dynabook is aimed at car manufacturers such as General Motors and Ford, and possible aero-space and business applications. Its value to the education community is also being considered. Dynabook retails for $4,995.

CD-ROM is quietly but steadily making inroads into the school library media center, where it satisfies information needs across the curriculum. It is a useful, educationally sound technology with many outstanding applications that promote higher-order thinking skills. At the secondary level, the need to access information on current trends and developments in social studies, science, foreign language, journalism, and English has made this an indispensable tool for forward-thinking library media specialists and educators. The school reform movement requires that administrators and teachers be current with changing educational philosophies and practices; CD-ROM technology can play a key role in the storage and dissemination of that information. The possible uses of CD-ROM technology in school offices, classrooms and library media centers are endless.

Roxanne Mendrinos is director of Library Media Services for the Westwood, Mass., public schools.

A Sampling of CD-ROM Discs

Here are some of the most widely used CD-ROM discs in schools today, as well as a listing of CD-ROM players that are compatible with each disc. Be aware that certain discs can only be used with certain players, as the chart below makes clear. Call the disc manufacturers for information about other compatible players that aren't listed.

GROLIER'S ACADEMIC AMERICAN ELECTRONIC ENCYCLOPEDIA

Sherman Turnpike, Danbury, Conn. 06816; (800) 356 5590

- The 1988 version includes 21 volumes of the Academic American Encyclopedia ($395). Subscribers to the 1986 version may send in the original school purchase order and for an additional $100 purchase the new version.

- **MS-DOS Version**
  COMPUTERS: IBM PC or compatible; 512K; DOS version 3.0 or later. CD-ROM DRIVERS: Hitachi 1502S, 1503S; Philips CM 100; Sony CDU 100; Amdek laser disc 2000. Packaged with the 5.25-inch diskette but includes a coupon for a 3.5-inch disk exchange.

- **Apple Version**
  COMPUTERS: Mac Plus, SE, Mac II; Operating System 4.1 or later; SCSI Interface; CD-ROM DRIVERS: Apple Drive CDSC; Hitachi CDR 1553S; Denon DRD 253; Toshiba XM 3201.

INFOTRAC

Information Access Co., 11 Davis Dr., Belmont, Calif. 94002; (800) 227-8431, (415) 591-2333

- Several distinct CD-ROM data bases are available including TOM, an index to 130 magazines; Magazine Index Select, an index to 212 magazines and the *New York Times:* National Newspaper Index which contains the *New York Times, Wall Street Journal, Los Angeles Times, Washington Post,* and the *Christian Science Monitor,* as well as Academic Index aimed at the university or academic journal audience. Microfiche of the full text articles is available with the indexes. Call for price information.

- **MS-DOS Version**
  COMPUTERS: IBM PC or compatible; 640K; a hard disk drive is recommended for future applications; DOS version 3.3 provided with software. CD-ROM DRIVES: Hitachi 1503S, 2500; Sony CDU 51012. INFOTRAC leases the above CD-ROM drives and computers.

- **Apple Version:** None.

WILSONDISC

H.W. Wilson Co., 950 University Ave., Bronx N.Y. 10542; (212) 588-8400

- A series of CD-ROM data base products. The most popular for schools include *Reader's Guide to Periodical Literature* (citations only), *Reader's Guide Abstracts, Applied Science and Technology Index, Business Periodicals Index,* and *Social Science Indexes* among others. There is a special school rate of $825 for the Reader's Guide CD-ROM discs. Access to on-line services for the specific data base is included in the rate. Annual and quarterly updates can be shared between schools.

- **MS-DOS Version**
COMPUTERS: IBM PS/2 Model 30; DOS 3.3 operation system—1MB of RAM, 20MB hard drive. CD-ROM DRIVES: Hitachi 1503S. H.W. Wilson sells the above CD-ROM drive and computers.

- **Apple Version:** None.

EBSCO MAGAZINE SUMMARIES

EBSCO Publishing, P.O. Box 1943, Birmingham, Ala. 35201; (800) 826-3024, (205) 991-1182

- A subscription service providing abstracts to 252 magazines. (The *New York Times* was added in 1989.) The annual CD-ROM laser disc costs $399; the quarterly service, $799; the nine-month service $1,199; and the monthly service, $1,599.

- **MS-DOS Version**
COMPUTERS: IBM PC/XT, PC/AT, or compatible; 640K. CD-ROM DRIVES: Hitachi 1503S, 3500 internal drive. EBSCO sells the above CD-ROM drives and computers.

- **Apple Version:** None.

SILVERPLATTER INFORMATION INC.

37 Walnut St., Wellesley, Mass. 02181; (800) 234-0064, (617) 329-0306

- A variety of CD-ROM products are available, the most widely used for schools include *ERIC, Occupation Health Information Data Base, Corporate Industry Research Report,* and *Computer Productivity Index.*

- **MS-DOS Version**
COMPUTERS: IBM PC or compatible: 640K; DOS 2.1 or higher, 20MB hard drive; MS DOS CD-ROM extensions. CD-ROM DRIVES: Hitachi 1502S, 1503S, 3500, Toshiba XM3201 B-Philips CM 100, CM 121, CM 201.

- **Apple Version**
COMPUTERS: Mac Plus, SE, Mac II; two 800K floppy disks or a hard drive; 1MB RAM (2MB are recommended); System 6.02 or higher. CD-ROM DRIVE: Toshiba XM 3201 with SCCI. (SilverPlatter sells selected CD-ROM drives.)

WHOLE EARTH CATALOG

Brøderbund, 17 Paul Dr., San Rafael, Calif. 94903; (800) 527-6263, (415) 492-3200

- A compendium of 2,500 entries covering a vast array of subjects including free resources such as public domain software, commercial products, reviews, insight into operating a small business, and more. Item descriptions provide detailed ordering information. The CD laser disc uses *Hypercard* and includes sound, graphics, and text. Price: $149.95.

- **MS-DOS Version:** None.

- **Apple Version** COMPUTERS: Mac Plus, SE, Mac II; 1MB. CD-ROM DRIVE: Apple CD SC.

SCIENCE HELPER K-8

PC Sig Inc., 1030 Duane Ave., Suite D, Sunnyvale, Calif. 94086; (401) 730-9291
- A science curriculum reference including 1,000 retrievable lesson plans. Price: $195.

- **MS-DOS Version**
  COMPUTERS: IBM PC or compatible;
  256K; DOS 3.1 or higher; MS DOS CD-
  ROM extensions. CD-ROM DRIVES:
  Hitachi 1503S, 3500 Internal.

- **Apple Version:** None.

McGRAW-Hill CD-ROM SCIENCE AND TECHNICAL REFERENCE SET

McGraw-Hill Book Co., New York, N.Y.
Distributed by EBSCO (see separate
entry); (800) 826-3024, (205) 991-1182

- Includes the 7,300 articles from the
  McGraw-Hill Concise Encyclopedia of
  Science and Technology and 98,500
  terms and 115,500 definitions of the
  McGraw-Hill Dictionary of Scientific
  and Technical Terms on one compact
  disc. Price: $300.

- **MS-DOS Version**
  COMPUTERS: IBM PC/XT, PC/AT
  or IBM compatible computer with keyboard DOS 2.0 or later; 640K memory.
  CD-ROM DRIVES: Hitachi 1503S or
  3500 Internal.

- **Apple Version:** None.

BIBLIOFILE

Library Corp., P.O. Box 40035, Washington, D.C. 20016; (800) 624-0559; (304)
229-0100

- Library of Congress holdings on CD-
  ROM laser discs. Price: $1,400.

- **MS-DOS Version**
  COMPUTERS: IBM PC or compatible: 640K; DOS 3.3, a 20MB hard
  dish is recommended. CD-ROM
  drives: Hitachi 1502S, 1503S. Library
  Corp. sells the above drives.

- **Apple Version:** None.

Interactive multimedia is the rage in educational technology these days. Most early examples that brought the benefits of multimedia to educators featured the laser videodisc—a 12-inch platter offering access to thousands of still images, up to an hour of video footage, and two parallel soundtracks. No doubt, interactive videodisc applications, which are making their way into classrooms in increasing numbers, will play an important role in education for years to come. But another medium is competing for the attention of those interested in interactive multimedia: the compact disc.

Compact disc technology, popularized by the audio CD in the mid-1980s, offers an advantage over laser videodisc: while the videodisc stores images and sounds in analog form (as do traditional videotapes and audio cassettes), the compact disc is a digital medium. This means that a CD can store computer programs (compact discs used in this manner are known as CD-ROMs), and that the images and information stored on the CD-ROM can be manipulated by the computer in the same way as other digital input. For example, unlike analog images that are sent unaltered from videodisc to monitor, digital images from a CD-ROM can be resized, modified, or combined with images and text from another source before they are displayed on the computer screen. And because of its digital format, data from CD-ROM can be sent via network or modem to a remote computer.

The second major appeal of the compact disc is its capacity. A CD-ROM can store over 600 megabytes of data—the equivalent of hundreds of floppy disks. The presence of all this information on a single disc opens up possibilities for multimedia applications.

As intriguing as the CD is to multimedia developers, it presents some challenges. In particular, there's motion video and the memory it requires. In a digital environment, one of the most straightforward methods of storing a screen image is to save information about the color of each dot ("pixel") on the screen so that the image can be recreated whenever necessary. However, since even a relatively low-resolution image is made up of close to 250,000 pixels and two bytes of memory are required to approximate the color of each one, a single image requires about 500K of memory. One second of "full-screen, full-motion video" (a full-screen video image changing at the speed of 30 frames per second) would require 30 times as much—nearly 20 megabytes. At that rate, an entire CD could hold little more than *half a minute* of motion video!

Fortunately, the problem is not insurmountable; a number of companies have demonstrated "compression" schemes that greatly reduce the amount of space required for full-motion video. However, it will be some time before such compression routines are perfected, necessary hardware and software tools completed, and a full range of applications

By
JUDY
SALPETER

519

that take advantage of compressed video developed. In the meantime, publishers aren't letting the lack of full-motion stop them. Instead, they are plunging ahead with CD-based multimedia titles that incorporate text, music, speech, and still images along with limited-screen animation.

What do these applications offer? And what will the machines they run on look like? That depends in part on which audience is targeted. There is a split between those who see the CD as a storage medium for business users looking to extend the computer's capabilities, and those who expect multimedia CDs to be the next consumer electronics craze. Neither camp sees education as its initial market; but both name educational institutions as the second group to benefit from their success. For this reason, it makes sense to watch carefully as the story unfolds.

CD-ROM: The Computer World's Approach

CD-ROM (Compact Disc-Read Only Memory) has been used as a storage medium for computers since 1984, two years after its relative, the audio CD, was introduced. Initially adopted by business to provide quick access to vast amounts of textual information (catalogs, statistics, etc.). CD-ROM has been used recently to deliver multimedia applications to a variety of end-users—including students.

There are now multimedia reference tools that present an entire encyclopedia on a single CD, complete with drawings or photos of images: realistic music and sound effects; and animated sequences to illustrate important concepts. Children can page through colorfully illustrated CD-ROM storybooks and hear words, phrases, or the entire story read aloud—in a choice of languages. And students of all ages can learn about music with the help of new CD-ROM applications that combine high-quality recordings with written commentary; animated scores; textual translations; glossaries that include examples the learner can listen to; and other illustrated lessons.

Such applications have received publicity during the past year, but are still a novelty. Few users (especially in school and home markets) own CD-ROM drives and few computer manufacturers offer the drives as standard. What will it take for CD-ROM to become "mainstream?" Some say it's a matter of time. But industry leaders are convinced that the key is to agree on a multimedia platform—a basic machine (with a built-in CD-ROM drive and other multimedia capabilities) that any developer can develop for, and any end-user with an interest in multimedia can buy, knowing that it will run most applications on the market.

In today's computer world an across-the-board standard is virtually impossible: Apple, Commodore, and MS-DOS companies will never agree on a single platform. But we can hope for consensus within a subgroup—producers of MS-DOS computers and software, for example. A group of companies, led by Microsoft Corporation, recently agreed on specifications for a PC that would include a CD-ROM drive, enough memory and power to deliver multimedia applications, and a new multimedia version of Microsoft *Windows 3.0*.

Tandy, one of the leading supporters of the standard, announced it would ship a computer that meets the specifications before 1992, and other MS-DOS computer manufacturers followed suit.

In addition, several companies announced tools that will make it easier for developers to produce titles for the platform, and others are promising upgrade kits to bring existing computers up to the new standards.

Will there be educational titles for the multimedia computers? Microsoft and Tandy both say "yes." The two companies are working with developers to convince them to create CD-ROM titles or enhance their existing ones to take advantage of the new platform and operating system.

What are other hardware players saying about standards? Although IBM is supportive of efforts to create tools and promote multimedia development, the company hasn't directly embraced the Microsoft guidelines; in fact, it is unlikely that Big Blue will deliver a "multimedia computer" that meets them exactly. However, IBM is assuring potential customers that all of the capabilities outlined in the standards are available for a number of its lower-end machines (either through third party upgrade kits or with help from one or more of IBM's own add-on cards).

Apple has even less need to agree with other manufacturers since, in the hardware arena, Apple sets its own standards. Nevertheless applications developers and end-users will be looking to the company for guidance about which machine it sees as the "multimedia computer" of the next few years and what role CD-ROM can play. So far, Apple has been relatively quiet about recommended hardware configurations but vocal about its commitment to multimedia development. In the K-12 market it's a safe bet that we'll soon see multimedia CD-ROM titles for the new Macintosh LC, the first color Mac aimed at the school market.

CD-I: A Multimedia Player for Every Home?

While the computer world hopes for standards, the consumer market insists on them. As the Beta/VHS battle in the VCR world demonstrated, it's hard for competing standards (both offering approximately the same capabilities) to survive. Consumers expect a device to be easy to use, reasonably priced, and able to run any application that comes along in the next few years.

Buoyed by their success with the audio CD player, the leading companies behind the compact disc, Philips and Sony, came together several years ago to define a standard for what they hope will be the next consumer rage: "Compact Disc-Interactive" (CD-I). Since then, CD-I has been endorsed by virtually all the leading Japanese consumer electronics companies. Players, which will retail for under $1,000, should be available in the U.S. by the end of 1991.

Although the CD-I player is built around the 68000 microprocessor found in older Macintoshes and Amigas, backers are not billing the machine as a computer. Convinced that consumers would reject a multimedia computer for the living-room, they are positioning the players as "home entertainment systems."

The players, when they ship, will look a lot like audio CD players—and will be able to play audio CDs. When plugged into a TV set, a CD-I player will offer much more: graphics, sound, text, animation, and interactivity. Although it is possible to connect a keyboard, disk drive, or printer to a CD-I player, the machine that will be featured in consumer stores will consist of the player, cables to connect it to your TV and stereo, and input device (a cross between a remote control and a joystick).

Knowing that CD-I cannot succeed without a pool of appealing applications, Philips has teamed with PolyGram record company to form an organization devoted to title development for the U.S. market. Known as American Interactive Media (AIM), this group has been working with developers to create applications for the home user. AIM promises around 50 titles at ship date—many of them educational.

How will these titles differ from those on CD-ROM? Some of the obvious differences relate to the different audiences being targeted. For example, CD-I titles will not assume that the user will be entering text, saving information, or printing; they will be designed for use by one or more family members sitting at a fair distance from the TV screen; and they will place a high priority on entertainment value.

Furthermore, while the technology behind the two approaches is the same, in building a system from the ground up, the creators of CD-I have been able to define more clearly the multimedia standards to be used by developers. Anyone interested in creating a CD-I title can license tools to create audio tracks at

Full Motion: Who Has It, Who's Working On It?

A number of developers have already succeeded in adding video-like effects to their CD-based applications. They've been able to do this in part by animating only a portion of the screen and also by changing the image far fewer than the standard 30 times per second. In addition, they are using certain "compression" techniques to decrease the amount of information that needs to be stored for each frame of motion. (A typical compression scheme might involve storing information about only the changes that occur from one screen to the next.)

Unfortunately, the amount of compression necessary for the storage of full-screen, full-motion video appears to be beyond the reach of even the most talented programmers; for such compression, special hardware is required. Special-purpose chips, now in the final stages of development, can provide developers with the computing power they need to compress video images before saving them on a compact disc. In turn, machines used to play back the com-pressed video will need to be equipped with special chips to handle the decompression process.

Here's a quick look at the progress being made with compression hardware for compact disc storage.

DVI

In the MS-DOS-based CD-ROM world, several compression schemes are currently in development. The best known is DVI (Digital Video Interactive), introduced by GE's RCA division in 1987 and now owned by Intel.

The DVI compression/decompression chips are already available to developers. They are also being licensed to hardware companies that want to build DVI capabilities into their machines, and to third parties that plan to create add on cards to allow existing machines to run DVI applications. In addition to the video compression capabilities for which DVI is best known, the chips also offer standards for the storage of still images, audio, and text.

three levels of sound quality (from AM radio broadcast to CD audio quality); still images at a range of resolutions; and partial-screen animations.

If all goes according to plan, CD-I players will enter American homes during 1991 and 1992 and will be marketed to schools in 1993. At that point, it is very possible that we will see applications that take advantage of computer-like features (keyboards, disk drives, etc.) added to the CD-I player. In the meantime, if the home education titles that assume a television set only are appealing enough, we may even see a few of them find their way into our nation's classrooms without trying.

CDTV: Commodore's Challenge

Philips and the Japanese consumer electronics companies are not the only players with an eye on the home market. Commodore has also announced a multimedia CD machine aimed at consumers. Formally introduced at the Consumer Electronics Show last month, CDTV ("Commodore Dynamic Total Vision") should be available within the next few months.

IBM is actively supporting DVI and we can expect others in the MS-DOS world to follow suit. At the same time, however, a number of other companies have announced alternative approaches to video compression for the CD-ROM world, some of which may turn out to be of higher quality or less expensive than DVI.

CD-I

The hardware manufacturers behind CDI have been scrambling to perfect compression/decompression chips for their CD-I players before they ship. At the time we went to press, it was unclear whether these companies would succeed. If they do not, add-on modules should be available before long to allow early purchasers of CD-I players to take advantage of full-motion applications once they appear on the market.

And Others

Both Apple and Commodore are working on their own compression schemes, although it's unclear how far along either company is.

Apple spokespeople have clearly stated that their eventual goal is to develop tools, hardware enhancements, and system software that will allow the Macintosh user to treat video as a standard data type like text, graphics, and sound) that can be captured, saved, edited, and added to files. However, the company will not comment on the compression technology to be used or the possible third parties involved.

In the meantime, some peripheral manufacturers are offering their own approach to compression for the Macintosh. For example, New Video (Venice, CA) is creating an add-on card for the Mac using DVI chips licensed from Intel.

In the Commodore world, we can also expect add-on cards that will allow CDTV players to display full-motion video. But as with Apple, Commodore's efforts appear to be in a relatively early stage.

—J.S.

CDTV will resemble CD-I in a number of ways. A CDTV player will plug into a TV set, be able to run audio CDs, be controlled by a device resembling a remote control, and offer a range of multimedia features based on the compact disc technology used to deliver the applications. CDTV differs from CD-I in one important way, however: it is more closely based on an existing machine—the Amiga 500 and on existing CD-ROM standards.

In a sense, CDTV is a hybrid—a home entertainment device that is essentially a disguised computer with a built-in CD-ROM drive. In fact, with a keyboard and disk drive connected, a CDTV player can run existing titles for the Amiga. And later this year Commodore plans to ship a CD-ROM drive and upgrade kit that will allow owners of Commodore computers to turn their computers into CDTV players.

The advantage of CDTV is that it is relatively easy for developers to port over floppy-disk applications already in existence for the Amiga and CD-ROM titles developed for other platforms. And, since fewer new hardware elements and software tools were required for the Commodore platform, CDTV was able to beat

---

The Microsoft/Tandy Multimedia Standards

Microsoft, Tandy, and other MS-DOS companies have agreed on standards for multimedia CD-ROM computers to be available by the end of 1991.

What the Multimedia Machines Will Include:
- A fast (10MHz) 80286 or 80386 microprocessor
- 2 Mb of RAM
- A 3.5-inch floppy drive and 30-Mb hard drive
- VGA graphics
- CD-ROM drive, digital audio outputs
- Audio subsystem including digital playback, music synthesis, sound input capabilities
- MIDI and joystick ports (plus standard serial and parallel ports)
- 101-key keyboard; two-button mouse
- Microsoft *Windows 3.0* with multimedia extensions

Availability and Cost

Tandy, Zenith Data Systems, and eight other computer manufacturers have announced plans to deliver fully configured multimedia machines by the end of this year. They will have a suggested retail price of less than $3,000.

Upgrade Kits

If you own MS-DOS computers that meet (or can be modified to meet) the basic microprocessor, memory, and graphics requirements outlined above, you will be able to purchase upgrade kits later this year that add the new features (extended audio capabilities, CD-ROM, the *Multimedia Windows* operating system, and so on) to your existing machines. The upgrade kits, which will be available from several sources, are expected to sell for less than $1,000.

CD-I to the market—even though CD-I development has been underway longer.

In the end, one of the two platforms (or perhaps a third?) is likely to win. It remains to be seen whether Commodore's head start, and the strong multimedia features of the Amiga on which CDTV is built, will prove sufficient against a team of consumer electronics giants with more marketing clout and a larger number of titles at launch.

If Commodore succeeds, schools will be targeted. The company's education division hopes eventually to market a specially priced K-12 CDTV bundle—offering schools a multimedia consumer device and an Amiga computer in one machine.

Not Etched in Stone

Reporting on emerging technologies is always hazardous. On one hand, announcements and breakthroughs seem to occur so fast that it's hard to stay current. On the other hand, delays are rampant, making it dangerous to announce a ship date for fear of reporting on "vaporware."

Nonetheless, after observing the progress of CD-ROM and related technologies, we have decided to take the plunge and report on what we know—accompanied by these words of warning:

• *Don't be surprised if ship dates change.* When we first heard about CD-I, it was supposed to be available early in 1990—almost two years earlier than the date being discussed today. And although when we went to press Commodore was promising CDTV players by March (six months later than planned), we can't guarantee they will be in the stores then.

• *Don't expect to purchase a CD-ROM application and hook it up to a computer network.* Although it is pos-

sible to use a CD-ROM drive on a network, if you allow networked users to access a CD-ROM application simultaneously, the results are likely to be painfully slow. Delays can be caused both by the CD-ROM itself (CD-ROM access time, while faster than a floppy disk, is slower than most hard disks) and by slow network operations. If you want to use an application over a network, therefore, it's important to purchase one created for that purpose; an example is the network version of *Compton's Multimedia Encyclopedia,* designed by Jostens, Inc.

• *Don't be surprised if some technologies described here resurface in different forms or by different names.* For example, DVI, originally positioned as a method for adding compressed video to CD-ROM applications, now looks as though it might show up in other forms—as a compression scheme for non-CD-ROM applications (e.g., delivered from a hard disk or over a network), or even at the core of a new multimedia consumer device.

• *Don't automatically expect titles on CD to take advantage of the new features offered by the compact disc.* Many publishers are using the new platforms to deliver collections of clip art and software that are already available on floppy disk. In such cases, the content may not be changed; the compact disc is simply more efficient than a huge stack of floppy disks.

• *Don't rule out the possibility of CD-ROM and videodisc technology living side by side in a single application.* Two recent Macintosh applications—*The Visual Almanac* and a school restructuring reference tool being developed by Apple and the American Federation of Teachers—make use of *both* videodisc and CD-ROM.

Are we likely to see more applications

like this? Unfortunately, although "omni" players that can run both videodisc and CD-ROM at the same time have been tried, this approach tends to be quite expensive. As an alternative, companies such as Pioneer are experimenting with ways of combining analog and digital information on a single disc. Pioneer's system, known as LD-ROM, might be daunting to publishers reluctant to develop for yet another standard, but if LD-ROM succeeds, it could deliver the best of both worlds.

• *Don't view the CD-based technologies described here as a comprehensive list.* There are already other devices on the market or in development based on the compact disc. For example, there's CD+G, which allows a user to listen to an audio CD while watching images sent to a TV screen; and CD-ROM XA (for eXtended Architecture), a standard Sony hopes others will license to deliver multimedia applications.

• *Don't be surprised if a few years from now developers are talking about moving beyond CD-ROM.* Just as the 5.25-inch floppy gave way to the 3.5-inch disk, CD-ROM and its equivalents will be replaced by something better before too long—probably a faster medium that allows the user not only to read but also to save and erase files. However, such offerings are several years away. In the meantime, we can be sure that progress made in solving challenges faced by today's machines will be incorporated into the next generation.

If it's difficult for a reporter to take an accurate snapshot of a rapidly moving field, it's even more difficult for a user to decide when to jump on board. It can feel especially risky when it's not clear whether all the competing standards and technologies will survive. You may be excited about the potential of CD-I but worried about its chance to win over consumers used to Nintendo. Or you may be enthusiastic about CD-ROM but concerned that the cost will remain too high for your school.

In the end, however, your decisions will probably be based on the range and quality of applications available. While it might be rash at this point to invest in large numbers of CD-I or CDTV players or to purchase computers with built-in CD-ROM drives for every classroom in your district, you may decide that at least one new application is exciting enough to try right now. If so, you stand a good chance of being one of the early adopters of next year's mainstream technology.

Judy Salpeter is the managing editor of Technology & Learning.

By
Michael N.
Milone, Jr.
and
Holly
Brady

Back in the 1950s, when television was coming out of the laboratory and into the living room, there was almost universal agreement that the new technology would change education forever. (There's still a lot of that going around, isn't there?) Educational television—ETV—promptly proved everyone wrong and almost sank into oblivion under the weight of cumbersome technical considerations, uninspired programming, and geeky professors who studied at the Matchbook School of Dullness.

ETV enthusiasts, however, did not throw in the towel. Instead, they refined their art, nurtured the technology, and worked assiduously to help the medium mature. Their efforts, though rarely recognized by either their professional colleagues or the media, have borne fruit, and to almost everyone's surprise, ETV in its many forms is today a seasoned technology that is perhaps the most versatile tool available to educators.

ETV now comprises a rich array of possibilities, ranging from the homebrew efforts of educators working in their own schools through network television. It also includes cable, satellite broadcasting, computer-based multimedia, statewide networks, university consortia, and, of course, video cassettes.

To gain an idea of the scope of ETV, consider this: with few exceptions, at least one member of every family in America is exposed to some form of ETV every week. If you doubt this claim, just examine a television guide—the airwaves are jammed with programming from the Discovery Channel, the Disney Channel, the Learning Channel, the Arts and Entertainment Network, Black Entertainment Television, Children's Television Workshop, The Family Channel, Nickelodeon, PBS, ABC, CBS, NBC, Fox, HBO, Showtime, USA, ESPN—you get the picture. And the shows that are in the ETV realm are not B-grade flicks viewed by small audiences. For every special on rain forest insects or seasonal lakes of Africa, there are true blockbusters such as *Sesame Street* or *This Old Home.*

If broadcast or cable TV doesn't meet your needs, you can rent a tape or point your dish at the sky to learn Japanese or take an advanced placement course, ski with the Mahre brothers, get the latest word on whole language teaching from Ken and Yetta Goodman, or brush up your veterinary surgical techniques. Professional associations, for-profit developers, universities, and government agencies offer video training on virtually every topic imaginable, and if the topic in which you are interested is not yet available, you can bet it will be shortly.

Why the Appeal?

There are several reasons why ETV has grown so much as an industry. Most obviously, for better or worse, we are a nation of TV viewers. Even if you are a "hardly" watcher, you know how to do it, you are accustomed to paying attention, and you don't have to work very hard. In other words, it's effective and easy on the mind.

527

Reprinted by permission of: *Technology & Learning* (Formerly Classroom Computer Learning)
© Peter Li, Inc. 2169 East Francisco Blvd., Suite A4, San Rafael, CA 94901

The ease associated with learning from a video is often criticized by traditional educators, but it isn't necessarily a bad thing. There are countless skills, from the cerebral to the physical, that can be assimilated faster and more efficiently through video-based learning. Besides, when writing was first invented, it was probably criticized in many of the same ways as TV is today. These criticisms include lack of socialization (writing made it unnecessary to attend tribal gatherings where oral traditions were shared), diminution of mental capacity (writing made memorization of oral history and traditions unnecessary), and transmission of shallow rather than in-depth knowledge (how could writing ever portray the deep meaning voice and actions can portray?)

A second reason for the growth of ETV is that once the equipment necessary to produce television programs has been acquired, creating programs can be relatively inexpensive. Certainly, you can spend a fortune to create a show, but you can also do a good job with a low budget. Some of the most popular PBS shows— *This Old House* or *Wall Street Week, for* example— are produced on surprisingly low budgets. Likewise, many fine technical programs, including those offered to medical practitioners, engineers, and the like, are simple voice-over videos of an expert demonstrating a new or modified technique.

The third reason for ETV's popularity has to do with response time. If the need arises for quick training, nothing is faster than video. When the current year's automobiles reach the showroom, they are often accompanied by a video for sales and service personnel. Car makers cannot afford to send a trainer to every dealership in the country. Another example of a video tool with quick turn-around is the commercially available computer-based videodisc from ABC News InterActive describing the last presidential election. *The '88 Vote,* a remarkably comprehensive documentary, became available within weeks of the election. A comparable book would have taken years and would have been far less effective simply because so much live footage was included on the disc.

But how are schools actually taking advantage of ETV? There are many answers to this question. Let's take a look at some of them.

Grassroots Efforts

Now that camcorders and other video equipment have become "consumer" items, costs have dropped to where most schools can afford such equipment. Consequently, many schools have made homebrewed video-based activities a regular part of the school day.

One of the most innovative projects we've seen is the morning news show done by the students at the North Elementary School in Hawley, PA. WNES, as the students have named their venture, is coordinated by two teachers, Sue and John Morgan, and in the course of a school year, involves every student. While a core group of students handles the equipment, the news anchors, reporters, and weatherpeople rotate on a weekly basis.

The morning news program is shot live and occupies approximately ten minutes at the beginning of the school day. Ten to 15 minutes of setup time are necessary, and about five minutes are spent after the broadcast "striking the set." The equipment includes an off-the-shelf camcorder, an Apple computer, and Brøderbund's VCR *Companion* software. Thanks to the foresight of principal Tom Kennedy, the school was wired for video in every room when constructed, and every classroom now has a TV to review the show.

The studio is a utility room decorated with backdrops created by students. The furniture includes tables and chairs for staff, students, and equipment; and a corner for students' stuff—they come right from the school bus to the studio. It's a squeeze but the size of the accommodations doesn't seem to affect the quality of the programming.

The broadcast includes school and local news, sports, birthdays, announcements, the lunch menu, lost and found, a weekly book report, student awards, and the weather. The last-mentioned feature, the only taped portion of the show is a real tickle. Just before the broadcast goes on the air, a camera crew and the weather person run outside. The "nowcast" is described in the student's own words, with no concessions to the traditions of network weather reports. If the temperature is near zero, for example, the description might be something like, "it's so cold that if you wet your fingers and touch metal it will stick."

The entire school community is pleased with WNES and what it has done for the students. Virtually no additional costs have been incurred by the school—the PTA donated the camcorder—and the teachers who coordinated the program have a regular workload. Other teachers handle their homerooms during broadcast time.

The success of the news program has prompted the staff to consider other applications of video technology including homebound instruction and advanced classes. Moreover, beginning this year WNES will be carried over a local cable network so friends and families can tune in. This is quite a coup for a small rural school, and opens up a whole new set of possibilities for making the home-school connection. For more information about this student news program, write to Thomas Kennedy, North Elementary School, Hawley, PA 18431; (717) 226-3894. If you are interested in obtaining a sample broadcast, send a blank videotape with your request.

Network and Cable TV

Commercial television was once described as a "vast wasteland" and is condemned regularly by educators for a host of reasons, only some of which are legitimate. Nonetheless, there are many fine shows on the airwaves, and broadcasters are making efforts to provide high-quality, educationally relevant programs to young viewers during the times they are most likely to watch TV.

Cable television has done an even better job than the major networks of developing programs that do more than simply entertain. In some subject areas, serious viewers of cable television would have little difficulty putting together a course of study to rival that offered in any school or university. Foreign languages, fine and practical arts, environmental studies, economics, and earth sciences are areas in which network and cable television have been most successful.

Making sense of the vast possibilities presented by broadcast and cable television can be overwhelming, but there is a shortcut available to educators. KIDSNET (6856 Eastern Avenue NW, Suite 208, Washington, DC 20012; (202) 291-1400) is a non-profit clearinghouse for children's television and radio that we recommend strongly for every school district. Karen Jaffe, the executive director of KIDSNET, and her staff do a marvelous job of previewing and organizing the dozens of shows each week that are of interest to educators and their students.

Among their services is a future bulletin that gives the date, time, and title of educationally relevant shows and a precis of the content. The best feature of the future bulletin is its timing: it appears several months before a show is aired, giving teachers enough time to work any given show into the curriculum, notify parents, and develop or acquire any supplemental materials that are necessary. (Many producers offer schools high-quality ancillary materials, at no cost for use with students.) The cost of subscribing to KIDSNET (about $375 per subscription), is relatively small for the huge benefit it provides, and we can't think of a better way to spend some of the money your PTA has raised.

Another interesting resource is Cable in the Classroom, a nonprofit organization the main goal of which is to help educators integrate cable programming into the curriculum. Cable in the Classroom is made up of over 30 cable distributors, serving over two-thirds of the national cable television audience, and 19 cable programmers. Members have promised to provide, by December 1992, free installation and basic cable service to *all* public junior and senior high schools located on a cable route. Some members also offer free cable installation to elementary schools; and others offer satellite dishes at cost for those public schools outside the cable delivery system. Members also promise to provide by December 1992 a free VCR and TV monitor to any school that doesn't already have one.

In addition, cable in the Classroom publishes a guide with listings and articles on educational programs available on cable. The guide is distributed by local cable stations, and will soon be available on a subscription basis (approximately $25 for 11 issues). To order a subscription to the guide or to find out whether your local cable operator is a member, contact Cable in the Classroom, 1900 N. Beauregard, Suite 108, Alexandria, VA 22311; (703) 845-1400.

Satellite Networks

The most versatile ETV format is satellite broadcasting. Although it is still relatively underdeveloped, satellite-based educational television has carved a special niche for itself among small and rural schools. Moreover, professional associations are looking at satellite broadcasting as a way of holding special-topic or international conferences without busting the budget.

One of the most successful educational satellite networks is TI-IN (1000 Central Parkway North, Suite 190, San Antonio, TX 78232; (800) 999-8446). It offers an impressive range of programs for teacher in-service and student instruction, and beginning this year, TI-IN courses will be available via cable through the Mind Extension University (ME/U), The Education Network. TI-IN also works through educational institutions such as the Education Satellite Network operated by the Missouri Schools Boards Association.

The typical TI-IN program is staged in the network's San Antonio studios. It is broadcast via satellite to subscribing schools around the country, where students and teachers can interact with the presenter through a satellite-transfer telephone system. The arrangement works well (barring high levels of sun spot activity), and there is often as much student-teacher interaction in a TI-IN course as there is in a regular classroom or live conference presentation.

TI-IN has been a boon for schools in which in-service and curriculum aspirations exceed their budgets. For a comparatively small subscription fee, teach ers can upgrade their skills through staff development sessions with noted educators such as Madeline Hunter and William Purkey, and students can bulk up their course of studies with calculus or Japanese. Given the rising costs associated with traditional education, the trend towards restructuring schools, and the pace of educational innovation, it is probable that satellite-based education, and its retransmission through cable networks, will play an increasingly important role in education at all levels.

In-School News Programs

A friend once commented that if she could get her students to watch and understand the news, she would die a happy teacher. Now, because of Whittle Communications' *Channel One* and Turner Broadcasting's *CNN Newsroom*, she has a chance to turn her students into newshounds.

Channel One and *CNN Newsrooms* are both in-school news programs, but their delivery systems differ, and their reception by the education community has been poles apart. *Channel One* (Whittle Communications, 505 Market St., Knoxville, TN 37902; (800 251-5002) is transmitted via satellite, with Whittle providing to participating schools free loan equipment (including satellite dish. TVs, and VCRs) for reception and distribution of *Channel One* and other programming. The only hitch is that commercial advertising underwrites the program, and two minutes of ads accompany each news broadcast. The response of some educators to this commercial tie has been so strong that you would think that

Satan himself were the anchor.

Commercial-free CNN Newsroom (c/o Media Management Services, 10 N. Main St., Yardley, PA 19067-9986; (800) 3446219) is the alternative. It is delivered over regular cable by Tele-Communications, Continental Cable, and Jones Intercable at no charge to schools. No equipment is included in the deal. The program is broadcast at 3:45 a.m. so schools can record and use it at their convenience. Turner Broadcasting has plans to expand the program to the summer months.

Both *Channel One* and *CNN Newsroom* open up enormous possibilities to educators. Beyond the obvious—the opportunity to foster the news habit among students—the two programs might trigger a new level of acceptance of television in education. To our way of thinking, nothing could offer more promise than to place teachers in a position of influencing students' television viewing.

Tuning Into the Future

As ETV continues to grow, we will surely see its influence expand from school to home. Even now many fine educational programs are available to the home viewer from such sources as The Discovery Channel, The Learning Channel, Showtime's *Familytime*, ABC's *After School Specials,* and CBS's *Schoolbreak Specials*. As the editors of Insider, a publication of the National School Board Association's Institute for the Transfer of Technology in Education, observe, "America's homes are evolving into a new kind of education institution: the wired household. This is an evolutionary path that

> The response of some educators to this commercial tie has been so strong that you would think that Satan himself were the anchor.

school leaders can and should influence, but cannot conquer. We argue that school leaders have a compelling interest in the education activities of 'wired households' and in how technologies—cable TV, VCRs, computers, radio, et al—are used educationally."

Patricia McGee of the TI-IN Network puts it another way: "Television in all its forms is the perfect medium to deliver instruction to students, in-service training to educators, and special interest learning to community members. The technology is present in almost every home, school, business, and community center, and, best of all, it is inexpensive. From restructuring middle school education to lifelong learning for retired adults, television has potentials that no other medium can match."

Michael N. Milone, Jr., is adjunct associate professor at Ohio State University and a freelance software developer. Holly Brady is editor-in-chief of Technology & Learning.

Distance Education in United States Schools

By
CHRIS
CLARK

Distance education involves situations where the learner and the teacher are separated by substantial distance, and the separation is bridged by a communications medium or combination of media. Until the end of the nineteenth century, printed correspondence study was the only method available, but audio telecommunication through electronic means now provides for live interaction. First telephones and then radio came into use, and now systems based on television or computers are becoming very popular.

Today's typical distance education system can involve a combination of media, including print, television, telephone, and computer; most rely very little on traditional face-to-face meetings between the learner and the teacher.

Distance education is practiced widely in the United States. While we are not leading practitioners of distance education at the adult learning level, a case could be made that this country is a leader at the school level.

Thirty-two state education departments reported funding distance learning projects last year; there are over seventy telecommunications projects in New York state alone. North Carolina budgeted three million dollars for distance learning efforts in small schools in 1987-88.

Educators should seriously explore the benefits of each technology as they consider alternatives to face-to-face instruction. The most advanced technologies are not always the most practical ones. Try not to think in terms of which single medium is the best for all schools, rather which combination of media is most appropriate in a given situation.

The use of these media differs from conventional education in a number of ways: groups are more heterogeneous, students are more independent, feedback is limited, learner support is crucial, and the instructor is more of a facilitator. Schools use distance education methods for a number of reasons, including shortage of teachers in certain areas, declining enrollments, geographical isolation, and limited course offerings. Distance delivery can provide enrichment programs and remediation, reduce scheduling conflicts, help individualize instruction, share expert teachers, and help serve migrant or home-bound students. Distance teaching efforts can be divided into three categories: EVENT—an individual session; PROJECT—supplementary instruction, a series of connected events; COURSE—basic instruction for one semester or more.

Correspondence Study

Some educators shun the practice of learning through the mails. In a national research survey of schools with less than 500 students, nearly half of the principals responding said counselors rarely or never recommended correspondence study. The same survey showed correspondence participants were seen as being mostly D or F students.

Correspondence study serves a respectably large segment of the learner population extremely well. The University of Nebraska-Lincoln Independent

533

Study High School (ISHS) is an accredited program which awarded seventy-four diplomas last school year and tallied over 12,000 course registrations. The school, which employs twenty—eight full- and part-time teachers, has issued nearly one thousand diplomas in the past sixteen years.

Besides Nebraska, at least two other states—Alaska and North Dakota—have complete secondary correspondence schools. A high school in Washington expanded its course offerings from fifteen to one hundred through the addition of supervised correspondence study.

Letter-writing projects, cousins of the correspondence course, have long been a favorite with learners. Teachers arrange for students to have pen pals with whom they can practice their writing skills and learn about other places and people. The print medium alone can meet the needs of some learning situations: but when combined with video, audio, and/or computer materials, writing projects can be extremely effective. Supervised correspondence study is a practice which schools would do well to consider. The other media categories involve electronic telecommunication. Figure 7.12.1 presents some of the advantages and disadvantages of the different technologies that are used for talking or "teleconferencing" with learners.

Telephone Audioconferencing

The telephone is a friendly, comfortable technology. Students in rural New York regularly conduct "electronic field trips," where they talk to rock musicians, actors, authors, and scientists. Such events

Figure 7.12.1

√

Some Characteristics of Four Types of Teleconferencing

Audio — Readily available, little delay in setting up a call, relatively inexpensive, little training required, participants are relatively anonymous, long conferences can be tiring.

Audiographic — Visual enhancement, greater sense of shared space, graphic information transmitted in real time, graphics must be carefully prepared.

Video — Intensity and emotionality, physical reactions are visible, visual cues are sometimes distorted, little anonymity, participation can be active, generally complex and expensive, limited in location.

Computer — Messages can be sent/received at any time, independent of participants' schedules, complete record of interactions, paperwork is reduced, difficult to convey nuances and subtleties, anonymity is very easy.

(Adapted from Kelleher and Cross, 1985)

are popular where it is not possible to bring a celebrity or expert into a classroom. The North Carolina School of Science and Mathematics has also used teleconferences to allow students to talk with historians and diplomats.

Telephones are also used to deliver basic instruction. Nebraska's ISHS sponsors a TeleLanguage program, now in its fifth year, which combines independent study and regular conference calls to teach French, Spanish, and German: twenty-four school districts participated in 1987-88. Telephone audio hookups offer high school math and science instruction in Louisiana, and in Tucson, Arizona the Homebound/Teleteaching Program has allowed seriously ill or handicapped students to participate in classes through phone hookups.

Computer Based Messaging

Electronic messaging, the use of computers equipped with modems and telephone lines to send and receive notes, is rapidly becoming a popular supplement to distance education course delivery methods such as correspondence study. Until two or three years ago, only a few schools were using this technology at all: five states report that last school year, over eighty percent of their high schools had at least one modem. A number of earlier *The Computing Teacher* articles discuss teachers' experiences with this medium.

Students in Hawaii combine audio and computer-based messaging in a technique called Multi-Mode Node (MMN) telecommunication to participate in scientific field studies, bring in guest speakers, and communicate with students in Massachusetts, Japan, and other locations.

Bulletin boards and information services (e.g., CompuServe) have been the center of attention for messaging until recently, but this past year the McGraw-Hill publishing company began a messaging service specifically for schools, MIX. AT&T is piloting a Long Distance Learning Network in hundreds of classrooms in six countries. The network is divided into "learning circles" where individuals carry out educational projects.

In Spring of 1988, four thousand children in grades 4-6 participated in a project to gather data on acid rain. Funded by the National Geographic Society, the National Science Foundation, and Apple Computer, *Kids Network* used electronic mail to receive data from two hundred sites across the country. The project was so successful that it will be repeated in 1989, and other areas for data collection are under discussion.

In the last few years, two notable pieces of computer software were released, which show some real promise as tools for distance education projects. Springboard's *The Newsroom* was released in the 1980s as a desktop publishing program, but included a component called *Wire Service* which allowed users to electronically exchange the materials they had created. A project in upstate New York had school children using the software to cooperatively produce a creative writing magazine.

Well known educational software author Tom Snyder produced the program *The Other Side* in the 1980s. It is a global conflict resolution simulation game, where each of two teams uses cooperation or treachery to build a bridge to the other side. It can be played by one computer in one room, on two computers in separate rooms joined with a wire, or by two teams anywhere in the world through the use of telephone modems. Soon after its introduction, network news carried pictures of teams in Massachusetts and the USSR playing *The Other Side*.

Audiographic Conferencing

There are different types of systems which use regular telephone lines to combine two-way audio and some kind of graphic image. The mechanical systems typically feature a light pen or graphics tablet, and allow for spontaneous, live drawing on the video screen. Separate phone lines can be used for the voice and the graphics, or a voice-to-modem will allow both to transmit at once. Audiographics is one of the least known of the new distance education media, in spite of the fact that a recent national study (Ellertson, et al. 1987) found it to be extremely cost effective.

The Delaware-Chenango BOCES (NY) Telelearning Program uses audiographics to connect as many as five rural schools at a time to deliver advanced high school courses. That program also provides minicourses and has recently added paper facsimile transmission to its system. Garfield County, Utah's Tele-Learning Network, and the Pennsylvania Teleteaching Project also use audiographics.

ITFS Broadcast

Many types of systems can deliver two-way interactive television: low power, cable, microwave, fiber optics, Interactive Television Fixed Service (ITFS), FM microwave, compressed video, and slow scan. Each technology has its strengths and limitations. ITFS is a relatively inexpensive system which uses low frequency, line-of-sight television broadcast; the signals can be received by a regular television set equipped with a converter. While the broadcast range is limited to forty miles, repeater towers can be used to extend service. Most ITFS stations are located in large urban areas.

Twenty-eight school districts in Virginia are linked through a combination of ITFS and open broadcast, and fourteen ITFS centers in South Carolina serve 380 schools. The St. Lawrence-Lewis BOCES (NY) uses two-way interactive ITFS with a repeater tower to reach remote districts in the Adirondack Mountain area; their system also allows paper copy to be exchanged with facsimile machines. Two large systems in Richardson and Houston, Texas serve a total of eighty schools; Houston's InterAct network alone covers seven counties.

Satellite Broadcast

In this type of system, video and audio signals are transmitted (uplinked) from a central studio, bounce off an orbiting satellite, and are received (downlinked) by dishes at remote sites. Over six hundred schools in the U.S. own satellite receiving equipment.

Kentucky Educational Television recently received funding to provide downlinks at all schools. The LearnAlaska network served 250 communities in that state, providing satellite video until the program fell victim to the economy of falling oil prices. A system in Utah delivers high school Spanish to more than two dozen schools.

In October 1988, the Department of Education announced the recipients of the Star Schools grants, demonstration efforts involving the use of satellites to deliver educational material. The first nineteen million of a hundred-million-dollar legislative package will be spent during the next three years on programs expected to reach nearly 500 schools in thirty-nine states. The four consortia and their base states are: TI-IN United STAR Network, Texas; Satellite Educational Resources Consortium, South

Carolina; the Midlands Consortium, Oklahoma; and Technical Education Research Centers, Massachusetts.

Other Technologies

Television programs broadcast by the Public Broadcast System have been used in schools for many years, and the commercial networks are beginning to offer more programs, such as the mini-series *The Winds of War*, complete with teacher support materials. As allowed by law, regional agencies and local schools often tape programs for delayed classroom use. The Chico campus of the University of California originates interactive video programs delivered to schools by fiber optics. Microwave technology has linked three small rural schools in Iowa and two in Michigan in separate interactive television programs. The Carroll Instructional Television Consortium is a cable-based system in Illinois that joined four districts to offer six courses in 1984-85.

There are techniques and systems not mentioned in this article—variations of old technologies, brand new inventions, and creative combinations of media. The purpose here has not been to describe all the available options in depth, but rather to mention a representative sample.

Issues

Among the problems faced by schools wishing to implement distance education are questions of certification and accreditation. Can a teacher who is certified in Texas legally deliver instruction using Texas-approved textbooks and curricula to students in Massachusetts? Other issues include class size, reception quality, supervision of students, job security, and equal access. Educational associations will become more concerned with these and other issues as distance education comes into greater use. A number of political questions will have to be answered as well: who pays for it? How much? Who leads? What courses are offered? When are they offered? Who is in charge?

Conclusion

Satellite technology is the fastest-growing medium for distance education in the United States, but correspondence study is very much alive; it is perhaps the most widely used and least expensive delivery system. Little-known audiographics is one of the most cost-effective technologies for providing education at a distance. A wide range of interactive television technologies offers lower-cost alternatives to costly satellite systems, and telephone and computer messaging techniques have been shown to be effective adjuncts to course delivery. Each medium has strengths and weaknesses to consider. The best advice is to consider using a variety of media in designing a distance education plan. Also remember that distance education can include learning experiences other than full-fledged courses. Special broadcast events and projects like cooperative creative writing are also part of distance education.

> Can a teacher who is certified in Texas legally deliver instruction using Texas-approved textbooks and curricula to students in Massachusetts?

Recommended Reading

Barker, Bruce O. (1987). *Interactive Distance Learning Technologies for Small Rural Schools: A Resource Guide*. Las Cruces, NM: ERIC Clearinghouse on Rural Education and Small Schools.

Bond, Sally L. (1987). *Telecommunications-based Distance Learning: A Guide For Local Educators*. Southeast Educational Improvement Laboratory. (ERIC Document Reproduction Service no. ED 287 474.)

Ellertson, E. Kent, Wydra, Dennis, and Jolley, Henry. (1987). *Report on Distance Learning: A National Effectiveness Study*. Mansfield, PA: Mansfield University. (Unpublished).

Kelleher, Kathleen and Cross, Thomas B. (1985). *Teleconferencing: Linking People Together Electronically*. Englewood Cliffs, NJ: Prentice-Hall.

Levinson, Cynthia Y. (1984). *The School Problem-solvers Guide to Distance Education*. Austin, TX: Southwest Educational Development Laboratory.

Norenberg, Curtis D. and Larry Lundblad. (1987). *Distance Delivery of Vocational Education: Technologies and Planning Matrices*. St. Paul, MN: Minnesota Research and Development Center for Vocational Education, University of Minnesota. (ERIC Document Reproduction Service no. ED 288 084.)

Pinsel, Jerry K. (1988). *Distance Learning: A Summary of Telecommunications Efforts Involving Education Service Agencies and Others*. Arlington, VA: American Association of Education Service Agencies.

G. Christopher Clark, The American Journal of Distance Education, *205 Rackley Bldg., Pennsylvania State University, University Park, PA 16802.*

By
THERESE
MAGEAU

Editor's Note: In this special report on telecommunications, we profile four teachers who differ in many ways: they are from vastly different geographic areas of the country (Oklahoma, New Jersey, Hawaii, California); one teaches in a Catholic school in the southwest; another teaches special education in a middle-class suburb of New York City; another teaches in a school located in the middle of a sugar cane plantation on an exotic island; and another teaches in a district that has the country's largest population of children of migrant farm workers.

Yet despite their differences, they all believe strongly in the value of telecommunications in education. Among their shared beliefs:

- telecommunications can be used to teach the curriculum; it does not have to be something "in addition" to what teachers are already charged to teach;
- telecommunications motivates children to learn because, in the words of one teacher, "it provides kids with an audience; it gives them a reason to write;"
- telecommunications promotes professional growth for teachers; as one teacher put it, "it breaks down the isolation of being in the classroom;"
- telecommunications helps teach children how to be citizens in the world of the future, because it gives them a skill they will be expected to know, and also because it helps children understand, in one teacher's words, "that the world is our community."

What follows are these teachers' stories: how they got started, some of their fascinating, curriculum-based projects, their tips for implementing a telecommunications program, and why they stay committed to keeping telecommunications alive in their classrooms, schools, and districts. We think you'll find their stories inspirational.

Kathy Rock, Tulsa, Okla.: From West Berlin to Beirut... Bringing the World to Students

"I feel very happy that they are Free now.... There have been very big parties 'cause they know that they can come to the 'west' and home every time if they want....Yes, me, I have relatives in GDR [German Democratic Republic]... We brought them fruits they couldn't get in GDR, clothes and food. You must know that they cannot get what they want. They have no fruits sometimes not enough meat... But now we invited them to visit us the next time... "

At the time the Berlin Wall was coming down, Kathy Rock's students at Sts. Peter and Paul School in Tulsa, Okla., received many letters like this over their computers. "We were in daily contact with children in West Berlin," reports Kathy. Through the AT&T Long Distance Learning Network, Kathy's students received letters from West Berlin students that discussed employment problems incurred from opening up the

539

wall, the lives of people who escaped into West Germany before the wall's opening, West Berlin children's opinions about East Germans moving to their country. Some of the letters were very moving. "They talked about going to the wall late at night and seeing all the candles and hearing the singing and seeing their moms and dads crying," says Kathy.

Kathy's students heard news of the Berlin Wall through professional sources as well. The XPress information news exchange sent her lab up-to-the-minute stories from seven different news services from around the world via a cable TV hook-up and a device called an infocipher hooked up to one of her IBM PCs. "I could print out news stories in English from both West Germany and East Germany," Kathy explains.

Interactive Simulations

"We have brought the world to our children," Kathy believes. And not just the western world. Last year Kathy and some of her eighth grade students took part in a worldwide telecommunications conference on the Middle East, sponsored by Interactive Communications and Simulations of the School of Education at the University of Michigan. Participating schools were assigned roles of real-life people in current middle eastern politics (Kathy and her students represented the Christian Lebanese leaders) and were charged with "making peace by finding compromises with all the other participating countries."

The Tulsa participants had to create a plan of action based on their country's needs and their understanding of the balance of power in the region. They made predictions about the outcomes of their plans, wrote press releases, did research, and communicated with other countries by following international protocol.

Offering A Choice Of Networks

Even the kindergartners at Sts. Peter and Paul are getting involved in worldwide communications. Through the Chimo Network (an Indian word that means "friendly trade"), her students are doing a cultural exchange with some Catholic schools in Canada, or, as Kathy puts it, "a kindergarten version" of a cultural exchange, which includes conducting a survey of favorite ice cream flavors.

Kathy believes in using a variety of networks because, "we're looking for different things to accomplish in school, and each network offers something unique." Offering a choice is especially important for encouraging more teachers to participate. "Because this is a new thing, because none of us learned this in college, it takes a while to get the teachers interested," says Kathy. "In the beginning, it's just another thing to fit into their day. We've got to find different projects that are going to excite each individual teacher so that they're willing to see how it can work in their classrooms."

Carol James, North Brunswick, NJ: Telecommunications' Special Role in Special Education

The idea of teaching telecommunications to special education children might have daunted some people, but not Carol James, a former teacher of neurologically impaired fourth, fifth, and sixth graders at the John Adams Elementary School in North Brunswick, N.J. "You find that special ed. kids frequently don't ever leave their town or state," says Carol, who is now one of two elementary computer lab teachers for her district. "I thought telecommunications would be a great opportunity for my students to expand their whole horizon."

Carol applied for and received a local district grant to start a modest telecommunications pilot program with her students. The pilot "grew beyond our expectations," says Carol. It in fact grew to the point where "every class in the school, including the preschool handicapped, participated in a telecommunications conference last year."

The Great Spring Vegetable Grow

Over the MIX network (McGraw-Hill's now defunct network which has more or less been replaced by MECC's Iris Network) John Adams Elementary participated last year in the "Great Spring Vegetable Grow," where classrooms around the country competed to grow the biggest vegetables and in the process learned various science skills such as measuring, plotting growth on graphs and charts, and experimenting with variables. Carol's students' job was to collect growth data from each class every week. Not surprisingly, considering Carol's students' infectious enthusiasm, John Adams Elementary won a nationwide competition for the heaviest radish, an honor the children still like to boast about.

First graders at Carol's school participated in a nationwide plotting of the migration of Canadian geese as they traveled the country. Little did the students know how pivotal their role would be in the siting process. Apparently, the geese love to congregate on the front lawn of the world headquarters of Johnson & Johnson, which is only a few miles away from John Adams Elementary. "We'd get messages from other schools saying, 'where are the geese? We haven't seen any.' And our kids would respond, 'that's because they're on the lawn of Johnson & Johnson!'"

Carol's special ed. students got to travel from the East to the West coast—telecommunicably, that is—courtesy of some mainstream seventh grade students in Oregon. The Oregon students were charged with taking Carol's students on a vacation from the East to the West coast. The seventh graders sent Carol's students an itinerary and Carol's students responded in "a language experience format about how they followed the itinerary: for example, 'we got to the top of the mountain, but so-and-so got sick from the altitude.'"

The days Carol's students received an itinerary, "they were ready with maps, atlases, travel guides, encyclopedias. They would *run* to the library." They learned about concepts such as inches per mile, altitude, the Continental Divide, even hydraulic dams. Carol reports that "it was one of the best examples of learning across the curriculum—math, language arts, science, history, geography."

Carol's students learned about their town history through an Iris network (MECC) conference entitled "Teleconnected Cultures." Using the library and conducting oral histories with town citizens, students collected information which they input in a data base and then shared with a culturally different school with which they had been matched. (They then used the data to create a town history timeline they gave to the mayor!) This project inspired the sixth grade class to research their families' immigrant histories to share with a school in California.

Perhaps one of the most successful conferences was the "Logo Pen Pal" exchange. The conference—which took place with a computer magnet school in St. Paul, Minn.—functioned like a simple pen pal exchange, but with a twist: students shared Logo programs instead of letters. This was particularly helpful for Carol's students who were unfamiliar with Logo. "The St. Paul students would write my kids saying, 'you're just learning Logo? You're going to love it! When you get to the lab next time, try this.' And they'd give them a program they'd written," says Carol. "Our kids were so excited and motivated to learn so that they could write their own LOGO programs to send out to Minnesota."

Buddy System Within The School

This kind of mentor system took place within Carol's school as well. Carol set up "buddy classes" where sixth graders team up with first graders, for example, to help them type their telecommunications correspondences. "A first grader could take an entire day to type a simple letter," explains Carol. "Not only does this system make the sixth graders feel good about themselves, it makes the first graders feel like they're connected."

The entire 1988-89 pilot was an immeasurable success, so much so that it

Helping Students Become Competent Researchers:
Using On-line Data Bases in the School Library

"Like many adults, I knew nothing about computers," recalls Joyce Sherman, the educational media specialist at Brunswick Acres School in South Brunswick, N.J. "I remember that once a month instead of a faculty meeting we all sat down at computers and tried to learn. I was the worst pupil," she adds laughing.

Worst pupil or not, when Joyce was approached by the districts computer coordinator to put a computer in her library and become part of the Dow Jones News Retrieval project, she reluctantly agreed. "Since then," says Joyce, "I've been an enthusiastic supporter. If I can do it, anyone can."

Dow Jones News Retrieval is an online network that provides access to data bases covering everything from the federal filings of the Security and Exchange Commission to movie reviews. Data bases for education include an on-line encyclopedia, news wire service, book reviews, newspapers, and nationwide weather information.

Joyce includes teaching how to use the data base retrieval service as a required part of the library skills curriculum she's designed for her K-6 school.

"What I consider my curriculum," says Joyce, "is to make students as competent researchers as I can before they leave the school. I want them to understand as we go into a whole new age that there are different ways of getting information not just from print. The aim of our whole program is to make kids comfortable finding things for themselves, to help them become independent learners."

Below are some of the on-line data base and information resource service available to educators:

Classmate
Dialog Information Services

was recognized by the state of New Jersey as one of the 10 best programs to exemplify the integration of technology into the curriculum. Carol's name was sent to the Computer Learning Foundation where winning projects from around the country will be compiled and disseminated.

Making A Community

It's clear from Carol's stories that telecommunications greatly benefits students, but Carol advocates telecommunications for the teacher's benefit as well. "Teachers get so stimulated and motivated by what other teachers are doing," says Carol. "Teachers tend to function in a cubicle. You're in your classroom. You might not even know what another teacher down the hall is doing. Yet here you have the opportunity to correspond with teachers from various parts of the country. I have seen with each exchange the work get better and better and better."

Carol has also seen her school become closer as a result of telecommunications projects. "What it does for the whole building is give us all such a sense of participating together, says Carol. "Telecommunications brings teachers together. It brings kids together. It makes for a community."

3460 Hillview Ave.
Palo Alto, Calif. 94304
(800) 334-2564

Users have access to 85 general interest data bases focusing on newspapers and magazines, general science, social studies, and the humanities. Curriculum materials include books, teacher guides, activity masters, transparencies, and a video. No subscription fee or monthly charge, just connect time. The phone call is free.

Dow Jones News Retrieval
Box 300
Princeton, N.J. 08543
(609) 452-1511

Allows access to 45 data bases of business, financial, general news weather, movie reviews, and an encyclopedia. An educator's guide contains a variety of lesson plans to supplement the service in a number of subject areas. A tutorial is also available. Flat monthly fee with unlimited connect time for most data bases.

X-Press Exchange
X-Press Information Services Ltd.
Regency Plaza One
4643 South Ulster St.,
Suite 340
Denver, CO 80237
(800) 772-6397

Provides "real time" news service from all over the world, including seven foreign press wires translated into English (information is also available in French and Spanish). One up-front charge for kit, which includes an "Infocipher" (a receiver that takes signal off a cable line and inputs it into a personal computer). Discount available to schools.

Maylene Siu, Kaipahu, Hawaii: Learning to Do Science... Over the Phone Lines

Maylene Siu's involvement with telecommunications took a fairly standard course: her students started out with pen pal letters, exchanging simple correspondence with children from other schools. Then she had them exchanging riddles and answers, "to practice getting on and off line," she explains. They then progressed to telecommunications research projects: using a data base to find information and then reporting it online to research partners at other schools.

What was unusual about Maylene's first telecommunications program, however, was that her K-6 students at Honowai Elementary School, just outside Honolulu on the island of Oahu, communicated not with students in Alaska or outer Mongolia, but with the high school students in the same town.

"We were essentially adopted by the local high school," says Maylene. "It was a mentor program where my students could try out telecommunications while gaining an understanding of what high school life is like." Each of Maylene's students had a high school partner they interviewed about life in high school. Eventually the younger students got to visit their partners at the high school and see their telecommunications and computing lab.

Starting At An Early Age

"It's important to expose children at an early age," believes Maylene. "Telecommunications is part of society and children become used to it when they're exposed to it. When my students went to the high school lab, they were able to say, 'Oh yeah, I know about this.' It wasn't something strange to them."

Maylene admits that when she was first learning about telecommunications it seemed very strange to her. "I was just like a child. How can information be transferred over the telephone lines, I wondered? Then we got a faster modem and it became a little more fascinating because the data was transmitted so quickly I couldn't read it fast enough on the screen."

Her fascination led Maylene to agree to participate in a pilot for National Geographic's *Kids Network,* a telecommunications program, sponsored by the National Science Foundation and now commercially available, that teaches elementary students science via a worldwide network.

Hands-On Science Projects

Kids Network, or *Kids Net* as it is referred to familiarly, is a unique program that combines an exploratory approach to the teaching of science (stressing skills such as original, hands-on research, careful observation, accurate recording and reporting of data, and drawing conclusions) with geography skills (such as map reading and plotting), and telecommunications. The first unit Maylene's school participated in, entitled *Hello* introduced students to data collecting and reporting by having them catalog their class pets, sharing and comparing their information nationwide, and drawing conclusions about how geography might play a role in the kinds of animals students have for pets.

The second unit, *Acid Rain* had students constructing rain collectors, using pH papers to test the rain water for its acidity, sharing and comparing their information with other schools from around the country, and again, drawing conclusions about the role geography might play in influencing the acidity level of rain water.

One of the great values of the project, according to Maylene, is that it helped her students see how the computer can be used as a science tool. "It was the first time they did science-related activities using the power of the computer," she reports. "It is a very good utilization of the whole system, because it helps a child not only understand telecommunications but how the computer can help them understand information they've collected. For other science activities, my students began to ask me, 'since the computer helped us graph the acid rain, could it also be able to take my data now?'"

Maylene shares the *Kids Net* philosophy of learning by doing. She gives her students complete control over their telecommunications and computers. "I don't do any of it at all, except to instruct with open-ended questions like, 'What do you think will happen?'"

Building Local Communication

Maylene is implementing a *Kids Net* kind of program on an island basis, using telecommunications to have local students compare data about pets. In fact, much of Maylene's telecommunications emphasis has been on improving communications at a local level. This may seem odd to people from other areas of the country who might assume that schools in Maylene's small island community would easily communicate with one another, but before telecommunications, Maylene reports, that wasn't necessarily so.

"Before, to talk to a teacher at another school, you had to wait to get a call through, which is always a problem because you call, leave a message, get a message back in return"—in effect, play telephone tag all day—"or you sent a note via the district mail truck. Now we use telecommunications among our teachers. We put the message on electronic mail and people can correspond daily. More and more teachers are getting on-line," says Maylene. The end result she says, is that "communication between schools is much better."

Yvonne Andres, Oceanside, Calif.: FrEd Mail Means Free Access to Fresh Ideas

Hundreds of FrEd Mail users around the country know her as OCNSIDE SYSOP. Others know her as the editor of *FrEd Mail News*. She is also known (by people in the know) as one of the original developers—along with Al Rogers and Nick Sayers—of FrEd Mail, the utterly affordable educational network. (FrEd Mail stands for "Free Educational Electronic Mail.")

But if you think Yvonne Andres—FrEd Mail "systems operator," unflagging reporter of FrEd Mail happenings, designer of FrEd Mail curricular projects, and all around FrEd Mail guru-enthusiast—started out as a computer hacker, think again.

"My background is psychology and sociology and I was mostly an English teacher," says the Jefferson Jr. High School, Oceanside, Calif., teacher. Yvonne had never even touched a computer until several years ago when someone donated an Apple II to her class of gifted sixth graders. "It was amazing to me to see the impact that one measly computer had on the students. They were so interested and so motivated that we expanded to a lab." In the process of expanding, they heard about how "computers could communicate with other computers. It was a real interesting idea at the time," says Yvonne. "And that's what did it. To be really honest, I'm not sure I would still be in teaching if I hadn't gotten involved with telecommunications. This is something that's exciting every day."

How FrEd Mail Works

How FrEd Mail works is also something that's exciting every day. As an example: suppose Yvonne's school wants to call a school in Troy, Mich. In the middle of the night, when phone rates are at their lowest, Yvonne's Mail would call SDCOE (San Diego Computer On-line Educators). FrEd Mail does it on its own; no one has to be there to do the dialing. The SDCOE, which works from grant money and therefore can afford to make longer distance calls, would then dial another FrEd Mail location (preferably another agency with a grant), perhaps in Wyoming, who would then dial another nearby FrEd Mail location. This piggyback calling system continues across the county until the destination school is reached; for the most part, all calls made are local or near-local calls, and grant money is spent on the longer distance calls. When the Michigan teacher comes in the next morning, Yvonne's message is waiting for her. Yvonne' s school only paid for the cost of calling San Diego in the middle of the night...pennies.

Kid Connections

But what's perhaps most exciting about FrEd Mail is the array of educational projects that Yvonne and other FrEd Mail users have designed, including The Soviet-American Space Bridge, Acid Rain, and the Idiom Project.

Yvonne's most current project is Kid Connections, a history/social science interactive network sponsored by the California Technology Project and based on the philosophy that "using technology will provide students with learning experiences that could not be duplicated within the confines of their own classrooms." Among the Kid Connections projects in the works: Commercially Speaking, where students survey and compare television commercials from different areas of the country: Original Opinions, where students exchange essays on contemporary, controversial issues; and The Experts Speak, where one group of students assumes personalities of non-living historical figures and another group interviews them to determine their identities.

(Yvonne is also adapting Kid Connections to work on other networks, such as Prodigy, AT&T Long Distance Learning Network, and CSU [California State University] Net.)

Yvonne finds that student enthusiasm is at an all-time high when she adapts something she's already teaching as part of the curriculum into a telecommunications project. "Students are much more motivated when they're going to be writing to another group of students and if they know they'll be getting feedback from them," says Yvonne. "They pay more attention to their spelling and punctuation and how they express themselves."

She also finds that, by and large, American students are not that knowledgeable about the larger world. She cites as an example how her students were communicating with Australian students, and the Australians wanted to hold a conference on world problems

"Our students couldn't even begin to talk about world problems," Yvonne says. "Most students, especially up until high school, don't have that much knowledge of the outside world. Their whole focus is on what's happening locally, in their school and community." Telecommunications gives students "building blocks" with which they can construct their world knowledge.

Having both a perspective on the rest of the world, as well as an understanding on how to communicate globally is crucial to today's students, believes Yvonne, because "electronic communications will become a necessity for business and education very soon as transportation and new buildings costs increase." These factors will affect how people work: "people will be telecommuting," Yvonne predicts, "working at home and commuting electronically." Therefore, giving students a background in telecommunication skills is imperative. "Any kind of base that you can give kids that they can use in their futures is important."

Therese Mageau is an Associate Editor for Teaching and Computers *and* Electronic Learning.

A Directory of Educational Networks and On-Line Projects

If you want to get involved with telecommunications, your options are practically limitless. Following is a list of just some of the networks and telecommunications projects available to teachers and students. In addition to a brief product or service description, we've included pricing structure and subscription information. Some networks are compatible with several computer types, while other are machine-specific. For further information, contact individual organizations.

America On-line
8619 Westwood Center Drive
Vienna, Va. 22182
(800) 227-6364
Formerly AppleLink, American On-line is a telecommunications service for the Apple community. Provides E-mail, updates for Apple II and Macintosh users, conferencing, and extensive reference library on product and technical information. Tutoring Center offers study materials and courses. Monthly fee and hourly connect charges.

CompuServe
5000 Arlington Centre Blvd.
P.O. Box 20212
Columbus, Ohio 43220
(800) 848-8199
Provides on-line access to news, financial services, travel reservations, forums, and live educational conferences. Extensive E-mail system and on-line "shopping mall." Sign-up fee and hourly connect charges.

Delphi
3 Blackstone St.

Cambridge, Mass. 02139
(800) 544-4005
(617) 491-3393 in Mass.
Provides E-mail, encyclopedia, news, games, shopping, groups and clubs, and travel information. Members come from over 40 countries. Sign-up fee and hourly connect charges.

FrEdMail Project
San Diego County Office of Education
Linda Vista Rd.
San Diego, Calif. 92111
(619) 292-3639
A cooperative educational messaging network in which participants contribute to the activities of the network. Two conferences are available: Ideas, a teaching ideas exchange; and Kidwire, a bulletin board to post student work. Software and connect time are free. Toll calls are necessary if there's no local bulletin board.

GEnie
Box 02B-C, 401 N. Washington St.
Rockville, Md. 20850
(800) 638-9636
Information services covering finance, travel, news, reference, shopping, computing, and entertainment. A Round Table special interest group on education is available. Sign-up fee and hourly connect charges.

GTE Education Services
2021 K St. NW, Suite 215
Washington, D.C. 20006
(202) 835-7311
The largest information and communications network servicing education. Among the many on-line services: *Ed-*

Line, data bases covering education management issues; *SciTech,* structured classroom activities that provide access to current scientific information; and *SpecialNet,* information exchange for special education. Pricing structure varies depending upon service.

Institute For Global Communications
3228 Sacramento St.
San Francisco, Calif. 94115
(415) 923-0900

A network dedicated to global peace and environment issues enables users in over 70 countries to communicate via E-mail and conferencing. Also offers data bases. Conferences include *PeaceNet, EcoNet, and ConflictNet.* Costs include a sign-up fee, connect time charge, and a monthly minimum.

Interactive Communications and Simulations
School of Education
University of Michigan
Ann Arbor, Mich. 48109-1259
(313) 763-6716

A worldwide network that offers role-playing simulations and conferences covering such issues as the Arab-Israeli conflict. An interactive poetry guild sponsors writing and sharing of verse. Eighteen different countries are participating members. One up-front registration fee.

Iris
MECC
3490 Lexington Ave. North
St. Paul, Minn. 55126
(800) 228-3504

Formerly the McGraw-Hill Information Exchange (MIX), Iris provides on-line curricular-based projects in language arts, social studies, math, and science for all grade levels. The Teacher Center promotes the exchange of ideas and col-

legiality. Annual subscription and hourly access fee.

Kids Network
National Geographic Society
17th and M Sts.
Washington, D.C. 20036
(202) 775-6580

Students perform hands-on, locally researched science projects (such as on acid rain) then share their results via the network with other schools across the country. An on-line scientific specialist helps students interpret and understand their results. One-time charge covers software, print and lab materials. Connect time is a flat fee that covers the duration of each project.

Learning Link
Learning Link National Consortium
356 W. 58th St.
New York, N.Y. 10019
(212) 560-6868

A full on-line system that features a variety of data bases and information resources, message centers and mail, threaded discussions, surveys, and gateways to remote data bases, and bulletin boards. Access is usually through local or toll-free calls. Costs range from no charge to a yearly flat fee which includes toll-free unlimited access.

Long Distance Learning Network
AT&T, P.O. Box 716
Basking Ridge, N.J. 07920-0716
(800) 367-7225, ext. 4158

Offers curriculum-based projects through "learning circles," six to nine classrooms who exchange and discuss work for a set period of time, then publish a report of their work. Single subscription rate covers membership in a learning circle, all access costs, curriculum guide, tutorial disk, software, technical support, and a newsletter.

News Access

Teachable Tech
2179 Hannah Lane
Tucker, Ga. 30084
(404) 939-4596

A joint project of the Cable News Network and Teachable Tech, the project centers around CNN's "Week in Review" news program. Schools videotape the broadcast and receive a classroom guide via E-mail. Annual fee includes video and print duplication rights. Network access available through GTE and X-Press Exchange.

NYCENET

N Y City Board of Education
Computer Information Services
Intermediate School #25
34-65 192nd St.
Flushing, N.Y. 11358
(718) 935-4040

New York City Educational Network offers a bulletin board, on-line curriculum guides, encyclopedia, a data base of software titles, and realtime conferencing. NYCENET recently hooked up with Unitex, the bulletin board of the United Nations. Connect time is free.

Personal Sharing Information Network Project (PSINet)

IBM Educational Systems
PO Box 2150
Atlanta, Ga. 30055
(800) IBM-2468

Software designed to help geographically distributed IBM PC and PS/2 users establish their own network and communicate with each other. Software contains E-mail, bulletin board, and conferencing capabilities. Price varies, depending on whether you purchase network server software or single workstation software.

Prodigy

445 Hamilton Ave.
White Plains, N.Y. 10601
(914) 993-8000

On-line information on weather, consumer and general news, and sports. Educational services include The Club, an electronic bulletin board for kids; The SmartKids quiz, in which children test their knowledge of history, geography and other subjects; science and rock and roll news, updated daily. Flat monthly fee, local access.

SchoolLink

Radio Shack Education Division
700 One Tandy Center
Fort Worth, Texas 76102
(817) 390-2967

A joint effort between Tandy/Radio Shack and GTE, SchoolLink is an international telecommunications project that explores integrated curricular activities in science and social studies and attempts to foster intercultural awareness among diverse student populations. One fee covers the first 10 hours of on-line time; additional 10 hour time blocks available at a discount. Sign-up closes June 15.

Unison Education Network

Unison Telecommunications Service
700 West Pete Rose Way
Cincinnati, Ohio 45203
(513) 723-1700

A large E-mail network that can exchange mail with more than 25 other on-line systems. The Education Network allows users to build private information and conferencing networks. Annual fee, hourly access charges.

Note: A modem is required to reach some of the phone numbers listed on this page.

Article #14
Distance Learning: What's Holding Back This Boundless System?

THERE ARE UNRESOLVED ISSUES THAT STUNT THE GROWTH OF DISTANCE LEARNING, BUT SPECIFIC EFFORTS MAY YET UNCHAIN ITS POTENTIAL.

BY
ISABELLE
BRUDER

The concept of "distance learning" really is as simple as it sounds: the learner in one location, the source of instruction in another.

But concepts fade without practical applications and, as can be expected, the application of this still relatively new educational delivery system incorporates countless concerns, possibilities, and some confusion.

Current definitions of distance learning usually refer to a situation where the learner and the educator use telecommunications or electronic devices (cable, satellite, fiber optics, broadcast, video, and computer technology) to interactively follow part or all of a course program.

For the purposes of this article, the definition of distance learning is one offered by the U.S. Department of Education's Office of Educational Research and Improvement: "the application of telecommunications and electronic devices which enable students and learners to receive instruction that originates from some distant location. Typically, the learner is given the capacity to interact with the instructor or program directly, and given the opportunity to meet with the instructor on a periodic basis."

Art Sheekey, acting director of the Information Resources division and the Information Technology branch of the OERI, points out that, "the key is that distance learning involve some electronic devices, and that it enable students to learn from instruction that originates someplace else. The difference between this and say, an open university tele-course or educational television, is that this is interactive, two-way technology."

Distance learning, or distance education, has evolved slowly, from mail order/ correspondence courses to interactive electronic mail. And that evolution will continue for some time because distance learning still has a long road to travel.

"I'll tell you what the biggest problem in trying to explain these things to people is," says Jason Ohler, director of the Educational Technology Program at the University of Alaska, Juneau. "It's the concept of the future. Most people think of the future in terms of their own lifespans, unconsciously. It's like this gate comes down shut and they can't get beyond that 70 or 80 years. I liken the origins of distance education in the United States, this period right now, to the installation of the first few steam engines in factories. Now, 200 years later, we see that it has totally revolutionized our roles, how people relate to each other."

Who Needs It

Helping people relate to each other and the world around them is exactly what distance learning is all about—bringing educational opportunities where none would otherwise exist.

551

So who is the distance learner? Although most often found in secondary and higher education (where a more flexible atmosphere lends itself to various applications), distance education knows no age limit—it may include anyone in K-12, higher education, or adult education. Ohler suggests that "the biggest misunderstanding in distance education" is identifying the student.

The distinction between distance and traditional learners is often more societal. The distance learner may be one of a number of people, says Ohler. Among them are:

- The geographically disadvantaged;
- The physically disabled;
- The financially disadvantaged ("because it's just a hell of a lot cheaper than building a school," he says);
- Those simply wanting to take advantage of the opportunities electronic media provides;
- Those in need of remediation;
- Those who want to avoid particular learning dynamics or particular content ("The federal government has estimated that of the half-million home learners in the U.S. most of them are at home to avoid secular content, says Ohler);
- Those wanting to protect cultural lifestyle and mobility (particularly among Native Americans, Ohler says, "it's a way to keep one foot in mainstream culture and another in their own").

The two major reasons to use distance learning as an educational delivery system, concludes Ohler, are to provide equity of educational opportunity, and to make up for the lack of conventional resources.

"Those, to a lot of people, would be essentially the same thing," he adds. "Let me put it this way: equity of enrichment. Because a lot of the schools buying into [distance learning] programs are the small schools that cannot afford the upper end of the education spectrum. So they have four students wanting calculus and they can't hire a calculus teacher, but they can afford to beam in a teacher via satellite."

Gregory Benson, director of the New York State Center for Learning Technologies Policy, Research and Development, Albany, agrees with Ohler's assessment of when distance education is best used.

"It's almost an inarguable situation [to use distance learning] if you can say, 'Look, these kids can't meet the minimum graduation requirements unless we do it this way.' And it's almost as strong to say, 'this kid has a skill and a propensity in this area and is highly motivated, and we can't offer advanced astronomy at our school unless we do it this way.' Because then the argument [to use distance learning] is not one of requirements or minimum requirements but one of whether or not we afford the learning opportunity in an individualized way for a student with the motive and enthusiasm to learn the topic. Are we going to keep that from him because of some regulation, or teacher certification or whatever?"

Identifying the Issues

Identifying the distance learner is, of course, just one battle of the war. There are virtually innumerable issues associated with establishing distance learning systems on a local, state, or national basis. Interwoven at all levels are policy issues that affect both faculty and learner.

Some of the issues are: the responsibility of instruction (which currently rests with state or local agencies); teacher certification (since distance learning may cross state boundaries) and career ladder concerns; course accreditation; and funding.

Benson, who oversees technology and telecommunications applications in elementary, secondary, post-secondary, public library, and cultural institutions in New York, offers another prospectus of the issues confronting distance learning.

"There's a general knee-jerk reaction within the profession, I think, to technology," he says. "That's not to say there aren't a whole lot of people out there who understand what needs to be done, what can be done and are willing to do it. But that group is still really at the forefront; it certainly doesn't represent the masses."

The generalized resistance to technology, he adds, is compounded "because anyone who speaks of offering a course remotely, in terms of the teacher's perception or in terms of the teachers' union's perception, is immediately talking about displacing a teacher. And then you raise the whole spectrum of job security." A way to resolve that, he says, has been to involve the teachers and, hopefully, the unions or collective bargaining agents, very early in the planning process. "So that, in fact, they understand that it's not displacing a teacher when a course is offered in, say, Latin I to five schools via cable system because the fact of the matter is those kids would not be able to take the course without it. There aren't teachers for it. And we've found that when projects have involved teachers early on, the teachers actually became advocates for this."

Another teacher-related issue, says Benson, involves salary and career ladder potential. If a teacher is given a larger workload with the addition of distance learning courses, would that teacher be financially compensated? And, in some cases, these teachers are referred to as "master" teachers because they serve multiple districts, when, in fact, they may not have reached that rung on the traditional career ladder yet.

"From a teacher's perspective, when she's at District A being beamed into Districts B, C, and D," says Benson, "it raises the question of why she can't be an employee of the district that has the better benefits. As you can see, there are a whole range of policy issues that you begin to confront."

The situation is different than any educational policy makers have known before, and that is evident when confronting the issue of certification—one of the hottest topics in distance learning today.

Lloyd Otterman, chairman and CEO of TI-IN, a Texas-based private satellite network which currently provides 23 states with math, science, and foreign language courses, and one of the Star Schools grant recipients (see Washington Report, Electronic Learning, Nov./Dec. 1988), agrees that certification justifiably rates high priority on distance learning issues.

"If there's anything that can really slow down the progress of distance learning," Otterman says, "it's these kinds of issues [such as certification] that states haven't thought through yet. Today there is no state that has really worked out its program in certification or curriculum to accommodate distance learning without a lot of provisional agreements. Because distance learning has just sort of sprung up, and they weren't ready for it."

Solutions to Certification?

Although TI-IN has not solved the certification issue, it does ensure that all its teachers (15-16) are certified in states where the courses are offered. To do this, the company seeks approval on credentials the teachers (recruited nationally) already have. In addition, all TI-IN teachers are certified in Texas and have passed other national tests. says Otterman.

"Unfortunately, in many cases we only end up with provisional credentials [provisional credentials are temporary and, in this case, must be reviewed yearly for renewal] because our teachers may not have had programs required by local classroom teachers, such as state history."

Such requirements imposed on telecourse teachers "pose a serious threat to the success of distance learning," Otterman says, "because the power of the medium lies in its wide applicability and use. To the extent that you limit it, you limit the effectiveness and economics of it. The promise of all this is to be able to bring first class instructional programs to America's schools in a cost-effective way."

Distance education opens up "a whole new sphere of knowledge," says George Rush, product manager, Technical and Information Systems for the Chief Council of State School Officers (CCSSO). "When you start talking about interstate certification, there are various kinds of expectations and standards that are established within a state, and people are reluctant to discontinue those."

Although there is currently no national certification, says Rush, "we're moving in that direction." CCSSO is currently working on a plan, to be released in November, concerning distance learning and the federal role.

What has happened up to this point in terms of distance learning is that most states have tended to operate under special exclusions. In other words, where there is some sort of policy that would prevent distance learning from occur-

ring [such as certification restrictions], there have been exceptions made, Rush says.

How realistic is national certification? "It depends on the definition," says Rush. "If we talk about national certification for a special set of circumstances, such as distance learning, that can occur much quicker than a set of criteria that all states accept for all teaching. It might take, if interest is sufficient, two years [to implement]. We're talking about a special set of circumstances and a desire to accommodate technology that is here and has the potential to have an impact on the delivery of instruction."

National certification is "a two-stage process," says Rush, "one that would address that special population [distance learners]; then a longer research and investigation period."

In fact, national certification may be necessary to further the distance learning effort, according to Rush. "I think it is something that will provide an opportunity for distance learning to be installed on an easier basis."

Curriculum Concerns

Even if teachers attain across-state certification, the curriculum must still meet two minimum requirements: first, it must either be tailored for the distance learning technology or the technology must be designed around the curricula (no one formula works for every program); and second, the curriculum must fit the standards in the given state.

Otterman of TI-IN says national telecourses should not be dependent on local or state requirements, because they should deal with subject areas national in scope. Eventually, he adds, "there's going to have to be a set of regulations developed in subject matter—such as math, science and foreign language—

that all states agree can be broadcast nationally. That's the only reasonable way to approach it, but it's not going to happen overnight."

For local telecourses, he adds, there should, of course, be an entirely different set of regulations.

As no new regulations on curriculum have yet been passed through legislature, Jason Ohler of Alaska voices a common perception of the way curriculum is currently handled in distance education. Namely, the importance, or danger, of cross-cultural distance education. How do you teach a wide area and keep a local angle? he asks.

"That is, if I am taking American history from a guy in Texas, there's a great chance he's not even going to mention Alaska," he says. "In a sense, whoever projects, dominates. So how do the facilitator and the people who develop the materials leave openings to personalize and localize that education? That's a critical issue. There are some theories on how to do that, but it's wide open at the moment. That's real important, especially when you're considering people like Native Americans.

"An interesting comment came from a Native woman," says Ohler, "who said the reason the missionaries that came to our community weren't successful is because they got us all together and they talked about the lion laying down with the lamb, and all the Natives looked at each other and said, 'What's a lion?' "

By the same token, says Greg Benson of New York, cross-cultural or "institutional ego" can be equally damaging to distance education curriculum.

"Some states have a lesser degree of, oh, institutional ego than others," says Benson. "Some states set up procedures to look at the curriculum programming [in other states] and determine if the content fits their requirements. But if,

as all these recent studies are saying, we've got to do something in math, then I think we ought to do something across the states, nationally, and not pretend that two plus two in Texas is six. It's four, period. The solutions of algebraic problems are the same no matter what state you're in."

Curriculum requirements, state to state, do vary in emphasis, he says, "and some of the Texas social studies courses, because some of the things emphasized are regionally based," aren't right for New York. "But there are areas where I think a lot of that is truly contrived." he asserts, "and it has to do with a 'not invented here' notion that we all have to get over."

Another part of the curriculum issue concerns staff development or training. Staff development is especially important in obvious "hot" areas—such as AIDS education and substance abuse—that have captured national attention over recent years and often require new curriculum.

In New York state, says Benson, "we've used, particularly in the AIDS education area, teleconferencing as a distance learning mechanism from the state to the regions. We did that a couple of years ago when we first got into the AIDS curriculum, and one of the outcomes was the creation of a local advisory council comprised of community members."

Developing Partnerships

The curriculum problems lead to another "issue within the issue," Benson says. That is, cooperative development related to curriculum programming.

"If we're going to address distance learning in an organized way and understand that many of the problems we have in New York are not much different than what's being faced in other districts in the state or in Florida or California or Texas, then what we really need are mechanisms for cooperatively developing materials, curriculum, and support materials for distance learning. That may mean cross-state development; it may mean universities working together. And you're beginning to see that."

One main example of cooperative ef-forts on the K-12 level is the recent Star School demonstration grants awarded to four consortia for distance learning efforts. The purpose of the Star Schools program is to encourage improved in-struction in math, science, foreign lan-guages, and other subjects among small or remote schools via satellite or other distance learning technologies.

Ten Tips for Statewide Distance Learning

1. Consider establishing a State Task Force on Distance Learning which can assist districts and institutions in planning, creating, and implement-ing distance learning programs. The Task Force may include leaders in the fields of education, communica-tions, government and business. *(An essential issue here is the development of relationships with collective bar-gaining agents, teacher's unions, or representation agents, in states where such organizations exist.)*

2. Officials, administrators, and edu-cators must keep abreast of the con-stant changes in technology and the advances in computer-aided instruc-tion. State grants could be provided to partially offset the cost of trips to conferences and subscriptions to the various learning journals as well. For institutions or districts without distance learning facilities and in-formation, such aid can help start the process

3. The Task Force can create and pro-duce a series of packaged training programs that instruct teachers, ad-ministrators, and technicians on the planning, design, operation, and analysis of distance learning projects. Videotaped instructional

packages can be loaned or sold, de-pending on need. Also, assistance may be provided by the state to de-termine whether it would be benefi-cial to implement a distance learn-ing system at all.

4. Rigorous evaluation procedures must be undertaken on a regular basis by participating districts and institutions. The evaluation process should be contemplated long before distance programs are implemented. Proper technological responses to students' needs, the cost-effective-ness of the program, resource avail-ability and management are impor-tant. The Task Force can help create evaluation standards for existing and planned programs.

5. The state could create the framework that determines how state funds should be distributed. In addition, the state must provide a leadership role in determining the most cost-effective means of transmitting edu-cational information. Also, determin-ing what are the best technical or operational systems that match the specific needs of the districts and in-stitutions is vital and something that can be accomplished at the state level.

6. There is a real need for wider and

Benson asserts that the Star Schools program, which awarded more than $19 million total, does not work as a cooperative effort.

"Unfortunately, it treated projects as separate. I know there are efforts for cooperative development now, but it's after the fact." Benson says the proposals for the Star School awards ought to have included a provision for some cooperative development between the four award winners, "so we didn't have four Star Schools awards to develop" four different projects.

"I know the problems they have with that from a political point of view and all that, but I think when we get down to it we need to begin looking more systemi-

more comprehensive planning involving a broader range of institutions and individuals. A greater spectrum of interested parties across all levels of the educational process, such as guidance counselors and others should be involved in the planning and implementation of projects. The scope and depth of planning must be increased and new groups brought into the planning, implementation and evaluation process.

7. It is imperative to build on distance learning systems currently existing and utilize these networks to their greatest capacity, as it makes no sense to create redundant systems. Therefore, the advantages of using currently operating systems to learners at all levels is that it will help prevent the waste of money and resources. Where the infrastructure is in place, what is needed is the insight to use the existing technology in a proper manner.

8. There is a need for more comprehensive state legislation and funding. In the past, legislative approaches have leaned toward specific regions or specific technologies. There is the need for greater systematic planning, integration, and coordination of available resources that meet specific needs. Without coordinated statewide planning, redundant, inflexible systems are created that cannot respond to the needs of the students.

9. Interested parties in distance learning networks must not become overly enamored with and interested in only the technology (hardware) of the system. Designing the actual programming, curriculum, and content of the courses being offered is vital. This "software" portion of the system takes a great deal of time and thought to design. Without the proper class materials and the correct style of pedagogy, all the hardware in the world means nothing.

10. There is a pressing need to create consistent reporting practices by the participating institutions to the appropriate authorities or the Task Force on Distance Learning. Details of the operating networks, as well as the strengths, weaknesses, and problems of operation should be reported on standardized forms to expedite the flow of information and the exchange of knowledge among all interested parties.

cally at education in this state, and across the states. In which case, there will have to be cooperative development and some incentive for that."

But these first demonstration grants awarded in the Star Schools program are the precursors to more extensive cooperative development," says Otterman of TI-IN. In that respect, the award winners ought to demonstrate a variety of developments in distance learning.

"This is a demonstration project," Otterman points out, "and one of the things it should do is find out the best mixes of [distance learning] products. Star Schools does that well. It's the differences that are important right now."

University Involvement

Not surprisingly, universities dominated the consortia make-up in the Star Schools awards. Universities are natural partners to choose for research and development of distance education programs. For one thing. says Greg Benson, "those conditions that we've identified so far that inhibit the application of distance learning at the secondary level—certification and curriculum issues—really don't exist at post-secondary levels. The other thing is that post-secondary institutions compete for students. And if distance learning allows colleges to better compete and extend campus offerings off the campus site, that has significant revenue implications [more students, more tuition coming in]."

Also, as Benson points out, because universities receive national accreditation, they are "already attuned to a far bigger geopolitical region...as opposed to the K-12 area which is clearly defined by a residency parameter."

Development partnerships at universities are not new, of course. One such partnership is the National University Teleconferencing Network (NUTN) begun in 1982 and housed at Oklahoma State University, Stillwater. NUTN is a consortium of 250 accredited higher education institutions, and offers programs and services to members and others.

Bill Dunn, assistant director of NUTN, says NUTN was created to act as an official association of the member universities, to share or exchange programming in the form of video teleconferencing via satellite.

NUTN offers over 100 (noncredit) programs a year to the general public through universities and exclusively to members. Programming varies (a recent subject, suggested by members and shown at 200 sites, was "date rape") and is developed by NUTN members, outside sources, and the NUTN home office at OSU. With a data base of 1,000 institutions throughout the U.S. who have downlinking facilities, NUTN offers a variety of training services.

Evidently, cooperative partnerships (and there are dozens) such as TI-IN and NUTN are a vital part of bringing distance education to the point of commonality.

Equally important is congressional support. That's one reason why the office of Technology Assessment, Washington, D.C., is in the process of conducting a study on distance learning technologies. [The results of the study are expected by late summer.]

Educating state, federal, and industry policy makers is undoubtedly the first step, says Benson. Educating them "in a very deliberate way. The problem is there's no continuity to it. You know, the OTA's responsibility is to do a report and move onto the next one. That's all well and good, but we need mechanisms that involve specific collaboration across public and private sectors, higher education, as well as in the whole range of public and private institutions that can play a role here. That really has to be done on a national basis."

Benson also asserts that learners must be presented with flexible educational delivery options. "I think we need to get away from the institutional structure of education. I'm not yet saying we need a revolution. I'm thinking deliberate and thoughtful evolution," he says. "We need to relax a little bit some of the traditional regulations in K-12."

Certainly, there are many concerns, and the possibilities of distance learning seem to be in the process of being addressed at most levels of policy-making. Yet, distance learning is still so new a concept it may require more time for experimentation, definition, and regulation before it effectively takes its place among educational delivery systems.

"I keep coming back, even in my own work," says Benson, "to the institutional motive versus the learner motive. And it's becoming a little discouraging that there is a discrepancy between the two of some inordinate magnitude."

Article #15
Breaking Down Classroom Walls:
Distance Learning Comes of Age

IT DOESN'T MATTER WHICH OF THE MANY AVAILABLE TECHNOLOGIES YOU
USE. THE GOAL IS THE SAME: TO TRANSPORT INFORMATION, NOT PEOPLE.

BY
GREGORY
JORDAHL

Peer into a high school classroom in any of a hundred rural towns across the country and you'll see a handful of teenagers watching TV, talking on the phone, or matching wits with a computer. But don't jump to conclusions. These students aren't simply entertaining themselves with adolescent pastimes; they are using their favorite media as tools for pursuing the knowledge needed to compete effectively in an increasingly complex world.

Televisions, telephones, and computers are currently playing leading roles in the rapidly evolving field of *distance learning*—the delivery of instruction from a central site to one or more remote locations. Taking advantage of recent advances in telecommunications, many rural—and some urban—educators are plugging into distant education networks in order to offer their students a broader range of high-quality, cost-effective instruction.

It wasn't too long ago that distance learning conjured up images of students sitting in front of a video screen listening to a one-way lecture from a talking head. There was no real interaction occurring between students and teacher, because there was no way to communicate with the image on the video screen.

Today, however, schools are taking advantage of newer technologies to build into their distance learning projects *crucial two-way communication links* between teachers and students. These links allow rural schools to simulate traditional classroom interaction—even though the teacher may be many miles away from the students.

Rapid Growth

In 1987, fewer than ten states were promoting distance learning. Today, virtually every state has some type of distance education plan. This rapid expansion in distance education is attributable to two major factors: declining rural populations and increased educational standards.

Declining rural populations, along with flagging economies and mounting teacher shortages, have forced many smaller, more isolated school districts to exclude from their curricula all but the most basic subjects. As a result, many rural high schools have had to graduate students without the background in foreign languages, higher-level math, and advanced science that today's colleges and careers require.

At the same time, state governments have responded to recent calls for educational reform by strengthening state educational standards. Many have toughened graduation requirements, while others have increased the curriculum standards for schools applying for state accreditation. As a result, many schools find themselves in the awkward situation of having to offer elective subjects for which neither funds nor teachers are available.

Faced with these circumstances, educators are tying into distance learning projects in record numbers. While projects vary greatly in both technologies used and geographical areas served, the goal of each is the same: to broaden educational opportunity by sharing scarce or costly instructional resources.

Two-Way TV

One of the most advanced applications of distance learning uses two-way television to connect instructors with students at remote sites. Rural school districts in Minnesota, for example, are using two-way television to transmit audio and video signals between participating classrooms located within instructional cooperatives. Depending on the location of each school, signals may be sent via cable, microwave, fiber optic, or low-power UHF transmission.

Under this system, every classroom is equipped with a group of television monitors and a video camera generally positioned to tape all the students in that class. The lead classroom may also have additional cameras for teacher use. The teacher (or a technician) controls the video images that appear on the monitors throughout the cooperative. For example, the teacher might transmit her image on one monitor and an image of the chalkboard, an overhead transparency, or a lab demo on another. When a question comes in from a remote site, the teacher can transmit an image of the student asking the question on yet another monitor. In effect, every participant can see and hear every other participant—just as they would if they were all in the same room.

What's more, some of the Minnesota schools have added other technologies to enhance student-teacher interaction. In Sibley County, for example, facsimile machines are being used to deliver tests and other class materials that were previously distributed by courier. This set-up trims turnaround time for student work submitted to the teacher, and permits the teacher to change assignments and tests at the last minute. Costs are kept to a minimum by transmitting the facsimile signals over the same cable facilities that deliver the video component of the instruction.

Through a series of federal, state, and private grants, over 100 Minnesota schools are now tied into two-way TV networks. These systems provide a wide variety of high school courses, including calculus, French, Spanish, speech, Russian history, and interior design. Teachers and administrators also use the facilities to conduct interdistrict meetings, thereby saving travel time and costs; and school officials make their networks available for community education and county extension workshops during after-school and weekend hours.

The effectiveness of two-way instructional television has attracted the attention of other states, too: Illinois, Iowa, Wisconsin, and New York all have successful projects underway. Moreover, a number of schools in these states have established partnerships with either cable or rural telephone companies to help defray direct equipment costs, which can range from $400,000 to $2 million per cooperative.

> In effect, every participant can see and hear every other participant—just as they would if they were all in the same room.

Audiographic Teleconferencing

Another approach finding favor among rural schools is audiographic teleconferencing, a system that connects teachers with students via a combination of computer and voice communications.

In this approach, a device called an audio bridge allows everyone in participating classrooms to hear one another, much as they would with two-way television. They also communicate via personal computers which are linked by modem and specially designed software

---

The Star Schools Project Gives Distance Learning a Big Push

Perhaps the single most powerful impetus for distance learning has come from the Star Schools Program, a grant project administered by the U.S. Department of Education (DOE). In 1988, the DOE awarded its first $19 million to four regional partnerships, each of which promised to develop high technology teaching networks that would reach elementary and secondary students in isolated, small, and disadvantaged schools. In the second year of the program, the DOE supplemented its initial grants with another $14.3 million, bringing the total for the two-year period to $33.3 million. The four original grantees are

- **The TI-IN Network,** based in San Antonio, Texas ($9.6 million);
- **The Technical Education Research Centers, Inc. (TERC),** based in Cambridge, Massachusetts ($4.4 million);
- **The Satellite Educational Resources Consortium (SERC),** based in Columbia, South Carolina ($9.7 million);
- **The Midland's Consortium,** based at Oklahoma State University, Stillwater ($9.6 million).

The four consortia have recently strengthened their projects by collaborating with one another and sharing resources. For example, students enrolled in TI-IN's physics course in 15 schools have experimented with the curriculum offered by TERC, and TI-IN viewers have also accessed satellite programs distributed by Midlands. To date, the partnerships have succeeded in delivering courses in math, science, foreign languages, and many other subjects to nearly 3,000 schools.

This past fall, the DOE began funding another round of two-year grants. A total of $14.8 million was awarded to four new partnerships, with each grantee contributing at least 25 percent in additional funds to their projects. The new grantees are

- **Central Education Telecommunications Consortium**, based in Washington, DC ($1.4 million);
- **Pacific Northwest Educational Telecommunications Partnership**, based in Spokane, Washington ($5 million);
- **Reach for the Stars: Massachusetts Corporation for Educational Telecommunications**, based in Cambridge ($4.9 million);
- **Telecommunications Education for Advances in Mathematics and Science Foundation**, administered by the Los Angeles County Office of Education ($3.5 million).

to the teacher's machine. Whatever is input into the teacher's computer—either via the keyboard or a graphics tablet—simultaneously appears on all the screens in the networked classrooms. In effect, the computer screen becomes an "electronic blackboard."

With this system, a math teacher can work through an equation while simultaneously clarifying the accompanying concepts over speaker phones installed at each site. Or a physics teacher can transmit animated graphics from her computer to each remote classroom while simultaneously delivering a lecture over the telephone. With special software, the system's computers can also send and receive information via a fax machine.

Since 1985, several schools in upstate New York have used audiographic teleconferencing to teach advanced placement courses in English, Spanish, history, chemistry, calculus, and music theory. This network, launched with a grant from various government and private sources, is one of over 200 projects that New York officials have designed that allow rural schools to offer low-enrollment elective courses by sharing qualified teachers.

The equipment required for audiographic teleconferencing—computer hardware, audio bridge, speaker phones, and associated software—averages between $6,000 and $13,000 per school. Participating schools normally share the long-distance charges incurred during the lessons. Until recently, audiographic systems required the use of two telephone lines, one for voice communications and the other for the data connection. Newer systems can combine both functions on one line, substantially reducing the on-going costs.

Satellite Networks

Two-way instructional television and audiographic teleconferencing are best suited for distance learning projects that span relatively small geographical areas. They also offer rural educators relatively strong control over educational programming, and consequently tend to be preferred by such educators.

However, many rural schools lack the resources to establish and manage the facilities to produce and deliver high-quality programming for such systems. As a result, an increasing number of schools have turned to a statewide or multi-state satellite network for delivery of effective distance learning programming. The centerpiece of these systems is a satellite dish or "uplink" that beams live instruction over a wide geographical area. Schools throughout the country receive these broadcasts via satellite reception dishes or "downlinks"—mounted on schoolhouse roofs or nearby.

One of the country's leading suppliers of satellite-delivered instructional programming for rural high schools is the Arts and Sciences Teleconferencing Service (ASTS), headquartered at Oklahoma State University in Stillwater. Serving over 6,000 students at 525 schools throughout the country, ASTS offers courses such as German, physics, and trigonometry taught by Oklahoma State professors.

During the twice-a-week ASTS class, students receive instruction via live video and interact with the teacher by toll-free telephone. On the remaining days of the school week, students use computers to practice recently introduced skills and concepts. The German course, for example, uses voice-enhanced software to test each student's grammar and pronunciation.

Students who have questions after class hours can either phone the professor or send questions by electronic mail. An adult classroom supervisor handles all the recordkeeping and on-site administrative duties at each outlying school.

The TI-IN network, another leading distance education supplier, currently transmits approximately 20 high school courses live to 6,000 students in 35 states. Headquartered near San Antonio, Texas, TI-IN uses live one-way video and two-way audio interaction via cordless telephones as its primary instructional vehicle. In addition to satellite delivery, TI-IN offers its courses over cable systems in several parts of the country.

A recent addition to TI-IN's technol-

New Video Supplements OTA's Distance Learning Study

Whoever said the government puts out nothing but dry, dull reports? When it comes to uses of technology in education, the Office of Technology Assessment continues to put out some of the most comprehensive, best researched, and most *readable* studies around.

In 1988, OTA produced the definitive report on educational technologies under the title *Power On! New Tools for Teaching and Learning.* Less than a year and a half later, the same agency came out with *Linking for Learning: A New Course for Education. Linking for Learning* is a 183-page softcover book that offers a comprehensive look at distance learning initiatives and projects across the country. It includes chapters on technologies used in the hybrid systems in place today, the effectiveness of various rural and non-rural projects, and state and federal roles in promoting distance learning within the educational community. It also has a useful appendix giving sample costs for various kinds of systems. "When we first published the report," says project director Linda Roberts, "we were a bit ahead of our time. We're getting more interest now—a year later—than we did when we first put the word out."

Currently, OTA is making available a two minute videotape to supplement *Linking for Learning.* The videotape is intended to illustrate certain aspects of the study that are better expressed through sound and pictures than in print. It examines the changes required in teaching methods when distance learning is employed in a district, and it explores the impact of distance learning on students' progress. It also looks at the future potential for distance learning technologies.

To purchase a VHS or BETA copy of the videotape *Linking for Learning: A New Course for Education,* send a check or purchase order for $30 to S.L. Productions, Box 1243, Manhasset, NY 11030. (New York State orders must add eight percent sales tax.) For a copy of the printed report, send $9 to Superintendent of Documents, Government Printing Office, Washington, DC 20402-9325; ask for *Linking for Learning: A New Course for Education,* GPO stock number 052-003-01170-1.

ogy repertoire is a voice mail system that handles overflow calls from students during the live video lessons. Questions recorded on the system are answered as soon as an instructor or instructional assistant is available. TI-IN officials predict that the system will eventually be used to record the foreign language exercises that students currently send on tape to TI-IN headquarters. This approach is expected to increase dramatically the speed with which students obtain feedback on their work.

Perhaps the most ambitious educational satellite system is Star Channels, developed by Kentucky Educational Television. From a communications center in Lexington, programming is beamed to the state's 1,300 elementary and secondary schools. Along with interactive courses, the network offers enrichment and staff development programs. Star Channels was initiated in 1986 with a $11.4 million appropriation from the Kentucky legislature.

Star Channels completed its demonstration year in the spring of 1990, with students in 150 Kentucky high schools taking classes titled Physics I and Probability and Statistics.

In addition to one-way live video and two-way interaction via telephone lines, Star Channels courses incorporate interactive keypads that resemble calculators with antennae. When the teacher asks a question, students use the keypads to enter answers. The data are transmitted over a telephone line to a computer at the studio, allowing the teacher to evaluate student performance within seconds. In addition, feedback is provided to each student via the screen on the keypad. The same screen also sometimes provides clues to help solve a particular problem. Instructional assistants are also available by telephone to help with homework two nights per week.

Other satellite-based distance learning projects include Washington state's Satellite Telecommunications Educational Network, which offers courses and staff development programming to over 100 school districts in eight states from its broadcast center at Eastern Washington University. Missouri offers similar programming to approximately 350 sites via its Education Satellite Network.

Funding Sources

Once districts become interested in distance learning programs, they must deal with finding funds for such programs. Fortunately, there is currently much activity within state departments of education and at the federal level to help underwrite the costs of starting distance learning projects.

States are funding distance learning projects with state appropriations, private foundation grants, and cooperative arrangements with private business. The Massachusetts legislature, for example, recently authorized $1.2 million for 50 satellite dishes as part of a statewide distance learning effort. In Missouri, the revenue from a tax on videotape rentals goes directly into a grant program designed to help local school

> Star Channels courses incorporate interactive keypads that resemble calculators with antennae. When the teacher asks a question, students use the keypads to enter answers.

districts purchase distance learning technology.

At the federal level, the most significant source of distance education funding has been the Star Schools Program, which was established in 1988 by Public Law 100297. Since the program's inception, over 100,000 students in 45 states have enrolled in courses funded at least in part by the Star School grants. In addition, numerous graduate credit courses and staff development programs have been made available to nearly 20,000 teachers.

And more federal money for distance education could become available through a recently introduced Congressional bill intended to promote foreign language instruction in public schools. The bill would allocate $10 million over four years for distance learning projects in needy areas.

With continued state and federal funding and steadily increasing interest among educators everywhere, distance education is likely to become an integral part of the classroom. As a result, technology may provide what today's small school students need most—a gateway to a new world of educational opportunity.

Gregory Jordahl is a freelance writer who specializes in new technology for education and business.

Visions of Future Educational Environments

Chapter

8

1. "Visions for the 90s." Terence Cannings. *CUE Newsletter,* April 1990. pg. 1.
2. "Visions of the Future." Isabelle Bruder. *Electronic Learning*, January 1990. pg. 24.
3. "Looking into the 1990s." Bobby Goodson. *Teaching and Computers,* September 1989. pg. 18.
4. "Empowering Environments, Hypermedia and Microworlds." Christopher J. Dede. *Computing Teacher*, November 1987. pg. 59
5. "The Next Decade: What the Future Holds." Daniel E. Kinnaman. *Technology & Learning*, September 1990. pg. 43.
6. "Restructuring With Technology." Robert Pearlman. *Technology & Learning*, January 1991. pg. 31.
7. "Technology is Imperative for School Restructuring." Albert Shanker. *The Electronic School*, September 1990. pg. A4.
8. "Restructuring and Technology Play Essential Role in New City School." Gwen Solomon. *Electronic Learning*, June 1990. pg. 16.
9. "Redefining the Textbook." Therese Mageau. *Electronic Learning*, February 1990. pg. 14.
10. "Electronic Highways and the Classroom of the Future." Edited by Fred D'Ignazio. *Computing Teacher*, May 1990. pg. 20.
11. "Learning to Use the Tools of the Future." Gwen Solomon. *Electronic Learning*, February 1990. pg. 14.
12. "The New Library/Media Center." Robert McCarthy. *Electronic Learning*, June 1990. pg. 25.
13. "MegaTech Makes the Grade." Don Broderson. *ComputerLand Magazine*, February 1991. pg. 19.
14. "Putting It All Together." Elizabeth Schultz. *Teacher Magazine*, January 1991. pg. 44.

"The future ain't what it used to be!" stated a well-known educator several years ago. It certainly isn't! Changes are occurring at an unprecedented rate. We are bombarded daily by changing values, life styles, relationships, products and emerging technologies. In fact, we have passed into a new era in the society — some call it the "Information Society," or the "Post Industrial Society" or as Toffler suggests, "The Third Wave" (the second wave being the "Industrial Society" and the first wave the "Agricultural Revolution"). No matter what book you read, all authors agree that the information era is here and that change will continue to impact our daily lives enormously. The only point of divergence is agreement as to when we entered this new era in our society.

What does this mean for teachers? Basically, we need to shift the teaching and learning paradigm from that relevant to an Industrial Age to the Information Age of today. Many of our schools are still organized to produce citizens who will fit an industrial era — the teacher is the information source and provider, the students are the "buckets" waiting to be filled with the teacher's knowledge which will be regurgitated on a test. Students often sit in rows facing the board and the teacher, and only speak when they raise their right hand. Are these the skills for 21st century citizens?

Today's Information Society requires people with different skills than that found in the Industrial Society. Students must be able to communicate, problem-solve, use a variety of strategies to access and analyze information and be able to work in a group situation. They must also be able to use the tools relevant to the Information Society and not simply view these tools as objects of study! We must integrate these information tools into our everyday classroom activities so that our students will view and use them as productivity instruments.

However, if schools are reactive (rather than proactive) in nature, it suggests that we will use the tools of the new society at a slower rate than the community at large. But it means we must find ways to use these tools — the society will demand it. We also know that educational institutions are reticent to change so we must discover and develop strategies to increase the adoption and adaptation of evolving technologies in the classroom.

One effective strategy requires each school creating its vision of education five to ten years from now. However, before a school can compile its own vision, each teacher must reflect and project their individual vision of future educational environments. This chapter will assist you to do that. Remember, if you have no vision of the future it is very difficult to create a mission strategy.

Many of the readings fall into three categories:
- future and evolving technologies;
- changing classroom paradigms;
- curriculum changes that reflect skills required of a 21st century citizen.

As you read the articles you will become aware that the first category is the focus for many writers. The other two areas require an appraisal of where schools are today and what it will take to change the paradigm of education. However, remember one fact: the students in our schools, and their parents, may change the paradigm for us! Students are telling us by their feet (AKA the "dropout" rate) that schools are not very relevant to today's world. At the other end of the spectrum, many students access international databases to obtain information and take technology tools for granted as they complete class assignments! How do we as educators bridge that gap?

In the first article, written by one of the editors of this book, you will learn some facts about the future and the type of skills students will need for survival in the next century. According to this article, *Interactive Multimedia* will provide important tools for today's learner. They will use a combination of computer, videodisc, videocassette, and software to construct image reports on topics selected by them and their teachers. The multimedia packages that are available enable teachers to present visual information very easily and efficiently. But we must also empower students to construct their own interpretations of events using this medium.

Chris Dede's article, "Empowering Environments, Hypermedia and Microworlds," illustrates the variety of cognitive enhancers that will have an impact on the next generation of educational software. The potential implications of these enhancers will be enormous but in applying them we must overcome two myths: the myth of "power" and "consolidation." Do you agree with these two myths? Do the four sequential stages of institutional input apply to schools you know? Are we just beginning the educational computing revolution that Dede envisages?

If you want to know what's in the pipeline for your technology-literate classroom in the 90s, the article by Daniel Kinnaman, "The Next Decade: What the Future Holds," visits several of the nation's think tanks and peeks at developing projects. Which project will have the greatest impact on tomorrow's classroom? How would you adapt these products for use in your classroom? Did you notice that most of the software mentioned is inquiry-based?

It appears that every school in the nation is "restructuring." The article by Robert Pearlman describes the relationship of technology and restructuring. Whatever your definition of restructuring, technology should be an important component according to this author. But remember, some schools are already offering programs similar to those proposed by the restructionists. In other words, an educational setting that promotes student-centeredness using technology tools can be implemented without being "restructured."

Videodiscs as textbooks? Has Texas begun a transformation of printed hardcopy to visuals that can be manipulated by teachers and students as a state adopted "text"? Remember, the state ranked the technology package #1 on their K-6 science adoption list! California also permits schools to use textbook funds to buy texts and associated videodiscs. Florida is moving in the same direction. These trends indicate that a radical change in the availability of additional instructional materials is occurring. School districts and teachers will be able to choose, for example, interactive multimedia packages that enable teachers to implement the core curriculum. Teachers can use these materials not as peripherals to the mandated curriculum, but as means for implementing the state frameworks. Therese Mageau's article describes developments in three states as they begin to transform the textbook adoption process from single texts to a combination of multiple media products.

Fred D'Ignazio's article, "Electronic Highways and the Classroom of the Future" challenges all educators to create a new paradigm for schools in which "a classroom won't be a stationary, isolated room, but a vehicle capable of traveling around the world, back into time, and out into the solar system and beyond." Certainly a visionary concept that will require radically different skills than used today. According to D'Ignazio, teachers will become, with their students, explorers, or knowledge navigators who can pilot their classrooms through the myriad of information and knowledge bases. How many teachers can become the type of educator suggested in this article? Why should we all try to emulate the model he proposes? Or should we?

The school's library/media center will be different, in many respects, as we move into the 21st century. In some schools that transformation is already taking place, but in others, much planning and visioning must occur before the library/media center will become an effective resource center. Robert McCarthy describes how this center will become a technology and information hub that is indispensable to students and staff. He shows how the use of optical storage devices will give more students instant access to more knowledge and reference bases than ever before.

Questions for Discussion

1. How will teachers create their own vision of education in the year 2000? How will they translate their personal vision into a shared vision at the school site?
2. Should teachers focus on technology in their visions or should they emphasize curriculum and instructional practices? In other words, what is the role of technology in creating visions of future classroom practices in education?
3. "The more things change the more they remain the same." Does this statement apply to educational uses of technology? Will classroom practices appear very different in the year 2000 than those found in many classrooms today? Why?
4. What are five major changes that could occur in schools between now and the year 2000? What strategies must be adopted for them to happen? What will be the two largest roadblocks?
5. What is your scenario or vision of a classroom in the future? Pick a year, say 2000 or 2010, and construct a one paragraph description of what you think a future classroom will be like. Share it with your colleagues. Any similarities?

Questions from the Readings

1. How will you organize your classroom to empower your students to use software programs such as *Mediaworks, MediaSpace, The Physics Explorer?*
2. Is the *Knowledge Navigator* a realistic concept for K-12 schools? Why?
3. What is the *Literature Explorer*? How would a teacher use it in their classroom?
4. What are some of the new roles teachers are adopting?
5. According to Fred D'Ignazio, what is a new paradigm for the use of the computer?
6. What is Cyberspace?
7. What is the "GUM" concept? Do you find the concept useful? Why?
8. What does "restructuring" mean to you? Why do educators link technology with restructuring?
9. What is unusual about the Saturn School of Tomorrow?
10. Will interactive multimedia packages replace textbooks in the American classroom? Why?

Article #1
Visions for the 90s

By
Dr.
Terence
Cannings

As we approach the year 2000, we know that many external factors are impinging on the classroom. We know that:

- we have entered the information age, the post-industrial society, the communications era, or as Toffler calls it, "The Third Wave." Depending on which book you have read, we entered this society 20 years ago, or we are still entering it today.
- children born in 2000 will live to be 81 years old on average compared with 75 for children born in 1986.
- graduates will have been exposed that year to more information than their grandparents were in a lifetime.
- 90% of information and knowledge required in year 2000 has yet to be invented.
- by 2000 service jobs will form 90% of the economy.
- employees will change professions, not just jobs, 4 or 5 times during their working lifetime.
- minorities will be majorities in 53 of the 100 largest US cities.
- women's salaries will have grown to within 10% of men's.
- 90% of labor force will work for companies employing fewer than 200 people.
- according to the Albuquerque Department of Education, the rate of change for the 4th grade child will be equivalent to 500 years of changing values, relationships, as you and I have known it.
- in Wurman's book, *Information Anxiety*, he states that "a weekday edition of the *New York Times* contains more information than the average person was likely to come across in a lifetime in 17th century England."
- the amount of information and knowledge in the world, according to John Naisbitt, doubles every 2.5 years.
- 6-7000 scientific articles are written every day in this country.
- when the class of 2000 graduates, according to Marv Cetron, the body of knowledge will have doubled four times since 1988.
- today, engineers find that half of their knowledge is obsolete within 5 years.

With those thoughts in mind, the question is, what are schools doing now to prepare our children for life in a world very different from the one in which we live today. What are these skills that will be needed? What are the responsibilities of teachers? Can technology help teachers in their role as facilitator, teacher, mentor? If you have a vision of what schools may look like in 2000, you may have defined your tasks to reach that vision. But, perhaps you are not sure of your vision; perhaps you feel that schools will not change significantly over the next 10 years?

In this article I will attempt to show that schools will be different from what they are today; that teachers will be asked to do more; and show that technology can assist teachers with their planning and instruction. I will present four different visions of the future and suggest some implications for teachers. In addition, I will describe some interactive multimedia examples that may decrease the amount of preparation time for teachers as they attempt to provide

571

an instructional environment for today's and tomorrow's learner.

The list on page one could continue, but you should now feel, even if you agree with only half of these facts, that the world will be a different place by the year 2000; children will require new skills than those necessitated by an industrial society, and teachers' roles will change to meet new demands on the teaching profession. If the amount of information that will bombard us in the future is so great, what skills will our students, and us for that matter, require just to survive? Will the Friday test in which students regurgitate facts, still be as important as it was for the industrial or "Second Wave" society? Or will process skills, often referred to as higher order or critical thinking skills, become a common element in the classroom as does the weekly spelling test of today?

Let me share with you four brief visions of the future—compare them with your vision.

> If the amount of information that will bombard us in the future is so great, what skills will our students, and us for that matter, require just to survive?

I. David Kearns (President/CEO Xerox Corporation) and Dennis Doyle, authors of *Winning the Brain Race.*

According to these authors, educational reform must be consistent with the fundamental values in our society: the American experiment in self-governance. However, they feel that for any reform to take place, business must take the lead. Yet they place great emphasis on the role of teachers as they become more involved in local decision-making. In their opinion, good teachers are not bureaucratic paper shufflers and good teachers do not fit into tidy bureaucra-

cies. They also suggest that teachers are "canny outlaws"—intellectual entrepreneurs, innovators, system beaters, and rule benders but acknowledge that teaching is hard work, and gratifying.

Their six point plan includes:
1. Schools of choice.
2. Abolition of traditional grade and grading structure.
3. Year round schools.
4. Granting teachers and principals more decision-making power: in the areas of curriculum, text selection, testing.
5. Restoring values of democracy and citizenship.
6. Federal responsibility for education.

They target the year 2000 for the effective implementation of their recommendations. Note that teachers will be expected to perform additional tasks but they will have more say on what goes on at their site. Will teachers find the time to undertake these additional responsibilities?

II. John Sculley's "The Knowledge Navigator"

Sculley acknowledges that the personal computer is not the panacea for educational reform but a TOOL around which solutions can be sought. He suggests that computers will make it possible for children to enjoy learning by making them explorers, active participants in educational adventures.

He states in his book *Odyssey* that optical media will be the technology behind the next big revolution in computing. Nowhere will this be more important than in public education. In our quest for innovation and respect for individual creativity, he feels we need a tool to stimulate human creativity, giving us access to more knowledge. Such a tool he calls the Knowledge Navigator—a discoverer of worlds; a tool as galvanizing as the printing press.

It will be a tool to drive through libraries, museums, data bases, and archives. According to Sculley, of greatest importance is how this new tool may change the way we learn, think, work, communicate, and live. Many of you have possibly viewed the visual representation of this tool in the popular Apple video of the same title. What are some characteristics of the learning environment in the video that could be applied to your classroom? Here is my list:

• personalized
• easy to use
• access to large databases
• reliance on visual imagery
• ability to explore, manipulate
• saves TIME for the teacher
• increases productivity of student and teacher
• simulates situations

Can we apply most of these characteristics to today's classroom? I believe we can and will give an example later in this article.

III. The Alhambra Model Technology Schools Project...

This project will attempt to show how a student-centered approach using technology as a tool, can be incorporated within state curriculum frameworks in typical suburban, multi-ethnic schools. This project will:

• empower students to be independent learners and creators;
• show the impact of technology on student learning over a 5 year period;
• provide technology tools to enable each student to reach his/her potential...

This is our vision for the students in this MTS project in Alhambra. We want

students to become more responsible for their own learning which necessitates teachers relinquishing some of their decision-making and involving students in discussions of classroom activities. To support these activities teachers and students have access to technology tools such as: computers, camcorders, videocassettes, telecommunications networks, satellite communications, laptop computers, laserdiscs, and video editing equipment. In this project, technology supports the philosophical approach: student centeredness. That is, an approach to learning and teaching drives the project; the technology becomes the support mechanism.

IV. Chiron Middle School

In a recent *Electronic Learning* article (June, 1989), Bob Pearlman described the vision of this school, located in Minneapolis. The planners for the 300 students in grades five through eight believe that "learning occurs best with great amounts of input and mental stimulation, and with many opportunities for students to learn by doing, inquiring, and discovering." Students participate in experiential learning activities at sites throughout the community. These learning centers include government agencies, communication centers, manufacturing and retailing industries, information processing centers, higher education institutions, and many more. Students work on projects in multi-age teams and present their experiences to other students, parents, and community members.

Each of the four visions described above represents an image of what educators and parents want for the children at a particular site. Not all visions mentioned technology per se but they stressed the importance of students as active learners, as participants in the educational process, not idle observers. These visions also highlighted the importance of the teacher in decision-making and the necessary resources that must be supplied if we are to achieve those visions.

How can technology promote and assist educators in the achievement of these visions? Enter Interactive Multimedia, the newest term in the educational technology vocabulary. It is heralded by many journals with banners such as "Interactive Multimedia—The Next Wave"; "*HyperCard* K-12: What's all the commotion?"; "Multimedia: What the excitement's all about"— can it meet all the promises that people exclaim? Probably not—it is just another tool that teachers and students can use to promote a better learning environment in classrooms. But, it has great potential, particularly as a planning and presentation tool.

What do I mean by interactive multimedia? Several interpretations of this term have been attempted but most people suggest it is the ability to combine text, graphics, audio, visuals, and video into a single learning system which is coordinated by a computer. For example, I can connect a laserdisc player to my Macintosh computer and through the use of *HyperCard,* select images and video clips from a laserdisc that I want to use for a presentation. Or I could use an Apple IIGS with *HyperStudio* or *Tutor-Tech,* or an IBM computer with *Linkway* connected to a laserdisc player.

Several interactive multimedia products are now available that teachers and students can use: *Vote 88* (ABC News), *In the Holy Land* (ABC News), *VideoCards* (Optical Data stacks for several science laserdiscs), *National Gallery of Art* and *Vincent Van Gogh Laserguides* (Voyager Company), *GTV: This Land is Our Land* (Lucas Film &

National Geographic), *Target Interactive Project* (Target/IBM). These laserdiscs and accompanying stacks are "topical" in approach (although Optical Data's *Windows on Science* series provides extensive learning and teaching materials). They require the teacher to select the appropriate program and integrate it into planned classroom activities. Teachers must be aware, first, that the programs exist, and second, spend time reviewing for appropriateness, and then select areas for teacher or student use. Not every teacher will have the time to complete all of these tasks.

If teachers will be required to undertake more decision-making tasks as suggested earlier, a more "integrated" approach to interactive multimedia tools may be very timely. That is, teachers will find useful a semester, term, month or year's course in which lessons are provided, activities are already aligned to a laserdisc, and lesson objectives are referenced to existing software, videocassettes, other laserdiscs, and any other instructional materials that a teacher would find useful. The teacher simply has to "point and click" when selecting lessons, activities, evaluation exercises, laserdiscs, examples, etc.

This type of planning and presentation tool is exemplified in "Learning Navigator," a *HyperCard* Resource Management program under development by a team at Pepperdine University, that when completed will provide the planning and presentation tools for an elementary or secondary science teacher.

Using "Learning Navigator," teachers could refer to the science framework, read the relevant district curriculum objectives, access software reviews relevant to the topic, implement activities listed for each lesson, use the critical thinking questions provided as well as the unit evaluation questions. Each lesson could access relevant sections from a science laserdisc which is aligned to the classroom activities. Most importantly, teachers could plan their own laserdisc presentations and lessons by using the built-in tools.

This concept will be developed further in the recently state-funded "Science 2000" project. This project will develop a one year course in 7th grade science, based on the new California Science Curriculum Framework, utilizing the power of the computer to select themes, topics, lessons, activities which will all be aligned to a laserdisc and other technologies. For example, a teacher will be able to trace a theme throughout several lesson units by isolating a particular theme (such as "patterns of change" or "energy") and let the computer select lessons that follow this theme. In other words, this integrated approach will save teachers TIME. But, it will be sufficiently flexible that teachers can change, edit, adapt, and create according to their students' needs.

A similar approach is being developed in another interactive multimedia tool called *The Literature Explorer*. This prototype is an attempt to implement the new California Language Arts Framework which is literature based. The tool lists language arts activities, aligns these to available laserdiscs, and lists the skills the teacher has incorporated in that lesson. The segments on the laserdisc (for example *Charlotte's Web)* have already been selected and aligned; all the teacher has to do is point and click on a *HyperCard* button! However, teachers will be able to add to the books in the stack by completing a template which automatically updates the skills and titles database.

In utilizing an integrated program approach, several points are important:

1. The tools must be simple to use, particularly if teachers want to modify, create or add to the existing database. Most teachers will not program in HyperTalk but will use templates and existing stacks in their planning and classroom activities. We have been through the "authoring" stage before with CAI and we know that the majority of teachers do not have the time to prepare this kind of material.

2. These integrated programs must be flexible so that a teacher can modify an existing lesson or activity, compose their own lessons or create their own navigational paths through the technologies. It is difficult to prepare sets of lessons that are appropriate for all teachers and all students so the ability to modify must be a high priority.

3. Student tools should accompany the teacher mode. Students, and teachers, will become so motivated through this medium that all participants in the learning process must have access to these tools. Students will prepare presentations, reports using (at least initially) the same hardware in the teacher's planning center and save their creation on their disk.

4. Interactive multimedia will not revolutionize schools. As Robert Pearlman points out in his article, schools first must appraise how they want to reorganize/restructure, as technology cannot perform that function: "technology implementation by itself will not change schools, but it can support teachers in designing student learning activities where students become 'active educational workers' and teachers expand their role from the front of the classroom to become facilitators and coaches of student learning."

In summary, whatever your vision for schools in the year 2000 may be, schools will be different from today. Students and teachers will incorporate new tools into the classroom to facilitate both teaching and learning tasks. As teachers become more involved in localized decision-making they will require assistance with instructional planning and delivery as the TIME element will become even more critical. Interactive multimedia is one of the tools that a teacher can use. This technology can "empower" teachers so that they can envision new ways to redesign their learning environment. Integrated interactive multimedia programs will save a teacher time, provide a more stimulating visual learning environment and give teachers and students tools relevant to an information society.

By
ISABELLE
BRUDER

Joan of Arc heard voices. Martin Luther King, Jr. had a dream. The educators you are about to meet on the next seven pages have devised a "wish list" of technologies—real or visions. Visions reflective of current conditions in U.S. schools and indicative of the directions education and educational technology might follow into the 1990s and beyond.

We've asked these 15 educators—among them, Christa McAuliff Educators, teachers, technologists, deans, and others—to share their concepts of education in two specific ways. First, we asked for their version of the "ideal" classroom for the upcoming decade. For that, they envision everything from a schooner to a computerized world library to a climate-controlled, inviting environment. Second, we asked them to devise a "wish list" of technologies—real of imagined—that they would like to see used in education in the 1990s. The list, includes an equally diverse range, from a solar-powered laptop to a heart on fire to an ordinary rotary telephone for every teacher's desk.

As educators, you know that the possibilities for learning and teaching in this next decade are endless. We hope, like us, you'll be surprised, amazed, amused, and especially attentive to the voices of these educators, who we believe represent a solid cross-section of American education.

Eileen Steele
Computer Resource Teacher, Lafayette Schools Corp. (K-12), Lafayette, Ind.

Ideal Classroom: "For me, the concept of the ideal classroom is...maybe 'classroom' is not the right terminology. I'd rather say a learning setting. Which includes students of various ages in one setting, working on themes or areas of common interest. It should provide an appreciation for individual differences and individual strengths, and utilize technology as tools to help students master those things they have difficulty with. But beyond that, the technology is used as tools for students to create and share their own information. The technology should not be a prominent feature. It is not something that should jump out at you. You should be able to walk into the classroom and say 'what a human environment this is!' I want it to be a warm, human, caring environment that happens to have technology that allows it to be that."

Technology Wish List: "I am most concerned with having tools that will allow students to be creative and to be able to produce. I envision technologies that make video recording, digitizing of sound, and editing at a personal

577

computer commonplace. The whole notion of hypermedia is absolutely essential for allowing people to pursue their interests and communicate their interests to others. And, I'm really excited about this whole notion of holographic teleconferencing: being able to bring images of people that can talk and speak to me and my students right into the room without them actually having to travel great distances."

Alan November

Computer Applications Specialist (K-12), Wellesley Middle School, Wellesley, Mass.

Ideal Classroom: "A schooner. Every kid ought to get on a boat and see the world; and have telecommunications there, of course. Short of that, I think schools ought to be open 365 days a year, 24 hours a day. And kids ought to be very involved in something called the 'Community Technology Consulting Office,' where they are lined up with clients from the community. Of course, the community could be anywhere in the world; kids in my community could be helping Native Americans figure out if something they are producing in Alaska will sell in Boston. So it's a Global Village. The role of kids completely changes from that of being 'warehoused' for 12 years while we feed them information, to one where they become essential to the community, and where they play an important role in helping people, especially with technology. And every classroom would be connected to that Consulting Office in some way. So that students can begin to appreciate that schools are places that truly value their contribu-

tions. Right now, students don't feel that. Also, I'm incredibly disappointed at how we haven't really applied technology to schools, to date.

Technology Wish List: "I need a cognitive map. I need to know how students make decisions, and how they think, and where they have problem areas. So I need a tool built into the software—I need a BIG computer for this. I need an artificial intelligence program that does cognitive mapping that can trace kids across time and subject; that will give me a helpful diagnosis of how to build a learning environment to stimulate each kid according to his or her learning needs. And, to help parents, the school would provide them with the diagnosis of their children's learning needs and what they can do to support, stimulate."

Isaac Asimov

Nightfall Inc., New York, N.Y.

Ideal Classroom: "My idea of the ideal classroom of the 1990s, or any period, is one in which each student gets individual attention and is taught at his natural speed and according to his natural bent. This cannot be done without access to a computerized library."

Technology Wish List: "My 'wish list' of technologies for education in the future, therefore, is a thoroughly computerized world library with access in the school and in the home. I don't expect any of this to come to pass in the 1990s. It would take a huge investment and Mr. Bush has 'more will than wallet' and, in my opinion, not much real will."

Barry Sponder

Associate Professor, Education, University of Alaska, Kuskokwim Campus, Bethel, Alaska

Ideal Classroom: "I really believe that you to have to have technology in the schools, but that it has to be technology with a heart. You have to combine the best of classical education with the best of technology. So that, ideally, in a classroom or education situation you want people to realize how things are connected.

"The ideal classroom in the 1990s, in a multicultural, multidimensional America, will help teachers and students learn where everyone fits in. And the ideal classroom should allow teachers to draw on local resources easily. So the technology of the 1990s will allow textbook publishers and local districts to create their own texts using universal concepts (i.e., the study of biology) and adapt them for schools and for districts."

Technology Wish List: "I think an aware heart in a teacher. We have all the external technology, but there's nothing like a heart on fire. I don't want the 1990s to lose the messages of the ages. I can just see it, in the year 2040...we find out that teacher training and making good teachers is really a function of making good people, moral people, or whatever. So I don't want to lose that."

Doris Ray

Director, Maine Computer Consortium, Maine Center for Educational Services, Auburn, Me.

Ideal Classroom: "In the ideal classroom or school we have to readmit kids into society. By that I mean that largely what happens between the walls of the school every day is unrelated to the world around us. We confuse school with education. We have isolated kids from the age of 5 to 18 and said, 'Go into this building and when you come out you're supposed to be educated.' And there are some real flaws with that, because actually their education occurs with technology—television, telephones, media, radio—all these things.

"So my concept of the ideal classroom puts the responsibility for learning and the means for learning and the incentive into the hands of kids again. And we [educators] validate their interest, we help guide them, but we let them take on real problems in the real world. There are a number of wonderful programs that do that. [National Geographic's] Kids Network is a good example. It admits kids into the larger society and lets them work on real problems, makes them active. So the ideal classroom opens all its windows and lets the real world in and lets kids take responsibility for some of the dilemmas."

Technology Wish List: "It is tantamount to child neglect and teacher abuse not to have a telephone in every classroom. How important is education? How can you defend that we have an 'education president' or that education is the number one priority on the national agenda and [not provide this service]? And of course a computer. Not every classroom has one and it should. I think every child ought to have one, ultimately. There ought to be access to one; we don't have equity in that respect. The computer is the tool of the age, the control panel for the world, at the moment. If we really believe what we say about children being our most important resource, then why doesn't every child have this tool?"

Jay Blanchard
Professor of Literacy, Arizona State University, Tempe, Ariz.

Ideal Classroom: "The curriculum is probably the most crucial [element] in what the classroom of the 1990s should be. It would be actual integration of technologies into all classes. Integration is the key word, because instead of stand-alone computer classes, everybody in the building would understand the role of technology in their own curriculum. [The technologies would consist of] integrated multimedia tools, including things like storage media, computers, CDs, VCRs, tapes, and TVs.

"Also, in this (ideal) classroom would be software that allows the teacher to change the content; the format doesn't have to change. If the teacher is working on reading and then switches to vocabulary, I'd like the teacher to be able to change the items."

Technology Wish List: "[Blanchard's technology wish list focuses on developing nations, and] it includes an emphasis on technologies to aid literacy efforts. For the most impoverished of the developing nations—for instance, Bangladesh, where there's no electricity—[there should be] wide dissemination of technologies devoid of electricity, including Dynamo Radio, a crank-powered radio, so that people in the village can crank this radio and actually receive information on health, agriculture, etc. Then literacy is integrated in their daily lives, it's not a stand-alone activity. So technology can do a lot, though it's not

the kind of technology you and I think about. It's not even battery, it's below battery."

Walt Tremer
Teacher/Director, Future Technology Center, Southern Lehigh High School, Center Valley, Pa.

Ideal Classroom: "The ideal classroom would be two things. First, where the curriculum is based on reality; the ultimate curriculum is reality, so the classroom has to reflect that, and not be isolated from the world. Second, it would reflect that the students are partners in learning, not just passive sponges; that they are actively involved in the process along with the teacher. So they are playing a part in research and problem solving and decision making, rather than just being lectured at.

Technology Wish List: "One technology would a be a visual link between kids of all groups, geographic areas, and economic levels. So my kids could sit in their classroom and could interact 'face-to-face' with kids all over the world. So the technology would have that capability, bringing a window on the world to my students.

"The second technology would deal with space, be it remote imaging, telescopes—something that allows us to reach beyond the earth's boundaries. It would emanate from the classrooms, from their own capacity to reach out, something real time, where the kids are participants. It all centers around the technology giving the mind capabilities, or stretching perspectives of the world and, consequently, their perspectives of themselves as players."

Bernajean Porter

Senior Technology Consultant, Colorado State Department of Education, Denver, Colo.

Ideal Classroom: "Where the learner has a lot of choices in how they want to learn and the materials they want to learn with. That obviously includes technology. But it includes additional things, not technology as an only selection, but certainly as a wonderful choice. And I do envision the information being available on all the modalities: visual, auditory, and print.

Technology Wish List: "I'd like to have media stations available to kids to produce their own documentaries and research papers. I would also like one [entire] wall of the classroom just as a production wall, like a large screen. And it would, of course, be the new Japanese one where you'd get the holographs, three-dimensional images. It'd be super to talk to authors or scientists and hear what they are thinking. And it might be vignettes of video that's stored, or it might be real time.

"The largest dream that comes out of this is the acceptability of showing your knowledge on [something] much larger than a printed test. That's our biggest void right now in making technology work well for us; when we finish we don't have a traditional product that people know how to grade.

"And one other thing I really envision is that we'll move away from prepackaged information, where someone else lines it up and decides exactly the way you'll be introduced to it and take steps through it. So learners will become knowledge builders, not just knowledge receivers."

Richard N. Sheets

Computer Coordinator/ Computer Services, Phoenix Union High School District, Phoenix, Ariz.

Ideal Classroom: "A classroom in which all the technology that can be installed in the curriculum is available to the teacher. For example, it could be a high-tech concept whereby the teacher would become a manager of information in such a way that we could direct the students, so students could pursue their own avenues for discovery."

Technology Wish List: "A solar-powered laptop. So the student (or anyone) is not limited by a situation that does not support a lab because of electrical requirements or whatever. The students would merely take this unit, carry it with them, much as they do a calculator right now, so they could have it in class to use all its functions: data base search, word processing, etc. Perhaps there could be a floppy with the assignments for each week and the students could just transfer that to their hard drive. Or they may have two computers: one at home and one in their locker and just carry the floppy back and forth."

Tom Snyder

Founder/Lead Designer, Tom Snyder Productions, Cambridge, Mass.

Ideal Classroom/Technology Wish List: "Every classroom would have an old-fashioned phone in it, that black one. Just an ordinary phone. Every teacher should have one. And every teacher should have a copying machine.

Every teacher will have a computer on their desk and it will be networked to other teachers in their school, and/or outside. And every teacher will have some sort of projection device for their computer, a big screen.

"I guess, too, we need a hookup through either the school library or other libraries to massive amounts of data through networks. And then every student would have some kind of low-cost word processing computer that they could hide in their desk. And that's it."

obtaining an accurate understanding of what the students have learned. And here I'm a little more skeptical of how technology will help. One can imagine some kind of computer-based expert system developed by recording actions, questions, and practices of teachers who are reputedly successful, then using those expert systems as an electronic lesson plan for other teachers to use. Or it could be as simple as videotaping model lessons presented by expert teachers for other teachers to use before (teaching) those same materials."

Henry J. Becker

Center for Research on Elementary and Middle Schools, Johns Hopkins University, Baltimore, Md.

Ideal Classroom: "The bane of classroom life is routine memorization drills. The best teachers enable students to accomplish that necessary learning, but in the context of getting them involved in activities that enable them to improve their written expression, their oral expression, their reasoning ability, and so forth. So that the ideal classroom, to me, is one where students who were previously failing or alienated are now really excited about doing academic tasks and, in the process, are mastering the routine skills that we all acknowledge are necessary but not the main purpose of schooling."

Technology Wish List: "Teachers have to have both skills and resource they don't [currently] have. And technology could provide some of the resources to make classroom learning more exciting and idea-focused. But the most obstinate impediment to instructional improvement is not [lack of] better materials, but providing teachers with more skills in using these resources more effectively and in

LeRoy Finkel

Instructional Technology Coordinator, San Mateo County Office of Education, Redwood City, Calif.

Ideal Classroom: "The ideal classroom of the 1990s has technology in place when and where it is appropriate, according to the learning style of the student and the teaching style of the teacher. Which means, in effect, there will continue to be classrooms that have no technology; there will be some that have only teacher desktop technology; there will be some that are riddled with technology."

Technology Wish List: "It seems to me that if we're really talking 1990s, the laserdisc is going to become commonplace—at least I hope so—with hypermedia. In addition, my wish list would [include] a reasonable cost for distance learning combined with in-class technology so that a child could receive instruction with worldwide colleagues and react with both the instructor and the worldwide colleagues, where appropriate. Along with the distance component—which is usually a television—would come both print materials and media materials (video and software), so it would all be tied into that integrated learning environment."

Zelia Frick

Computer Coordinator, Rowan County Schools, Salisbury, N.C.

Ideal Classroom: "What I'd really like is good air-conditioning, new furniture, and carpeting—a good learning environment, so we can feel good about ourselves while we're learning. And a computer on every desk.

"The computer will more or less break down the walls of schools. We need to rethink the phase of having computers in labs reserved for one department; they should be in every classroom. I'd hope all students could have their own personal computer that they can carry from class to class, that they could possibly plug into a network when they come in. In that network, they could be tied into reference materials, other classrooms, whatever. I think they will be tied into a data bank of basic-skills software, so they can be retrieved easily whatever the subject area might be.

"For the teacher, each should have a station that is used more as a presentation manager system, maybe tied to the administrative offices. Maybe software will be correlated with textbooks. Maybe have a large screen, to use the computer as a chalkboard replacement."

Technology Wish List: "A tool that will help everyone read and communicate. Maybe we could call it the 'Barrier Dissolver.' It would be portable, a pop-up notebook kind of thing, to carry around. It could help students so they will not be confronted with a language barrier. We see a great influx of students from other countries. It's important that

we have a solution to the problem of language barriers between students and school and each other. We need to help the student become a fluent writer, no matter what the first language is; maybe they could use this to write in their language and it would type out in English. And for students who cannot read, it could have a device to scan in printed text and the computer would have audio input, so as you read, each word is highlighted, and the computer reads along with you. As you come to a word you don't know, the computer would speak it and define it. It could also break down the barrier of having to be connected to telephone lines by having its own microsatellite dish to send and receive information."

Allen Glenn

Dean, College of Education, University of Washington, Seattle, Wash.

Ideal Classroom: "Our classrooms in the next decade may change more than they ever have before. We're always going to have schools, because of their tremendous socialization functions. We're not going to have kids sitting home alone studying with the television. The school needs to prepare the student for life as a citizen: an economic citizen, a political citizen, a social citizen—that's critical. We have to teach the basic skills. I'd like to see the classroom become an open window to the world, its people, and its knowledge. What do I mean by an open window? An opportunity through technology to explore not only what's bound between the covers of a textbook, but to reach out to communities all across the world. So that means what we teach and how we teach shifts dramatically. And I think we're going to move away from a reliance upon set time periods—history for 50 minutes a day—to a more flexible schedule. Move away from large group instruction to more small and individualized instruction, in which the teacher is a facilitator and works with students. It also means that the classroom is linked with a variety of other, what we would consider non-school agencies, like businesses, community agencies. So maybe the goal for our ideal classroom is that (although) it may physically be isolated, intellectually and in other ways it is not, via the technology."

Technology Wish List: "The ability to link me with people in other places. So that I can link into a data base without all the hassle I go through now with modems and so on. And we're talking about a quantum leap, because we can't even get telephones to teachers now. But the telecommunications (one-way and two-way) will be enhanced. And the technology will be part of the curriculum. That's kind of a dream, I guess, but if it's going to become a part of kids' lives to ask questions and analyze data, we have to have better access to that technology."

Carol Kelnow
Director, Information Resources, Oakland Schools, Pontiac, Mich.

Ideal Classroom: "If I were looking at what needs to change most, I would look at the relationships: students to students and students to teachers. And I'd like to see the classroom more like an office or research facility; so that we use technology to support cooperative work and view kids more as information workers. They need to learn to generate questions, to learn to design and create. Be-

cause obviously as we move forward, rock-solid knowledge is gone; everything is in a constant state of flux. The only thing you can count on is your own creative process. In the [ideal] classroom we value leading and participating; we value things like working together, instead of sitting quietly and following instructions; we value solutions to problems that are found by a group, rather than by an individual. [Currently] if students talk to solve a problem, it's cheating. When you get into the workplace, that's not the case; at work you'd be foolish not to talk to other people.

And the relationship of teacher/student: this is where technology can have some catalyst effect [because] kids need to have some more control and responsibility over their learning. So, then, the management role of the teacher changes, and the way we measure student success changes."

Technology Wish List: "Whatever 'it' is, it's small, light and powerful. My first wish is for an incredible battery, and this battery would be driving this small-screen powerful device—let's say it's a 'Cognition Enhancer.' This device would 'magically' go from home to school, but it would be designed with an open computing system so that even if the school building or district was networked or had some kind of global information system, this device could go to a specialized workstation where you could either print your work, modem it, fax it, whatever. In other words, it would have some kind of standard input/output so that you could show evidence of your work in a number of ways. And you could have compatibility with various storage devices, such as CDs or whatever. And it has to be, not cheap, but affordable. That's not asking for much, is it?"

Snapshot of the 21st Century

Editor's Note: The National Foundation for the Improvement of Education (NFIE) is in the midst of conducting a multi-year initiative aimed at uncovering the potential of technology to improve education in U.S. schools.

The five-stage program is called "Learning Tomorrow," and the outcome of the first stage was published last summer in a report titled "Images of Potential." This first stage—scenario-building—brought together 38 professionals, including classroom teachers, facilities and design people, members of industry, hardware and software producers, school improvement and restructuring advocates, and researchers. The group broke into six subgroups and independently devised six scenarios of what schools might look like with the integral use of technology in the 21st century. The following excerpt is a portion of one of the six "Images of Potential" envisioned by the NFIE groups. The scenarios described learning environments in rural, urban/suburban elementary, middle and high schools. Each scenario, says the NFIE, should be "viewed as a snapshot, as one point in time," providing alternate images of the future while illustrating common underlying elements or themes.

Urban/Suburban High School

Diana's day begins with Introspection. This time is allotted for the student to center, meditate, reflect on past, current, or future activities, clear the mind, etc.

Diana then begins the knowledge portion of her day. She attends multi-disciplinary, integrated subject classes, where multiple subjects are taught based on a theme. This week, the students discovered several artifacts out on the research fields of the northwest section of the school grounds. They began an archaeological dig site and have uncovered several peculiar objects that have given them clues to a civilization which existed here many years ago.

Diana's Social Sciences class is studying about past civilizations and cultures. Diana's class is using telecommunications to search data bases on topics and artifacts they have discovered. She has just sent a message through her laptop computer at her student workstation to a student in the foreign-language class to help translate a script found scrawled on one of the objects. She then calls up the interactive videodisc surrogate field trip of Cancun. She travels through the ruins, choosing many different paths. She selects in-depth information on digging techniques.

Diana's Math class is working on designing the three-dimensional computer graphics simulation of the dig site. They are working closely with the science class to determine the appropriate dating techniques to ascertain the age of the artifacts. They are also studying the site's geological formations to incorporate the appropriate physical and chemical characteristics into the simulator, which will allow them to manipulate the environment. Diana spends some time with the expert system tutorial for the 3-D simulation, which helps give her instruction and advice as she learns to use the technology. Diana finishes class by sending a picture of the dig site to Mario, who is home with the flu. Mario has been keeping up with classwork through the curriculum data base connection.

In her language arts class, Diana is preparing the newspaper reports of the class' recent activities and sending her draft story to the local newspaper, with hopes for its publication. Her classmates are also storyboarding the video story they are producing as a documentary, which will air on the Student Educational Television Network for a news spot. This afternoon her class is conducting an interactive videoconference, with other classes in the Soviet Union and La Paz, Bolivia, to discuss their latest finds. Students have already interpreted the press release, and are completing the sequence. Other classmates are putting the finishing touches on the community newsletter which gets mailed to parents and community members. The deadline is now only two hours away....

All before lunch, and all for the 21st century.

The NFIE says it hopes the scenarios in Images of Potential—which "do not always consider the problems encountered or the multiple contexts in which learning takes place"—will stimulate more teachers "to employ technology as a tool in their teaching." We hope so too.

For additional information, write:
**The National Foundation for the Improvement of Education
1201 Sixteenth St., N.W.
Washington, D.C. 20036-3290.**

A PIONEER IN CLASSROOM COMPUTING REFLECTS ON WHAT'S
HERE AND WHAT'S AHEAD FOR TECHNOLOGY-USING TEACHERS.

By
Bobby
Goodson

With this school year comes a turning point: the end of the beginning of educational computing, and the dawn of a whole new era.

Those of us who have been teaching with computers for the duration have seen a lot of changes, and not all of them have been technological. Sure, the hardware and software have gotten flashier. more flexible, and lots easier to use. But the more important changes have come in how teachers have looked at computers: from a subject to teach about, to engaging electronic workbooks to tools for enhancing the existing curriculum, to aids in creating a whole new pedagogy for the next century.

Over the past year, discussions about technology in the classroom have begun to dovetail with national debates about education and the teaching profession in general. A consensus seems to be growing around these key points: that citizens of the 21st century will need different kinds of skills than our schools currently provide, that teachers of the 21st century will fulfill different roles than they currently do, and that technology has a part to play in both of these transformations. (See the box called "Guides to the 1990s" for a list of reports on these topics.)

Whether you're a veteran computer-using teacher or are just beginning to work with technology, you will be uniquely well-equipped to thrive through all of the changes that the next decade brings. Before we peek into the 1990s and beyond, however, let's look back on the lessons of educational computing's brief history.

Where We've Been And What We've Learned

Although we have all arrived at our own place with technology, there are startling similarities in the path taken by otherwise diverse schools, districts, or groups of teachers. It does not seem to matter whether they started with the first microcomputers in the late 1970s, jumped on the bandwagon in the 1980s, or are just getting started now, on the cusp of the 1990s (and there are many who are at that point!).

The Teacher's Key Role

Most often the first computer entered the elementary school of the 1980s with a curious, imaginative teacher who was ready to try out some new ideas with equally curious students! That teacher was one who "learned computers" with a book or friend, through trial and error and all-nighters. In the end, that teacher became the mentor, the guide for the rest of the school. Even in cases where computers came into the school on the tide of a grant or master plan, someone in the school had to accept the role of guide and mentor—if the technology was to be used successfully, once the initial excitement wore off.

The 1980s also taught us, however, that technology implementations that

587

work do not remain identified with just one teacher, however enthusiastic. Success is insured when there is a sense of ownership, pride, and involvement by the larger group of colleagues within any school setting.

The Importance of Planning

Another hallmark of successful technology programs has been the existence of a special kind of plan—a plan that starts with a sincere vision of what is needed, rather than just what is perceived as possible. A successful plan may start small but eventually broadens out to involve all students, all departments, and multiple applications. As the National Education Association report on educational technology (see box below) concludes, "a plan must focus on the individual educational needs of students and how educators meet those needs rather than on the technology" as an end in itself.

The Question of Readiness

The OTA report, *Power On!* refers to information technology as the "catalyst for change." Almost always, the use of technology in our profession starts new ideas flowing: new ways to present information, to challenge or to encourage students, to streamline time-consuming tasks. We've seen clearly, however, that technology alone cannot produce change. There really seems to be a point of "readiness" for each of us—a particular state of mind. When teachers are ready to learn something completely new, they are ready to start along their own path toward use of technology in their teaching.

Once they reach this point of readiness, teachers are often surprised to discover that they already have most of the skills they need to use technology. They know how to type, so the keyboard is no problem. They are used to teacher's

---

Guides to the Future
Reports about teachers and technology

Power On! New Tools for Teaching and Learning (September 1988). An exhaustive study of educational technology in the United States today, with thoughtful recommendations for correcting gaps and redressing inequities. U.S. Congress Office of Technology Assessment, OTA-SET-379, Washington, D.C. 20402-9325.

Report of the National Education Association's Special Committee on Educational Technology (August 1989). Reviews the status of technology in the public schools and

offers recommendations for building on the teacher's central role in successful use of technology. NEA Communications, 1201 16th St. NW, Washington, D.C. 20036.

Images of Potential (Spring 1989). The first product of the National Foundation for the Improvement of Education's "Learning Tomorrow" initiative, this report contains imaginative scenarios brainstormed by groups of forward-looking educators. NFIE Publications, P.O. Box 509, West Haven, CT 06516; Stock No. A701-00355.

manuals and, once they master the language, the computer manuals aren't much worse. Teachers are used to putting ideas on the blackboard or the overhead projector, so putting ideas on the screen is not that different. Very quickly, these days, technology-ready teachers find themselves "up to speed" with computers.

The Myths We've Outgrown

There was a collection of "myths" about technology that arose in the 1980s— things that we may have believed at one time but are happy to leave by the wayside as we progress toward the 1990s. We no longer fear that computers will replace teachers. We no longer feel that everyone must learn BASIC, or for that matter even learn to program. We no longer think that teachers will write all of the necessary software (but we do have new hypermedia tools to make it easier for those who do want to develop their own material). We no longer expect a school or a district to select one type of hardware and stick to that choice forever, for everything. We no longer assume that there is one best way to implement a technology program in every school, just as there is no best way to teach every student. Most importantly, we no longer see inservice technology training as something we can "finish," because we know now that for every possibility we explore, two more wait just over the horizon.

What's Ahead and How We'll Get There

If we accept the fact of change and realize that change will occur at different rates and at different times in every school and district... if we work toward what we think is needed and not get

"hung-up" on what we see as merely possible... what might our classrooms be like in the 1990s?

Mix and Match Technology

All three of our key reports speak of a convergence of existing technologies: computers, facsimile machines, hypermedia, multimedia, interactive video, telecommunications, voice synthesis, microwaves, satellites (see "Glossary for the 1990s"). Students will have access to technology for exploration, expression, and reinforcement. Teachers will have access for lesson development, record-keeping, and communications. Classrooms of varying sizes and configurations will be equipped with technology for presentation and investigation. Libraries will become information centers with access to all types of media and with connections to a world of knowledge beyond their four walls.

This array of tools is not so far removed from what is available today. With the continuing development of versatile hardware and software, we're already beginning to mix and match the pieces to suit our individual teaching styles, the demands of the subject at hand, and the specific needs of each student.

New Roles for Teachers

The NEA report describes one of our future options as a "value added model" where technology is used to "enrich human capital," to expand the ability to process information, to allow modeling and creativity, to free the imagination to enhance (rather than merely streamline) the learning process. All this means a change in the role of the teacher. Most technology-using teachers are finding themselves becoming co-explorers with their students, guides to the learning processes, rather than the sole deliverers of knowledge and instruction. For most, this is an exciting and rewarding transition. However, that new role seems to be too often restricted by the existing structure of schools and classrooms, so we need to look at eliminating requirements that restrict the freedom to explore and learn in the new environment (see "Flexibility and Diversity," below).

Renewed Innovations

Many of the educational innovations of the past have "withered on the vine"—not because they were not valid but because at the time they were introduced, they were not practical for the average classroom teacher to implement. If we review some of those ideas we may find several "old friends" to bring along into the technology-aided 1990s. For example, with the ability of the computer to manage information, the individualization of instruction becomes not only possible but practical and desirable. With the changing roles for teachers, there needs to be a fresh look at differentiated staffing. The availability of a broad selection of resources through telecommunications makes true discovery learning possible, even in remote sites, and breathes new life into the ideal of socially relevant, crosscultural instruction. The multimedia aspect of

Glossary for the 1990s

Key technology terms and tools, adapted from *Images of Potential*

Camcorder: Combination of camera and recorder. Contains the video camera and recorder all in one unit.

Compact disc: Generally refers to five-inch discs (CD-ROM) that are read by laser beam. Most people are familiar with digitally recorded audio CDs. Similar discs are also used in CD-ROM drives for computers, and can hold a great deal of information.

Computer synthetic voice translation: Refers to the technology of converting text into artificial speech using a computer. Also known as voice synthesis.

Desktop publishing: The capability of using computers and laser printers to combine text and graphics into publication-quality documents.

Electronic mail: Sending and receiving messages over telephone lines.

Fax (facsimile) machine: Scans a document (text or graphics), converts it into code, sends it through the telephone line to a machine at another location which decodes the digitized message and converts it back into its original form.

Fiber optics: A bundle of many glass fibers that transports light across the length of the fibers. Computer data and phone conversations can both be carried through these fibers.

Hologram: A thin, flat piece of glass or film through which can be viewed a three-dimensional projected image.

Interactive videodisc: A combination program using a computer and videodisc player, which allows the user to interact with the events occurring on the screen. The user can stop the video, search for other information and pictures, and create his or her own "path" through the material.

Laserdisc or videodisc: The 12-inch

technology fits naturally with a "learning modalities" approach and interdisciplinary connections. And the ability of students to create tangible polished output—from word processed stories to multimedia presentations—opens new vistas of "hands-on" mastery and self-esteem.

Flexibility and Diversity

To really work, the technology-enriched classroom of the 1990s must empower the student and the teacher to learn and to explore in many directions. What we really want is a learning-centered classroom, where the teacher is free to use whatever material and method is most appropriate to the student and the subject matter at hand. We are looking for a technology-assisted classroom that allows for flexible groupings of students and for a teaching staff of wide ranging skills, working most often in their own areas of expertise. To realize these goals, we must be free of some of the current restrictions—of grade level, of sequence of skills, of time, and of resources. The NEA report makes its strongest recommendations for the decentralization of the learning environment and the individualization of objectives for each learner.

discs which are read by laser on a videodisc player. Each side of these large discs may hold 54,000 frames of information in the form of still pictures, text, graphics, or full motion video/film segments.

Microwave: The extremely high frequency wavelength which the major television networks use to transmit their programs. The transmissions are broadcast to satellites which amplify and retransmit the signal to many other locations, which receive with their own satellite dish. Cellular phones and all kinds of radar equipment also use microwaves.

Modem: A "computer telephone" which converts information generated on a computer into tones that can be transmitted over telephone lines.

Multimedia: The use of more than one technology to develop a presentation, lesson, or production. Possible combinations include computer with text and animation, videodisc player, CD-ROM player, synthesizer, and so on.

Overhead projection panel: Connected to a computer and placed on an overhead projector, this device allows a computer user to display "live data" on a large film screen.

Robotics: The technology related to machines that can be programmed to do physical tasks or activities, such as manipulating materials, tools, and special devices.

Scanner: A machine which can "read" the dark and light images of a document (text or graphics), and convert them into digitized information which can be seen and used on a computer.

VCR: Video cassette recorder, allows users to record and play videotapes on a television screen.

Voice recognition unit: A device which is programmed to recognize and respond to commands spoken by a person.

Access, Support, and Training

In the school we envision for the 1990s, teachers have adequate access to technology—to do their own work and to meet each student's needs in the most effective and efficient way. At the very minimum, each teacher will have a computer on his or her own desk. Teachers will have adequate and on-going training to use the equipment they have and, more importantly, to develop the ability to match the technology to the curriculum and create a diverse and exciting pedagogy where technology becomes a partner, not a subject. Teachers will be encouraged to take instructional risks, to share information with each other, and to constantly inventory their own professional development needs and goals.

Creative New Curricula

The curriculum for our 1990s classroom will be determined, not by tradition, but by a careful investigation of the needs of a citizen in the 1990s. In *Images of Potential,* for example, the imagined curriculum of the future contains many of the traditional subjects (as well as such "new" skills as critical thinking and collaboration) presented and combined in new ways, using a variety of methods. The end result—mastery of well-defined, predetermined objectives and skills—may be the same, but the roads to mastery may be very diverse.

The classroom of the 1990s, then, will foster a lifelong love of learning—for teachers and students alike. It teaches skills more often than facts: for example, writing skills more than word processing; problem solving, not just multiplication tables: and research skills with access to the world's greatest libraries.

It will present diverse options and acknowledge individual differences. All learners will be accepted where they are in their own development and guided toward the acquisition of the skills they need.

The Road to Tomorrow

Although many of the elements of this imagined future are currently within our grasp, our 1990s school is not a 1980s school with fresh paint. It is restructured to take advantage of the best we know now. It is, to quote the NEA report, "a restructured school environment, not piecemeal appendages grafted onto the current school structure and curriculum."

We know this school will not materialize on January 1, 1990, but with a plan that charts the direction in which we want to go, it will take shape in the years to come. If our foundation is solid and our vision is clear, it will happen more quickly than we dare hope. With the help of state and national policy makers, with district and school administration and staff working together with their communities, the school of the 1990s can become a reality in any community.

Bobby Goodson was a pioneering computer using teacher in the Cupertino California public schools and a founding advisor of Teaching and Computers. *Today her Sunnyvale, California-based firm. Bobby Goodson and Associates, assists teachers and schools in making the best use of technology.*

Unlike other necessities of life, information technologies are rapidly increasing in power while dropping in price. In another five years, schools will be able to purchase devices with greater capabilities than large research computers had five years ago. What new types of educational software will this next generation of hardware make possible? What will be the implications for students and teachers?

The Evolution of Instructional Devices

For over four decades, the capabilities of computers to process, store and transmit information have steadily increased, while their costs have decreased. For example, 10 years ago, $3,500 could buy an Apple II with an eight-bit, one-megahertz processor, 48K of RAM, eight K of ROM, a 40-character by 24-line uppercase display, high-resolution graphics (280 by 192, 16 colors), two 140K disk drives with a controller, and an RF Modulator to connect with a television set. Adjusting for 10 years of inflation, an equivalent amount of buying power today is $6,800. For that price, one can buy a Macintosh II with a 16-megahertz 32-bit processor, one megabyte of RAM, 170K of ROM, two 800K disk drives, a 20-megabyte internal hard disk, and a 640 by 480 RGB display with 256 colors!

Comparable increases in computers' power/cost ratio are expected for another 10 to 15 years. By the 1990s, schools will be able to afford the equivalent of today's advanced engineering workstations. (However, by the early 21st century, physical barriers such as the speed of light, the second law of thermodynamics, and quantum mechanical tunneling of electrons will constrain the evolution of electronics. A shift to optical or biological architectures for computers will be required to push this trend further still.)

The external memory that computers can access has also been growing rapidly. A digital optical disk (CD-ROM) the size of a 45 rpm phonograph record now can store about 500 megabytes (250,000 pages) of information. This is equivalent to what a secretary could generate typing 80 words per minute, eight hours per day, for eight years! When stamped in quantities of more than 100, these discs cost less than $5 each to produce, reducing the cost of "publishing" by three orders of magnitude.

In addition to lowering the price of accessing information, digital storage greatly increases the speed with which specific data can be found. As an illustration, one company, Quantum Access, has published on a CD-ROM a "State Educational Encyclopedia" for Texas school administrators: 100,000 pages of information (federal and state education codes, attorney generals' opinions, commissioners' rulings, etc.) updated every three months. The unified index to this information is itself over 70,000 pages in length and includes all words in the documents except universal terms (such as "and,"

By
CHRISTOPHER
J. DEDE

593

"or," "the")! As a result, a search can find in three seconds every paragraph in the 100,000 pages that contains a group of specified phrases (e.g., "handicapped," "reading scores," and "Montessori"). Such an information utility can save many hours of tedious scanning.

Numerous emerging hardware developments have implications for educational technologies. For example, the next generation of information technologies will synthesize the attributes of computers and telecommunications. Devices will emerge to combine the capabilities of the telephone, television, radio, printing press, computer, and copier. Already, real-time digitization and storage of high-resolution images (30 frames per second) are available for personal computers.

These advances in fusing the information technologies are proceeding very rapidly, driven by scientific breakthroughs, the global marketplace, and competition between vendors who previously had separate market niches (computers, telecommunications and media). The resultant decreases in cost are truly incredible—three years ago an optical scanning element capable of 300 dots-per-inch resolution sold for over $2,000; now it retails for less than $7.

However, all this increased power has little meaning unless software takes advantage of its capabilities. After all, what does it matter if a word processor can paste in 1/1,000 instead of 1/10th of a second? Fortunately, simultaneous with these hardware advances, our understanding of the potential of computers has expanded from number crunching to data processing to symbol manipulation. New types of applications have been created as our conceptions have become more sophisticated and as the power to support more advanced functions has become available.

The Next Generation of Educational Software

Historically, instructional usage of computers has evolved through different stages: from computer literacy to programming languages, computer-assisted instruction, and computers as tools (e.g., word processor, data base, spreadsheet, graphics). Researchers in artificial intelligence and cognitive science are now developing two additional types of educational software: intelligent tutoring systems and "cognition enhancers." Here I discuss emerging cognition enhancers such as empowering environments, hypermedia, and microworlds (Brown, 1985). (A synthesis of recent research in intelligent tutoring systems is given in Dede [1986].)

The concept underlying a cognition enhancer is that the complementary cognitive strengths of a person and an information technology can be used in partnership. For example, computers have large short-term memories (megabytes of RAM), while human beings are limited to an immediate storage capacity of less than 10 chunks of information (Anderson, 1983). Computers can also execute complex "algorithms" (precise recipes for solving one class of problem) more rapidly than people. For tasks involving manipulation of successive symbolic results (e.g., involved mathematical calculations), these two cognitive attributes give computers an advantage over humans. In general, computers are becoming superior at all forms of standardized problem solving.

However, people store information over the long term in rich "semantic networks" containing webs of associationally related textual, temporal and visual imagery. For example, in human memory the word "apple" conjures up religious, corporate, computational, botanic and gustatory dimensions. At present, computers are much more limited in how their information can be interrelated, as anyone who uses a data base knows! The cognitive attributes of human beings give them an advantage over computers at applying peripheral real-world knowledge to ill-structured problems (such as diagnosing the source of a student's motivational difficulties). In general, people are still much better than computers at problem recognition, at metacognition (thinking about thinking), and at non-standardized problem solving.

Some researchers are working to develop intelligent devices which could teach a student a particular topic without the help of a human instructor. For example, a machine-based tutor could show a pupil the steps to follow for subtraction, guide the student through examples, give sample problems to test comprehension, diagnose errors, and provide remedial instruction (VanLehn, 1983). A computerized coach could monitor a pupil playing an educational game, looking for patterns of suboptimal moves and occasionally intervening to suggest a better strategy (Brown & Burton, 1982). This mirrors the one-on-one instruction a human teacher could provide. Research suggests that such an approach is very powerful (Bloom, 1984).

However, because of current limitations of computers, cognitive science, and artificial intelligence, developing devices capable of independent instruction is very difficult. While intelligent machine-based tutors and coaches will gradually become useful in school settings, cognition enhancers designed to combine the cognitive strengths of humans and computers will evolve much more rapidly. These tools are still in their infancy, but so far three kinds seem to be emerging: empowering environments, hypermedia, and microworlds.

Empowering Environments

This type of cognition enhancer utilizes the computer's strengths in structured symbolic manipulation to empower human accomplishment through a division of labor: the machine handles the routine mechanics of a task while the person is immersed in its higher-order meanings. For example, I once took an oil painting course. My goal was to faithfully convey to a canvas the images in my mind so that viewers could share my experiences and emotions. However, rather than pondering form and composition and aesthetics, I spent my time trying to mix colors that remotely resembled my visualizations, trying to keep the paint from running all over the canvas, and trying to keep the turpentine out of my hair. Now I can use a graphics construction set to choose from a huge palette of colors; to alter, pixel by pixel, the contour of an image; and to instantly undo my failures. I am involved with the deep semantics of art, while the empowering environment handles the mechanics. (However, my accomplishments are still ultimately limited by my own talents and knowledge as an artist.)

Researchers are just beginning to understand how to design this type of cognition enhancer. On one level, a rich comprehension of a domain is necessary to generate an optional menu of manipulable symbols and processes for the user. For example, in building an empowering environment for a programming language, an array of debugging aids and compilers and code generators must be chosen for inclusion.

Di Sessa's (1986) work on Boxer illustrates the evolution of an educational empowering environment for programming. The fundamental unit of information in this programming language is a "box" just as more conventional languages have units which are lines of code). Each box is a window on screen which contains part of a program. Boxes can be hierarchically nested; for example, Boxer program is a box which contains different types of internal boxes. These include boxes for input and output variables and other boxes which determine how variables are processed. Boxer's integrated functionalities include text processing and structured filing, the ability to use and modify prewritten programs, data base features, graphics capabilities, and tools for programming from scratch. Boxer also has hypermedia capabilities (discussed in the next section).

A second type of design issue is the range of tasks for which empowering environments would be useful. For example, would a "myth construction set" aid anthropologists? Similar elements underlie the myths in all cultures, and many societies have closely related myth structures. An empowering environment might be useful for building, comparing and tailoring a cultural mythos, just as a word processor allows the manipulation of words and word structures.

As a third design issue, what capabilities should empowering environments possess? Intelligent coaches with embedded models of expertise could monitor a user's work, intervening to improve patterns of suboptimal performance. For example, a graphics environment with an intelligent coach might beep when I used eight keystrokes to modify a picture and display a message, asking if I wanted to learn how to accomplish the same result with only two keystrokes.

Similarly, empowering environments could save "cognitive audit trails" of user operations, so that later a person could review his/her sequence of actions, looking for patterns of errors and ways to improve performance. Connecting indi-

vidual workstations could create shared computational environments to allow cooperative work (e.g., several people simultaneously composing music) and to aid group decision making through tools which structure the dynamics of meetings. Consciousness sensors which monitor the user's motivation and mood through tracking respiration, skin conductivity, heart rate, and other physiological measures are another possibility. Research into how to make individual empowering environments more versatile is producing some very interesting ideas (*Proceedings: Computer-Supported Cooperative Work,* 1986).

Primitive empowering environments are beginning to be used in education. A word processor with spelling checker, thesaurus, typing tutor, and graphics tools is the beginning of an empowering environment for writing. Even the early versions of this type of cognition enhancer have an interesting property: Their usage by a person unconsciously alters the *style* of task performance!

For example, as a result of using a word processor, I no longer can write well with paper and pencil. I used to compose a sentence by thinking for a couple of minutes and setting down a final version that was about 90 percent of optimal; I took my one best shot because making changes later would involve massive physical cutting and pasting. Now I write by thinking for half a minute and typing a sentence that is perhaps 40 percent of optimal, think for another 15 seconds and make a change (now at 50 percent), make another change a few seconds later (65 percent), and so on. The same amount of time is required to get to the 90 percent level, but now my psychological momentum is behind revision and polishing rather than producing a single finished product, and no cognitive dissonance bars the sentence from eventually evolving to optimal.

However, when I try to write with a pencil using this new, superior strategy—disaster! Most people who use word processors (or music tools, data bases or spreadsheets) experience the same unconscious shift in style. In a world of intelligent empowering environments, the ways we accomplish many tasks may alter.

Hypermedia

Even with a sophisticated empowering environment for desktop publishing, I can still get writer's block. A second type of cognition enhancer is needed: Hypermedia is a framework for non-linear representation of symbols (text, graphics, images, software code) in the computer. As discussed earlier, long-term human memory is a storage system of associational semantic networks; I can know everything I want to write, but not have my ideas in the linear stream required for written or oral communication. I need an "idea processor," a way of externally creating a multidimensional construct which mirrors the concepts and links forming the material in my memory. With my knowledge externalized into a hypermedia system, I can traverse this network along alternative paths through nodes and links, seeking the right sequential stream for my intended content, audience and goals. The computer is working in cognitive partnership to eliminate the overload involved in transferring long-term to short-term memory. Also, a person's access to long-term memory may be enhanced by the process of building and using hypermedia.

Hypermedia is a general tool that can be utilized in several different ways. In addition to serving as an externalized

associational memory for an individual, hypermedia could be an alternative representational system for a large, shared data base (such as an integrated textbook series for the entire curriculum). Such an approach would encourage group interdisciplinary exploration by explicitly interconnecting similar ideas in different subjects. Hypermedia as a knowledge representation format empowers instructional design based on cognitive principles of learning such as active structural networks, schema theory, web teaching, and generative learning (Jonassen, 1986).

The Intermedia project at Brown University (Yankelovitch, 1986) is one illustration of educational applications of hypermedia. Intermedia enables browsing through information which is linked, cross-referenced, and annotated. System authors can access an integrated set of tools which includes a text processor, a graphics editor, a timeline editor, a scanned-image viewer, and an application to view three-dimensional models. Maps which present visual representations of the network are used to guide viewers through the system. Intermedia materials are used as a resource in several courses on the Brown campus, so the system is designed to handle a multi-user environment of workstations connected by local area networks. Future plans include the development of segment, map, video, and animation editors, as well as access to CD-ROM data.

An "inference engine" (the part of an expert system which supports reasoning about data) can be built onto a hypermedia framework. For example, some software engineering projects use a "truth maintenance system" to propagate changes made in one part of the code into their consequent impacts on other sections of the program and documentation (Narayanaswamy & Scacchi, 1987). In this way, programmers can avoid making a change that introduces more bugs than it fixes, since the system will force the user to examine all the consequences of altering one part of the code.

The emergence of primitive hypermedia systems on personal computers is likely to unleash a variety of new ideas about uses for this type of cognition enhancer. For example, the hypermedia version of this paper, done on Guide, places each fundamental concept together by providing icons, buttons or highlighted words on which the user can click to bring up windows of related text (e.g., the material on semantic nets in the "cognition enhancers" section links to the "hypermedia" section). Such modularity and juxtapositions might increase comprehension over the force delinearity of textual presentations. Perhaps new styles of remembering and knowledge transfer will evolve as well!

Microworlds

This third type of cognition enhancer allows the user to explore and manipulate limited artificial realities. A problem that learners constantly experience is how to relate abstract, formal knowledge to specific real-world situations. For example, if I were teaching how Einstein's theories of general and special relativity had altered our understanding of gravity, I could approach this task by explaining the appropriate equations and formulas to my students. However, even if they had the logical reasoning skills and the background in physics and calculus to understand my exposition, few would be able to link their abstract comprehension to real-world applications (such as why water swirls down drains in opposite directions in the Northern and South-ern hemispheres).

What I need is a microworld, an artificial reality in which I can vary gravity's fundamental properties. The students could use the computer to explore some activity (say, baseball) at earth's gravity; even a very short game at zero gravity! Varying one item at a time, we could work through the constants and variables in the equations, altering each in turn to see how the game of baseball would change. Then students would have both formal and applied knowledge of the theories underlying gravity.

The concept of microworlds extends to "surrogate travel" and "surrogate experience." Taking advantage of the merging synthesis between telecommunications and computers, interactive videodiscs could allow an individualized "trip" to be taken to the Louvre in Paris. The student could "walk" through the museum examining art objects in any order, at different angles, for any duration, with or without commentary, with hypermedia links to related subjects. This experience would not be the same as actually visiting the Louvre, but it would be far more instructive and motivating than group viewing of art history slides!

Surrogate experience could be gained in a profession (say, medicine) by having students use an interactive videodisc to interview a "patient," make a diagnosis, and prescribe a therapy. This experience would be far different than a structured problem at the back of a text chapter; the student would need to spot visual cues, elicit information essential to the diagnosis, and determine the accuracy of the patient's responses. As with computational microworlds, key variables could be manipulated in surrogate travel and experience to encompass the range of situations in which a particular chunk of abstract, formal knowledge is useful.

Users find microworlds very motivating; in fact, researchers are studying video games as an example of artificial realities to determine what makes some of them so interesting and how to generalize this reinforcement to educational situations (Lepper & Malone, 1987). Learning environments such as the Logo language and the simulations now used in classrooms are the beginnings of microworlds. The work of Smith, O'Shea and Scanlon (1987) on the Alternate Reality Kit (ARK) illustrates a more advanced educational microworld. Users can manipulate the laws of physics and experience how everyday activities (such as throwing a ball) change in different environments.

Summary

Empowering environments, hyper-media, and microworlds illustrate the variety of cognition enhancers under development. Further exploration is needed to learn more about how partnerships between people and intelligent tools can improve learning, additional research is required to comprehend how best to design cognition enhancers; and the emergence of powerful, inexpensive information technologies is necessary to empower their usage in schools. All of these initiatives are underway, but what will be the ultimate effects of moving education in this direction?

Implications for Educators of Cognition Enhancers

Science and science fiction writer Isaac Asimov once said that the important thing to forecast is not the automobile, but the parking problem; not the income tax, but the expense account; not the television, but the soap opera. Similarly, the fundamental issue is not how many empowering environments, hypermedia systems and microworlds will be in classrooms and homes in decade, but how they will change the relationship between student and teacher, school and society. Illustrative potential impacts of the wide-spread long-term usage of cognition enhancers are listed below.

- Human strengths in partnerships between people and cognition enhancers involve skills such a creativity, flexibility, decision making given incomplete data, complex pattern recognition information evaluation/synthesis, and holistic thinking. Such higher-order mental attributes might become a new definition of human intelligence, as basic cognitive skills would increasingly shift to the intelligent tool's portion of the partnership. Polishing students' mastery of lower-level skills would be like grooming John Henry to compete with the steam engine!

- Students would still need fundamental descriptive and procedural knowledge—one cannot master higher-order skills without a foundation of lower-order concepts and processes—but the goal of teaching the basics would shift from performance fluency to providing a cognitive underpinning for sophisticated problem recognition and unusual problem solving. Methods of educational assessment would alter from charting mastery of descriptive knowledge to evaluating attainment of higher-order skills. Fortunately, cognition enhancers can aid in collecting the detailed individual data necessary, as well as empowering more sophisticated empirical educational research.

- "Learning while doing" would become a more significant component of education because combined computer and telecommunication technologies allow delivery of instructional services in a decentralized manner. To allow credit for occupational accomplishments, workplace tools may include intelligent devices that act as job performance aids while simultaneously collecting a cognitive audit trail of user skill improvements, creating increasingly informal systems of credentialization. Occupational roles will alter rapidly as the evolution of information technologies drives the knowledge-based economy, and adults may become a major clientele of schools (Office of Technology Assessment, 1984).

- Widespread use of cognition enhancers would facilitate the participation of every person associated with the educational process—learner, teacher, administrator, employer or parent—in shaping instructional outcomes. Society's five primary educational agents (schools, family, community, media and workplace) could act in a more coordinated fashion to shape the learning environments of individuals through the use of interlinked educational information utilities which supply access to a variety of data, courseware, tools, and training.

- Productivity gains from a mature, technology-intensive educational approach could enable a higher overall ratio of students to teachers, but smaller class sizes for group instruction through supplementary use of intelligent technologies and non-school instructional agents (Melmed, 1986). Teacher salaries would be better and the total educational workforce might increase due to a wider range of clients. Given equivalent expenditures, instructional outcomes would

be significantly higher.

- Over the long term, the effects of intelligent technologies on cognitive style, personality, and social skills may be profound (Turkle, 1984). The television and the computer have each demonstrated the capability to shape the attributes of youngsters immersed in their usage. The deliberate tailoring of individualized, information-intensive environments could produce a generation radically different in its characteristics from any previous one. For example, a technology-intensive model could incorporate interactive learning situations designed to build the affective skills of cooperation, compromise, and group decision making essential in a knowledge-based economy.

- Educational equity could increase through the power of intelligent systems to individualize instruction. Because the economic strength of a knowledge-based democracy is dependent on universally excellent performance by workers and citizens, each member of society would have a strong self-interest in promoting optimal educational achievement by all learners.

More detailed expositions of the widespread, long-term use of cognition enhancers are given in Dede (1987) and Dede and Freiberg (1986).

Conclusion

The potential implications for civilization of intelligent educational environments could be profound. The next generation of information technologies could become history's first "knowledge medium": humanity's conscious mechanism for tailoring its cognitive evolution (Stefik, 1986). For example, in the final chapter of his book *The Selfish Gene,* Richard Dawkins suggests that ideas (he calls them "memes") are like genes. This opens up a myriad of analogies: meme pools, mimetic drift, mutation, displacement, and even recombinant memes. Education would be a crucial component in a society's attempt to increase knowledge and wisdom through intelligent tools which aid in the collecting, filtering, modeling and sharing of massive amounts of data and information.

To accomplish such a transformation, we need to overcome two myths in instructional computing. The *Myth of Power* states that novices need less powerful devices than expert users. This article has argued the opposite: Rapid computational speed and large amounts of memory are required to support the self-explicating interfaces, multiple mental models, and alternative knowledge representations helpful to beginners. Experienced users actually need less power to run complex but non-explanatory versions of the same applications. The Apple IIGS, the IBM System 2 Model 25, and similar machines from other vendors are too limited to support the next generation of advanced learning environments; but educators are being sold these machines to create the "school of the future!"

The **Myth of Consolidation** states that the wave of innovation in instructional computing is over: that we now know what computers can do for students and, based on this summative evaluation, we can tailor our educational investments to more of the same machines, software, and teacher training. This article argues the opposite: Much more powerful tools are emerging, attempts to judge how computers can improve learning are premature, and the real wave of technological change in schools is just beginning.

The two most common errors in technology assessment are overestimating the speed of diffusion of an innovation and underestimating its eventual consequences and side effects. Typically, new information technologies have their impact on societal institutions in four sequential stages (Coates, 1977):

Stage One: The new technology is adopted by an institution to carry out existing functions more efficiently.

Stage Two: The institution changes internally (work roles, organizational structures) to take better advantage of these new efficiencies.

Stage Three: Institutions develop new functions and activities enabled by additional capabilities of the technology. As the roles of different types of institutions expand, new competitive relationships emerge.

Stage Four: The original role of the institution may become obsolete, be displaced, or be radically transformed as new goals dominate the institution's activities.

Current instructional computing is still in Stages One and Two. Workplace tools are beginning to enter Stage Three. Schools must follow by implementing more advanced learning environments or they will once again risk preparing a generation of students for the past rather than the future. Far from consolidation, we are just at the beginning of our exploration into education, cognition and computation.

References

Anderson, John R. (1983) *The Architecture of Cognition,* Cambridge, Mass.: Harvard University Press.

Bloom, Benjamin S. (1984) "The 2 Sigma Problem: The Search for Methods of Group Instruction as Effective as One-On-One Tutoring." *Educational Researcher,* 13, pp. 3-16.

Brown, John S. and Burton, Richard R. (1982) "An Investigation of Computer Coaching for Informal Learning Activities." In D. Slecman and J. Brown (Eds.), *Intelligent Tutoring Systems.* New York: Academic Press.

Brown, John S. (1985) "Process Versus Product: A Perspective on Tools for Communal and Informal Electronic Learning." *Journal of Educational Computing Research*, 1, pp. 179-202.

Coates, Joseph F. (1977) "Aspects of Innovation: Public Policy Issues in Telecommunications Development." *Telecommunications Policy*, 1, 3, pp. 11-23.

Dawkins, Richard. (1976) *The Selfish Gene.* New York: Oxford University Press.

Dede, Christopher J. (1985) "Assessing the Potential of Educational Information Utilities." *Library High Technology*, 3, 4, pp. 115-119.

Dede, Christopher J. (1986) "A Review and Synthesis of Recent Research in Intelligent Computer-Assisted Instruction." *International Journal of Man-Machine Studies*, 24, 4, pp. 329-353.

Dede, Christopher J. and Freiberg, Jerome P. (1986) "The Long Term Evolution of School Effectiveness." *Educational Forum*, 51, 1, pp. 65-80.

Dede, Christopher J. (1987) *Implementation of Artificial Intelligence in Education: Two Scenarios.* Austin, Texas: Center for Research on Communication Technology and Society, University of Texas.

DiSessa, Andrea A. (1986) "The Future of Programming: Breaking the Utility Barrier." In D.A. Norman & S.W. Draper (Eds.), *User Centered System Design: New Perspectives on Computer-Human Interaction.* Hillsdale, N.J.: Lawrence Erlbaum.

Jonassen, David H. (1986) "Hypertext Principles for Text and Courseware Design." *Educational Psychologist,* 21, 4, pp. 269-292.

Lepper, Mark R. and Malone, Thomas W. (1987) "Intrinsic Motivation and Instructional Effectiveness in Computer-based Education." In R.E. Snow and M.J. Farr (Eds.) *Aptitude, Learning, and Instruction III: Cognitive and Affective Process Analyses.* Hillsdale, N.J.: Lawrence Erlbaum.

Melmed, Arthur. (1986) "The Technology of American Education: Problem and Opportunity." *T.H.E. Journal,* 14, 2. pp. 77-81.

Narayanaswamy, K. and Scacchi, Walt. (1987) "A Database Foundation to Support Software System Evolution." *The Journal of Systems and Software,* 7, pp. 37-49.

Office of Technology Assessment, U.S. Congress. (1984) *Computerized Manufacturing Automation: Education, Employment, and the Workplace.* Washington, D.C.: USGPO.

Proceedings: Computer-Supported Cooperative Work. (1986) Austin, Texas: Software Technology Program, Microelectronics and Computer Technology Consortium.

Smith, Randal B., O'Shea, Tim, and Scanlon, Eileen. (1987) *Building and Using Alternate Realities for Physics Education.* Palo Alto, Calif.: Xerox Palo Alto Research Center.

Stefik, Mark. (1986) "The Next Knowledge Medium." *The AI Magazine,* 7, 1, pp. 34-46.

Turkle, Sherry. (1984) *The Second Self: Computers and the Human Spirit.* New York: Simon & Schuster.

VanLehn, Kurt. (1983) "Human Procedural Skill Acquisition: Theory, Model, and Psychological Validation." *Proceedings of the American Association for Artificial Intelligence,* pp. 420-423.

Yankelovitch, Nicole. (1986) *Intermedia: A System for Linking Multimedia Documents.* Providence, R.I.: Institute for Research on Information and Scholarship, Brown University.

Article #5
The Next Decade: What the Future Holds

By
Daniel E.
Kinnaman

For better or worse we've left the "industrial age" behind and we're racing full-speed through the information age." Yesterday's science fiction is rapidly becoming today's reality. Electric cars, notebook-size computers, and "smart" appliances are no longer just dreams. Worldwide interactive communication links that simultaneously transmit audio, video, and hard copy are already in place. Today's personal computers have hundreds of times as much memory and processing power as those introduced into our schools just ten years ago. And the world's knowledge base is growing at an exponential rate.

How are schools reacting? We seem to be caught between the inertia of traditional educational practice and growing demands for reform and restructuring. How should we change? What should we emphasize? What role should technology play in education over the next decade?

To help you sort through these issues, we visited several of America's top think tanks in search of the most promising projects, products, and ideas for technology's future role in the classroom. And we spoke with many of the best known thinkers in educational computing, interestingly, many of these thinkers hold similar perspectives on the uses of technology in schools, perspectives that strongly influence their development efforts. These common beliefs include the following:

- All of education, from the physical organization of schools to instructional methods and assessment, needs to be open to review and change.
- Inquiry-centered, process-oriented learning environments in which students are active participants on an academic adventure are heavily favored over the traditional classroom setting.
- There is a decided emphasis, at least presently, on improving math and science education.
- In the '90s schools will look to technology more than ever before for educational solutions.
- Although computer power will continue to increase at astounding rates, technology is still just a vehicle. It isn't a destination. It can be a critical ingredient of successful school experience for children, but its usefulness is dependent upon the context in which it is used.

As you read about the individual projects described on the following pages, you will encounter these themes from a variety of vantage points, integrated in various ways and implemented through a range of technology applications.

Dr. Robert Tinker and the Technical Education Research Centers (TERC)

Now in its 25th year as an educational research and development center, TERC focuses primarily on improving mathematics and science education. Central to TERC's vision for education is direct involvement of students, especially as researchers collecting and analyzing real data in meaningful contexts. In several of TERC's projects, this involves electronically connecting large numbers of

604

students and their teachers with scientists and others in the research community. TERC calls this "network science."

Two of TERC's best-known network science projects are the National Geographic Kids Network (see *CCL*, October '89, pg. 30) and the TERC Star Schools project that is part of the larger U.S. Department of Education Star Schools Program (see *CCL*, January '89, pg. 12). Two other exciting new network science projects at the Cambridge, Massachusetts-based research center are described below.

Global Laboratory: This project is designed to involve students and teachers from around the world in conducting global ecology research with full-time scientists. Project goals include establishing an international network that promotes collaborative scientific investigation among students, teachers, and scientists who are widely dispersed geographically, developing inexpensive technology tools for monitoring and modeling various aspects of the environment, as well as for data analysis and representation; and developing strategies for integrating global studies into the science curriculum.

LabNet: LabNet is a telecommunications-based "teacher enhancement" project for secondary school science teachers. The project is designed to support teachers in successfully using microcomputer-based laboratory tools (MBLs) to help their students participate in collaborative, hands-on science investigations. Through the nationwide telecommunications network, teachers are able to share ideas, collaborate on the development of MBL activities and support each other in modifying their curricula to involve students in more experimental, project-based instruction.

What's ahead at TERC? In the '90s Tinker hopes to see the development of an international telecommunications network for K-12 education. But he points out that to use telecommunications successfully today, teachers need to understand too much technical jargon such as "baud rate," "handshaking," "parity," and "protocol." The telecommunications interface in NGS Kids Network represents a first attempt to overcome this problem. Currently, TERC is working on a new user-friendly, general telecommunications interface code-named "Alice." According to Tinker, TERC will be ready to begin testing prototypes of Alice in October.

Another obstacle to the widespread use of telecommunications in schools is the difficulty faced by the average classroom teacher in gaining access to telephone and network services. To overcome this obstacle, Tinker and others— including Senator Albert Gore (D-Tenn) who chairs the Senate Committee on Science Technology and Space—are calling for federal funding for an international K-12 education network. According to Tinker, the costs of the network might ultimately be covered by a number of funding sources (e.g. federal, corporate, state, and local education agencies). To the end users (i.e., teachers and students) however, access to the network would be free. In many ways this network would operate similarly to BitNet, the highly successful international network for higher education.

Once such a network is established, Tinker envisions schools and classrooms forming relationships with others locally, nationally, and internationally. However, for an international network to become truly useful, Tinker believes we will need to develop "computer-aided natural language translators." Such software would allow students on one network node to enter data in their native language and would digitally convert it into the native language of the students at the receiving wire. Sound farfetched? Tinker expects to see a "free" telecommunications network for K-12 education by 1995 and computer-aided language translators in use by the end of the decade.

Dr. Seymour Papert and the MIT Media Lab:

"There's not going to be any technology fix for education," says Seymour Papert. "Change," he says, "has to start with a new perspective on education. Our present system is fundamentally wrong. It's out of date: it's obsolete. Technology can help us to think in a bolder way about alternative education, but [there are] still too many people thinking only about how to use technology within the present system. They're treating the symptoms while the patient is dying."

According to Papert, educational technology will fulfill its potential only as fundamental changes occur in schooling over the long term. In that regard, he believes that there are several significant developments to look forward to in the coming decade. "First," he says, "the computer is going to be established as an integral part of learning in the '90s." This, he says, will help to "create an atmosphere in which really radical and novel ideas can be born."

In grappling with the fundamental issues of teaching and learning, Papert and his colleagues at the Media Lab are experimenting with a number of new educational uses of technology. One exciting project involves the development of robotic kits that allow children to build computer intelligence into a robot. (Most existing kits require the robot to be attached to a standard computer.) The Media Lab has already developed a matchbook-sized computer, equivalent

in power to an Apple II that resides within a LEGO brick. This on-board computer, which will run Logo, has the potential to extend the power and flexibility of products such as *LogoWriter* and *LEGO TC Logo*, creating an even richer set of construction elements.

Papert and his colleagues are also working on a post-Logo programming language. "Current programming languages," he says, "still reflect the basic programming structures of the '60s and '70s. In the '90s we'll need to develop programming structures that can take advantage of advanced hardware." One practical example, says Papert, is multiprocessing. "Multiprocessing is important because it makes it easy for children to work interactively with several objects at once." Researchers at the Media Lab are working on a post-Logo prototype in which a child can have 1,000 different turtles, each simultaneously running a different program. Such a language allows a user to program a colony of ants, for example, with each ant programmed to interact with many other programmable objects.

Unfortunately, such languages require more sophisticated hardware than that currently found in schools. But Papert is optimistic that machines with the power of today's Macintosh IIs and high-end IBM PS/2s will become widely affordable to schools within the next two to three years.

In addition to hardware and software developments. Papert is very interested in "empowering teachers to be bold enough to think about and be open to change. We can't create a new education without people who will do it," he claims. He sees his group's projects not so much as products that will change schools, but as ideas that will help "change the minds of enough teachers to begin a movement that will ultimately change education."

Dr. Judah Schwartz and Harvard's Educational Technology Center (ETC)

Judah Schwartz, Harvard professor and co-director of ETC, says that "raising a generation of people who know how to think" is a guiding principle for the work done at ETC and should be central to the mission of all schools. He emphasizes that learners should not be expected to function like sheep, but instead should be challenged to create and to develop the skills of taste and judgment in every content area.

According to Schwartz, the *Geometric Supposer* software series (published by Sunburst Communications), which has been the focus of a good deal of ETC's recent research and development, represents "a small step down that road." A mathematics education specialist, Schwartz believes that we need to "rethink the intellectual storyline in mathematics." That is, we need to restructure the math curriculum, taking content areas such as algebra, trigonometry, geometry, probability, and calculus which have traditionally been taught in isolation from one another, and integrating them in a way that takes advantage of the "extraordinary possibilities computer technology offers."

Schwartz sees new software development as a critical component of this process, and he stresses that good math software must be more than just a tool for symbolic manipulation; it must also be rich in the content of mathematics. He adamantly opposes building the curriculum around hardware and software that just do math chores and don't engage students with the content of math.

New software, he argues, needs to go beyond what is represented by today's graphing packages which he refers to as "wonderful half-tools." Half-tools are those that are primarily designed to draw a graph of a function entered in its symbolic form. To be a full tool the software also needs to allow students to enter a graph and see the corresponding changes in the symbolic form of the function. The function, he points out, is a fundamental object of algebra, and software should enable students to work directly with it in either its symbolic or its graphic form.

Based on these principles, Schwartz is currently working on the development of a new software series called *Visualizing Algebra*. Part one of the four-part series is called the *Function Supposer* and was released last year. It comes in MS-DOS format and is published by Sunburst Communications. The *Function Supposer,* part two in the series, is scheduled for release at the beginning of this school year, and the final two parts, *Equations* and *Inequalities,* are due out sometime in 1991.

Like the *Geometric Supposer, Visualizing Algebra* is software designed to provide students with "intellectual minors," says Schwartz. That is it provides them with a content-rich environment in which they can explore their understanding of mathematical principles and concepts. It gives students opportunities to gain ownership of content and to reason with and about mathematics.

"But, developing the software is the easy part," warns Schwartz. "Changing the school structure is the hard part."

> "But, developing the software is the easy part," warns Schwartz. "Changing the school structure is the hard part."

For instance, ETC research into classroom use of the *Geometric Supposer* has shown that students' roles don't normally include inventing and creating. And just because a software package enables a student to develop and explore conjectures and make evaluative judgments, there's no insurance that the teachers will use it for such purposes.

At ETC in the 1990s, lots of attention will be focused on conducting research that will help schools through the process of restructuring and toward the type of math education envisioned by Schwartz and his colleagues. He is confident that software such as the *Visualizing Algebra* series can provide opportunities to rethink and significantly improve the teaching and learning of mathematics. With the current price of hardware and software development, and with our increasing knowledge of cognition and learning, Schwartz says, "it is immoral for us to spend 200 hours teaching someone to be a poor imitation of a five-dollar calculator."

Institute for Research on Learning (IRL)

Every high school science textbook is filled with diagrams. And every student has spent time poring over the captions to these diagrams trying to understand the scientific principles behind them. But what if the diagrams themselves were manipulable? What if a student could change the parameters of the diagram to see how the effects changed? What if that student could actually "perform experiments" with the diagram just as in the real world and receive scientifically accurate results?

These are the questions being asked by researchers working on the "Dynagrams" project at the Institute for Research on Learning (IRL). At the Palo Alto-based think tank, which was recently established with a $5 million grant from Xerox, research scientist Dr. Miriam Reiner and her colleagues, under the direction of senior research scientist Dr. Roy D. Pea, are building dynamic diagrams, or "dynagrams," on the computer screen that simulate the physical properties of light as it interacts with matter. For example, a student can focus a "ray of light" (line) on a representation of a certain kind of lens and observe the scientifically accurate refraction or reflection of the ray. By altering the qualities of the lens, he or she can see how the ray of light is refracted or reflected in different ways.

The point of the study is to give students tools to experiment and communicate with one another better about physical principles without getting bogged down in the mathematical equations that represent them. "We want to see how students reason with these diagrams," says Reiner, "and how they collaborate with one another as they experiment." Reiner and her colleagues hope to add a video component in the project that shows students the actual phenomena modeled in the dynagrams. Who knows? Perhaps someday every science textbook will come with similar software.

IRL, with the help of Apple Computer Inc., is also funding the *MediaWorks* project, an examination of students' use of multimedia tools to create their own reports and other documents, IRL researchers began this project by building a multimedia tool call MediaWorks, designed to help students research and create computer-based multimedia compositions that incorporate text, digitized images, video, sound effects, and music. At the same time, they also created *MediaSpace*, a database of science-related text (news stories, glossaries, etc.), pictures, graphics animations, and sounds for students to use in composing their reports. Then they invited a class of eighth-graders to try out the materials.

"The kids went through our stuff pretty quickly," says researcher Michael Chenok, "and it was soon clear that they didn't like being constrained by the database we built." So the researchers modified the materials giving students' the capabilities to scan in their own photos and sounds and to save them as "click art" in *MediaSpace*. The results? One group of students created a document—studded with video clips, photos, and digitized sounds collected from a visit to a local zoo that persuasively argues for preservation of endangered species. The project continues to investigate the cognitive, social, and technological issues involved when kids learn to compose using multimedia tools.

Bolt Beranek and Newman, Inc. (BBN)

The educational technology group at BBN laboratories in Cambridge, Massachusetts strongly believes that technology has the potential to help us teach some things far more effectively than could be accomplished by other methods. For example, sophisticated computer models can be designed, they say, to provide students with opportunities for real-time interaction with both the process and content of science and mathematics.

The Physics Explorer, which BBN co-developed with LOGAL of Israel, is one such product. It provides teachers and students with mathematically accurate, highly interactive models for exploring the physical sciences. It takes full advantage of the power of today's Macintosh computers, and is designed to grow with the complexity and power of student workstations of the future.

The *Physics Explorer* series is being published by Wings for Learning, the new subsidiary of Sunburst Communications. The first four *Physics Explorer* models (*Gravity, Harmonic Motion, One Body,* and *Waves*) will be available by the end of October, and more will follow at regular intervals over the next few years. (There are currently about 20 models under development.)

The models are designed on a special software platform that includes a set of underlying analytic and display tools, which include everything from dynamic graphing and integrated spreadsheets to on-screen buttons and slide controls.

Like the dynagrams software developed at IRL, the *Physics Explorer* helps students learns physics by doing physics. It is full of materials that enable students to have concrete experiences with subject matter that would otherwise be very abstract and difficult to understand. Each model is an open-ended, content-rich environment that encourages exploration and experimentation. According to Dr. John Richards, director of the project for BBN, the software is designed to engage students with the process of science, inviting them to observe, predict, invent, analyze, and create.

One activity in *Gravity*, for example, involves experimenting with circular orbits. Students control such variables as mass, initial height, and initial speed of an orbiting object. The *Physics Explorer's* supercomputer-like modeling then brings the science of gravitational orbits to life, enabling students to view the orbit from vantage points that provide them with a wealth of integrated pictorial, graphic, and numeric data to analyze and make conjectures about. They can make modifications (they can even change the force of gravity) and restart the simulation as often as they wish, conducting lots of "what if" experiments as a natural part of their learning.

Another exciting BBN project is called *Function Machines*. Like the *Physics Explorer,* it is destined to take advantage of the powerful graphics computers which will become standard during the '90s. *Function Machines* is referred to as a "visual programming environment." According to BBN developers, the "original intent in developing *Functions Machines* was to create a visual isomorph to the Logo programming language with the goal of eliminating some common conceptual barriers" (e.g. the output primitive, the naming of variables, and the mechanism of recursion).

In *Function Machines* all data flow and control are performed through the machine metaphor. Each function machine can be represented as a screen icon with features such as "input hoppers," "output spouts," "connecting pipes," "sockets," and "wires." There are two basic types of machines: doers and testers. Doers produce actions such as calculations, graphics, or cursor movements. Testers affect program control flow. Additionally, all machines are either primitive or composite. As in Logo, the primitives are defined by the language. Composite machines are the equivalent of Logo procedures.

However *Function Machines* is more than just an iconic Logo. Not only does it represent an attempt to improve Logo's semantic clarity, it also extends Logo's capabilities and power, specifically in the areas of parallel control strategies. For example, a function machine may have more than one output spout, and output may be simultaneously passed to more than one machine. By default a function machine "fires" when all of its input hoppers are full. Thus it is natural to the language to have several machines (i.e., procedures or programs) operating simultaneously. And while on present-day Macintosh computers (which have only a single processor), no processing speed advantage is realized, this feature will represent an important programming structure as hardware advances continue.

Education Development Center, Inc. (EDC)

The focus for EDC's Center for Learning Technology (CLT) in Newton, Massachusetts, is to "make technology central to the curriculum." For technology to contribute positively to education reform, "it has to become a fundamental part of what teaching and learning are about," says CLT director Myles Gordon.

Toward this end, two types of educational technology development are underway at EDC. The first involves developing curriculum and materials that will encourage and enable the effective use of *current technologies* by much larger numbers of teachers and students. The second is to contribute to the development of *advanced technologies* that will open new opportunities for teaching and learning. Both areas of development involve helping students "redefine that path they take through a body of knowledge," says Gordon.

With regard to present-day technologies, one of the EDC's most significant new projects is *Journeys in Mathematics: A Model for a New Elementary Mathematics Curriculum.* The curriculum is consistent with the new NCTM standards for mathematics education, and is designed to help teachers and students "change the rules of math class." The goal is to move away from the worksheet drill approach and its underlying assumptions, such as 1) there is a single, easy-to-attain answer for every problem, and 2) doing math with computers or calculators is cheating.

Journeys includes a number of new software packages designed to help students use computers to explore mathematics. There is more emphasis on geometry, statistics, communication, and problem solving than has been the rule with K-8 math curricula, and students are involved regularly in using mathematics to represent ideas, to reason, and to connect content areas. In one (not yet available) software package, for example, students travel with the classic character Gulliver, using math as they write descriptive stories about their encounters and observations.

Other software development activities designed for today's hardware include IBM's *Exploring Measurement, Time, and Money*, and co-development work on the *Geometric Supposer* series. (EDC is also co-developing the *Visualizing Algebra* series mentioned earlier in this article.) According to EDC developers, these projects help to mold the current curriculum into a form that's more problem-driven (i.e., students learn math concepts as they are exposed to them while solving problems).

EDC plans to continue the push toward inquiry learning and problem-centered curricula by taking advantage of advanced technologies such as networks, hypermedia, and CD-ROM, which they believe will become widely available to classrooms over the next few years. The following are among their current projects under development.

Multimedia in Education: Two interactive video products for early reading are being developed and are designed for a new digital video system called CDI (Compact Disk Interactive). CDI is expected to be available by 1991.

Resources for Mathematics Reform: The goal of this project is to create a CD-ROM-based resource of exemplary materials in mathematics education. The CD will link the NCTM standards to a large library of classroom lessons and supplemental resources.

The Geometric Workstation: This advanced version of the *Geometric Supposer* will include software tools for doing geometry, and some form (probably CD-ROM) of on-line geometry encyclopedia that can be used as a reference in making inquiries and solving problems.

Seeing Beauty in Mathematics: These secondary school materials include software tools to help students visualize such concepts as rate of change (calculus) and explore new content domains such as fractal geometry.

Text Browser: This is a management/assessment tool being developed in anticipation of the widespread use of classroom computer networks. It allows teachers to collect and assess student work in ways that have traditionally been difficult, and more easily to modify the curriculum for individual students based on their individual work.

The '90s will undoubtedly be a pivotal point in American education. We can avoid reform and simply use technology further to entrench the traditional approach in which teachers (or computers) deliver information for students to memorize and recite. Or we can embrace reform and use technology to develop inquiry-centered, process-oriented, project-based, interdisciplinary learning environments in which every student has numerous opportunities for direct involvement. If the work being done at these think tanks is any indication, the emphasis will surely be on the later. And if that's true, there may never have been a better time to be a part of it all.

Daniel E. Kinnaman is News Editor for Technology & Learning. *He is also computer education coordinator for Windham Public Schools in Willimantic, CT.*

Article #6
Restructuring With Technology

WHAT IF YOU COULD LOOK INSIDE TWO DOZEN SCHOOLS ACROSS THE
COUNTRY TO SEE HOW THEY ARE USING TECHNOLOGY TO RESTRUCTURE?
WHAT WOULD YOU FIND? AND HOW MANY OF THEIR IDEAS COULD YOU USE IN YOUR OWN DISTRICT?

BY
ROBERT
PEARLMAN

Restructuring has become such a buzzword in American education that some are pasting it on any and every small change or reform in schooling. But those who advocate restructuring our nation's schools say that the process involves deep and profound changes in the way the schools function.

There are numerous definitions of the term "restructuring," but virtually all of them revolve around two central areas that require change. First, restructuring involves defining what goes on within classrooms and schools—rethinking the way teachers teach and students learn as well as the methods we use for assessment.

Second, restructuring involves a change in the way schools are organized. Such reorganization requires redefining the roles of teachers, administrators, parents, and students in the governance and management of schools. As Phillip Schlechty of the Center of Leadership in School Reform puts it, restructuring entails changes in "rules, roles, and responsibilities." These organizational changes might also lead to physical changes in the way classrooms and schools are set up—and even in where those schools are located.

But beyond general definitions, what does restructuring look like in the schools and classrooms that are attempting it? And what are the technologies and technology applications that forward-looking schools are using to support these changes?

In the pages that follow, we will take you into a number of schools and school districts that are restructuring with the help of technology.

Redefining Learning

Many of the principles central to restructuring are not new. Many of the schools involved in restructuring draw a number of their ideas from constructivist thinkers and other educational innovators who, over the years, have advocated "learning by doing." However, when combined with the organizational changes key to restructuring and when aided by new technologies, active learning takes on a new look in today's schools.

Following are some examples of the changes that are occurring in the way teaching and learning can take place when schools restructure.

Restructuring schools strive to help students become more active educational workers. In such classrooms, students are not simply receivers of knowledge; instead, they are engaged in project-oriented activity that often results in products or exhibitions.

At Cincinnati Country Day School (CCDS), computer co-coordinator Joyce Rudowski explains that two principles underlie CCDS's commitment to restructuring: "First, that learning is best achieved by doing, and second, that technology—better than anything else so

612

far—promotes principle number one." Art and music rooms at CCDS's high school division now contain high-tech composition workstations. The student artists' compositions have been published in national art magazines, and the music students, using the new tools, have become active composers, not just players of music.

In the "Teaching and Learning with Technology" classrooms at Spring Mills Elementary School in Highland, Michigan, 45 minutes of writing time takes place daily. Bill Devers' fifth-graders produce a monthly newspaper for the entire school community. They also share their ideas, activities, and information with a group of six schools (including one outside the U.S.) via AT&T's Long Distance Learning Circle telecommunication network. These students are writers and authors with products and audience.

Students at restructuring schools are using new tools for knowledge production. Multimedia technologies are providing new and more powerful ways for students to engage in what Gwen Solomon, principal of New York City's School of the Future, refers to as the GUM process—getting, understanding and manipulating information.

Eliot Wiggington's Foxfire student authors at Rabun Gap High School in Appalachian Georgia have for more than 20 years published books and magazines about their families and their communities. Today they use desktop publishing to do their production work. And students at Davidson Middle School in San Rafael, California, working with Apple and LucasFilm, have added multimedia to the Foxfire idea, capturing the images and sounds of their community and assembling them into videodisc and videotaped stories.

At Kendom Elementary School in Lansing, Michigan, children and Michigan State graduate students are working together, under a grant from the W.K. Kellogg Foundation, to develop a videodisc almanac with pictures and video clips of the school and the community. The students will then write about their homes and neighborhoods to add to a *Hypercard* database that drives the videodisc.

Students in restructuring schools don't just watch television, they make it. While many schools and school districts are barring classroom television because, they say, students have already learned to watch TV at home, restructuring schools are seeing television's many forms—broadcast, cable, satellite, and videocassette—as vital, new global learning resources.

Students at Penn-Madison High School in Osceola, Indiana, capture video from CNN cable and satellite broadcasts and repurpose it into video essays on contemporary social and political issues. They also welcome opportunities such as those offered by *CNN Newsroom* to contribute their own video segments for national viewing.

And, at Forest Hills Central High School in Grand Rapids, Michigan, the students in Ann Layton's communications class produce a weekly news program and broadcast it over their school's video distribution system.

Restructuring schools go beyond the boundaries created by school walls or national borders. At restructuring schools, students not only spend time outside of the school building learning about their local community, they also use satellite and telecommunications technology to stay in touch with people and events in faraway places.

In Honolulu, Hawaii, students at McKinley High School use video telephones (made available through a project called TeleClass International) to communicate with students at Kanazawa Commercial High School in Kanazawa, Japan. Students in both classes prepare talks about themselves and their culture and then present them live (in the language of the receiving class) over the video phones.

Restructuring schools also take advantage of activities such as the Jason project, which enabled 250,000 students around the world to see and talk daily via satellite with scientists on an expedition to recover the ancient ship *Argo*. This ability to "travel" without leaving the classroom is referred to as "telepresence" by Jason Foundation leader Robert Ballard, who plans future scientific expeditions in the Galapagos Islands and the Great Lakes.

A similar project, offered by the Mass Learnpike, allowed students at 50 schools in Massachusetts to tour the Soviet Space exhibit at the Boston Museum of Science and discuss issues with Soviet cosmonauts and space scientists— all from within their classrooms.

Restructuring schools aim to explore knowledge in an integrated, real-life manner. Project-oriented education quickly transgresses formal academic boundaries. Integrated curriculum becomes the norm.

Restructuring schools are becoming involved in international, multi-disciplinary projects such as the expedition last June sponsored by the Institute of New Technologies in Moscow, which sent teachers and students to the Arctic Circle to collect data on the solar eclipse and telecommunicate them to students in the U.S. and other countries. Next June the Soviet team will pair with a school in Hawaii, the best viewing site for the next solar eclipse, to compare their findings and communicate the results. Should such expeditions and exchanges be classified as hands-on science, geography, sociology, political science, or all of the above?

Restructuring schools seek to promote behaviors for independent learning. St. Paul's Saturn School uses several Integrated Learning Systems not as remedial tools but, instead, as stations for independent learning. At meetings with parent and teacher advisors, each student sets goals and determines the methods and materials (which might include portions of an ILS curriculum) to be used to reach those goals.

Distance learning is another tool with enormous potential for students engaged in independent learning. Self-directed students at restructuring schools can use distance learning courses such as those offered through the TI-IN satellite network to meet their own personal learning goals.

Restructuring schools are making cooperative learning a norm. At Aurora, Colorado's, Cherry Creek Elementary School, team teachers Judy Bird and Karen Peterson use videodiscs and computers primarily as tools to encourage cooperative learning. For example, when using an instructional software package or videodisc, students in Bird and Peterson's class work together in teams, dividing up the tasks normally performed by an individual user (one student might be the record-keeper, another in charge of operating the videodisc, etc.) and reaching consensus on each response before it is input.

At New York City's Ralph Bunche School, educators use microcomputer networks not for delivering individualized instruction, but for cooperative work. They use the Earth Lab network system (developed by Denis Newman of Bolt, Beranek and Newman) to engage students in group scientific projects involving shared data collection and on-line idea exchanges.

Restructuring schools are seeking new ways to assess student performance. This year the state of Vermont is piloting in 135 schools the use of math and writing student portfolios to measure student abilities. And in Gorham, Maine, technology coordinator Wally Ziko, principal Cynthia O'Shea, and teachers at the Narrangansett school are adding technology to the equation, pioneering the use of the computer and various multimedia devices to develop "electronic portfolios" of students' work. Teachers and students will add to these portfolios every year, and at graduation, each student will receive a compact disc containing his or her entire portfolio.

Changing Rules, Roles, and Responsibilities

In restructuring schools educators are actively involved in planning the future. At some sites they are redesigning schools to make them more effective; in other communities, entirely new schools are being designed from the ground up.

Many restructuring districts are committed to "school-based management/ shared decision making," which places decision-making power in the hands of those who care most and know most about what is happening at each school: teachers, building-level administrators, parents, and students.

In general, teachers at restructuring schools are being given more of a say in the day-to-day running of schools. They are regrouping into work teams and clusters involved in the daily planning and coordinating of schools.

Let's look more closely at some of these reorganization efforts and how technology is helping.

Educators engaged in the restructuring movement are breaking down communication barriers and exchanging ideas with colleagues nationwide. Computer-based conferencing is one way that educators around the country are helping one another in the restructuring process. IRIS, a national telecommunications network, offers a variety of on-line forums for teachers and administrators including the "Technology and Restructuring Roundtable" conference where restructuring educators can exchange ideas, information, frustrations, and visions.

Live national satellite conferences, such as the nine-session teleconference on restructuring organized last year by the North Central Regional Education Lab, are another way that teachers and administrators are sharing visions, plans, and concerns.

Another technology-based resource for sharing restructuring ideas has been created by the American Federation of Teachers and the Apple Multimedia Lab using both videodisc and CD-ROM. This multimedia program includes interviews with educators, policy-makers, business people, parents, and community members involved in the restructuring process; over 100 articles and documents; case studies and stories from out in the field; as well as roundtable discussions about controversial issues. Users will be able to explore various topics, create their own personalized videotapes, and print out articles and documents.

Technology can also be useful on a local level for exchanging ideas about restructuring. For example, teachers at

Forest Hills Central High School in Grand Rapids, Michigan, are currently using desktop publishing to publish *Metafile*, a restructuring newsletter for their entire school community.

Restructuring districts are investing in their teachers as resources and equipping them with the tools necessary to increase their productivity and effectiveness in the classroom. This past fall the state of Michigan's Classroom of Tomorrow program issued a request for proposals from teachers who wanted computers for their own use in the classroom. Of the state's 72,000 teachers, 20,000 submitted proposals indicating how they would use the computers, and 10,000 of them were awarded the hardware.

At the Cuyahoga Valley Regional Vocational Technical School outside Cleveland, Ohio, teachers contracted to participate in 100 hours of in-service training in exchange for receiving computers and printers for their own personal use at home. If the teachers failed to conclude the training, the agreement they signed with the school district stipulated the computer would be paid for through pro-rated payroll deductions.

In year one of the program (instituted in 1987), 100 percent of the faculty took part in and successfully completed the program. These vocational/technical teachers then researched the sorts of technology being used in their areas of expertise in the "real world" and chose which hardware, software, and auxiliary equipment to purchase for use with their students during year two of the program.

Restructuring districts recognize that technology expertise and leadership skills must go hand in hand. Teachers and administrators who are trained in the uses of technology may be able to *support* school restructuring efforts, but only those educators who also have leadership skills will truly make a difference.

This was the philosophy behind Washington State's third SLICE (Symposium on Leadership in Computer Education) conference, held last year for 100 leading educators. The two-day conference didn't just offer participants new technology skill; instead, working in small groups with assistance from resident technical experts, attendees employed a variety of technologies to develop and share multimedia presentations of their visions of restructured schooling.

Teachers from throughout the state of Michigan can learn about both technology and restructuring by spending a few days with multimedia pioneer Fred D'Ignazio at the Teacher Explorer Center in East Lansing High School. In this model classroom the teachers learn, through hands-on experience, how to use technology to create an active learning environment in which all learners are "knowledge producers."

Restructuring schools are building community among teachers, students, and parents. Minneapolis' Public School Academy experienced between 50 to 95 percent active parent involvement in its first year of operation. How was this achieved? A year-one evaluation suggests that small classes and a 100-year-old technology—the telephone—on every teacher's desk facilitated close collaboration of teachers and parents.

Burlington, Massachusetts, makes available its local community cable channel for teachers who want to post homework assignments. This helps parents keep track of their children's assignments.

At Miami, Florida's William Jennings Bryan elementary school, the school-based management team this fall installed a voice mail system. Using this system, teachers can leave voice messages for parents, and parents can leave questions and concerns for teachers.

St. Paul's Saturn school is one of several pilot sites for the *Personalized Education Management System* (PEMS) network software developed by the W.C. Norris Institute's Transformed Learning Consortium. PEMS is designed to help students, parents, and teachers work together to develop and manage students' personalized learning plans, goals, and schedules.

In restructuring schools, portfolios and student exhibitions—both produced more effectively with the help of technology—are used not only to assess student abilities but also to communicate with parents. Cougar Valley Elementary in Silverdale, Washington holds "curriculum carnivals" for parents where student demonstrate their work and parents are able to view their children's portfolios.

In restructuring schools the shape and look of learning environments are changing. Some of the changes involve the size and location of entire schools. For example, in New York City's District 4, schools are no longer synonymous with buildings. Rather, a building might house up to five separate schools, making it easier for each school to build community. And Minneapolis' Chiron School has students rotate among three sites (near the art museum, in the business district, and on the farm campus of the University of Minnesota) in order to link their curriculum to real-life projects.

Within the school buildings, classrooms are beginning to look like workrooms and desks are giving way to workstations filled with a variety of technological tools. Lake Washington's one-year-old Laura Ingalls Wilder Elementary School has large triangular rooms with a teacher presentation area in the center of each room and several nooks and crannies serving as cooperative learning stations. The presentation area is equipped with a computer, projection display, videodisc, VCR, and monitor, and is linked to the school's satellite dish.

Other restructuring schools provide students and teachers with a number of shared production stations and production rooms. For instance, Lafayette, Indiana's Project Slice has set up production rooms for desktop publishing and desktop video, while Cincinnati Country Day School's computer lab looks like a large workroom with several distinct multimedia and desktop publishing workstations.

Restructuring schools are changing in a variety of ways. Restructuring educators are rethinking the ways teachers teach and students learn; they are reorganizing to share decision making and build community; and they are changing the way classrooms and schools look. By supporting all of these changes new educational technologies are playing—and will increasingly play—a key facilitative role in restructuring process.

Robert Pearlman is the National Consultant on Educational Technology for the American Federation of Teachers.

Article #7
Technology Is Imperative for School Restructuring

By
Albert
Shanker

A teacher, as Socrates, noted, is only a midwife to students, who must carry out the labor of learning themselves. There is no learning unless the student is the worker. The student learns by listening, by writing, by thinking, by arguing, by imagining, by building, by drawing, by experiencing. If the student isn't engaged in work, no learning takes place.

But if students learn by working, what kind of workers are they? Classrooms are much like offices: in both, people sit at desks; use books, pencils, pens, and typewriters; read and write reports; give and listen to oral reports; and manipulate words and numbers. But no office in the world is organized the way a school is organized, with 30 desks at which everyone is doing the same thing; with no one allowed to talk to one another; with everyone going to different rooms and different desks at the sound of a bell to do new work with a new boss. In an office, you wouldn't change a person's task every 45 minutes—and you certainly wouldn't have workers switch rooms and bosses seven or eight times a day. It's not productive.

Why did we ever organize schools this way? Because the traditional organization of schools is based on the assumption that students aren't workers but raw material—like automobiles on an assembly line. In the first period of the day, the math teacher drills mathematics into them, 50 minutes later, the assembly line moves them into English class where the English teacher hammers English into them. It's a factory approach, and it's a problem technology can help us overcome through customizing education. Indeed, technology can help us transform our age-old rhetoric about individualizing instruction into reality.

What we need is a school where children don't have to sit still and be quiet, where they can be actively engaged. And that means getting away from a didactic system of lecturing and listening. We need schools where kids can proceed at their own rate, where those who learn in different ways can find different ways of learning. We need a system in which kids can learn in relative privacy, either individually or in small groups. This is where technology comes in. Today, all kinds of technology exist that can make individualized learning possible; what's more, it is commercially available and relatively inexpensive.

Technology contributes to teacher professionalism as well. Teachers today can communicate nationally with ease, directly, and at low cost through telecommunications and electronic data

> What we need is a school where children don't have to sit still and be quiet, where they can be actively engaged. And that means getting away from a didactic system of lecturing and listening.

618

bases. For example, outstanding social studies teachers across the country can now review all sorts of software, textbooks, pictures, magazines, videotapes, computer software, and multimedia—even questions for cooperative study groups—via computer, saving themselves hundreds of hours of research.

No professionalism is possible without such communication. Now teachers can talk to parents and say, "here are the six different ways in which most kids are able to learn this. I suggested to Johnny that he do it this way; that didn't work, so I'm trying this other method." That is the same kind of discussion lawyers and doctors and dentists have with clients.

We now have the possibility for the radical transformation and customization of education.

But most school districts in this country aren't turning to technology for help. In private business, it's exactly the opposite. Everyone turns for help to technology because it expands and diversifies the ways and means of doing one's work, it promotes efficiency and productivity, and it can free up human intelligence for creative tasks.

We need to create a similar kind of attitude toward technology in the world of public education. The work today's school leaders are doing with technology should not be an add-on or peripheral. American public education will not survive without rethinking what teaching means and how kids learn. And there is no way of doing that without an appropriate use of technology.

Albert Shanker is president of the American Federation of Teachers. This article is excerpted from a presentation made at NSBA's conference, "Making Schools More Productive: Technology and Learning," November 1989.

Article #8
Restructuring and Technology Play Essential Role in New City School

THE AUTHOR OF THIS COLUMN SHARES SOME OF HER IDEAS ON EDUCATION, TECHNOLOGY, AND REFORM AS SHE PREPARES TO OPEN THE SCHOOL OF THE FUTURE IN NEW YORK CITY.

BY
GWEN
SOLOMON

Since March 1988, when the Technology Solutions column first appeared, you've read about successful classroom examples of teachers using technology to help students learn. The focus has been on the solution, not on the technology.

This month's column is about a school that will concentrate on new methods of learning, one in which technology will be an important tool. The School of the Future in New York City's Community School District 2 is an alternative secondary school for grades 7 through 12 that is scheduled to open with 75 seventh graders this September. It's a school that Gwen's not just reporting about; she became its director on February 1, and she wants to share its vision with you.

Starting a school is a little like putting together a giant jigsaw puzzle, one where many pieces are outside the box. It's exciting and challenging, but it's not easy making all the pieces fit.

Picture a place where students in grades 7-12 work collaboratively in small groups with university students and staff, who act as mentors, interns, and project leaders. Master teachers supervise and guide the process.

In one corner, a group working with ABC Interactive's videodisc *In the Holy Land* watches Israeli and Palestinian youngsters discuss the Middle East. They study geography, history, conflict resolution, and psychology as they progress.

Another group uses desktop publishing to prepare publications: a school newspaper, a literary magazine, a yearbook, and mock newspapers of various periods of history the students are interested in.

Using CD-ROM and telecommunications, some students access data bases for reports, some contact students in other U.S. cities to compare conditions of their homeless population and even brainstorm with each other to come up with solutions, some prepare stories for an on-line newsletter produced cooperatively with youngsters from other countries.

Another group of youngsters sit comfortably on couches and discuss media ethics. They've run Tom Snyder's simulation *Television,* and will analyze local media based on criteria they've selected in the discussion. They'll contact the press for input.

These groups don't exist yet, but beginning in September, students at the School of the Future will participate in many projects like those described above. We'll also place computers in students' homes so they can write, design, conduct research, and communicate with others at any hour of the day.

The Reality

Many of those projects will take place thanks to a three-year federal grant

620

from the U.S. Secretary of Education's Fund for Innovation in Education and the commitment of district superintendent Anthony Alvarado, New York City's new chancellor Dr. Joseph Fernandez, and other administrators and teachers.

We're working on restructuring the curriculum to make it student centered rather than teacher dominated. The process is difficult because we've all been trained in the old ways. We're creating new schedules for the school day; planning to transport youngsters to New York University, museums, companies, and other off-site learning centers; and determining how and when to bring in experts in various fields.

Eager parents and residents in the community who have experience in video production, journalism, drama, and dance also want to help. But how do we balance these wonderful opportunities with state-mandated requirements?

The GUM Theory

The School of the Future will teach students the skills necessary for success in the 21st century. This is the Information Age; we'll all have to be able to Get, Understand, and Manipulate (GUM) information to succeed.

To Get information, students must learn how to search for it read the material they find, and communicate about it with others (including telecommunication to students and teachers around the globe).

To Understand information, students must develop thinking skills visualize outcomes, solve problems creatively, and learn cooperatively.

To Manipulate information, students must "learn" how to learn (so that each new piece of information is integrated into what they already know), adapt to changes, and ask questions.

Information is power if you know what to do with it. If students learn to manage information successfully, they will be that much closer to achieving self-actualization, and one day they will become leaders in society.

Let's think of a sphere as a metaphor for information. If the sphere represents all knowledge, currently we send children around the circumference chasing superficial facts. Occasionally, they get below the surface to some level of understanding. The deeper they go, the more they understand the topic and the process of learning. We intend to help students find the points on the circumference from which they can begin to dig—and then help them learn how to dig.

> This is the Information Age; we'll all have to be able to Get, Understand, and Manipulate (GUM) information to succeed.

New Approaches to Learning

Instead of taking subjects for 45 minutes each day, students will learn in larger blocks of time to allow them to fully investigate issues. The traditional boundaries of subject disciplines will often be ignored; any issue worthy of investigation deserves to be looked at from all perspectives.

Students will work collaboratively in small groups on projects. They'll define problems, set goals, explore possible alternatives, apply the most practical solutions, and analyze and evaluate the results. They will understand that all decisions have consequences. The advantage of the small group approach is that students develop trust for one another and take intellectual risks.

In addition, we want students to become not only learners but also mentors—both to other students and teachers. In some cases, traditional roles will be reversed. One youngster who will attend the school wants to be an astrophysicist; he knows more about the topic at age 11 than I will ever know. We will encourage students to share their expertise and special interests with us.

Education must be humane. The school will provide the students with a safe, secure environment; personalized education plans; dedicated, caring professionals; and emotional security. Students will get individual desks and the necessary psychological space.

Students will be evaluated on performance rather than on standardized tests. They are responsible for keeping a portfolio of work (on or off computer) that demonstrates skills and knowledge mastered. We've contracted with an outside evaluator to make sure we measure success properly. In addition, we will evaluate students on how much learning they encourage in one another. We are an educational family; we'll acquire 21st-century skills only by working together.

Many of the projects we'll implement are ones I wrote about in my Technology Solutions column. Many other ideas came from *Electronic Learning* readers who have written or called me. And I have no doubt that our students will be another creative source.

If education is to be successful, the way decisions are made in schools must change. All participants at the School of the Future will share in the decision making. Teachers will decide many educational matters, and staff, parents, and students together will design youngsters' personalized education plans. In addition, a school-based management team made up of teachers, administrators, parents, and students will make administrative decisions. In shared decision making, it is most important for everyone to have respect for the other participants and for the process itself.

U.S. Education Secretary Lauro Cavazos said, "our education system must be restructured. We need a revolution in teaching and learning." At the School of the Future, we hope to be at the cutting edge of that revolution and create the conditions in which learning will thrive.

Article #9
Redefining the Textbook

TEXAS, FLORIDA, AND CALIFORNIA HAVE CHANGED TEXTBOOK ADOPTION PROCEDURES TO ACCOMMODATE TECHNOLOGY-BASED PRODUCTS. FOR EDUCATORS, TEXTBOOK PUBLISHERS, AND TECHNOLOGY PUBLISHERS, THE RAMIFICATIONS COULD BE FAR-REACHING.

BY THERESE MAGEAU

The recent decision in Texas to adopt a videodisc based product as a textbook was, to many educators and software publishers, the handwriting on the wall. When a conservative state like Texas radically changes the time-honored tradition of textbook adoptions, chances are it's a signal that larger changes are to come. In fact, many industry and education leaders believe that during the next decade a growing number of states will officially adopt technology for basal curriculum instruction. And incorporating technology into the adoption process, they predict, will affect software companies, textbook publishers and education itself.

"The text will support the technology in the classroom," believes Texas School Board Association (TSBA) executive director Obrey Holden. "We're always going to have printed material, but it's clear there are better ways to teach than the way we're currently teaching."

In addition to Texas, California has formally adopted technology in their textbook process, and Florida's laws permit it to do the same. But it's become evident that the current "textbook adoption" process in many states needs to change if states are going to equitably and judiciously use adoption as a means of getting technology into schools. *Electronic Learning* looks at some of the concerns about incorporating technology in the textbook adoption process, and examines the ramifications on educational publishing.

The Adopting States

Texas has received the most media coverage for its technology adoption because, according to Geoffrey Fletcher, Texas Education Agency assistant commissioner, "…we have redefined the textbook." In November 1990, the Texas State Board of Education gave final approval to a decision made the previous August by the state textbook committee: schools can use money earmarked for elementary science textbooks to buy Optical Data's elementary science videodisc series, *Windows on Science.* (Two traditional textbooks were also adopted.) The definition of a textbook now is expanded to mean any instructional materials that meet curriculum requirements. "We have to move beyond relying on the textbook as the primary instructional tool," Fletcher says.

Being adopted doesn't guarantee sales, however, and it remains to be seen if Texas schools will abandon textbooks and buy a product most teachers have no experience with. Optical Data president Bill Clark thinks they will. "We're the differentiated product," he says. "Textbooks have been demonstrated not to work. We've seen the declining test scores in science. We believe we're giving teachers strategies and resources that have a chance of improving student performance."

There is no indication yet how many Texas districts will purchase Optical

623

Data's videodisc series; at press time, no districts had begun buying materials for the 1991-92 school year.

In October, California adopted three textbook/videodisc packages—consisting of Houghton Mifflin texts and ABC News Interactive videodiscs—for the state's fifth, sixth, seventh, and eighth grade history curricula. California schools may use textbook funds to buy the texts and videodiscs.

Florida's laws permit it to adopt technology in the textbook process, according to Jorge Ortega, the administrator of instructional technology services for the Florida Department of Education, but it has yet to receive a technology submission. "We want to adopt a media-based product for a course," says Ortega. "But we can't adopt what publishers won't submit."

Obstacles to Adoption

The fact that technology publishers aren't submitting products to Florida's $110 million textbook market (the nationwide textbook adoption fund is estimated at $200 billion a year) seems surprising. However, industry leaders claim that there are a number of obstacles that prevent software publishers from submitting products for adoption. The adoption process needs to radically change, these leaders say, or few companies can take advantage of it.

Chief among the obstacles is cost. Most adoptions use a process called sampling, which requires publishers to provide, free of charge, copies of their instructional materials under consideration to all adoption committee and subcommittee members. This can mean supplying to the state anywhere from 75 to 100 copies of a product.

To complicate matters, in Texas and California software publishers are also required to supply hardware if the evaluators don't have the requisite equipment on which to run the software. Florida eventually may have the same requirement, state officials say.

And, in most state adoptions, representatives from the publishers must pay calls on all the evaluators to make presentations and answer questions. Evaluators are dispersed throughout a state, requiring the resources of a large sales force. With the exception of integrated learning system (ILS) publishers, most software companies do not have sales forces.

All of that is required just to make the adoption list. Once a company's on the list, the process begins all over again. But, this time publishers must make enough material available to let every school district in the state sample the product. The cost of this requirement has always been a major—even debilitating—expense for textbook publishing houses. For technology publishers, the expense of supplying their product—particularly a videodisc or network-based product—could be minimally 15 times the cost of supplying a textbook.

Publishers are also encouraged to visit the districts that are considering their materials. That might not be easy in a state like Texas, where there are 1,100 school districts.

All this translates into one thing: a publisher potentially has to dish out hundreds of thousands of dollars. Several years ago, Sunburst Communications contemplated submitting a textbook and a software program to Texas. "We figured out that to get adopted it would cost us $30,000," says Sunburst vice president Marge Cappo. "If we made the list, it would have cost us an additional $150,000 to $200,000 to send our product to all the districts." To a small publishing house like Sunburst, which had only one salesperson, "It just wasn't worth it," says Cappo.

In fact, it's debatable whether Optical Data could have managed the Texas adoption without Jostens Learning Corp.'s recent equity investment in the company, because now Jostens' considerable sales force in Texas will be able to sell *Windows on Science* for Optical Data.

Changing the Process

Texas was aware of these logistical problems when it decided to include technology in the adoption process. So when it changed the law defining textbooks, it changed another law that defined the adoption procedure. For the elementary science adoption, 15 members were appointed to the textbook committee, instead of the traditional 90 committee and subcommittee members. In place of sending publishers' representatives to each committee member, all members convened in Austin to review the products under consideration.

This new procedure cut down on the cost of providing materials and eliminated the need for a large sales staff. It enabled Optical Data to compete on equal footing with textbook powerhouses like Scott, Foresman Inc. and Silver, Burdett & Ginn.

In addition, Texas has decided that Optical Data does not have to send the entire, costly *Windows on Science* product to each of its 1,100 districts. Instead, Optical Data is sending a videotape describing the product, a sampler videodisc, and sample reading materials. The cost of such a package will run $40, considerably less than it would cost to send the actual program.

California's review process has also changed to accommodate technology. On any given instructional materials review committee (California's equivalent of a textbook committee), only a chosen number of the members will actually look at the technology materials. They then report on the products to the other members of the committee. For instance, when California adopted the Houghton Mifflin texts and ABC News Interactive videodiscs, only five members of a panel of 25 actually reviewed the videodisc materials. They recommended to the rest of the committee that the packages be adopted. These approved materials are now on display for schools' review in the 12 instructional materials display centers (there are 30 such centers) around the state that are outfitted with the appropriate technology.

Is the New Process Fair?

These changes make the adoption process a bit more fair to technology publishers. But is it fair to competing textbook publishers, who must win the approval of entire committees, not just select members, and whose entire product, not just representative portions of it, is under scrutiny by schools? And, more important, is the process fair to schools?

Most people feel it is not. "It's a problem," says Donovan Merck, director of the Office of Educational Technology for the California Department of Education. "I don't think you can get a fair review of a product by looking at it summarized on videotape. But it's doggone difficult to review a technology-based product," he says, particularly one that will use a variety of media to present content.

While everyone agrees that the process is still flawed, there are few ideas on how to change it to make it work for technology publishers, textbook publishers, and schools alike. One suggestion comes from Sunburst's Marge Cappo, who recommends that review committees and schools agree to return the product to the publisher once the review process is over. This would substantially cut down on the high cost of providing expensive review materials.

But how do schools in adoption states review the approved software if they don't have the right hardware? The kinds of products that might be eligible for adoption are not likely to run on a 64K Apple IIe, one of the most common computers in schools today. The technology-based products that can meet the vast curriculum requirements of a statewide adoption must be big. They will probably reside on networks, videodiscs, CD-ROMs, or large hard drives. If schools are going to fairly evaluate all the products on the adoption list, who can be expected to provide the necessary hardware?

IBM's John Frey, who manages the company's reading and language arts division, looks at many of IBM's products that are designed specifically for network use and asks, "How can we provide a network, computers, and full complement of software to every school reviewing materials? It's impossible."

Frey believes, as do other technology publishers, that states looking to include technology in their adoption process must be prepared to buy the hardware these large curricular packages are designed for. This is not an inexpensive proposition.

It is, however, a necessary proposition if adopting technology is to have any real impact in schools, believes the Texas School Board Association. "The textbook adoption process is only a minor part of the picture," says TSBA executive director Holden. "You also have to have a way for people to buy computers, networks, and provide for teacher training."

That's why the TSBA formed an alliance with Texas business leaders and lobbied to pass legislation that will provide, starting in 1992-93, a student technology allotment at $30 per student. This money constitutes a fund separate from textbook monies, and districts may spend it solely on hardware, courseware, and teacher training. The total cost, for the first year alone, will be somewhere around a billion dollars. That's a tremendous amount of money, but Holden believes that "when you start talking about adopting technology, you have to look at the bigger picture, and that means investing money in hardware and training."

Old Boys' Network

You can't talk about adoption without talking about politics. Statewide adoptions are infamous for their political entanglements—whether it's satisfying special interest groups or getting shut out of what some software publishers refer to as the "old boys' network." Richard Erdmann, chairman of the board for Wasatch Education Systems, worries that the politics of adoption will compromise technology's ability to bring about curriculum change, much in the same way that adoption has led to a "watering down" of the textbook. "Technology has a golden opportunity to challenge the curriculum today because it's not embroiled in the politics of adoption," Erdmann says. "My fear is that 10 years from now it's all going to end up in adoption, and that's probably not a good thing."

Sunburst's Cappo is skeptical as well. "The products that challenge the curriculum are unlikely to be the products that are adopted," she says. But Cappo also believes that even if adoption doesn't encourage innovation in technology, educational software will not lose its creativity as long as software publishers continue to market directly to the teacher as well. "When you're selling to the teacher, rather than a committee, you're likely to sell a more innovative product."

Cappo's concerns about the adoption process, however, are not preventing her from looking at upcoming adoptions. Wings for Learning, a Sunburst subsidiary, is aiming for the California grades 4-8 mathematics adoption in 1994.

Most people in the industry believe, however, that stand-alone software companies like Wings for Learning have an uphill battle. The heavy investment it takes to submit to an adoption leads many stand-alone publishers to the same conclusion made by Scholastic Software publisher Peter Kelman: "We are much better off selling around an adoption, rather than submitting," he says, meaning that software publishers can be more successful promoting their programs as worthy ancillary products to adopted materials.

Jan Davidson, president of Davidson & Associates, believes, however, that there's a tremendous opportunity in technology adoptions. "It's clear to me that this is the direction we're moving in," she says. "More and more states are going to specify what they want in technology, and I want Davidson to be a player in that process."

Davidson points out that smaller technology publishers can build strategic alliances with larger companies, such as ILS publishers, and contribute components of larger electronic systems to submit for adoption.

ILS Publishers

ILS publishers are in an excellent position to submit to adoptions because their products are already designed to cover complete curriculum objectives in math and language arts. Computer Curriculum Corp. (CCC) president Ron Fortune says that "ILS companies, as compared to stand-alone software companies, are clearly much better suited to a statewide adoption." Where CCC doesn't have any "immediate plans" to submit its program for adoption, Fortune says that "we pay attention to adoption requirements In our product development. It would be quite easy for us to move in that direction."

Jostens Learning Corp. CEO, John Kernan, says that one of the reasons why Jostens was formed (via a merger between ESC and Prescription Learning Corp. and a subsequent buy-out by Jostens Inc.), "was because we believed that, during the 1990s, states would be routinely interested in adopting technology as basals. We needed to create an organization that would be big enough to build an electronic basal."

Is Jostens interested in submitting their product for adoption? "We're looking at adoption in every state that's interested in trying an electronic product," says Kernan.

Educators have their own concerns about adopting technology. For one, there's the issue of accessibility. "It's important that every student have equal access to the primary deliverer of information, whether they're at home, in the classroom, in the library, or study hall," says Shirley McCandless, a former technology consultant to the Florida Department of Education. With textbooks, that accessibility is possible. But schools are not at the point where every child can take home a videodisc or other computer product.

Technology publishers interested in adoption know this, and build into their products some component that is portable. For instance, Windows on Science includes booklets—one for every child—

that contain articles and stories pertinent to the science concepts covered on disc.

Some educators are also concerned about the way the adoption issue is being framed: textbook vs. technology. Will technology replace textbooks? Is that what educators really want?

"We need multiple media," says Florida DOE's Ortega. "We need software, textbooks, videodiscs, CD-ROM. We need a more holistic approach to instructional materials."

Fletcher of Texas agrees. "We have the potential to change instruction in the classroom," he says. "But we need to look at a combination of tools."

Textbook Technology Synergy

Technology and textbook publishers alike support a multiple media environment. "The future [of educational publishing]," says Simon and Schuster Education Group president Patrick Donaghy, "will become a kind of joint venture. Media companies, [textbook] publishing companies, high-technology companies, and telecommunications companies will increasingly work together."

The focus on adopting multiple media products "is causing a tremendous amount of synergy between textbook and technology publishers," says IBM's Frey. "Over time, these alliances will be very important to the survival of traditional textbook publishers. They will also be important to exploiting technology's true potential."

Jostens' Kernan believes that one of the great potentials of technology is its ability to enable individual states to adopt a curriculum that's truly specific to their instructional needs. "There is a trend to move away from the national curriculum that textbook publishers have more or less forced on us," he says.

"If you're a smaller state, you pretty much have to go along with what California, Texas, and Florida have told the basal textbook publishers to print."

But if curriculum comes in an electronic form, the state adoption committee or the district's curriculum review committee can customize it. Kernan points to new technologies like "intelligent documents" and hydra technology, which allow schools to create a "customized curriculum."

TSBA's Holden also looks to a future where curriculum is delivered electronically and "schools can produce what they want locally. Right now, we're hamstrung with what's in the textbook," he says. To Holden, and other educators as well, the Texas adoption was an important first step, but in his mind, it didn't really tap the potential of technology in the classroom. "We're not truly using technology yet," he says. "You're going to see a lot of changes in the adoption process. We've only scratched the surface of what needs to change."

Adoption States Respond to the Texas Decision

Electronic Learning contacted officials in 10 textbook adoption states and asked the following questions. Their responses are below.

Q: What is your reaction to the Texas decision to adopt technolgy as a textbook?

Q: Do you see your state moving in that direction?

ALABAMA

Harry Toothaker, Information Specialist, Department of Education (DOE)

- "Right now we're just concerned with getting adequate funding for textbooks. With the amount of funding currently appropriated for textbooks, the state can only fund book purchases for grades K-8."

GEORGIA

Jerry Pace, Textbook Administrator, DOE

- "We think the Texas decision is great. For the past three years we've had the option for publishers to submit technology products for textbook adoption. No publishers have submitted technology so far, and we don't know why. We're looking forward to technology-based text book submissions."

LOUISIANA

Wilmer Cody, State Superintendent of Education

- "We applaud the decision made in Texas. I expect Louisiana to be considering the same type of proposal within the next one to two years. I would expect that we will see the continuation of traditional printed materials, but also a variety of electronic materials that would be considered appropriate as texts for instruction. I would hope to see software and videodisc publishers summit a proposal to Louisiana to our next textbook adoption."

MISSISSIPPI

Richard Thompson, State Superintendent of Education

- "The decision is something I want to know more about, but I think it makes a lot of sense. I see great implications for the future. I've heard objections that kids can't take videodiscs home, but I don't know if that's a valid criticism. The technological implications are so great that it's a distinct possibility at some point in the near future that videodisc and other technology will be in all the homes. Mississippi isn't rushing into adopting technology, but it is an issue we will bring before the board. We believe it has an awful lot of potential to change instruction."

NEVADA

Frank South, Educational Technology Consultant, DOE

- "I see no reason why technology shouldn't be adopted as a textbook. Our adoption process involves instructional materials being trial tested in districts. Then districts request what textbooks they would like. Generally the state department approves what the districts want. To adopt technology, the district would have to demonstrate that it works, that it's as effective or better than what they are currently using. I can't see who would oppose the idea."

NORTH CAROLINA
Elsie Brumback, Director, Media and Technology, DOE

- "The impetus to adopt technology has got to come from the local districts—right now they want their local autonomy. It will be a few years before we adopt technology on a state level. We need to first pass Senate Bill 2, which would authorize $27.8 million to buy computers statewide. We need that installed base of computers out there first."

OREGON
Don Erickson, Director, Instructional Technology/Media, DOE

- "As a technology person, of course I'm excited about the Texas decision. At this point there have been no discussions in Oregon about adopting technology. Technology is still considered supplemental and not instructional in our state. We don't have a technology plan nor do we mandate that schools teach technology skills. I think it's going to take a real paradigm shift for Oregon to go that way."

SOUTH CAROLINA
Pamela Pritchet, Chief Supervisor for Utilization, Office of Instructional Technology, DOE

- "We are most definitely interested in adopting technology. Our philosophy supports resource-based instruction—where instruction is not based on one, but on many resources. There is nothing in the law to prohibit technology submissions. Our problems have to do with finances. We've had problems providing enough funds to schools to purchase textbooks."

UTAH
George Brown, Coordinator of Educational Technology, State Office of Education

- "Adopting technology is inequitable. Software will be as common in the classroom as textbooks, maybe more so. In order for it to have credibility and integrity, it must go through an adoption process. Utah isn't moving rapidly in this direction at the moment, but it's simply going to have to happen."

WEST VIRGINIA
Henry Marocki, State Superintendent of Schools

- "I think it's an excellent decision. We have adopted traditional language arts texts and given schools the option to buy either *Writing to Read* or Jostens *Basic Learning System* as a supplement to those texts. I think that as soon as our teachers become comfortable with the technology, there will be an abundance of requests to have those products adopted as we adopt texts."

Customized Text for K-12? Not Now, But Maybe Soon

The Technology to create customized textbooks exists today, but it is not being used for grades K-12. Predictions abound, however, that in the not too distant future states will be able to order from a publisher—or even create themselves—a textbook that's designed specifically to meet their state K-12 curriculum requirements.

How do customized texts work? Two relatively new technologies, known as "intelligent" documents and "hydra" machines, play key roles. Intelligent document technology consists of, in part, a hard drive or CD-ROM that holds a tremendous amount of text-based material (textbooks, trade books, pamphlets, reference books, and so on). Each paragraph in every publication on disk is designated as an object, so when a user requests all material on a certain subject, the system can efficiently pull together pertinent text from all the available resources.

The user then can create a personalized bound book by using a hydra, a high-speed "copying" machine that digitally stores both images and text. The hydra can laser print and bind the user's book in a matter of minutes, depending on the size of the book.

MacMillan/McGraw-Hill has already begun a customized textbook operation in the McGraw-Hill college division. Individual college professors call an 800 number to choose material from a data base relevant to their course. The system then selects the articles, creates a table of contents, copies, and binds the books. The K-12 division is "seriously investigating customizing texts as well," according to James Levy, president and CEO of MacMillan/McGraw-Hill. Ken Komoski, executive director of the EPIE Institute, a New York-based educational "consumer's union," believes that the need for customized text books is an urgent one. EPIE helps school districts align their textbooks more efficiently to their objectives, and it has discovered that "more than 50 percent of a textbook typically contains material that's over and above a district's curriculum objectives," Komoski says. But teachers tend to equate the text with the curriculum, he says, and, in an effort to cover the entire text, end up inadequately addressing the objectives their students need to master. Customization could address this problem by delivering to the teacher books that only cover state and district objectives.

Komoski believes that states are already headed in the direction of customization. He points to a recent elementary math textbook adoption in Texas, where the requirements were so specific to the Texas math curriculum, that, in essence, they ended up calling for a somewhat customized text."

Komoski feels that states are only "intrigued" by the idea of customized curriculum. "Once they understand the potential of the technology," he says, "I think they'll all move in that direction."

Article #10
Electronic Highways and the Classroom of the Future

Edited By
Fred
D'Ignazio

In this column we've explored the concept of *desktop fusion*. All major knowledge, information, and communication industries are converging around the digital desktop computer. New, faster, more powerful microcomputers will soon have the ability to capture, process, store, and communicate all forms of knowledge—including words, still photos, video, speeches, hi-fi music, and animations.

Planetary Fusion

Desktop fusion resembles the process of planetary formation. Many scientists believe our planets were formed from motes of dust that combined into clouds. The clouds combined to form boulders, the boulders combined to form still larger boulders. The mega-boulders eventually combined to form planets.

Similarly, small electronic devices are starting to combine into more complex devices. Instead of the force of gravity (and centrifugal force) we have the power of the *integrated circuit* acting to draw different devices together. Microprocessors and memory chips have become the "souls" of all kinds of communication machines, such as telephones, TVs, fax machines, and CD-ROM drives. Now we see the machines themselves beginning to combine. Video cameras and VCRs have combined to form *camcorders*. TVs and VCRs are combining to form *TVCRs*. Boom boxes now commonly carry several "on-board" information appliances, including a radio, a cassette player/recorder, a compact disc player, and a TV. Sony recently announced the "Face to Face" picture phone, consisting of a tiny TV screen and a camera attached to a telephone. Casio makes a tiny musical keyboard, the *SK-1,* that has stored sounds from real instruments and voices, and a microphone and memory chip that allow you to digitally record and store additional sounds, including your students' voices.

In the process of planetary formation, small units combine to form bigger units. Due to the miniaturization of solid-state components and electrical motors, large, heavy units are combining to form smaller units. Sony's *Video Walkman* combines a color TV screen and an 8mm VCR into a TVCR the size of a paperback novel. The *10th Anniversary Walkman* includes a stereo radio and auto-reverse cassette player that you can slip into a shirt pocket. Transportable computers have become portables. Portables have become laptops. Laptops are turning into *notebook computers* and *memo pads*. And as they shrink, they are being combined with scanners, bar code readers, and faxmodems!

Tiny tech means more features, more devices fused together on a smaller piece of electronic real estate. And it usually means better quality. The Sony player may be the size of a box of crayons, but its *Mega Bass* delivers room-sized stereo sound!

Electronic Highways

All of society's information producers are busily converting their specialized knowledge into a digital format. In addition, they are furiously constructing new

632

channels that have the speed, capacity, and reliability to rush their knowledge to its next destination. *These channels are the electronic highways of the 21st century:*

- Communication satellites
- Fiber optic lines
- Cable TV
- Microwave transmissions
- Cellular phones
- Computer modems
- Fax machines
- Broadcast television
- Radio

Who is building these highways? Who are the users? Businesses, government agencies, and higher-education institutions. Even drug lords, spies, and terrorists are on these highways. Everyone, in fact, is a builder or a user of electronic highways—except *schools!* With a few notable exceptions, K-12 schools are *not building, using, or planning to use* the electronic highways of tomorrow.

After all, what educational purpose do these highways serve? They carry news broadcasts, scientists' research findings, academic studies, government reports, banking and financial information, people's voices, data, and images. This may be the electronic buzz of an entire planet, but how does it fit into curriculum? And even if schools saw a way to incorporate it into a teacher's lessons, how would they *capture* it? How would they *transform* it into something useful in the classroom?

Electronic Dirt Roads

This attitude reflects the prevailing orthodoxy of how knowledge enters the classroom and how that knowledge is used. It has created an odd variant of the electronic highways that might be called the *electronic dirt roads.* Some pioneering schools are aware of the importance of electronic (increasingly digital) methods of capturing and communicating knowledge. Unfortunately, most of their efforts are in developing road systems that are walled off and insulated from the highways and byways of the larger world.

Many of today's current and planned distance-learning networks consist almost entirely of professors and teachers broadcasting their lectures to students in remote locations. In many cases, the students can respond to the teacher via a two-way audio link or a two-way video link.

The names *teleclassroom* and *distance learning* have the ring of "high tech," "innovation," and "the future." But we may be using electronic methods to reinforce a teaching environment better suited to the past.

Much of the educational research of the last decade has been critical of the "frontal lecture" method of teaching. New methods of learning are being developed as supplements and alternatives to the lecture style, including cooperative learning, apprenticeship, peer teaching and peer coaching, thematic learning, community problem-solving, and inter-generational learning. In classrooms of the future, today's educational leaders see students in active, problem-solving roles, working closely with their classmates to develop a "hands-on" understanding of curriculum topics.

In this context, is a distance-learning network that features an electronic "talking head" a road into the future—or a dead end? Few in business, government, or even higher education will wish to climb aboard and ride these roads alongside us. These K-12 networks may become electronic alleyways that have no role to play in the larger network of electronic highways that will carry almost all of the new knowledge of the 21st century.

A New Paradigm for "Classroom"

How does knowledge enter the classroom? What role does the teacher play in carrying that knowledge to the student? If the paradigm for a classroom shows knowledge entering the classroom through "teachers" and through "textbooks," then schools will try to extend that paradigm into the electronic age. Schools will create their own electronic networks. And the only travelers along those networks will be tele-teachers and tele-textbooks.

This model of the classroom has electronic trappings, but it doesn't turn the classroom into a *vehicle* that teachers *and* students can use to travel the *real* electronic highways in order to experience new knowledge for themselves.

It is 1990, and we are on the threshold of a new century. To prepare for the new century we need to create a new paradigm for "classroom." *In the 21st century a classroom won't be a stationary, isolated room, but a vehicle capable of traveling around the world, back into time, and out into the solar system and beyond.* The tools to turn today's classrooms from stationary boxes into sleek ships for knowledge exploration are already at hand. But we will never use them until we begin dreaming boldly and start imagining a new kind of "classroom" where we might teach.

Just in Time Training

In the classroom of the 19th century, the pace of emerging knowledge and the need for retraining was slow enough to permit a "trickle-down" method of dissemination. Educational publishers could take their time, digest the highlights of new discoveries, file them into appropriate subject headings and taxonomies, and distribute them as worksheets and textbooks to thousands of classrooms. Teachers played the role of "switchmen" on the railroad. They routed these curricular materials, slotted them into the daily schedule of their school, and paced and measured their students' progress.

As we make the final jog to the next century, things are changing rapidly. New knowledge is exploding and growing more complex. The need for training and retraining is no longer occasional, it is constant. The whole notion of training is being redefined from an alternative track that a worker enters only once or twice a year to "on-demand" training and "just-in-time" training in which a worker receives training almost continuously, in order to cope with a constantly changing work environment. If the workplace changes from week to week, then a worker needs training in small, customized bites, right on the job, rather than on weeklong sabbaticals to special "training classrooms."

And what does the worker's workplace look like? It has real people. But there are also more and more machines whose job it is to take the worker to all the *virtual people* with whom he or she does business. Webster's dictionary defines "virtual" as not physically real but having the effect of being real. Computers, fax machines, telephones, and video monitors are becoming commonplace in the workplace. These machines are transforming the physical workplace into a *virtual workplace* that includes remote customers, suppliers, lenders, reference sources, and other business contacts that a worker interacts with on a daily basis. Work groups are not just the folks around you. *Virtual work groups* link workers in far-flung locations who communicate instantaneously in order to do business.

This is all made possible through desktop fusion. The computer hub and its constellation of electronic devices are becoming a vehicle that can carry workers to distant locations in order to transact their business. As corporations, government agencies, and higher-education institutions go through restructuring and modernization, they are equipping their workers with vehicles that can travel on small secondary roads and, increasingly, on the electronic highways of the wide, wide world. This is a lead that schools should follow.

The Old Paradigm
for "Computer"

You are a computing teacher. Therefore you must use a computer. How do you see your computer? Most teachers see the computer as a kind of electronic Cuisinart. You pour information into the computer and—it slices, it dices, it blends, it whips, it purees.

And then it disgorges—onto its display screen, onto a noisy, buzzing printer, or into some peripheral device that blinks a hot red as its innards are flooded with computer output.

Teachers also see the computer as a device that stands still. It may be even bolted to the table that it rests on. Information travels through the computer, and people sit down and talk with the computer. But the computer stands still. It is stationary, fixed, and immobile.

A New Paradigm
for "Computer"

The standalone, standstill computer is an old paradigm. This paradigm fits inside the old paradigm for "classroom," but it has less and less to do with the outside world. A new paradigm for "computer" is suddenly emerging. Associated with this paradigm are the concepts: *network, communication, connectivity, multimedia,* and *vehicle.*

We are, overnight, crossing the threshold from personal computing to *interpersonal computing.* In tomorrow's workplace, we will all be using *workstations* instead of mere computers. The word "workstation" implies *communication.* The workstation must talk with the other people and the other machines in the workplace, and it must talk with distant people and distant machines—down the hallway and around the world.

If we couple this concept of a communicating workstation with multimedia, we can see how the computer is no longer a stationary device, but a *vehicle.* Workers can ride that vehicle to a virtual workplace to communicate with their customers and colleagues. Students and teachers can ride that vehicle to the furthest reaches of human knowledge and imagination.

The Computer as Vehicle

In his award-winning novel *Neuromancer* (New York: Ace, 1984), science fiction writer William Gibson sees computers of the future as spaceships that carry hotshot pilots through *cyberspace.* "Cyberspace" is the invisible world of computer data. In the cyberspace of today, most of that data is at a primitive symbolic level, barely above the ones and zeros, on-and-off voltages that form the building blocks of digital code. But in the future, with desktop fusion, computers will transmit photographs, people's voices, movie clips, dazzling three-dimensional models, and animations that appear lifelike and realistic.

Cyberspace will be a virtual, electronic re-creation of the real world, with shocking richness, realism, and authenticity. Laserdisc and software authors face a formidable challenge in ensuring the accuracy and completeness of the sounds and images that will make up this virtual world. As on the recent magazine covers that placed Oprah Winfrey's head on Ann-Margaret's body, and digitally moved the Sphinx closer to its neighboring pyramids, the boundary line between the real world and the virtual will become increasingly transparent.

We are talking of nothing short of "instant electronic publishing." With the right tools from far-sighted educational publishers, teachers and students can pilot their computer vehicles onto landing strips located in Prague, Czechoslovakia, underneath the Mediterranean Sea, atop the Galileo spacecraft orbiting Jupiter, or onto the small, bobbing boats that carried the American soldiers across the icy Delaware River during the Revolutionary War.

Sounds like a good PBS documentary? It is far more.

At the helm of a multimedia computer, students aren't looking at reality but at *virtual reality*. They can pause any event and instantly replay it. They can capture a video "window," resize it to a quarter of the display screen, and play a second video alongside it. Meanwhile, they can look up an encyclopedia reference and put it into a third window. They can make contact with a professor, policy maker, or architect, and, through multimedia E-mail, ask them to comment on the materials they are assembling. They can capture the first words of Nelson Mandela the moment he is released from prison, or the sounds of picks chipping away at the Berlin Wall, or the whoosh of helicopter blades as federal drug officials snare a drug runner just off the coast of South America. All these fragments of the real world can be cut and pasted into an interactive *virtual field trip* that the student team is assembling for their classmates, teacher, and local community.

A virtual field trip is an *immersion learning* experience. It reinforces and accelerates learning by placing learners in a rich, multilevel, real-world environment that they can experience with all their senses and that they can analyze using all the tools on the computer.

These tools are already available, and they soon will become inexpensive enough for any school. But they can only be used to their fullest potential if we rethink our notions of "computer" and "classroom." Schools must begin planning now to implement these new paradigms. After all, to travel the electronic highways of the future, students must first have a roadworthy vehicle. Such a machine must be able to communicate, and it must be able to process multimedia data (images, text, sounds, animations, etc.). It must be fast. It must be capable of high-volume (e.g., magnetic and optical) storage. But even with all these features, the machine is still just a box. It does not by itself create a classroom environment that allows teachers and students to use the computer to maximize learning and human development.

A Teacher Explorer Center

Two months ago this column described an inquiry-centered "classroom of the future." The classroom would run on multimedia "wheels" and be capable of carrying teachers and students anywhere they cared to go. It would be based on the new paradigm for "computer" and the new paradigm for "classroom" discussed in this month's column.

Such a classroom is now being created at East Lansing High School, just outside Michigan's state capital. The classroom is known as a "Teacher Explorer Center." It is a pilot training site for Governor Blanchard's "Classrooms of Tomorrow," a program that is designed to put computers and other multimedia devices into the hands of more than 20,000 Michigan teachers over the next two years. We hope that many of the Classroom of Tomorrow teachers will come to the Explorer Center for training, along with government policy makers, business leaders, and representatives from higher education.

In the Teacher Explorer Center we are focusing on training teachers as *teacher explorers*—as knowledge navigators who can pilot their classrooms out onto the edge of human knowledge. Teacher explorers will make journeys to places, events, and especially to people. They will reach out and touch experts in the community, in the state, and around the world, and try to see critical areas of knowledge—math, science, geography, writing—through the experts' eyes, as pioneers on knowledge's frontiers and as "hands-on" practitioners who have knowledge not found in any textbook. Teachers will begin their journey by electronically linking up with experts in East Lansing, the nearby state capital, and local universities and community colleges.

Poles of Power

We are now scavenging resources in East Lansing to assemble multimedia "inquiry centers" for teams of teachers and students to use. We are hoping to set up five centers in the classroom: a teacher center and four student centers. Each center sits beside a *power pole*. We think of the power pole as the *entry ramp* onto the electronic highway. Physically, the power poles are simple aluminum poles—hollow shells. Inside the poles are wires and cables for electrical power, local area networking, video networking, cable TV, fiber optics, and telephone lines. Each cable represents a lane onto a different electronic highway.

The Starship Enterprise

Each of the five workstations can take its own entry ramp onto a different electronic highway. One team of explorers can go to Jupiter, another to ancient Rome, a third to the Amazon rain forest, a fourth to an archaeological dig in Asia, and a fifth on a whale watch in the North Atlantic. Each team goes on their journey as "mapmakers" armed with gear (camcorders, VCRs, still-image cameras, etc.) to capture bits and pieces of the real world so they can later analyze, organize, and re-create their journey for others to experience.

Teams are also encouraged to leave their workstation and make journeys to real places and interview real people in the local community.

Each journey is focused on important umbrella themes that organize the inquiry, give it a real-world context, and force the explorers to make decisions faced by real-world experts.

The explorer teams can journey separately, or they can journey together. Imagine the teacher as Captain Kirk on the bridge of the starship Enterprise. Around the teacher are teams of student explorers clustered together at their workstations. Together the teacher and students are on a mission to "boldly go where no one has gone before"—for example, to the future to calculate the effect of global warming on the earth's societies.

> Imagine the teacher as Captain Kirk on the bridge of the Starship Enterprise.

All the teams are mapmakers, playing a supporting role in the classroom mission. One team, the math and science team, creates diagrams to analyze the effect of pollution on global warming. Another team, the imaging team, gathers satellite images from NOAA, aerial photos, video clips, and magazine photos documenting the extent of temperature changes and worldwide pollution. A third team, the Journal Writers, supervises the first two teams and creates a written and verbal journal describing the class' journey. The fourth team journeys out onto electronic highways and contacts leading experts in the local community, a government agency, and a citizen's action group. They interview the experts and create miniature "expert systems" that simulate the experts' point of view, priorities, and key decisions.

At the end of the class' journey, the teacher has assembled a multimedia database and several problem-solving simulations related to global warming. The class is planning to present their findings as a virtual field trip to other classes and to their parents at the next Open House. They plan to publish their findings on the local public-access cable channel and by sending their findings to the experts they interviewed and to local news organizations.

A Multimedia Skateboard

The Teacher Explorer Center in East Lansing is a pilot classroom of the future that will serve the entire state of Michigan. Not every classroom needs to be this elaborate. The important thing is to begin thinking of your classroom as a room whose walls become "the world all around" (Maurice Sendak, *Where the Wild Things Are,* New York: Harper & Row, 1963). And think of your computer as a vehicle, not as a stationary box that processes data. If you can't afford a high-powered vehicle, don't despair. In fact, it's prob-

ably best to begin with something more like a skateboard. You can scavenge your multimedia from around the school. You can create a do-it-yourself version of desktop fusion by putting a camera, keyboard, computer, tape recorder, VCR, and TV together on one desktop. (See earlier "Multimedia Sandbox" columns in *The Computing Teacher* for details.) Next, find yourself a modem. Ask for a phone outlet into your classroom. Or try to get your principal to install cable TV. There are several levels of multimedia, each tailored to a certain size school budget. You can:

1. Set up a scavenged multimedia inquiry center in the library as a resource for the entire school.
2. Set up a rolling inquiry center that can visit different classrooms for different curriculum units.
3. Set up a shared inquiry center for two or three classrooms.
4. Set up an inquiry center in each classroom or in a single demonstration classroom.
5. Set up a multimedia "teacher explorer center" classroom with lots of workstations. Teachers and students can schedule visits to the center for special projects and "journeys."
6. Set up a cluster of multimedia inquiry centers in each classroom in the school.

Number one is the least expensive option; number six is the most expensive. However, as you can see, setting up a simple, scavenged inquiry center is affordable even for schools accustomed to operating on a shoestring. It is time to rethink computers. It is time to rethink classrooms. Look to the year 2000 and create a long-range strategy for your classroom and your school. The year 2000 is still ten years away. You have a whole decade to make your dreams come true. The important thing is to begin.

Learning to Use the Tools of the Future

STUDENTS IN A PENNSYLVANIA HIGH SCHOOL SPEND A LOT OF TIME IN THE FUTURE TECH LAB, WHERE THEY USE EVERYTHING FROM COMPUTERS TO ROBOTS TO LASERS.

"The ultimate curriculum is reality," says Walt Tremer, director of the Future Tech Lab in the Southern Lehigh School District, Center Valley, Pa. Students here attend a traditional high school, but many spend their study halls, lunch periods, and after-school hours preparing for careers in the 21st Century.

The district's $200,000 Future Tech Lab is run by Tremer, who is also director of the district's gifted program. Installed in December 1989, the lab covers six areas of technology robotics, fiber optics, holographic research, computer-aided design, space studies, and artificial intelligence. "Students are really touching the future," Tremer says.

The lab is new to the district, but technology is not. The Future Tech project is six years old, and during that time period Tremer and his students have been experimenting with everything from computers to robots to lasers.

Ten years ago the district began with a single Radio Shack computer in the high school. Today the computer-to-student ratio is 1 to 7. With computers integrated into the curriculum at every grade level, students began to ask, "what's next? Where do we go from here?" Many students were no longer satisfied to use only computers.

Robots

For these students, Tremer introduced the Hero 1, a robot that has arms, a body, and can be programmed to move, carry things, avoid obstacles, and much more. Tremer bought Hero 1 unassembled to save money, and took the package to the county's vocational technical school, where students put together the 4,000-part robot.

Hero 1 worked throughout the district. Not only did the high school students learn about robotics, but youngsters in the four elementary schools learned phonetics with the robot's help. They used the keyboard on the robot's head to program it to say their names. Once the students figured out the sequence of phonemes, they progressed to programming in brief messages.

Students at the middle school programmed the robot to recite passages in foreign languages, which in turn helped students learn about inflections and intonations and how to speak precisely. Hero 1 also spent the year performing public relations duties. Looking in every sense like a robot, Hero 1 became a popular addition to the district. It cut ribbons at technology fairs and visited school board and parent association meetings. Tremer and a core group of students took their technology show on the road with live demonstrations and videotapes of projects in progress.

Through Hero 1, the district saw how technology can be used across curriculum areas, and can benefit students at many grade levels.

The district has also added a Microbot Teachmover robot to the program. Microbot looks and acts like an indus-

By
Gwen
Solomon

trial robot and helped Tremer's technology students learn about real-world automation. Students built a conveyor belt and programmed the robot to sort blocks. One project had Microbot wrapping the school cafeteria's plastic utensils.

Another involved product testing. Students had Microbot pull on the eyeballs of dolls thousands of times to check product safety.

Tremer's students eventually connected the robot to an Apple IIe's game port and attached an optic sensor to the robot's arm. They moved into the area of artificial intelligence by programming the computer to discriminate among colors, sense and respond to levels of light, and to sort objects.

Tremer and his students visited the New York Holographic Museum, and read up on creating their own holograms. They made a 2,000-pound sandbox and borrowed a laser from the science department. The first holograms were a little Buddha, a porcelain horse, and a Moravian star.

The project was so successful that by the time Tremer returned the laser, the school district was already planning to buy one. "The district is committed to preparing students for the future," says Tremer. "The ideas the district implements are on the forefront, so it can provide youngsters with an awareness of what's coming. It's hands-on contact with the future."

The Lab

Students have been planning for the new lab and equipment for the last two years. When the high school had to un-

> ... this lab is "an oasis where youngsters can brainstorm ideas and build on them. The structure isn't formal; it's not a whole class, so it engenders creativity."

dergo asbestos removal, the district decided to renovate the 35-year-old building. Since the Future Tech project had been so successful and could also be used for industrial arts and technology education, the district decided to add the large, new lab as part of the renovation.

A visitor to the lab may find 15-20 students actively doing projects alone or in groups. Tremer says this lab is "an oasis where youngsters can brainstorm ideas and build on them. The structure isn't formal; it's not a whole class, so it engenders creativity."

Student Daniel Deschu, for example, is interested in aeronautical design. He builds rockets in the lab, and will launch a scale rocket complete with payload. He's also helping to design an airplane's wing and build a wind tunnel for test purposes.

Krista Walter is concerned with human adaptation in space; she has run simulations of space deprivation and studied the effect of calcium loss.

Emil Lerch is studying the causes of the 1986 Challenger space shuttle accident.

Other students use an Apple IIe to monitor weather conditions for a Philadelphia television station. They use Brøderbund's Science Toolkit thermisters to measure temperature and photo cells to monitor light. They also have designed software to keep track of weather patterns and regularly report their statistics to the station.

"The rationale for investing in the equipment," says Tremer, "is that the more real the curriculum is, the better." Some students have gone on to study related subjects at college. One recent graduate is at the Massachussetts Institute of Technology majoring in aeronautical engineering. Another is at Carnegie-Mellon University studying robotics.

The Teacher

Tremer himself is an inspiration to his students. An archeology major in college, he worked as both a Chinese and Russian interpreter in the Far East and taught anthropology at a high school and at Muhlenberg College. He has worked for the Southern Lehigh School District since 1978. In 1985 Tremer was selected as Pennsylvania's representative to the Teacher in Space program and has been a liaison between NASA and the public since then as a NASA Space Ambassador. He lectures on integrating space science into the mainstream of education.

This year Tremer is a Christa McAuliffe Institute Educator. (See EL October 1989.) Says Tremer, "I've gone from someone with no technical base to a person who carries a computer on an airplane when I travel. I've come that far. And anyone can do that; anyone can use the benefits of technology along with the students."

Gwen Solomon is the author of a software program and two books on improving writing with computers. She is currently computer coordinator at Adlai Stevenson High School in the Bronx, N.Y.

Article #12
The New Library/Media Center

THE SCHOOL LIBRARY/MEDIA CENTER IS BEING TRANSFORMED INTO A
TECHNOLOGY AND INFORMATION HUB THAT IS INDISPENSABLE TO STUDENTS AND STAFF.

BY
ROBERT
MCCARTHY

The topic of Billy's report is the political career of John F. Kennedy. To find information, he sits down at a computer in the library/media center's computer lab and instantly finds magazine and book citations and prints out several complete articles about Kennedy. Using a videodisc player that's connected to his computer, he watches several of Kennedy's speeches and news clips on his assassination. He then accesses a word processor and begins taking notes, and soon he finishes a first draft of his report. Is this library/media center a fantasy? In fact, it's a reality in many schools.

Today's K-12 school library/media center is quite often a hive of activity, as well as one of the school's technological hubs.

In some schools, for example, library circulation is computer controlled, and thus vastly speeded up. Books with bar codes and library cards with barcoded student identifications can be scanned across optical readers just like packages at the supermarket checkout. Often the familiar card-catalogue drawers are gone, replaced by computer-terminal search stations. Using key words, students perform searches until they come up with a focused bibliography on the selected topic. They can then instruct the computer to print out a hard copy of the bibliographic list on the selected topic. In addition, the status of the library materials—whether the book is in the stacks or checked out—is indicated on the terminal screen. With some cata-logue systems, a map of the library will appear indicating the location of the book or books required.

Laser-disc technology (CD-ROMs and videodiscs) is also an important component of today's library/media center. With CD-ROM drives or players attached to computers, students can access numerous electronic resource tools. These may include *The Electronic Encyclopedia* (Grolier, Danbury, Conn.) and Newsbank (Newsbank Electronic Index, New Canaan, Conn.), an index to more than 2 million newspaper articles. A popular reference videodisc is *The Video Encyclopedia of the 20th Century* (CEL Educational Resources, New York, N.Y.), a 4-volume videodisc set with film and/or still photographs of every major news story that occurred this century.

Using computers and modems, students in today's library/media centers can access on-line information data bases like Dialog Classmate (Dialog Information Services Inc., Palo Alto, Calif.) or Dow Jones News Retrieval (Princeton, N.J.). Some of these data bases contain only book and article references, but with others it's possible to get full texts, and to make hard copies of these texts.

Today's library/media center may contain a computer lab. Students can use the computers to take notes as they do research and, if the computers are networked into the library catalogue system, search for resources as they write.

"The next step," says Hannah Hollifield, media coordinator at Central

Senior Davidson High School, in Lexington, N.C., "is to establish search stations throughout the school, all networked to the library—and not only to the collections catalogue, but to the CD-ROM resources as well. Then, from your workstation in the computer lab, you can call up an article in Grolier's *The Electronic Encyclopedia* and even get a printout."

In short, say some educators, the library/media center is beginning to rival the computer lab as a focus of educational technology. According to Don Adcock, coordinator for program support for the American Association of School Librarians (AASL), conference sessions on school-library automation have been among the hottest tickets in town for the past three years.

The Benefits

"Automating the library is a very hot issue right now, a growing trend," says Bob Skapura, librarian at Clayton Valley High School, in Concord, Calif. Skapura chairs the AASL technology committee and has spoken about automation to many state conferences of school librarians. "Automation can help with circulation and assist you in keeping your collections intact," he says. "And then there's the replacement of the card catalogue. Every librarian who's ever worked with kids knows that the card catalogue has never been more than a partially successful search tool. It's just hard for a kid to use. Consequently, librarians have long dreamed of a magic tool whereby a student just types in a key word, like 'cars,' and immediately the system begins listing everything in the collection on cars. And then subsets of that—like 'American cars' or 'classic American cars.' "

Library automation is a much-discussed topic, agrees Mary Holloway, computer and media consultant with the North Carolina Department of Public Instruction, "because of the many advantages it provides. For one thing, it largely eliminates time-consuming drudge work. With an automated system updating overdue books, a task that used to take a day-and-a-half, now takes just a few hours. That frees up additional time that can be devoted to the librarian's instructional program."

Also, she says, "an on-line catalogue search system can model computer literacy for the student. If a student can do on-line searches, then he is indeed computer literate." And, she continues, "an automated circulation system also gives you much better inventory control. And when you know what you have and where it is you are better able to estimate your future needs." She concludes: "The on-line catalog is a success because it motivates students to do research. It eliminates the drudgery of manual searching. You don't have to flip through the card catalogue, jot down titles and call numbers, attempt to do your own cross-referencing, etc. All you have to do is prompt the system and it will do the searching. The bottom line for education is that students do more research."

Holloway believes that as students learn how to manipulate the search technology more successfully, they will gain a better understanding of what research means, how to make connections among bodies of knowledge, and how to refine topics. "Traditionally, school librarians have stressed how to find the information," she says. "But, as we automate, more and more we'll be stressing how to use the information that you have found. And that means higher-level thinking skills growing out of the search technology."

At schools where some library automation is already in place, librarians have pinpointed a number of positive developments. "There's something about a computer that makes a student simply want to use it," says Karen Schaffer, librarian at Torrington High School, Torrington, Conn. "Whereas it was difficult to teach children to use the card catalogue and the print version of *Readers' Guide to Periodical Literature,* they will go to the computer and search the on-line catalogue and the CD-ROM version of *Readers' Guide* and do it without very much trouble."

"The primary value is educational," says Melvin Stirsman, computer-contact teacher in the Evansville-Vanderberg School Corporation, Evansville, Ind. "Student work is coming out better, with more sources and better research. More time is spent on reading and note-taking and writing, because less time is spent on raw searching. More time with the books, instead of with book-finding."

CD-ROM technology gets positive marks from many teachers. Melvin Stirsman points out that with Grolier's *The Electronic Encyclopedia,* students can now do more than simply take notes on relevant encyclopedia articles. "The student can now print out the entire article for study and for further reference. When you're writing the paper it's much better to have the entire source at your fingertips, and not simply handwritten notes of an article."

"Our CD-ROM stations are getting a lot of use," says Janet Leistner, media specialist at Central High School, Evansville, Ind. "Using Microsoft's *Bookshelf* disc, for example, students are able to make use of a lot more statistical information in their papers than ever before. The *McGraw-Hill Science and Technical Reference Set* discs are useful be-

cause they facilitate cross-references; everybody can now get a different 'take' on the same topic."

Some schools use modems to hook up with outside data bases. "We've done pilot projects where we've allowed students to access both citation-only and full-text data bases," says Mary Holloway. "We've used Dow Jones News Retrieval and Dialog Classmate. Students can search, find what they need, and call up the full text—either for printing out or for saving on a floppy disk. We've found that such resources have been especially effective with lower-level students, for whom the main problem has always been getting them past the drudgery of research."

Technology has also made library management a little easier. Barbara Regan, librarian/media specialist at Jackson Memorial High School in Jackson, N.J., marvels at how easy inventorying her collections has become—thanks to catalogue and circulation software. "Now that the books all have bar codes," she says, I just take the light wand and wave it over the stacks and everything on the shelves is in the computer. Then all I have to do is compare what I have to what I'm supposed to have."

"Our system has helped quite a lot in terms of reducing losses and overdues," says Janet Leistner. "The automated circulation, plus our ability to track overdues easily, has meant a reduction in losses from 400 items two years ago to only 30 items last year." But the biggest benefit for Leistner has been the increase in utilization. Since her on-line system has been in place she estimates that library use has quadrupled.

Hannah Hollifield of Lexington, N.C., has noticed that static portions of her collection are more active with automated searching. "In part," she says, "that's because the on-screen book reference gives you more information about what's in the book than you would ever find in the card catalogue. So books that might not have seemed relevant to certain topics are now seen to be useful."

The Problems

But even the proponents of the automated library admit that getting there, and staying there, is not without problems. Perhaps the biggest hurdle is the need to do a retrospective conversion of your inventory, which simply means transferring the information contained in the card catalogue to the computer. The old-fashioned way, of course, is to take the cards from your catalogue and type the information they contain into the computer. "There are companies that will do that for you," says Bob Skapura. "You just box up your card catalogue and, for a healthy fee, someone else will do the typing."

An easier, yet somewhat time-consuming, way to complete the conversion is with programs such as *Bibliofile* (Library Corp., Inwood, W.Va.), a software program that is used in conjunction with a compact disc containing bibliographic records of the Library of Congress. Using an inventory listing of your own collection, you scan the CD-ROM listings for matches. Then you simply transfer the bibliographical information from the CD-ROM onto your catalogue software.

"The conversion problem is the biggest one right now," admits Skapura. "But even when you decide how to solve it that doesn't mean your automated library is home free. Consider this: right now I have a 90 drawer card catalogue," he says. "Theoretically, as many as 90 students can search simultaneously. Now, suppose I replace the card cata-logue with an automated system that comes with three search stations. Well, instead of 90 students being able to search simultaneously, no more than three can. And because the process is new, and students usually don't type fast, you can very quickly find enormous queues backing up around the search stations. Of course, the solution is to buy more search stations. But at a cost of about $1,800 a piece, how many can you afford to buy?"

Similar problems exist for the CD-ROM resources. Skapura cautions library/media specialists not to toss out their *World Books* and *Encyclopedia Americanas*, just because they've installed one CD-ROM station and a disc-based encyclopedia.

"Outside data bases can be another problem," he adds. "These can be very seductive items. They are lightning fast (if used with some know-how), large, and various. But oftentimes what you get at the end of your search is merely a list of citations. And what good is that if you don't carry the material in your library? As for the full-text data bases, they can be extremely expensive. Don't forget, all the while the student is browsing through the material, making sure he can use it, etc., you're on-line and the cost is mounting."

Veterans of library automation, like Janet Leistner, acknowledge the relevance of Skapura's caveats. "The first year we automated," she says, "we had only one search station, so we did see some lines backing up. But now, with seven terminals available, that's not such a problem. Students are also becoming more adept at making searches getting their print outs, and freeing up the computer."

But Leistner does still have a back-up problem with the CD-ROM resources. Since her library has only two CD-ROM stations, she often comes in early to give students more time with the machines. Or she will have students make lists of the materials they want, and she will print it out between classes.

Endless Possibilities

Yet another possibility for library automation is the linking of many libraries to a single catalogue/circulation system. In Carmel, Ind., for example, the high school library, and the libraries of two elementary schools and two junior highs are networked to the town's public library. "The public library's mainframe controls the network," explains Ann Daniels, media department chairman at Carmel High School. "Using a terminal in any of the schools, or in the public library, you are plugged into a catalogue of all of the items contained in the six libraries. Our teachers are amazed at some of the resources their students find."

In Hawaii, the state's entire public-library system is computerized and networked; in addition, 12 school libraries located in rural school districts are plugged into the public-library network. "Besides the search stations," says Tahirih Foster, head librarian at the Lanai Public Library, Lanai, Hawaii, "each public library also has microcomputers available for public use, plus a production-room center staffed by an audio/visual technician. School classes often come in and are trained by the A/V tech on how to develop photographs, how to make videos, etc."

But perhaps the most interesting—and dare one say bravest?—of the library/media center automation innovators are those who are operating without the print card catalogue. Such a person is Pat Foster, media coordinator at Broadcreek Middle School, Newport, N.C.

"Ours is a relatively new school," says Foster, "so we went directly to the online catalogue system." The middle-school library has four IBM PS/2 computers that serve as search stations, and a 15-station Apple II lab. In addition, there is a Macintosh attached to a laser printer.

"The school library is getting more use than I'm used to seeing," says Foster. "We've had as many as 100 students at a time using the library facilities. The students love not having to thumb through a bunch of cards to find the references they need. And the electronic catalogue has been a benefit for me, since students in our schools used to be famous for finding the reference they needed in the card catalogue, and then simply tearing the card out of the drawer and taking it with them while they searched for the book—which made it rather difficult for anyone else to find that particular reference.

"Plus, having a computer lab on the premises has also stimulated library usage. Sometimes a teacher will preempt the lab, if his or her class has a special assignment. But often the computers are available to anyone who comes in. The students use them to write assignments, or they sit down with books from the stacks and take notes electronically, saving them on a disk or printing them out."

In Fort Lauderdale, Fla., the Parkway Middle School is part of a "magnet school" program that uses high technology to lure students back to underutilized inner-city schools.

In addition to computerized catalogue and circulation, says Debra Klein, coordinator of the magnet program, the school is making use of videodisc technology in the media center. "For instance, we have all 40 volumes of *The Video Encyclopedia of the 20th Century,* which has visual data on just about every major news event that's been filmed or photographed. A student accesses it by going to an index and looking up, say, the Challenger explosion. He will get a date and a reference number that tells him which disc and which chapter on the disc to go to. The student then goes to the multimedia station, loads the disc, instructs the computer as to the appropriate chapter and up comes film on the Challenger explosion. Right now we have a videodisc setup in the media center, in the computer lab, and I've just ordered two additional units. Besides *The Video Encyclopedia,* we also have *Vote '88* from ABC News Interactive/Optical Data (Warren, N.J.), and a set of earth-science discs."

Klein's media center is also connected to WilsonLine (H.W. Wilson Co., Bronx, N.Y.), an on-line service that provides access to the *Readers' Guide to Periodical Literature* and 19 other data bases. Using WilsonLine, students are able to get resource citations and, if the material cited is not available in the Parkway library, they can use WilsonLine to get printouts of abstracts of the resources cited.

But perhaps the most dynamic feature of the Parkway magnet program is the availability of laptop computers in the media center. "Right now we have about 150 laptops," says Klein, "a mixture of Toshibas and Tandys at a ratio of about one computer for every two students. Next year we hope to have a laptop for every student. The students can sign out for the laptops, take them to class, even take them home," she says. "We also have modems available, so the students can talk to each other via computer/modem hookup. But most often the students use the laptops in the library for note-taking purposes. We've found that the students take better and more legible notes using the computer; hence, their notes are more useful when it comes time to prepare their assignments. The improved content of their work indicates they are spending more time on it."

Klein's next project is to participate in a county-wide, multimillion-dollar bid that will result in the purchase of 75 new computers for each school in the Fort Lauderdale area. "All the computers will be networked," she says. "About half of them will be designated for CAI use and the remainder will be earmarked for a reading/writing skills lab. Now, many of the schools in Broward County will be installing the reading/writing lab in the library/media center which, more and more, seems to be the logical location. What that indicates to me is that the library/media center is coming to be as much of a technology center as the computer lab."

Robert McCarthy is a Weehawken, NJ-based freelance writer.

Article #13
MegaTech Makes the Grade:
High School of the Future

By
Don
Broderson

Two years ago, when Steve Cogorno was in eighth grade and had to choose a high school, he selected one located eight miles across town from his home and with "a bad reputation." But he had quite a compelling reason for doing so: he was drawn to William C. Overfelt High School in San Jose, California, by MegaTech, a magnet program in computers and technology within the high school. Now, he says, "I'm at school more than I'm at home. I leave the house at 6:15 a.m. and get back at 6:30 p.m. I'm even at school on the weekends, and so are my friends."

Magnet programs, which focus on particular areas such as art or vocational training, are a fairly new and widely used strategy to cope with many of the problems—from racial imbalance to low motivation—facing today's schools. Students in "choice" systems or magnet districts are free to select a school appropriate to their individual interests. The idea is that the program will be so engaging it will attract and hold students—like a magnet.

Now three years old, MegaTech is a work-in-progress, an evolving effort to create the school of the future. Its slogan is "computers and technology across the curriculum," and the program comes very close to fulfilling that promise. What has enabled MegaTech to succeed where other school-based technology programs have failed is its unique combination of faculty enthusiasm, business support, and an exciting curriculum.

Although computers have been used in classrooms for about ten years, the results have sometimes been more depressing than impressive. Forty machines isolated in a lab and supported by a stock of software about as imaginative as an electronic ditto sheet is a typical scenario. Add to that a budget that doesn't allow for upgrading of equipment and a staff of technophobic teachers who have not been trained or even informed about the potential of the machines as learning tools, and disaster is assured.

At MegaTech there are more than 300 computers on campus, most in clusters of 15 or 16 machines in a room. Cogorno says he uses computers in almost all his classes. Every room has a television monitor. Two dishes bring international programming in from 30 satellites. The MegaTech video production classes transmit their own programs on this system twice a week. There is an elaborate media center open to all classes that contains an array of electronic equipment including videodiscs, VCRs, FM radios, audio tapes, televisions, films, slides, and computer projection systems. A central resource pool, being established in the library, will include software, videodisc curricula, and about 2,000 hours of videotape. This material will be available to all teachers, whether or not they are in the MegaTech program.

This saturation of the environment is part of the plan as MegaTech tries to

648

prepare students for the world of the future. Art Darin, MegaTech's coordinator, says, "We feel that technology is going to touch all our lives in every profession. So we show students they need to be aware of the uses of technology no matter what career they go into, and we give them hands-on experience." Cogorno and his friends, for example, put out the school's award-winning newspaper in the MegaTech desktop publishing lab.

> "You have to get people excited about the technology—you need to take away their fear and demonstrate applications."

Not all Overfelt's faculty were eager to become involved in the new magnet curriculum, and some even found it downright intimidating. Like most teachers, they were comfortable with their familiar methods and reluctant to invest time in learning one so totally different. Some teachers who were not in the magnet program were resentful of the amount of money spent on goodies they would not use.

After a rocky start, the administration brought Darin in to be MegaTech coordinator. Formerly a successful football coach, Darin knew how to build a team and how to motivate people. With a core of inspired teachers and the indispensable backing of Principal Elias Chamorro and Superintendent Joe Coto, Darin set about making the program work. "You have to get people excited about the technology—you need to take away their fear and demonstrate applications."

The core group set up the media center for all teachers to use. Then it set aside money for in-service training for all of the staff and showed them what the high-tech goodies could do. It broadened access to computers on campus and let teachers take computers and software home. Contrary to popular practice, the group decided against the model of computer labs. Says Darin, "The lab can kill you if it just sits there. That's why we put the computers in the classrooms. We want teachers using them and kids getting their hands on them every day." To further motivate teachers, special efforts were made to match programs with the interests of the staff.

The home economics department was having trouble attracting enough students to stay afloat. Theresa McRae, the department chair, had a background in design but knew little about computers. MegaTech, in collaboration with McRae and Apple Computer corporation, put together a fashion and interior design course that not only is a success but has had the unexpected dividend of attracting boys to the classes. The course uses computer-aided design (CAD) software on Macintosh computers, which are set up next to the sewing machines. The students design patterns on the computers and are able to see what garments will look like before scissors ever touch cloth.

Another program lets the students design entire rooms. They use kits to build model rooms then design the interiors on the computer. Robotics, laser, computer-assisted technology, studio fashion photography, synthesized music, and computer programming are some of the other courses offered at MegaTech. (For the basics—English, math, social studies, etc.—MegaTech students take classes with the regular Overfelt students.)

Assembling the hardware and developing the curriculum was successfully accomplished through a fruitful collaboration between MegaTech and several representatives from business and industry. Darin put together an advisory board comprised of officials from some of the biggest names in Silicon Valley: Apple, Hewlett-Packard, IBM, and Pacific Bell. Local business people, professionals, and union representatives serve on the board.

Although MegaTech receives considerable material support from these companies, Darin emphasizes that "you can't go to industry saying 'give me, give me.' You must ask, 'what can we do as a team to make this interesting to both sides, so we both have rewards?'" From the corporate perspective, says Sonia Lopez, of Pacific Bell's Latino Professional Association, "business recognizes the need for an educated workforce in the future."

Darin looks to industry for guidance and inspiration. In his view, industry can not only help design a school that will fit the needs of future job markets, but it can do a lot to motivate students. IBM, for its part, has adopted the school; the company sends tutors to help students, and it runs a program aimed at keeping potential dropouts in school. Lopez's Pacific Bell group started a one-on-one mentor program at the school through which students visit different workplaces, thereby gaining a powerful image of the possibilities of a future in telecommunications. "Industry can create the excitement. It can show how these technologies carry over into the real world," says Darin. "Education is going to change radically in the next ten years, and industry has to be a big part of that."

Darin's dreams for MegaTech's future include a terminal on every teacher's desk that could be used for routine work, roll call, and grading, as well as E-mail between teachers, communication with counselors, and helping students with questions about their programs. He also envisions teacher learning centers with multimedia stations for curriculum development and teacher training, and he would like to see portable computers available for students to check out and take home. With Darin's winning strategies, it seems very likely that his dreams will be realized.

Don Broderson is a veteran high school teacher in Richmond, California.

The buildings resemble a high-tech corporate headquarters. On the roof of the sprawling glass-and-red-brick structure sits a gleaming white satellite dish, which catches sunlight like a dewed spider web. Inside, a secretary answers the phone and types a command into a computer, bringing up the information needed to answer the caller's question. In another room, a person about to give a slide presentation pushes a button and a screen slides down from the ceiling with a hum. In the hall, a rectangular board spells out a silent message with moving red lights that look like stock tickers on Wall Street.

But the message on the electronic board has nothing to do with the price of equities; it announces that class rings are on sale in the cafeteria. A bell peals, shattering the corporate atmosphere and sending scores of teenagers out of classrooms and into the hallways.

The building, located in Eagan, Minn., some 15 miles from downtown St. Paul, houses Dakota Hills Middle School and Eagan High School. The schools, which fully opened last fall, make use of technologies that the rest of the working world takes for granted. A visitor will find televisions, videocassette recorders, and telephones in most classrooms, and a sizable inventory of video cameras, videodisc players, and other high-tech gadgets, which are wheeled around on metal carts from room to room.

But at these two schools, the focus is not on the technology; it's on learning. Thomas Wilson, Eagan High's principal, compares the technology in the school to a phone in a home: "you have a telephone in your home, but your home doesn't focus around the telephone. The phone is just a part of what you do every day; it gets absorbed into the fabric of your life."

Wilson knew that the technology would only become part of the fabric of school life if teachers used it frequently. He also knew that teachers would only use it frequently if it was helpful and simple to use. All too often, he'd heard teachers say, "I don't think I'll use that video tape. It's too clumsy." So, to avoid turning teachers into "scientists of wires," Wilson equipped each classroom with one electronic switchboard that enables the teacher to orchestrate the use of many machines.

Wilson points to the simple configuration of switches and outlets to describe his brainchild. Need the lights off to watch a video on the overhead television? Just flick the switch. Want to watch a conference on global warming beamed down by satellite? Simply change the channel on the VCR. Need help? Lift the phone and call for support.

Just putting simple devices like telephones in every classroom has revolutionized the school, connecting teachers to each other, to administrators, and to the outside world. Rita Anderson, an English teacher who has a class of rambunctious 10th graders, found that the phone has a remarkable effect on her students. Once, when a student got out of hand, she picked up the phone and called home.

651

"That blows them away," she says. "They say, 'You can call mom?' They are much more aware of immediate repercussions." Other teachers use the phone in class to arrange field trips or to have students talk to experts in the community.

A building-wide "voice mail" system, which works like an answering machine and takes messages for each teacher, further encourages communication. Teachers can pick up their messages from any phone in the school—or anywhere in the world, for that matter. "If you have a quick question," says Susan Brooks, who teaches English at Dakota Hills, "you lift up the phone, and leave a message for someone. They can get back to you and say, 'Yes, that's OK,' or 'No, that's not,' then you're done. You aren't chasing someone all over or writing notes."

Voice mail also helps parents track teachers down when they have a problem or concern. Some teachers send notes home every three weeks with an update on class activities and their voice-mail number. That way, parents feel informed and know that the teachers are accessible. Mike Vruno, a social studies teacher at the middle school, says voice mail has helped him become more responsive to parents. "I find myself worrying less about talking to parents because there's less time involved," he says. "I'm already on the phone, so it's easy to take care of the problem right then. If I get notes in my box, I put them on the bulletin board and there they stay for a week."

One thing this "school of the future" doesn't have is a computer on every student's desk. Why not? Because software doesn't teach, teachers teach, according to Brad Johnson, middle school teacher and resident computer guru. Of course, teachers use computers, but only when they're needed.

Teachers have a number of computer options available to them. Both schools have large, centrally located computer labs, with PCs lined up back to back like tightly packed rows of corn. Unlike most schools, computer use isn't restricted to word processing and computer programming; students also work on spreadsheets, foreign languages, computer-aided design, and desktop publishing, as well as other applications.

Teachers generally use computers to supplement classroom instruction. For example, geometry teacher Jane Lee presents a unit on geometrical perspective in her classroom and then brings her students into the labs for some three-dimensional simulations that let them flip and rotate triangles and lines. "Kids need to see things," she says. "It's hard for them to always read theorems and words. On computer, they make conclusions on their own, without me leading them to it. It allows them to discover."

In addition to the central labs, both schools have computers that teachers can wheel in for classroom use; in the middle school, teachers can borrow as many as eight computers at a time. In one classroom, a group of kids who normally bolt for the door at the end of class are so caught up in the scary stories they are writing on computers that they don't even notice the bell has sounded. "You guys need to shut these babies down," the teacher yells as little fingers type furiously.

Plenty of additional computers are located in teachers' offices and in the library. Those in the labs, classrooms, and library are networked, so teachers and students can call up something they are working on from almost any computer in the building.

The Eagan and Dakota Hills libraries are located in the center of each school, like ancient Roman atriums. But that's their only connection to ancient times.

The libraries—also known as "media centers"—are a grand departure from the days when students rifled through the card catalogs and *Readers' Guide*, scribbling notes on scrap paper. Instead, young researchers belly up to an IBM computer and type in a topic, author, or book title for an instant on-line search. An electronic card catalog tells them if a book is checked out, so they don't have to waste time looking for it.

Thanks to CD-ROM technology, which enables volumes of information to be housed on a small disc, students can touch a few buttons and get computer printouts of magazine and newspaper articles published in the past five years. They can also take notes and write papers on the computers. And when it's time to check out a book, a laser gun, like a grocery store scanner, simply reads the bar code on the book and the student's ID number.

These research tools and a number of other high-tech devices allow students to go beyond writing traditional term papers. With video cameras, state-of-the-art editing equipment, and Apple Computer's HyperCard, students can prepare video reports that meld spoken scripts, taped footage, and segments from a visual almanac that has video clips on everything from speeches by Martin Luther King Jr. to physics experiments.

Students aren't the only ones who know that video cameras are good for more than just home video. In her speech class Brooks tapes students so they can see for themselves if they speak too quickly or avoid eye contact. "Even though we've told them 18 times that they need more eye contact they say they begin to believe it when they actually see it. One teacher even tapes all of her lectures that cover new material so students who missed class or didn't understand a topic can view them again."

In the belly of the building far from the rows of desks and chalkboards, is a nerve center of microchips and megabytes. It's a room that whispers mission control rather than "teacher control." The "switch room" houses the building bell and P.A. system and energy-management system. It is also the central feed for the telephone wires, TV cables, and the instructional computing network. It is packed with a tangle of wires, boards lit up with scores of red lights and nearly a dozen glowing computer monitors.

When there's a problem in the building, whether it involves ventilation or voice mail, the custodian or administrator will probably solve it from this room. "Before the custodian reaches for his tools," says Greg Utecht, teacher and technology coordinator for the high school, he sits down in front of the computer, dials up a graphic of the building, and scans through to find out what's wrong. Then he gets his tool belt to fix it."

The automation makes life easier in the administration office, as well. "This office is run as a business," says secretary Judith Palmateer. "Information is readily accessible, well-organized, and easy to find." Palmateer is often the first person people talk to at the school. And the memos, calendars, and personnel files stored on her computer help her answer their questions right away. "There's less filing, and information is right at your fingertips," she says, typing away at her keyboard.

Computers also keep track of student attendance. For the moment teachers pencil in little ovals on class rosters and the computer reads them and quickly compiles the data. Utecht hopes that in the future, teachers will be able to enter attendance figures directly into the computer. A software program also helps teachers calculate their students' grades. When parent-teacher conference time came this year teachers printed out individual progress reports for each student, complete with class standing and comments.

But the real boon for teachers is the way computers have helped them cut their load of daily paperwork; they can use the machines to prepare lesson plans, work sheets, tests and memos. After a teacher has prepared a ditto he or she

---

Teacher-Approved

Like many Minnesotans, he speaks with a question mark hanging on the end of every sentence. But accents are deceiving; Thomas Wilson is a confident man. He knows that Eagan High School and Dakota Hills Middle School will work because they were built with teachers in mind. In fact, teachers helped plan the school every step of the way.

Two months after local voters approved a $47.5 million bond issue that included $34.6 million needed to build the two schools, Wilson was chosen as the high school's principal. During the two years before construction began he recruited more than 80 district teachers, administrators, secretaries, and custodians to brainstorm on the design and ways to integrate technology into the schools. "They told me, 'if I had my choice, this is what I would have, and this is how I would design it. Here's how I would use the space; this is where I would put the door,'" Wilson recounts.

The notes from these meetings—enough to fill several boxes—helped architects make preliminary sketches and final blueprints, which also received the teachers' stamp of approval.

Greg Utecht, a physics and chemistry teacher at the high school, remembers clearly what he and other teachers asked for in the early meetings

because most of their requests have become part of the schools. "We wanted the ability to be in one part of the building and talk to teachers in other parts of the building," he says. "We wanted video capabilities right there in our rooms. We didn't want to wander all over creation to find a computer or video or other technology. We wanted to have it where we are—accessible, easy, let's go."

To help him turn the teachers' dream school into reality, Wilson brought in local experts and consultants from firms in Boston and Houston. One thing—teachers were intrigued by, for example was a "voice mail" system, but they feared the system would be no better than messages in a mail box unless they could tell at a glance when someone had called. Wilson's idea was to put boards in a central area of the schools with a number for each teacher that would light up when he or she had a message. The consultant simplified the idea; now, computer monitors throughout the building list people who have voice messages. Melding the phone system and computer monitors required a tremendous amount of cooperation from the engineers, the phone company, and computer people. But, according to Wilson and the teachers who now work there, it was worth the effort.

can send it electronically to a resource room with instructions for the secretaries. A secretary then prints out the document, makes copies, and sends the computer file back to the teacher's personal electronic file cabinet. "We've gotten spoiled because we can spend more time on teaching and less time running errands," says Brooks. "We're getting to the heart of the things faster."

The Eagan Schools have abandoned the traditional classroom with four walls and a door. Most classrooms in the schools have three walls and one open side facing the library or a hallway.

A teacher walking by can see other teachers in action. Although some admit that the less-than-private classrooms have taken some getting used to, most say the open environment has helped them pick up new ideas. "If I had my own classroom, where I shut the door, I would never get to see how the teacher next door uses the computer," Vruno says. "Anytime I see something appropriate for my kids, I take it."

The middle school is broken into interdisciplinary "houses," each with four rooms. Some rooms open to the hallway, and some walls between rooms are movable. The English, science, social studies, and math teachers who share the four rooms have a common planning time. This interdisciplinary approach supports the use of technology since teachers aren't confined by the traditional structure of the school day. "If teachers want, to use technology to do something," says Johnson, "they don't have to be limited by a 40-minute period."

Before the new school opened, teachers had a week of training with the phone, audiovisual, and computer equipment. Periodically, special in-service sessions are held to bring the staff up to date on new software or hardware. But training alone doesn't explain the relaxed, eager attitude of faculty members, most of whom came from traditional schools in the district.

The other two-thirds of the credit goes to Greg Utecht and Brad Johnson, two teachers-turned-coordinators who agreed to spend most of their time helping the schools' teachers use technology. Utecht teaches only two high school courses and Johnson spends his entire day making the high-tech tools work.

"We can go to Brad and say, 'we want to do something with charts,' and he makes it happen," Brooks explains. "We say, 'We want our kids to design their own space station on Mars,' and he'll show us what we need and how to do it." Middle school principal Patrick Sullivan says that Johnson often helps a teacher with a new skill during first or second period. And by the end of the day, he says, the teacher has it mastered.

Teachers say this kind of support gives them more control over their teaching. "In this school, we have a lot more power over what we want to do," Brooks says. "I feel like I can try something. If I get stuck, I have a resource."

Utecht tries to nudge his colleagues along gently: "one thing we do with both teachers and kids is to say, 'We don't care how we hook you, we just want to hook you.' So, if we hook a kid using the computer after school on the yearbook, and the kid thinks, 'hey, it would be great to do my social studies paper on this,' we've got 'em."

During one training session, Utecht tried to hook a 50-year-old admitted "computerphobe" who insisted he would never use the machines. Utecht showed the man, the school's baseball coach, a graphics program, and he seemed mildly interested. So, Utecht called up a file that included some baseball clip art. All of a sudden, Utecht couldn't get rid of him, the computer whiz recounts with a smile. Now, the teacher takes a computer home every weekend.

"You keep a hand at their backs," Utecht says. "You never shove somebody over the cliff, but you won't let them back away. You know they'll get there eventually because the world's going to make them go there."

At both schools, the process has not been without difficulties. Some teachers have mastered the technology, but others need more practice. Utecht and Johnson have been battling computer viruses and other incapacitating ailments in the equipment. And overeager secretaries and administrators have put too much information on computer disks, making it more difficult for people to find what they really need.

Teachers say the technology has shaken up their lives. "Teachers are much busier now because nothing stays the same," says high school teacher Suevonne Carlson. "You have new approaches and new software; you have to make changes and revisions. It takes more planning, and you have to be open to new ideas and committed to working with technology."

Despite the problems and the challenges, the teachers say they have no intention of giving up. Technology, they say, is a tool whose time has come. "I can't help but think these kids are going to be better prepared for the real world," says Anderson of the high school. "One, because they know the power of technology. And two, because it helps me teach them the skills they need."

INDEX

A

B

C